MARS:
The Monuments At Risk Survey of England, 1995

Main Report

Timothy Darvill and Andrew K Fulton

Assisted by Mark Bell and Bronwen Russell

And with contributions from Kate Anderson, Michael Baxter, Hugh Beamish, Jeffrey Chartrand, Karen Gracie-Langrick, Robert Haslam, Nicola King and Melanie Pomeroy

School of Conservation Sciences, Bournemouth University
and
English Heritage
Bournemouth and London
1998

The MARS Project was commissioned by English Heritage from the School of Conservation Sciences, Bournemouth University, and was undertaken in association with the Royal Commission on the Historical Monuments of England.

First published 1998 by the School of Conservation Sciences, Bournemouth University, Fern Barrow, Poole, Dorset BH12 5BB in association with the Historic Buildings and Monuments Commission for England, 23 Savile Row, London W1X 1AB

English Heritage product code: XC20007

Layout and origination by Colourgraphic Arts, Bordon, Hampshire.
Printed in England by Riverside Printing Company, Romsey, Hampshire.

British Library Cataloguing in Publication Data

Darvill, T. C. (Timothy C.)
MARS : the monuments at risk survey, England 1995 : main report
1.Monuments - England 2.Historic sites - England 3.Historic buildings - England 4.Archaeological
surveying - England 5.England - Antiquities
I.Title II.Fulton, Andrew K.
936.2

ISBN 1 85899 049 1

Front cover: Aerial view of the A14 east of Brampton, Huntingdon, Cambridgeshire, looking north-east in 1995. The view illustrates some of the many hazards facing England's archaeological remains, and shows the high level of risk facing what survives. The newly constructed dual-carriageway cuts through arable fields which reveal buried archaeological monuments as cropmarks in ripening cereals. Gravel extraction and housing development beside the road have also reduced the number and extent of surviving monuments. *[Photograph: Chris Cox, Air Photo Services Ltd. Copyright reserved]*

Contents

List of Figures

List of Tables

Foreword

G J Wainwright

England was first colonized by our predecessors half a million years ago when Britain was still joined to the continent and elephants, lions and wolves roamed the South Downs. Two thousand years ago, the Romans invaded Britain and it is only from that comparatively recent time that we have the remains of masonry buildings, written script and the names of kings and queens. The evidence of our past then becomes accessible through visible structures and documents which can be read and analysed. In addition to what can be derived from archaeology, this accessibility becomes more pronounced with the passing years so that for many people our past is equated with the built heritage of the last two or three centuries. This material can readily be experienced, assessed through a variety of architectural tastes, and is vociferously defended by a number of special interest groups and national bodies.

Yet the evidence for 500,000 years of our past lies largely beneath our feet, visible only as 'humps and bumps' and accessible only through the work of archaeologists who have had varied success in bringing the importance and interest of their subject matter before the public. That latent public interest is there in abundance. The finding of the shin-bone of the earliest European, the debate over the future of Stonehenge, the Temple of Mithras and the fate of Tudor theatres in London are all issues guaranteed to receive wide publicity. The reason is not solely the universal interest which exists in finding something which adds a new chapter to what we know of our origins, but a recognition by the public at large that we are dealing with irreplaceable fragments equivalent in importance to the historical archives of the last 2000 years, some of which will be recorded before they are destroyed and some of which will be handed down to future generations.

Throughout my career, I have been asked how many archaeological sites we have in the country, what is their variety, and what do they tell us about our past. Equally importantly, I have been asked what sort of condition are these remains in, how much is being lost, what are the agencies of destruction and what is the trajectory of that decay? Hitherto, my answers to those questions have been largely guesswork and yet, in order to progress and mature, we need to put our knowledge on a secure footing. This need led to the *Monuments at Risk Survey* (MARS) - the first general census of the archaeological resource in England. The concept of MARS was ambitious and I am indebted to David Morgan-Evans and Tim Darvill for their vision and determination in steering it to a successful conclusion.

The vision is of a general census of archaeological sites in England which will be a baseline for future reports at appropriate intervals, thus providing us with an overview of the changing state of our heritage. The implementation of that vision was complex because an acceptable sampling framework had to be devised which would be repeatable and applicable to the whole country. MARS is the first survey of its kind. Other environmental resource surveys are in their third generation and, as a result, have weeded out sampling, technical and definition problems which appeared at the beginning. These issues were faced in numerous peer review meetings and will no doubt be encountered again when MARS 2 is planned.

It needs to be emphasized that MARS was not designed to identify specific monuments which are at risk. MARS is concerned with the national picture and with large categories and groupings. The aim of the project was to look for general patterns which can be used in the development of strategic policies. The census year for the project is 1995. This report, which is accompanied by an illustrated Summary Report, is intended for three key audiences: archaeologists wishing to understand something about what is happening to the material they are charged with looking after or which provides the raw material for their work of documenting the past; professional planners, heritage and conservation officers and local and national government administrators whose work embraces an interest in the preservation and management of England's archaeology; and politicians seeking detailed facts and figures as the context for continuing support of existing programmes and developing new ones.

Inevitably, since 1995, some important initiatives have been concluded - or may still be in progress - the results of which will substantially change the picture of the archaeological resource post-1995. These changes will be accommodated when MARS is repeated at some future date. For the foreseeable future though, the MARS report and its archive will be the source for anyone wishing to comment on the condition and future of England's archaeological heritage.

London
January 1998

Summary

MARS, the Monuments at Risk Survey, is the first census of England's rich and diverse archaeological resource. The project was commissioned by English Heritage, the government's statutory adviser on archaeology, from the School of Conservation Sciences in Bournemouth University. The survey was carried out in association with the Royal Commission on the Historical Monuments of England between July 1994 and November 1996.

MARS had two primary aims: first to provide a general picture of the survival and condition of England's archaeological monuments; and, second, to set benchmarks against which future changes can be monitored. The census date for the survey is 1995. The Main Report contains a full account of the survey, with chapters covering: the background and theoretical perspectives; methodology and implementation; the nature of the recorded resource and the way it has built up; survival patterns over the last 50 years; the condition of the resource in 1995; land-use in relation to surviving monuments; the effects of designations; and patterns of risk that monuments currently face. A series of conclusions and proposals are presented. A Summary Report is also available.

The starting point for MARS was the information held in local and national archaeological records. A representative sample of 14,591 monuments distributed through 1297 randomly selected sample transects was examined. Work was carried out through four linked programmes: **Field Survey** to record the survival and current land-use of all MARS Monuments; **Aerial Photography** to examine land-use change and monument decay for a sub-sample of 7005 MARS Monuments in 646 transects; **National Survey** to collate information about existing local and national archaeological records; and **Case Study Research** to investigate the archaeological history of select monuments and landscapes.

Records of England's archaeological monuments have been compiled since the later nineteenth century. MARS found that in 1995 local sites and monuments records held 937,484 separate entries, 657,619 as retrievable items and a further 279,865 awaiting input. Estimates based on current rates of growth suggest that there will be more than 1 million entries by the end of the millennium.

Not all entries in local Sites and Monuments Records refer directly to archaeological monuments. MARS defined monuments in general terms as: any definable structure, building or work that has archaeological integrity because it represents the contemporary embodiment of the physical context, setting or result of one or more activities that took place in the past. Extrapolating from the MARS sample there are approximately 300,000 monuments recorded in England. Collectively, these cover about 6.5% of the country's land area. No account is taken of monuments not yet discovered.

About 12% of recorded monuments are of prehistoric date, 7% Roman, 22% medieval, and 37% post-medieval and modern; the remainder are of unknown date. Over half of all monuments are small single monuments (e.g. barrows and enclosures under 3ha in extent), 9% are large single monuments (e.g. hillforts, deserted villages), 22% are standing buildings and structures, 8% are linear monuments (e.g. roads, boundaries), and 5% are field systems. About 49% of monuments were visible at ground level. There is public access to about 25% of monuments; payment for access was recorded for only 1% of monuments.

The destruction of archaeological monuments has been considerable and widespread. Numerically, 16% of recorded monuments had been completely destroyed prior to 1995, 8% within the last 50 years. In real terms this represents the loss of one recorded monument every day. Piecemeal destruction was recorded at all but 5% of surviving monuments. In total, piecemeal losses amounted to 35% of recorded archaeologically sensitive land. Five main hazards account for over 80% of losses: agriculture, urbanization and development, mineral extraction, demolition and building works, and road construction.

Over the last 50 years there have been considerable changes in monument survival. It was estimated that 95% of earthwork monuments had very good survival in the 1940s; by 1995 only 76% of monuments fell into this category, a decrease of nearly 20%.

Land-use is a critical factor for the survival of archaeological remains. Together, arable, pasture, developed land, semi-natural land and forestry contain about 95% of recorded monuments. Some 87% of monuments lie under a single land-use regime, but only 58% have the same land-use around about as over the monument itself. About 43% of monuments which survived in 1995 had changed land-use at least once since 1945. Attention is given to the implications of projected land-use changes in relation to the survival of the archaeological resource.

About 6% of monuments are protected in law as Scheduled Monuments. They were found to have suffered a lower than average rate of destruction. Consideration is given to other site-based and area-based designations. It was found that many extensive area-based designations, for example National Parks and Areas of Outstanding Natural Beauty, contain some of the best-surviving monuments in the country.

Risk is defined in terms of the probability of particular hazards having a detrimental effect in relation to the impact of such effects. All surviving monuments were assessed. Nationally, about 2% of monuments were found to be at high risk and are considered likely to suffer destruction or serious damage in the next three to five years.

MARS concludes that while there are positive aspects to the current condition and survival of archaeological monuments, for example their visibility and accessibility, the overall picture is bleak. Much of what has been meticulously recorded has already been lost, and while important progress has been made with strengthening controls on development in recent years, attention must now focus on the other two main hazards: agriculture and natural erosion. In making a series of detailed proposals three general needs are identified: strategic policy that is concerted and integrated with other allied interests and at all levels; practical implementation of initiatives at appropriate levels within the range of local, regional and national archaeological organizations; and the increasing application of theoretically informed approaches to the formulation, modelling, application and monitoring of archaeological resource management in England.

Résumé

MARS, Monuments At Risk Survey (Etude sur les monuments en péril) est le premier recensement des riches et diverses ressources archéologiques dAngleterre. Le projet a été commandité par English Heritage (Patrimoine anglais), le conseiller officiel du gouvernement en matière darchéologie, qui fait partie de la Faculté des Sciences de la préservation de lenvironnement de lUniversité de Bournemouth. Létude a été menée en association avec la Royal Commission on the Historical Monuments of England (Commission royale sur les monuments historiques dAngleterre) entre juillet 1994 et novembre 1996.

MARS avait deux buts principaux: fournir une vue densemble de la survie et de létat des vestiges archéologiques dAngleterre et établir des points de référence suivant lesquels les futurs changements pourraient être contrôlés. Le recensement date de 1995. Le rapport principal contient un compte-rendu complet de létude, avec des chapitres couvrant les domaines suivants: contexte de base et perspectives théoriques; méthodologie et réalisation; nature des ressources prises en compte et manières dont elles se sont développées; caractéristiques de la survie lors des cinquante années passées; état des ressources en 1995; utilisation du territoire relativement aux monuments subsistants; effets des désignations; types de risques actuellement encourus par les vestiges. Une série de conclusions et de propositions est présentée. Un récapitulatif illustré est également disponible.

Le point de départ de MARS se trouve dans les sources dinformations locales et nationales des archives archéologiques. Un échantillon représentatif de 14 591 monuments répartis à travers 1 297 segments déchantillons sélectionnés au hasard a été examiné. La mission a été menée à travers quatre programmes liés: Field-survey (Etude du terrain) pour enregistrer la survie et lutilisation actuelle du terrain de tous les monuments MARS. Aerial Photography (Photographie aérienne) pour examiner les changements dans lutilisation du territoire et le délabrement des monuments dans un sous-échantillonnage de 7005 monuments MARS dans 646 segments. National Survey (Etude nationale) pour rassembler les informations sur les archives archéologiques locales et nationales existantes. Case Study Research (Recherche par létude de cas) pour enquêter sur le passé archéologique des monuments et paysages sélectionnés.

Des archives des vestiges archéologiques dAngleterre ont été regroupées depuis la fin du XIXe siècle. MARS a découvert quen 1995, les archives des sites et monuments contenaient 937 484 données distinctes, dont 657 619 éléments inscrits et 279 865en attente denregistrement. Les estimations basées sur les taux de croissance actuels montrent quil y aura plus dun million dinscriptions dici à lan 2000.

Toutes les inscriptions dans les archives des sites et monuments ne font pas directement référence aux vestiges archéologiques. MARS a donné une définition générale du monument: toute structure, bâtiment ou ouvrage pouvant être défini et ayant une intégrité archéologique puisquétant aujourdhui lincarnation du contexte physique et des évènements du passé. En extrapolant, il y a approximativement 300 000 monuments enregistrés en Angleterre. Ensemble, ils couvrent environ 6,5 % du territoire national. Nont pas été pris en compte les monuments non-découverts à ce jour.

Environ 12 % des monuments enregistrés datent de lépoque préhistorique, 7 % de la période romaine, 22 % datent du Moyen-Age et 37 % sont postérieurs à la période médiévale et moderne. La part restante ne peut être datée. Plus de la moitié de tous les monuments sont de petits monuments isolés (par exemple, tumulus et enclos de moins de trois hectares de superficie), 9 % sont de grands monuments isolés (par exemple, châteaux forts, villages désertés), 22 % sont des structures et des bâtiments levés, 8 % sont des monuments linéaires (par exemple, routes, frontières) et 5 % sont des champs. Environ 49 % des monuments étaient visibles au niveau du sol. Environ 25 % des monuments sont accessibles au public, accès payant enregistré pour seulement 1 % de ces vestiges.

La destruction des vestiges archéologiques est considérable et très répandue. En valeurs chiffrées, cest, en 1995, 16% des vestiges répertoriés qui ont disparu, dont 8% durant les cinquante dernières années. Concrètement, cela représente la disparition dun site par jour. Les résultats enregistrés montrent que 95% des sites subsistant aujourd'hui sont touchés par une détérioration partielle qui, globalement, touche 35% des terrains archéologiquement fragiles. L'agriculture, l'urbanisation, l'exploitation minière, les travaux de construction et de démolition, et la construction des routes sont les cinq principaux facteurs qui expliquent 80% des pertes archéologiques.

On remarque une évolution certaine dans le nombre des sites détériorés au cours des cinquante dernières années: dans les années quarante, on évaluait à 95% la part des sites en très bonne condition, ce qui n'était le cas que pour 76% d'entre eux en 1995, on constate donc une baisse de 20%.

Le type d'exploitation des terres est un facteur crucial pour la survie des vestiges archéologiques. 95% des sites répertoriés se trouvent sur des terres arables, pâturages, zônes construites, terres semi-exploitées ou boisées. Environ 87% des vestiges se trouvent sur des terres entrant dans une seule de ces catégories; mais pour seulement 58% d'entre eux, les terres environnantes bénéficient du même type d'exploitation que celles-là même où on les trouve. 43% des vestiges subsistant en 1995 se trouvent sur des terres dont le type d'exploitation a changé au moins une fois depuis 1945. Une attention particulière est donc accordée à ce que l'exploitation future des terres impliquerait sur la conservation du patrimoine archéologique.

Environ 6% des sites sont protégés par la loi, classés monuments historiques. On constate qu'ils ont subi un taux de dégradation inférieur à la moyenne. Une importance particulière est donc donnée à la dénomination des sites et des régions. On a constaté que c'est dans les régions classées, comme par exemple les "National Parks" (parcs nationaux) et les "Areas of Outstanding Natural Beauty" (zones de grande beauté naturelle) que l'on trouve les vestiges archéologiques parmi les mieux conservés du pays.

Le niveau de risque est déterminé selon la probabilité d'occurence de causes bien précises qui auraient un effet destructeur. Tous les vestiges subsistant ont été étudiés selon ces critères. Sur la totalité du territoire, il a été constaté qu'environ 20% des sites étaient en grand danger et considérés comme ayant de fortes chances d'être détruits ou de subir de sérieux dommages dans les trois à cinq ans à venir.

En conclusion, MARS remarque que malgré les aspects positifs concernant la condition et l'entretien des sites archéologiques, comme par exemple les possibilités d'y accéder et de les visiter, la situation est dans l'ensemble plutôt désespérée. Beaucoup de ce qui a déja été méticuleusement répertorié a disparu, et alors que de gros progrès ont été faits en vue d'une plus grande matrise du développement urbain ces dernières années, une importance particulière doit être accordée à deux aspects fondamentaux: l'agriculture et l'érosion naturelle. Si l'on établit une liste détaillée des actions nécessaires, ce sont trois points principaux qui dominent: une politique d'action réfléchie et compatible avec les intérêts parallèles; une mise en place d'initiatives à tous les niveaux d'action, à la portée des organismes archéologiques locaux, régionaux et nationaux; et plus de mise en pratique des approches théoriques sur la formulation, l'élaboration, l'utilisation et le suivi de la gestion du patrimoine archéologique anglais.

Zusammenfassung

MARS (Monuments at Risk Survey) ist die erste Zusammenfassung von Englands reichen und vielseitigen archäologischen Ressourcen. Die English Heritage, das beratende Institut der Regierung in archäologischen Fragen, beauftragte die Abteilung für Erhaltende Wissenschaften der Universität in Bournemouth mit diesem Projekt. Die Untersuchung wurde in Zusammenarbeit mit der Royal Commission für geschichtliche Denkmäler Englands im Zeitraum von Juli 1994 bis November 1996 durchgeführt.

MARS hat zwei grundsätzliche Ziele: erstens die Erstellung eines Überblicks der noch existierenden archäologischen Funde und Denkmäler Englands und deren Zustand; und, zweitens das Setzen von Maßstäben dahingehend, welche zukünftigen Veränderungen beobachtet werden können. Für die Zusammenfassung der Untersuchung wurden Daten von 1995 herangezogen. Der Hauptreport umfaßt die gesamten Zahlen der Untersuchung. Die einzelnen Kapitel beinhalten: den Hintergrund und die theoretischen Perspektiven; das methodische Vorgehen und die Umsetzung; die Beschaffenheit der erhaltenen Ressourcen und die Art und Weise, wie sie erbaut worden sind; Erhaltungsmaßnahmen über die letzten 50 Jahre; der Zustand der Ressourcen 1995; die Landnutzung in Relation zur Erhaltung der Denkmäler; die Effekte durch die Einführung von bestimmten Bezeichnungen; die Risiken, denen Denkmäler derzeit ausgesetzt sind. Eine Reihe von Schlußfolgerungen und Vorschläge werden präsentiert. Ein illustrierter, zusammenfassender Report ist ebenfalls erhältlich.

Der Ausgangspunkt für MARS waren Informationen, die in regionalen und nationalen archäoligischen Aufzeichnungen festgehalten sind. Eine repräsentative Auswahl von 14.591 Denkmälern, die sich in 1297 wahllos selektierte Gebieten befinden, wurden untersucht. Die Arbeit wurde durch vier zusammenhängende Programme durchgeführt: Felduntersuchungen, um festzustellen in welchem Zustand und die derzeitige Landnutzung aller MARS Denkmäler sind. Fotografien aus der Luft lassen die Veränderungen der Landnutzung erkennen und den Verfall von Denkmälern für eine Unterauswahl von 7005 MARS Denkmälern in 646 Gebieten. Die Nationale Untersuchung stellt alle Informationen zusammen über die existierenden lokalen und nationalen archäologischen Aufzeichnungen. Fallstudienuntersuchungen ermitteln die archäologische Geschichte von aussortierten Denkmälern und Landschaften.

Aufzeichnungen von Englands archäologischen Denkmälern wurden seit dem späten 19ten Jahrhundert gesammelt. MARS fand heraus, daß 1995 lokale Grabstätten und Denkmal-Aufzeichnungen aus 937.484 verschiedenen Elementen besteht, 657.619 sind bereits registriert und weitere 279.865 warten noch auf eine Erfassung. Nach Schätzungen, die mit einem weiterem Anstieg rechnen, wird es zum Ende dieses Jahrtausends mehr als 1 Millionen Aufzeichnungen geben.

Nicht alle Eintragungen von lokalen Gebieten und Denkmälern beziehen sich direkt auf archäologische Funde. MARS definiert Denkmal oder Fund in allgemeinen Umschreibungen als: jede definierbare Struktur, Gebäude oder Arbeit, die archäologische Echtheit hat, weil es den zeitgenössischen Inbegriff des physikalischen Kontexts repräsentiert, Schauplatz oder Ergebnis von einer oder mehrer Aktivitäten ist, die in der Vergangenheit stattfanden. Ausgehend von der MARS Auswahl gibt es ungefähr 300.000 registrierte Denkmäler in England. Alle zusammengenommen decken sie 6,5% der Landesfläche ab. Dabei wurden die noch nicht freigelegten Denkmäler nicht mitgezählt.

Rund 12% der registrierten Denkmäler sind prähistorischen Datums, 7% sind Romanisch, 22% Mittelalterlich und 37% Post-Mittelalter und Moderne; der Rest ist unbekannten Datums. Mehr als die Hälfte aller Denkmäler sind kleine, einzelne Denkmäler (wie z.B. Hügelgräber und eingefriedete Bereiche mit einer geringeren Ausdehnung von 3ha), 22% sind stehende Gebäude und Bauwerk, 8% lineare Denkmäler (wie Straßen und Grenzen) und 5% sind Feldsysteme. Etwa 49% der Denkmäler waren sichtbar auf ebener Erde. Der Öffentlichkeit zugänglich sind ungefähr 25% der Denkmäler; Eintrittsgelder besteht nur für 1% der Denkmäler, wurde ermittelt.

Die Zerstörung von archäologischen Denkmälern ist beträchtlich und weitreichend. In Zahlen ausgedrückt, bis 1995 waren 16% der aufgezeichneten Denkmäler vollständig zerstört, 8% davon in den letzten 50 Jahren. Klar ausgedrückt, das bedeutet, daß an jedem Tag ein Denkmal verschwindet. Eine stückchenweise Zerstörung wude bei allen festgestellt außer bei 5% der erhaltenen Denkmäler. Insgesamt bedeutet das, der stückchenhafte Schwund addiert sich zu 35% der aufgezeichneten archäologisch interessanten Fläche. Die fünf größten Gefahren, die für über 80% des Verlusts verantwortlich sind, sind: die Landwirtschaft, die Verstädterung und Erschließung, Förderung von Mineralien, Abriß und Gebäudebau sowie Straßenbau.

In den letzen 50 Jahren sind beträchtliche Veränderungen bezüglich Denkmalschutz zu verzeichnen. Es wird geschätzt, daß 95% der Denkmäler einen sehr guten Schutz hatten in den 40er Jahren; 1995 fielen nur noch 76% der Denkmäler unter diese Kategorie, ein Rückgang von 20%.

Die Landnutzung spielt eine entscheidende Rolle zum Überleben von archäologischen Denkmälern. Landwirtschaftlich genutzes, Weide- und erschlossenes Land, halb-natürliche Flächen und Wälder umfassen zusammen über 95% der registrierten Denkmäler. 87% davon befinden sich auf dem Land der gleichen Kategorie, aber nur bei 58% dieser Denkmäler erstreckt sich das Land der gleichen Kategorie über weite Teile der Denkmalfläche hinaus. Bei 43% der Denkmäler, die 1995 erhalten waren, änderte sich die Landnutzung mindestens einmal seit 1945. Die Aufmerksamkeit muß auf geplante Veränderungen der Landnutzung gerichtet und in Bezug auf das Überleben von archäologischen Resourcen gesetzt werden.

Ungefähr 6% der Denkmäler sind laut Gesetz geschützt, stehen unter Denkmalschutz. Diese sind weniger von der Zerstörung betroffen als der Durchschnitt. Überlegungen gehen dahin, andere grundstück- oder gebietsbezogene Bezeichnungen zu finden. Es wurde herausgefunden, das in vielen ausgedehnten Gebieten mit entsprechenden Bezeichnungen, wie zum Beispiel "Nationalparks" und "Gebiete von außergewöhnlich natürlicher Schönheit", sich einige der besterhaltenen Denkmäler befinden.

Das Risiko besteht in der Feststellung der Wahrscheinlichkeit von bestimmten Gefahren, die einen schädlichen Einfluß haben bzw. die Auswirkungen dieser. Landesweit wurden über 2% der Denkmäler ermittelt, die einem hohen Risiko ausgesetzt sind und die in den nächsten 3 bis 5 Jahren entweder zerstört oder erheblichen Schaden nehmen werden.`

MARS faßt zusammen daß, troz dem es positive Aspekte zum gegenwärtigen Erhalt und Überleben von archäologischen Funden gibt, wie z.B. deren Sichbarkeit und Zugänglichkeit, ist deren Gesamtblick eher düster. Viele der registrierten Funde sind schon verloren gegangen und obwohl in den vergangenen Jahren bedeutende Fortschritte gemacht wurden in Bezug auf strengere Kontrollen bei der Landerschließung, muß die Aufmerksamkeit nun auf die zwei anderen Hauptgefahren gelegt werden: die Landwirtschaft und die natürliche Erosion. Eine Serie von detaillierten Vorschlägen hat drei allgemeine Bedürfnisse identifiziert: eine strategische Vorgehensweise, die gemeinsam und integriert mit anderen Interessenten auf allen Ebenen verbündetet ist; eine praktische Umsetzung der Initiativen auf geeigneten Ebenen in Zusammenarbeit mit lokalen, regionalen und nationalen archäologischen Organisationen; und die verbreitete praktische Anwendung der Theorien zu Formulierungen, Modellieren, Anwenden und Überwachen von archäologischen Resourcen Management in England.

Sommario

MARS (Monuments at Risk Survey, cioè lindagine sui monumenti in pericolo) rappresenta il primo censimento delle risorse archeologiche dellInghilterra, così ricche e diverse. Il progetto venne commissionato alla School of Conservation Sciences della Bournemouth University da English Heritage, lente statutario che funge da consulente del governo sullarcheologia. Lindagine fu eseguita tra luglio 1994 e novembre 1996 assieme alla Royal Commission on the Historical Monuments of England.

Lo scopo di MARS è duplice: prima di tutto provvedere unidea generale di come sopravvivono i monumenti archeologici inglesi e le loro condizioni; e, secondo, stabilire dei punti di riferimento contro i quali poter paragonare i cambiamenti futuri. La data del censimento per lindagine è 1995. La relazione principale contiene un resoconto completo dellindagine, con capitoli che coprono: lo sfondo e le prospettive teoriche; la metodologia e limplementazione; la natura delle risorse prese in considerazione ed il metodo in cui è stata stabilita; i modi in cui sono sopravvissuti; metodi di sopravvivenza negli ultimi 50 anni; la condizione delle risorse nel 1995; luso del terreno per quanto riguarda i monumenti che hanno sopravvissuto; gli effetti delle designazioni e i tipi di rischi a cui sono esposti i monumenti in questo momento. Vengono presentate diverse conclusioni e proposte ed esiste anche una relazione sommario illustrata.

Il punto dinizio per MARS fu linformazione contenuta in documenti archeologici nazionali e locali. Venne esaminato un campione rappresentativo di 14.591 monumenti distribuiti in 1297 transetti campione scelti a caso. La ricerca fu eseguita attraverso quattro programmi collegati: **indagine sul campo** per annotare la sopravvivenza e luso corrente del terreno di tutti i monumenti MARS; **fotografia aerea** per esaminare i cambiamenti nelluso del terreno e la decadenza dei monumenti per un sotto campione di 7005 monumenti MARS in 646 transetti; **indagine su un campo nazionale** per raccogliere le informazioni sui documenti archeologici esistenti nazionali e locali; **ricerca su un caso particolare** per ricercare la storia archeologica di monumenti e siti archeologici.

Studi di monumenti archeologici sono stati compilati sin dalla seconda parte del 19esimo secolo. I compilatori di MARS trovarono che nel 1995 gli archivi di siti e monumenti locali vantavano 937.484 voci individuali: 657.619 come informazioni già catalogate e altre 279.865 in attesa di essere catalogate. Da preventivi basati sul tasso di crescita del momento, si anticipa che ci sarà oltre 1 milioni di voci per la fine del Millennio.

Non tutte le voci negli archivi di siti e monumenti locali si riferiscono direttamente a monumenti archeologici. Per MARS i monumenti vengono definiti in termini generali come: qualsiasi struttura, edificio o opera definibile che possieda unintegrità archeologica dato che rappresenta la personificazione contemporanea del contesto fisico, ambientale o risultato di una o più attività svoltesi nel passato. Estrapolando dal campione

MARS esistono circa 300.000 monumenti documentati in Inghilterra. Collettivamente, coprono circa 6,5% del terreno nazionale, ma non si sono presi in considerazione monumenti non ancora scoperti.

Circa il 12% dei monumenti annotati provengono dalla preistoria; il 7% è romano; il 22% medievale e il 37% post-medievale e moderno. Le date del resto sono sconosciute. Oltre la metà è rappresentata da un monumento piccolo singolo (per esempio tumuli e recinzioni elencate sotto 3ha nellestensione), il 9% da monumenti singoli larghi (cioè fortini su colline, villaggi deserti), il 22% da edifici e strutture ancora in piedi, il 9% da monumenti lineari (cioè strade e confini) ed il 5% da sistemi agricoli. Circa il 49% dei monumenti sono visibili a livello del suolo. Il pubblico può accedere a circa il 25% dei monumenti, ma si annotò che era necessario pagare soltanto nell1%.

La distruzione dei monumenti archeologici è stata considerevole e molto diffusa. Numericamente, il 16% dei monumenti catalogati fu completamente distrutto prima del 1995, mentre 18 negli ultimi 50 anni. In termini reali ciò rappresenta la perdita di un monumento catalogato ogni giorno. La distruzione un po per volta fu notata in tutti i monumenti sopravvissuti, eccetto il 5%. In totale, le perdite pezzo per pezzo ammontarono al 35% del terreno catalogato archeologicamente sensibile. Cinque pericoli principali stanno a significare oltre 180% delle perdite: lagricoltura, lurbanizzazione e lo sviluppo, lestrazione minerale, i lavori di demolizione e edilizia e la costruzione delle strade.

Negli ultimi 50 anni si sono verificati considerevoli cambiamenti nella sopravvivenza dei monumenti. Nel decennio del 1940 si credeva che il 95% dei monumenti fossero sopravvissuti molto bene, mentre nel 1995 soltanto il 76% è stato classificato in questa categoria: una riduzione del 20%.

Luso del terreno rappresenta un fattore critico per la sopravvivenza di resti archeologici. Oltre il 95% dei monumenti catalogati sono contenuti in terreni arabili, coltivati e semi-naturali, pascoli e boschi. Circa 187% dei monumenti si trova in un terreno ad uso singolo, ma soltanto il 58% in una zona usata tuttintorno allo stesso modo di quella in cui giace il monumento. Luso del terreno su cui si trova il 43% dei monumenti sopravvissuti nel 1995 è cambiato almeno una volta dal 1945. E necessario prestare attenzione alle implicazioni dei cambiamenti nelluso anticipato del terreno in relazione alla sopravvivenza della risorsa archeologica.

La legge protegge circa il 6% dei monumenti come Scheduled Monuments (cioè elencati). Si trovò che avevano sofferto un grado di distruzione inferiore a quello medio. Si prendono in considerazione altre identificazioni basandosi sul sito e zona. Si constatò che molte identificazioni basate su zone estensive, come National Parks e Areas of Outstanding Natural Beauty (cioè parchi nazionali e luoghi di eccezionale bellezza) contengono diversi monumenti tra i più speciali sopravvissuti nella nazione.

Il rischio viene definito secondo la probabilità

che particolari pericoli possano avere un effetto negativo in relazione allimpatto di tali effetti. Vennero presi in considerazione tutti i monumenti. Nellintera nazione, circa il 2% dei monumenti vennero definiti ad alto rischio, cioè si anticipa che probabilmente verranno distrutti o considerevolmente danneggiati nei prossimi 3-5 anni.

La conclusione a cui giunse MARS è che, mentre esistono aspetti positivi per la condizione corrente e la sopravvivenza dei monumenti archeologici, per esempio la loro visibilità e possibilità di accesso, il quadro in generale è deprimente. Una gran parte di quanto fu meticolosamente catalogato è stato già perduto e, mentre negli ultimi anni si sono fatti considerevoli progressi nellintensificare i controlli sullo sviluppo del terreno, ora è necessario prestare attenzione agli altri due principali pericoli: lagricoltura e lerosione naturale. Nel fare una serie di proposte dettagliate, vengono identificati tre aspetti essenziali: una politica strategica concordata ed integrata ad altri interessi ed a tutti i livelli; unimplementazione pratica delle iniziative ai livelli appropriati nella gamma di organizzazioni archeologiche locali, regionali e nazionali; e una maggior applicazione di un approccio teoreticamente informato alla formulazione, modellatura, applicazione e monitoraggio della gestione delle risorse archeologiche in Inghilterra.

Resumen

El Estudio de Monumentos en Peligro MARS (*Monuments at Risk Survey*) es el primer censo de los ricos y diversos recursos arqueológicos de Inglaterra. El proyecto fue encargado por *English Heritage*, el asesor legal del gobierno en arqueología, a la Facultad de Ciencias de la Conservación (*School of Conservation Sciences*) de la Universidad de Bournemouth, y se ha realizado en colaboración con la Real Comisión de Monumentos Históricos de Inglaterra (*Royal Commission on the Historical Monuments of England*) entre julio de 1994 y noviembre de 1996.

MARS tiene dos objetivos principales: en primer lugar proporcionar un panorama general de la supervivencia y estado en que se encuentran los monumentos arqueológicos del país y, en segundo, fijar los parámetros necesarios para poder medir futuras variaciones en dichas condiciones. La fecha de la realización del censo es la de 1995. El Informe Principal constituye el estudio completo dividido en capítulos sobre los antecedentes y marco teórico, metodología y su aplicación, naturaleza de los recursos evaluados y cómo han progresado éstos; modelos de supervivencia durante los últimos 50 años; el estado de los recursos en 1995; el uso del terreno en relación con los monumentos supervivientes; el efecto que causan los distintos niveles de protección legal; los modelos de riesgo a los que están expuestos los monumentos actualmente; y para concluir, una serie de conclusiones y propuestas. También se ha realizado un resumen ilustrado del estudio.

El punto de partida del proyecto MARS se basó en la información proporcionada por los registros arqueológicos locales y nacionales, examinando una muestra representativa de 14.591 monumentos en 1.297 secciones del país elegidas al azar. El trabajo se realizó a través de cuatro programas relacionados entre sí: el **estudio de campo** para comprobar el grado de supervivencia y el uso actual del terreno de todos los monumentos del MARS, la **fotografía aérea** para identificar cambios en el uso del terreno y deterioro de los monumentos en una selección de 7005 monumentos del MARS en 646 secciones, el **estudio a nivel nacional** para recoger la información aportada por los registros arqueológicos locales y nacionales, y **estudios monográficos** sobre la historia arqueológica de una selección de monumentos y paisajes.

La recogida de datos o registros de monumentos y yacimientos arqueológicos de Inglaterra se ha venido realizando desde el siglo XIX. Según los datos estudiados por MARS, en 1995 los registros locales contenían 937.484 entradas, de las cuales 657.619 estaban disponibles y 279.865 estaban pendientes de registro. Según el ritmo de crecimiento actual se estima que el número de entradas a finales del milenio será de un millón.

No todas las entradas en los registros locales se refieren directamente a monumentos arqueológicos como tales. En MARS el término monumento arqueológico se define como cualquier estructura, edificio u otro tipo de obra con integridad arqueológica, es decir representando actualmente el contexto y los hechos de una o más actividades del pasado. Extrapolando los resultados de MARS se calcula que hay unos 300.000 monumentos registrados en todo el país, ocupando alrededor del 6.5% del área del mismo, sin contar con aquéllos que todavía están por descubrir.

Sobre un 12% de los monumentos registrados pertenecen a la etapa prehistórica, un 7% a la romana, un 22% a la medieval, un 37% a la post-medieval y moderna, y el resto sin identificar. Más de la mitad de todos ellos son monumentos pequeños (ej túmulos y cercamientos de menos de 3 ha), 9% son grandes (ej poblados fortificados, despoblados), 22% son edificios y estructuras verticales, 8% son monumentos lineales (ej vías y carreteras, líneas de demarcación) y 5% son campos. Aproximadamente el 49% son visibles a nivel del suelo; un 25% tiene acceso público y un 1% exige pago por entrada.

La destrucción de monumentos arqueológicos ha sido considerable y generalizada; el 16% de los monumentos registrados ha sido destruído antes de 1995, con un 8% en los últimos 50 años, lo que representa la pérdida de un monumento registrado cada día. Un 95% de los monumentos padece deterioro parcial, deterioro que causa la desaparición de un 35% de los recursos arqueológicos clasificados como frágiles. El 80% de las pérdidas se debe a cinco factores principales de riesgo: agricultura, urbanización, extracción mineral, demolición y obras de construcción, y construcción de carreteras.

Durante los últimos 50 años se han producido cambios considerables en la supervivencia de los monumentos, ya que del 95% de los monumentos que se estimaba se encontraban en buen estado en los años 40, se ha pasado a un mero 76% en 1995, es decir, se ha producido una reducción del 20%.

El uso del terreno es un factor clave en la supervivencia de los restos arqueológicos, y su impacto en la conservación de los restos arqueológicos ha sido analizado en MARS. El 95% de los monumentos registrados se encuentran en terreno cultivable, pastos, terreno urbanizado, semi-urbanizado o bosques. Alrededor del 87% de los monumentos se encuentran en tierras destinadas a un solo uso, pero sólo un 58% tiene un terreno destinado al mismo uso tanto en el monumento como en las tierras que lo circundan. El uso del terreno del 43% de los monumentos conservados hasta 1995 ha cambiado al menos una vez desde 1945.

Los monumentos que están protegidos por la ley al ser declarados patrimonio histórico (cerca de un 6%) tienen un índice de deterioro inferior a la media. El estudio también considera otros yacimientos y áreas protegidas, como parques nacionales y zonas de belleza natural excepcional (*Areas of Outstanding Natural Beauty*) donde se encuentran algunos de los monumentos mejor conservados del país.

El nivel de riego se define considerando la probabilidad de aparición de ciertos factores y el impacto negativo de los mismos. Dicho nivel fue examinado para todos los monumentos conservados, concluyendo que a nivel nacional el 2% de los monumentos estaban en alto riesgo, es decir, se podía esperar que sufrirían daños serios o destrucción total en los próximos 3 ó 5 años.

MARS concluye estableciendo que aunque hay aspectos positivos en cuanto al estado actual y la conservación de los monumentos arqueológicos, como por ejemplo su visibilidad y accesibilidad, el panorama general no es muy alentador. Muchos de los restos que fueron meticulosamente registrados ya se han perdido y aunque se ha progresado enormemente en los últimos años al aumentar el control sobre el desarrollo urbano, es necesario centrar la atención en los otros dos principales factores de riesgo: la agricultura y la erosión natural. En dicho sentido MARS sugiere una serie de propuestas divididas en tres áreas: política estratégica concertada e integrada a todos los niveles con otras entidades interesadas, puesta en práctica de iniciativas a los niveles adecuados en las organizaciones arqueológicas locales, regionales y nacionales, e impulsar la aplicación de enfoques teóricos en la formulación, elaboración, aplicación y control de la gestión de recursos arqueológicos en Inglaterra.

Резюме

MARS (МАРС) - Проект обзора памятников под угрозой - это первая попытка проведения учета богатых и разнообразных археологических ресурсов Англии. Проект был заказан статутным консультантом правительства в области археологии, English Heritage, в Школе консервации университета в Борнемуте. Перепись памятников была осуществлена вместе с Королевской комиссией по историческим памятникам Англии в период с июля 1994 по январь 1996 г.

Перед проектом МАРС были поставлены две цели: во-первых, представить общую картину «выживания» и состояния английских археологических памятников, и во-вторых, установить эталоны для отслеживания будущих изменений. Дата переписи для обзора - 1995 г. Основной доклад содержит полный отчет обзора, с разделами, посвященными следующим темам: фоновая информация и теоретические перспективы; методология и внедрение; характер учтенных ресурсов и методика их накопления; схемы выживания за последние 50 лет; состояние ресурсов в 1995 г.; землепользование в отношении к уцелевшим памятникам; воздействие статуса особоохраняемого объекта и схемы риска, угрожающие памятникам в настоящий момент. В докладе также представлен ряд заключений и предложений. Имеется также краткий иллюстрированный отчет.

Отправной точкой для МАРС стала информация, содержащаяся в местных и национальных археологических записях. Было проведено исследование представительной выборки, включавшей 14.951 памятник, распределенных на 1297 случайно выбранных конкретных участках. Работа проводилась на основе 4 взаимосвязанных программ: **полевое исследование** - для учета выживания и нынешнего землепользования всех памятников, охваченных проектом МАРС. **Аэрофотосъемки** - для изучения изменений в землепользовании и обветшания памятников в под-выборке из 7005 памятников из проекта МАРС на 646 конкретных участках. **Национальный обзор** - для сбора информации о существующих местных и национальных археологических записях. **Изучение отдельных случаев** - для исследования археологической истории выбранных памятников и ландшафтов.

Записи об археологических памятниках в Англии ведутся с конца 19-ого века. В ходе работы над проектом МАРС оказалось, что в 1995 г. местные достопримечательности и записи о памятниках содержали 937.484 отдельных единиц (на компьютере). 657.619 позиций доступны для выборки, а еще 279.865 ожидают ввода. На основе оценок текущих темпов роста можно предположить, что к концу тысячелетия их число перевалит за миллион.

Не все единицы записи о местных достопримечательностях и записях о памятниках связаны напрямую с археологическими памятниками. Памятники в проекте МАРС определяются общими терминами как: любое поддающееся определению сооружение, здание или предмет, обладающий археологической целостностью, так как он представляет современное ему воплощение физического контекста, обстановки или является результатом одного или более видов деятельности, происходивших в прошлом. Экстраполируя из выборки проекта, в Англии имеется около 300.000 учтенных памятников. Сообща они охватывают около 6.5% территории страны. Не были приняты во внимание еще не открытые памятники.

Около 12% учтенных памятников являются доисторическими, 7% - это памятники времен древнего Рима, 22% - средневековые, и 37% - пост средневековые и современные. Даты создания остальных неизвестны. Более половины всех памятников - это небольшие индивидуальные памятники (например курганы и огороженные участки площадью меньше 3 га), 9% -это крупные индивидуальные памятники (например крепости на холмах или возвышенностях, покинутые деревни), 22% - это здания и сооружения, которые еще стоят, 9% - линейные памятники (т.е. дороги и границы), и 5% - полевые системы. Около 49% памятников видны на уровне земли, к 25% памятников публика имеет доступ. Администрация лишь 1% памятников взимает оплату за доступ.

Уничтожение археологических памятников - это значительное и широко распространенное явление. В процентном выражении 16% учтенных памятников было полностью уничтожено до 1995 г., 8% из них за последние 50 лет. В действительности, это означает ежедневную потерю одного учтенного памятника. Частичное уничтожение было зафиксировано во всех кроме 5% уцелевших памятников. Всего частичные потери составили 35% учтенной археологически чувствительной земли. 80% потерь приходится на долю 5 основных видов рисков: сельское хозяйство, урбанизация и застройка, добыча полезных ископаемых, слом и строительное работы, строительство дорог.

За последние 50 лет произошли значительные перемены в выживании памятников. По проведенным оценкам памятники очень хорошо сохранялись до 1940-х годов. К 1995 г. только 75% памятников можно включить в эту категорию, т.е. произошло 20% сокращение.

Землепользование является критическим фактором для выживания археологических остатков. Совместно пахотная земля, луга, застроенные земли, полу-натуральные земли и лесные массивы содержат более 95% учтенных памятников. Около 87% памятников расположены в зоне одного режима землепользования, но только в случае 58% памятников режим землепользования вокруг и над памятником является идентичным. Режим землепользования в местах, где расположено 43% памятников, сохранившихся до 1995 г., изменился по крайней мере один раз с 1945 г. Уделяется внимание последствиям планируемых изменений в землепользовании в их связи с выживанием археологических памятников.

Около 6% памятников находятся под защитой закона, как представляющие особый интерес. Оказалось, что степень их уничтожения ниже, чем у других памятников. Рассматриваются другие специальные назначения, основанные на местоположении и области, например Национальные парки и участки, отличающиеся необычной красотой, где расположены некоторые из лучших памятников в стране.

Риск определяется как вероятность того, что данный риск будет иметь негативный эффект, что касается воздействия таких эффектов. Была проведена оценка всех уцелевших памятников. По всей стране оказалось, что в категорию высокого риска входят 2% памятников, и считается вероятным, что они будут уничтожены или серьезно повреждены в течение следующих 3-5 лет.

Заключение проекта МАРС следующее: хотя существуют положительные аспекты в нынешнем состоянии и выживании археологических памятников, например их видимость и доступность, общая картина довольно мрачная. Многие памятники, тщательно зафиксированные в документах, уже потеряны, и хотя за последние годы был достигнут важный прогресс в усилении контроля над застройкой, теперь необходимо сосредоточить внимание на двух других важнейших рисках: сельском хозяйстве и натуральной эрозии. В целом ряде подробных предложений, были выявлены три общие потребности: стратегическая политика - слаженная и интегрированная с другими связанными интересами, действующая на всех уровнях, практическое внедрение инициатив на соответствующих уровнях в ряде местных, региональных и национальных археологических организаций и все возрастающее применение теоретически обоснованных подходов к формулированию, моделированию, использованию и мониторингу управления археологическими ресурсами в Англии.

概説： MARSプロジェクト

MARSプロジェクト(MARS: The Monuments at Risk Survey の略)は、イングランド(スコットランド、ウェールズ、北アイルランドをのぞく)に残る遺跡の最初の国勢調査である。このプロジェクトは、イギリスの考古学的国家資産においての政府の助言者の役目にあたるイングリッシュ・ヘリテージの任命により、ボーンマス大学保存科学学部が王室歴史遺物委員会(RCHME: Royal Commission on the Historical Monuments of England)と共同で1994年7月から1996年11月にわたって行ったものである。このプロジェクトが目指すものは、イングランドに残る古代史遺跡の残存状態を明らかにすること共に、それをもとに遺跡のこれからの変化を観察するための一定の基準を規定することである。このために1995年が調査履行の年とされた。この調査についての詳細は以下の8項目から成る報告書に記されている。

1) 調査の背景と眺望
2) 調査の方法と履行
3) 保護遺跡と指定された遺跡の特質
4) 過去50年の遺跡の残存のパターン
5) 1995年時点の遺跡の残存状態
6) 土地利用の遺跡残存との関係
7) 政府団体による遺跡保護の影響
8) 古代史跡の瀕する危機の現状

このプロジェクトの出発点は全国及び各地方当局レベルで行われた記録からであった。1,927回に及ぶ無作為抽出法によって選ばれた14,591の遺跡が調査の対象として研究された。この調査は次の4つの関連作業を通して行われた。

1) マーズ・プロジェクトの調査対象となった遺跡の残存状況と近年の土地利用を調べるための現地調査
2) 土地利用の変遷と遺跡の残存及び腐敗状況を調べるための航空写真撮影
3) マーズ・プロジェクトによる遺跡調査記録と各地方当局そして全国レベルでかってこれまでに行われた記録との比較照合のための過去の記録の全国からの収集
4) 遺跡とその土地利用の考古学的歴史を調べるためのサンプルとして選ばれた遺跡の事例研究

イングランドにおける埋蔵文化財の記録は19世紀の後半から行われてきた。1995年における全国各地の記録によると、修復可能な埋蔵文化財の数はあわせて937,488にものぼることがこの度のMARSの調査でわかった。この数は今世紀の終わりまでに100万に達するもの予想される。

しかし、ここで注意すべきことは記録されたものすべて古代のものとは限らない点である。MARSプロジェクトでは過去の出来事、姿を近世に知らせるものとして、包括的に「遺跡、」とよばれるものを定義づけている。このように考えると、MARSの推測では、これまでに見つかったものだけでもイングランド内の遺跡の数は300万にまで及び、イングランド全土の面積の6.5%に相当することになる。

これらの遺跡の年代については、12%が先史、7%がイングランドがローマ帝国の支配下におかれていた頃（5世紀初め）のもの、22%が中世、37%が中世以降から近代にかけてのもの、残り初め年代不明という内訳になっている。

遺跡の規模という点から見ると、過半数が小規模なもの、9%が集落跡や砦のような大規模のもの、21%が建物跡などの遺構9%が道路といった平面的、比立体的なもの、そして5%が地形である。また50%の遺跡層は地上に露見している。25%に当たる遺跡は公衆に公開されており、そのうち見物に有料なのはわずか1%である。

埋蔵文化財の荒廃は深刻かつ大規模である。数字でいうと1995年までに16%が完全に破壊され、うち8%は過去50年以内のあいだに破壊された。これは1日1つの割合で遺跡荒廃が起きてきたことになる。微細な荒廃も含むと、35%の遺跡が失われたことになる。これらの荒廃は、1）農業、2）都市化などの土地開発、3）鉱物抽出、4）建設作業、5）土木作業の5つが主な原因として考えられる。

遺跡の残存状況には、ここ50年年余りのあいだに著しい変化が見られる。95%の遺跡がよい状態で残っていたにも関わらず、その後1995年までの間に25%減少し、75%まで落ち込んだ。このような変化は遺跡の残る土地の利用法との関連があると考えられる。遺跡の眠っている地帯の土地の利用法は、その遺跡の残存状態を決定づける重要な要素である。95%の遺跡は農場、牧場、自然地形、森林地形で見つかった。約87%の遺跡はある単一の地形の形で残り、58%は一つの地形の部分的な形で残った。また、1995年の調査の対象となった遺跡の43%の土地の利用法が、1945年以来、最低2種類以上の異なった目的で利用された地形の下に眠っていた。土地利用の変化の埋蔵文化財の残存に及ぼす影響に関心が集められている。

イングランドの遺跡の6%が重要埋蔵文化財に指定により、法的に保護されている。これらの遺跡は損傷の少ないよい状態で残ったものである。このような法的保護は遺跡及び地域レベルで指定される。国立公園や自然地形といった広大な地形に遺跡がよく残っていることからこのような国の保護の恩恵を受けている。

今日残っている遺跡は、その腐敗及び腐敗による影響の可能性をもとに残存状態の程度が判定されている。全国の2%の遺跡がこの先3年から5年の内に破壊されてしまう危険性をはらんでいる。

MARSプロジェクトは、現在のイングランドに残る遺跡に関して、そのプラス面を認める一方で、全体像としてはかなり深刻な状況にあるという結論をこの調査結果からだした。この調査で得たことから広範囲、かつ詳細にこれからの史跡保護・研究のための必須条件として、以下の3点を上げている。

1) 考古学のみにとどまらず、自然科学など、他の分野の専門家との広範囲に及ぶ協力による研究調査の促進。
2) 各地域・全国レベルで行われる遺跡調査が、考古学者などの専門家の指揮の下で行われること。
3) 最新の学説・技術をイングランドがもつ考古学的・歴史的資産の調査研究に適用すること。

Preface and acknowledgements

The MARS Project was managed by a Project Steering Committee comprising: Dr Geoffrey Wainwright (Chairman), Professor Timothy Darvill (Project Director), Andrew Fulton (Project Manager), Dr Bob Bewley (RCHME), Roy Canham (ACAO), Amanda Chadburn (English Heritage), Graham Fairclough (English Heritage), Vicki Fenner (RCHME), Raymond Foster (English Heritage), Neil Lang (RCHME), Nicola Nuttall (ADAO) and Bill Startin (English Heritage). Special thanks are due to the English Heritage Project Officers Tim Williams, Chris Scull and Keith May for all their help and guidance during the Project. Bob Croft (ACAO and ALGAO) provided much useful liaison and feedback from local authority archaeological officers.

Project staff comprised: T C Darvill (Director); A K Fulton (Project Manager); M Bell (Data Co-ordinator), K Anderson (Assistant Data Co-ordinator; N King (National Survey and Research Programme Supervisor); R Haslam, M Pomeroy, D O'Regan and M Robinson (Field Survey Programme Supervisors); J Lawrence and L Thomson (AP Programme Supervisors); K Walke, P Newman and B Russell (National Survey Programme Research Assistants); H Beamish, K Gracie-Langrick, P Emberson (Case Study Programme Research Assistants); R Barton, I Baxter, S Buckham, N Cohen, J Ecclestone, A Gascoyne, T Goldring, K Graham, D Hart, N Herepath, D Keene, L Pallister, D Radford, S Robertson, H Sherlock, B Stephenson and L White (Field Survey Research Assistants); K Gillies, J Hogan, P Jones and L Thomson (AP Programme Researcher Assistants); G Driver, D Evans, S Carlyle-Lancaster, A J Hunt, J Spencer, G Talbot and B Williams (Research Assistants) and J McMullen, A Smith and M Tubbs (Secretarial and Administrative Assistants).

Collection of the data for MARS was only possible with the kind help and assistance of many people and organizations too numerous to mention here individually. Special thanks go to all the county archaeological officers, district archaeological officers, National Park archaeological officers, Sites and Monuments Records officers, and the other staff of archaeological curatorial offices who provided information, discussed sites they knew, and answered what must at times have seemed trifling queries. Caroline Hardy (Northumberland), Simon Timms (Devon), David Baker (Bedfordshire), Roy Canham (Wiltshire), Peter Wade-Martins (Norfolk) and Glenn Foard (Northamptonshire) kindly cross-checked MARS data from a selection of sample transects as an aid to the data validation process. Steve Stead advised on and assisted with computer programming for accessing data which were available in electronic form. Nigel Clubb, Neil Lang and Simon Walton provided data for the sample transects held in the National Monuments Record and advised on its interpretation and usage. Special thanks are also due to all the private and corporate landowners, occupiers, tenants and estate managers who kindly allowed MARS field survey teams to visit monuments on their land or in their care. Without their help MARS would not have been

possible; their generosity is illustrated by the fact that more than 92% of monuments recorded in the sample transects were able to be examined on the ground.

The compilation of this report draws on contributions from many members of the Project staff and outside advisers, as listed on the title page and credited, where appropriate, with work on particular sections. Special mention may be made of the work of Mark Bell in looking after the databases, compiling the numerous data-sets from which the tables and graphs were constructed and, especially for Chapter 7, providing interpretative commentaries to accompany them; and Bronwen Russell for formatting and editing the tables and graphs.

Help and assistance from many other members of the School of Conservation Sciences at Bournemouth University is also gratefully acknowledged, especially: Bryan Brown (Head of School), Kevin Andrews, Brian Astin, John Beavis, Mark Brisbane, Stephen Burrow, Margaret Cox, Paul Kneller, Vince May, Miles Russell and Carole Ryan.

Mike Baxter (Nottingham Trent University) provided valuable critical comment on the sampling scheme and approaches to the statistical analysis of the data. Chris Cox and Rog Palmer (AP Critique), Sue Lindley (Bournemouth University), I Maitland (Bournemouth University School of Design, Engineering and Computing), Glenne Mitchell (Thalla Partnership), David Wilson (Cambridge University Committee for Aerial Photography) and Bud Young (Landscape Overview) provided much valuable help and assistance on a variety of matters.

Thanks to the following for help with the preparation of case studies for single monuments: Hugh Beamish, Paul Bidwell, H M W Borrill, M J Dearne, Jane Downes, J G Evans, Julie Gardiner, F Griffith, David Hopkins, Julie Lancley, Jacqueline A Nowakowski, L H Pontin, Clare de Rouffignac, D D A Simpson, S Timms, K A Tinniswood, Heather Wallis, Jason Woods; and for landscape-based case studies: Clare Attridge, Ian Ayris, Bob Bearley, Nicola Beech, Alison Bennett, B Bewley, H M W Borrill, Rosemary Braithwaite, Martin Brown, Gareth Browning, Richard Brunning, Norman Cadge, S J Catney, Helena Cave-Penney, R J Chapman, D Coe, Rosemary C Dunhill, Jane Edwards, Graham Fairclough, Keith Falconer, Veronica Fiorato, Katie Fretwell, J A Gorner, John Graham, Stuart Graham, David Graty, Geoff Hann, Caroline Hardie, G Heard, G Hey, Bettie Hopkins, Brian Hopper, Peter D Horne, Dilwyn Jones, Louis King, Graham Lee, Fiona Matthews, Linda McAinley, Peter McCrone, Janet Morgan, Richard Newman, J Parker, John Parker, A Pattison, David Pearce, Colin Pendleton, Claire Pinder, Mike Ponsford, Patrick Randell, Steve Rippon, Irwin Scollar, Linda Seery, Carol Somper, Tony Squires, Jane Waite, Chris Webster, Linda Weeks, Jason Wood, Robert White, Liz Williams and Simon Woodiwiss. In preparing notes on the history of record development Mark Bowden, Martin Fletcher, David Graty, Donnie Mackay, Joy Sutton and Cyril Wardale kindly provided much useful comment and guidance.

Numerous inquires were made of individuals and organizations to check details and obtain information. Special thanks are extended to Frances Cambrook and Matt Holland (Bournemouth University Library Services); Tony Evans (British Geological Survey); Bob Monks (Countryside Commission); David Wilson and the staff of CUCAP; Tom Simpson (DETR Minerals Planning Office); Graham Fairclough, Gerry Friell, Philip Ellis, Bill Startin and Roger Thomas (English Heritage); Philip Biss and Simon Scott (English Nature); Simon Gillam, Alister Henderson and Tim Yarnell (Forestry Commission); Phillipa Swanton (FRCA/ADAS); David Wardrop (Friends of UNESCO); Colin Barr (ITE); Dave Boulton (MAFF); Philip Claris, Chris Gingell and David Thackray (National Trust); Caroline Hardy (Northumberland County Council); T Parker (Ordnance Survey); Alan Pickett (Highways Agency); Neil Lang, Bob Bewley and Dawn Abercromby (RCHME); and Jane Jackson (Wrekin District Council).

While preparing this report many people kindly read and commented on draft chapters and sections, among them: Dawn Abercromby, David Baker, Mike Baxter, Hugh Beamish, Bob Bewley, Roy Canham, Amanda Chadburn, Timothy Champion, Graham Fairclough, Alex Hunt, Nicola King, Francis Pryor, Ellen Macadam, Dai Morgan-Evans, Richard Morris, Bill Startin, Geoff Wainwright and Tim Williams. Translating the English summary into other languages was undertaken by Itsuko Andrews (neé Shibata), Irena Arjantseva, Olivier Dumousseau, Chris Gerrard, Stéphanie Guillemet, Alejandra Gutierrez, Steffi Horstmann, Vince May, Louisella Mount, Ester Pellejero, Praetorius Language Services Ltd, and Donald Rayfield. Rob Wilson assisted with the preparation and formatting of figures and tables.

Acknowledgements for individual figures and plates are included in the captions, but special thanks are due to John Allan (Exeter City Museum), Paul Ashbee, Martin Bell (Reading University), Alison Bennett (Essex County Council), Bob Bewley (RCHME), T Carlton (MoD Crown Copyright Office), Jill Collins (Cheshire County Council), Andrew Fitzpatrick (Wessex Archaeology), Clare King, Sharon Soutar, Fiona Mathews, Lindsay Jones, Chris Chandler and Carolyn Dyer (RCHME National Monuments Record - Public Services), J Lloyd and M Perera (Ordnance Survey), Donnie Mackay (RCHME), David Miles (Oxford Archaeological Unit), John Schofield (Museum of London Archaeology Service), Celia Sterne (English Heritage), David Wilson and Rose Desmond (CUCAP Library in Cambridge) and Stuart Wrathmell (West Yorkshire Archaeology Service) for their help in selecting illustrations, tracking down sources, and making appropriate arrangements for their use.

Ellen Macadam (English Heritage) provided valuable editorial assistance with the preparation of the final text. Frances Brown copy-edited the manuscript. Design and lay out is by Grant Campbell with assistance from Kynan Webb (Bournemouth University Design Unit). Cover design is by Sam Armstrong. The cover photograph, which embraces in one image so many of the things that MARS was concerned with, was kindly provided by Chris Cox of Air Photo Services Ltd.

Finally, on a personal note, very special thanks

are extended to Jane and Jemma, and to Bronwen and Miles, for putting up with some late nights and early mornings during the weeks while we were getting this report off to the printers.

Timothy Darvill and Andrew Fulton
Easter 1998

Key abbreviations and acronyms

AAI	Area of Archaeological Importance
AARG	Aerial Archaeology Research Group
ACAO	Association of County Archaeological Officers
ADAS	Agricultural Development and Advisory Service
ADS	Archaeological Data Service
AGM	Annual General Meeting
ALGAO	Association of Local Government Archaeological Officers
AMIC	*Ancient Monuments in the Countryside* (Darvill 1987)
AONB	Area of Outstanding Natural Beauty
AP	Aerial Photograph
APA	Aerial Photographs Available
APN	Aerial Photographs Not Available
APU	Aerial Photographic Unit (of RCHME)
ARM	Archaeological Resource Management
Anon	Anonymous
BAR	British Archaeological Report
BARS	Buildings at Risk Survey
BTA	British Tourist Authority
CA	Current Area
CAP	Common Agricultural Policy
CAS	Congress of Archaeological Societies
CBA	Council for British Archaeology
CBI	Confederation of British Industry
CCD	Countryside Commission Document
CCP	Countryside Commission Publication
CIS	Countryside Information System
CMH	Current Maximum Height
CNP	Council for National Parks
CoE	Council of Europe
Col	Column
CPRE	Council for the Protection of Rural England
CRAAGS	Committee for Rescue Archaeology in Avon, Gloucestershire and Somerset
CS1990	Countryside Survey 1990
CS2000	Countryside Survey 2000
CUCAP	Cambridge University Committee for Aerial Photography
DAMHB	Directorate of Ancient Monuments and Historic Buildings (of DoE)
DAS	Devon Archaeological Society
DCMS	Department of Culture, Media and Sport
DCRA	Devon Committee for Rescue Archaeology
DDF	Decade Decay Function
DETR	Department of Environment, Transport and the Regions
DNH	Department of National Heritage
DNHAS	Dorset Natural History and Archaeological Society
DoE	Department of Environment
DTp	Department of Transport
EC	European Commission (of the EU)
ECVAST	European Council for the Village and Small Town
EH	English Heritage
EM	East Midlands
EN	English Nature
ENAR	Extended National Archaeological Record
EOA	Estimated Original Area
EOE	Estimated Original Extent
ERL	Environmental Resources Limited
ESA	Environmentally Sensitive Area
ETB	English Tourist Board
EU	European Union
FMW	Field Monument Warden
FRCA	Farming and Rural Conservation Agency

FS	Field system
GDO	General Development Order
GIS	Geographical Information System
GPS	Global Positioning System
GRA	Greatest Recorded Area
HMG	Her Majesty's Government
HMSO	Her Majesty's Stationery Office
HSE	Health and Safety Executive
IAM	Inspectorate of Ancient Monuments
IFE	Institute of Freshwater Ecology
ITE	Institute of Terrestrial Ecology
LAC	Local Advisory Committee
LB	Listed Building
LM	Linear Monument
LSM	Large Single Monument
LUC	Land Use Consultants
LUSAG	Land Use Statistics Advisory Group
LUSS	Land Use Stock System
MAFF	Ministry of Agriculture, Fisheries and Food
MAP2	*Management of Archaeological Projects* (2nd edition)
MARS	Monuments at Risk Survey
MHLG	Ministry of Housing and Local Government
MIDAS	Monument Inventories Data Standard
MoD	Ministry of Defence
MPBW	Ministry of Public Building and Works
MPP	Monuments Protection Programme
NAR	National Archaeological Record
NBR	National Buildings Record
NCC	Nature Conservancy Council
NE	North East
NHC	National Heritage Committee
NHTPC	National Housing and Town Planning Council
NLAP	National Library of Aerial Photographs
NLUSS	National Land Use Stock System
NMP	National Mapping Programme
NMR	National Monuments Record
NNR	National Nature Reserve
NS	New Series
NW	North West
OAP	Ove Arup and Partners
OS	Ordnance Survey
PAE	Projected Archaeological Extent
PAL	Percentage Area Loss
PC	Personal Computer
PHL	Percentage Height Loss
PPG	Planning Policy Guidance
PPG16	Planning Policy Guidance Note number 16: *Archaeology and Planning* (DoE 1990a)
PRN	Primary Record Number
PS	Policy Statement
PVL	Percentage Volume Loss
QA	Quality Assurance
RCHME	Royal Commission on the Historical Monuments of England
RSM	Record of Scheduled Monuments
SAM	Scheduled Ancient Monument
SB	Standing Building
SCAUM	Standing Conference of Archaeological Unit Managers
SE	South East
SEP	Scheduling Enhancement Programme
SERRL	South East Regional Research Laboratory
SI	Statutory Instrument
SM	Scheduled Monument
SMC	Scheduled Monument Consent
SMR	Sites and Monuments Record
SSM	Small Single Monument
SSSI	Site of Special Scientific Interest

SW	South West
TRRU	Tourism and Recreation Research Unit
UAD	Urban Archaeology Database
UDC	Urban Development Corporation
UK	United Kingdom
UNESCO	United Nations Educational Scientific and Cultural Organization
VDU	Video Display Unit
WARP	Wetland Archaeological Research Project
WAT	Western Archaeological Trust
WCSP	Wildlife Conservation Special Committee
WM	West Midlands

Glossary

Accelerated decay: Deterioration of the structural integrity of an archaeological monument at a more rapid rate than would be expected given its situation, environment, and the prevailing land-use. Accelerated decay is usually caused by the onset of an archaeologically damaging factor (hazard) such as dewatering, cultivation, road-building or development.

Amelioration: Deliberate or intentional actions which have the effect of reducing the speed at which a monument is decaying or deteriorating. This often involves changing the land-use regimes both on and around a monument or carrying out capital works to limit or remove destructive forces.

Ancient monument: Legally defined in the *Ancient Monuments and Archaeological Areas Act 1979* (Section 61(12)) as: '(a) any scheduled monument; and (b) any other monument which in the opinion of the Secretary of State is of public interest by reason of the historic, architectural, traditional, artistic or archaeological interest attaching to it'. In the *National Heritage Act 1983* (Section 33(8)) the same term is defined as 'any structure, work, site, garden or area which in the Commission's opinion is of historic, architectural, traditional, artistic or archaeological interest'. See also MONUMENT.

Archaeological excavation: The systematic investigation, recording and analysis of archaeological deposits according to recognized methodologies and practices. See also RESCUE EXCAVATION.

Archaeological monument: see MONUMENT.

Archaeological resource: The sum total of physically constituted evidence relevant to the understanding of human communities and their activities in past times, as defined by archaeologists at any given point in time. The archaeological resource is a sub-set of the original population of things that might potentially be relevant to archaeology as a discipline. The archaeological resource can be divided into an extant resource (i.e. that part which survives at any given point in time) and the extinct resource (i.e. that which does not survive at a defined point in time). It can also be divided into the recorded resource (i.e. those components listed or itemized on a recognized register of some kind) and the unrecorded resource. See also EXTANT RESOURCE, EXTINCT RESOURCE, RECORDED RESOURCE, UNRECORDED RESOURCE.

Archaeological resource management (ARM): Making proper and appropriate use of archaeological sites and monuments, for common benefit, through the manipulation and control of their destiny.

Archaeological site: see SITE.

Areal extent: The area or spatial coverage of an archaeological monument, usually measured in square metres, hectares or square kilometres.

Areal survival: An expression of the physical survival of monuments in terms of their spatial extent as a series of five broad categories: very good, good, medium, poor, very poor. Ascription to one of these categories is based on the calculation of Percentage Area Loss (q.v.).

Bronze Age: Subdivision of prehistory traditionally characterized in technological terms by the extensive use of bronze for tools and weapons etc. Broadly, *c.*2400-700 BC.

Building / buildings and structures: One of the defined categories of monument character (q.v.) and form (q.v.). In MARS, buildings and structures are defined as comprising either a permanent fixed construction forming an enclosed space and providing protection from the elements or a construction of some other sort. Such monuments may be complete, roofless or ruinous. They are generally made mainly of stone, wood, brick, daub, or a combination of these, typically with lesser quantities of other materials too (e.g. iron, steel, cement, plaster etc.). See also CHARACTER, FORM.

Character: The general qualities of a monument that distinguish its outwardly visible archaeological qualities. Three, not wholly discrete, categories of monument character were defined for MARS: earthworks (q.v.), buildings and structures (q.v.) and landcuts (q.v.).

Class Consent: General permission granted by Statutory Instrument (SI 1994 No. 1381) for the continuation or undertaking of defined works and activities at Scheduled Monuments that would otherwise require Scheduled Monument Consent. The following consents are granted for England: Class 1 for agricultural, horticultural or forestry works; Class 2 for works by coal mining operations; Class 3 for works executed by the British Waterways Board; Class 4 for works for the repair or maintenance of machinery; Class 5 for works urgently necessary for safety or health; Class 6 for works carried out by the Historic Buildings and Monuments Commission for England; Class 7 for works relating to an archaeological evaluation; Class 8 for works carried out under certain agreements concerning ancient monuments; Class 9 for works grant-aided under Section 24 of the 1979 Act; Class 10 for certain works carried out by the Royal Commission on the Historical Monuments of England.

Condition: The general circumstances of a monument at a given point in time.

Cropmark: Particular colourations and discolourations, observable at ground level and/or from the air, in growing field-crops and pasture that broadly reflect, in a variety of ways, the position, extent and character of buried features such as walls, ditches, pits or geomorphological structures.

Curatorial management: The maintenance of ancient monuments with the intention of preserving them for as long as possible.

Current Area (CA): The estimated, measured or calculated spatial extent of surviving archaeological remains or deposits representing a given monument at a defined point in time.

Current Maximum Height (CMH): The greatest estimated, measured or calculated distance from the ground surface to the top of the highest recorded feature of a monument at a defined point in time.

Decay: The deterioration of a monument in terms of its stratigraphic and structural integrity and its artefactual and ecofactual content. See also ACCELERATED DECAY and NATURAL DECAY.

Designated land: A piece of ground, which may be of any size from a few square metres to many square kilometres, that is subject to one or more legally imposed constraints or controls over its use or treatment.

Destroyed: One of three defined states (q.v.) in which archaeological monuments are recognized. In MARS a destroyed monument is one at which more than 95% of its recorded physical extent has been lost to a form of land-use whose creation will have removed archaeological deposits (e.g. road-construction, gravel extraction). A monument has experienced wholesale destruction when the complete monument, as recognized, has been lost; piecemeal destruction refers to the loss of a part of a monument.

Development control: The process whereby the Town and Country Planning system is implemented to require prior permission for development in the form of demolition, construction, quarrying, dumping or flooding works and for changes to the use of land or buildings.

Earthwork: One or more archaeological features, such as a bank, ditch, wall, mound or setting of some kind, that appears in topographical relief in the ground surface, usually as a rise, projection or a series of 'humps and bumps'. An earthwork is not necessarily made of soil; it may comprise stones and other materials too. An earthwork normally represents the decayed remains of some kind of structure. See CHARACTER.

English Heritage: The popular name of the Historic Buildings and Monuments Commission for England which was established under the *National Heritage Act 1983* to secure the preservation of ancient monuments and historic buildings situated in England, to promote the preservation and enhancement of the character and appearance of conservation areas situated in England, and to promote the public's enjoyment of, and advance their knowledge of, ancient monuments and historic buildings situated in England and their preservation.

Estimated Original Extent (EOE): Best approximation of the area occupied by a monument when first constructed, or at a distinctive stage in its development. The estimate is based on available information about a particular monument, and a general knowledge of the characteristics and features of other examples of the class to which it belongs.

Exploitative management: The controlled use of archaeological deposits or monuments for some specific purpose or gain, for example as tourist attractions, leisure facilities, or the advancement of knowledge about the past (academic or research excavation).

Extant recorded resource: That part of the extant resource (q.v.) that is recorded on a recognized register or list of archaeological monuments, for example a local SMR, the NMR, or a published inventory of some kind.

Extant resource: That part of the archaeological resource that remains in existence (i.e. physically extant as against destroyed or extinct) at a given point in time. The extant resource can be subdivided into the extant recorded resource and the extant unrecorded resource (q.v.).

Extant unrecorded resource: That part of the extant resource (q.v.) that is not recorded on a recognized register, list or published inventory of some kind and therefore effectively remains unknown as an archaeological monument. This sector of the archaeological resource is the target of many mapping and discovery projects.

Extended National Archaeological Record (ENAR): A cover-term used by RCHME to describe the contents of the numerous local SMRs in England.

Extinct recorded resource: That part of the extinct resource (q.v.) that is recorded on a recognized register or list of archaeological monuments, for example a local SMR, the NMR or a published inventory of some kind.

Extinct resource: That part of the archaeological resource that has been destroyed or lost prior to a defined point in time. The extinct resource can be subdivided into the extinct recorded resource and the extinct unrecorded resource (q.v.).

Extinct unrecorded resource: That part of the extinct resource (q.v.) that is not recorded on a recognized register, list or published inventory of some kind and therefore effectively remains unknown as an archaeological monument. A monument in this sector of the archaeological resource is unlikely to be discovered through fieldwork or research of any kind unless there exists some previously unknown account or picture of it prior to its destruction or loss (as in the case of some unanalysed aerial photographs for example).

Flat / flattened: One of three defined states (q.v.) in which archaeological remains survive. In MARS a flat monument is one in which upstanding (q.v.) features have been peneplained by human or natural agency, thus creating a flat or levelled ground surface that is totally or nearly indistinguishable from the natural topography of its situation. There may be other kinds of surface indications other than topography, for example the presence of distinctive materials or artefacts in the topsoil. It is also likely that archaeological deposits still remain within or below the topsoil at levelled monuments, but, equally, facets of their vertical dimension will have been lost.

Flight line: The mapped representation of the central flight track as taken by an aircraft when taking vertical or near vertical aerial photographs.

Form: The basic shape, outward aspect or arrangement of archaeological features. Five principal monument forms were defined for MARS: field systems (FS), large single monuments (LSM), linear monuments (LM), small single monuments (SSM), and standing buildings (SB).

Greatest Recorded Area (GRA): See PROJECTED ARCHAEOLOGICAL EXTENT.

Guardianship: Direct or indirect ownership or interest in an ancient monument by the state or a local authority for the purposes of maintaining it and ensuring its proper protection and preservation as established by Sections 12-14 of the *Ancient Monuments and Archaeological Areas Act 1979* (as amended for England).

Hazard: A potential cause of harm or threat to an archaeological monument. In archaeology hazards can most easily be identified as the main erosive and destructive forces that potentially place monuments in a lower survival band.

Historic building: A building or structure (q.v.) that has some historical interest by virtue of its age, distinctive architectural or constructional style, or historical associations with people or events.

Impact: The extent and disposition of damage inflicted upon or caused to archaeological monuments in relation to the size and form of a monument. For MARS five types of impact were defined: neighbourhood; peripheral, localized, widespread, and segmenting.

Iron Age: Cultural-historical phase of prehistory traditionally defined in technological terms by the introduction and common use of iron. Broadly *c*.800 BC to AD 50 in southern England, extending rather later in northern and western areas where Roman occupation began later and was less intensive.

Landcut: Archaeological monument comprising one or more archaeological features whose creation mainly involved, or resulted from, digging down into the ground, thus forming some kind of hole, void, cavity, shaft or depression. Natural holes, caves or depressions which were utilized for some purpose also come into this category. Landcut monuments may contain structures or built-up elements too. Examples include: ponds, quarries, wells, mines, shafts and limekilns. See CHARACTER.

Land-cover: The vegetation, habitat, materials or structures that occupy the ground surface of the land. These are typically classified into broad groups or categories that may be further subdivided into narrow classes of various sorts, for example: Woodland (conifer woodland, deciduous woodland, mixed woodland etc.); Developed land (car-parks, residential houses, factories etc.).

Land-type: Broad, and not necessarily spatially discrete, subdivisions of the countryside and urban areas according to general topographical, physiological, geological, historical characteristics. MARS draws upon and expands the land-types defined for the publication *Ancient monuments in the countryside* (Darvill 1987): wetland; coastland and estuaries; rivers lakes and alluvium spreads; woodland; lowland heath; arable land; parkland and ornamental gardens; upland moor; urban developed land; industrial land; and unclassified.

Land-use: A categorization of land based on the main activities taking place on or over it and which give it certain distinctive characteristics in terms of vegetation cover or the presence of buildings or constructions. In many ways the definition of land-use combines characteristics of land-cover and land-type. For MARS use was made of the Land Use Stock System (LUSS) of land-use classification developed for the Department of the Environment during the early 1990s. APPENDIX H provides a full listing of the broad and narrow land-use classes used when recording the prevailing conditions at archaeological monuments.

Levelled: see FLAT

MARS Monument: A monument (q.v.), whether Scheduled or not, information about which was supplied to MARS by a local SMR and/or the MNR because it lay within one of the 1297 defined sample units used in the MARS study. In validating the lists of records as supplied to the project a number of exclusions were made, principally the removal of all buildings in domestic use post-dating *c*.AD 1700, all buildings constructed after *c*.AD 1900, records of stray finds, single human burials, non-archaeological material, records of place-names, unlocated sites, and what appeared to be duplicate records. In all, 14,591 MARS Monuments were defined. (see Figure 3.4 for a schematic representation of how MARS Monuments were arrived at)

Management agreement: A fixed term arrangement for sympathetic land-use (and related capital works where relevant) between a land-owner / tenant and English Heritage or another public authority in order to control land-use practices and thus the rate of decay at a monument. The duration of most agreements is between five and ten years.

Management option: A preferred course of action or policy, selected as appropriate for a given situation.

Mesolithic: Culture-historical phase of prehistory traditionally defined on technological grounds (extensive use of microlithic flint industries) and lifestyle (hunter-gather economies). Broadly *c*.10,000-4500 BC.

Monument: Legally defined in the *Ancient Monuments and Archaeological Areas Act 1979* (Section 61(7) as: '(a) any building, structure or work, whether above or below the surface of the land, and any cave or excavation; (b) any site comprising the remains of any such building, structure or work or of any cave or excavation; and (c) any site comprising, or comprising the remains of, any vehicle, vessel, aircraft or other movable structure or part thereof which neither constitutes nor forms part of any work which is a monument in paragraph (a) above'. More generally in archaeology, a monument is taken to be a definable building, structure or work that has archaeological integrity because it represents the contemporary embodiment of the physical context, setting, or result of one or more activities that took place in the past.

Monument character: see CHARACTER.

Monument form: see FORM.

Multi-option (or multi-purpose) management strategy: Two or more management options taken together, in series or parallel, to provide a coherent and unified approach to the control of change within a defined area of land. The options selected to be part of the strategy will usually relate to a range of different activities, for example archaeological resource management, nature conservation, forestry, water management, agriculture and so on.

National Archaeological Record (NAR): The central index or register of all terrestrial and offshore maritime sites of archaeological significance dating from the earliest times to 1945. It is maintained by the Royal Commission on the Historical Monuments of England and, at the MARS census date, was an integral part of the National Monuments Record (q.v.).

National Buildings Record (NBR): An archive of photographs, plans, and other material relating to historic buildings in England. It is maintained by the Royal Commission on the Historical Monuments of England and is an integral part of the National Monuments Record (q.v.).

National Monuments Record (NMR): Permanent publicly accessible source of information about the archaeological and built heritage of England, maintained in Swindon (Wiltshire) by the Royal Commission on the Historical Monuments of England. The NMR comprises three main parts: the National Buildings record (NBR), the National Archaeological Record (NAR) and the National Library of Air Photographs (NLAP).

Natural Area: A parcel of land identified by English Nature as having individual and characteristic traits of geological, topography, climate and vegetation. Ninety-two Natural Areas have been defined for England.

Natural decay: A cover-term to describe the progress of an archaeological monument from the time of its creation or abandonment through to the present day assuming that there is no human interference with the processes of decay. In reality in England such a pattern is unlikely, although for older monuments there may be long periods of its history when natural decay obtained. See ACCELERATED DECAY.

Natural erosion: The wearing away of archaeological remains below, on or above the surface of the ground by the action of environmental forces such as rain, river action, wind, frost, the sea, and ice.

Neolithic: Cultural-historic phase of prehistory traditionally characterized in technological terms by the presence of pottery and polished stone tools, and in terms of lifestyle as pre metal-using farming economies. Broadly c.4500-2400 BC.

Non-archaeological designation: A constrain or control placed over the way a piece of ground is used or treated which does not explicitly include archaeological considerations (e.g. Site of Special Scientific Interest).

Non-MARS monument: A monument (q.v.) situated in England and forming part of the recorded resource that was not part of the sample of 14,591 MARS Monuments studied during the project.

Original population: An unknown and unknowable quantity of material which represents the sum total of all deposits, structures and monuments that have ever been created or formed and which could potentially be of interest to archaeology. A sub-set of this original population is, at any one time, defined as the archaeological resource (q.v.).

Palaeolithic: Cultural-historical phase of prehistory representing the earliest period of occupation in northern Europe. Traditionally characterized on technological grounds by reference to distinctive flaked stone tools and by the presence of hunter-gatherer lifestyles. The period embraces the dominance of a number of early hominid species and spans the last Ice Age in Europe. In Britain broadly c.500,000 BC to 10,000 BC.

Percentage Area Loss (PAL): A measure of monument survival. The visible or implied destruction of a geographically or spatially definable (and thus measurable) portion of the areal extent of a monument (up to 100% of its areal extent) determined by calculating as a percentage the difference between the Projected Archaeological Extent (PAE) of a monument and its Current Area (CA). It is assumed that all archaeological deposits whether above or below the ground will have been lost within the area identified as having been destroyed.

Prehistory: A cover-term for the earlier part of England's past, generally taken to mean the period before the existence of written records. In practice, however, prehistory in England is taken to end with the Roman invasion in the mid first century AD. Prehistory is conventionally divided into five broad phases: Palaeolithic, Mesolithic, Neolithic, Bronze Age and Iron Age (q.v.).

Primary Record Number (PRN): Unique index number assigned to individual records (items) held by local SMRs and the NMR.

Projected Archaeological Extent (PAE): An estimate of the land area of an archaeological monument that includes or included archaeological remains below, on or above ground level as documented by information included in the records and supporting archives which relate to the monument.

Record enhancement: The process of checking, validating and expanding the record of an archaeological site or monument through the integration of new or previously under-utilized sources of information.

Record mode: Subdivision of the recorded resource according to the kind of things represented by individual record items held by local SMRs and the NMR. The following modes were defined for use by MARS: monuments (q.v.), urban areas; archaeological landscapes or relict cultural landscapes; stray finds (q.v.); and miscellaneous records.

Recorded resource: That part of the archaeological resource (q.v.) that has been itemized on a recognized register or list of archaeological monuments, for example a local SMR, the NMR or a published inventory of some kind.

Rescue excavation: The investigation of a site by archaeological excavation in advance of its destruction. In this sense the site is being 'rescued' from destruction by being recorded.

Retrievable records: Items or record units (however defined) held in manual or machine-based systems within local SMRs and the NMR that can be retrieved from them using a defined and fairly exact query or search routine.

Risk: In general risk is the idea that there is a chance or possibility of danger, loss, injury or some other adverse consequences as a result of natural processes or the intentional or unintentional actions of individuals or groups. More particularly, the degree of risk that any monument may be exposed to is the combination of the probability or frequency of the occurrence of a recognized hazard in relation to the magnitude of the consequences. MARS defined three categories of risk: high, medium, and low.

Royal Commission on the Historical Monuments of England (RCHME): The national body for archaeological and architectural survey and record in England. Created in 1908, its Royal Warrant has been revised several times, most recently in 1992. One of its primary responsibilities is the maintenance of the National Monuments Record (q.v.).

Sacrificial layer: A deposit of inert material laid over the eroded surface of an archaeological or architectural monument or structure for the purpose of protecting the underlying object or structure by allowing the imposed to be eroded away in place of the original ancient materials.

Sample unit / sample transect: The basic frame of study within which recorded archaeological monuments were investigated by MARS; 1297 sample units were randomly selected from within England. Each unit is 1km x 5km, orientated north to south or east to west and aligned with the National Grid.

Schedule of Monuments: A list of monuments (q.v.) considered to be of national importance that is compiled and maintained by the Secretary of State. The list is usually called 'The Schedule'.

Scheduled Monument (SM): Any monument (q.v.) for the time being included on the Schedule of Monuments (q.v.) and therefore subject to various controls and measures contained in the *Ancient Monuments and Archaeological Areas Act 1979* (as amended for England).

Site: (1) A geographically definable place where a monument formerly existed (as in: 'long barrow, site of'); (2) an area of land, which may be anything from a few square metres to many hectares, within which some kind of archaeological intervention or 'event' (e.g. an archaeological excavation) has taken place that has resulted in the observation and recording of some aspect of the archaeological resource.

Sites and Monuments Record (SMR): A register or inventory of archaeologically relevant items (records) mainly created and maintained by local authorities (mostly counties, but some districts and unitary authorities).

State: General appearance of a monument relative to its original appearance. Three principal states were defined for MARS: upstanding; flattened; and destroyed.

Stray find: An object or small group of objects discovered by chance, often during engineering or agricultural operations, although increasingly by users of metal detectors and individuals out walking in the countryside. As a rule, stray finds lack archaeological context; most also lack adequate geo-referencing. However, stray finds are important because of the information they provide about the possibility of more substantial deposits in the same area.

Surface geology: The bedrock type or drift deposit found immediately below the topsoil and representing the parent material in the formation of the soil profile.

Survival: A point-in-time measure of the prevailing state or condition of a monument relative to some former state; a reflection of the cumulative effects of all the natural and humanly induced processes that have come to bear on the monument. In MARS this was mainly determined with reference to areal survival (q.v.).

Threat: See HAZARD.

Unrecorded resource: That part of the archaeological resource (q.v.) that has not been itemized on a recognized register or list of archaeological monuments, for example a local SMR, the NMR or a published inventory of some kind. The unrecorded resource can be subdivided into the extant unrecorded resource (q.v.) and the extinct unrecorded resource (q.v.).

Upstanding: One of three defined states (q.v.) in which archaeological remains survive. For MARS taken as referring to monuments with visible surface topography reflecting, in the vertical plane, details of sub-surface features. In this sense, upstanding may include archaeological features that extend downwards into the ground as well as those projective above ground level.

Visibility: Discernible physical remains of a monument that can be recognized at ground level in normal conditions by a reasonably competent archaeologist equipped with appropriate information about the whereabouts and distinguishing characteristics of the monument such as might typically be available from the relevant local SMR.

Wholesale destruction: The physical eradication of all or most (over 95%) of the archaeological remains and deposits, both above and below the surface of the ground, that previously formed a discrete monument, thus rendering the monument effectively useless as a source of archaeological information.

1 Introduction

It sometimes occurs to me that the British have more heritage than is good for them. In a country where there is so astonishingly much of everything, it is easy to look on it as some kind of inexhaustible resource ... In fact the country is being nibbled to death.

(Bill Bryson 1996, 103-4)

1.1 Setting the scene

England is an old country that embodies, within its towns and countryside, numerous traces of its past. These archaeological remains relate not only to the last few centuries, after England became a nation-state, but also to much earlier times, as far back as the first colonization of northern Europe by human communities about half a million years ago. Together, these archaeological remains represent a veritably significant dimension of today's environment. They are not simply bits of the past that happen to have become stranded in the present: they are components of our contemporary world whose significance to modern society derives from their antiquity.

Archaeological remains are represented in many different forms and guises: earthworks, ruins, buried deposits, historic buildings and structures, cuttings made into the ground surface, finds or scatters of ancient objects, and patterns in the very lay-out and structure of our countryside, towns and cities. Collectively, these are the raw materials from which archaeologists develop an understanding of the past. They also represent the inheritance that we of today have received from our forebears, parts of which we will hand down to future generations. The archaeological heritage stands alongside, and complements, the archives of historical documents, maps and illustrations which are usually preserved in libraries, record offices and galleries. But the archaeological evidence is also much more: some of it relates to periods for which no surviving historical documentation exists, and all of it provides the basis for taking our knowledge of the past well beyond what is covered by written records.

England's archaeological monuments therefore represent a treasure-house of information and inspiration. But how much is there? Where is it recorded? What sort of condition is it in? How is it changing? And how much are we losing each year to the many other demands of modern life such as property development, urbanization, road-building, and hostile land-uses? These and other questions are critical in planning the future. They are raised time and time again whenever important archaeological remains are threatened with destruction and it becomes necessary to provide a context for what is happening. Back in 1966 it was just such concerns that caused the government of the day to set up a Committee of Enquiry into arrangements for the protection of field monuments (Walsh 1969), and they reappeared again more recently in deliberations about Scheduled Monuments by the House of Commons Environment Committee (Environment Committee 1987, xxiv-xxv).

There are no simple answers to any of these questions, although many guesses have been made. Change is an inexorable process whether propelled by natural forces or driven forward by human intervention. Some changes are obvious, highly visible and patently bad for the things affected; other changes are more subtle and their effects difficult to appreciate (Figure 1.1). For archaeology, some changes have the dual effect of bringing new evidence of the past to light for recording and new interpretation, while simultaneously destroying things that have survived for hundreds or thousands of years. It is this complicated web of relationships in which change diminishes what is known while revealing a little more of the unknown that makes archaeological resource management such an interesting, unpredictable, and sometimes controversial, field of endeavour.

In musing on the matter of Britain's heritage, American travel writer Bill Bryson perceptively puts his finger on two key issues which lie behind much thinking about the way archaeological remains stand in relation to the modern world. In his travelogue *Notes from a Small Island* he recognizes the common perception that the supply of heritage is inexhaustible (incidentally, it is remarkable that in this popular book, which by May 1997 had sold over 630,000 copies in the United Kingdom, Bryson refers to Britain's heritage as a 'resource'). So far as the archaeological heritage goes this, of course, is a misunderstanding born of the way in which archaeologists lament the loss or damage of one or two sites while almost simultaneously announcing a mass of important new discoveries. Two examples taken more or less at random from the magazine *British Archaeology* illustrate the problem. The October 1995 issue lamented the construction of three new houses inside a hillfort in the Stonehenge World Heritage Site with the consequent loss of part of the interior of the monument (Anon 1995a); opposite was a report entitled '"Best year ever" for air photography' which told readers that 2000 sites had been recorded by RCHME fliers in the summer of 1995, 'a large proportion of which were new' (Anon 1995b). Similarly, the May 1997 issue juxtaposed a story headlined 'New 7th century remains found at Ripon' with one proclaiming 'Sussex "Flag Fen" decays without record' (Anon 1997a; 1997b).

Such reports are often taken at face value, and it is not necessary to be an accountant to know that a balance sheet on which income exceeds expenditure and gains exceed losses, superficially at least, appears to be a healthy one. Looked at this way, is it really a problem if a few archaeological sites are lost? Bryson's second point

Figure 1.1 - The changing situation, environment and preservation of Whitehawk Camp, near Brighton, East Sussex. This Neolithic causewayed enclosure constructed about 3500 BC was first recorded in 1923. (Top) Aerial photograph of the site in 1946 with the enclosure visible as a series of concentric earthworks. (Bottom) Looking south-west in 1995. Comparison of the two pictures reveals significant changes in land-use across the monument, some of which have been hostile to its preservation with the consequent diminution of the earthworks: some changes of land-use had resulted in the complete destruction of parts of the site. In 1991 and 1993, selective excavations in advance of the construction of the housing development (top left) and road improvements to Manor Hill revealed previously unrecorded features which significantly increased the understanding of the monument. See also Figure 6.38. *[Photographs: RCHME. Copyright reserved]*

provides an answer: yes it is, he suggests, because the very resource itself is being 'nibbled to death'.

Effectively, the role of MARS - the Monuments at Risk Survey - is to examine in some depth the issues that Bryson articulates so well and that form the focus from which other more wide-ranging questions radiate. As such, MARS is the first piece of extensive consolidated research to investigate what archaeological resources there are, and what is happening to them. Put simply, it is a general census of the archaeological resource in England for the mid 1990s which combines an historical overview of the developing record of the resource, a position statement, preliminary analysis, and suggestions for future directions in managing our common archaeological inheritance.

As the first study of this kind in archaeology it is appropriate right at the outset to consider whether the balance-sheet approach, using simple quantifications of gains and losses, is either appropriate or meaningful in relation to archaeological remains. It is a matter that, in a general sense, has received considerable attention in recent years, not least in relation to other environmental resources and the application of the principle of sustainability (Bromley 1995; HMG 1994, 88). In the jargon of eco-economists, the archaeological resource is non-renewable 'critical environmental capital' (Comeren 1994; Toman and Walls 1995; English Heritage 1997a). In other words, there is a finite quantity of what is regarded as a valuable raw material, and while the efforts of prospectors may continue to increase reserves for the foreseeable future it is in the nature of the material itself that this cannot continue indefinitely. Consumption of the raw material, through whatever means and whether consciously or otherwise, reduces not simply the stock of raw material already known about, but the total resource, that is the sum of what is known about plus any which is still unknown and which exists to be recorded in the future. The problem therefore, and the factor that makes accounting for 'gains and losses' so inappropriate to this kind of material, is the fact that in archaeology we can only be certain of what has already been recorded, and really only guess at what has not. Environmental capital in general, and archaeological resources in particular, does not behave in the same way as other assets, nor is it valued by society with the same standards and points of reference (Darvill 1993b; 1995; Kristiansen 1993; Carver 1996; Allison *et al.* 1996; CAG 1997).

Thus in developing MARS there was a conscious attempt to move away from simplistic tabulations of gains and losses and instead to look at models based on the idea of a total resource base which could be quantified in terms of increasing knowledge about its nature and extent set against the effects of natural and humanly induced processes of decay and change.

As it has turned out, MARS was undertaken at a critical moment for archaeology in England. In the year or so during which the results were being processed and analysed (1996-7) a series of five fundamental changes have taken place, or been signalled, and there may be more to come. These deserve brief mention here because to some extent they have influenced the way that this report has been written, and because they will certainly affect the way the results of MARS are used over the coming years.

First, central government funding of archaeological work has started to decline significantly after nearly three decades of increase. This is most clearly seen in the archaeology grants budget expended by English Heritage, the largest public funding agency in this field. After climbing steadily from less than £500,000 in 1972-3 up to £5.64 million in 1993-4 it peaked at £7.51 million following arrangements for special expenditure on archaeology in 1994-5. Since then it has fallen back to £5.35 million in 1995-6, and £4.87 million in 1996-7 (English Heritage 1985, 2; Olivier 1996a, 76; 1997, 100).

Second, set against these reductions in public expenditure there are increasing contributions from private-sector sources, mainly attained through the application of policies set out in PPG 16 (DoE 1990a), in which developers pay for archaeological works connected with construction projects falling within the town and country planning regulations. It has been estimated that in 1990-1 developer funding of archaeological work amounted to approximately £15.5 million (Speorry 1992, 32), a figure that by 1996-7 had risen to an estimated £35 million (*The Times*, 24:2:1998).

Third, public interest in archaeology and an informed awareness of the heritage appear to be undergoing a renaissance: witness the huge public debate about the fate of the Rose Theatre in London (Wainwright 1989; Biddle 1989); the increase in visitor numbers to historic houses and monuments, calculated to be in the order of +4% in 1994-5 alone (BTA 1996, 5); and the success of television programmes such as *Time Team* and *Meet the Ancestors* (Richards 1998).

The fourth change is in approaches to the recording and classification of the material record of the past itself. After more than 100 years focusing on discrete and definable monuments as units of study, more holistic notions of 'historic landscapes' and the 'historic environment' are beginning to be translated into new ways of defining and managing the archaeological resource (Greeves 1989; Macinnes and Wickham-Jones 1992; Wainwright 1993; Countryside Commission 1994a).

Finally, organizational and administrative arrangements which provide the context for looking after archaeological remains are changing on several levels at once. Locally, throughout England, local government reorganization is being implemented through the creation of unitary authorities for some areas, changes to county council boundaries, and the granting of independence to National Park Authorities who also have a new duty to protect the cultural heritage (ALGAO 1998). On a wider scale, there is increasing devolution of central government responsibilities to offices and agencies in a series of ten defined regions (DETR 1997, 52-3), a move that has been mirrored in the restructuring of English Heritage as the government agency charged with looking after the country's archaeological monuments and built heritage (Alexander 1998). At the European scale, plans to develop a framework for land-use planning decisions through the European Spatial Development Perspective are already well advanced (Darvill 1997b; Anon 1998, 4-5) and, when operational, will have an important role to play in trans-national strategic planning.

Thus, at a time when public expenditure on the archaeological heritage is reducing, private expenditure and public interest is expanding, archaeologists are refocusing their attention, and administrative arrangements are being reorganized, the need to take stock of what there is as a prelude to targeting funding and developing strategic approaches to conservation policy and management has never been greater.

This, the main published report of the project's findings, is aimed at those with a professional interest, archaeological or otherwise, in the nature and extent of the archaeological resource and England's historic environment. It should be of particular use to all those who deal regularly with archaeological resource management issues, and to those who handle strategic initiatives and policy developments that include archaeological considerations. The report is technical in nature, and accordingly there is an extended glossary to explain the terminology used in MARS together with other specialist vocabulary that is drawn upon. A non-technical summary of the project and its findings has also been published (Darvill and Fulton 1998) to provide a guide to the more detailed information discussed here.

1.2 Purpose and aims

The overarching purpose of MARS was to provide up-to-date information on the general characteristics of the archaeological resource in England, specific details about its past and current state, and projections about its future. The advantage of carrying out such a survey on a nation-wide scale lies in the level of consistency that will be achieved in providing such information, attaining a truly national picture of what has happened and is happening to the resource, while picking up regional trends wherever possible.

To this end, two principal aims for the MARS Project were defined:

1   A systematic quantification of England's archaeological resource in terms of:

- the changing state of knowledge about the scale and nature of the archaeological resource, including single monuments, archaeologically defined landscapes and historic urban areas;

- the scale and rate of physical impact on monuments since 1945 and the reasons and causes for this;

- the present condition and survival of the recorded resource and future projections of it; and

- the effect of measures introduced to improve management of individual monuments, especially the role of site and area specific designations.

2   An investigation into the implications of monument decay for different classes of monument in terms of the information preserved at different scales of survival.

A third aim, partially fulfilled by this report, was defined in the project design as: 'the preparation of appropriate publications and presentation materials to convey the results of the Project to a range of audiences'.

1.3 Background and history of MARS

The recognition of the need to carry out resource surveys such as MARS goes back a long way. By the late nineteenth century several authorities (notably archaeological societies) were concerned at the lack of general information available, and the antiquarian David Murray published a detailed proposal to carry out an archaeological survey of the United Kingdom (Murray 1896). His suggestions came to nothing at the time, although the principles he discussed, subsequently elaborated by Baldwin Brown (1905), remain the basis of much archaeological resource management in England.

In the late 1960s the Walsh Committee identified the need to survey the condition and survival of field monuments in order to develop appropriate policies for preserving and protecting them (Walsh 1969, 26 and 58). As a result, numerous local and regional studies of monument decay and condition were carried out, some targeting particular classes of monument, others covering specific geographical regions or urban areas. Today these studies would be called 'resource assessments'; APPENDIX A provides a select bibliography of those identified by MARS. Many were published and circulated only as ephemeral typescript reports, but collectively they represent a major contribution to the establishment of frameworks within which research, rescue excavation programmes, and management and conservation schemes can be developed. It is especially notable that in large urban areas some of these resource assessments have passed through second and third iterations, and in many a further programme of study has been announced (Croft *et al.* 1996).

The need for a nationwide survey remained. In 1983 a rapid quantification exercise was undertaken by the Inspectorate of Ancient Monuments to provide information about the relationship between the Schedule of Ancient Monuments and the archaeological resource as recorded on local Sites and Monuments Records (IAM 1984). Among other things, this survey highlighted inadequacies in the nature of general information about England's archaeological resource. Ironically, the information gathered by this survey is the only reliable point-in-time data available for comparison with the MARS data.

The 1987 policy statement and review *Ancient monuments in the countryside* (Darvill 1987) identified the main landscape types in which archaeological evidence is found and the threats to the archaeological resource characteristic of each type, based on predominant land-use and management practice. This work also linked on-going management works to landscape type and prevailing land-use, while recognizing that the history of land-use is responsible for the state and condition of monuments today. Again, the poverty of general information was identified as a stumbling block to the development of strategic policy on monument management initiatives.

Two years later, the idea of a national survey of monument condition was articulated in the form of a draft project design and method statement commissioned by English Heritage (Darvill 1989). This proposal set out a scheme for the collection, analysis and presentation of information on the survival and decay of England's archaeological heritage since 1945. A pilot study to test the general feasibility and methodology of such a project was suggested, and this was carried out in the county of Wiltshire during 1989 and 1990, under the title *England's archaeological resource: the survival assessment programme.* Wiltshire was chosen for the pilot study because of the range of different land-use types present, the availability of contrasting data-sets involving well and poorly studied regions, the wide range of pressures likely to contribute to monument decay, and the general accessibility of relevant data.

A professional seminar attended by members of English Heritage, RCHME, ACAO and others was held in Trowbridge, Wiltshire, on 1st May 1990 to examine the initial results and implications of the work to date. The full results of the pilot study were published in early 1991 (Darvill 1991). A period of critical reflection on the results and methodologies ensued.

Drawing on the recognized success of the Wiltshire pilot study, the policy document *Exploring our past: strategies for the archaeology of England* (English Heritage 1991a) confirmed the importance and desirability of collecting baseline data about the condition of the archaeological resource. Within the framework of strategic decision-making, the identification, recording and understanding of monuments and historic landscapes was recognized as being critical for informing management, achieving accurate resource allocation and defining research strategies (English Heritage 1991a, 34).

In the light of discussions and comments received over two years, a draft research proposal for the main study was produced in early 1993. The proposal outlined a set of objectives and incorporated revisions based on the practical experience of the field staff involved in the Wiltshire pilot study (Darvill 1993a). Modelled on MAP2 (English Heritage 1991b), this new proposal outlined a carefully staged approach, the first stage involving the construction of a detailed project design. This took place between September 1993 and February 1994, the project design (Darvill *et al.* 1994) being the basis of the MARS Project reported here. Throughout the drafting of the project design there were extensive discussions with interested parties, and a professional seminar attended by over 40 invited individuals was held in London on 17th November 1995. A paper entitled *Monuments At Risk Survey: briefing paper 1* was widely circulated prior to the seminar, and a number of written and verbal comments were subsequently received and taken into account.

1.4 Needs, objectives and applications

By the start of the MARS Project the need for it was widely recognized, as too was the fact that its results would be important for everyone involved in archaeological resource management at national level (i.e. English Heritage; RCHME; the National Trust), and more locally (i.e. county archaeological officers; unitary authority archaeology officers; SMR officers; National Park archaeological officers; district / city archaeological officers; archaeological units and trusts; and consultants). The stated aims of the project included measures to overcome some of the difficulties faced by those concerned with archaeological resource management, as follows:

1   Lack of quantified information on the condition of archaeological remains nationally, the relative rates of decay that monuments of different kinds in different regions have been subject to over recent decades, and the degree to which ongoing land-use, land-use change and other impacts influence the nature and extent of monument decay.

2   Inadequacies in information about the resource, such as the absence of accurate figures for the number of monuments recorded to date in England, the proportion of recorded monuments which have been surveyed and documented, and the relationship between the recorded resource and the extant resource.

3   Absence of baseline data for predictive studies on the likely fate of monuments in individual landscape types, and the resources needed for future conservation and management initiatives.

The challenge faced by the project was thus to quantify some of the basic characteristics of the archaeological resource, while reflecting the complicated links that exist between the main elements of the resource and variables such as landscape, monument form, survival, the influence of protective designations, and many more besides; links which represent the parameters for effective archaeological resource management. The urgency with which results were needed was highlighted by the increasing frequency of parliamentary questions about such subjects, for example one posed by Simon Hughes MP on the matter of ancient monuments under threat from ploughing on the eve of MARS getting under way (*Hansard*: Written Answers 6th May 1993, col 201).

Meeting the challenge required the fulfilment of a series of subsidiary objectives which are outlined in the following sub-sections.

1.4.1 Academic and intellectual
As a discipline, archaeological resource management is still developing, and requires information about, and an enhanced understanding of, the fundamental nature and extent of the material it is dealing with. To date, archaeological resource management has generated very little in the way of theoretical or conceptual literature, with the result that there were few models from which to build an approach for MARS. This is one reason why Chapters 2-4 of this report include detailed discussion of conceptual and definitional issues.

1.4.2 Practical and functional
A factual statement of the state of the resource is not only of academic interest, it is also necessary as a basis on which resource managers can develop, and present with professional confidence, positive approaches to preservation and protection. This is especially important where justification is needed for continued private and public sector expenditure on archaeology. Also, as archaeological considerations become increasingly important in environmental assessment, land-use planning, development control and estate management, it is crucial that robust information about the resource as a whole is available to allow comparisons and contrasts between the general and the particular.

Figure 1.2 - England's archaeology old and new. (Left) Excavations at Boxgrove, West Sussex, which revealed the earliest recorded evidence for human occupation in England, estimated at about half a million years ago. The site was discovered during gravel extraction. (Below) Second World War pill-box at Old Berwick, Northumberland, overlooking the valley of the River Till. The pill-box has been constructed inside a prehistoric fortification, the banks of which are visible behind the concrete pill-box. *[Photographs: (Left) English Heritage; (Below) Timothy Darvill. Copyright reserved]*

Various approaches to the classification and study of change to the archaeological resource have been undertaken in the past, and part of the MARS Project involved establishing what had been done and with what result. Care has been taken to relate these results, which were often based on small data-sets, to the wider picture drawn by MARS. Care is also required on the part of the reader. Different levels of analysis carry different implications: for example representative analyses will portray something of the picture over England, while definitive analyses involve a more accurate quantification. Information is drawn from thematic works researched by MARS and these are used as signposts, indicating many of the concepts addressed by the project. These local, regional and monument-specific studies of erosion and decay needed to be consolidated and placed in some sort of context.

1.4.3 Progressive and developmental

Identifying a baseline means that it will be possible to monitor future changes to the archaeological resource more effectively. However, this requires the recognition that change is worth recording systematically, and for this to happen it is necessary to establish and adopt agreed measures.

1.4.4 Relations and linkages

The results of MARS will contribute to the growing national picture of England's heritage resources, and furnish related environmental studies with data about the situation as far as archaeology is concerned. Equally, it must be recognized that any patterns that can be seen in the archaeological data are likely to be related, although not exclusively so, to wider social and economic trends and patterns. These deserve to be investigated.

1.5 Scope and coverage

MARS cannot be everything to everyone; there were limits to its scope. Geographically, MARS covered the land area and coastal fringe (i.e. foreshore) of England, estimated at a total area of $131,035km^2$, excluding offshore islands (Ordnance Survey 1995; Wisniewski 1997, 4). Offshore deep water archaeology was not included in the MARS Project.

The chronological coverage represented by the archaeological resource is very broad (Figure 1.2). At one end of the scale is the earliest evidence of human presence in England dated to about half a million years ago; at the other end are buildings and structures less than a century old. Indeed, it is now recognized that some archaeological records will include items of even more recent date, for example First and Second World War defences and emplacements, and occasionally still more modern structures.

In general, the archaeological resource was defined pragmatically as anything which has been reported to and recorded by archaeologists as being part of that resource during the systematic assembly of Sites and Monuments Records. Part of the MARS Project involved an examination of what that set of records actually comprised, and for this a specialist vocabulary was developed (see Chapter 2). However, one category of evidence which stood on the borderline of the project was

historic buildings. MARS was planned and executed before the computerization of the lists of buildings of special architectural and historical interest. At the time of data transfer between RCHME and MARS the lists of buildings of special architectural and historic interest had not been fully computerized; it was agreed that consulting the printed lists at that time would be too lengthy a process for MARS, but that in future this material would be an important additional source. All domestically occupied buildings whose construction post-dated *c*.AD 1700 were excluded from both the field survey and aerial photographic programmes, but included in the national survey of SMRs. Earlier buildings and later non-domestic unoccupied buildings and structures itemized on archaeological records were included in the MARS Project, although for some there were restrictions on the recording of certain information sets. These are considered further in Chapter 3. It should be emphasized, however, that the focus of the MARS Project was on the archaeological resource, and in the case of historic buildings it is these dimensions to which attention is directed.

Two other kinds of archaeological evidence were also only partly covered by MARS. For historic parks and gardens, the issue of aesthetic qualities and their overall contribution to 'landscape' in its wider sense was not encompassed by MARS, although the structures and remains that parks and gardens comprise were included. Hedgerows also would not traditionally be regarded as part of the archaeological resource, but during the early 1990s the historical significance of many boundaries became more widely understood, and, in 1997, protection for historic hedges was provided by the *Hedgerow Regulations 1997* (SI 1997 No. 1160). The regulations apply only to 'important' hedgerows, regarded as any hedgerow over 30 years old and satisfying at least one of the criteria listed in Part II of Schedule 1 to the regulations (e.g. marking the boundary of at least one historic parish or township, incorporating an archaeological feature or containing certain specified species). Since the introduction of these regulations, but too late for inclusion in the MARS Project, a number of archaeological records have been expanded to include details of historic boundaries of various sorts.

In summary, MARS was concerned with what are most conveniently described as 'monuments' as the main units of analysis because these represent the principal currency dealt with by local Sites and Monuments Records in the decades leading up to the survey. It will be interesting to see whether a future iteration of MARS finds a shift in emphasis towards the more holistic definitions of the archaeological resource being talked about at the time of survey (see above, 1.1), for example the developing emphasis on historic landscapes as units of analysis.

Although MARS is a census or snapshot of the archaeological resource at one point in time it is important to emphasize that it was achieved by examining a sample of what was known. The methodology adopted will be discussed further in Chapter 3. The census date is taken to be 1995, but in practice the various surveys that were carried out to collect data for MARS were all of slightly different duration. Further details are given in Chapter 3, but the National Survey took place in 1994-5, the Field Survey in 1994-6, the Aerial Photographic Survey in

1994-6 and the Case Study Research in 1994-6.

The timescale over which change is considered is from *c*.AD 1945 to 1995 (i.e. the census date of the project). This, of course, is the merest twinkling of an eye in comparison with the antiquity of many of the sites studied. For example, it represents just 1% of the time over which a typical Neolithic long barrow constructed *c*.3000 BC has survived, or 2.7% of the existence of a Roman villa constructed in AD 150, and still only 18% of the lifespan of a building constructed as recently as AD 1700. It is, however, the longest timescale that can reasonably be examined using the available sources of data.

1.6 Other environmental resource surveys

MARS does not stand alone. By its very nature it is connected, in a variety of ways, to recent or ongoing studies both within other areas of cultural resource management and in related environmental disciplines. Wherever possible contact has been made with these other initiatives, and information exchanged. Reference is made to results from most of these studies in later chapters; the following notes provide only a brief outline of their scope and coverage.

1.6.1 The archaeological and built heritage

The two programmes most closely related to MARS were undertaken by English Heritage and related to historic buildings and Scheduled Monuments:

Buildings at Risk Survey. This study was undertaken by English Heritage between 1990 and 1991 with the aim of establishing a picture of the general condition of Listed Buildings, and particularly the extent to which repairs were urgently required. A total of 43,794 Listed Buildings were surveyed (about 8.8% of the 500,000 Listed Buildings in England), although the sample was not statistically constituted (English Heritage 1992a).

Monuments Protection Programme. This long-term project aims to review and up-date the Schedule of protected ancient monuments. It was one of English Heritage's major ambitions when the new organization was set up in 1984. The MPP commenced in 1986 and has three aims (English Heritage 1997b):

1   The evaluation by monument class, taking account of regional diversity, of all known monuments, using SMR data where available and commissioning new national overviews in other cases.

2   The identification, confirmation and description of nationally important monuments with the definition of viable management regimes, notably but not exclusively through the use of Scheduling.

3   The dissemination of its results to inform the work of local government and others in protecting the historic environment through the planning process.

The first two of these aims are the most advanced. Over half of the recorded resource has been evaluated, and the Schedule has been increased in size from 12,500 to 17,000 monuments, a figure representing perhaps 32,000 individual sites or components of archaeological interest.

The MPP, like the MARS Project, involves visiting and documenting a sample of monuments. The MPP sample is not, however, spatially restricted but instead is defined by qualitative measures of significance based on criteria defining national importance (Darvill *et al.* 1987). These criteria take some account of condition and survival, but focus mainly on the archaeological attributes of monuments. The MPP does not include a measure of risk nor of the rate of recent decay; its data on the current condition of Scheduled Monuments are more detailed than those collected by MARS but do not readily support extrapolation to the national level. Finally, the MPP is planned to take place over a longer timescale, about two decades, and cannot provide a snapshot of the resource and its condition at any one time. There is thus no overlap in the objectives of the two programmes or duplication of effort between them. Indeed, MPP data have provided one of the frameworks within which to interpret MARS data, while MARS conclusions will help to target the MPP's scheduling work in terms of risk. The two programmes are therefore mutually supportive.

1.6.2 Studies in land-use change

Land-use changes provide a fundamental backdrop against which to view the changing state of preservation of archaeological monuments. In recent years land-use changes have also been a matter of considerable concern for other environmental disciplines and accordingly have been the subject of several parallel programmes of research and investigation:

Landscape Changes in Britain. This study was based on periodic surveys of the countryside in 1977-8 and 1984 by the Institute of Terrestrial Ecology (ITE). The aim was to determine the extent of recent changes taking place within characteristic land-uses and extrapolate this to a view of landscape as a whole. The methodology adopted involved measuring variables in a representative series of 384 1km by 1km sample units throughout Great Britain (Barr *et al.* 1986). This programme was continued for the turn of the decade as the Countryside Survey 1990, and a fourth iteration, Countryside Survey 2000, is planned.

Countryside Survey 1990. This integrated programme of field survey and remote sensing was completed by the Institute of Terrestrial Ecology to provided information on land cover and countryside features in Great Britain. The Countryside Survey used a stratified sampling strategy based on land-type. A total of 508 units, each of 1km², was used to sample the whole of Great Britain. Each unit was intensively examined, field survey being used to gain information on land cover and linear features, vegetation plots, freshwater fauna and soils. The survey incorporated land cover and land classification mapping based on information from ITE satellite imagery (Barr *et al.* 1993). The study forms the basis of the Countryside Information System.

Monitoring Landscape Change. Hunting Surveys and Consultants Limited undertook this detailed survey in 1986 to review current and past distributions of landscape features, and provide a quantification of the type of features and the rate of change they were undergoing. Aerial photography was used to measure change; information was gathered on the extent of features at around 1951, 1971 and 1981. The survey divided features into two main types: area features of more than 5km^2 and linear features. The project sampled approximately 2.4% of the land area of England and Wales for area features and 1.1% for linear features (Countryside Commission 1990a).

1.6.3 Resource mapping

Four studies that focus on mapping the incidence and distribution of environmental resources and habitats at national and local levels are more distantly relevant to MARS:

Natural Areas Map. English Nature undertook this mapping exercise, identifying land and coastal areas with distinct geological, geomorphological and habitat type zones. The work was based on interpreting Land Utilization Maps, Board of Agriculture reports and soil surveys, and identified and characterized 92 areas (English Nature 1993).

Phase 1 and 2 Habitat Surveys. English Nature co-ordinated these surveys, carried out at local level, with the aim of charting semi-natural vegetation types and wildlife habitats over large areas of countryside (NCC 1990; 1991). The work involved a combination of map inspection and rapid field survey. Coverage varied in completeness for different counties and it is currently unlikely that a complete national coverage will be created. The purpose, however, is to produce a rapid habitat mapping system. The next stage (known as Phase 2) will be the detailed botanical description of each habitat.

New Map of England. A proposal was made by the Countryside Commission to identify all the pieces that make up today's landscape, map their extent, describe the character of each piece, and link them together to paint a portrait of the English countryside in the 1990s (Gilder 1994). A pilot study was undertaken in the south-west of England, but the project was continued under the title 'The Countryside Character of England'.

Countryside Character Map. A partnership between the Countryside Commission, English Nature and English Heritage, this project developed map-based coverage depicting the natural and cultural dimensions of the English landscape by creating distinct and characteristic groupings of the landscape, wildlife, archaeological and natural features. Four different organizations compiled the information used for the archaeological overlays: Bournemouth University (Neolithic and Bronze Age archaeology); the Royal Commission on the Historical Monuments of England (earthwork survival); Lancaster University Field Archaeology Unit (industrial archaeology); and the Oxford Archaeological Unit (historic landscape patterns). In all, the project defined 181 discrete character areas and correlated them with the 92 Natural Areas defined by English Nature (Countryside Commission 1996a).

In addition, a series of summary statements has already been published, and detailed character descriptions are being prepared during 1997 for each of the character areas. The latter will provide a more comprehensive description and corpus of natural, historical and archaeological information, for example through species and habitat plans and settlement patterns / archaeological distributions.

1.6.4 Statistical surveys

The Environment Agency has brought together a survey of the state of the environment as a whole from official statistics under the title:

The Environment of England and Wales. A Snapshot. This study by the Environment Agency was designed to increase public awareness of the various pressures that exist on the environment. The topics covered include climate, population, land-use and crop production, water abstraction, flooding, energy consumption, transport, the atmosphere, water quality, waste management and radioactive materials (Environment Agency 1996).

1.6.5 Overview

Together these various reports and studies present a wide-ranging and detailed insight into the landscape and natural heritage of England, but none deals directly with the full range of cultural heritage represented by archaeological monuments. This was the purpose of MARS. During the time that MARS was being planned and executed, however, resource assessments concerned with monument condition and survival were carried out on a national scale in other countries and states, including, for example, Wales (Burnham 1991; Rees 1994), the Netherlands (Groenewoudt *et al.* 1994; Groenewoudt and Bloemers 1997), and parts of the United States of America (C Mathers pers. comm.).

1.7 Arrangement and contents of this report

MARS did not aim to identify specific monuments which were at more or less risk, rather it was directed at looking for general patterns which could be used in the development of strategic policies. As set out in this report, the findings follow closely the aims identified earlier in this chapter.

Chapters 2-4 preface the detailed results and findings with a general introduction to some of the issues and principles that underlie much of what MARS set out to achieve. In particular, Chapter 2 considers the underlying theory, conceptualization and terminology relevant to MARS. Chapter 3 deals with the methodology and implementation of MARS. Chapter 4 looks at the existing record of England's archaeological resource, what it contains and the way it has built up: this is critical to an appreciation of the interpretations which can be placed on quantified data.

Chapter 5 looks at what MARS revealed about the state of the resource at the census date. Chapter 6 then considers how the recorded archaeological resource has changed over the last half-century, noting especially the extent of damage and destruction. Chapter 7 explores the effects of land-use on archaeological remains, and Chapter 8 considers designations and their effect. The matter of risk is given detailed treatment in Chapter 9.

Finally, Chapter 10 summarizes some of the main points and develops some conclusions and recommendations under a series of key themes. Specialist and technical appendices support the text and are cross-referenced where appropriate. Three case studies have been included (in Chapters 2 and 3) in order to illustrate, especially for non-archaeologists, some of the characteristics of the material that MARS was concerned with.

Before embarking on the core chapters of this report, it is, however, appropriate and necessary to deal briefly with a number of limitations and constraints relating to what MARS achieved.

1.8 Limitations and constraints on MARS data

Carrying out the MARS Project was never easy, and every part of it was subject to numerous constraints and limitations. In presenting the results, therefore, great caution must be exercised in the way some of the data can be and should be used. First, MARS is the first general census of the archaeological resource in England. As already noted, some environmental resource surveys are in their second and third iterations, and, in consequence, have ironed out the sampling, technical and definitional problems which cannot be foreseen at the outset but which appear all too clearly during the first run. With no real history of monitoring or measuring change within the discipline of archaeology, the MARS Project started from

a very low experience base. Part of the MARS Project involved setting out baseline data (e.g. Chapters 4 and 5) of sorts which to some readers may seem obvious, but which have never previously been systematically collected or summarized on a national scale (Figure 1.3). In doing so a series of new terms and measures have been created which it is hoped can be developed and used in future. Baseline data are useful only as a starting point for future studies, and the work of MARS 1995 was partly intended to set the scene for a future iteration, perhaps in 2015.

Second, a good deal of what interests archaeologists cannot quickly and easily be measured. For example, the sub-surface survival of deposits is very important in determining the value of an archaeological site, yet the only practical way to obtain information on the subject is through field evaluation, a practice which is both expensive and time-consuming. The MARS findings must be set against the fact that they are based on visual observations and field inspection, although the field surveyors attempted to visualize and take into account the effects of land-use on buried deposits wherever they could.

Third, there are many variations in the definition of what constitutes archaeological material. Although a liberal and pragmatic definition has been adopted as the starting point for MARS (see above, 1.1) its application may not satisfy everyone. Moreover, as already noted, explicit definitions have had to be developed for many terms in order to build a working vocabulary with which to describe and discuss the archaeological material examined by MARS. Account has been taken of legal

Figure 1.3 - A systematic survey. MARS field survey team measuring a small round barrow on open moorland on Exmoor, Devon. *[Photograph: MARS Archive]*

definitions where appropriate, but in developing new definitions the guiding principle has always been the idea of producing interpretive statements about the past based on the application of general archaeological theory. It is recognized, however, that some of the data which are of interest to archaeologists with wider environmental concerns may extend beyond what is strictly relevant to the core needs of the discipline of archaeology.

Fourth, MARS is concerned with a national picture, broken down into regional blocks. It therefore deals mainly with large categories and groupings. The extent to which these can be broken down into smaller units depends on the nature of the analysis and the level of confidence that would be acceptable.

Fifth, MARS had to work with what there was at the census date of 1995 in terms of the best retrievable information in SMRs and, to a lesser extent, the National Monuments Record. In bringing together information on about 15,000 monuments from a range of sources a number of gaps and inconsistencies within and between records have inevitably come to light. It would be easy to play down the implications of such irregularities, but they are important. As discussed at greater length in Chapter 3, the main problem is non-random missing data, which means that most analyses must be descriptive rather than quantitative in a statistical sense. Examples of these incomplete data-sets include detailed geological coverage for England (some maps have never been published, so the information is not available equally for all areas), the poverty of aerial photographic coverage for some decades for sites in the MARS sample, and incorrect or mistranscribed information from earlier records. MARS researchers made strenuous efforts to reduce the number of errors in the MARS database, but with a data-set of this size drawn from so many different sources some inconsistencies will inevitably remain.

Sixth, archaeological resource management is a continuing process that is driven forward by studies and projects with typical durations of two to five years. Inevitably, in 1995, numerous initiatives were in train or were imminent and the results of these will, in some cases at least, have changed the picture of the archaeological resource, in a few cases rather drastically. However, the point of MARS was to examine the situation as at the census date; what is added or discovered after the census date will be the subject of analysis if and when MARS is repeated in the future. It will then be possible to judge the impact of these new pieces of work in a way which has simply not been possible hitherto.

Seventh, as already noted, MARS is concerned with broad patterns of change and risk. Detailed studies of, for example, changes to soil chemistry are certainly of interest, but cannot be dealt with in a study whose focus is the national picture. However, general theories of decay and change based on detailed case studies and experiments underpin much of the thinking behind MARS, and it is to these matters that attention is directed in the next chapter.

2 An archaeological perspective

Theoretical discussion involves defining terms, starting positions, setting up categorical boundaries. ... Our practices always necessarily employ generalities in order to make sense of what we find and do. What we measure and how we measure it are theoretical.

(Ian Hodder 1992, 2-5)

2.1 *Method and theory*

Archaeological resource management is now a well-established sector of archaeological endeavour in Britain (Fowler 1978; Baker 1983; Wainwright 1984; Hunter and Ralston 1993), other European countries (Cleere 1984; Willems *et al.* 1997), America (McGimsey 1972; Schiffer and Gumerman 1977; Nickens 1991), and many other parts of the world too (Cleere 1989). The principles which guide the practice of archaeological resource management have been evolving and developing over the last century or so, but relatively little attention has been devoted to the underpinning conceptual and theoretical frameworks. In the context of developing the MARS Project this epistemological lacuna was recognized as critical, because it has resulted in a general dearth of accepted models and perspectives through which to approach such subjects as the nature of the archaeological resource, decay patterns and the central concept of risk.

As practised in Britain during the 1990s, archaeological resource management is empiricist, in that empirical data derived mainly from controlled observation provide the basis for knowledge. Its philosophical outlook is essentially positivist, again taking empirically derived data as the basis for testing current understandings. Such an outlook naturally causes conflicts of interest, especially among potential users of data generated under the broad banner of archaeological resource management. On the one hand, conservationists and those most closely involved with the management of archaeological monuments operate within a mix of two not unrelated approaches. The first relates closely to what Popper (1959) described with enthusiasm as 'methodological nominalism', where the focus of attention is the form, patterning, behaviour and regularity of the objects or materials under study, leading in many cases to a rather vaguely conceptualized 'holistic' understanding of the place of the objects of attention in relation to their broader context. The second, grounded in capitalist ideology, involves the 'commodification' of the resource so that selected elements of it are identified for special and discrete treatment, often in a way that abstracts them from the contexts and relationships that make them what they are.

On the other hand, much archaeological research is constantly pulling in several directions at once. Amid a theoretically and philosophically pluralist mêlée of debate and argument that is fast-moving and keenly pursued, showers of disapproval sometimes rain down on the actions of those conservationist archaeologists whose primary role it is to look after the archaeological remains themselves. Even the positivists among those engaged in archaeological research have argued that overly zealous conservationism dampens progress in archaeology by limiting opportunities for excavation as the principal means of testing ideas and expanding knowledge (Biddle 1994; Carver 1994, 9; Morris 1994, 9).

In this chapter an attempt is made to address some of the main theoretical underpinnings of the MARS Project, not in terms of debating the merits or otherwise of the fundamental philosophies and approaches that inform archaeological resource management, but rather, as Ian Hodder enjoins us to do, to set out and examine the starting positions and categorical boundaries necessary to develop a methodology. In some respects these statements are simply the consolidation of thinking that is current within archaeological resource management but rarely articulated. There are five main sections which move from the general to the particular. First, attention is directed towards defining the general character of the archaeological resource and its broad subdivisions. Second, consideration is given to the components of the archaeological resource that form the subject of MARS: here termed archaeological sites and monuments. Third, there is some discussion of the idea of decay processes and their effect on the archaeological resource, considering two sets of case studies, long barrows and small Roman villas, in some detail. Fourth, the idea of amelioration as a counterpoint to decay is examined briefly, and finally the question of how to measure archaeological monuments and the related concepts of survival and risk is considered.

2.2 *The nature of the archaeological resource*

The body of material regularly referred to as the 'archaeological resource' comprises an extremely complicated set of data that has accumulated over a long period of time through the efforts (and therefore with the biases) of many individuals and organizations. What it currently comprises is discussed in Chapter 4, but as a prelude to that discussion it is necessary to formalize some concepts that allow the totality of the resource to be explored and analysed.

There is no easy definition of what the archaeological resource is, or how it is constituted, because, in practice, the resource is whatever data archaeologists take to be relevant to their discipline at a given point in time. In this sense it is an expanding universe, because in general more classes of material are drawn into the domain of archaeological research as time

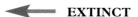

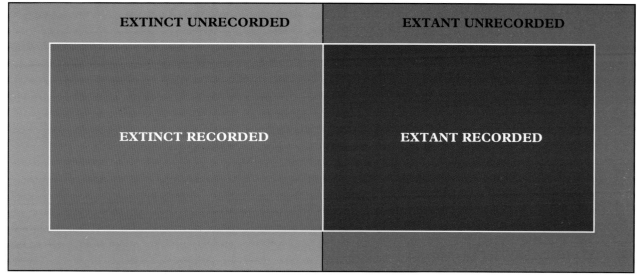

Figure 2.1 - Diagram showing a conceptual model of the archaeological resource split into its main components.

goes by. Recent extensions to the range of material considered relevant to archaeological work include the wealth of Second World War defensive structures dotted across the countryside and in our towns (Brown *et al.* 1995), numerous remains of the industrial past (Buchanan 1972; Major 1975), and parks and gardens (Taylor 1983; McRobie 1996a). Not all additions are necessarily of recent date, as shown by the identification of natural boulders propped up by stones that formed the focus of attention in prehistoric times (Bender *et al.* 1997, 152-3), and work which demonstrates the antiquity and significance of field boundaries and hedgerows (Fleming and Ralph 1982; Wildgoose 1991) which since 1997 are being added to local SMRs in some areas (e.g. Anon 1997c).

Changing the limits of what is considered archaeological does not have any effect on the scale of what was previously included within the definition of the archaeological resource. Taking the current definition of what is regarded as being archaeological as the main parameter, the resource so delimited can be arranged in a series of logical categories which serve to conceptualize the relationships between what is actually known (i.e. recorded) and remains that might potentially be known. Figure 2.1 attempts to show diagrammatically something of these interrelations between different categories or sectors of the archaeological resource, and to provide some vocabulary to start talking about them.

The starting point is what is here called the **original population.** This is an unknown and unknowable quantity which represents the sum total of all deposits, structures, monuments and other data that have ever been created or formed and which could potentially be of interest to archaeologists. Peter Fowler, among others, has suggested a way round the problem of defining the original population by accepting that the whole of England, an area of about 130,035km², is actually one single enormous archaeological site (Fowler 1977a, 48). And in the sense that people in the past occupied, and had

knowledge of, an area that was broadly speaking the same size then as it is now, this is true. However, it is widely recognized that not every piece of ground contains tangible archaeological deposits, and that for this reason the original population must in areal extent be less than the total land area.

Allied to the concept of the original population is the idea that although its components, however defined or recognized, had some kind of existence in the past they can only be experienced in the present. In archaeological interpretation there is thus a critical tension between what was and what is, while for archaeological resource management there is a tension between what there is and what there might be.

That part of the original population which is currently defined as interesting and relevant to archaeological study is, in pragmatic terms, definable as the **archaeological resource.** This is represented as the outer box on Figure 2.1. As already noted, the constant redefinition of what is considered relevant to the discipline of archaeology means that the frame of reference for the 'archaeological resource' is always changing its shape and size. In crude terms, the collective view of what the archaeological resource represents can be visualized as a sort of pastry-cutter chopping into the layer of all that could potentially be relevant (the original resource). At any point in time, therefore, the archaeological resource represents a finite, although in practice largely unknowable, quantity which is a sub-set of something which is, theoretically at least, infinite.

There are two reasons why recognizing the existence of the archaeological resource as a finite quantity is important. First, it allows estimates to be made of the size of recognizable sub-sets within some kind of context. Second, it offers a basis from which general estimates can be made of its size and characteristics. There are two main ways of estimating the overall size of the archaeological resource, although in practice both are severely restricted in their application. One way is to subdivide the archaeological resource into component parts, about which it is possible to say, with greater or lesser certainty, how many examples of a particular kind were created. Such information is rare, and is mostly confined to relatively recent times, when historical records provide detailed information. An obvious example is monastic houses, for which detailed documentary evidence exists (Roberts 1949). Another way of gauging the extent of the archaeological resource for any chosen measure is through estimates based on samples. By understanding the distribution patterns of past settlement strategies, and of depositional and post-depositional formation processes, it is possible to make inferences from the sampled population to the target population (in this case the archaeological resource), even if that target population no longer exists in its entirety. This kind of regional sampling has been widely used (Judge *et al.* 1975; Cherry *et al.* 1978), most notably in Britain in a study of east Hampshire (Shennan 1985).

There are many other ways of partitioning the archaeological resource, some of which will be considered later in this study. Two binary divisions are particularly relevant at this stage, however: the extent to which it is extant or destroyed, and whether it has been recorded or not. Figure 2.1 summarizes these divisions.

At any given point in time the archaeological resource will comprise elements which have physical existence, the **extant resource**, and other elements which have been lost or destroyed some time before this point, the **extinct resource**. The proportion of the archaeological resource which survives or has been destroyed is a time-specific statistic, and the balance is constantly changing with the moving present.

Archaeologists will know a portion of the archaeological resource, including both surviving and destroyed elements, in more or less detail. This may be termed the **recorded resource**, and it is this portion of the archaeological resource that forms the subject of MARS. In practical terms, the recorded resource is the sum total of all that has been registered, catalogued and itemized to date. The National Monuments Record (NMR) and numerous local Sites and Monuments Records (SMRs) based in local authorities throughout England have been assembling this data over the last 30 years or so, although the origins of such records go back much further (see Chapter 4). Of course, much valuable and important information about sites, monuments and the archaeological resource in general also exists in places other than SMRs. Sources such as private collections, museum-based records, and unconsolidated data in primary and secondary sources will inevitably yield new material to expand the record in breadth or depth. However, for logistical reasons these additional sources and archives were outside the remit of MARS, although as Chapter 4 highlights there is a great deal of scope for using these sources in future.

The **extant recorded resource** is that part of the archaeological resource that has been recorded and which still exists as recognizable features, whether above or below ground. This too is a point-in-time figure, the difference between the recorded resource and the extant recorded resource being the number of recorded monuments lost since being recorded, the latter being the **extinct recorded resource**.

That part of the archaeological resource not itemized on recognized archaeological records is the **unrecorded resource**. Part of this is extinct, the **extinct unrecorded resource**, and can never be recorded or understood (one exception to this may be where an independent record of it was created before its destruction but the content of this record has not yet been brought into the archaeological domain; obvious examples include old aerial photographs which show features that have long since gone). The other part is extant, the **extant unrecorded resource**, but not yet recognized for what it is; this is the sector of the archaeological resource that forms the subject of surveys to discover and identify it. Wherever studies have been carried out to compare the extant recorded resource with the extant unrecorded resource it is clear that much more exists to be found than is known already, in many cases between five and ten times more (Richards 1978, 11; Darvill 1986, 19).

Within these broad subdivisions of the archaeological resource more detailed analysis requires the definition of more precise categories of entity.

2.3 Archaeological sites and monuments

Within archaeology there is nothing equivalent to the taxonomies available in the biological sciences, or the habitat definitions used in ecology, for the classification and categorization of remains and deposits. Two general terms in widespread usage - 'sites' and 'monuments' - provide the basic generic vocabulary, although when MARS began both terms were the subject of considerable discussion.

The term **site** has a general usage as a place where archaeological remains have been found, sometimes with the implication that they are no longer there any more (as in 'Roman Villa, site of' on Ordnance Survey maps). The same term, **site** or sometimes **site event**, has also developed a more stringent technical usage in the course of the development of new approaches to the construction and compilation of archaeological record systems. Here the term is used to refer explicitly and exclusively to an area of land, which may be any size from a few square meters upwards to several square kilometres or more, within or over which an event involving the structured observation of some aspect of the archaeological content of that land has taken place (Darvill and Gerrard 1994, 8-9; Foard 1997). A site is really thus a 'sight' or window onto the archaeological resource which lies in, on or above the ground. The most common kinds of site include excavations, study areas covered by various kinds of watching brief or survey (e.g. geophysical survey, aerial photographic interpretation and mapping unit), places where objects are found, whether by accident (stray finds) or design (fieldwalking etc.), places where visible features can be observed directly (e.g. descriptions, pictures, map depictions), and places where tradition identifies the former existence of visible features (e.g. place-names). The limits of a site are defined by those carrying out the events or structured observations. Obviously, a site cannot exist within an archaeological record system unless some kind of record of the structured observations also exists. By the same token, there will be variations in the quality and precision of the records made and thus in the value of sites in terms of their contribution to the discipline of archaeology. Thus a critical appreciation of the data represented by a site is essential.

This technical definition of a site provides a valuable cover-term to deal with a wide range of archaeological operations that in themselves cannot be regarded as elements of the archaeological resource but which are essential to the development of an understanding of the resource, for example the use of geophysical prospection as a method of exploring apparently sterile ground. It is in this technical sense that the term site is generally used within the MARS Project. But how is the archaeological resource itself defined?

Traditionally, the term used to refer in a generic sense to the principal components of the archaeological resource is **monument**. In some ways it is a strange term, meaning 'anything enduring that serves to commemorate or make celebrated' *(Concise Oxford Dictionary of Current English,* 1990 edition), from the Latin *monumentum.* Disquiet with the term has a long history: Baldwin Brown (1905, 16) discussed its meaning at some length in the early years of the century, and a number of authorities have suggested abandoning its use in relation to archaeology, for example Greeves (1989, 664). However, abandonment would be difficult, since it has a clearly established legal meaning as well as an increasingly well-defined technical usage.

Legal usage stems back to the first ancient monuments legislation, the *Ancient Monuments Protection Act 1882* (Ch.73, S11). Subsequent re-enactments perpetuated the term. It is defined closely for the first time in the *Ancient Monuments Act 1931* (Ch.16, S15(1)). In current legislation, the *Ancient Monuments and Archaeological Areas Act 1979,* the word 'monument' is both retained in the title and given precise definition in the text (Ch.46, S61(7)) as being:

(A)   any building, structure or work, whether above or below the surface of the land, and any cave or excavation;

(B)   any site comprising the remains of any such building, structure or work or of any cave or excavation; and

(C)   any site comprising, or comprising the remains of, any vehicle, vessel, aircraft or other movable structure or part thereof which neither constitutes nor forms part of any work which is a monument within paragraph (A) above; and any machinery attached to a monument shall be regarded as part of the monument if it could not be detached without being dismantled.

Subject to certain restrictions, any monument (as defined above) that is considered to be of national importance can be included on a Schedule maintained by the Secretary of State (Ch.46, S2(4)); while it remains on that list such a monument is known as a Scheduled Monument. Scheduled Monuments are subject to the protective measures which apply to such monuments under the *Ancient Monuments and Archaeological Areas Act 1979.* Moreover, all Scheduled Monuments, and any other monuments which in the opinion of the Secretary of State are of public interest by reason of the historic, architectural, traditional, artistic or archaeological interest

attaching to them, are defined in the 1979 Act as Ancient Monuments (Ch.46, S61(12)). This category is further expanded for England by the *National Heritage Act 1983* (Ch.47, S33(8)), which also allows 'any structure, work, site, garden or area which in the Commission's [i.e. the Historic Buildings and Monuments Commission, usually referred to as English Heritage] opinion is of historic, architectural, traditional, artistic or archaeological interest' to be an ancient monument. Curiously, the term 'site' is not defined in the legislation, although it is widely used in contexts which imply something very similar to that described above, namely a place where remains have been discovered by some means or other, without necessarily implying that anything is extant or that the site itself represents the complete entity.

Technical use of the term monument increasingly draws on the post-processualist theoretical axiom that the past can exist only in the present. Thus a monument as a definable building, structure or work can have archaeological integrity because it represents the contemporary embodiment of the physical context, setting or result of one or more activities that took place in the past. This raises an interesting philosophical dilemma concerning the definition and recognition of monuments, however: although they are believed to have a quasi-autonomous existence in the sense that they have substance before being recognized and defined, discovery is itself an interpretive process based on contemporary meanings and understandings. The solution to the dilemma is to accept that what are now called monuments are created twice. The first time, in the past, mainly involved a physical process. What was created was not in itself the monument but rather something or some arrangement that had meaning and relevance to its builders and users. The second creation takes place in the present and is an intellectual process involving the interpretation and formal categorization of a transformed variation of the original creation as what can now be called a monument. In relating this to the technical definition of a site we may note that the basis for making these interpretations will essentially be information generated from structured observations. A single site, because it has spatial definition, may of course provide data on one or more monuments. Equally, a monument may be known through data from one or more sites.

If this line of argument is accepted it has two crucial corollaries. First, and rather obviously, physical remains formed in the past, which allow the creation of monuments in the present, exist out in the world to be found. This is also central to the idea that the archaeological resource at any one time is a sub-set of the original population. Second, and perhaps less obviously, the intellectual process of defining and understanding monuments is never complete, because of the dialectical nature of the research process and the fact that the present is always moving on. Thus any statement about a monument must be regarded as provisional.

MARS took as its starting point the legal definitions of the term 'monument' as set out in the 1979 and 1983 Acts, although in doing so we recognize the technical demands of defining monuments in terms that move beyond simple equations between past and present states of existence. For practical reasons a number of phenomena that fall within the broad legal definition of

Figure 2.2

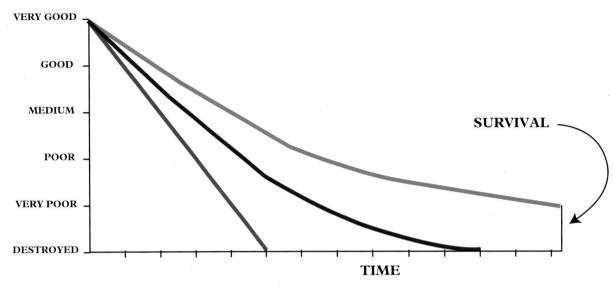

Figure 2.2 - Specimen decay profiles for archaeological materials.

'monuments' were excluded; these are dealt with in Chapter 3 which considers the methodology in detail.

Whether seen as a legal entity or purely as the building blocks of the archaeological resource, monuments have certain characteristics that are critical for MARS. First is the idea that what is defined as a monument at any point in time represents the interpretation of a physical entity that is itself a transformed variation of something that existed previously. In making interpretations of the past, archaeologists are constantly wrestling with the way in which such transformations contort and modify the data at their disposal. The operation and control of these transformations is the primary concern of archaeological resource managers. Secondly, monuments have spatial boundaries to their existence, both horizontally and vertically, and these can provide a way to define them and to monitor, somewhat crudely, the processes of transformation.

2.4 A model of transformations: decay processes and archaeological monuments

The archaeological record is a product of human activities, both at the time of its creation and through the changes that have occurred since. But the transmission of archaeological materials from their formation down to the present is a process which is subject to various transformations, and these are particular to individual monuments. Schiffer (1976; 1987) provides a useful framework for considering the changing circumstances of information in the archaeological record at the monument level, subdividing the formation processes into 'systemic contexts', relating to the initial creation of deposits, and 'archaeological contexts', which relate to the formation of the entities which archaeologists actually deal with.

In simplistic terms these transformations can be used to develop a sort of 'life-cycle' for any given monument, best characterized as a series of stages or

biographical episodes: construction, use, re-use, adapted use, desertion, dereliction (?monumental status), decomposition, deterioration and disappearance. The later stages of this cycle provide a rough measure of the general state of a monument and the way it is represented archaeologically (upstanding, flattened or destroyed), and these stages are considered in later chapters. The concept of a life-cycle provides a model of how monuments change, a decay model which works through time.

Inevitably, individual parts of the archaeological record, for example earthworks, timber buildings, bone needles or ironwork, begin to change and decay from the moment of deposition or creation. However, the rate at which decay occurs depends upon a wide range of factors, principal among which are:

- the durability of the components and materials
- the environment of deposition
- the environment after deposition
- the processes of attrition (e.g. chemical, physical etc.)
- the effects of subsequent and on-going human activities.

As Les Groube proposed, the life-cycle of a given monument, or part of a monument (e.g. a specific artefact or ecofact), can be visualized graphically as a decay curve extending along an axis representing time as calculable from the point of construction of a monument or the deposition of material (Groube and Bowden 1982, 15; Darvill 1986, 46). Characteristically, such a decay curve begins steeply, as the archaeological components become acclimatized to their surroundings, followed by a shallower fall-off as the components, now more stable, gradually change and stabilize in relation to their surroundings. Figure 2.2 shows a series of specimen decay profiles for archaeological materials modelled in this way.

Within any given monument, some remains of the activities originally undertaken there will be more durable than others, while some monuments are more robust than others. In exceptional circumstances materials will be preserved in particularly favourable environments on either a micro- or macro-scale. Thus the decay curves describing the transformation of some monuments, and even the different components within a monument, will be so short and steep that nothing survives into the present day, while others will, by comparison, be long and shallow, with much evidence still surviving.

The mechanics of the decay process affecting archaeological deposits are not yet well understood. Scientific and technical studies relevant to this matter are being undertaken, but this is only a beginning. APPENDIX B provides a select bibliography for this field and illustrates something of the diversity of the work being done. At one end of the scale studies of the behaviour of artefacts are especially important for the understanding and interpretation of patterns of structured deposition. It is also possible that in future the study of a sample of artefacts from a monument will allow general statements to be made about its general condition and preservation. What is already clear, however, is that localized environments within monuments give rise to considerable variations in the decay of different kinds of materials. The same applies to ecofacts and environmental materials, where again both physical and chemical agencies affect survival.

At the other end of the scale research is being undertaken on the decay of whole structures, and here the results from the study of experimental earthworks are especially important. The two earthworks constructed in the early 1960s under a programme established by the British Association for the Advancement of Science (Jewell 1963) at Overton Down, Wiltshire, and Morden Bog, Wareham, Dorset (Figure 2.3), provide information

at all levels from artefacts and materials through to structure and stratigraphy (Fowler 1989; Bell *et al.* 1996). Differences in the decay rates represented at the two earthworks can already be seen and are considerable. At Overton Down, on chalk, the bank reduced in height from its maximum of 1.52m in 1960 to 1.22m in 1992 (19% reduction in 32 years), while the centre of the ditch silted up from an original depth of 1.75m to 1.55m over the same period. The bank did not spread very much during this erosion, not at all on the north side and by only 0.3m on the south. In contrast, at Wareham, on lowland sandy heath, the bank diminished from 1.52m in 1963 to 1.14m in 1980 (25% reduction in 17 years), while the ditch silted from its original depth of 1.75m to 1.47m over the same period. There was also noticeably more spread of the earthwork, 0.9m to the south and 1.3m to the north. These very general figures disguise a great deal of detailed information about the way in which this erosion took place and changes to the profiles of the banks and ditches as a result. The quality of this kind of data, and its implications for monument management and conservation, make it highly desirable that further experimental work be started soon, so that comparable information can be generated for other kinds of environment, for example clayland, gravel and open upland moor.

The results of monitoring *in situ* preservation schemes to see how management actions affect the decay profiles of artefacts, ecofacts, stratigraphy and structures are also of great potential importance. Most of these projects are still at an early stage and it would be premature to make judgements from the results to date. Many more carefully conceived monitoring programmes are needed, however, to reflect the diversity and range of

Figure 2.3 - View of the experimental earthwork at Overton Down, Wiltshire. (Left) As constructed in 1960. (Right) After 32 years of decay in 1992 showing the ditch sediments and buried soil. This and other experimental earthworks illustrate decay processes at work. *[Photographs courtesy of Martin Bell and the Experimental Earthworks Committee. Copyright reserved]*

situations represented by the archaeological resource as a whole.

If natural processes alone were responsible for shaping the decay curves of archaeological monuments then, excepting the effects of natural disasters such as landslips, floods and so on, the profiles of some curves would be of smooth inverse exponential form. In fact, human intervention has undoubtedly been one of the most significant factors in shaping the decay curves of most monuments and these variations in human intervention through time make the profiles uneven and irregular.

Looked at over a long-term perspective, the patterning and regularity of the impact of such human influences are closely related to the nature of the landscape in which the monuments are set. Thus in upland areas the decay curves are probably stepped, each step corresponding with an identifiable episode of colonization, expansion, exploitation and retreat. In lowland areas, which have been subject to prolonged arable cultivation, steepening of the decay curves can be postulated to coincide with major phases of agricultural intensification such as those known in the later Iron Age, the Roman period, early medieval times, and the enclosure movement of the seventeenth and eighteenth centuries AD.

Thus in trying to measure and understand the patterns of change through which monuments pass it is first necessary to acknowledge that 'decay' is an ongoing process that affects all monuments. In speaking of damage or loss through human intervention, be it ploughing, quarrying or some other process, we are actually talking of an acceleration of the 'natural decay' process - in short, 'accelerated decay'. The following case studies show how the biographies of a selection of monuments reflect the decay processes and how different elements of the archaeological record at each are affected.

2.5 Case Study 1: long barrows [1]

Long barrows represent one of the earliest and most widespread classes of field monuments recorded in England. They date mainly to the middle Neolithic period, about 4000-3000 BC, and consist of a rectangular or trapezoidal mound with a length, generally in the range of 25 to 120m, of over twice the greatest width. The mound may be constructed primarily of stone, turf or soil or a mixture of these, and may be revetted internally and/or externally by timber, turf or stone. Key components include internal cell-like chambers of stone or wood, quarry pits or flanking ditches, a façade at the highest and widest end, and sometimes a forecourt. Examples are widely scattered over England with major regional groupings in the Cotswolds, Wessex, East Anglia and the Yorkshire and Lincolnshire Wolds. Other smaller groups include the Medway Valley (Kent), the Peak District (Derbyshire) and Bodmin Moor (Cornwall). Stone was widely used in their construction in the north and west, while timber was mainly used for structural elements in the south and east. Figure 2.4 shows a reconstruction drawing of the Fussell's Lodge long barrow near Salisbury in Wiltshire (Ashbee 1966).

The survival of long barrows varies tremendously according to topography, geology, land-use and, in particular, the materials of construction, leading to an equal variety of decay curves. Three excavated examples in differing states of survival at the time of their excavation serve to illustrate something of this variety (see Figure 3.2

Figure 2.4 - Reconstruction drawing showing an interpretation of the original appearance of the Fussell's Lodge long barrow, Wiltshire. *[Drawing by Elizabeth Meikle for the Ministry of Public Building and Works. Reproduced by permission of Paul Ashbee. Copyright reserved]*

Figure 2.5 - Long barrows. (Top left) Hazleton North, Gloucestershire, in 1979; (Right) Giants' Hills 1 and 2, Lincolnshire, in 1961; (Below left) Tiverton, Devon, in 1985. *[Photographs: (Top left) Timothy Darvill; (Right) Cambridge University Collection of Air Photographs; (Below left) Exeter City Museum. Copyright reserved]*

for the position of the monuments considered here):

Hazleton North, Gloucestershire, was in good condition (equivalent to 'Good' areal survival as defined below in 2.9) at the time of its excavation between 1979 and 1982 (Saville 1990).

Giants' Hills 2, Lincolnshire, was in medium condition

(equivalent to 'Medium' / 'Good' areal survival as defined below in 2.9) when excavated in 1975-6 (Evans and Simpson 1991).

Tiverton, Devon, was in poor condition (equivalent to 'Poor' / 'Medium' areal survival as defined below in 2.9) when excavated in 1985 by the Central Excavation Unit (Smith 1990).

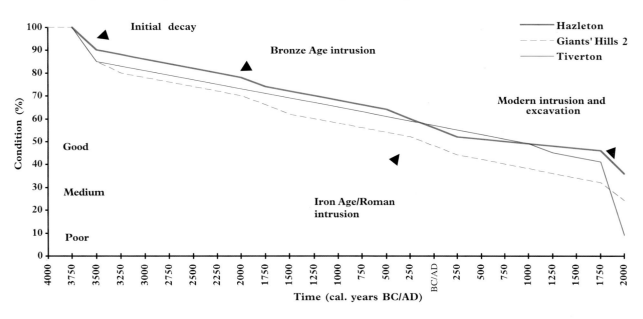

Figure 2.6 - Specimen decay profiles for three excavated long barrows.

Figure 2.5 shows a view of each of the three barrows shortly before they were excavated. Figure 2.6 shows specimen decay profiles for each, based on what is known from the excavations about its history and use. In the following sub-sections attention focuses on four major data categories: monument scale, features and components, artefacts, and ecofacts.

2.5.1 Monument scale

The boundaries of long barrows are conventionally defined by the mound or cairn, but other components such as forecourt features or deposits, ditches, quarry pits and eroded portions of the mound may lie outside or adjacent.

The Hazleton mound was well defined as relatively little material had eroded from the monument, apart from the collapse of the external revetting at some time during the later Neolithic. The original dimensions of the cairn were easily determined from the basal courses of the revetment, which was still largely *in situ* except at the eastern end where ploughing had removed all traces of it. When excavated, the cairn had a maximum height of 1.70m, and was 19m wide and 56m long. The original height was postulated to be in the region of 2.80m. Erosion of the mound can be calculated with reference to various rather precise historical accounts. When visited in 1883 the mound stood some 2.75m tall (Witts 1883, 79). O G S Crawford estimated the mound to be the same height on 20th November 1920 but noted that the monument was then under the plough (Crawford 1925, 102); on 28th September 1959 the height had been reduced to 1.90m (O'Neil and Grinsell 1960, 81). With a height in September 1979 of 1.70m, this represents an estimated loss of 1.1m (40% of its height) over 60 years. It is estimated that about 30% of the volume of the mound has been lost since the barrow was constructed. The collapse in antiquity of the revetment walls, and the consequent spread of the mound, helped to preserve deposits such as those of the forecourt from dispersal by recent ploughing.

Quarry pits lay beside the barrow, but were not recognized prior to the excavation. Both quarries were found to be about 2.5m deep and their upper fills showed shallow plough disturbance.

Some intrusion was noted in the body of the cairn, probably casual investigation and limited stone robbing in the eighteenth and nineteenth centuries AD. The south chamber showed more serious and determined intrusion, with the removal of stone blocking and paving stones from the passage, possibly during the Roman period to judge from the find of a large, unabraded sherd of Severn Valley ware. The excavator postulated that ploughing since the nineteenth century was likely to have contributed substantially to the collapse and infilling of some internal spaces.

The Giants' Hills 2 long barrow showed a significant degree of erosion to the mound, which was 65m long, 13m wide and up to 0.9m high when excavated. It was estimated to have originally been about 77m long and 19m wide; it was probably about 2m high. Some 45% of the area of the mound had been eroded and it is estimated that about 60% of the volume of the mound has been lost. Where it survived, on the north edge, the mound was clearly delimited by a line of chalk blocks, probably representing external revetting. Forecourt and façade features were preserved beneath soils partially derived from the eroded mound. The ditches were wholly infilled, up to 2m deep, and had clearly encircled the entire mound.

Giants' Hills 2 suffered attrition to its stratigraphy and integrity from tillage and ploughing in the Beaker, Roman and medieval periods. The monument was constructed on chalk bedrock and overlain by an alkaline topsoil up to 0.4m deep. The mound sealed a buried soil averaging about 0.1m in depth. The mound, which was composed of soils and chalk rubble derived from the quarry ditch, had been substantially eroded and survived to a height of 0.90m at the eastern end. The quarry ditch was unusual in having been partially backfilled and extended some 10m further to the west. The infilling of the ditch was composed of eroded material from the mound including ploughsoils of Roman and medieval origin. These episodes of ploughing had caused the greatest damage to the mound, but the use of the monument as a boundary marker, forming the corner of a field, caused increased erosion of the south and west sides, so that some 60% of the mound had been destroyed by the time of excavation. During the excavation the old field boundary was found to be a linear zone of tree root intrusion. In addition, three pits of indeterminate date and function had been cut into the chalk bedrock on the south and west sides of the monument.

The Tiverton long barrow showed considerable erosion of the mound, and at least 40% was lost when the eastern end was bulldozed in 1985. At the time of excavation, the monument stood up to 0.60m high, 12m wide and about 50m long. The original dimensions of the mound could not be defined because no kerbing or revetment features were noted; the excavator suggested an original length of about 90m. It is estimated that about 80% by volume of the monument had been lost before the excavation began. No forecourt, façade or mortuary features were observed. The ditch was clearly visible and was investigated in seven places; up to 3.25m deep, the fill showed a simple sequence of primarily natural silting with little interruption.

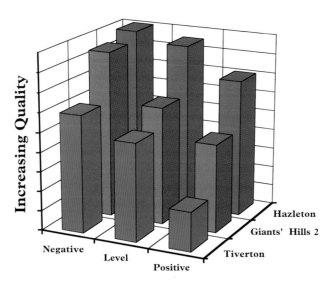

Figure 2.7 - Quality of archaeological features recorded at three excavated long barrows.

Before the bulldozing, ploughing appears to have almost levelled the mound so that by 1985 it stood only 0.60m above the surrounding ground level. An old mill leat may also have intruded upon the monument; it apparently followed part of the southern edge of the mound and possibly re-used a stretch of the ditch. Cartographic evidence suggested the monument was also used as a reference point for field systems and was probably damaged as a result.

2.5.2 Features and components

Long barrows are complicated structures with a wide range of features and components. In addition to those already mentioned in the preceding sub-section, almost all contain stone or wooden chambers, internal revetting and revetment walls, and forecourt features such as pits and hearths, while some will also have a façade, and perhaps negative features cutting the mound and its surroundings. Beneath the mound there will be a buried land surface which may itself contain features. Figure 2.7 shows graphically, and in highly simplified form, the survival patterns for positive, negative and level (e.g. surfaces and spreads) features as revealed during the excavations.

Hazleton North revealed much information about the construction of the mound. It had clearly been marked out by dumps of soils placed in a line. Internal cells of dry-stone revetting were built to contain less coherent dumps of limestone, which made up the bulk of the cairn. The orthostats of the passages and chambers were put in place early in this sequence of events and their corbelled walling was probably constructed as the main body of the cairn was raised. The whole of the cairn was encircled with an outer revetment of dry-stone walling which was interrupted by the entrances to the chamber passages and probably built up higher in the area of the forecourt horns. Mortuary deposits and a small quantity of artefacts were placed or perhaps processed in the passages and chambers. The forecourt area included two deposits of soils with animal bone, overlying the pre-cairn soil and apparently related to use of the monument.

Beneath the cairn was an old land surface with deposits and features relating to a possible earlier Neolithic settlement. The quarry pits were filled with a sequence of primary, secondary and tertiary fills, having been left open when the monument was completed. A hearth and deposits of pottery and animal bone were noted in the primary fills and related to activity soon after the completion of the monument.

The mound at Giants' Hills 2 was substantially eroded, which meant that only a little of the construction sequence could be recovered. Bays defined by timber fences were infilled with a basal layer of chalk rubble and topped with an upper layer of chalky soil. The loss of most of the upper strata precluded the preservation of secondary inhumations. Under the mound was evidence for a timber structure, built around a pair of large postholes, and a façade constructed of timber uprights bedded in a trench and packed with chalk. The façade was burnt down before the mound was built. All this activity took place over a buried soil, the structure of which indicated that tillage had taken place.

Severe damage to the mound at Tiverton precluded the recovery of all but the most basic data. A central core of sandstone slabs was overlain by layers of gravel and loam with some evidence for turf, but nothing could be said about the upper mound or its edge. No features associated with pre-cairn activity or primary burial survived apart from occasional and scattered patches of buried soil in slight hollows. The only major component which survived in anything approaching reasonable condition was the ditch, although it had been cut by modern drainage features. The fills showed a natural silting sequence with no backfilling or deposits of cultural material.

2.5.3 Artefacts

In general, the condition of the artefacts recovered at Hazleton North was good, although pottery with calcareous inclusions did suffer some decay in the decalcified sub-cairn soil. Bone artefacts were concentrated in calcareous burial contexts, a relatively protected micro-environment. Certain contexts within and under the barrow contained most of the artefactual evidence: the sub-cairn soil and the burial deposits were key artefactual components.

The quality and size of the pottery assemblage permitted detailed analysis to focus on fabrics and forms, and thus allowed meaningful comparisons with other assemblages. The flint assemblage was also of a quality and quantity which permitted detailed analysis and dating parallels. Some 20 pieces of flint were found associated with the burials, including two arrowheads and four cores. One of these cores was deposited with Skeleton 1 in the entrance to the north chamber. Stone artefacts were also recovered including hammerstone pebbles and quern or rubber stone fragments. Six bone artefacts, four beads and two points, were recovered, mainly from the burial deposits. Among a small quantity of fired clay fragments was one positively identified as daub, with clear wattle impressions, a particularly rare find in early and middle Neolithic contexts.

Most of the early Neolithic pottery from Giants' Hills 2 came from the buried ground surface under the mound. Other pottery strongly suggests later re-use of the monument: Roman and medieval sherds were found in the upper ditch fills and within the ploughsoil. Sixteen pieces of worked flint were found, all but one from the buried soil.

The only prehistoric artefacts from Tiverton were 24 pieces of worked flint and chert. Most were from the upper ditch fills and were interpreted as residual. One was a gun flint. One piece was securely stratified in a Neolithic context. A few sherds of post-medieval pottery were found in the upper ditch fills.

2.5.4 Ecofacts

Over 9,000 human bones or fragments were recovered from Hazleton North. The overwhelming majority came from the chambers, representing the remains of 22 adults, at least 13 pre-adults, and 2 foetuses. One adult and a pre-adult were represented by cremation deposits. The condition of the skeletal material was generally good, with limited damage caused by the collapse of corbelling and roofing into the chambers, and only a few instances of animal toothmarks. The condition, quantity and distribution of the skeletal material allowed detailed analysis of age, sex, pairing, articulation and pathology (injury, infections, inflammatory disease, joint disease).

A substantial assemblage of animal bone was also collected at Hazleton, 2813 fragments in various states of preservation. Bone from basal quarry fills and upper cairn contexts showed severe weathering and pitting while bone from the sub-cairn soil or the basal cairn showed little weathering or decay. A small quantity of randomly scattered bone was found within the fabric of the cairn and 55 antler picks were found abandoned in the quarries. The forecourt included deposits of bone, principally of pig and cattle, which apparently represented primary butchery waste.

Both molluscan and pollen samples were poorly preserved, largely owing to the strongly decalcified nature of the sub-cairn soils. Charcoal fragments and carbonized grain were recovered in good condition from the pre-cairn soil, and together with the limited pollen and molluscan evidence produced a general picture of the immediate environment of the monument.

At Giants' Hills 2, 44 pieces of human bone were recovered, representing a minimum of three or four individuals. The condition of the bone was mixed: where little or no disturbance had taken place, the bone was relatively well preserved but most showed a degree of damage from various sources. The physio-chemical weathering of surfaces indicated pre-deposition disturbance, as did damage by scavenging animals and obvious disarticulation. Post-deposition damage was noted and assumed to have occurred during the collapse of the timber chamber, resulting in the crushing of the skulls and breakage of long bones in particular. The condition of the human bone severely restricted the level

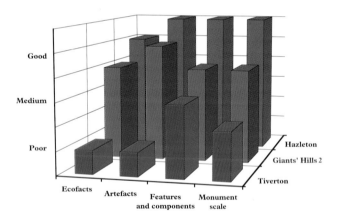

Figure 2.8 - Quality of data categories recovered from three excavated long barrows.

of analysis possible; no metrical analysis to help definition of age and sex was possible. Evidence for pathology was limited to one incidence of interdental abscess (temporomandibular) and one incidence of joint disease.

Over 400 pieces of animal bone were recovered, the majority (70%) from later Neolithic or Beaker ditch contexts. Small quantities were recovered from the mound (2.1%), the façade trench (0.7%) and the buried soil (3.4%). Condition was generally poor, with few complete bones and very few long bones with complete articular surfaces. Much physio-chemical weathering was evident: bone surfaces were often heavily pitted.

Other ecofactual evidence included charcoal and molluscan remains recovered primarily from column

samples. The combination of charcoal and molluscan evidence presented a full profile of the local environment before, during and after the active life of the monument.

No human bone was recovered from Tiverton. The ecofactual evidence is derived entirely from the buried soil which provided information about the pre-barrow environment. Primary woodland clearance was succeeded by an open grassland environment, possibly maintained by grazing animals from a nearby settlement. The absence of human remains is attributable to the destruction of the eastern portion of the barrow rather than degradation in acid soils.

2.5.5 Discussion

These three barrows illustrate both the complexity of circumstances at different monuments, and also the close relationship between the survival of the monument as a whole and the quality of the information that can be derived from it. Figure 2.8 shows in summary form the survival characteristics of all four factors considered in the foregoing sub-sections. It is clear that the best-preserved barrow contains a wealth of information. Investigations of Hazleton North radically changed views on the construction, dating and use of long barrows. It is estimated that at the time of its excavation it had lost perhaps 30% of its original volume and a commensurate degree of archaeological integrity. The excavation report shows that information about the original appearance of the structure is missing, as is evidence which would provide insights into the initial decay of the upper mound. Giants' Hills 2 was less complete, having lost perhaps 60% of its original volume by the time of excavation, although the differences in the level of information which could be recovered were not especially marked, except in respect of the quality and condition of the burial deposits. In part, however, this relates to the nature of the original construction (timber rather than stone) and the less intensive use of the chamber areas.

The greatest difference in information yield can be seen by comparing Hazleton North and Giants' Hills 2 with the Tiverton long barrow. The last site had lost about 80% of its original volume by the time of excavation, and as a result yielded little more than evidence for its former existence and information from the ditches.

All long barrows, no matter how poor their survival, contain some valuable information; indeed some kinds of inquiry (for example studies of quarry fill processes or pre-cairn environments) may be better based on a poorly preserved example than a well-preserved example. However, taking the monument as a whole, the critical point on the decay curve for long barrows is when more than 50-60% of the volume of the monument is lost. At about this point the information content relating to the main features (especially burials and chamber structure) begins to be compromised and very careful attention needs to be given to the potential of long barrows on a monument by monument basis according to the precise circumstances which obtain. Moreover, it is important that the matter of survival is not confused with the concept of archaeological value or importance. The two are quite different, the latter being based on a wide range of factors of which survival might be one element.

Figure 2.9 - Reconstruction drawing showing an interpretation of the original appearance of the Gorhambury Roman villa, St Albans, Hertfordshire. *[Drawing by Frank Gardiner. Reproduced by permission of English Heritage. Copyright reserved]*

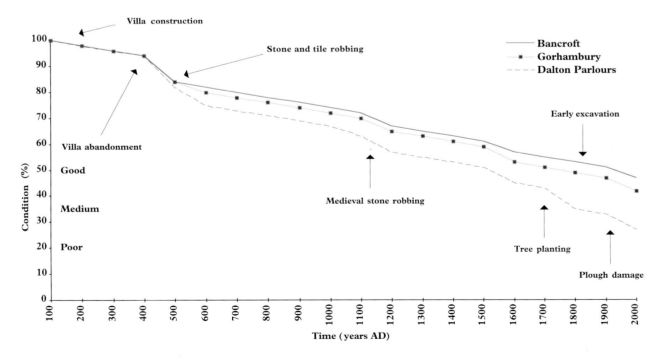

Figure 2.10 - Specimen decay profiles for three excavated minor Roman villas.

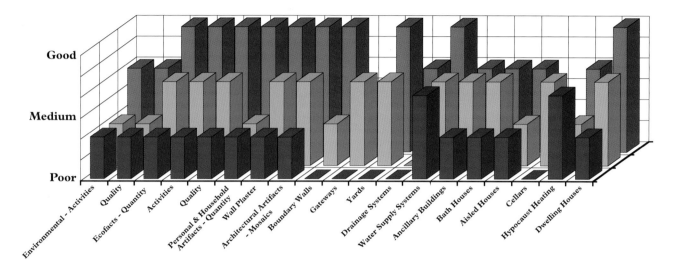

Figure 2.11 - Quality of components represented at three excavated minor Roman villas.

2.6 Case study 2: minor Roman villas [2]

Minor Romano-British villas are among the most numerous and widespread monuments of the early first century AD. Archaeologically, they comprise groups of integrated domestic and agricultural/industrial buildings originally constructed of stone, timber and cob. Abundant examples are known in all the south-eastern counties, and they are more thinly scattered in western and northern counties. Figure 2.9 shows a reconstruction drawing representing the perceived original appearance of the Gorhambury Villa, St Albans, Hertfordshire.

The natural decay curve of these monuments is likely to show a distinctive sharp drop during the first 200 years or so after their initial abandonment, a reflection of the collapse and robbing of the main buildings and structures, or decomposition and dereliction in Schiffer's terms (1987). In consequence, even the best-preserved examples appear very diminished by comparison with their original appearance, although their areal extent may remain constant. Three examples show something of the range of possibilities.

Bancroft Villa, Milton Keynes, Buckinghamshire, was considered to be in fairly good condition (equivalent to 'good' areal survival as defined in 2.9 below) at the time of its excavation in 1971-8 and again in 1983-6 (Williams and Zeepvat 1994). The excavated area covered some 14,000m².

Gorhambury, Hertfordshire, was considered to be in a medium to poor condition (equivalent to 'medium' areal survival as defined in 2.9 below) when excavated extensively during the late 1950s and again in 1972-82 (Neal *et al.* 1990). A total area of about 3ha was examined.

Dalton Parlours, West Yorkshire, was considered to be in a poor condition (equivalent to 'poor' areal survival as defined in 2.9 below) when excavated in 1976-9 (Wrathmell and Nicholson 1990); about 1.43ha was examined.

Figure 3.2 shows the location of these case studies in England; Figure 2.10 shows specimen decay profiles for each. In the following sub-sections attention is focused on four main data categories: monument extent and structure, features and components, artefacts, and ecofacts.

2.6.1 Monument extent and structure

The scale of Roman villas is such that any idea of total excavation is not really practical. Even the most extensively examined examples allow only a relatively restricted glimpse of the extent of these monuments. All three villas considered here had a complex stratigraphy which was mainly the result of building alterations and re-use over a long period of time. In broad terms, the stratigraphic evidence of many examples suggests a chronological and topological development from a simple to a complicated structure. Factors which affect preservation and stratigraphic integrity are almost all related to stone and tile robbing in the late Roman and medieval periods. This reduced the level of the standing structures to less than 1m in height and often opened the way for further diminution through cultivation or some other fairly intensive land-use.

Both Bancroft and Gorhambury produced a broad range of dating evidence, including stratigraphy and artefacts, which showed prolonged and apparently continuous usage during the Roman period. A composite plan was achieved for both villas, representing most of the key physical components.

By contrast, Dalton Parlours was found to have been heavily ploughed, with the result that most finds were unstratified and poorly preserved. Although little horizontal displacement had been caused, there had been vertical displacements and excessive artefact damage. The floor surfaces were also poorly preserved and the only complete mosaic had been unearthed and lifted during a nineteenth-century excavation. The architectural materials were too depleted to provide any chronological indications on structural or stylistic grounds. Although the site was too badly damaged to provide much evidence of function a basic plan was recovered.

2.6.2 Features and components

The main components/key features of minor Romano-British villas are: dwelling houses, including bath suite and hypocausts; aisled houses; ancillary buildings including barns and yards; gateways and trackways; water supply systems including wells, ponds and drainage systems; and gardens.

Figure 2.11 shows graphically, and in highly simplified form, the presence and quality of these various components at each of the three monuments considered here.

Although the villa at Bancroft had been disturbed by ploughing and subject to extensive stone robbing, it showed a significant number of surviving key features, and five phases of Roman occupation were established. In its early phase it comprised a house, with an associated farmyard and trackway, numerous outbuildings and two walled gardens. These were later replaced by a small but well-appointed house, which was further rebuilt in the mid fourth century. By this time there as an ornamental garden, fishpond and other associated buildings.

At Bancroft very few of the walls were extant above floor level, but there were ample structural clues to suggest sequences of remodelling. The recovery of mosaics in three of the rooms in building 1 and the corridor suggests that floor surfaces remained intact. The farmyard area, although slightly damaged, was also well stratified in the area of a cobbled trackway. While much of the rest of the farmyard evidence had been destroyed as a result of ridge and furrow ploughing in medieval times, the area between buildings 2, 3 and 9 was offered some protection by a surface layer of loosely packed limestone cobbling.

Gorhambury had been subject to ploughing and extensive stone robbing, but it retained a high-level, intact stratigraphy and surfaces, datable finds in sealed contexts, and building phases. The site saw several phases of construction. First was a timber building replaced in masonry c.AD 100 after a fire. After a series of changes, it was rebuilt to become a working farm in the later fourth century. The principal dwelling house, building 27, showed three phases of development, beginning as a rectangular block of three rooms and being extended to form a more sophisticated structure with five rooms and a cross-passage, measuring 6.50m by 22.50m. In the third phase the villa was extended 3m further north and provided with a channelled hypocaust.

At Dalton Parlours the extent of the damage caused by ploughing, stone robbing and tree planting since 1777 was so severe that most of the stratification had been removed, except in a few isolated patches, and the standing structures had been reduced to the lowest wall foundations or footings. The soil cover on the site had been reduced to as little as 0.35m over the limestone bedrock. The widespread evidence of early agricultural activity on the site and the proximity of important Roman roads and settlements indicate that there was continuity on the site and set a context for the nearby Iron Age farmsteads and Romanized villa. There were also signs that the villa had been deliberately levelled, suggesting that there was later occupation on the site. Since the removal of the Medusa mosaic pavement in the nineteenth century no further complete mosaics have been found, only pieces of tesserae in the ploughsoil. Very few of the Roman floor levels survived. The evidence of robber trenches has, however, allowed a ground plan of

structure J to be recovered. Structure M, the best preserved of the major buildings, reflects the most complicated structural sequence with three phases. On a site where the stratigraphy has been almost totally destroyed by ploughing, the closed group of finds represented by the assemblage in Well 1 (over 16m in depth) has proven to be of most value and significance.

2.6.3 Artefacts

Finds from minor Roman villa sites tend to fall into three main categories: pieces with architectural associations (e.g. mosaics and painted wall-plaster); personal effects such as jewellery and coins; and household objects (e.g. pottery and tools in a variety of materials). Overall, artefactual remains are best preserved in contexts such as the matrices of walls and floors, foundation trenches, occupation or destruction layers, and the fills of pits, pools, ditches and drains.

A wealth of artefactual material was retrieved from Bancroft. During the 1982-6 excavations a total of 741 coins was recovered, one of the largest assemblages known from a Roman villa. They were mainly found in building 1, the farmyard area and the adjacent stream. The ceramic finds amounted to over 800kg of stratified Roman pottery (over 57,000 sherds). Most of this material was of suitable quality for dating and phasing of the structures and the majority of the features. The villa also produced 3600kg of tile and brick in a variety of fabrics. Tiles used as roofing material were restricted to buildings 1, 6, 7 (the bath suite) and 8. There was evidence for the re-use of tiles. Building 1 also revealed several large assemblages of wall-plaster which have been ascribed to structural alterations made to the principal dwelling. Perhaps the most striking piece of wall-plaster, a large intact fragment of a marine scene, was found at the bottom of the fishpond and may have come from the walls of the bath suite in building 1. There were also intact mosaic floors in three rooms and the corridor of building 1. Some small mosaics were thought to represent 'door mats'. Metalwork included objects for personal adornment, furniture fittings, domestic items (for cooking and toiletry) and tools; 25.6kg of slag was also recovered. The 355 small finds included leather shoe fragments, objects of bone such as hairpins and needles, glass bottles, beakers and beads, wooden fragments, and stone querns.

As a group, the variety of small finds from Gorhambury, more than 1000 in all, reflected the life of a flourishing villa estate, although individually the objects were not of outstanding quality. They included personal possessions, agricultural tools such as ploughshare tips, spade sheaths, scythes and sickles, tools and implements representing other economic activities on the estate, structural fittings, cosmetic implements, and decorative items, some with military associations. The site also produced painted wall-plaster and stucco in the form of a human torso. Building 27 room 1 produced evidence for three mosaics, and the west corridor of building 37 also contained a mosaic which had been damaged by ploughing: it was dated AD 175 to 250. The late Iron Age and Roman ceramic finds totalled 1337kg (1290 sherds). Other key finds included 530 fragments of glass, the majority of vessel and window glass but including decorative objects such as pins, gaming pieces and beads. Metal objects included structural fittings of lead such as hinges, domestic objects of iron such as keys and handles, and items with military associations, such as the vine leaf pendant. The bone finds included objects of personal adornment and cosmetic and domestic implements: there appears to have been a concentration of bone pins and needles in levels associated with the second-century villa. In general, these small finds were distributed widely over the site. There was also a high level of smithing slag and metal offcuts, suggesting that there was a forge on the site.

At Dalton Parlours, only 87 coins were found, a small number for a such a prosperous site. The comprehensive area excavation produced 14,840 sherds of pottery, 13% from ploughsoil, 40% in well 1, and 47% from the villa building. Although ploughing in this area had caused little horizontal displacement, and each excavated group showed a chronological mix which spanned the Antonine period to the mid-fourth century, there had been considerable and damaging vertical displacement. The sherds were all small and abraded. There were few sealed deposits and the limited information obtained could not be used to date successive phases of building modifications. Although the overall preservation of the finds was poor, the site was of high status, with military associations indicated by copper alloy objects, military equipment and the Medusa mosaic.

Metal objects were mainly silver or copper alloy: only 6 complete objects were recovered, with 90 fragments. Less than a third of these were found in stratified contexts such as ditch fills and destruction deposits and they had little value for dating. The range of these objects included personal ornaments, toilet implements, furniture fittings and military equipment such as belt plates and buckle loops. The most important group of iron objects came from well 1. There were 271 glass finds from the Roman period, including 138 vessel fragments and 103 pieces of window pane. The surviving finds assemblage was very small for a site of this size and status and may reflect an efficient recycling regime or scavenging, plough loss and destruction post-dating the Roman occupation. However, the site produced one of the largest collections of quern stones to be found on a Yorkshire villa site, from a variety of contexts from the second to the fourth century. They included saddle querns, 37 beehive querns, fragments of lava querns and pieces from 36 rotary querns.

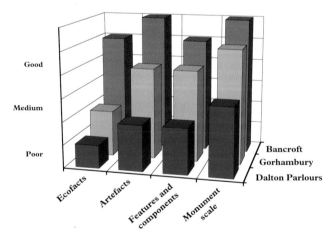

Figure 2.12 - Quality of data categories recovered from three excavated minor Roman villas.

2.6.4 Ecofacts

Bancroft yielded nearly 15,000 animal bones, of which two-thirds were selected for analysis. The majority came from Phase 4 (fourth century) and consisted mainly of cattle, sheep/goat, pig and horse. The age and sex of the animals were determined, as were butchery practices. The plant remains consisted of seeds, fruits, chaff and charcoal fragments, concentrated in the eastern area of the farm buildings. Samples were also examined from waterlogged remains close to the Bradwell Brook and from the fourth-century ornamental fish pond. Radiocarbon determinations were obtained for a skeleton found on the mosaic floor in room 1 and indicated a date at the end of the fourth century.

At Gorhambury about 14,000 mammal bones were recovered from the Roman period, goats/sheep being the commonest. The loss of environmental evidence due to the acidity of the soil was reduced by the presence of alkaline building materials, and molluscan evidence was preserved. Only a small quantity of carbonized seeds was retrieved from the floor surfaces and most of these were in very poor condition.

At Dalton Parlours only half of the 2622 animal bones could be positively identified by species and most were unsuitable for ageing, sexing and determining butchery practices. Because of heavy ploughing over the site the plant remains were subject to contamination and contributed little to the understanding of the economy and environment.

2.6.5 Discussion

The successful analysis of minor Romano-British villas depends on the quality of the excavation process, the scientific téchniques employed, and the condition / preservation of the key components, artefacts and ecofacts in relation to the soil types and land-use. The effects of soil chemistry do not appear to have had a major impact either on the survival of the later masonry villa buildings or for determining the overall site plan. Soil chemistry does, however, affect the survival of artefacts and ecofacts and must be considered a significant factor in estimating and influencing the survival and condition of these monuments. Assessing survival is extremely difficult because the range of possible contexts is enormous and the variability in survival even within a single monument considerable. Even superficially poor sites may have some features with exceptional preservation which can yield real and substantial contributions to knowledge.

Site definition and integrity may be perceived in two dimensions, horizontal and vertical. Poor definition in the horizontal dimension results from the partial removal of the key villa components or from physical restrictions on the scale of investigation. Degradation in the vertical dimension (e.g. through stone robbing and ploughing) affects the interpretation of the stratigraphic relationships of the key components and removes artefactual and ecofactual remains from their original contexts.

Figure 2.12 shows graphically a comparison between the survival characteristics of the four main data-sets considered above for each of the three case study monuments. In summary, the examples which have not been substantially disturbed by stone robbing and ploughing, and whose key components are sufficiently complete to allow structural analysis and permit alterations and continuity to be observed and analysed, may be characterized as having good survival. These sites also have a high level of intact stratigraphy, with composite floor surfaces and large numbers of well-preserved artefacts and ecofacts.

The key moment in the decay curve for small Roman villas is the point at which they move from being in medium condition to poor condition. At this point their overall information yield is considerably reduced and their information value lies in the contents and structure of protected, but probably isolated, features such as wells and deeply cut structures. As with long barrows, of course, poor survival does not equate with low value or importance (see above 2.5.5).

2.7 Amelioration

The idea of amelioration is closely connected with the idea of accelerated decay. Amelioration may be said to occur when the decay curve flattens out over a period of time. The decay trajectories of monuments which have reverted to natural decay, excepting the extreme examples which have been wholly destroyed, are likely to be less steep than for those suffering accelerated decay. This apparent improvement cannot relate to the first three factors causing decay described above because once archaeological deposits have gone they are lost for ever, but the conditions for preservation and the pattern of surrounding land-use and support can improve, for example by the abandonment of cultivation over a monument turned over to long-term grassland, the backfilling of a quarry which threatened to swallow up a monument through the expansion of the quarry face, or the re-watering of a traditionally wet monument that was drying out. Amelioration may thus be defined as the levelling off of an otherwise steep downward profile on a decay curve. Chapter 6.11 briefly explores the incidence of amelioration, while Chapter 7 explores some of these issues more deeply in relation to land-use. However, recognizing amelioration requires the careful observation of monuments and, where possible, the measurement of characteristics that relate to a monument's decay.

2.8 Measuring monuments

There are no established standard measures available to quantify archaeological monuments in England. The Monuments Protection Programme has developed a numerically based scoring system to aid judgements made for the identification of monuments of national importance (Darvill *et al.* 1987), but it is specific to the needs of the programme and deals only with the question of importance. Although one of the criteria used in determining importance is 'survival', its application is based on a simple three-level scale. Carver (1996, 53-5) has suggested that the value of archaeological deposits (and by implication monuments too) to the discipline of archaeology is measurable in terms of their quality, and their potential to be read, and thereby to contribute to current research agendas. This he calls 'archaeological legibility' (Carver 1987a, 124), but determining legibility is neither easy nor direct. In many respects it must depend on the reader's ability and skill as much as on the archaeological record's inherent ability to be read. Both of these systems are intuitive judgement-based approaches which fit their purpose but do not provide a satisfactory basis for the more general questions posed by MARS.

It was thus necessary to define new measures at the outset of the MARS Project. APPENDIX C lists the key dimensions that were regarded as relevant and possible. There are three groups of measurements: those concerned with the horizontal extent or area of a monument; those concerned with its height and/or depth; and those relating to its volume. In other words, a monument is a three-dimensional entity with width, length and thickness, and these attributes can be measured in metres, square metres, hectares, cubic metres and so on. In MARS square metres (m^2) and square kilometres (km^2) were used for area measurements and metres (m) for linear measurements.

Within each group of measurements three main parameters were recognized as possible for comparative purposes. These were constructed in the light of the thinking set out above:

- characteristics of the original shape and form of a monument (i.e. how it was in the past when created or in use)

- the extent of archaeologically recorded characteristics using all available records past and present

- the current characteristics of the monument at a defined point in time based on data obtained by observation.

Measuring an archaeological monument involves both conceptual and practical problems. It can be difficult to replicate measurements unless there are well-established fixed datum points to hand (*cf.* Reynolds and Schadla-Hall 1980, 116). These do not exist for any but a very small number of monuments. Even with sketches and extensive notes it can be difficult to be sure that measurements are being made between the same points, and when some of those points have been destroyed or have changed position the situation is complicated further. Global Positioning Systems may eliminate this difficulty in the future: the datum points are satellites whose elevated position means that they can be used for all monuments, provided a direct line of sight to the satellites is available. The present state of GPS technology would permit some analysis of the horizontal extent of monuments, but further refinements are needed before it can be used successfully for vertical (height-related) measurements.

Not all the measurements set out in APPENDIX C were applied to the monuments examined during the MARS Project, although all are theoretically possible. Practical experience during the early stages of the project, the level of information retrievable from existing sources, and constraints on the time available for researching and validating details of individual monuments, meant that only Projected Archaeological Extent (PAE), Current Area (CA) for a series of points in time and Current Maximum Height (CMH) were systematically recorded wherever possible. The time period covered was essentially 1945-95. Sometimes measurements were used to reflect particular decades (e.g. 1940-50, 1950-60 etc.); in other cases mid-decade points ±4 years were used (e.g. 1945, 1955, 1965 etc.). Estimated Original Extent (EOE) was also recorded for some monuments but was not used in the analyses. Even with the simplest measurements, however, the important issue of survival can be approached.

2.9 *Measuring survival as Percentage Area Loss*

Decay is a process the consequences of which can be recorded for any defined point in time: this is the concept of survival. There are no absolute measures of survival that can be applied to monuments because the concept is a relative one, in which the situation at one point in time is compared with that at another: even the statement that a monument has been totally destroyed is only a relative statement based on the assumption that something once existed but now does not.

Thus survival is a point-in-time measure of the current state or condition of a monument relative to some former state, a reflection of the cumulative effects of all the natural and man-induced processes that have operated on it. Figure 2.2 shows this graphically, survival being the distance between the decay curve and the bottom axis of the graph, representing the total loss of a monument.

In order to determine survival, MARS used the physical measurements of individual monuments as set out above. Ideally, survival should be measured with reference to the original characteristics of the monument (e.g. EOE), but in practical terms it was difficult to determine the original state of all but a few particularly well-recorded, and usually relatively recent, monuments. County Archaeological Officers in particular were averse to MARS placing any reliance on estimated measurements of volume or of original extent, and on their advice these were largely excluded from the range of measurements used in the analyses presented here; further research in conjunction with County Archaeological Officers to validate estimates of volume and original extent could bring these estimates into a more usable form. However, for the first iteration of MARS attention focused on the identification of areal survival: the changing physical extent of monuments in the horizontal plane. One main reason for doing this was that it allowed effective use of the evidence from aerial photographs. Here, as in the field, measurements of horizontal distances and areas are relatively reliable provided that the remains to be measured can be located. Thus in quantifying areal survival, PAE and CA have to be used to calculate a Percentage Area Loss (PAL) value as the main indicator using the following formula:

$$PAL = \left(\frac{PAE - CA_1}{PAE}\right) \times 100$$

in which PAE is the Projected Archaeological Extent of a monuments and CA is the Current Area at defined time 1 (e.g. CA1995).

The PAL score relating to the time of the work that defined the Current Area can be translated into general categories of areal survival as follows:

Very good	PAL <20%
Good	PAL 21–40%
Medium	PAL 41–60%
Poor	PAL 61–80%
Very poor	PAL >80%

2.10 *The concept of risk*

If survival is taken to provide a measure of how monuments have fared to date, then risk must be regarded as the measure of how a monument is likely to fare in the future. As a parameter of change, risk is not as easy to quantify as survival because the events that are of interest have not yet happened. At a general level, risk can be seen very simply in terms of a relationship between a monument and its environment. This is the perspective that most archaeological surveys have used to date (see APPENDIX A), and it is the approach developed in Chapters 5-8 of this report. But the examination of risk, especially in the context of environmental assessment, is becoming increasingly widespread, more scientifically based, and ever more sophisticated in its conceptualization of the issues (Fortlage and Catharine 1990; Lambrick 1993). In Chapter 9, a rather different approach is adopted in which risk is itself seen as a variable that can be quantified.

The concept of risk in relation to archaeological monuments concerns the chance or possibility of future danger, loss, injury or some other adverse consequences as a result of natural processes or the intentional or unintentional actions of individuals or groups. In this sense all archaeological monuments are at risk because it is impossible to predict either the source or the timing of damaging actions in the future. However, some monuments can be identified as being at greater risk than others because of their identifiable exposure to potentially harmful circumstances.

In the language of risk assessment, a potential cause of harm is known as a hazard, and for archaeology such hazards can most easily be identified as the main erosive and destructive forces that reduce the survival of monuments. These are dealt with in detail in Chapter 6. It is important to recognize, however, that hazards are context-specific, or in other words a hazard will cause harm only under specific sets of circumstances, with the corollary that changing those circumstances will alter the degree of harm, for better or worse.

The distinction between hazard and risk can best be illustrated by an example. Many engineering works are hazardous in relation to archaeological monuments: for example, pile-driving during the construction of foundations will displace materials, distort stratigraphy, and sever relationships. However, the works are only a risk to archaeological survival in so far as archaeological deposits or monuments are exposed to them. The degree of harm caused by the exposure will depend on the specific degree of exposure. If only a small percentage of an archaeological deposit is pierced by small-bore piling then the risk of harm is minimal compared with the effect of using large-diameter piles, even though the hazardous properties of the works themselves remain unchanged.

In developing a meaningful application of the concept of risk for MARS it is appropriate to elaborate the basic definition with contingent relationships between probability, anticipated hazards, and the actual impact those hazards might have on the archaeological deposits and monuments. For MARS, risk is therefore defined as:

> The combination of the probability or frequency of the occurrence of a recognized hazard in relation to the magnitude of the consequences.

This broadly follows the Department of the Environment's definition of risk in a draft guidance note on contaminated land (DoE *et al.* 1996, 28).

The determination of risk therefore requires a basic risk assessment which addresses the source and character of a potential hazard (e.g. quarrying, road scheme, livestock, visitors etc.), the nature and extent of its likely impact (e.g. one-off, recurrent, ground-breaking, extensive, intensive), and the nature of the target it might affect (i.e. the characteristics of the archaeological monument itself). Thus the risk posed by a new road scheme to a small monument which will be completely destroyed is clearly far higher than the risk posed by the same road to a very extensive monument where only a small proportion lies in the corridor of destruction. Equally, the risk to a monument presented by a small number of visitors may be regarded as negligible, but the risk posed by heavy and frequent visitor usage is far greater. The same applies to arable cultivation, where the risk posed by a single ploughing of an already cultivated monument is minimal in contrast to the risk posed by frequent and continued cultivation.

Approaching the future of archaeological monuments in this way moves away from traditional and rather simplistic hazard-based approaches (anything happening to a monument must be bad) to a risk-based perspective in which it is recognized that a level of zero-risk is unobtainable or simply impractical, and that a certain level of risk in a given set of circumstances may be deemed acceptable after the benefits have been taken into account. This is essentially the approach argued for the management of the archaeological resource in relation to continuing development in York (OAP 1991). The key to successful archaeological resource management is to deal effectively with risk management, risk perception and risk communication, all of which are discussed further in Chapter 9. First, however, these theoretical perspectives need to be developed into a methodology, the subject of the next chapter.

3 MARS methodology and implementation

This heritage of landscape ... represents a large part of our collective memory. It provides roots for people, a sense of place, a link with the past, a storehouse for ideas on how we can use the land, a vital source of culture and spiritual creation. It represents a massive inherited capital of human effort, which we may (to our cost) ignore or waste or we may choose to use or adapt.

(ECVST 1991)

3.1 Theory into practice

Building on the theoretical foundation outlined in the last chapter, the methodology developed for MARS attempted simultaneously to embrace a range of different facets of what was defined in the last chapter as the archaeological resource. This was achieved by looking at the recorded resource, both extinct and extant, from two perspectives: first, that offered by a general study of the development and content of the records which collectively represented the recorded resource at the MARS census date of 1995; second, through a detailed examination of a sample of the recorded resource to see what it was like and what was happening to it. The former was carried out by the National Survey Programme and the results form the basis of Chapter 4; the latter was carried out by the Field Survey Programme and the Aerial Photographic Survey Programme and the results are used in Chapters 5-9.

Because very different data collection procedures were used, and the data themselves were handled in different ways, the pictures created for these two scales of analysis cannot directly be compared with each other, even though, in a general sense, they both relate to the same body of material. How and why this is so will become apparent in later chapters.

This chapter focuses on the practical organization, execution and management of the MARS Project. It is divided into nine main sections. The first looks at the definition of 'monuments' by building on the legal definitions offered in Chapter 2 to show how the concept was applied within MARS. The second section describes the four MARS programmes that together formed the project as a whole. This is followed by a consideration of the sampling scheme that was used, and how the sample was constructed. In the fourth section attention is directed to the definition and identification of MARS Monuments as a sub-set of all monuments, and this is followed by the definition of a series of MARS Regions which provide the basic geographical units for data analysis. The sixth section reports on an independent review of the success and integrity of the sampling scheme and the data it generated, a review carried out during the data assessment stage of the project. This work is included here to show both the strengths and weaknesses of what has been achieved. The last three sections deal with the structure and content of the MARS databases, the organization and management of the project, and the content of the MARS archives. Several of the sections in this chapter are supported by appendices which appear at the end of the report.

Before considering in detail how MARS was carried out, two points touched upon at the end of Chapter 1 deserve elaboration. First, MARS was the first study of this kind ever undertaken in England. When MARS began there was very little experience to draw upon apart from the 1989-90 Wiltshire pilot study. In retrospect it is easy to see aspects of the work that could or should have been done differently. The experience of the MARS Steering Committee that reviewed the progress of the project and determined the way forward at each stage may best be likened to a journey to an unknown destination along unlit streets.

Second, as Chapter 2 intimated and the citation at the head of the chapter underlines, the nature and range of subjects that are recognized to have a bearing on the past, the heritage, are enormous. No single containable project could hope to deal with everything. Parameters have to be set and limits defined. In making decisions about how to carry out MARS two guiding principles were applied. First, whatever approaches were adopted had to be theoretically sustainable but practical. Second, the focus had always to be on the interests of the archaeological profession as represented in prevailing theory and practice.

3.2 Monuments and MARS Monuments

As the name of the project suggests, and as earlier chapters note, the concept of the archaeological 'monument' lies at the heart of MARS. It is a term that has enjoyed a long and widespread use in archaeological resource management, perpetuated in large measure by its central place in ancient monuments legislation since the later nineteenth century. As was discussed in Chapter 2, the term monument has both legal and general definitions. MARS follows the basic elements of the legal definition, with some reinforcement of the boundaries to retain a sharp archaeological focus and clearly differentiate what is covered from the English Heritage Buildings at Risk Survey, a quite separate project.

For MARS, a monument was taken to be any definable building, structure or work, that has archaeological integrity because it represents the contemporary embodiment of the physical context, setting or result of one or more activities that took place in the past. This of course includes remains both above and below the surface of the land, caves and excavations, and the remains of vehicles, vessels, aircraft or other movable structures.

For general studies of the recorded resource this broad definition provides a useful working model which is inclusive rather than exclusive. It is recognized, however, that such a broad definition can be interpreted to include structures and remains with little real archaeological interest and which the survey was not originally intended to cover (e.g. recent dwelling houses). Accordingly, for detailed studies of the resource, a more rigorous definition was developed, the following being excluded from the range of all monuments:

- monuments whose location is unknown

- stray archaeological finds and single human burials

- suggestions of the former existence of some kind of monument in the form of place-names or historical sources

- buildings in domestic use constructed after *c.*AD 1700

- all buildings constructed after *c.*AD 1900.

The sub-set of all monuments filtered in this way is referred to in this report as MARS Monuments; these are only found within defined MARS sample transects as the latter are the only areas for which data have been systematically scrutinized and sorted (see below 3.5).

It should be emphasized that nothing was excluded from MARS because it was considered unimportant: in the first three cases listed above there was the pragmatic imperative that these kinds of material simply could not be visited in the field or identified on aerial photographs, and could not therefore provide meaningful observational data about such parameters as land-use or size. It is fully recognized that, in particular, stray finds and single human burials make important contributions to understanding the past, and often provide the first hints that extensive monuments exist in an area.

Unlocated monuments with imprecise NGRs were a particular problem in some areas, mainly where the Ordnance Survey Record's quarter-sheets provided the sole source of geo-referencing for individual records. Most derived from the so-called 'margin entries' relating to items known to have been located somewhere on a quarter-sheet details of which were written on the margin of the map. Records referenced only by OS quarter-sheet number (i.e. a grid reference in the following form: ST 08 NW, equal to ST 0080) can only be tied to a 5km by 5km square, an area five times more extensive than a MARS sample transect and accordingly of little use in this study.

Buildings, including historic buildings and relatively recent standing structures, posed a rather different problem. Some SMRs record them systematically, while others do not. Moreover, just before MARS data were extracted from the NMR the former National Archaeological Record (NAR) and National Buildings Record (NBR) were combined within the MONARCH system. This produced a massive duplication of records, since some standing structures are both archaeological monuments and historic buildings. Items in the National Buildings Record were located primarily by postal address, grid references being given to four figures only. A

meeting of the Steering Committee in November 1994 decided to exclude from MARS all monuments whose origin was the NBR records only. MARS was not primarily concerned with historic buildings, not least because a complementary study of Buildings at Risk was carried out in 1990-1 (English Heritage 1992a). Specifically excluded therefore were all buildings in domestic use constructed after *c.*AD 1700 and all buildings of whatever purpose constructed after *c.*AD 1900. Despite these exclusions, most twentieth-century structures such as Second World War defences (e.g. gun emplacements, pill-boxes etc.) were included in MARS if they were recorded on the NMR or a local SMR. All early buildings with an SMR or NMR entry were included in the MARS Project, although the focus of interest in these buildings and structures was of course their archaeological elements.

Formulated in this way, and given the above-mentioned exclusions, the definition of MARS Monuments provides a template with which to achieve a degree of consistency in what is considered in this study. MARS Monuments form the focus of attention in two out of the four interconnected data collection programmes established within MARS: the Field Survey and the Aerial Photographic Survey.

3.3 The MARS programmes

Data collection and analysis were carried out through a series of four main programmes. The purpose and operation of each is reviewed in the following sub-sections. The data collected fell into three main categories: gross counts of what has been recorded; sample counts to estimate defined populations; and qualitative data based on what could be seen and identified.

3.3.1 National Survey

The purpose of the National Survey Programme was to acquire data about the content of local Sites and Monuments Records, and in particular to develop a general picture of the recorded resource as it stood in 1995. Some comparative analysis of this picture in relation to earlier studies is possible, for example the studies by the Inspectorate of Ancient Monuments in 1983-4 (IAM 1984) and English Heritage in 1987-8 (Chadburn 1989). Accordingly, the content and scope of these earlier studies in part determined the range of questions asked and data collected. Data from the RCHME's National Monuments Record were used for only one of the sections in the National Survey, dealing with a sample of 40 monument classes and the counts of entries in the NMR for each.

The National Survey also examined the development of national and local Sites and Monuments Records in two ways: first by exploring the history of the early sources and the inspirations that resulted in much of the record as it now stands, and second by looking at the way that the records of individual MARS Monuments within the sample transects have developed over time, for example how they were discovered, when they were added to the record, and whether or not the records have been enhanced in some way.

The first task of the National Survey was to identify the definitive local Sites and Monuments Record for each area. This was achieved through telephone calls, letters

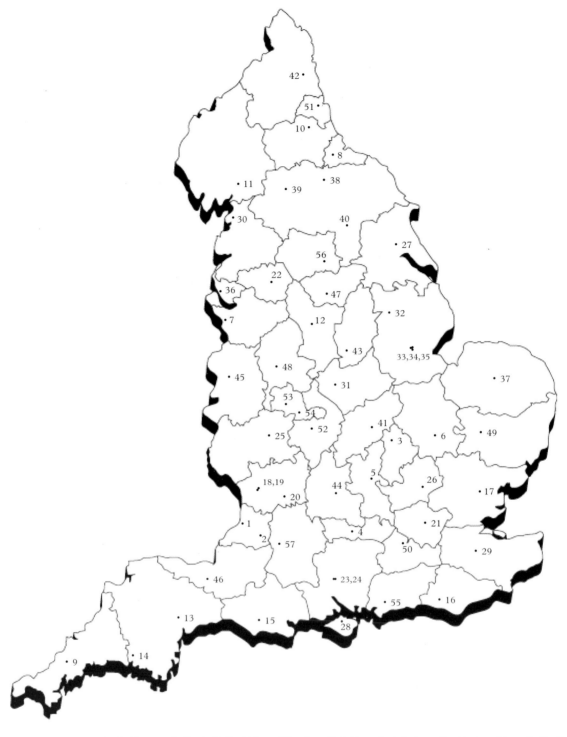

1.Bristol, Avon. 2. Bath, Bath City. 3. Bedford, Bedfordshire. 4.Reading, Berkshire. 5. Aylesbury, Buckinghamshire. 6. Cambridge, Cambridgeshire. 7. Chester, Cheshire. 8. Middlesborough, Cleveland. 9. Truro, Cornwall. 10. Durham, County Durham. 11. Kendal, Cumbria. 12. Matlock, Derbyshire. 13. Exeter, Devon. 14. Plymouth, Plymouth City. 15. Dorchester, Dorset. 16. Lewes, East Sussex. 17. Chelmsford, Essex. 18. Gloucester, Gloucestershire. 19. Gloucester, Gloucester City 20. Cirencester, Cirencester UAD 21. London, Greater London. 22. Manchester, Greater Manchester 23. Winchester, Hampshire. 24. Winchester, Winchester City. 25. Worcester, Hereford & Worcester. 26. Hertford, Hertfordshire. 27. Beverley, Humberside. 28. Newport, Isle of Wight. 29. Maidstone, Kent. 30. Lancaster, Lancashire. 31. Leicester, Leicestershire. 32. Lincoln, Lincolnshire. 33. Heckington, North Kesteven district. 34. Heckington, South Kesteven district. 35. Heckington, Boston district. 36. Liverpool, Merseyside. 37. Dereham, Norfolk. 38. Northallerton, North Yorkshire. 39. Bainbridge, Yorkshire Dales National Park. 40. York, York City. 41. Northampton, Northamptonshire. 42. Morpeth, Northumberland. 43. Nottingham, Nottinghamshire. 44. Oxford, Oxfordshire. 45. Shrewsbury, Shropshire. 46. Taunton, Somerset. 47. Sheffield, South Yorkshire. 48. Stafford, Staffordshire. 49. Bury St. Edmonds, Suffolk. 50. Kingston-upon-Thames, Surrey. 51. Newcastle, Tyne & Wear. 52. Warwick, Warwickshire. 53. Solihull, West Midlands. 54. Birmingham, Birmingham City. 55. Chichester, West Sussex. 56. Wakefield, West Yorkshire 57. Trowbridge, Wiltshire.

Figure 3.1 - The position and catchment of the 57 local SMRs providing data for the National Survey and the definition of MARS Monuments within the sample transects.

and visits to individual archives. The sources identified were the most up-to-date cumulative records and those where coverage was greatest, in most cases county council-based SMR records. However, in seven counties it was found that district or city council SMRs were more complete for their areas of coverage, and accordingly these were used. In counting record items in these counties, all those record items held at county level which referred to the sub-area (e.g. town or district) were subtracted, and then the counts from the sub-areas added to give aggregate counts. In this way a total of 59 SMRs were contacted; 57 were able to provide data, and 54 were eventually included in the analyses undertaken as in three cases it was impossible to gauge accurately the degree of overlap and duplication between records. APPENDIX D lists the records used for each county. Figure 3.1 shows the position of SMRs and the catchment areas over which the MARS Project regarded them as the definitive local record.

Throughout the National Survey there was an emphasis on local records. There were inevitably differences in the quality and range of data held by different records. It was also recognized that museums, National Parks and some private bodies hold SMR-type information, but following discussions with a selection of such sources they were not brought into the survey, either because the information they contained was wholly or largely duplicated by the local SMRs as a result of data exchanges, or because the data held were incompatible with those required for MARS. The exception to this was North Yorkshire, where the Yorkshire Dales National Park record created by RCHME was, at the census date, the most comprehensive record for that area; a combination of the North Yorkshire County Council and the Yorkshire Dales National Park data was therefore used throughout MARS. Visits were also made to the National Trust and the Ministry of Defence to assess the scope of their records, but neither was eventually accessed.

Museums hold a range of data relevant to archaeology, but they were not systematically assessed within the MARS Project because computerization of these sources was still in its infancy and the data not yet at a stage where they could easily submit to the kind of analysis MARS demanded.

Information collected by the National Survey falls into five broad categories:

● SMR details and background information

● record composition and period divisions

● simple counts for 40 sample monument classes designation data in the SMR

● progress in data accessioning and SMR history

● data on land-use and monument condition.

APPENDIX E provides a full listing of the defined fields used by the National Survey.

In order to gather data for the National Survey in a structured way, a *pro forma* data recording form was developed. The form was circulated in stages between September and November 1994, in all cases after telephone contact was made with the appropriate SMR

officer. In order to assist compilers, the form was accompanied by a guidance note which explained in greater detail how the information requested should be compiled. At the same time the National Survey team offered help to SMR officers through visits from MARS staff to explain the purpose of the survey, or to assist in the completion of the form. The offer included the possibility of MARS staff working on the SMR while the SMR officer was occupied in completing the MARS forms. Overall, it was felt that MARS staff made a great contribution towards the profession's understanding of MARS at this stage by personally contacting all the SMR officers concerned, and by visiting some to assist in the completion of the forms. In a few cases MARS staff completed the forms themselves from the sources made available to them by the SMR. In all cases, however, there was assistance and guidance from the SMR officer and County Archaeological Officer. APPENDIX D identifies the SMRs visited by MARS staff in connection with the National Survey.

The MARS National Survey relied upon SMR officers being able to interrogate their systems and access information. One dramatic change since the first comparable survey in 1983 is the number of SMRs which now have machine-readable systems. In 1983 Fraser used five methods of data retrieval (IAM 1984, 26):

● manual search of primary data, i.e. card index systems

● unpublished summaries, i.e. summary lists or analyses of the SMR prepared by the SMR officer

● published summaries, i.e. summary lists prepared as a public statements of holdings

● optical coincidence cards, i.e. the system developed in the 1970s using punched cards

● computer-based storage and retrieval system.

Little more than ten years later, in 1995, MARS used just two methods:

● computer searches of machine-based systems

● tallying of paper records.

Reviewing the 1983 retrieval methods, it was found that optical coincidence card systems had almost gone out of use, although Oxford County Council was still using such a system at the time of the MARS visit. Unpublished summary lists were available at some records, mainly as a back-up for computerized records, and these were used where appropriate. Published inventories of archaeological monuments remain rare in England even though modern information technology theoretically makes them easier to produce than ever before. This contrasts with the situation for historic buildings, where gazetteers of Listed Buildings of all grades (over 500,000 items in all for England) are available in published and electronic form. There are also published registers of historic parks and gardens (English Heritage 1984-8) and battlefields (English Heritage 1995a). For archaeology only lists of Scheduled Monuments are published on a county by county basis. The situation in Ireland may also be noted, as here the development of a National Archaeological Record by the Office of Public Works includes the publication of county inventories (Moore 1992).

Most of the data for MARS were provided by searches using computer systems, the majority of which were PC or mainframe-based and situated within, or networked to, the individual record offices concerned. In some cases reviewing data on a screen coupled with manual tallying was the only available method for extracting the necessary information. Not all systems could be interrogated in ways which allowed the MARS research questions to be answered, and not all SMR officers were sufficiently proficient in the query languages used on their systems to generate counts involving combinations of record fields or tables.

Some recipients of the questionnaires commented on the unsuitability of the MARS *pro forma* for data held in computerized systems. Naturally, there is sympathy for these complaints since any questionnaire will be easier to deal with on some systems than others. As the RCHME has demonstrated, the plurality of systems now in use provides a very uneven platform for the extended national archaeological record and levels of satisfaction with existing systems among SMR officers seem rather low (RCHME 1993a, table 5).

MARS also recognized that all local SMRs are supported by map-based information, and in many cases by files of data not destined to be entered into the computer system. Information in operational computer systems formed the focus of the MARS Project, but questions about backlog data-entry were asked, as were questions about migration between systems since some records were upgrading to new software at the time. Allowances were made in the responses from West Yorkshire for the fact that some data were held on paper, and these were easily retrieved for MARS. Data was collected from East Sussex using manual reference cards.

Table 3.1 shows an analysis of the range of systems in use at the time of the MARS Project. About one third of the records used systems based on Superfile, developed by English Heritage and installed as part of a massive SMR development and enhancement programme during the 1980s (see Chapter 4). The mainframe systems use a wide range of software, including Oracle and bespoke in-house data management systems; they have been grouped

Table 3.1 - Summary of recording systems used by the local SMRs providing data for MARS at the time of the National Survey (1994-5). *[Source: MARS National Survey Programme]*

Record System	Frequency
Foxpro	3
Monarch/Oracle	6
Paper based	6
Mainframe	7
dBase III, IV	8
Other commercial	8
English Heritage (Various)	19
Total	**57**

together in the table because the responsibility for the management of the system is held outside the archaeology group. It may be noted, however, that at the time when MARS was collecting data for the National Survey a number of local SMRs were in the process of moving over to GIS-based computer systems which combine map-based and text-based records.

3.3.2 Field Survey

The purpose of the Field Survey Programme was to provide point-in-time data about a sample of recorded monuments. Special attention was given to recording land-use over and around monuments, the scale and extent of visible damage (i.e. destruction), survival, risk, accessibility and visibility. Project staff visited and checked a total of 13,488 monuments in 1297 separate sample transects scattered across England between September 1994 and March 1996. Details of how the sample was determined and MARS Monuments identified are set out in 3.4 and 3.5 below.

The Field Survey was carried out by six field teams, each comprising two members of the MARS staff. The teams were organized into two groups, each group managed by a regional supervisor. In general, each field team worked within a defined region (see 3.6 below) in order to build up local knowledge and contacts. However, in the later stages of the Field Survey it was necessary to move teams around between regions in order to cover the remaining areas efficiently and effectively. This also had the effect of helping to reduce to a minimum any regional biases brought about by operator differences. APPENDIX F lists the periods during which each county was surveyed.

Each field team was equipped with a portable computer for data entry using the MARS database. Briefly, the procedure fell into three main stages (with some inevitable local variations).

First, a MARS folder was established for each sample transect; inside was a provisional list of the MARS Monuments, a map of the transect (usually at 1:10,000 scale) as supplied by the local SMR, print-outs of all information for monuments in the transect supplied by the local SMR (usually long reports), and print-outs of all information for the monuments in the transect supplied by the NMR. The importance of these print-outs in locating and identifying monuments is hard to underestimate, and those counties for which documentation was poor naturally represent sources of weakness in the overall data-set obtained for the MARS Project.

Second, the regional supervisor and/or members of the field team who were to survey the transect discussed the position and extents of the monuments with the relevant SMR officer and, if possible, the County Archaeological Officer. One specific aim of this work was to mark up the maps and agree on the Projected Archaeological Extents of the monuments represented. These were marked with red lines on the map. Not all counties were willing to mark up maps in this way, arguing that the archaeology was not sufficiently well known. In such cases MARS staff added the lines on the basis of information in the records provided.

Third, once the records had been checked and maps marked, the folders were taken over by the field teams, who arranged a programme of visits to check the marked monuments. Wherever possible and necessary, the teams contacted landowners in advance and made appointments to visit monuments. Access was denied to a few MARS Monuments, others were out of bounds in sensitive areas, and a few could not be located because of incorrect grid references. Out of a total of 14,591 defined MARS Monuments, 13,488 (92%) were visited. This field checking took approximately 4500 person days; the overall average rate of checking was therefore three MARS Monuments per person day, taking into account data entry and first-level validation. Some data are available for the 1165 MARS Monuments which could not be field checked. APPENDIX G lists the data fields recorded during the field survey, including fields common to other databases for cross-referencing.

It should be emphasized that the field survey was concerned only with checking MARS Monuments derived from existing records. There was no attempt to 'survey' the transects in the sense of looking for unrecorded archaeology. However, during the survey work the field teams identified a few monuments not present on the MARS lists, and these were notified to the appropriate SMR using a standard MARS *pro forma*.

During the field survey some additional information was added to the transect maps concerning the definition of the areal extent of monuments. Green lines were used to denote the extent of visible archaeological remains within the red line; green shading was used to denote areas of visible archaeology outside the red lines. Orange lines were used to show parts of the red-lined areas which had been totally destroyed (e.g. by the construction of a road or the expansion of a quarry). Current Area 1995 (CA95) was taken to be the area within the red line where archaeology was believed to remain (i.e. PAE less any land defined by the orange line). Throughout, it was assumed that if the ground remained intact then some archaeological deposits would exist even if they were not visible on the surface.

The glossaries used in completing the database during and following field survey were mainly standard lists of categories drawn from, or based upon, published guidance (e.g. RCHME 1992; RCHME and EH 1995). Land-use was a critical issue for MARS, and here use was made of the LUSAG classification developed by the Department of the Environment for eventual application across the UK as the basis for determining land-use stock and patterns of change (LUSAG 1993). The system involves 12 broad groups subdivided into 53 narrow classes. APPENDIX H provides a summary of the system. It is believed that MARS was the first national study to make extensive use of this classification.

During and immediately after the field survey, the data were subjected to a number of checks and validations. At regional level, the regional supervisor checked information before it was returned to Bournemouth for incorporation in the master database. The Project Manager and Project Director visited field teams during their fieldwork, checking data categorization for inter-regional consistency. Once returned to Bournemouth, all data were checked by the project's Data Co-ordinator, who identified omissions and inconsistencies. Where necessary these were referred back to the supervisors and surveyors to rectify. Three data-sets proved especially difficult.

Some data fields were relatively unproblematic and could be completed quickly and easily. Others could not.

Field measurements are very difficult to take and almost impossible to replicate (Reynolds and Schadla-Hall 1980). Small monuments were measured using hand-tapes and ranging rods. Larger monuments were measured using detailed maps and surveys modified with field observations. Throughout, professional judgements had to be made about the dimensions recorded and how they could best be physically measured, scaled or calculated. Inevitably, the field teams found it difficult to establish what measurements held in SMR records, mainly measurements derived from OS survey records or the work of earlier fieldworkers such as Leslie Grinsell, actually referred to. No doubt future fieldworkers will have the same problem with some recorded MARS information!

Background information on underlying drift geology was also problematic. Some SMRs record this information consistently and made it available to the project. Others do not record it at all, or do so only when it has been supplied to them with source material. Sometimes geology can relatively easily be determined at the monument itself (e.g. chalk bedrock in arable countryside), but often this is not the case. The situation is complicated by the absence for England of a complete coverage, at a reasonable scale, of accurately mapped geological data. Eventually, geology was validated by checking MARS Monuments against 1:50,000, 1:63,360 or 1:253,440 scale solid and drift series sheets, whichever were available in published form from the British Geological Survey.

Designations and management agreements also proved extremely difficult to identify and verify. Again, SMR information was inconsistent across the country, especially for non-archaeological designations such as National Parks and AONBs. Even the agencies responsible for maintaining records on such matters were unable to provide nationally consistent information at suitable scales to check against digitized transect and MARS Monument information. Most checking had to be done visually using digitized maps and scaled overlays.

3.3.3 Aerial Photographic Survey

The purpose of the Aerial Photographic Survey Programme was to provide observational data on MARS Monuments for earlier decades, wherever possible back to the 1940s. In particular, information about land-use, survival and visibility was recorded. The Aerial Photographic Survey examined a sub-sample of transects, 646 in all, containing 7005 MARS Monuments. Because not all the transects in the sub-sample had usable aerial photographs, and some monuments could not be located on available prints (mainly because the monuments were too small to pin-point), the success rate in recording data about MARS Monuments back in time was much less good than for work by the Field Survey Programme. In all, 4474 MARS Monuments (64% of those in the defined sub-sample transects) were recorded by the Aerial Photographic Programme, some of them several times over for different decades.

As explained below, the transects covered by the Aerial Photographic Survey represent a randomly drawn sub-set of the overall sample. Of the 4474 MARS Monuments examined by the Aerial Photographic Survey, 4152 (92%) were also field checked. It should be noted, however, that the range of MARS Monuments examined by the Aerial Photographic Survey was more restricted than was possible for the Field Survey because of the difficulties inherent in identifying small structures on aerial photographs. It is inherent to vertical aerial photographs, typically available as prints at scales of between 1:7500 and 1:12,000, that remains less than about 10m across are difficult to see in sufficient detail to record, for example the nature of the land-use on the monument itself. This constraint mostly affected what are defined below as small single monuments (e.g. standing stones, crosses), and standing buildings and structures.

Land-use and damage identification from aerial photography is a well-established skill, initially developed during the Second World War for the assessment of bomb damage (Nesbit 1996). It has successfully been applied in other fields (St Joseph 1977), but the identification of the condition of monuments from aerial photographs, unless they were taken under suitable conditions, is sometimes unreliable. For MARS all but the best available coverage was filtered out before interpretation work was undertaken.

The Aerial Photographic Survey was carried out by a core team of three interpreters and a programme supervisor between September 1994 and November 1996. Approximately 1800 person days were expended on the work, giving a rate of 2.5 MARS Monuments examined per person day. This includes data entry and checking, but hides the fact that some monuments may be covered by a large number of individual photographs while others have relatively little coverage. The Aerial Photographic Programme examined approximately 14,841 individual photographs during the course of its work. Approximately 100,000 images were sifted in order to find the optimum cover for the work in hand. All work for this programme was carried out in liaison with the Aerial Survey Team of the Royal Commission on the Historical Monuments of England. APPENDIX G sets out the fields recorded for the Aerial Photographic Survey.

The basic analysis and recording were done in two stages. First, a search was made using a computerized index system (PHOTONET) to identify all available vertical and oblique photographic coverage held by the RCHME. With the transect folders for those sample units to be covered by the Aerial Photographic Survey to hand, the flight-lines for available coverage were plotted, and intersections with MARS Monuments recorded. All available photographs of reasonable quality were then assembled and sorted for analysis.

Second, photographs relating to as many decades as possible for each MARS Monument in each sample transect were examined, although monuments with only one decade represented were ignored unless it was the 1940s. For each decade, a blue line was added to the main transect plan showing the extent of visible archaeology within the area previously outlined in red. Blue hatching was used to show areas of visible archaeology not included within the red line. An orange line was used to show the extent of land within the area outlined in red which had been destroyed. Thus the Current Area for earlier decades (e.g. CA65; CA45) is represented as the PAE less those areas recognized from the photographs as having been destroyed. Areas were measured using planimeters. As in the Field Survey, if the land appeared to be intact then it was assumed that some archaeology remained below the surface. With aerial photographs it is not possible to

Table 3.2 - Analysis of MARS Monuments with associated aerial photography for one or more decade 1940s to 1980s. *[Source: MARS Aerial Photographic Survey. Sample: n= 4474]*

Number of decades for which aerial photographs available	Number of MARS Monuments
1	145
2	855
3	1540
4	1331
5	603
Total	**4474**

determine height measurements very accurately so only data relating to areal extent were recorded.

The Aerial Photographic Survey was interested in all MARS Monuments recorded as at the census date of 1995. The aerial photographs themselves provide the best available objective record of what those monuments were like in the past, at least in terms of land-use and survival. The survey was retrospective, examining change by working back from the present. Thus the fact that some of the monuments under study were not part of the recorded resource at the time the photographs were taken is irrelevant; the photographs were simply used as a date-specific source of information about the recorded resource as definable in 1995. Table 3.2 shows a breakdown of the number of MARS Monuments with photography for one or more decades.

Although the RCHME's National Monuments Record Air Photographs Library contains over 4 million pictures, it was not the only collection available. Where possible, and time permitting, use was also made of photographs from the collection of the Cambridge University Committee on Aerial Photography. These were mainly oblique views. No attempt was made to draw on the aerial photographic collections held by individual local authorities, most of which date from the 1970s onwards.

3.3.4 Case Study Research

The purpose of the Case Study Research Programme was to provide insights into the way monuments are discovered in different kinds of landscape, how they decay, and what, in archaeological terms, different states of survival mean for the recovery of information. The intention was to provide a sidelight on the results of the quantitative studies forming the core of the MARS Project. The work was carried out between September 1994 and July 1996 by two research assistants, helped from time to time by the National Survey Co-ordinator and the Project Manager.

The work involved the examination and re-analysis of the findings from excavated monuments, and the study of the archaeological record in a series of areas representing recognizable land-types. APPENDIX I lists the studies carried out; the MARS archive contains a draft report on each. Figure 3.2 shows the location of the monuments and landscape areas considered. This report presents three case studies in some detail, two in Chapter 2 and one in Chapter 4, and draws on the results of others

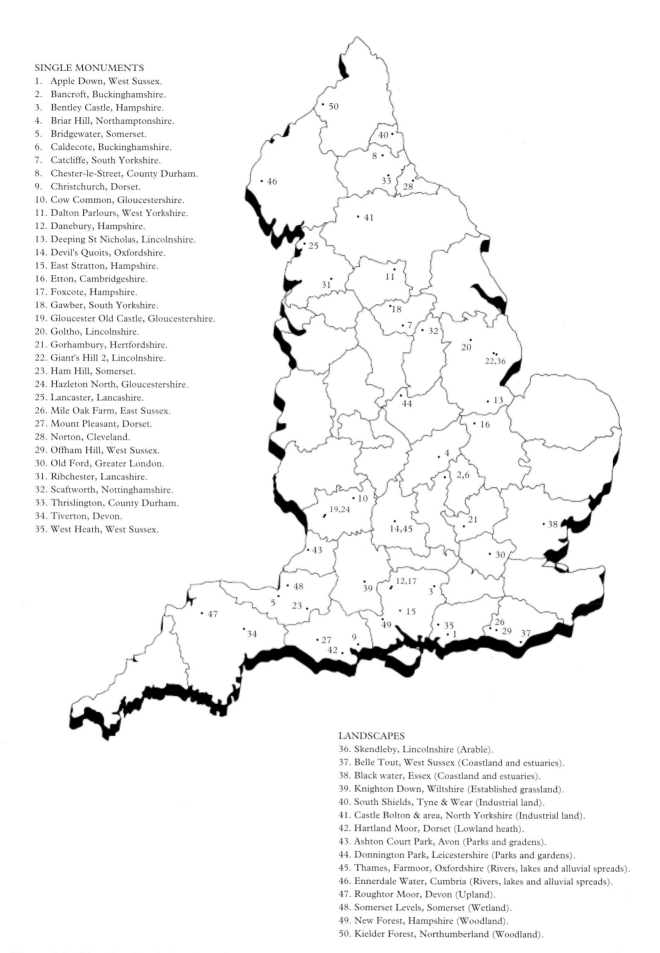

SINGLE MONUMENTS
1. Apple Down, West Sussex.
2. Bancroft, Buckinghamshire.
3. Bentley Castle, Hampshire.
4. Briar Hill, Northamptonshire.
5. Bridgewater, Somerset.
6. Caldecote, Buckinghamshire.
7. Catcliffe, South Yorkshire.
8. Chester-le-Street, County Durham.
9. Christchurch, Dorset.
10. Cow Common, Gloucestershire.
11. Dalton Parlours, West Yorkshire.
12. Danebury, Hampshire.
13. Deeping St Nicholas, Lincolnshire.
14. Devil's Quoits, Oxfordshire.
15. East Stratton, Hampshire.
16. Etton, Cambridgeshire.
17. Foxcote, Hampshire.
18. Gawber, South Yorkshire.
19. Gloucester Old Castle, Gloucestershire.
20. Goltho, Lincolnshire.
21. Gorhambury, Hertfordshire.
22. Giant's Hill 2, Lincolnshire.
23. Ham Hill, Somerset.
24. Hazleton North, Gloucestershire.
25. Lancaster, Lancashire.
26. Mile Oak Farm, East Sussex.
27. Mount Pleasant, Dorset.
28. Norton, Cleveland.
29. Offham Hill, West Sussex.
30. Old Ford, Greater London.
31. Ribchester, Lancashire.
32. Scaftworth, Nottinghamshire.
33. Thrislington, County Durham.
34. Tiverton, Devon.
35. West Heath, West Sussex.

LANDSCAPES
36. Skendleby, Lincolnshire (Arable).
37. Belle Tout, West Sussex (Coastland and estuaries).
38. Black water, Essex (Coastland and estuaries).
39. Knighton Down, Wiltshire (Established grassland).
40. South Shields, Tyne & Wear (Industrial land).
41. Castle Bolton & area, North Yorkshire (Industrial land).
42. Hartland Moor, Dorset (Lowland heath).
43. Ashton Court Park, Avon (Parks and gradens).
44. Donnington Park, Leicestershire (Parks and gardens).
45. Thames, Farmoor, Oxfordshire (Rivers, lakes and alluvial spreads).
46. Ennerdale Water, Cumbria (Rivers, lakes and alluvial spreads).
47. Roughtor Moor, Devon (Upland).
48. Somerset Levels, Somerset (Wetland).
49. New Forest, Hampshire (Woodland).
50. Kielder Forest, Northumberland (Woodland).

Figure 3.2 - Map showing the location of monuments and landscape areas used in the Case Study Research Programme.

as appropriate.

Twelve monument classes were selected for study, collectively representing a wide chronological range and considerable variety in size, scale and the type of archaeological deposits represented. In each case relatively recently excavated examples were examined in some detail, the examples being chosen to reflect what, at the time they were excavated, may be regarded as having 'good', 'medium' and 'poor' survival.

Ten studies of specific land-types were undertaken, the types selected being those discussed in *Ancient monuments in the countryside* (Darvill 1987). One or two representative areas, each covering between 4km^2 and 8km^2, were selected for study. In all cases the land-type forming the core of the study comprised at least 80% of the study area in 1995.

3.4 The MARS sampling scheme

Mark Bell

Although it might seem desirable to have examined all recorded archaeological monuments in England for the MARS Project, this would have been impractical on grounds of both cost and timescale. Moreover, standard sampling theory makes this unnecessary as it is perfectly feasible to identify patterns and trends in large data-sets from properly constituted samples. In developing an appropriate sampling scheme for MARS, the overarching aim was to obtain the best information about England's archaeological monuments from the smallest data-set. The scheme was developed on the basis of the knowledge gained from the pilot study; it had to be straightforward in practice, soundly based, and repeatable in future.

The simplest method of sampling would have been to select an appropriate number of monuments at random from an established list. However, when MARS began no such list existed in a form that could be used as a sampling frame. Instead, land area was used as the sampling frame. This had the advantage that future iterations of MARS could use the same basic sample to document changes in the recorded resource as well as in the condition of the extant resource. One concern raised as a result of the Wiltshire Pilot Study was that sample units should be aligned in different directions to take account of geological trends that tend to run from north-east to south-west. To check whether localized geological trends had an effect on various aspects of the recorded resource the decision was taken to split the sample into two parts, with one set of transects oriented east to west and the other north to south. This meant that sample units had to be rectangular in shape.

The selection of the sample size was based on information from the Wiltshire pilot study. This suggested that while a 1% sample of monuments would be large enough to give an accurate picture of the current state of the resource, it would be insufficient to show change over the last five decades because of the relatively small proportion of monuments shown in at least one aerial photograph during an earlier decade. A 1% sample with information from the 1940s was regarded as the minimum necessary to make inferences about change in the resource. The Wiltshire Pilot Study suggested that a 5% land area sample would contain 1% of monuments with photographs from the 1940s.

The sample units were oriented on the Ordnance Survey's National Grid so that monuments within each unit could be easily located in SMR records and on the ground. For practical reasons it was decided to use sample units of 1km by 5km, a selection of monuments spread over an area of 5km^2 being relatively easy to check in one day. As noted above, the sample units had to be rectangular in outline so that the sample could be split into two differently oriented sub-samples. It was also believed that, in this case, a large number of small sample units was preferable to fewer larger units, since the coverage of the former is more dispersed.

Estimates of the land area of England vary, partly because of different measuring procedures and partly because the coastline is a dynamic and constantly changing boundary. For MARS, England's land area was taken as 130,035km^2, a figure based on the estimates made in 1981 (Wisniewski 1997, 4), adjusted to exclude offshore islands as these could not be accommodated within the sampling scheme. A 5% sample of land area would thus be approximately 6502km^2, or about 1301 transects each of 5km^2.

Using these parameters a sample selection programme was written in BASIC. Each Ordnance Survey quarter-sheet (i.e. a 5km by 5km cartographic unit) was assigned a number. All possible quarter-sheets were used but no account was taken of the quantity or distribution of monuments recorded in each sheet or sample transect. North to south transects were selected first and then the east to west units. The RND function was used to generate a list of random numbers after initializing the RANDOMIZE function with a suitable random number seed. Once a quarter-sheet was selected, one of the five possible north-south strips was selected at random using a second random number. This was repeated for the east-west transects. Any overlapping units were eliminated by visual search, as were those sample units in which 50% or more of their area lay in the sea. To allow for a margin of error, more than the required 1301 units were initially selected. Since this left more than the required number, a random number generator was again used to eliminate excess units until the correct number of units were left.

Out of the 1301 sample units selected in this way, four were later rejected for technical reasons, leaving a total sample of 1297 1km by 5km units. Of the four sample units rejected, one was left out on the advice of the county SMR officer; transect 895 turned out to have the same co-ordinates as transect 900; the wrong data were sent for transect 1013 and the mistake was not discovered until both programmes were complete; and transect 1148 overlaps with part of another transect in Lincolnshire and was missed during the visual search to weed out such overlaps.

Initially, the same sample was to be used for both the Aerial Photographic Survey and the Field Survey Programmes. However, the Aerial Photographic Survey was subsequently reduced in scale because sorting and interpreting photographs took longer than expected and because more photographs were available for each sample unit than had been expected. The number of sample units in the Aerial Photographic Survey Programme was therefore reduced by half to 646 transects using a random number generator to identify sample units for exclusion.

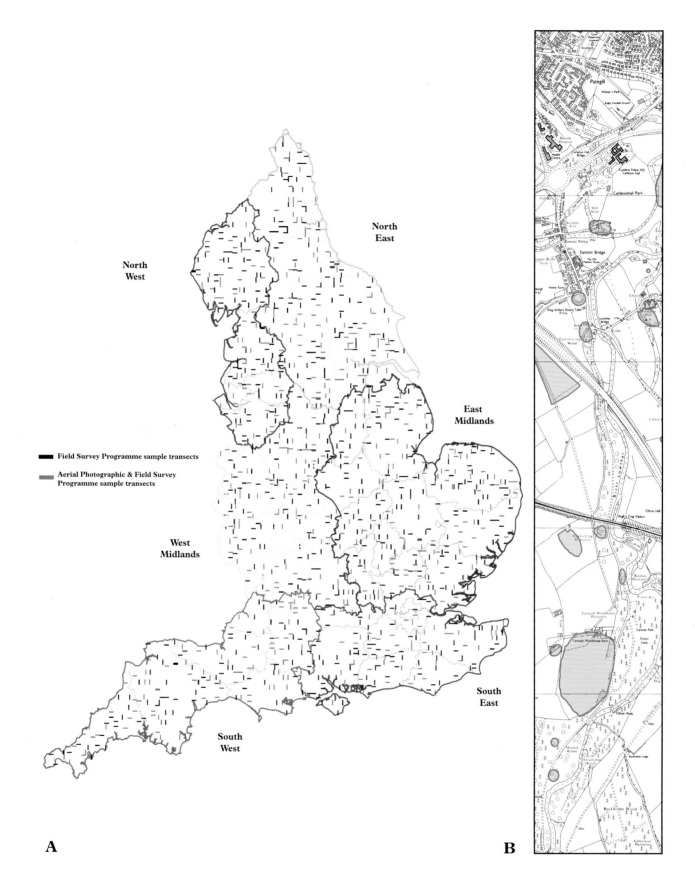

Figure 3.3 - (A) Map showing the distribution of MARS sample transects. Sample transects used in the Aerial Photographic Survey programme are highlighted in red. (B) Map showing a specimen sample transect 1km by 5km in extent. The Projected Archaeological Extent (PAE) of recorded monuments is shaded red. *[Map A created by J Chartrand; Map B reproduced from Ordnance Survey mapping with the permission of the Controller of Her Majesty's Stationery Office. Crown copyright licence number GD03093G/1/98]*

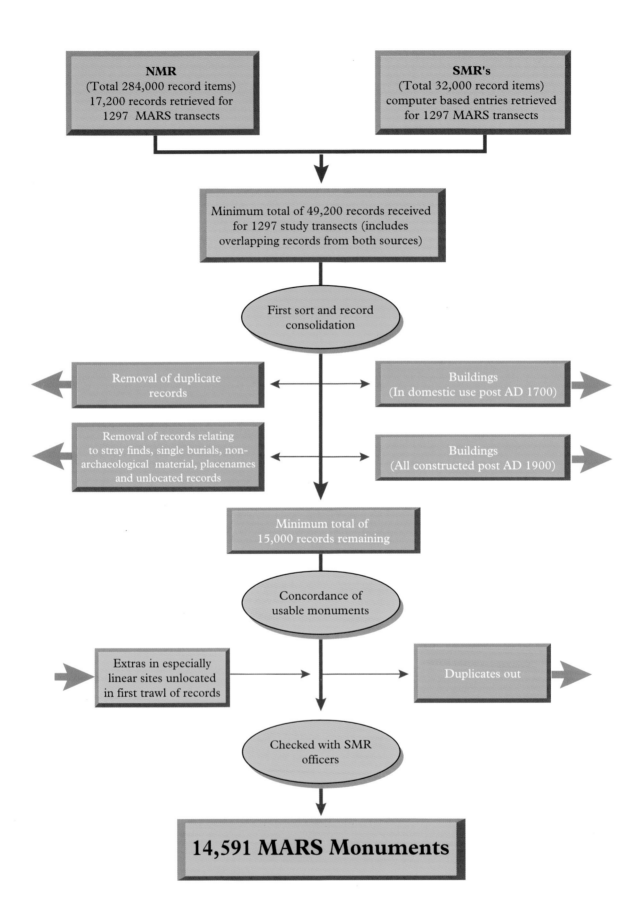

Figure 3.4 - Schematic representation of the data flow used to capture, validate and consolidate information about the recorded resource relating to each MARS transect and for the definition of MARS Monuments.

The result was a reduced sample of 324 east-west units and 322 north-south units. Figure 3.3A shows the national distribution of sample transects and indicates those included in the Aerial Photographic Survey Programme. Figure 3.3B shows a specimen sample transect maked-up with MARS Monuments.

3.5 MARS Monuments and their identification

MARS Monuments were defined above (3.2) as being the sub-set of all monuments that fell within the MARS sample transects, subject to a number of exclusions in order to sharpen the focus of what was covered by MARS at the detailed scale of analysis and to overcome inconsistencies in what was recorded in different records. Before work could begin on either the Field Survey Programme or the Aerial Photographic Survey Programme a definitive list of MARS Monuments had to be assembled. The starting point for identifying MARS Monuments was the assembly of detailed information about the recorded resource for all the sample transects.

Two main sources were used: Sites and Monuments Records, and the National Monuments Record maintained by the RCHME. Figure 3.4 shows a flow chart which summarizes the way that data from these two sources were treated.

Approximately 32,000 records relating to the 1297 transects derived from local SMRs, the majority of which were transferred electronically to the MARS master database, while the remainder were input manually from paper records. Some local SMRs were able to filter out the kinds of record that MARS was not interested in before sending their data, so this figure probably under-represents the true number of records relating to the transects held by local SMRs.

Approximately 17,200 records relating to the sample transects were supplied by RCHME from the NMR's MONARCH database. To obtain data from MONARCH an external consultant was engaged to develop a customized query and down-loading routine.

The total number of records assembled from the primary sources was therefore about 49,200. During the first sorting and record consolidation, all recognizable duplicate records were removed. These mostly arose from the same item being recorded in both the NMR and a local SMR, some because monuments were recorded twice in the same record system. Also removed were recognizable examples of the explicit exclusions discussed in section 3.2 above. At the end of this process about 15,000 records remained.

The production of a draft list of MARS Monuments for each transect involved making a concordance to link the MARS numbers with records held by the NMR or local SMR. At this stage a certain amount of 'splitting and lumping' of records was necessary to iron out local variations in the way that records for individual monuments had been constructed. As an example, consider the case of a Bronze Age round barrow cemetery which in some records would appear as numerous separate entries, one for each barrow, while the same thing in another record would appear as a single entry for the whole monument. Other difficult cases included flint and pottery scatters. For these, multiple finds in a concentration spread over a fair-sized area were included as a monument, but small numbers of sparsely scattered fragments were excluded.

Naturally, the process of producing a concordance revealed further duplicate records, especially where transects crossed county boundaries or where two records had been given different NGRs or names for the same entity. These were excluded.

A special problem was encountered with linear monuments such as Roman roads, canals and railway lines which ran over several map sheets. These might have grid references outside of the transect and hence were not always detected during computer searches and as a result were missing from the electronic records supplied to MARS. Accordingly, these monuments were added to the database during the creation of the concordance, or as a result of work by the Aerial Photographic Survey team or of the Field Survey teams finding them marked on NMR or local SMR maps.

Wherever possible the final review of the list of MARS Monuments was done by the field team supervisors during discussions with SMR Officers and the spatial delineation of the PAE with red lines. Only a few changes were necessary in the light of experience by the Field Survey teams and Aerial Photographic Survey teams.

Overall, 14,591 MARS Monuments were defined, scattered among the 1297 sample transects. Of these, 7005 lie within the 646 transects used for the aerial photographic study.

Although rigorously defined and validated as outlined above, it should be emphasized that MARS Monuments accord closely with both the theoretical concept and the legal definition of a 'monument' as discussed in Chapter 2. Equally, in considering the results of analyses presented in later chapters, it must be remembered that the list of MARS Monuments (i.e. the sample) can only be as good and complete as the original data supplied by the various national and local records.

3.6 The MARS Regions

For practical and analytical purposes MARS divided England into six regions, the position and extent of each being shown on Figure 3.5. In all cases, the boundaries of these regions are formed by county boundaries as they obtained between 1974 and 1995. The post-1974 local government administrative boundaries for districts, counties and metropolitan counties were used throughout the MARS Project. The definitive map used in the project was the Ordnance Survey's 1:625,000 map of Great Britain showing Local Government administrative areas (Ordnance Survey 1986). It is recognized, however, that the reorganization of the metropolitan counties by 1995 and the shire counties in 1995-6 means that some of the administrative units used in MARS no longer exist. APPENDIX J provides a concordance of MARS Regions with counties and other defined regions.

Table 3.3 shows the size of each region, the number of sample transects represented, the area represented by the transects, and the number of MARS Monuments represented in the transects. From the table it can be seen that the regions do not vary greatly in area; the range is between 11% and 26% of the land area of England with a

Figure 3.5 - Map showing the disposition and extent of MARS Regions.

Table 3.3 - Key statistics for MARS Regions in relation to estimated land area, the distribution of MARS sample transects, the recorded resource revealed by the National Survey, and the distribution of MARS Monuments. *[Source: MARS National Survey Programme]*

Region	Land area (Sq km)	% land area	Number of sample units	Land areas of sample units	% of sample (by sample units)	Number of archeological records	% of archeological records	Number of Monuments	% of Monuments	Number of MARS Monuments	% of MARS Monuments
North West	14382	11%	171	855	13%	46138	7%	38752	9%	1928	13%
North East	23866	18%	221	1105	17%	108087	16%	72826	17%	2532	18%
West Midlands	20713	16%	206	1030	16%	78850	12%	45175	10%	2088	14%
East Midlands	33814	26%	346	1730	27%	156067	24%	114938	27%	3210	22%
South West	21245	16%	190	950	15%	130574	20%	59154	14%	2955	20%
South East	16015	13%	163	815	12%	137903	21%	101346	23%	1878	13%
Total	**130035**	**100%**	**1297**	**6485**	**100%**	**657619**	**100%**	**432191**	**100%**	**14591**	**100%**

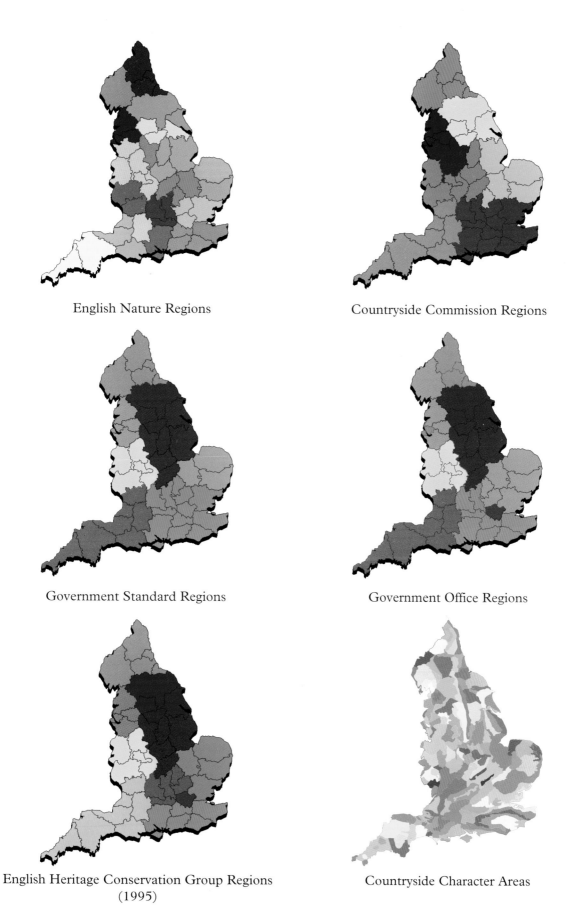

English Nature Regions

Countryside Commission Regions

Government Standard Regions

Government Office Regions

English Heritage Conservation Group Regions
(1995)

Countryside Character Areas

Figure 3.6 - Maps showing the regional subdivisions used by other organizations: English Nature, Countryside Commission, Government Standard Statistical Regions, Government Office Regions, English Heritage Conservation Group Regions as in 1995, and the Countryside Character Areas. *[Sources: various]*

mean of 16%. There are slightly greater discrepancies in the distribution of archaeological records between regions, the range here is between 7% in the North West through to 24% in the East Midlands. The distribution of MARS Monuments between regions is more equitable, and ranges from 13% in the North West to 22% in the East Midlands. No attempt has been made to even up the size of regions as this would only introduce other imbalances.

All the MARS Regions included acceptable samples for the purposes of quantifying the resource, and the fact that some have more than others is a function of using a random sampling scheme. Moreover, the regions were chosen to reflect broad geo-topographic regions within England and thus to have a degree of integrity in their own right. The North West region, for example, covers the exposed uplands and coastal plain of the Lake District and ground west of the Pennines. The East Midlands, the biggest region, reflects the relatively low-lying ground of East Anglia, the Fens and the London Basin. In general, the defined regions also tend to encompass distinctive patterns of land-use, economy and climate, all relevant factors for the future management of monuments.

Figure 3.6 shows, for comparison, regional subdivisions used by other organizations, namely the Countryside Commission, English Nature, Government Standard Statistical Regions, the Government Office Regions as announced in August 1997 (DETR 1997), and the operating areas of English Heritage's Conservation Group at the time of MARS in 1995. Of these, only the Government Office Regions are used for analyses later in this report. APPENDIX J summarizes, as far as possible, the relationships between MARS Regions, Government Statistical Regions and the Government Office Regions.

Attention may also be drawn, however, to the Countryside Character Areas as defined by the Countryside Commission and English Nature as a result of a study published in 1996 (Countryside Commission 1996a). This set of defined areas takes account of, among other factors, natural, historical and archaeological data. The areas are too small in themselves to be studied by MARS because the samples falling within each would be so small, but there is considerable correspondence between broad blocks of Countryside Character Areas and the MARS Regions. APPENDIX J includes a concordance of Countryside Character Areas in relation to MARS Regions.

3.7 How good is the sample?

Mike Baxter

An independent technical assessment of the approach to, effectiveness of and validity of the project's sampling strategy was undertaken in 1996-7 during the assessment and analysis phase of the project. Discussions were held to establish basic information and a series of statistical tests were carried out. There is no single way in which 'validity' or 'goodness' can be defined in this context, and accordingly six aspects of sample collection and interpretation were examined:

1   A critique of the original sampling design was undertaken. This included a re-analysis of various

tests undertaken during the pilot phase of the main project (carried out for Wiltshire). Their outcomes were to influence decisions about the overall sample design.

2   In the light of this, a review was carried out of the sampling theory that could be used to estimate quantities of interest, and the statistical errors associated with them.

3   The critique suggested that the achieved sample consists of two distinct samples, defined by the orientation of sample transects. The validity of combining the two samples was examined, and in the course of this the application of the sampling theory was illustrated.

4   The extent to which missing data in the sample could determine the usefulness of results was also examined.

5   The extent to which sample estimates are consistent with selected 'population' values determined from the National Survey was examined.

6   The validity of data from the aerial photography programme was examined.

These matters are dealt with seriatim in the following sub-sections.

3.7.1 A critique of the sample design
Detailed information about the recorded archaeological resource in England was not available at the outset of the Project so a 'surrogate' sampling frame was used. This frame was the 26,000 1km by 5km transects covering the land area of England, a 5% sample of which was selected for study.

In terms of standard sampling theory the sample can be viewed in different ways. A simple random sample of transects was intended, and analysis could be conducted at the level of the transect. Equivalently, the sample may be viewed as a one-stage cluster sample, with the monument the basic unit of record. It is argued later that the achieved sample is not precisely the simple random sample which was intended, and that in some ways it mimics a two-stage cluster sample.

A stratified sample could have been selected, for example based on defined land-use regimes, but this would have added greatly to the complexity of sample selection. It could be argued that this added complexity militates against the use of a stratified sample, especially in view of the fact that no detailed information on the distribution of land-use was available. Moreover, if transects are used as the sampling unit there is the problem of multiple land-uses. Defining strata to consist of uniform land-uses is not a trivial problem and would have added considerably to the cost and complexity of both sampling and analysis. There is, additionally, the fact that stratification suitable for one variable may be unsuitable for others. Thus, despite the fact that there is probably an association between land-use and condition, the use here of a simple random sample of transects is supported on grounds of cost, simplicity and ease of analysis.

The precise method of transect selection is discussed above (3.4). In general, selection of transects was based on the random selection of a 5km by 5km National Grid square followed by a randomly sampled transect from within the selected square. Sampling of squares was with replacement; sampling of transects was without replacement. In the project design it was noted that 'England has a natural "grain" of geology running north-east to south-west' which might influence the preservation and condition of monuments (Darvill *et al.* 1994, 42). To overcome this perceived problem half the transects were oriented north-south and half east-west. North-south transects were selected first, and the grid squares containing them were excluded in the selection of the east-west transects. It was noted that any grid square could potentially have up to five transects selected from it.

This procedure causes problems of various kinds. There are approximately 26,000 1km by 5km transects in the population, and therefore approximately 5200 5km by 5km grid squares. The 651 north-south transects selected were from 649 of these, with just two squares being sampled for more than one transect. Since these 649 squares are excluded from sampling for east-west transects, such transects are being sampled from approximately three-quarters of England's land area, with the remaining quarter 'missing' randomly. In other words, the north-south transects constitute a 2.5% sample of England's land area while the 650 east-west transects constitute a 2.9% sample of three-quarters of the land area.

Thus, rather than a single simple random sample of transects, two simple random samples have been selected. If the rationale for making the north-south / east-west distinction is correct then the possibility exists that these samples will display different properties. Since they are both random samples of the same land area, or a randomly selected portion thereof, both should lead to statistically similar estimates of means and totals, but may differ in their variability. This possibility has been investigated (see below 3.7.7).

Combining the two samples, even if valid, produces a single sample that does not possess some of the properties to be expected of a simple random sample. Had a simple random sample of 1301 transects been selected one would have expected that about 34 squares would be sampled for two or more transects. In the event, only six such squares have been selected. This is a demonstrably predictable result of the selection procedure adopted. The sample achieved looks almost identical, apart from 6 squares, to that which would be obtained using two-stage cluster sampling. That is, the combined sample looks very close to one obtained by first selecting a National Grid square without replacement and then selecting a transect within the square.

To summarize, there is a concern about the legitimacy of amalgamating the north-south and east-west transect samples, if the legitimacy of making this distinction is valid in the first place. If amalgamation is valid, and this will be examined later, then the sample achieved is not the simple random sample of transects originally envisaged.

The use of a 5% sample was determined on a pragmatic basis. Analysis of the pilot data on monument condition suggested that a 1% sample allowed an estimate of monument condition that did not differ significantly from the known population distribution. From the pilot study it is known that there were aerial photographs from the 1940s for only about one in four monuments, so to achieve a sample size that allowed a reasonable estimation of condition in the 1940s it was argued that at least a 4% sample was needed. This was increased to 5% to allow for uncertainty in the estimate of the proportion of monuments covered by aerial photographs in other parts of England. This led to 1301 transects being sampled. This essentially pragmatic approach seems reasonable, but in retrospect it can be seen that aerial photographic coverage of Wiltshire is atypical. Furthermore, many more aerial photographs from the 1940s became available after the survey started as a result of further accessions to the RCHME's library of aerial photographs. Of the monument forms selected for the Aerial Photographic Survey, 1940s photographs were found for about 75%.

Sample units that did not contain any previously recorded monuments were, quite properly, recorded in the main survey and were not subsequently replaced.

3.7.2 Sampling theory

Estimates of means and their precision can now be used to compare results for the two samples collected, of north-south and east-west transects. These estimates can be obtained using standard simple random sampling theory. It emerges that there are no important differences between the samples, which can thus be merged into a single combined sample. However, this single sample does not have all the properties that a single random sample should have, and does not quite conform to any of the standard designs covered by authorities such as Cochran (1977). In many ways the combined sample mimics a two-stage cluster sample. If it is treated as such, however, it is not possible to estimate standard errors, because at the second stage of sampling only one unit is sampled. This is discussed later, where it is argued that a safe way to proceed is to treat the sample as a simple random sample. In other words, although the sample does not have all the characteristics that a simple random sample should have it can be treated as such: the achieved sample is not quite what was intended, but it can be safely treated as if it were. An example of the calculations is given here, drawing on the results set out below. This raises other practical issues, and introduces the later analysis of the comparison between north-south and east-west transects.

The 1297 usable sampled transects each contain between 0 and 159 MARS Monuments. Figure 3.7 shows the cumulative distribution of MARS Monuments per transect, separated according to whether the transect was north-south or east-west. First, it may be noted that for practical purposes the results for the two kinds of transect are almost indistinguishable. Second, some east-west transects clearly contain more monuments than any north-south transect. The maximum number of monuments for a north-south transect was 76. Three east-west transects had noticeably greater numbers: 94, 110 and 159. This has consequences for the comparison of results below.

After amalgamating the two samples the distribution of MARS Monuments per transect is shown in Figure 3.8. The most striking characteristic of this figure is its positive skewness. Such skewness can

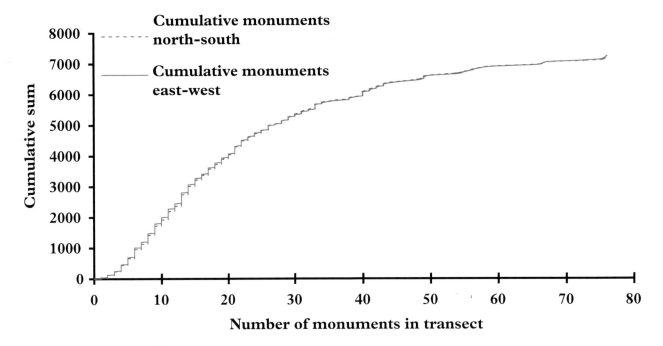

Figure 3.7 - Cumulative distribution of MARS Monuments per transect, grouped by north-south oriented transects (dotted line) and east-west oriented transects (solid red line).

compromise the integrity of the normal approximations used to construct confidence intervals for means etc. Cochran (1977, 39-44) suggests, as a crude rule of thumb, that $n>25G^2$ (where G is a particular measure of skewness) should be satisfied for the approximations to be reasonable. In the present case the rule gives a value of 320. The actual sample size is comfortably in excess of this, so that the results to follow are reasonable.

The mean number of MARS Monuments from 1297 sampled transects is 11.27. Under the two proposals for estimating the standard deviation given below the first,

which is an underestimate, gives 0.295. The second estimate, assuming simple random sampling, is 0.340. Dividing these numbers by 5 converts to the estimated density per km². Thus, under the first proposal, the estimated density is 2.254 with estimated standard deviation 0.059 and an approximate 95% confidence interval for the true density is (2.138, 2.370). For the second proposal the corresponding limits are (2.121, 2.387). Estimated totals may be treated in a similar way. For example, under the second proposal, assuming a population of 26,000 transects, the estimated total

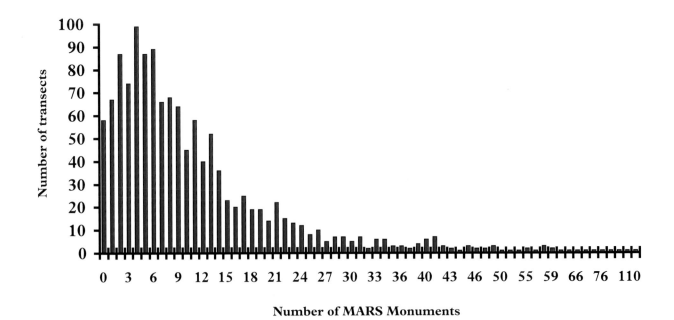

Figure 3.8 - Distribution of MARS Monuments per transect.

number of MARS Monuments is 293,036 and the 95% confidence interval is (275,695 310,377).

3.7.3 A comparison of north-south and east-west transect samples

As the distinction between north-south and east-west transects is drawn in the project design, and as this has unintended consequences for the nature of the achieved sample, it is prudent to establish that they give similar results. The data relating to monument form have been analysed (see Chapter 5.3 for definitions of forms), one of the few variables for which information is complete. This also serves to demonstrate a number of data-analytical issues that need to be borne in mind in analysis and interpretation. Analyses for other variables are summarized. The overall conclusion is that, for practical purposes, results from the two samples are statistically indistinguishable. It has already been argued that two separate simple random samples have, in fact, been selected. One is of north-south samples from England's total land area, and the second is of east-west samples taken from about three-quarters of the land area (randomly determined). Standard simple random sampling theory can be used to get estimates from these samples. Missing information is not a problem for monument form; the consequences of missing data for other variables is discussed later. In the results to follow finite population corrections are ignored, as the sampling fractions are small.

In calculating statistics, 1297 sample transects are used, including those for which there are no recorded MARS Monuments. For monument form there are 14,591 monuments. The data can be presented in various ways, based on the counts given in Table 3.4. To get a feel for the similarity of the two sample conversions to percentages, which are also estimates of population percentages, it is probably most effective to view the data as proportions. Rounding to the nearest whole number gives the figures in Table 3.5. Results for the two samples are very similar, and if all that is needed is to demonstrate that such estimates are much the same for both samples this would suffice.

To examine the reliability of estimates it is easiest, in terms of standard sampling theory, to work with the mean numbers of monuments (totals or proportions could also be used). These are given in Table 3.6. The main reason for working with means is that calculation of their estimated standard errors is straightforward. These are given in Table 3.7. There are two points to notice here. The first is that the means for the two samples, whatever the monument form, are separated by less than the larger of the standard errors of the means for the two samples. This demonstrates, without the need for formal testing, that the estimates of the means are statistically similar. The second point is that the estimates of the standard errors are generally similar, but differ more than might be expected for field systems and small single monuments. This is mainly due to the fact that the distribution of numbers of monuments of a particular form within transects is highly skew, with extreme outliers in some cases. This is investigated further below.

In summary, and subject to the caveat about relative sizes of standard errors, amalgamation of the two samples seems justified for monument form. The combined sample can then be treated as if it is a single simple random sample from the population, at least approximately (see below).

Data of the kind in the previous section allow statements of the form 'an approximate 95% confidence interval for the mean number of small single monuments per transect, in the population, is (5.90, 6.86)'. The above calculation ignores finite population corrections, and assumes that use of approximations based on the normal distribution are valid. A critical value of 2 rather than 1.96 has been used. As with numbers of monuments per transect the skewness of the distribution is potentially a problem. Using the rule of thumb given in the section on sampling theory a sample of 555 is needed for the approximation to be valid; there is therefore no problem.

To arrive at population totals the means can be multiplied by the total number of 1km by 5km transects in the population. It is similarly straightforward to convert to a figure for estimated density per square kilometre. It is marginally more difficult to assign confidence limits to proportions. The estimated proportion of small single monuments is 0.57, and this is a ratio estimate. Using the theory outlined below, this gives an estimated standard error for this of 0.02 and hence an approximate 95%

Table 3.4 - MARS Monuments by monument form and transect orientation. *[Source: MARS Field Survey Programme. Sample: n= 14,591]*

Sample	Field system	Large single monument	Linear monument	Small single monument	Standing building
North-South	389	584	634	4035	1549
East-West	362	659	609	4241	1528
Total	**751**	**1243**	**1243**	**8276**	**3077**

Table 3.5 - Percentage of MARS Monuments by monument form and transect orientation. *[Source: MARS Field Survey Programme. Sample: n= 14,591]*

Sample	Field system %	Large single monument %	Linear monument %	Small single monument %	Standing building %	Total %
North-South	5	8	9	56	22	100
East-West	5	9	8	57	21	100
All	**5**	**9**	**8**	**57**	**21**	**100**

Table 3.6 - Mean number of MARS Monuments per sample transect, by monument form and transect orientation. *[Source: MARS Field Survey Programme. Sample: n= 14,591]*

Sample	Field system	Large single monument	Linear monument	Small single monument	Standing building
North-South	0.60	0.90	0.98	6.23	2.39
East-West	0.56	1.02	0.94	6.53	2.35
All	**0.58**	**0.96**	**0.96**	**6.38**	**2.37**

Table 3.7 - Standard errors for the mean number of MARS Monuments per transect, by monument form and transect orientation. *[Source: MARS Field Survey Programme. Sample: n= 14,591]*

Sample	Field system	Large single monument	Linear monument	Small single monument	Standing building
North-South	0.08	0.05	0.07	0.29	0.17
East-West	0.05	0.06	0.07	0.38	0.17
All	**0.05**	**0.04**	**0.05**	**0.24**	**0.12**

Table 3.8 - Distribution of monument form within 'inaccessible' and 'accessible' transects. *[Source: MARS Field Survey Programme. Sample: n= 14,591]*

Sample	Field system %	Large single monument %	Linear monument %	Small single monument %	Standing building %	Total %
Inaccessible	2	10	7	71	10	100
Accessible	5	8	8	57	22	100
All	**5**	**9**	**8**	**57**	**21**	**100**

confidence interval of 0.53, 0.61. Table 3.5 shows the same data as percentages.

One problem related to skewness is the effect of extremes in the data. It was noted from Table 3.7 that two of the pairs of standard errors were not as close as would be expected if east-west and north-south transects were both random samples from the same population. In both cases there is an extreme observation. Thus, for east-west transects and small single monuments, one transect has 131 monuments and the next largest 61. This will inflate the estimate of the standard error. If the transect is omitted from calculations the standard error is reduced from 0.38 to 0.33, which is closer to that for the north-south transects.

Analyses for other variables have been undertaken in a similar way. The variables used were geology, access, amelioration, risk, management, visibility, impact, sub-surface damage, land-use on and around the monument, and cause of damage. A slightly different form of analysis was undertaken for area loss above and below ground. For most of these data there are missing values, and the estimates of means will be biased. This does not affect the comparison of north-south and east-west statistics, since they will be biased in a similar way. The more general problem of missing data is discussed below.

3.7.4 Missing data and their consequences

There are a total of 14,591 MARS Monuments in the sample, of which 13,488 were surveyed. Except for monument form and geology, for which information for all MARS Monuments was available, at least 7.6% of data is missing for other variables used in the survey. For particular variables the percentage missing may be higher if, for example, a monument was surveyed but the variable

of interest could not be, or was not, recorded. Data can be 'missing' or 'not there' for different reasons, and some care needs to be exercised in the treatment and evaluation of the consequences. The following problems have been recognized:

1   Of the 1301 transects selected for sampling four could not be used for a variety of reasons. This number is so small as not to constitute a problem.

2   Fifty-eight sample units devoid of archaeology were included in any calculations of estimates and their precision.

3   Some monuments could not be surveyed.

Suppose (although this was not the case) that either all or none of the MARS Monuments in a transect could be surveyed. Quantities such as means, densities etc. could then be estimated from those transects for which data were available. Under the questionable assumption that data were missing randomly these would then be unbiased estimates of population values. The true situation is not so simple, since the 1103 monuments not surveyed were distributed over 412 transects, only 20 of which could not be surveyed at all. The obvious approach, again assuming that data were missing at random, is to apply a simple correction factor. This is best illustrated by example.

The numbers of monuments in four risk categories were 244, 5807, 3460 and 3978, totalling 13,489. There were 1103 monuments for which data were missing. Scaling these figures up, on the assumption that these

1103 were distributed among the categories in the proportions observed, involves multiplying the numbers in each risk category by 1.082 (= 14591, the sum total of MARS Monuments, divided by 13489) to give 264, 6281, 3744 and 4304. Dividing by 1297, the number of transects, then gives the estimated mean densities per transect of 0.20, 4.84, 2.89 and 3.32. If proportions, or relative proportions, are required no rescaling is necessary, but it must still be assumed that data are missing randomly.

However, the assumption that the data are missing randomly is not a safe one. Some indication of this can be seen if transects are separated into those with 50% or more of the MARS Monuments within them unaccessed, and the rest.

Table 3.8 shows the distribution of monument form within the 'inaccessible' transects and the accessible remainder. The main difference is that small single monuments are more likely to be inaccessible than standing buildings. These figures are indicative only; the numbers of 'inaccessible' transects are small, and no account is taken of standard errors. The main point is to suggest that it cannot be assumed that data are missing randomly. A similar analysis was undertaken for geology, the other variable for which full information is available. There is some suggestion that calcareous and igneous / metamorphic rocks are over-represented in the 'missing' transects, and that clay and sandstone / sedimentary rocks are under-represented.

There is little that can be done about this. Fortunately for this study, the amount of missing data is in most cases small, so that scaled figures based on the assumption of randomly missing data are unlikely to be seriously misleading for the field survey data. If necessary, 'worst case' figures could be calculated, by assigning all missing data to a single class to see the difference in results this generates; however, the 'worst case' is highly unlikely to be the true one. The aerial photography data are discussed elsewhere, and present a different problem. In particular, the programme required data for at least two distinct decades, and for most pairs of decades over 50% of the data are missing. In consequence it is unsafe to treat the available data as a random sample, although this does not preclude analysis, provided that suitable caveats are entered.

3.7.5 Comparison with National Survey data

The purpose of sampling is usually to arrive at an estimate of population quantities that are unknown. Usually, therefore, the 'validity' of sample results cannot be checked against known population figures. This is generally true of the field survey results. Some 'population' figures are, however, available from the National Survey for monument class, and it is interesting to compare these with the estimates derived from the MARS sample. Table 3.9 shows comparative figures for nine monument classes whose definitions were initially thought to be compatible between the two surveys. The second column gives the gross 'population' counts derived from the National Survey, ordered by magnitude. The third column gives the numbers of each monument class in the MARS sample. Multiplying these by 20 would give an estimate of the population total and thus represent the picture for all recorded examples in each monument class.

An immediately apparent feature of the sample data is that for five out of the nine classes there is a different ordering by magnitude of count compared with the National Survey data. This suggests that the results from the two surveys may not be compatible. This suggestion can be examined more precisely by calculating 95% confidence intervals for estimates of population totals based on MARS Monuments; the final column of Table 3.9 shows the results. For each of the five commonest classes the National Survey figure is not contained in the confidence interval. The differences between the two surveys are considerable in some cases; for example, the National Survey recorded more than twice as many field systems as were estimated from the MARS sample.

Given the apparent lack of comparability between the National and MARS sample data, what conclusions can be drawn concerning sample validity? The basic sampling scheme used for MARS is sound, so very gross levels of mis-classification, non-recording or inconsistency in the sample would be necessary to explain the differences if the National Survey figures are 'correct'. It seems much more likely that the differences arise because the ways in which monument classes were defined and recorded during the collation and validation of data for the two surveys were not as comparable as was hoped. It is beyond the scope of this report to speculate further on what the precise differences might be, but it is notable that the four classes of monument where the National Survey

Table 3.9 - Population figures for the National Survey compared to MARS sampled number for nine monument classes with lower and upper estimates of the population size at 95% confidence limits based on MARS Monuments in the sample transects. *[Source: MARS National Survey Programme. Sample: as shown]*

Class	Population (National Survey)	MARS Monuments in sample transects	Lower estimate	Upper estimate
Field systems	7760	180	2873	4326
Deserted villages	5565	222	3753	5126
Roads	3264	261	4439	6001
Villas	1157	43	584	1136
Pottery kilns	586	11	79	369
Mottes	556	29	371	789
Windmill mounds	365	24	282	678
Stone circles	311	12	105	375
Henges	192	17	145	535

and the MARS sample agree closely (shaded on Table 3.9) are all well-defined, easily recognized and relatively small groups. The implication is that any extrapolations or forecasts made from the MARS sample must be clearly understood in terms of the definitions used within MARS, rather than of definitions used elsewhere.

3.7.6 The Aerial Photographic Survey sample

The Aerial Photographic Survey sample was selected randomly from total sample to comprise half of the transects covered by the Field Survey. The selected sample contained 7005 monuments in 646 transects. This resulted from a redesign of the scheme for this element of the project and was undertaken for practical reasons of time and resources. As already noted, the difference between the anticipated number of aerial photographs for the 1940s and the actual number was very marked (see above 3.7.1). The figures for aerial photographic coverage of the sample used by MARS are as follows: 1940s = 76%; 1950s = 51%; 1960s = 55%; 1970s = 54%; and 1980s = 29%. This mismatch between expectation and actuality has obvious implications for the proposed analytical programme.

Some consequences of the mismatch in relation to the original aims are outlined in the next sub-section. The validity of the aerial photographic sample, in the sense that it is a good random sample from the population, is not an issue. The problems lie in the extent to which data are missing and the extent of this problem for different decades. The most constructive approach was to try to assess what might be done with the data obtained, and this is addressed below in the context of what was initially proposed.

A major theme of MARS was to document and understand the nature of change in the resource, and the Aerial Photographic Survey was crucial for this. From the outset there was a reasonable expectation that aerial photographic coverage would increase with time. The fact that the opposite appears to be the case confounded expectation and caused problems for the intended analysis.

1   For any pair of decades the maximum number of monuments for which a decay measure may be obtained is less than the minimum of the number of aerial photographs in each of the two decades. The two decades for which most data are available are the 1990s (Field Survey data), and the 1940s. The coverage will be less than 76%, since some monuments for which aerial photographs are available were not surveyed in the 1990s.

2   For all other pairs of decades the corresponding figure is likely to be somewhat less than 50%, and somewhat less than 30% in comparisons involving the 1980s.

The conclusion to be drawn from this is that for most pairs of decades the missing data problem precludes the rigorous statistical analysis of change that was envisaged at the outset. This does not rule out the descriptive use of the data, but means that any conclusions need to be carefully assessed qualitatively rather than quantitatively. In other words, those monuments for which the full set of structured data exists, however that is defined, cannot be regarded as a random sample of the population, and they therefore cannot validly be used for statistical inferential purposes such as the estimation of unbiased estimates and of the precision of such estimates. These observations apply directly to the aerial photographic data. One implication is that, for the earlier decades at least, the Aerial Photographic Survey could not

Table 3.10 - Proportions of monument form (%) by decade for MARS Monuments with an available aerial photograph. 1990 figures derived from field survey. *[Source: MARS Aerial Photographic Survey and Field Survey Programmes. Sample: n is the sample size of available aerial photographs where the maximum possible is 5600]*

Decade	Field system %	Large single monument %	Linear monument %	Small single monument %	No. of aerial photographs available
1940s	9	12	12	67	4282
1950s	8	12	11	68	2826
1960s	7	13	11	69	3062
1970s	8	13	12	66	3035
1980s	8	13	13	67	1598
1990s	7	11	11	72	~

Table 3.11 - Percentages showing the distribution of current visibility categories for MARS monuments for which 1940s aerial photographs available and not available. *[Source: MARS Aerial Photographic Survey Programme. Sample: as shown]*

Status on aerial photograph	Available (APA) %	Not available (APN) %
Visible	32	24
Barely visible	6	3
Not visible	58	71
Obscured	4	2

be used for generating reliable, in the sense of statistically unbiased, information about the population.

In the event, and paradoxically, it is the earliest decade covered, the 1940s, that holds out most hope of a reliable comparison with the Field Survey data of the 1990s. For other inter-decade comparisons the missing data problem precludes rigorous comparisons. For the 1940s and 1990s the number of aerial photographs is large enough to generate statistics which may be reasonably reliable, provided that they are interpreted with due caution and that not too much is read into small differences or minor 'trends'. The sample is subject to bias.

Monuments may be divided into those for which aerial photographs are available (APA) from the 1940s and those for which aerial photographs are not available (APN). Apart from monuments that were not inspected in the Field Survey, APA and APN monuments have been monitored and their present state is known. If APN monuments are missing at random then, for any variable, results should be similar to those for APA monuments apart from sampling fluctuations.

Table 3.10 shows the distribution of monument form for the aerial photographs in each decade, compared with that for the Field Survey sample, used as the baseline for comparison. One feature of these figures is the stability of the distribution from one decade to the next. Relative to the Field Survey figures, which are an estimate of the population percentages, small single monuments seem slightly under-represented in the aerial photographic sample. This does not of course take account of standard errors, but the pattern is consistent.

The stability is comforting but conceals the fact that biases nevertheless exist. This may be demonstrated using a slightly different form of presentation for the 1940s and 1990s data only. Table 3.11 compares the APA and APN monuments in terms of their current visibility. It is clear that monuments for which aerial photographs from the 1940s are not available are currently more likely to be non-visible than monuments for which aerial photographs are available. This indicates that APNs are not 'missing' randomly. A similar phenomenon can be seen if current land-use on the monument is examined. To highlight the most obvious differences, a comparison of the number of monuments identified as being under agricultural land-use is over-represented in the APA sample (48% compared to 34% for the APN sample), while residential use (8% and 17% respectively) and industrial and commercial use (3% and 10% respectively) are under-represented. The main reason for this is considered to be the fact that small monuments in built-up areas could not be securely identified on the photographs and were thus omitted from the analysis.

Finally, the 'cause of damage' variable was examined. Again, to highlight the most obvious differences, agriculture is over-represented in the APA sample (40% compared to 26% for the APN sample) as are natural processes (19%, 14%). Unknown causes (9%, 16%) and urbanization (3%, 10%) are under-represented. The bias towards agricultural causes of damage is clearly correlated with the similar bias towards land-use on monument.

The main purpose of quoting these figures is to demonstrate that the aerial photographic sample clearly is subject to bias, because the missing data are demonstrably

not missing randomly. However, the APA sample for the 1940s is also large enough to contain useful information. While the size of the bias for any given comparison with the 1990s cannot easily be quantified a mental adjustment of 8-10% (the sort of adjustment an experienced poll-watcher might make to a General Election poll) would almost certainly err on the side of caution and avoid over-interpretation of any set of figures.

3.7.7 Overall conclusions

The rationale for the original sampling design was limited in some respects, and aspects of the design and intended treatment could have been strengthened. Despite this, and because of what was actually done, the achieved sample can be treated, approximately, as the simple random sample of transects intended. From this point of view the sample is valid, and internal evidence such as the comparison of the north-south and east-west transects suggests it behaves as a simple random sample.

As demonstrated, simple random sampling theory can be applied to obtain estimates of population quantities and their precision. Potential practical problems arise from the skewness of much of the data, outliers and missing data. The sample size is such that the first two problems are not serious for any of the analyses described here, though they would need to be evaluated for any analyses focusing on a small sub-set of the data.

Missing data are a more serious problem, since it cannot be assumed that data are missing at random. For the Field Survey data, however, the scale of the problem is not great, and assuming that data are missing randomly is unlikely to be seriously misleading.

Comparisons of Field Survey estimates of totals in different monument classes with National Survey figures show them to be incompatible for the larger classes for which comparisons were made. Several reasons for this discrepancy could be advanced. There is no obvious reason why the Field Survey results should be seriously in error, so that the discrepancies are more likely to have arisen because of the unintended use of different definitions of monument class between the two surveys.

It is unlikely that the Aerial Photographic Survey data can be used in the manner originally intended, because of the extent of missing data. It was always anticipated that data would be missing, but it was thought that this would mostly be a problem for earlier decades. In the event, the only pair of decades for which there is less than about 50% missing data are the 1940s and 1990s, for which about 25% of data are missing in a manner that is demonstrably biased. This does not prevent the use of the data for comparative purposes, but it does militate against the use of rigorous inferential statistical procedures for assessing the statistical significance of differences.

In summary, four main conclusions were reached. First, the most important practical consequence of the original sample design is that the achieved sample really consists of two separate simple random samples, rather than the intended single simple random sample. Nevertheless, standard sampling theory can be applied as an approximation to the total sample to obtain estimates of quantities of interest and their precision.

Second, there are missing data problems associated with the Field Survey data, but these do not appear to be serious.

Third, the estimates from the Field Survey do not,

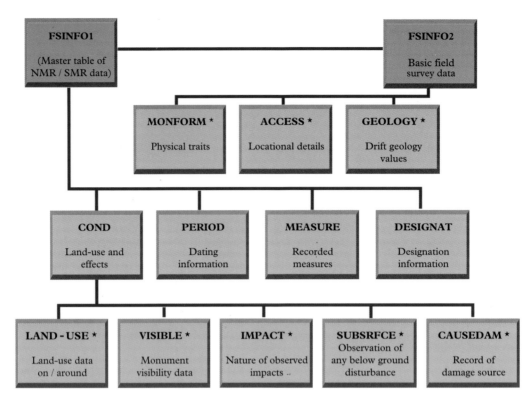

Figure 3.9 – Schematic structure of MARS Field Survey database (* indicates table of controlled vocabulary).

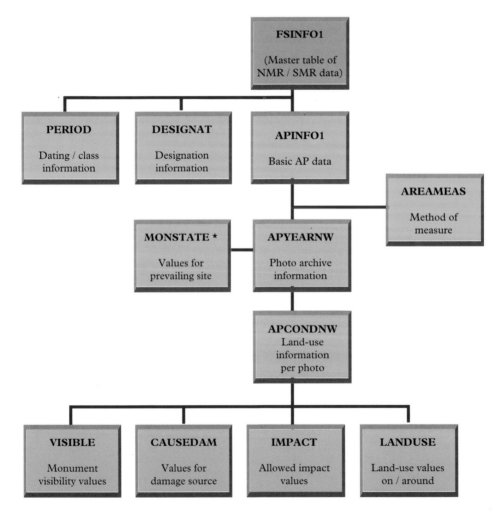

Figure 3.10 – Schematic structure of MARS Aerial Photographic Survey database (* indicates table of controlled vocabulary).

in general, seem compatible with 'population' quantities derived from the National Survey, where these are available.

Fourth, the nature of the aerial photography data is different from that originally envisaged. In particular, and contrary to expectations, the only decade with enough data to offer hope for a rigorous statistical comparison with the Field Survey data is the 1940s. Even here there are enough missing data, with a demonstrable bias, to suggest that the data are best used descriptively rather than inferentially.

3.8 The MARS databases and their analysis

Mark Bell

The master database for the MARS Project was constructed in Paradox for Windows. Figures 3.9 and 3.10 show the schematic structure of the database tables holding Field Survey and Aerial Photographic Survey data.

Overall, the MARS database consists of 31 separate tables. In addition to the 21 database tables shown on Figures 3.9 and 3.10, there are tables containing secondary information such as the size of counties and the number of sample units in each county. For several database fields, notably land-use and related information such as impact, cause of damage and visibility, more than one value could be recorded for each MARS Monument.

Altogether, three main kinds of quantification were used in the analyses in this report: counts based on the number of MARS Monuments with defined traits; counts based on the number of observations of defined traits (which may exceed the number of MARS Monuments); and estimates of land area according to defined characteristics. The majority of analyses presented in the report are straightforward descriptive studies using single or paired variables to produce simple charts and graphs. The aim was to provide straightforward information uncomplicated by statistical expression and manipulation.

3.9 MARS organization and project management

The project design (Darvill *et al.* 1994) not only considered the aims, objectives and needs of the project but also focused on how to achieve them in a structured, flexible and efficient way. It was as important to recruit the right staff for the various field- and desk-based assignments as to enforce an appropriate management and operational structure. The project management

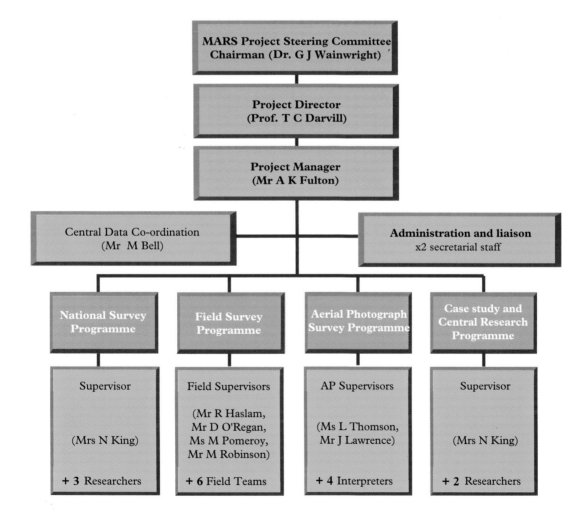

Figure 3.11 - Organizational model of MARS programmes and staff structure.

Figure 3.12 - The MARS team together with Geoffrey Wainwright and Tim Williams at the launch of the Field Survey Programme in August 1994. *[Photograph: MARS Archive]*

model was taken from *Management of archaeological projects* (commonly referred to as MAP2: English Heritage 1991b). This revolves around the principle that at each project stage, no matter how small, there should be a four fold cycle of proposal, decision, data-collection and review.

The project design, also based on the MAP2 model, was prepared during the autumn of 1993, submitted in February 1994 and agreed after consultation in April 1994. It formed the basis for all the necessary working documentation for each activity (e.g. data collection manuals and operational procedures). Given the timescale over which MARS took place, and the size of elements of the work (for example the scale of the aerial photographic reference collection used), it was necessary to update parts of the project design towards the end of each defined phase. Updates for each of the key activities were submitted (March 1995, May 1995, September 1995, January 1996) and consolidated in a revised document in May 1996 (Fulton 1996).

The MARS Project was divided into nine phases - pilot, review, proposal, decision, set-up, data collection, data assessment, analysis and publication - each of which was distinguished by different activities within a logical sequence of events. The advantage of this model was that it enabled monitoring at a variety of scales. The overall project was therefore a set of four interconnected programmes pursued in series.

The main phases of the project were split into task-sets with appropriate constraints (times, activities, budgets, reporting and quality assurance) and procedures (health and safety, reporting, daily routines, data transfer, and recording methodology) for each.

The Steering Committee, which had overall direction and management of the project, met on ten occasions between July 1994 and June 1997. Dr. G J Wainwright of English Heritage chaired the Committee, which included senior members of the project staff, and representatives from English Heritage, the Royal Commission on the Historical Monuments of England, the Association of County Archaeological Officers and the Association of District Archaeological Officers (subsequently amalgamated to one representative from the Association of Local Government Archaeological

Officers). The Project Director was Professor Timothy Darvill, and the Project Manager, Andrew K Fulton, was responsible for day to day management. A tier of supervisory staff reporting to the Project Manager oversaw the four distinct programmes (see 3.3 above) and managed the various data collection, administrative and central staff employed within specific regions and research areas. Figure 3.11 shows the core activities of the project and its staffing structure.

All the component parts of MARS were undertaken by dedicated project staff, although on a few occasions external specialist and technical staff were brought in. The Field Survey Programme and National Survey Programme in particular drew upon the local knowledge of curatorial staff in the counties and districts visited, and the Aerial Photographic Survey benefited greatly from the experience of aerial photographic interpreters working for the RCHME.

A team of 30 research, field, administrative and supervisory staff was established at Bournemouth University in July 1994 (Figure 3.12). The project began with a period of intensive training in the background and workings of the project, recording techniques, interpersonal skills, information systems, first aid and health and safety procedures, driving technique, and reporting/quality control in data collection. Throughout the period of data collection, September 1994 to March 1996, four major reviews were held in Bournemouth. For the Aerial Photographic Survey based in Swindon, surgeries were held by staff of the National Library of Aerial Photographs (RCHME) to help solve interpretive problems raised by difficult photographs.

A system of data transfer, field visits, sample checking and team reviews was established to ensure that appropriate and corrected data were being recorded. Inevitably, during the first month or so of work, particularly during the Field Survey, adjustments had to be made to the scope of several of the data fields to encompass the wide range of monument classes and situations actually encountered by the field teams. Old data were revisited to correct information according to these updates. Specimen field survey and aerial photographic sample data were circulated to a group of county-based curators for comment.

The archaeological profession, interested parties and the wider public were kept in touch with progress through a series of leaflets, bulletins, meetings, seminars and media reports (APPENDIX K). A promotional video was prepared during the set-up phase as an introduction for landowners, project staff and the wider profession. The success and scale of the fieldwork was largely due to the kindness and goodwill of many landowners and occupiers, without whose co-operation things would have been exceedingly difficult.

3.10 The project archive

Data collection and the assembly of materials from the various elements of the survey have created a substantial archive comprising many different forms of information: computerized records, original data, map-based evidence, images, research reports, and notes and additional information. APPENDIX L provides a preliminary listing of the main items.

The archive is the copyright of Bournemouth University and English Heritage. It is curated with the primary purpose of acting as a baseline statement about England's archaeological resource in the 1990s for use in due course when a comparable study is carried out to measure further changes. Copies of the data-sets relating to individual administrative areas have been returned to the relevant participating SMRs, and a security copy of the master database has been deposited with the National Monuments Record (RCHME, Swindon). Figure 3.13 shows the main components of the archive.

In forming the benchmark for future studies, the MARS achieve reflects the state of the archaeological record and the extent of the recorded resource at the census date. The development of these archaeological records, and the nature of the information they contain, is the result of many complicated and interlocking historical processes. Unravelling this history as the context for understanding the present shape and size of the record is the subject of the next chapter.

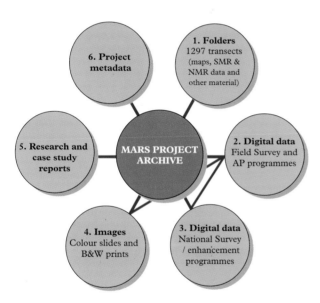

Figure 3.13 - Representation of components held in the MARS archive.

4 Data accumulation and the recorded resource

Mr Austin concluded by making suggestions as to the form of the lists and as to the buildings and objects which should be included in them ... The compilation of such lists would, he was sure, be welcomed by the planning authorities, who would be glad to have reliable information for use in preparing the maps to accompany official schemes.

(CAS 1938, 8)

4.1 Recording the resource

England's recorded archaeological resource has gradually been brought together, piece by piece, over a very long time and through the efforts of many individuals and organizations. Ironically, the practical implications of the ever-changing conceptual basis of what the archaeological resource actually includes, as discussed in detail in Chapter 2.2, mean that some of the archaeological entities now considered integral to the resource were not regarded as archaeologically interesting or relevant, or had not even been created, when records began; the growing recognition of the importance of remains from the Second World War and the Cold War are perhaps the most poignant (Schofield and Lake 1995).

One of the greatest achievements of archaeology in England in the 1970s and 1980s was the unification of much scattered and disparate material to create a national system of archaeological records. However, the idea and practice of doing this was not new to the later twentieth century, nor indeed was it new to archaeologists like Mr Austin working in the earlier twentieth century. The creation of inventories and indexes of known remains goes back to the very early days of field archaeology in England in the sixteenth century, and almost invariably one of the reasons for building, publishing and using such records was concern about the destruction of monuments and the definition of the risks they face.

This chapter is concerned with the way in which the recorded resource represented on local SMRs and the NMR has developed, and what it comprised in 1995. Because the recorded resource is cumulative, the way it has built up and the biases and imbalances that are inherent to it are themselves part of the overall picture of the recorded resource. Thus in the first main section attention focuses on the history of record development in Britain. Five main phases are identified, but special attention is devoted to the period 1930 to 1972 and the role of the Ordnance Survey Archaeology Division in creating an archaeological index that later became the foundation upon which most current local SMRs, and indeed the archaeological element of the NMR Inventory, were built. After looking at the history of the recorded resource, quantified information is introduced from the work of the National Survey Programme. In this, attention is first focused on the scale of the recorded resource in 1995, the way in which it has grown over the last decade or so, and how it might continue to evolve into the early years of the next century. The nature of the items represented in the recorded resource (record mode) is then examined, followed by a more detailed examination of those records which can be regarded as monuments according to the definitions given in Chapters 2.3 and 3.2. Here the aim is to explore what led to the discovery and recording of these remains, and how records relating to them have subsequently been enhanced. A case study is presented to illustrate the process of record development.

Exploring the history and development of the recorded resource is important because it represents the starting point for the more detailed analysis of MARS Monuments in Chapters 5-9. Biases in the patterns of data assembly will inevitably be reflected in the MARS sample of the recorded resource simply because the sample reflects the situation as it actually was, not how it might have been in an ideal world.

4.2 Building the recorded resource [1]

No comprehensively researched history of England's archaeological record systems has ever been published, although there are accounts of specific elements of it, for example the Ordnance Survey· (Phillips 1980), the development of the Royal Commission on the Historical Monuments of England (Fowler 1981; Croad and Fowler 1984), the development of the national archaeological record (Croad 1992; Aberg and Leech 1992), recent history of local government-based records (Burrow 1985), the development of computer systems applied to archaeological records (Evans 1984; 1985; Leech 1986; Hart and Leech 1989; Clubb and Lang 1996), and accounts of the formation of numerous local SMRs (e.g. Allden 1984; Clubb and James 1985). The rest has to be pieced together from fragmentary sources. What is clear, however, is that the idea of having a consolidated accessible record of archaeological remains goes back a long way, and that early endeavour shaped a number of key traditions which find expression in the formative period of record development during the 1970s and early 1980s; indeed, some are still echoed in even the most up-to-date systems in place today. Five main phases in record development can be recognized and these are consider briefly in the following sub-sections.

4.2.1 Antiquaries, maps and the first inventories

The creation of itineraries and inventories of archaeological monuments can be traced back to the very beginnings of the antiquarian traditions in the sixteenth century. John Leland (1506?-1552), the first and only person ever to hold the post of King's Antiquary, was given a commission to search the length and breadth of the kingdom of England and Wales for surviving antiquities and monuments of all types. His brief included a Royal Command that scholars of every subsequent generation have envied: to search all the libraries of monasteries and colleges in the realm for information about the remains of the past (Marsden 1983, 1). Leland's *Itinerary* was not published until the present century (Toulmin Smith 1906-10), but the tradition of recording monuments through research backed by fieldwork was closely followed by others, many operating at a county level. Ashbee (1972, 41) draws particular attention to the work of John Norden, whose *Survey of Cornwall* was compiled in about 1584 and includes a map of the county, detailed engravings of the separate hundreds, and lists of antiquities arranged and designated according to their hundred locations.

By the early nineteenth century the art of making and publishing inventories was well established. Sir Richard Colt Hoare's magisterial two-volume set *The history of ancient Wiltshire* perhaps exemplifies the apogee of the craft, representing 12 years of dedicated fieldwork and recording not only the opening of hundreds of barrows (classified according to a system still in use today) but also the description of dozens of earthworks, enclosures and findspots (Colt Hoare 1810; 1819).

Research was one function of inventories. Another was to form a record of remains in the countryside that were disappearing as a result of development and agriculture. William Stukeley should be remembered as one of the first conservation-minded archaeologists, lamenting on the first page of his treatise on Stonehenge the damage caused to surrounding monuments by continued cultivation (1740, 1; Figure 4.1). Similar themes can be detected in the writings of other antiquaries (Fawcett 1976). Indeed, the same concerns became a focus of interest for the Congress of Archaeological Societies founded in 1888, which met for the first time in 1889 (O'Neil 1946). The Congress comprised representatives from the numerous county and regional archaeological societies that had sprung up around the

country during the middle decades of the nineteenth century (Piggott 1974). Its objects, were to promote:

- the better organization of antiquarian research

- the preservation of ancient monuments and records.

The records referred to in the second clause were documentary and historical records of various sorts, and the Congress, with others, was instrumental in establishing County Record Offices, by means of a series of negotiations and published papers (e.g. Copinger 1907). In the strictly archaeological domain the Congress took forward two main initiatives: first, publishing annual bibliographies and surveys of archaeological work, and second, promoting the idea of a nationwide archaeological survey. The first was in part achieved by listings in the Congress's annual reports from 1891 down to 1910, and the latter was promoted by a publication issued by the Society of Antiquaries of London in 1894, entitled *Archaeological survey of Britain arranged by counties*. The Society of Antiquaries subsequently began publishing a series of county surveys, some of which were included in the *Archaeologia* while others were separately printed. Indeed, the idea of undertaking a nationwide survey of the antiquities of Britain had been discussed in detail by a Scottish antiquary, David Murray, in 1896 (Murray 1896). By 1921, seven surveys had been produced, covering the counties of Cumberland, Westmorland, Lancashire, Herefordshire, Hertfordshire, Kent, Northamptonshire and Oxfordshire. They were of varying quality, but all included a map at a scale of 1:250,000 and a listing of monuments and finds arranged by parish/place with details of the date, the nature of discovery and a bibliographic reference. The last to be published was for Oxfordshire (Manning and Leeds 1921) and contained approximately 820 entries ranging from stray finds of Palaeolithic handaxes through prehistoric and later earthworks to Anglo-Saxon burial grounds.

Antiquities were depicted on early published maps in Britain, especially those produced by the Ordnance Survey from its creation in 1791 (it was given formal

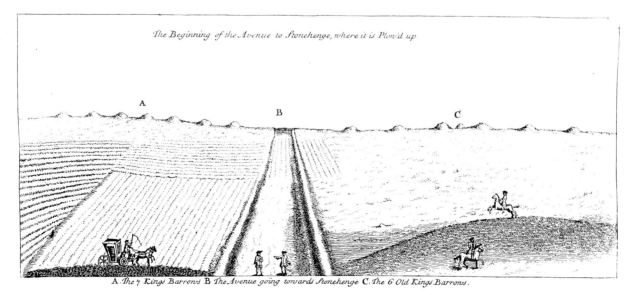

The Beginning of the Avenue to Stonehenge, where it is Plow'd up.

A. *The 7 Kings Barrows* B. *The Avenue going towards Stonehenge* C. *The 6 Old Kings Barrows.*

Figure 4.1 - A view of the Stonehenge Avenue and King Barrow Ridge, Amesbury, Wiltshire, drawn in *c*.AD 1720. The encroachment of cultivated land onto the earthworks of the monument can clearly be seen. *[After Stukeley 1740, 52]*

status by Parliament in the *Ordnance Survey Act 1841*). However, the work which led to antiquities appearing on nineteenth-century Ordnance Survey maps was largely uncoordinated, and the results were somewhat variable. Information was recorded onto field survey maps and into 'Name Books' during the process of basic map-making. Many of the original Name Books that recorded archaeological and topographical details alongside the various spellings of place-names were lost during the Second World War, and only those for Cumberland, Durham, Hampshire and Northumberland are still extant. A few books of later series have also survived, containing some parishes for Devon, Derbyshire, East Sussex, Essex, Gloucestershire, Herefordshire, Kent, Lincolnshire, Norfolk, Oxfordshire and Worcestershire. Both groups are held by the Public Record Office at Kew.

With the turn of the nineteenth century, however, attitudes towards mapping, inventories and the classification of remains changed, and with them approaches to archaeological records.

4.2.2 The early twentieth century

The Congress of Archaeological Societies continued its interest in the creation of archaeological records, encouraging its members to carry out work in their own counties, providing some general national guidance, and encouraging the Ordnance Survey to record fully ancient sites and earthworks on its maps (O'Neil 1946, 64). In 1901 the Congress established an Earthworks Committee under the chairmanship of Professor Windle. In the words of O G S Crawford, 'the modern phase of field archaeology began with the Earthworks Committee and the workers inspired by it' (1960, 45). From 1903 through to 1931 this Committee published an annual report which included notes on the preservation, destruction and exploration of earthworks during the preceding year (O'Neil 1946, 65). Special reports were also published, including the *Report of the Special Committee on the cataloguing of local antiquities* (CAS 1926), the *Report on linear earthworks* (CAS 1927), and the *Report on lynchets and grass ridges* (CAS 1931). All of these were influential documents and began to put in place the vocabulary and working definitions used for the recording of field monuments. The most influential publication, however, was the *Scheme for recording earthworks*, first published in 1902 but revised and updated several times over the following 30 years (best known through the later revised editions, e.g. CAS 1910). The scheme appears to have been well received and was adopted by the Victoria County History as the basis for preparing its articles on ancient earthworks. It was also a major influence on Hadrian Allcroft, whose book *Earthwork of England* (Allcroft 1908) represents one of the first attempts to write an account of early times using field monuments as the main line of evidence. In some parts of the country there was considerable interest in the creation of archaeological records and the registration of finds (e.g. Law 1914).

In parallel with these initiatives, the first decade of the twentieth century saw the creation of three separate Royal Commissions to inventorize ancient and historical monuments for England, Wales and Scotland respectively. The Royal Warrant for the English Commission was signed on 27th October 1908 and set out the aims succinctly, stating that the King had:

deemed it expedient that a Commission should forthwith issue to make an inventory of the Ancient and Historical Monuments and Constructions connected with or illustrative of the contemporary culture, civilization and conditions of life of the people in England, excluding Monmouthshire, from the earliest times to the year 1700, and to specify those which seem most worthy of preservation. (quoted in Fowler 1984, 8)

Following earlier traditions it was decided that the county should be the unit of publication and the parish the unit of study. Hertfordshire was the first county surveyed and the inventory was published in 1910 (RCHME 1910), only 18 years after the same county had been covered by no less an authority than John Evans for the Society of Antiquaries (Evans 1892). Between 1910 and 1920 two further inventories, both for counties in the south-east of England, were published by the Commission, Buckinghamshire (1912-13 in two volumes) and Essex (1916-24 in four volumes).

By 1920, therefore, a number of trends had already emerged in the way archaeological records were prepared. Key elements include the county-by-county basis of their construction, the use of parishes and local places as the geographical referencing system, the incorporation of bibliographic information, the development of classifications and promulgation of accepted definitions and vocabulary, and the combined use of maps and lists as the main elements of the record. Behind these lists and maps there was to be a bigger research archive of source material such as plans, descriptions and photographs (Croad and Fowler 1984, 8).

In retrospect, 1920 was a critical moment in the history of archaeological records, a watershed between the old world and the new (Ashbee 1972, 63). The event which now seems so significant was the appointment in October 1920 of O G S Crawford to the staff of the Ordnance Survey as their Archaeological Officer, putting archaeology on a professional footing within the Ordnance Survey. Crawford himself has provided a very personal account of the trials and tribulations of beginning work and setting up what was to become the Archaeological Section:

My arrival at the Ordnance Survey was (to put it mildly) not greeted with any enthusiasm ... At the outset I had nothing but an empty room and a table. There was not even a chair, and I had to steal one from the library opposite. (1955, 154-65)

Maps were the *raison d'être* of the Ordnance Survey, and they soon became vehicles for archaeological information over and above the traditional depiction of antiquities (Crawford 1926). The purpose of the Ordnance Survey record was to provide systematic information for use in conventional map-making, although Crawford quickly recognized the research value of his material and used it to publish period maps and synthetic reports (e.g. Crawford 1925; 1926).

4.2.3 1930-72

During the inter-war period the role of local authorities in planning and economic development grew considerably, a fact not lost on archaeologists. Discussion took place within the Congress of Archaeological Societies on the opportunity of recording county antiquities with special reference to Section 17 of the *Town and Country Planning Act 1932* (CAS 1938: later repealed by the *Town and Country Planning Act 1947*). The important point of this legislation, as far as archaeologists were concerned, was that the planning authorities (at this time urban and rural councils) were empowered, subject to the approval of the Minister of Health, to provide in their schemes for the protection of buildings and other monuments of archaeological interest and importance. It was here, Austin argued (CAS 1938, 8), that the preparation of lists of monuments was of paramount importance, because sooner or later the planning authority would need this information.

Little use was made of the powers available through the 1932 Act, and the immediate effect of the discussion that Austin promoted was little more than an exercise in letter-writing in order to encourage the creation of local records. But the long-term effects were considerable. For the first time, a link was forged between local records, local authorities and planning. In many ways this was the catalyst for the creation of the modern SMR system, but it is important here to note two points. First, the need for these records was being recognized by the members of amateur societies concerned with their own regions. Second, and related to the first, many of the traditions established before 1920 were perpetuated in this recording, especially the use of counties and local authority areas as the geographical units of study.

Museums also recognized the need to develop a role in the creation of archives and inventories. In his anniversary address to the Society of Antiquaries of London on 23rd April 1945 Sir Cyril Fox called for the creation of a National Card Index of museum collections to allow the study of artefacts and their distributions (Fox 1945, 114). In practice, however, the various proposed indexes were constructed piecemeal and remained largely in the hands of local societies and local museums. Other opportunities, such as the potential for a national air-photograph library (Steer 1947), were also ignored until much later. The most significant development of this period was in the work of the Ordnance Survey, with an expansion of its involvement in archaeological recording.

It was not until after the Second World War that a systematic indexing system was created within the Ordnance Survey under the supervision of C W Phillips (Phillips 1949a; 1949b; Harley 1975, 145), an earlier card index started by Crawford and mainly related to long barrows having been destroyed during the war (Crawford 1955, 161). The Archaeology Division was established in 1947 as a response to the need for urgent mapping and recording of antiquities during the immediate post-war developments (*cf.* O'Neil 1948). The main purpose of the collection of data by the Ordnance Survey was to enhance its mapping, both specialist period-based maps and the normal topographical maps available at a range of scales.

The Ordnance Survey Archaeology Division included three main groups, each of which had sub-groups: Revision, Recording and Examination (fieldwork). The Revision Section was the entry and exit point of archaeological information from the Archaeology Division to the Ordnance Survey proper, and the

Recording Section had numerous sub-sections which trawled through books, inspected aerial photographs and edited material from the fieldwork teams. The results of this work were set down on record cards, which later went to the field teams for field enhancement, and were added to a set of 1:10,625 maps, the smallest scale which covers the whole of the country. A unique numbering system was developed in which all sites and finds were marked on a quarter-sheet map of the 1:10,625 coverage and assigned the map sheet number (e.g. ST45SE) followed by a record number in an established sequence unique to that map sheet (e.g. ST45SE/20). Simple and effective, this system is still in use in some local SMRs. Most significantly, the system was tied to the Ordnance Survey's National Grid rather than to local government administrative units. The Examination Section (field survey teams), which was launched later than the others in August 1950, undertook the systematic inspection of all known antiquities, ensuring correct classification and providing a survey at the appropriate scale for publication.

The first task of the sections was recording and indexing. Record sheets, topographic cards and a classified index were considered essential at the outset, although the classified index was later abandoned. A policy statement issued in September 1951 (Ordnance Survey 1951) gives Archaeology Division three main tasks:

1   To collect, compile and maintain systematic topographic and period records of items or archaeological interest covering the whole of Great Britain. Information collected by responsible individuals, learned bodies and societies and other Government Departments to be used to the maximum extent practicable.

2   To include on standard maps and plans on all scales from 1:250 to 1:1,000,000 selected appropriate items of archaeological interest.

3   To compile and revise as necessary such period maps covering Great Britain as have been approved for publication.

Initially a date of AD 1714 was adopted as the latest date for which items would be recorded, reflecting the practice of the RCHME. This date replaced the previous latest date of AD 1688 which appears on the older maps (Harley 1975, 146). The date range was later expanded to include items of interest over 100 years old in the later 1950s, and this date range appears in later Policy Statements (e.g. Ordnance Survey 1965). Thus the early days of the record did not include the large numbers of post-medieval and industrial remains which, as will be seen, form such a big proportion of SMRs today.

Work on the cards and maps was not standardized until 1951, when the system underwent a radical overhaul and the decision was taken to include the results of systematic bibliographic searches.

The 1951 overhaul also included the addition of NGRs, and by the first quarter of 1951 some 40,000 cards had to be amended. The classified index allowed cross-referencing by period and type of archaeological find, whether site, building or artefact. The classified index was abandoned in 1956 because the cost of copying cards was too high at that time. Some 60,000 cards had been created for this index, although there was a lag between the topographic and classified indexes and the topographic index then totalled around 80,000 cards.

Archaeological field surveying and recording were undertaken on a county by county basis until 1958. Two levels of field survey were used: full surveys and extant site only surveys. Six counties were completed by the end of 1958. Full survey field recording included the examination of known sites, the identification of new sites, and surveying sites for archive and publication. The extant sites only surveys examined only those sites already known to and previously recorded by the Ordnance Survey. By 1958 the counties of Dorset, Hampshire and Northumberland had been fully surveyed, while Lancashire, Durham and Staffordshire had been subject to surveys of the extant sites only. After the completion of the first county surveys, information was sent out from the Archaeology Division to other bodies.

In 1965 a revised Policy Statement was introduced. This illustrates the commitment of the Ordnance Survey to recording all archaeological entities, whether visible on the ground or known only through methods such as aerial photography, defining the brief of the Archaeology Division as being:

> To identify, assess and describe all 'monuments and sites' which can be recognised in the field either by ground inspection or with the help of aids such as aerial photography. 'Monuments and sites' will normally be recorded only if they are at least 100 years old, but exceptionally examples of more recent date may be included. The terms include places which are or have been associated with popular custom and belief, and trees with historical or folk-lore traditions. (Ordnance Survey 1965)

This brief was wide in scope and was undoubtedly interpreted in different ways by the individual researchers. Throughout the 1960s, the Archaeology Division continually tried to understand the nature of what it was producing: what is called here the recorded resource. The information produced for various purposes included assessments of the number of different types of field monument, and statements about the density of the recorded archaeological resource. By 1966 there were 350 different categories of field monument recorded in the Ordnance Survey index. It was also noted that there were differences in densities of sites throughout Britain, and that such variations might be due to past and present land-use (Ordnance Survey 1966). Density was easy to assess at this time: the number of cards in a particular area could easily be extracted from the topographical index and counted, weighed or measured.

During 1972 there was a change in the level of recording by the Archaeology Division. It was decided to suspend recording of non-visible and thus non-publishable antiquities. This introduced yet another bias into the range of material entered onto the archaeological index during the 1970s. There was an outcry from the archaeological profession, channelled through the Archaeological Advisory Committee and the Grimes Working Group on Archaeological Records, which asked

that non-visible antiquities continue to be recorded for the index, even if nothing was ever to be published (Ordnance Survey 1975). The Grimes Working Group had recommended that the DoE should pay for the non-intensive archaeological record which included the non-publishable antiquities (Ordnance Survey 1975).

In 1975 the Ordnance Survey undertook an evaluation of the archaeology record before renewing the Policy Statement relating to archaeology. Four categories of the record were identified at this time: counties completed on a county basis, mainly between 1962 and 1972; counties fully recorded on a county basis, mainly between 1962 and 1972, but in general without field investigation; counties with records compiled for the most part between 1954 and 1962; and counties never fully recorded even to the level of those falling within the previous grouping. The Archaeology Division's commitment to the 'Basic Scales Field Programme' was completed in 1981.

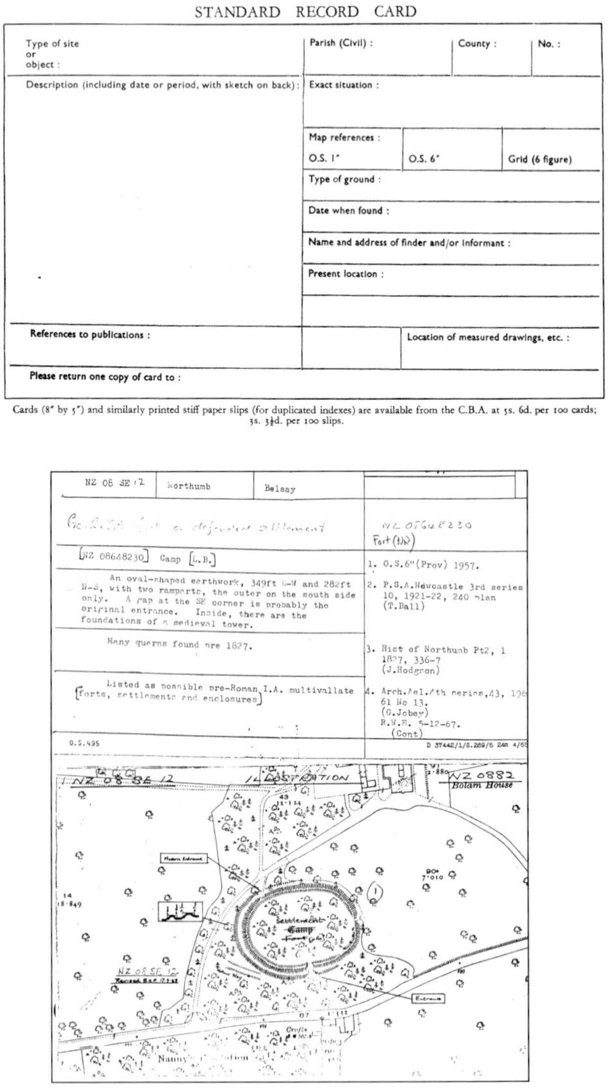

Figure 4.2 - Archaeological record cards. (Top) *Pro forma* card produced by the Council for British Archaeology in 1952; (Bottom) completed card as used in the Ordnance Survey Archaeological Index *c*.1962. *[(Top) From CBA 1952, 44; (Bottom) From OS Record cards held by Bournemouth University]*

In 1975 the categories of antiquities to be recorded were made explicit for the first time in a Policy Statement (Ordnance Survey 1975, para. 4):

1   Prehistoric and Romano-British
- extant remains
- identified sites which are no longer extant
- objects found without structural associations.

2   Dark Ages to 1714
- earthworks
- buildings of outstanding importance
- objects of outstanding importance
- scenes of sociological or political events of major significance (e.g. Runnymede)
- battlefields and scenes of conflict
- natural features associated with major historical characters, folklore, celebrities or saints.

3   1714 to 100 years before present
- major sites of the Industrial Revolution
- other important features such as deserted townships and military roads.

Public use of the Ordnance Survey's archaeological record was an important aspect of this work. The indexes were accessible to visitors in Southampton, and quarterly bulletins and a visitors' book record the people who drew on the resource or visited to appreciate the resource available. One notable regular visitor was Phyllis Ireland of the National Trust, who used the Ordnance Survey's information to build archaeological records for National Trust estates, but many others went to seek information for local, regional or period studies.

Alongside the development of archaeological recording in the Ordnance Survey the post-war period saw a number of other changes taking place. In particular, the massive elaboration of the town and country planning system in Britain provided the impetus to realize and recognize officially the gist of the discussion introduced in the inter-war period by the Congress of Archaeological Societies and others. Local archaeological societies continued to work away in the background and the Council for British Archaeology carried out a survey of their activities in 1951-2 with the help of its regional Groups. This revealed 'considerable activity, but little uniformity in the kind of information recorded' (CBA 1952, 10). As a result, a 'standard record card' was devised on which local societies could record archaeological monuments; the card (Figure 4.2) was published in the CBA's Annual Report for the year ended 31 July 1952 (CBA 1952, 44). The cards (8 inches by 5 inches) were available from the CBA price 5s 6d per 100.

The Royal Commission on Historical Monuments (England) continued to produce county inventories, many of which focused especially on historical buildings, and between 1920 and 1975 published inventories for six counties: Huntingdonshire (1926); Herefordshire (1931-4 in three volumes); Westmorland (1936); Middlesex (1937); Dorset (1952-76 in eight parts comprising five volumes); and Cambridgeshire (1969-72 in two volumes). Surveys of four historic towns were also produced: London (1924-30 in five volumes); Oxford (1939); Cambridge (1959); and York (1962-81 in five volumes). Over this period, the pace of work on the inventories was slowing down, while the scale was increasing in proportion to the breadth and depth of coverage achieved.

After 1956, the Commission took on additional responsibilities, including the 'task of recording prehistoric and other early earthworks threatened with destruction by afforestation, opencast mining and above all by improved methods of agriculture and other recent technical developments affecting the countryside' (RCHME 1960, 3).

The first report resulting directly from these new tasks was published in 1960 under the title *A matter of time: an archaeological survey of the river gravels of England* (RCHME 1960). It comprised a survey of the river gravels of England, highlighting the impact of gravel extraction and its destructive effect on archaeological monuments. It was followed in 1963 by a report entitled *Monuments threatened or destroyed. A select list: 1956-1962*, which provided summary accounts of recording work in advance of destruction carried out at 187 earthwork monuments.

Both these studies were reactive, but in 1969 the Commission published *Peterborough New Town. A study of the antiquities in the areas of development* in advance of the construction of a new urban centre. That report provided the basis for archaeological research and investigations on a massive scale, notably in connection with the establishment of industrial estates at Fengate to the south-east of the town (Pryor 1984 with earlier references), and around Longthorpe for the construction of the western primary road and a golf source (Dannell and Wild 1987). It also set the pattern which others have followed in preparing threat-based resource assessments and archaeological surveys of various kinds (APPENDIX A).

In 1963, under the terms of a new Royal Warrant, the Commission received additional responsibilities, the maintenance of the National Buildings Record which had been founded in 1940, and the creation of a National Monuments Record for England. At the time the Commission's role was that of an archive, holding copies of its own surveys and the Ordnance Survey cards (Burrow 1985, 8). The Ordnance Survey cards could thus be referred to in two locations, Southampton and London.

Further changes in the pattern of England's archaeological records came as a direct result of the findings of the Walsh Enquiry into the protection of field monuments, published in 1969 (Walsh 1969). In compiling this report, a series of three studies was undertaken in Wiltshire to appraise the degree of damage and destruction that archaeological monuments were facing. A total of 640 monuments were visited, of which 250 (39%) were found to have been destroyed or seriously damaged and 150 others (23%) less seriously damaged over a ten-year period (Walsh 1969, 6). Appendix 5 to the report contained short accounts of reported damage to monuments by way of illustrating the diversity of what was happening. In its conclusions, the Walsh Committee picked up the critical connection between damage, risk, and the need for detailed records of the recorded resource as the starting point for action. Section 7 of the report recommended that:

> a consolidated record of all known field monuments should be held by the County Planning Authorities so that they may be aware of all such monuments in their areas

while Section 37 recommended that:

> County Councils which have not already done so should consider whether adequate professional archaeological assistance is available to them and should examine whether the appointment of an archaeological officer on a full-time or part-time basis as called for in their areas.

One of the reasons for making these proposals was the fact that the Ordnance Survey did not consider that their work of verifying monuments on the ground would be completed until after 1980, over ten years into the future, but the problem of destruction through ignorance, or to put it another way through inadequate records, needed to be addressed (Walsh 1969, para. 76). Widespread ignorance was one of the four categories of threats identified by the Walsh report (Walsh 1969, para. 18) and included ignorance among archaeologists as well as members of the general public, landowners, contractors, etc. The need, identified in the Walsh Report, for these records to be locally based was in line with earlier perceptions of the importance of the link with planning authorities, but what was different was the emphasis placed on their management and use by professional staff. Unlike earlier calls for such records, the Walsh Committee recommendations were acted upon.

4.2.3 The first modern SMRs

Some of the comments in the Walsh report were undoubtedly prompted by developments in Oxfordshire during the late 1960s. In 1965, immediately following its creation, the Oxford City and County Museum Service acquired a set of the Ordnance Survey's archaeological records for the county and set about developing a more elaborate local record to serve local needs. The first of the modern generation of Sites and Monuments Records in England was thereby created.

The initial thinking behind this system has been set out by its principal architect Don Benson (1972), the aims and objectives of creating the record being to bring together diverse sources of information and to provide a short cut to all other records whether held locally or nationally. The Record would also provide a centre to which information could be sent (Benson 1972, 226).

In the wake of the Walsh report a number of other counties appointed archaeological officers and began to develop local record systems, so that by 1975 nearly half the counties in England had direct access to a local SMR (Burrow 1985, 9; RCHME 1978).

During the 1960s and 1970s the Ordnance Survey recognized the value to the planning system of the availability of archaeological information which would allow the preservation of antiquities. Accordingly, local authorities, county record offices and others were offered copies of the relevant index cards, building on earlier distributions. Because sets of cards were copied and circulated at different times there are several different OS card indexes for some counties. Only one quarter of the authorities requested copies at this time (Ordnance Survey 1975), although it is not known exactly how many copies were made, or who received them (D Graty pers. comm.).

Mid-way through the 1970s the future for archaeological records therefore looked bright, with the prospect of comprehensive and multi-tiered records, even if the purpose of the records at each tier was seen as being rather different. Three levels could be clearly recognized. At the top of the pyramid was the UK-wide record maintained by the Ordnance Survey for mapping and research purposes. It covered England, Wales, Scotland and the Isle of Man. It was systematically enhanced through field-checking and searches through published works. The vast scale of the operation was described by C W Phillips, Archaeology Officer at the Ordnance Survey between 1947 and 1965, in a series of publications (e.g. Phillips 1961; 1980) and in a letter to the editor of *Antiquity* in 1978 (Daniel 1978, 1-3).

Next in scale and coverage was the work of the RCHME, which had been working in parallel with the Ordnance Survey throughout the first half of the twentieth century. Although the National Monuments Record created in 1963 at first incorporated only the archive derived from all of the Commission's previous surveys and the National Buildings Record (Croad and Fowler 1984, 13), it soon developed its own structure with separate sections for architectural records, archaeological records and aerial photography, and was promoted as the definitive 'national' record (Fowler 1981, 108-9).

Below this again were the emerging county-based records, whose role was increasingly identified with planning and conservation (ACAO 1978). The urgency of this was underlined by a series of national and local resource assessment studies that were compiled at this time (see APPENDIX A), expanding on the earlier studies such as the RCHME's *A matter of time*. One of the most influential resource assessments of the early 1970s was *The erosion of history*, prepared by Carolyn Heighway for the Council for British Archaeology's Urban Research Committee (Heighway 1972). The conclusion of this study was that:

> Of those historic towns which remain for study, the archaeological value of one-fifth will most probably have been entirely destroyed in the next twenty years; another two-fifths will be re-developed in lesser ways. The archaeology of the most important sites under-lying these towns must be recorded and so should the structure of any buildings of architectural or historical interest, particularly those which are due for complete demolition. (Heighway 1972, 2)

4.2.4 1975-94: system growth and diversification

One of the reasons for the rapid growth of local SMRs during the late 1970s and early 1980s was central government support for archaeology within local authorities, clarified and emphasized in a circular to county councils in 1972 (DoE 1972), and through a tapered funding scheme introduced by the Inspectorate of Ancient Monuments in the Department of the Environment, and continued by English Heritage. Under this scheme, county councils, and latterly district councils, were grant-aided to appoint an archaeological officer, the level of grant reducing as a proportion of salary costs over a period of years until the post was firmly established and taken over by the host organization. The strategy was remarkably successful and is undoubtedly the main reason for the present national coverage of local archaeological records and advisors.

The mid 1970s was a period when policies and approaches to the development of Sites and Monuments Records started to become more diverse. In 1972 an Association of County Archaeological Officers was formed, and in 1978 published its own *Guide to the establishment of Sites and Monuments Records*. The distinction between local and national records became more marked as the 1970s progressed, with increasing recognition of national policy. The CBA and RESCUE statement entitled *Archaeology and government* published in 1974 was intended to provide a blueprint for all archaeological work in Britain. It advocated a centralized state archaeological service with regional offices linked to county-based archaeological units and trusts. It was at the county level that the Sites and Monuments Records would be created and maintained, but the proposed national archaeological service would also maintain a national archaeological archive (CBA and RESCUE 1974, 10-13). More realistically, the 1977 CBA working party on survey and archaeology identified that the local records represented the 'intensive' record of archaeology, while the national records were 'non-intensive' and could be regarded as an index to the local holdings (CBA 1978, 56)

Surveys of various sorts had been a major element of field archaeology in England during the period between 1950 and 1975, building on earlier traditions (Fowler 1980), and should have provided major contributions to the development of the recorded resource in England. But did they? In 1978 RCHME published a report entitled *A survey of surveys* which presented the results of a study aimed at documenting what was going on and reviewing the state of the various organizations funded or assisted by central or local government and concerned with archaeological field survey and recording in England. The study was carried out by Frances Griffith using questionnaires and interviews. It gathered information on the staffing levels, organization, funding and methods of work of the organizations concerned. The data are largely qualitative in nature and provide little statistical information for comparison with later surveys. Overall the report painted a rather bleak picture, but its recommendations were highly influential in the development of existing SMRs and the creation of new ones. In particular it endorsed the earlier view that county-based SMRs should be the major detailed archive for their areas (RCHME 1978, 10).

The development of SMRs during the 1980s has been well documented (e.g. Burrow 1985; Lang and Stead 1992). Figure 4.3 shows graphically the numerical increase in the number of local-authority-based SMRs through to 1995.

The developing picture is further elaborated by two extensive surveys of record content and structure by English Heritage and its predecessors, one in August 1983 and one in 1987. The primary aim of the 1983 survey carried out by David Fraser (IAM 1984) was to assess the extent to which the Schedule of Ancient Monuments was a representative sample of England's archaeological resource. To achieve this the IAM had to quantify this resource and it selected the county SMRs as the best available database for the purpose. The survey looked closely at the state of SMRs across the

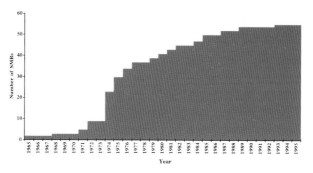

Figure 4.3 - Cumulative increase in the number of archaeological Sites and Monuments Records within local authorities in England 1965-95. *[Source: MARS National Survey]*

country and at the contents of their records, visiting 52 organizations in 46 counties. On the strength of its findings the report proposed a Scheduling Enhancement Programme (SEP) to increase the number of SAMs from 12,600 to 52,500.

The 1987 survey undertaken by Amanda Chadburn and others in the English Heritage Records Office (Chadburn 1989) differed from the 1983 survey in being a direct assessment of the state of SMRs in preparation for their use as the primary database for the Monuments Protection Programme (MPP). It was primarily concerned with SMRs as record management systems and dealt predominantly with the computerization of the records, providing only limited information about the records themselves. It does, however, allow the quantification of the national archaeological resource at this time and provides another benchmark against which the MARS results can be compared.

While local records were expanding and enjoying increased funding and greater recognition during the 1980s, the two national records were in crisis. The Ordnance Survey Archaeological Record was maintained in Southampton by a dedicated staff of investigators until 1983. At that time it consisted of approximately 130,000 records (for the whole of Great Britain). However, in reviewing the functions and role of the Ordnance Survey, the Serpell Committee recommended that the archaeological records should more appropriately be maintained by the Royal Commissions for England, Wales and Scotland respectively (Serpell 1979). Despite appeals against the proposals (Daniel 1978, 1-3; Darvill *et al.* 1978, iv) the Archaeology Division was duly disbanded, the record itself being partitioned and transferred to the appropriate authorities (the section relating to the Isle of Man, also part of the Ordnance Survey's operating area at the time, was transferred to Manx National Heritage, where it now forms the core of the island's NMR). This change meant that for the first time in nearly half a century there was no systematic archaeological record covering Great Britain.

In England the National Monuments Record maintained by the RCHME was supplemented by the transfer of the former Ordnance Survey Archaeological Record. Discussions for the transfer of recording duties to the three Royal Commissions began in 1981 (Cleere 1982, 25), and the transfer occurred during 1983. The national non-intensive record contained around 250,000 archaeological items in 1982, around one-third of which were known to be finds or sites of features no longer extant, the other two-thirds comprising upstanding field monuments including some buildings (Cleere 1983, 25-6). After the RCHME took over the role of maintaining the Ordnance Survey records, both cards and maps, copies were circulated to all SMRs (except Norfolk; H Borrill pers. comm.). The RCHME began computerizing the Ordnance Survey record cards in 1983; at which time there were about 400,000 separate cards relating to archaeological sites, Grade I and II* listed buildings, and Grade A churches in England (CBA 1984, 24).

Immediately before this, however, the Commission had been redefining its own role in relation to surveys, record keeping and publication. In 1981 it announced that the programme of publishing county inventories would come to an end (Fowler 1981, 112-13) and that the terms of the Royal Warrant would be fulfilled through the 'publication' of work by placing it in the National Monuments Record. The NMR came to have increased prominence and importance in the work of the Commission:

> In 100 years' time the worth of the Record should reflect not just the Commission's input, but the quality of work by others in the field. Indeed one of our priorities must be to stimulate and encourage such work, by example and sometimes by training others, so that, with time, the overall quality of the Record as well as the extent of its coverage is improved.
>
> By and large, far too many low-grade records exist at the moment. One of RCHM's functions through the NMR must be to reduce their proportions by increasing the quality of the record overall, and perhaps by defining a minimum standard of site record acceptable for accessioning in the National Record. This is not to advocate record for record's sake but to anticipate to the next century when, sadly, scholarship and the popular perception of the national past will be very much dependent on records as a surrogate for vanished field evidence. RCHM is not then merely in the business of archives; our aim must be a continuous, cyclical enhancement of the national monumental record, quantitatively as much as qualitatively. (Fowler 1981, 109)

The task of creating and maintaining the NMR was perhaps more monumental than Fowler could have anticipated. Taking over the Ordnance Survey record added an enormous quantity of material, but the resources were inadequate to deal with it (Fowler 1984, 2).

In 1989 the Government transferred responsibility for taking the 'lead role' in relation to local SMRs from English Heritage to the RCHME. Shortly afterwards the principles set out in earlier reports (e.g. CBA 1975; RCHME 1978, 10) were re-affirmed and fully activated, the RCHME noting that:

> it is neither feasible nor desirable for all of this information to be held centrally within the

NMR. In future the national heritage database should be seen as an extended record, some elements of which will be curated centrally ... other elements will be curated locally by SMRs. (RCHME 1993a, 40)

Thus, within a decade, the twin pillars of the national archaeological record (the Ordnance Survey's Archaeological Record and RCHME's National Monuments Record) had become one: a centrally held core data-set (the NMR Inventory) and a series of geographically defined independent local records (the local SMRs), which collectively form the 'Extended National Record'.

In 1995, the three previously defined elements of the NMR (National Archaeological Record, National Buildings Record and the National Library of Aerial Photography) were brought together under a unified management structure, replacing previous arrangements in which there had been separate divisions representing the archaeological and architectural disciplines. The unified NMR Inventory seeks to make available a basic accurate and consistent computerized core record of England's historic environment. Thus it provides not only a guide to the Commission's own archive (the NMR Collections) but also an index to parallel records by English Heritage, local SMRs and other partners in the heritage community (RCHME 1996a, 6; 1996b, 16). In April 1993, RCHME launched a new computer system known as MONARCH in preparation for the unification of the NMR (RCHME 1993c); at the time of writing plans were being developed for a second generation of this software.

After a period in which the records of England's archaeological resource seemed to become increasingly fragmented the tide now seems to be turning and greater attention is being given to integration, access and data standards (RCHME 1993b; 1998). The unification of the various strands of what is now the National Monuments Record was a first tentative step. New technology perhaps holds the key to the creation of wider networks between RCHME, English Heritage, local authorities and the rest of the world (Clubb and Lang 1996). A joint statement on co-operation between RCHME, English Heritage and the Association of Local Government Archaeological Officers provides the organizational framework for future development and a potential bid to the Heritage Lottery Fund for financial assistance to achieve it (RCHME *et al.* 1998). RCHME and English Heritage hope to develop a joint GIS system. RCHME is sponsoring new software for SMRs. What these possibilities will achieve will be the subject of a future iteration of MARS; the focus now is to look at the recorded resource in the light of the events that have shaped its creation hitherto.

4.3 The scale and growth of England's archaeological records

In 1995 local-authority-based SMRs in England collectively held approximately 657,619 **retrievable records** in their main systems, with a further 279,865 **anticipated records** awaiting input or in the process of creation. The total number of items represented in England's archaeological records is

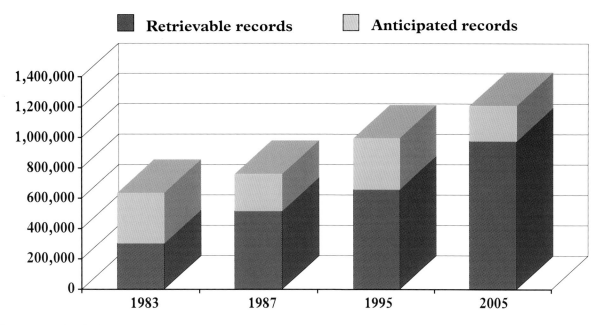

Figure 4.4 - Stacked bar chart showing increases in the number of retrievable and anticipated records held in local SMRs in England 1983-95, and projected forward to 2005. *[Sources: IAM 1984; Chadburn 1989; MARS National Survey Programme]*

therefore approximately 937,484.

A survey of the National Archaeological Record in 1992 revealed the presence of approximately 284,000 records retrievable in computerized form or by manual searches, with a further 100,000 records awaiting input (RCHME 1993a, 29; but see also 4.3.2 below). The fact that there are fewer records in the National Archaeological Record than in the SMRs is partly explained by the way in which its records are structured, with many records including information on several different components.

Relatively few comparative data are available to estimate the overall number of retrievable records in earlier decades. For local authority SMRs the main source is the study carried out by David Fraser in 1983 (IAM 1984) and the follow-up survey by Amanda Chadburn in 1987 (Chadburn 1989). For the NAR there are estimates of holdings in 1978 and 1983 to set alongside the 1992 census, together with information of the situation when the MONARCH database went live in 1993.

4.3.1 The SMRs

Figure 4.4 shows a stacked bar chart for retrievable and anticipated records held by local SMRs in England over the period 1984 to 1995, with projections forward to 2005 on the basis of anticipated records. On the basis of changes over the past decade, a steady growth in the number of retrievable records is predicted for local authority SMRs. The total number stood at 302,519 in 1983; by 1988 this had risen to 516,341, an increase of 70.7%. By 1995 the number of retrievable records had risen still further to 657,619, an increase of 27.4%. Thus the total increase in retrievable records between 1983 and 1995 was 117%. Over the 11-year period between the surveys of 1983 and 1995 the average rate of accumulation amounted to about 32,000 per year, or nearly 100 records per day. This represents a very considerable achievement and a great deal of commitment on the part of those doing the work.

In all surveys to date the number of retrievable records is generally taken to be the number of PRNs (Primary Record Numbers) assigned by the system. There are, however, variations, especially where manual tallies are necessary, and achieving precise numbers is inevitably very difficult.

Estimates of known records not yet transferred to established computer systems are still more difficult to determine, mainly because of difficulties in estimating the quantity of records that will be generated by material not yet examined. The 1983 survey estimated a national total of 635,676 records, comprising 302,519 retrievable records and 333,157 records awaiting formal accession. By 1995 this had risen to a total of 937,484 records, of which 279,865 could be regarded as anticipated records. A comparison of the 1983 figures with those for 1995 reveals that some local SMRs showed exceptionally high increases in their estimates, most notably in Avon, Greater London and East Sussex, with rises of 1567%, 560% and 275% respectively. These increases most probably result from the recasting of SMRs in the late 1980s and early 1990s, the revision of the sources used to compile the record, for example aerial photographs, and the inclusion of records on buildings for the first time. The extension into the mid twentieth century of the date range for records compiled by some SMRs may also contribute to these increases (see below section 4.5).

The 1988 survey did not take into account Cheshire, Dorset, Hertfordshire, Lancashire, Oxfordshire, West Midlands and West Sussex, all of which were unable to provide estimates at that time; thus to allow a comparison with the other surveys the total numbers of records in 1988 were used in place of estimates for these counties.

Care must be exercised when interpreting this data because the mechanism and principles used in estimating the 'anticipated' number of records over and above those already retrievable differed from county to county and from survey to survey. Most counties appear to have arrived at the estimate by adding the current number of records to the backlog of uncomputerized records, or to have followed the 1983 survey's definition of the estimate by including other secondary sources (e.g. LBs, APs and SMs) not yet incorporated into the SMR. This is what they were asked to do. Others, however, believed the instructions asked them to estimate what broadly equates to the 'archaeological resource' as defined in Chapter 2.2.

It is extremely noteworthy that the total number of known records in 1983 (635,676) had been comfortably realized in terms of the number of retrievable records by 1995 (quantified as 657,619). This suggests that forward projections for record assimilation over periods of perhaps a decade are fairly realistic, and implies that estimates of the number of anticipated records made in 1995 can be used with confidence in planning record development over the next five to ten years.

Assuming that the rate at which retrievable records accumulate continues at about 32,000 per year, by the year 2000 the number of retrievable records will be approximately 820,000 items, only just short of 1 million records (977,600) by the year 2005. In large measure this represents the backlog of material that is already identified as anticipated records and will migrate into electronically retrievable form. It is more difficult to predict the extent to which previously unknown material will come to attention for eventual addition to the record. It is this material that is represented among the anticipated records. Assuming the flow of this material continues at the same rate (estimated at 27,500 per year), and there is no reason to think it will slow down, the total number of records known will exceed 1 million by the year 2000 (1,074,984) and by 2005 will have reached about 1.2 million items (1,212,484).

Figure 4.4 also represents another trend. This concerns the proportion of retrievable records to anticipated records. In 1984 this ratio was about 1:1.10,

but by 1995 it had narrowed considerably to 1:0.42. The trend looks set to continue as recording systems are more fully computerized: by AD 2005 the proportion may be as low as 1:0.25.

If these predictions are correct, there are major implications not only for resourcing the continued work of assembling records and keeping them up to date with new information, but also for the curation of the records themselves through the maintenance and upgrading of the computer systems that store the information. Clearly there is much to do just to continue the process of turning anticipated records into retrievable records. It is impossible to predict who, in organizational terms, will be developing and curating these records in ten years time, because much will depend on local government reorganization and the role of regional agencies. However, Table 4.1 shows the distribution of records in relation to organizations which appeared in 1995 to be the definitive records-holders for a discrete geographical area. As can be seen, county councils collectively hold over 92% of records, the second biggest holdings being those for National Parks. In this analysis duplicated records were excluded where they could be recognized, but it should be noted that many duplicate records exist where organizations have geographically overlapping areas of interest.

4.3.2 The NMR

Over broadly the same period, the expansion of the NAR has been continuing too. Figure 4.5 shows these changes in a form comparable to that presented for local SMRs, although the census dates are slightly different. The upward trend, however, is very similar even if not quite so steep. In 1978 there were about 130,000 retrievable records in the portion of the Ordnance Survey record relating to England, about the same as when it was transferred to RCHME in 1983. The merger served to expand the record, so that by 1984 there were about

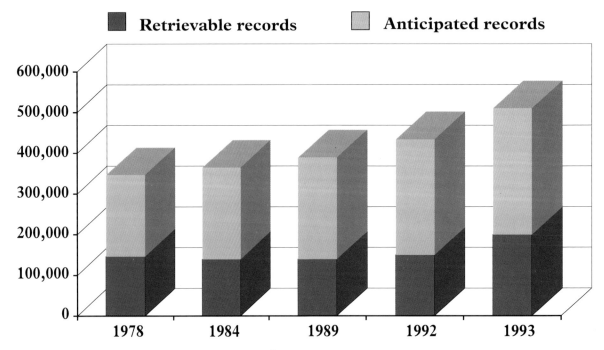

Figure 4.5 - Bar chart showing increases in the number of retrievable and anticipated archaeological records held by the National Monuments Record 1978-93. *[Source: MARS National Survey Programme using data supplied by RCHME]*

Table 4.1 - Distribution of retrievable records in 1995 by organizational location of the SMR. *[Source: MARS National Survey. Sample: as shown]*

SMR type	Number	Percentage of total
County Council	610918	92.3
District Council	7949	1.2
Borough Council	609	0.1
City Council	8468	1.3
National Park	33682	5.1
Total	**661626**	**100%**

140,000 entries. Published estimates of approximately 150,000 entries in 1992-3 (RCHME 1993a, 29) are now known to be rather on the low side as when the MONARCH database was opened in 1993 there were found to be about 200,000 archaeological entries. This represents a 65% increase over a 15-year period.

4.3.3 Record density

Looking at the quantity of records accumulated to date another way, the total number (i.e. retrievable and anticipated) in local SMRs in 1983 represented an average density of 2.34 items per square kilometre across England; just over a decade later the average density had risen to 5.04 records per square kilometre.

However, this general national picture hides a great deal of regional variation. Figure 4.6 shows the distribution of records (retrievable and anticipated), standardized as density per square kilometre, for the counties in England in 1984. It shows that many blocks of adjacent counties have similar densities, especially in midland and south-western England. Only five counties

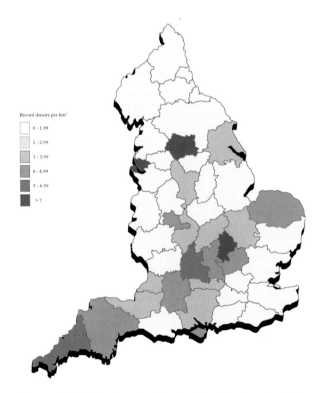

Figure 4.6 - Map showing the density of archaeological records in England by county in 1983. *[Source: IAM 1984]*

had densities of more than 5 records per square kilometre.

Figure 4.7 shows the situation in 1995 based on the MARS National Survey data. Nineteen counties now have record densities in excess of 5 records per square kilometre. Many others have increased their overall density. Blocks of counties with broadly similar densities are still apparent, although the high spots have shifted slightly, and now include Greater London.

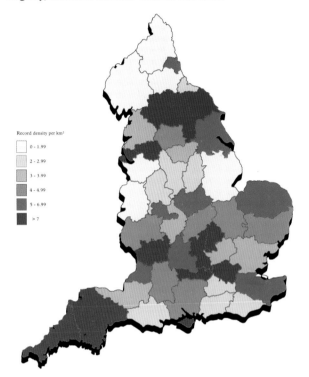

Figure 4.7 - Map showing the density of archaeological records in England by county in 1995. *[Source: MARS National Survey]*

At first sight these maps may be taken to reflect the actual density of archaeology across the country, but this is not necessarily the case, as they show differences only in the cumulative record of data. Counties with the highest densities tend to be urban areas, such as Greater London and Merseyside, with high proportions of buildings, or small counties which have been intensively studied for the purposes of record creation (e.g. the Isle of Wight, which has risen from 3 to nearly 17 records per square kilometre). Large rural counties such as Cumbria, Lincolnshire and Northumberland tend to have relatively low densities. Another factor in the changing picture is the way that individual records have been developing, those already well established in 1984 remaining fairly constant over the decade, while those only just starting up in 1984 show massive increases.

There is also an historical dimension. Looking at the counties with more than 4 records per square kilometre it is notable that they include five out of the seven counties included in the *Archaeological survey of Britain arranged by counties* noted earlier in this chapter, and a high proportion of the counties were covered by the RCHME inventories or early surveys by the Ordnance Survey Archaeology Division.

4.3.4 Changes at county level 1983-95

Table 4.2 shows a county by county comparison between

Table 4.2 - Retrievable and anticipated records by county for 1983 and 1995 with percentage increases in retrievable records 1983-1995. *[Source: for 1993, IAM 1984; for 1995, MARS National Survey Programme. Sample: as shown]*

COUNTY	Date SMR established	Records 1983 retrievable	Records 1983 anticipated	Records 1995 retrievable	Records 1995 retrieveable and anticipated	% increase in retrievable record 1983-95
Avon - county / Bath City	1977/1981	3200	6000	9704	59704	203
Bedfordshire	1971	12356	12356	14085	39085	14
Berkshire	1970s	4000	7000	16437	16437	311
Buckinghamshire	1972	6018	6018	21618	21624	259
Cambridgeshire	1975	10000	20000	13744	13744	37
Cheshire	1974	2703	4000	4520	14520	67
Cleveland	post 1970	1079	2000	1843	3114	71
Cornwall	1976	24000	50000	33535	33535	40
Cumbria	1974	6000	25000	13530	13530	126
Derbyshire	1982	5623	8000	5467	6967	-3
Devon - county / Plymouth City	1976/1993	20919	20919	53750	54030	157
Dorset	1972	4500	20000	7458	7558	66
Durham	1989	2000	20000	3500	25000	75
East Sussex	1979	2300	4000	4236	15000	84
Essex	1972	5319	5319	12997	18897	144
Gloucestershire	1982/1989	1000	7000	19303	19303	1830
Greater London	1984	2000	10000	65994	65994	3200
Greater Manchester	1980	1700	5000	9510	11510	459
Hampshire - county / Winchester city	1975/1974	10624	15000	15653	16153	47
Hereford & Worcester - two counties	1968/1974	5300	40000	16083	66083	203
Hertfordshire	1976	6532	11000	6480	13780	-1
Humberside	1984	7500	15000	18315	18315	144
Isle of Wight	pre-1965	1319	4000	6460	15460	390
Kent	1989	3526	10000	19728	20228	460
Lancashire	1979	3600	36000	10965	10965	205
Leicestershire	pre-1965	3000	6000	14386	14466	380
Lincolnshire - county / N & S Kesteven	1985/1987/1987	6300	10000	10224	27724	62
Merseyside	1977	7000	10000	7613	19613	9
Norfolk	1974	19000	19000	30403	33403	60
Northamptonshire	1974	5500	22000	10967	11167	99
Northumberland	1985	4055	40000	7119	22119	76
North Yorkshire - county / Dales NP / York City	1970s/1970s/1985	9383	40000	58384	59918	522
Nottinghamshire	1974	3200	10000	5963	5963	86
Oxfordshire	1965	13500	13500	13935	13935	3
Shropshire	1976	3735	3735	5168	8848	38
Somerset	?1974	8600	10000	10354	10354	20
South Yorkshire	1974	3018	4000	5496	5726	82
Staffordshire	1965	3600	3600	6265	6265	74
Suffolk	1974	4500	9000	15200	22200	238
Surrey	1972	2200	5000	4341	6341	97
Tyne & Wear	1975	331	3000	3679	7679	1011
Warwickshire	1977	4250	15000	7117	19117	67
West Midlands - county / Birmingham City	1980s/c1981	3000	3000	5512	5532	84
West Sussex	1971	3429	3429	5054	10554	47
West Yorkshire	1975	30000	30000	9751	9751	-67
Wiltshire	1975	11800	11800	15773	16273	34
Total		**302519**	**635676**	**657619**	**937484**	**117%**

the situation in 1983 and in 1995, with the percentage change over the period calculated on the basis of retrievable records. Clearly, patterns of change and rates of growth vary across the country, but most SMRs show consistent growth, albeit at different rates. Wiltshire, for example, is fairly typical, expanding from 11,800 retrievable records in 1983 to 14,200 in 1988, reaching 15,773 in 1995; a total increase of 34%. By contrast, during the same period, the SMR for Greater London increased by 3200%, largely accounted for by the migration of records relating to Listed Buildings and Scheduled Monuments to the SMR. SMRs in other counties, for example Berkshire and Dorset, appear to have increased rapidly between 1983 and 1988, only to diminish in size slightly by 1994. This results from early overestimates of size matched against later, more accurate, quantification. Only three SMRs, Derbyshire, Hertfordshire and West Yorkshire, show decreases between 1983 and 1995, again because of early overestimations of the number of retrievable records.

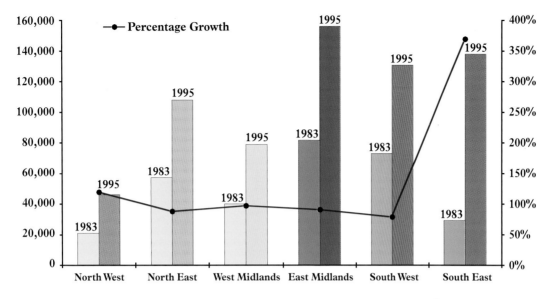

Figure 4.8 - Bar chart showing trends in retrievable record accumulation 1983-95 by MARS Region. *[Sources: IAM 1984, table 7 and MARS National Survey. Samples: 1983 n= 302,519; 1995 n= 657,619]*

4.3.5 Changes by region 1983-95

Figure 4.8 shows the situation according to MARS Regions. All show healthy increases in the number of retrievable records, the greatest increases being 369% in the South East, powered by the development of detailed records for Greater London and Kent, and 120% in the North West. Increases in the remaining four regions are consistent at between 79% and 97%.

4.3.6 Changes to the period breakdown of records

There is also considerable variability in the increases in the number of records in relation to defined periods. This is difficult to measure, because there is surprisingly little consistency in the application of periods to archaeological data between Sites and Monuments Records, and there is

considerable variation in the upper cut-off dates for the accessioning of records which will affect quantification for the more recent periods. Between 1988 and 1994 there was extensive revision of the cut-off dates used by SMRs (*cf.* Chadburn 1989, 2). Of the 46 surveyed, 24 have no defined cut-off date and 16 use AD 1945 as a terminal date. Five use a variety of dates later than AD 1600: Cheshire was in the process of extending its date range to include all remains before AD 1900 (formerly 1700), and the same cut-off had been selected by the SMR for the Isle of Wight. Norfolk had opted for 1962. Greater Manchester had decided on a 'floating' cut-off date to include anything over 30 years old. Wiltshire maintained its traditional cut-off date of AD 1600, but included later Scheduled Monuments in its record. At the time of the survey Dorset remained distinctive in having subjective,

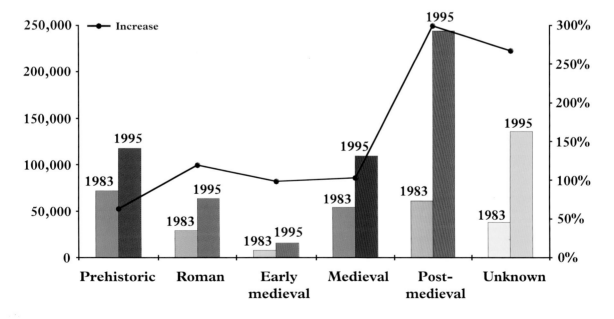

Figure 4.9 - Bar chart showing patterns of record accumulation for retrievable records in local SMRs by archaeological period, 1983-95. *[Sources: IAM 1984, table 7 and MARS National Survey. Samples: 1983 n= 261,388; 1995 n= 685,406]*

unspecified criteria for the inclusion of sites in its SMR.

Figure 4.9 shows the distribution of retrievable records according to a series of broad chronological divisions. In 1983 it was thought that most SMRs gave low priority to post-medieval (i.e. post AD 1540) material, given the relatively low number of records relating to that period (IAM 1984, 25). The percentage increase in the number of records per archaeological period since 1984 shows that this situation has altered considerably. There has been a threefold increase in the number of records relating to the period AD 1540 to present, the largest single increase for any one period by a long way. In part this suggests the targeting of resources to the development of this sector of the record, even if only by trawling the sorts of sources that would lead to the incorporation of this kind of material.

There are, however, regional variations too: the South East and North East both increased records relating to the post-medieval period by more than 200%, whereas in the North West the increase in post-medieval records was only 22% over the same period.

Records relating to prehistoric periods increased nationally by only 63%, the lowest level of increase, while records relating to Roman material rose by 119%. Again, however, there are regional variations, with the South East and North East showing the greatest increases, perhaps as a result of major record development in these areas. Records of uncertain date increased by 267% nationally, despite advances in the application of absolute and relative dating and better understanding of the chronological range of field monuments. Both the North East and the South East again show the greatest increases in these records. One explanation is that record compilers are being more cautious in assigning period

1983

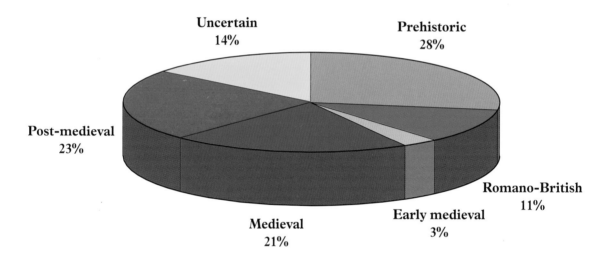

1995

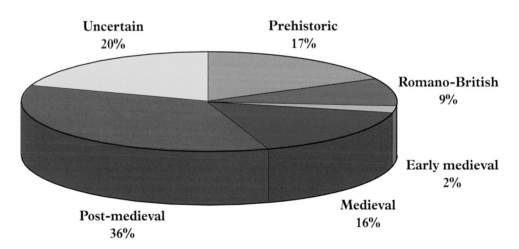

Figure 4.10 - Pie charts showing the breakdown of retrievable archaeological records in local SMRs by archaeological period, 1983 and 1995. *[Sources: IAM 1984, table 10 and MARS National Survey Programme. Samples: 1983 n= 261,388; 1995 n= 685,406]*

classifications to new records because archaeological research has called into question the dating of many classes of monuments that were thought to be securely dated, as for example standing stones, rock art and regular field systems.

Nationally, the effect of all these changes has been to change considerably the chronological balance of the range of retrievable records. Figure 4.10 shows a pair of pie charts which summarize the composition of retrievable records in 1983 and 1995 by period. Although the number of records relating to the prehistoric, Roman, early medieval and medieval periods has increased, their contribution to the overall make-up of the record has diminished considerably.

4.4 Record mode

The number of known records is a very crude measure of the archaeological resource because of the range of entities that can be identified as a unit of record. There have been many discussions about what SMRs consider appropriate entities as the basis for record creation (e.g. Benson 1985, 32), most of them rather unproductive because they were not tied to secure and explicit theoretical or conceptual underpinnings. Neither the 1983 nor the 1987 studies comprehensively addressed the matter of record content, although Fraser collected some information about the incidence of records relating to findspots and buildings (IAM 1984, 23-5). In 1995 the content of SMRs was explored in terms of the kinds of records represented in considerable detail for each county, combining where necessary data from each principal SMR in a county to provide an overall picture.

Six main 'modes' of record were defined, as follows:

Monuments (excluding buildings). These records conform to the broad definition of monument discussed in Chapter 2.3, and includes all Scheduled Monuments. Forty-three out of 46 counties were able to interrogate their systems to determine the number of records which related to monuments. Devon, Gloucestershire and West Sussex were unable to make these counts at the time of the survey, although within Devon figures were available for Plymouth City. The total number of retrievable records relating to monuments was 299,140.

Buildings. These represent a sub-set of the broad category of monument defined in Chapter 2.3, but were identified separately in this section of the survey because of their special position in relation to the archaeological record as a whole. Forty of the 46 counties were able to determine the number of records relating to buildings of early medieval, medieval, post-medieval, modern or unknown date; gaps in the data are caused either because the records themselves do not distinguish buildings in a way that allows queries to be formulated, or because no suitable query routine could be developed. Berkshire, Cornwall, Dorset, Kent, Staffordshire and West Sussex were unable to quantify the number of records which related to buildings. The total number of retrievable records relating to buildings was 133,051.

Urban areas. These were defined as records which relate to historic towns and cities of various sorts, mainly Roman, medieval, post-medieval and modern. This follows the definition of the concept of such archaeological entities within the Monuments Protection Programme (Darvill 1992b) and initiatives to create Urban Area databases (English Heritage 1992c). Despite the fact that the idea of an urban area has been a fundamental part of archaeological thinking for many years, only 18 counties out of 46 include records relating to urban areas, the total being just 267 such records.

Archaeological landscapes. These were defined as records which applied to complexes of monuments or extensive groups of monuments related because of their preservation, co-existence, or functional integrity. Again this follows the definition of the concept of such entities within the Monuments Protection Programme (Darvill 1992a) and the very considerable interest in historic and ancient landscapes in both theoretical and practical archaeology for more than two decades. Only 21 of the 46 counties include records relating to archaeological landscapes, collectively reporting a total of 1117 such retrievable records. However, most of these appear to relate to historic parks and gardens as one element of the broader picture of archaeological landscapes.

Stray finds. Stray finds mainly include objects (e.g. potsherds, stone axes, flints, coins etc.) and materials (e.g. ancient glass, brick, stone etc.) with no precise provenance or certain association with a recorded monument. Information about stray finds is available from 44 out of the 46 counties, although some had trouble distinguishing between sites and stray finds or between finds from excavations and stray finds. No information is available from Gloucestershire and West Sussex. For Devon, information is available only for Plymouth City. Quantifications for Lancashire, Leicestershire, Northumberland and North Yorkshire (county information) included all finds. Nottinghamshire listed find spots. The Norfolk quantification included counts for each type of material included within any given find, and was therefore inflated. Staffordshire was unable to distinguish prehistoric records from later records of stray finds. Suffolk expressed a lack of confidence in their figures for Neolithic, Bronze Age and Iron Age stray finds. A total of 131,246 retrievable records relating to stray finds have been reported.

Miscellaneous records. These records relate to items not covered by the other modes, and mainly comprise entries established to deal with information from local legends, non-antiquities, place-names without archaeological substance, or geological features. Thirty-four counties out of 46 have data relating to miscellaneous records; other SMRs were unable to supply data because they either could not retrieve it or did not include such things in their system. Buckinghamshire retrieved data on historic and prehistoric records only. Cornwall, Humberside, Norfolk and North Yorkshire (county SMR) may have over-estimated the data-set slightly because of the inclusion of information relating to known monuments. Suffolk regards the number of prehistoric records in this count as being inexplicably high. Wiltshire included some undated or dubious monuments in this count. A total of 36,705 retrievable records relating to

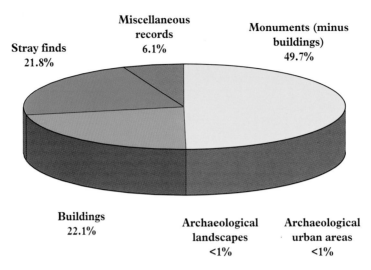

Figure 4.11 - Pie chart showing the breakdown of retrievable archaeological records in local SMRs in 1995 by record mode. *[Source: MARS National Survey Programme. Sample: n= 601,526]*

miscellaneous finds were reported.

Figure 4.11 shows a pie chart which summarizes the overall breakdown of record modes for England as a whole. Approximately three-quarters of all current retrievable records in England relate to archaeological monuments that conform fairly comfortably with the broad definition offered in earlier chapters. About half of all records relate to monuments that are not buildings; about a quarter of all records relate to monuments that can be considered to be buildings. Of the remainder, about one-fifth of records are currently stray finds. Only about 6% of records fall into the miscellaneous category. Urban areas and archaeological landscapes are each represented by less than 1% of records.

The apparently low percentage of records relating to urban areas is not terribly surprising as there are numerically rather few examples: Wacher (1974), for example, identified 21 major Roman towns, and Burnham and Wacher (1990) 53 small towns; while Heighway (1972) lists 778 towns and cities of medieval or earlier origin.

At first sight the apparently low percentage of archaeological landscapes (also called 'historic landscapes' or 'relict cultural landscapes') represented is perhaps more surprising, especially given the high level of interest in defining them and using them as the basis for discussions of conservation and management programmes (Timms 1993; Darvill 1997a). However, it can be suggested that archaeological landscapes are not easily recorded in SMRs using conventional systems, and that the concept of the archaeological landscape is currently being deployed as a cover-term to refer to groups of monuments which appear on the record as single items. Existing record systems include most of the kinds of things they were designed for, and which are well understood by those who run them and use them. Making the systems adaptive to the introduction of fundamentally new kinds of data may require structural changes to their architecture.

4.4.1 Record mode by region

Within this general picture there are considerable regional variations. Figure 4.12 shows a series of pie charts reflecting record modes by MARS Region. From this it is clear that monuments (excluding buildings) represent the highest percentage of records in all six regions, but that representation varies from 74% in the South West to just over 60% in both the northern regions and about 40% in the South East and East Midlands. Buildings generally fall between 12% and 22%, apart from in the South West where the figure is only 5%. This is largely due to the dominance of prehistoric records in the South West.

Stray finds are proportionally higher in the South East and East Midlands, probably because of both the predominant land-type in the region (arable regimes, most notably in the East Midlands) and the potentially higher levels of successful fieldwork (especially fieldwalking). Fewest miscellaneous records occur in the North West; in the remaining regions they are of similar proportions.

4.4.2 Record mode by period

Period-based variations are also important. Figure 4.13 shows an analysis of the records according to six broad periods. There are no buildings dated to the prehistoric period, archaeological landscapes being the smallest record mode followed by miscellaneous records, monuments and stray finds (the largest record mode, representing nearly half of all prehistoric records). Unsurprisingly, the earlier prehistoric periods in particular are dominated by stray finds rather than monument-based records. Records relating to the Romano-British period are likewise dominated by stray finds (54%), and the pattern for the remaining modes is largely the same, excepting the presence of archaeological urban areas. It is only for the early medieval and later periods that buildings appear as a significant component of the recorded resource, increasing to a proportion of nearly 70% for post-medieval records.

Certain periods are better represented by particular modes of record than others, as Figure 4.14 shows. For monuments, 10% are of post-medieval date, and a further 26% medieval. Only 11% of recorded monuments are Romano-British and 23% prehistoric. The biggest single group, amounting to 27% of all records classifiable as

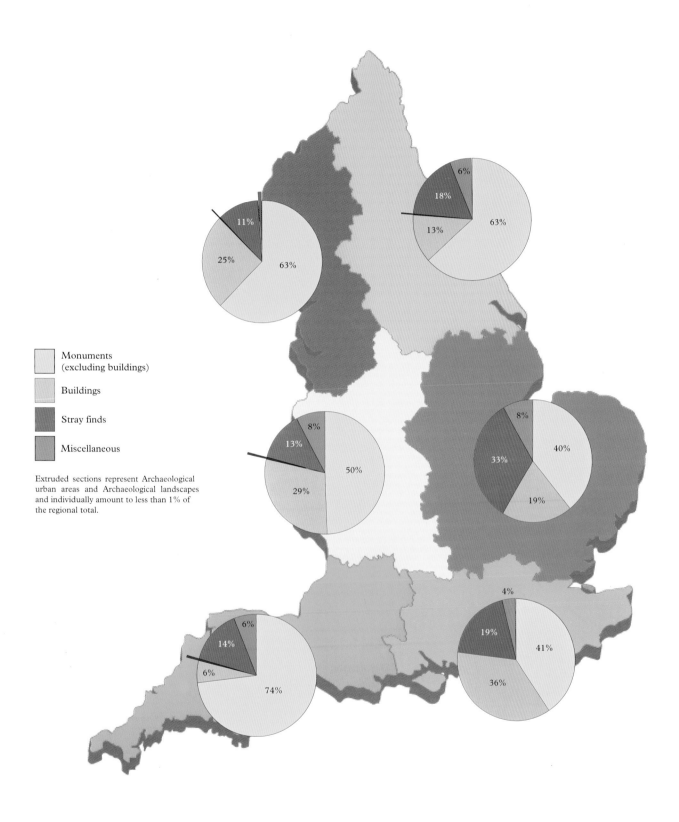

Figure 4.12 - Pie charts showing the breakdown of retrievable archaeological records in local SMRs in 1995 by record mode for the MARS Regions. *[Source: MARS National Survey Programme. Sample: n= 601,526]*

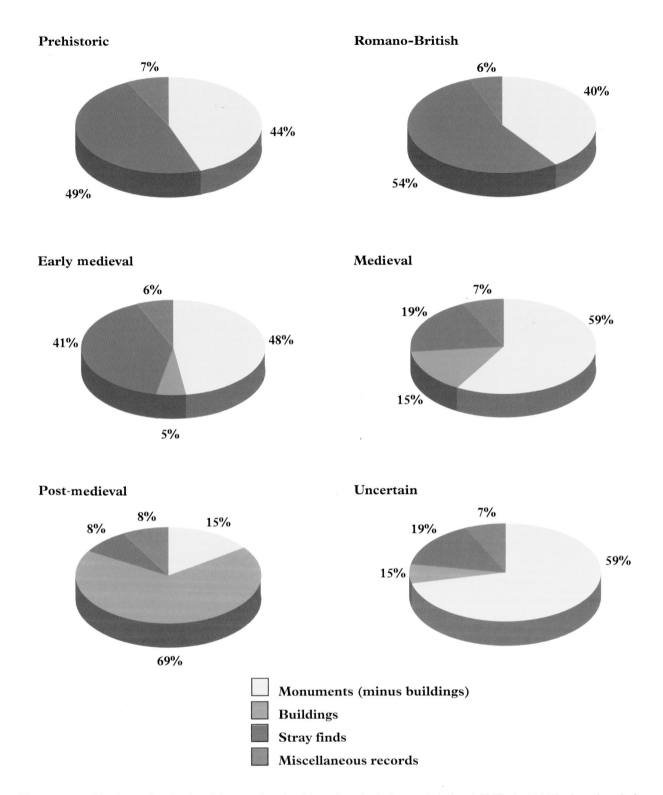

Figure 4.13 - Pie charts showing breakdowns of retrievable archaeological records in local SMRs in 1995 by broad period classified by record mode. *[Source: MARS National Survey Programme. Sample: n= 601,526]*

monuments, are of unknown date.

Buildings are by definition of post-Roman date, the majority (83%) being post-medieval. The majority of urban areas are of medieval date, although it is clear that many more medieval towns have still to be added to the records. Heighway (1972, 123-6) listed 57 potential urban areas in England where archaeological potential was yet to

be investigated or where no archaeological work was being undertaken. By contrast, the majority of substantial Romano-British towns are present on the record, at least 30 out of the 70 or so recorded in England (Wacher 1974; Burnham and Wacher 1990).

The majority of archaeological landscapes are of medieval and post-medieval date, as indicated above,

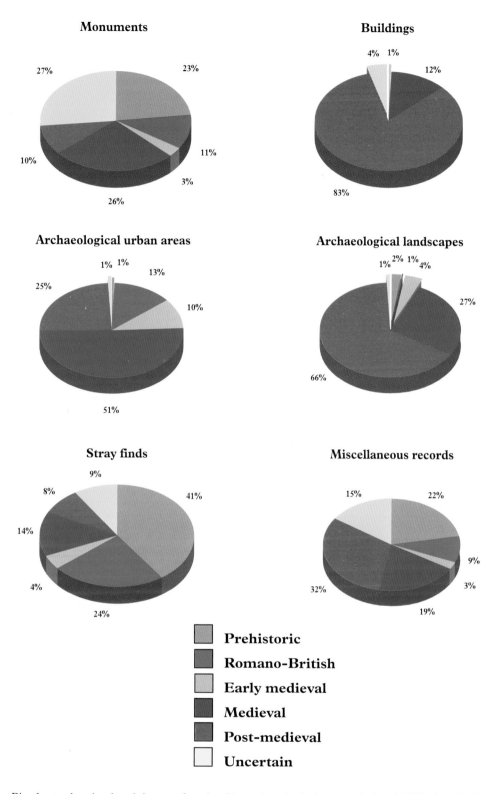

Figure 4.14 - Pie charts showing breakdowns of retrievable archaeological records in local SMRs in 1995 by record mode classified by broad period. *[Source: MARS National Survey Programme. Sample: n= 601,526]*

most being parks and gardens from the English Heritage Register of Historic Parks and Gardens. Others mainly consist of medieval field systems and industrial landscapes. However, there is a small but important number of prehistoric landscapes, most of which include field systems as well as related monuments.

Stray finds show a different pattern. The majority

are of prehistoric date, possibly because it is often difficult to connect finds with monuments for these early periods.

One additional mode which was not included in the MARS Project, but which could be considered in future, is records relating to negative evidence. These will mostly be site records in the sense discussed in Chapter 2.3, but a number of SMRs already include such records as a result of the increasing number of assessment and field-evaluation projects.

4.5 Rates of growth in the recorded resource

The 72% of records which can be classified as monuments (including those relating to buildings) can be regarded as a gross estimate of the recorded resource. In an effort to investigate the way that records relating to these monuments had been created and development a detailed study of MARS Monuments was undertaken. The aim was to find out when these monuments first appeared on established archaeological inventories / records, how they were first discovered, and what had happened to their records in terms of enhancement and validation since they were added to the record.

The source information for this study comprised the reports provided for each MARS Monument by SMRs and the NMR. Full particulars were not available for all MARS Monuments, so the sample used in these studies is less than the number of MARS Monuments cited elsewhere.

Figure 4.15 shows cumulative frequency graphs for the development of the recorded resource represented by MARS Monuments. The steepening upward slope of the curve during the 1970s and 1980s is especially notable and can be compared with the development of SMRs in England (*cf.* Figure 4.3). There is also a clear difference in the rate at which buildings have been added to the record. It should be emphasized, however, that since these profiles reflect MARS Monuments a proportion of buildings and structures of recent date have been excluded; what remain are essentially buildings of the greatest archaeological interest.

The percentage increases by decade also show some important trends (Figure 4.16), both standing buildings and archaeological monuments being added to the record in similar proportions each decade. Of particular note is the fact that 21% of the recorded resource currently known, mostly monuments which are not buildings, was already listed in inventories and catalogues before 1940. Broken down by period, this early recorded resource is contains a relatively high percentage of prehistoric monuments (24%) which represents a major part of the prehistoric section of the recorded resource even today. The steady increase in the percentage of additions in later decades is clear, falling off slightly during the 1990s if the first five years are a guide to the eventual total (the bar shown on the chart is a projection based on data for the period 1990-5).

Regional variations in the rate of development are also apparent, as Figure 4.17 shows. The two northern regions are particularly striking, with high proportions of monuments apparently being brought onto the record in recent times, in the North West during the 1980s and in the North East during the 1990s. The three counties contributing to the North West region have SMRs dating back to the 1970s, while in the North East region three major contributing SMRs originated in the 1980s and the rest have a history dating back to the 1970s. However, the establishment of the Yorkshire Dales National Park SMR in North Yorkshire may have had a considerable impact on the number of previously unrecorded monuments brought into the recorded resource.

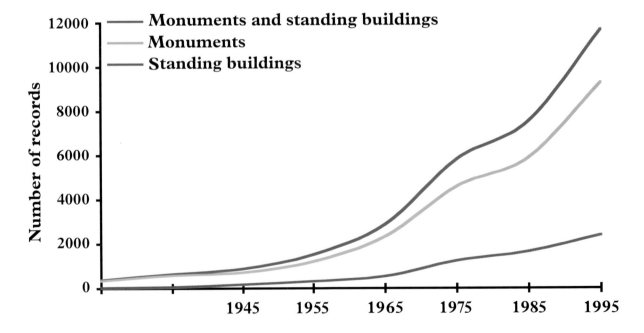

Figure 4.15 - Cumulative frequency graph showing the increasing number of MARS Monuments brought onto the recorded resource over the period pre-1940 to 1995. *[Source: MARS National Survey using records for MARS Monuments. Sample: n= 11,700]*

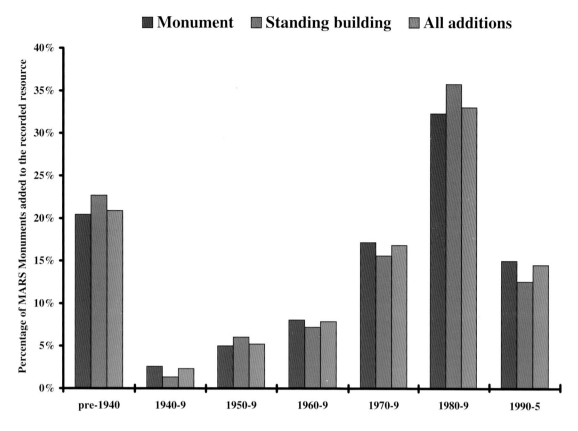

Figure 4.16 - Multiple bar chart showing the proportion of all MARS Monuments added to the recorded resource prior to 1940 and by decade to the 1990s. *[Source: MARS National Survey Programme using records for MARS Monuments. Sample: n= 11,700]*

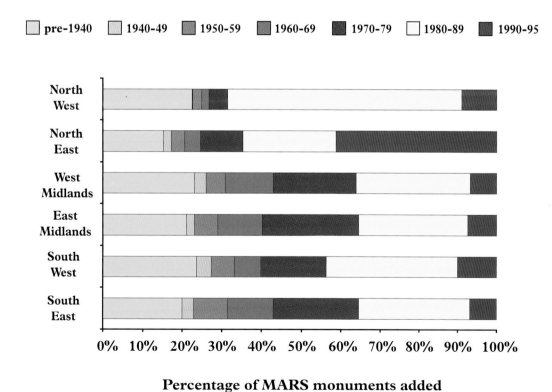

Percentage of MARS monuments added

Figure 4.17 - Horizontal stacked bar chart showing regional trends in the growth of the recorded resource represented by MARS Monuments. The bars are calculated as additions per decade as a proportion of all MARS Monuments. *[Source: MARS National Survey Programme using records for MARS Monuments. Sample: n= 11,700]*

Table 4.3 - Monument discovery event types pre-1940 and by decade to the 1990s for MARS Monuments. *[Source: MARS National Survey Programme using MARS Monuments. Sample: n= 11,700]*

Method/Event Type	No date recorded	% of time frame	pre-1940	% of time frame	1940-9	% of time frame	1950-9	% of time frame	1960-9	% of time frame	1970-9	% of time frame	1980-9	% of time frame	1990-5	% of time frame	Sample	% of total sample
Direct observation	28	7.4	802	38.8	82	29.8	336	54.9	374	40.6	746	37.9	929	24.0	213	13.2	3510	30.0
Documentary research	44	11.7	458	22.1	39	14.2	87	14.2	165	17.9	363	18.4	533	13.8	446	27.7	2135	18.2
Old maps	48	12.8	293	14.2	0	0	14	2.3	17	1.8	79	4.0	1148	29.7	467	29.0	2066	17.7
Aerial photography new pictures	101	26.9	10	<1	115	41.8	44	7.2	77	8.4	303	15.4	285	7.4	83	5.1	1018	8.7
Aerial photography old pictures	89	23.7	7	<1	7	2.5	14	2.3	23	2.5	137	7.0	367	9.5	85	5.3	729	6.2
Compilation of record	6	1.6	182	8.8	9	3.3	21	3.4	67	7.3	75	3.8	181	4.7	124	7.7	665	5.7
Systematic surface reconnaissance	1	<1	78	3.8	1	<1	31	5.1	82	8.9	67	3.4	162	4.2	118	7.3	540	4.6
Excavation (modern)	12	3.2	59	2.9	9	3.3	34	5.6	40	4.3	76	3.9	67	1.7	29	1.8	326	2.8
Secondary sources	5	1.3	10	<1	0	0	1	<1	11	1.2	45	2.3	114	2.9	13	<1	199	1.7
In course of destruction	2	<1	35	1.7	4	1.5	16	2.6	27	2.9	46	2.3	32	<1	7	<1	169	1.4
Chance finds	2	<1	36	1.7	7	2.5	9	1.5	21	2.3	9	<1	5	<1	3	<1	92	<1
Excavation (antiquarian)	2	<1	74	3.6	0	0	0	0	0	0	0	0	0	0	0	0	76	<1
No method identified	33	8.8	4	<1	0	0	1	<1	1	<1	3	<1	6	<1	2	<1	50	<1
Modern evaluation project	0	0	0	0	0	0	0	0	5	0.5	6	<1	18	<1	13	<1	42	<1
Systematic field-walking	2	<1	0	0	0	0	0	0	2	<1	4	<1	14	<1	8	<1	30	<1
Place-name evidence	1	<1	11	<1	0	0	0	0	7	<1	3	<1	1	<1	0	0	23	<1
Unsystematic surface reconnaissance	0	0	3	<1	1	<1	2	<1	1	<1	4	<1	2	<1	1	<1	14	<1
Private papers of antiquarians	0	0	6	<1	1	<1	1	<1	0	0	2	<1	1	<1	1	<1	12	<1
Unsystematic field-walking	0	0	0	0	0	0	1	<1	0	0	1	<1	0	0	0	0	2	<1
Geophysical survey	0	0	0	0	0	0	0	0	1	<1	0	0	0	0	0	0	1	<1
Recasting of SMR	0	0	1	<1	0	0	0	0	0	0	0	0	0	0	0	0	1	<1
Total	376	100%	2069	100%	275	100%	612	100%	921	100%	1969	100%	3865	100%	1613	100%	11700	100%

Table 4.4 - Monument discovery event types pre-1940 and by decade to the 1990s for MARS Monuments. *[Source: MARS National Survey Programme using MARS Monuments. Sample: n= 11,700]*

Method/Event Type	North West	% of region	North East	% of region	West Midlands	% of region	East Midlands	% of region	South West	% of region	South East	% of region	Sample	% of total sample
Direct observation	175	11.1	543	27.2	513	40.8	639	23.4	913	34.9	727	47.7	3510	30.0
Documentary research	159	10.1	502	25.2	341	27.1	355	13.0	581	22.2	197	12.9	2135	18.2
Old maps	835	52.8	589	29.6	77	6.1	231	8.5	309	11.8	25	1.6	2066	17.7
Aerial photography (new pictures)	38	2.4	178	8.9	103	8.2	410	15.0	214	8.2	75	4.9	1018	8.7
Aerial photography (old pictures)	105	6.6	47	2.4	45	3.6	188	6.9	218	8.3	126	8.3	729	6.2
Compilation of record	134	8.5	12	<1	8	<1	464	17.0	21	<1	26	1.7	665	5.7
Systematic surface reconnaissance	55	3.5	50	2.5	92	7.3	153	5.6	130	5.0	60	3.9	540	4.6
Excavation (modern)	14	<1	18	<1	24	1.9	84	3.1	47	1.8	139	9.1	326	2.8
Secondary sources	46	2.9	3	<1	24	1.9	18	<1	98	3.7	10	<1	199	1.7
In course of destruction	1	<1	5	<1	6	<1	70	2.6	10	<1	77	5.1	169	1.4
Chance finds	3	<1	7	<1	1	<1	67	2.5	2	<1	12	<1	92	<1
Excavation (antiquarian)	4	<1	22	1.1	13	1.0	9	<1	16	<1	12	<1	76	<1
No method identified	2	<1	3	<1	7	<1	0	0	33	1.3	5	<1	50	<1
Modern evaluation project	0	0	2	<1	1	<1	17	<1	8	<1	14	<1	42	<1
Systematic field-walking	6	<1	5	<1	0	0	7	<1	2	<1	10	<1	30	<1
Place-name evidence	0	0	5	<1	0	0	4	<1	11	<1	3	<1	23	<1
Unsystematic surface reconnaissance	1	<1	0	0	1	<1	8	<1	0	0	4	<1	14	<1
Private papers of antiquarians	3	<1	2	<1	1	<1	6	<1	0	0	0	0	12	<1
Unsystematic field-walking	0	0	0	0	0	0	1	0	0	0	1	<1	2	<1
Geophysical survey	0	0	0	0	0	0	0	0	1	<1	0	0	1	<1
Recasting of SMR	0	0	0	0	0	0	0	0	1	<1	0	0	1	<1
Total	1581	100%	1993	100%	1257	100%	2731	100%	2615	100%	1523	100%	11700	100%

4.6 Monument discovery

In resource management terms, the events or methods which give rise to the initial discovery of archaeological monuments is very important. An analysis of 11,700 MARS Monuments provides a detailed picture. The NMR was not separately consulted for this exercise, or for that relating to enhancement activities, but MARS found the information supplied in print-outs from MONARCH to be most valuable in determining discovery and enhancement episodes. This is probably because it incorporates information from Ordnance Survey record cards and RCHME surveys.

Twenty main event types or methods of monument discovery were identified and the discovery of each monument assigned to one of these on the basis of information included in the SMR or NMR records. These records rarely record the discovery event outright, and so it is necessary to work from the free text descriptions, record sources (to find the earliest) and bibliographic references. Table 4.3 shows an analysis of the national picture overall (right-hand column) and by date of discovery.

In all, over 46% of monuments in the sample were identified through some kind of fieldwork, direct observation being predominant and accounting for 30% of all monuments. Field surveys of various types account for 5% and excavation for 3.4%. Aerial photographic studies using old and new photographs together account for the discovery of 15% of monuments. About 40% of monuments were identified through various historical studies, including the use of cartographic sources.

In looking at these figures, however, there are a number of peculiarities which are probably functions of the fact that records have been constructed with little regard to what happened to prompt identification (the relationship between sites and monuments discussed in Chapter 2.3). For example, unsystematic fieldwalking must account for more than two monuments being discovered in the sample units; the problem here is that such data were probably recorded as stray finds. Equally, excavations are probably over-represented, and this raises two points. First, because of their intrinsically archaeological nature, excavations will be recorded on the SMR. Second, they rarely discover new monuments; they tend to be following up discoveries made through other methods in order to verify and expand the initial discovery.

Archaeological evaluations and assessment programmes appear to contribute relatively little to the new monuments discovered in the 1990s, although this can in part be explained by the poor integration of such material into local SMRs (Darvill *et al.* 1995, 39); they are thus assumed to be among the anticipated records referred to and quantified above. The same probably applies to geophysical surveys.

The decade in which discoveries were made is often related to the event types involved. In general there is a move away from field-based discovery methods towards paper-based sources, but more subtle trends can be seen too. For example, the 1950s saw very extensive fieldwork carried out by Ordnance Survey field investigators (see above); this is clearly reflected in the high number of monuments first recorded by direct observation, nearly 55% of all discoveries in the 1950s. The steady rise in the use of secondary sources through time is an interesting reflection on both the production of such works and their influence on record-makers.

Aerial photography remains important, although from the evidence of record numbers identified with it in SMRs appears to be declining in its overall contribution. This may be linked to declining funds for this kind of work and the focus of attention by the RCHME on the National Mapping Programme, which would not have made much impact on SMR records at the MARS census date. Equally, it is possible that the process of record creation is tending to conflate results from aerial reconnaissance by making a single monument out of palimpsests where several separate monuments might have been defined in the past (*cf.* Whimster 1989, 7 on interpretation and mapping units).

It is also noticeable that while in early decades a relatively small number of methods contributed to the development of the recorded resource, in recent decades the range of methods has clearly increased (11 in 1946-56, 16 in 1986-95).

The regional pattern is also important, as Table 4.4 shows. The national trend in the frequency of key discovery events is broadly matched in each of the six regions, although in the North West map evidence has contributed most discoveries. The national figure for discoveries made as a result of modern excavation is partly skewed by the 129 of these events in the South East. Record compilation in the East Midlands has also contributed a greater number of discoveries than the national average and this may be due simply to the ways in which the SMRs of the region record monuments.

What is clear from all available information about the recognition of monuments and their recording in local and national records is that the sequence of identification, description and recording is complicated and highly variable, resulting from a mixture of happenstance, opportunity and deliberate investigation. In addition to the factors that can be measured by MARS, account needs to be taken of local circumstances, land-use, and the extent and purpose of archaeological activity. These things are explored and illustrated at the level of a particular area of countryside through the following case study. It illustrates the process with reference to an archaeologically important and distinct land-type.

4.7 Case study 3: Hartland Moor, Dorset [2]

According to a 1989 study, Hartland Moor is the sixth-largest block of heathland in Dorset (Chapman *et al.* 1989). A 2km by 4km transect within the Moor was selected for detailed study, the south-west corner being at NGR SY 9384. The majority of the transect falls within the parish of Arne, with small parts in Wareham, Holy Trinity and Corfe Castle, on the northern edge of the Isle of Purbeck to the south of Wareham. The dominant landscape type is ericaceous heathland, currently around 50% of the study area, with pasture and plantations as subsidiary components.

Dorset County SMR has 17 records that relate to the remains in the study area, all of which can be regarded as monuments in the context of MARS. Three records have a number of chronologically distinct entries under a

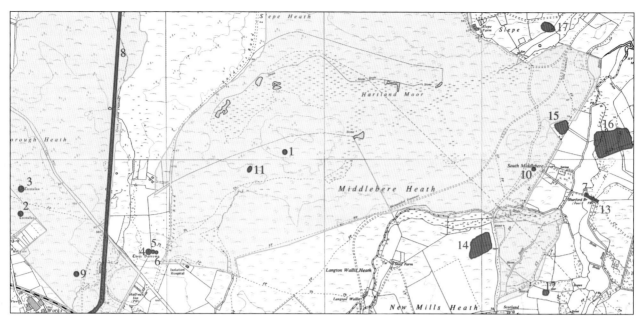

Figure 4.18 - Map showing the position and extent of archaeological monuments recorded in the Hartland Moor heathland study area, Dorset. The numbers refer to Table 4.5. *[Reproduced from Ordnance Survey mapping with the permission of The Controller of Her Majesty's Stationery Office. Crown copyright licence number GD03093G/2/98]*

single record; separated out these give a total of approximately 24 monuments for the area, equal to 3 per square kilometre. This is only very slightly above the national average noted above; there is no reason to believe that Hartland Moor is atypical of other heathland areas in the region.

Figure 4.18 shows the position and estimated extents of the archaeological monuments in the study area. A range of large and small monuments are represented, the area covered by the monuments amounting to approximately 0.2km², equal to 2.5% of study area. This is below the national average indicated by the MARS National Survey Programme (see below Chapter 5.2.3), suggesting that the archaeology is dominated by relatively small and discrete monuments with some non-extensive areas of dispersed features. The chronological range of the monuments represented spans the period from the late third millennium BC through to the later second millennium AD (i.e. post-medieval time), although the record is dominated by monuments of two main periods, the second millennium BC and the post-medieval period from AD 1700.

The archaeological record as currently known has developed since the early nineteenth century. Table 4.5 shows in chronological order the recognition and recording of the monuments. Three main phases may be identified, each closely tied to the implementation of a range of event types. There are several monuments that have always been visible, including the upstanding bowl barrows and the stone bridge at Sharford, but which were identified as archaeological monuments at different times. The earliest recorded barrow is Record 1 in the middle of the heath; 1811 is given as its date of first recording because it was shown on the earliest Ordnance Survey map of the area as a mound. The Three Barrows were also shown on early maps, but they were not included in public sources until they were surveyed by Leslie Grinsell at an unknown date between 1930 and the mid 1950s; the results of his work were published in 1959 (Grinsell

1959). Grinsell included surveys of three round barrows (Records 1, 2 and 3), which were also shown on early maps. The year 1959 marks the end of the first phase of archaeological discovery on the heath.

A subsequent survey of the Isle of Purbeck by the Trust for Wessex Archaeology in the 1980s added several features visible only on aerial photographs, as well as some monuments visible on the ground.

Finally, the Wytch Farm Oilfield project examined infra-red aerial photographic sources not previously available, as well as undertaking excavation and watching-brief studies (Cox and Hearne 1991). All of these methods were new to the heathland area and contributed significantly to the understanding of the nature of archaeology on the heath.

The range of techniques deployed in assembling the record is interesting. Documentary research and fieldwork each contributed significantly, although it was not until the mid 1980s that any intervention took place. Stray finds are notable by their absence, perhaps because of the poverty of opportunity for research and because compiling the SMR has not involved carrying out a systematic appraisal of local museum collections. Neither has it been possible within the scope of this survey to trawl museum accessions to identify stray finds from the area. Miscellaneous records such as place-names are also missing, which here might contribute to understanding the medieval and later development and use of the heath.

Factors affecting the format of the record for Hartland Moor, as currently known, are clearly very varied and numerous. Figure 4.19 provides a cumulative frequency plot showing the increase in recorded monuments against the decrease in the extent of heathland since the early nineteenth century. At first sight there appears to be a fairly close relationship between heathland loss and monument discovery, but this is illusory. Only 5% of the known archaeology exists within the distinctively heathland parts of the area.

The highest rate of discovery post-dates the greatest

Table 4.5 - Summary details of recorded archaeological monuments in the Hartland Moor study-area, Dorset. *[Source: Dorset County Council SMR, with additions]*

Reference No.	Date of first recording	Land-use in 1846	Monument type	Estimated area m²	Land-use at first earliest recording and dimensions	Land-use 1994 and most recent dimensions	Land-use predicted after 1994
1	1811	Heath	Probable bowl barrow	95	Heath; crossed by parish boundary bank	Gorse and heather covered; diameter 11.0m, height 1.2m (1983)	Heath
2	1959	Heath	Bowl barrow	308	Heath; diameter 66.7 feet, height 7 feet (diameter 20.3m height 2.1m)	Heath; diameter 19.8m, height 2.4m (1983)	Heath
3	1959	Heath	Bowl barrow	221	Heath; diameter 60.6 feet, height 6 feet (diameter 18.5m height 1.8m)	Heath; diameter 16.8m, height 1.7m	Heath
4	1959	Heath	Bowl barrow (one of three barrows)	514	Heath; possibly with ploughed land to the south of the group. Diameter 81.8 feet, height 6.5 feet (diameter 25m height 2.0m)	Under gorse; group surrounded by ploughed land; diameter 25.6m, height 2.0m	On National Trust owned farm bordering on regenerated heathland
5	1959	Heath	Bowl barrow (one of three barrows)	201	Heath; diameter 48.5 feet, height 6 feet (diameter 14.8m height 1.8m)	Under gorse; diameter 16.0m, height 1.8m	On National Trust owned farm bordering on regenerated heathland
6	1959	Heath	Bowl barrow (one of three barrows)	132	Heath diameter 39.4 feet, height 2 feet (diameter 12.0m height 0.6m)	Under gorse; diameter 13.0m, height 0.6m	On National Trust owned farm bordering on regenerated heathland
7	1970	Footpath	Stone bridge	10	Footpath	Footpath	Footpath
8	1983	Heath	19th century tramway	10000	Heath	Heather and gorse covered heathland and as boundary between pastures.	RSPB Reserve as heath, heathland and boundary between pastures
9	1983	Heath	Possible bowl barrow	80	Heath	Heath	RSPB Reserve heath
10	1983	Arable	Ring ditch	80	Grassland/Heath	Grass / pasture	Pasture
11	1983	Heath	Probable bowl barrow	314	Heath; diameter 15-20m, height 0.5m	Heather covered / heathland	Heath
12	1985	Heath	Enclosure on AP	1000	Pasture / occasionally ploughed	Pasture	Regenerated heathland under English Nature management
13	1985	Heath	Sunken trackway to bridge	600	Pasture / occasionally ploughed	Pasture	Pasture
14	1985	Heath	Possible Medieval/Post Medieval field boundaries on AP in area defined on SMR map. Late Neolithic artefacts in topsoil Bronze Age field system identified in Wytch Farm survey	125000	Pasture / occasionally ploughed	Pasture	Regenerated heathland under Stewardship scheme
15	1988	Heath	Iron Age features and pottery including industrial evidence (excavated)	18000	Pasture	Pasture	Pasture
16	1988	Pasture	Bronze Age field system; mid Bronze Age burial deposits; late Iron Age industrial settlement; Romano-British field system; Medieval and post-medieval field systems (excavated)	40000	Pasture	Pasture	Pasture
17	1989	Pasture	Unidentified feature in trial pit	2500	Pasture	Grass / Pasture	Pasture

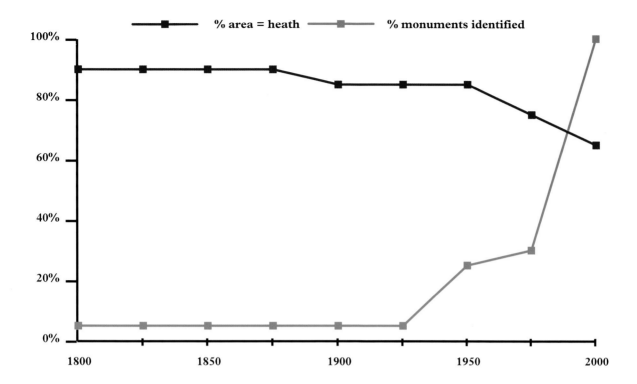

Figure 4.19 - Cumulative frequency chart showing additions to the recorded resource for Hartland Moor, Dorset, in relation to the decrease in heathland cover. *[Sources: MARS Case Study Research Programme using Dorset SMR data with additions]*

losses of heath. The seven monuments recorded before 1970 result from research-oriented survey work, related in part to mapping and in part to a systematic study of a single category of monument, the round barrow. Investigations related to development proposals in the period 1983-9 effectively quadrupled the number of monuments recorded, even though the extent of the work was confined to relatively small parts of the heath which were to be affected by development. This included the discovery and recording of two further barrows and a ring-ditch, which increased the number of recorded round barrows by 50%. The survey work connected with these development-prompted studies included a process of archaeological assessment and field evaluation. The field evaluation identified the multi-period monuments East of Corfe River (Record 16) and West of Corfe River (Record 15). The examination of infra-red photographs held by the National Rivers Authority revealed unknown features, probably relating to prehistoric field systems (Record 14). Their contribution to the recorded resource in the area is considerable and important because they expanded the range of both chronology and archaeological monument classes. Although no environmental sequences were established for the study area, some were carried out nearby. It can be estimated that had these various surveys been applied to the whole of the study area, an overall density of about 6 monuments per square kilometre would now obtain.

4.8 Monument record enhancement

The discovery and initial inventorizing of monuments is widely recognized as the first stage in a continuing process

of maintaining an adequate record of the recorded resource. The periodic checking or enhancement of records relating to defined monuments is important in keeping them up to date and current.

Looking again at MARS Monuments, there is evidence of over 30,000 enhancement events since before 1945, an average of nearly three events per record over the period. Figure 4.20 shows how the proportion of the recorded resource subject to some form of enhancement has changed over recent decades. The cumulative percentage of the resource on record is shown on the top line and the number of monuments added as a percentage of the resource known in that decade as the lower line. It can be seen that a considerable percentage of the total number of monuments in any decade had their records enhanced and that the proportion enhanced increased between 1940 and 1995. In the 1980s and 1990s the proportion enhanced exceeded the proportion added.

Table 4.6 presents an analysis of the recorded enhancement event types in relation to the methods used by region. All of the methods used in the discovery of monuments were also found in the enhancement work represented. The least frequently used method was unsystematic field walking (method 10), with just 8 instances; record compilation (method 20) was the most frequent, with 13,640 examples. This typically involved the recasting of records during computerization, and provided the opportunity to check details and update information.

Changes are apparent in the application of different methods to record enhancement over time, as Table 4.7 highlights. As with monument discovery, the 1940s were for obvious reasons a low period for record enhancement,

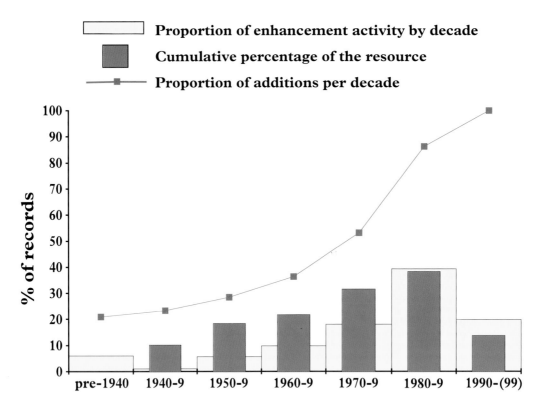

Figure 4.20 - Charts showing the extent of record enhancement events prior to 1940 and per decade to the 1990s in relation to the additions made to the recorded resource and the scale of the recorded resource. Based on MARS Monuments. *[Sources: MARS National Survey using records for MARS Monuments. Sample: n= 11,700]*

but thereafter enhancement increases by an average of 100% for each subsequent decade. The trend for the 1990s apparently shows this rate slowing down, but this is based on incomplete data relating to the first five years of the decade, a time of general recession and cut-backs in public expenditure. After 1940 the use of old maps as a means of enhancement tails off to a low of 1.5% in the 1950s. Today the use of old maps accounts for only 3% of all enhancements. The trend among other, less frequently, used methods (e.g. the use of place-name evidence or the trawling of private papers) shows a steady decline. The use of old and new air photographs fluctuates around the 2% mark, but the figures do not reflect the efforts of the RCHME's National Mapping Programme.

The discovery and enhancement of archaeological records is a major element of the work carried out by staff of the SMRs and the NMR. It is essential for maintaining the integrity, relevance and accuracy of the records themselves, although as the size of the total record grows the task of enhancement and maintenance will inevitably use up an increasing proportion of available time and resources. In recent years greater attention has been given to the compilation of metadata as part of a record (that is, information relating to the processes of creation and maintenance), and no doubt further improvements could be made in this area in future. For the time being, however, the record as it stands is clearly the product of a complicated and convoluted set of processes which extend a long way back in time and which may never be fully understood or documented.

One of the things that enhancement work regularly has to deal with is the matter of keeping information up to date. Individual monuments are constantly changing, as too, as this chapter shows, is the very nature and extent of the recorded resource itself. This theme is developed further in the next chapter, which focuses on the distribution and condition of England's archaeology in the 1990s.

Table 4.6 - Record enhancement event types by region for MARS Monuments. *[Source: MARS National Survey Programme using MARS Monuments. Sample: n= 30,998 documented events]*

Method/ Event type	North West	% of region	North East	% of region	West Midlands	% of region	East Midlands	% of region	South West	% of region	South East	% of region	Sample	% of total sample
Compilation of record	1883	55.0	1982	46.0	1168	36.6	4039	49.9	2836	34.3	1732	46.6	13640	44.0
Documentary research	699	20.4	1050	24.4	1011	31.7	1678	20.7	2437	29.5	751	20.2	7626	24.6
Direct observation	296	8.6	832	19.3	696	21.8	1055	13.0	1500	18.2	853	22.9	5232	16.9
Old maps	333	9.7	109	2.5	43	1.3	238	2.9	296	3.6	26	<1	1045	3.4
Systematic surface reconnaissance	47	1.4	68	1.6	36	1.1	168	2.1	432	5.2	48	1.3	799	2.6
Aerial photography (old pictures)	46	1.3	64	1.5	77	2.4	213	2.6	294	3.6	63	1.7	757	2.4
Aerial photography (new pictures)	16	<1	111	2.6	62	1.9	303	3.7	187	2.3	69	1.9	748	2.4
Excavation (modern)	14	<1	32	<1	40	1.3	123	1.5	44	<1	109	2.9	362	1.2
Secondary sources	35	1.0	21	<1	33	1.0	20	<1	159	1.9	6	<1	274	<1
Recasting of SMR	17	<1	11	<1	4	<1	80	1.0	0	0	8	<1	120	<1
In course of destruction	2	<1	4	<1	0	0	41	<1	9	<1	20	<1	76	<1
Place-name evidence	3	<1	9	<1	5	<1	12	<1	32	<1	2	<1	63	<1
Chance finds	0	0	0	0	0	0	50	<1	4	0	5	<1	59	<1
Modern evaluation project	2	<1	6	<1	12	<1	23	<1	7	<1	7	<1	57	<1
Systematic field-walking	26	<1	4	<1	0	0	12	<1	4	0	3	<1	49	<1
Excavation (antiquarian)	0	0	4	<1	2	<1	7	<1	14	<1	8	<1	35	<1
Private papers of antiquarians	3	<1	2	0	0	0	13	<1	3	0	1	0	22	<1
Geophysical survey	1	0	1	0	3	<1	6	<1	2	0	3	<1	16	<1
Unsystematic surface reconnaissance	1	0	0	0	0	0	4	0	0	0	5	<1	10	<1
Unsystematic field-walking	0	2	0	0	0	5	<1	1	0	0	0	8	0	<1
Total	**3424**	**100%**	**4312**	**100%**	**3192**	**100%**	**8090**	**100%**	**8261**	**100%**	**3719**	**100%**	**30998**	**100%**

Table 4.7 - Record enhancement event types pre-1940 and by decade to the 1990s for MARS Monuments. *[Source: MARS National Survey using MARS Monuments. Sample: n= 31,583 documented events]*

Method/ Event type	Pre 1940	% of time frame	1940-9	% of time frame	1950-9	% of time frame	1960-9	% of time frame	1970-9	% of time frame	1980-9	% of time frame	1990-5	% of time frame	Sample	% of total sample
Compilation of record	644	33.4	109	32.0	678	38.9	989	32.4	1947	34.8	5955	48.9	3317	54.0	13859	43.9
Documentary research	529	27.5	76	22.3	323	18.5	667	21.9	1263	22.6	3075	25.2	1693	27.5	7764	24.6
Direct observation	360	18.7	71	20.8	572	32.8	1027	33.7	1487	26.6	1342	11.0	374	6.1	5377	17.0
Old maps	240	12.5	8	2.3	26	1.5	42	1.4	117	2.1	407	3.3	205	3.3	1068	3.4
Systematic surface reconnaissance	23	1.2	1	<1	25	1.4	101	3.3	145	2.6	338	2.8	166	2.7	810	2.6
Aerial photography (new pictures)	5	<1	38	11.1	27	1.5	56	1.8	277	4.9	280	2.3	65	1.1	770	2.4
Aerial photography (old pictures)	2	<1	4	1.2	14	<1	38	1.2	160	2.9	421	3.5	118	1.9	766	2.4
Excavation (modern)	32	1.7	14	4.1	46	2.6	69	2.3	91	1.6	85	<1	25	<1	374	1.2
Secondary sources	18	<1	7	2.1	12	<1	18	<1	55	<1	116	<1	48	<1	276	<1
Recasting of SMR	0	0	0	0	3	<1	5	<1	2	<1	70	<1	40	<1	120	<1
In course of destruction	10	<1	2	<1	4	<1	9	<1	21	<1	17	<1	13	<1	76	<1
Place-name evidence	9	<1	7	2.1	2	<1	4	<1	5	<1	25	<1	11	<1	65	<1
Chance finds	16	<1	1	<1	7	<1	10	<1	10	<1	13	<1	2	<1	59	<1
Modern evaluation project	0	0	0	0	0	0	2	<1	3	<1	20	<1	32	<1	57	<1
Systematic field-walking	1	<1	0	0	1	<1	3	<1	8	<1	8	<1	28	<1	49	<1
Excavation (antiquarian)	35	1.8	0	0	0	0.0	0	0	0	0	0	0	0	0	37	<1
Private papers of antiquarians	3	<1	2	<1	2	<1	2	<1	4	<1	3	<1	6	<1	22	<1
Geophysical survey	0	0	0	0	0	0	3	<1	4	<1	4	<1	5	<1	16	<1
Unsystematic surface reconnaissance	0	0	0	0	3	<1	1	<1	0	0	6	<1	0	0	10	<1
Unsystematic field-walking	0	0	1	<1	0	0	5	<1	0	0	2	<1	0	0.0	8	<1
Total	**1927**	**100%**	**341**	**100%**	**1745**	**100%**	**3051**	**100%**	**5599**	**100%**	**12187**	**100%**	**6148**	**100%**	**31583**	**100%**

5 Distribution and condition: England's archaeology in the 1990s

The more the past is destroyed or left behind, the stronger the urge to preserve and restore. Threatened by technology, pollution and popularity, surviving vestiges command attention as never before...

(David Lowenthal 1990, 399)

5.1 Records and monuments: places and spaces

Records of archaeological remains considered in Chapter 4 are one thing, the reality that exists in the countryside and towns of England quite another. Archaeological monuments are not simple to count and measure. It is relatively straightforward, and perfectly acceptable, to make a list of places where archaeological remains are known to exist and tally the number of entries to give a grand total. Equally, from another perspective, each monument occupies a space that can be measured, even if only approximately, so that the total space occupied by recorded monuments can be calculated.

Far more difficult is determining precisely which attributes of recorded monuments should be counted and measured; this issue must be considered in the context of two great uncertainties. First is that the starting point for any review of what really exists is the record of sites and monuments itself, complete with its biases and anachronisms. Second, as every archaeologist knows, raw numbers do not very adequately reflect the complexity of archaeological remains and that however the recorded resource is quantified it represents only a fraction of the whole resource. As Lowenthal suggests above, when the remains of the past are threatened they tend to be more highly valued; inevitably it is the recorded remains that command attention, but given this situation it is sometimes possible to lose sight of the bigger picture.

Despite these reservations, however, decisions, resource allocations and future initiatives must be based on what is known to exist rather than what might exist. This chapter looks at the general character of England's recorded resource as known in the mid-1990s, focusing first on the total recorded resource and then on the extant (or surviving) recorded resource. Thus section 5.2 looks at the size, distribution and extent of the recorded resource; this is followed in subsequent sections by discussion of the forms of monuments represented and the periods of the past to which they relate. Attention then shifts to the extant recorded resource, first, in section 5.5, to consider its scale and then to look in turn at its overall condition, visibility and accessibility.

5.2 The size, distribution and extent of the recorded resource

As shown in Chapter 4.4, the MARS National Survey revealed that approximately 50% of all records held by local SMRs could be classified in broad terms as relating to archaeological monuments, and a further 22% to standing buildings. With about 657,619 retrievable records in the SMRs around the country, these percentages translate in numerical terms into a recorded resource of approximately 328,800 archaeological monuments and approximately 144,700 standing buildings.

Both these figures of course derive from counts made in 57 separate local SMRs which have then been brought together without any formal validation such as checking for duplicate entries relating to the same thing (a special problem with linear monuments such as Roman roads that run through several modern administrative areas), or cross-checking the definitions applied when making the original counts. In this connection it may also be noted that the figure for standing buildings is low compared with other estimates of the number of historic buildings in England; there are, for example, 500,000 Listed Buildings (English Heritage 1992a, 3). However, this can be explained by the fact that local SMRs treat historic buildings in widely differing ways: some include as monuments those considered to have archaeological relevance, others only include older buildings, and many exclude from the SMR information from the historic buildings registers altogether because it is held in other parallel record systems.

5.2.1 Estimating the recorded resource with MARS Monuments

Another way of exploring the size of the recorded resource is through the MARS sample transects. For these 1297 units the available archaeological records were carefully checked and validated against the definitions set out in Chapter 3.2. As a result 14,591 MARS Monuments were identified. Extrapolating from this sample, the total population of similarly defined monuments in the whole of England (i.e. the recorded resource) can be estimated at 293,036 with a 95% confidence interval of 275,695-310,377. Thus in round figures, MARS shows that at the census date of 1995 there were 300,000 archaeological monuments recorded in England. In providing this estimate it should of course be emphasized again that it relates to the fairly precisely defined range of archaeological remains defined as being MARS Monuments, and that of course it takes no account of known archaeological remains awaiting registration on established record systems (i.e. anticipated records, see Chapter 4.3.1), or of unrecorded remains awaiting discovery.

Accepting the difficulties inherent in taking consistent account of standing buildings, the two quantifications just considered are very similar and comfortably within 10% of each other. Monuments defined in the general sense by the local SMRs include some buildings and structures, as too does the definition of MARS Monuments. Both definitions exclude most relatively modern buildings, especially modern domestic buildings. The coincidence of these two estimates serves to endorse the validity of the sample of MARS Monuments as fairly reflecting the recorded archaeological resource in England.

5.2.2 Counts and areas

The number of monuments is one dimension of the recorded resource. The area of land occupied by these 300,000 recorded monuments is perhaps a more significant statistic for land-use planning and management, and is also more relevant in relation to recorded archaeology that is inherently difficult to classify in conventional terms, for example the much debated cropmark complexes revealed by aerial photography (Edis *et al.* 1989; Hingley 1991; Palmer 1991), and urban deposits (Carver 1987b; Schofield 1987). Such remains will be numerically under-represented in counts of monuments because of their physical size and complexity. The danger, therefore, is that simple counts will lead to them being under-valued in relation to their overall contribution to archaeological knowledge.

MARS attempted to overcome some of the problems with simple counts by quantifying the recorded resource by area. This was not easy because most existing record systems rely on point-data when it comes to mapping the archaeological resource; very few had begun to translate information contained in the records into geo-referenced spatial representations. Nonetheless, area measurements were attempted for all MARS Monuments, starting with the Projected Archaeological Extent (PAE) which reflects the land area which is currently believed to contain, or formerly to have contained, recorded archaeology. The methodology for doing this, and the limitations on what could be achieved, were discussed in Chapter 3.3.2.

Within the MARS sample area of 6485km^2, the total PAE of MARS Monuments was 425km^2. By extrapolation, it is estimated that in 1995, for England as a whole, some 8500km^2 of land area was recorded as containing archaeological deposits. Based on the MARS sample, about 6.5% of the land area of England contains recorded archaeological monuments.

Naturally, this estimate of land area known to contain archaeological deposits must be considered provisional until the recording of areal extents is more developed.[1] The present calculations include estimates for large single monuments and monuments of complex shape whose areal extent is unlikely to have been estimated as accurately as for smaller monuments with a more regular outline. The more extensive application of GIS technology to archaeological records will, in due course, improve the accuracy of estimating areas.

A figure of 6.5% containing archaeological remains is, however, of the right order of magnitude. Completely independent of MARS, preliminary results from the National Mapping Programme being carried out by the RCHME broadly support a figure of 6.5% of land area

Table 5.1 - Incidence of MARS Monuments in relation to broad geological types. *[Source: MARS Field Survey Programme. Sample: n= 14,591]*

Geology	Mars Monuments		Natural distribution by land area %
	number	%	
Clay	3863	26.5	16.7
Calcareous rock	3754	25.7	16.8
Sandstone/ sedimentary rock	3273	22.4	27.5
Gravel/sand	1779	12.2	12.3
Igneous/ metamorphic rock	958	6.6	2.7
Alluvium	806	5.5	12.1
Organic material	158	1.1	11.9
Total	**14591**	**100%**	**100%**

containing recorded archaeology in the areas looked at so far (H Welfare pers. comm. 2nd May 1997). Set in context, this coverage amounts to more than six times the land area of England currently classified as wetland, and is not far short of the percentage of England under forestry (see Chapter 7.3). It must also be remembered, however, that the estimate is an average for the whole country. There will be many areas where the percentage of land recorded as containing archaeological remains is much higher.

5.2.3 Monument densities

Considerable variation was found in the numbers of MARS Monuments in the sample units. Out of the 1297 MARS sample transects, 58 contained no recorded MARS Monuments at all, while, at the other extreme, one transect contained 158 MARS Monuments. The mean number of MARS Monuments per transect was 11.25, allowing the mean density to be estimated at 2.25 per km^2 with a 95% confidence interval of.2.138-2.370. This is an important figure, because it represents a rough measure of the number of monuments likely to be encountered in archaeological assessments and field evaluations.

Regional and local variations in the density of monuments should be expected. Figure 5.1 shows the national picture extrapolated from the MARS sample transects to reflect the density of MARS Monuments by county (*cf.* Figure 4.7 showing record density by county). High-density areas (darker colours) are notably restricted in extent, being scattered through most regions. The blocking together of counties with similar densities is also interesting, and allows two large blocks with slightly above-average densities to be identified, one south-west of a line from Cheshire to West Sussex, the other coast-to-coast across northern England.

From a slightly different perspective, Figure 5.2 shows an extrapolation of monument density, based again on MARS Monuments, but without being consolidated to fit county boundaries. The high-spots can now be seen more clearly. Geographically, all of them are fairly restricted, and many can be related to major programmes of field survey. Thus, for example, the high-spots in the South West coincide with work in West Penwith (Johnson and Rose 1983; Johnson 1985), on Bodmin Moor (Johnson and Rose 1994) and on Dartmoor (Fleming 1988). For comparison, Figure 5.3 shows the distribution of major recent survey projects aimed at the identification,

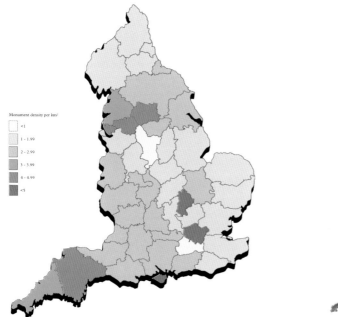

Figure 5.1 - Density of monuments for counties in England in 1995 (in monuments per km²) extrapolated from MARS Monuments. *[Source: MARS National Survey using MARS sample transects]*

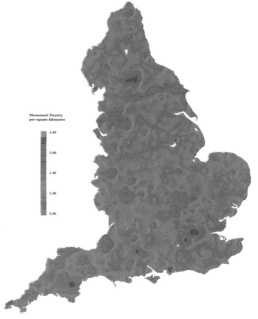

Figure 5.2 - Generalized density of monuments in England in 1995, extrapolated from the distribution of MARS Monuments. *[Source: MARS National Survey using MARS sample transects. Plot prepared by J Chartrand]*

Figure 5.3 - Map showing the position and approximate extent of recent major archaeological survey programmes in England. *[Source: Annual Reports and review documents published by English Heritage and RCHME 1985-95]*

characterization and recording of archaeological monuments, some of which had fed results into local SMRs at the MARS census date.

These generalized density plots also raise important questions about the meaning of areas identified as having a low density of recorded archaeology. Are these cold-spots real lacunae in the distribution of remains or simply caused by low levels of field survey and reconnaissance? When complete, the National Mapping Programme (RCHME 1996b, 32-3) may be able to answer this question for some regions, and no doubt redress the balance in others. It will not, however, provide a complete answer because it is based on mapping aerial photographs which themselves carry limitations related to the responsiveness of different kinds of countryside and patterns of land-use. Fieldwork in the form of sample-surveys are also needed in these cold-spots in order to verify the existing records and gaps, and assess the likely contribution from aerial photography.

5.2.4 Monument distribution and geology

One of the factors known to affect the discovery of monuments, especially through techniques such as aerial photography, is surface geology and the related overlying soils (Riley 1983). England has a very varied geological base, from the ancient pre-Cambrian and igneous rocks of the west and north through to the recent alluvial and glacial drift deposits in major river valleys and down the east coast. Table 5.1 shows the distribution of MARS Monuments in relation to seven broad surface geologies.

About three-quarters of all MARS Monuments lie on three geological types: clays, calcareous rocks, and sandstones and sedimentary rocks. On three geologies, calcareous rock, sandstone and sedimentary rock, and gravel/sand deposits, archaeological monuments are slightly over-represented in comparison with the true distribution of these types. On the other geologies archaeological monuments are under-represented. In part this may reflect the location and distribution of preferred settlement areas in the past, but, given that it is based on all kinds of monuments grouped together, it tends to support the premise that geology has affected monument discovery. Sampling strategies that cross-cut geological variations should, in future, be able to overcome this kind of problem (e.g. Shennan 1985).

5.3 Form and the recorded resource

Archaeological monuments come in a range of shapes and sizes. They can be classified in functional or operational terms by monument class or category, as is currently being done for the Monuments Protection Programme through the systematic preparation of monuments class descriptions (English Heritage 1997b, 13-14), for example co-axial field systems, bowl barrows or monuments representing extractive industries. However, these are relatively small-scale divisions and depend on understanding something of the nature of the monuments in question. For MARS, five broad categories of monument form were used to measure diversity within the resource. In fact, these reflect definitions which can, in part at least, be traced back to early archaeological recording (Chapter 4.2.1), and widespread usage can be tied easily to recognized classes such as those listed in the

Thesaurus of monument types (RCHME and EH 1995). The five categories of monument form are:

Small single monuments: small discrete monuments whose area rarely exceeds 3ha. Examples include long barrows, bowl barrows, henges, small enclosures, stone circles, Roman villas, moats, moot mounds, castles, farmsteads etc. (Figure 5.4).

Figure 5.4 - Small single monument. Prehistoric barrow at The Hyde, Minchinhampton, Gloucestershire. The monument is currently under grass within an arable field. A small tree is growing on the mound. *[Photograph: Timothy Darvill. Copyright reserved]*

Large single monuments: substantial and extensive monuments, sometimes overlapping or spatially related, whose total area generally exceeds 3ha. Some are discrete and well defined, but more often they are irregular, with imprecisely defined limits. Examples include causewayed camps, large enclosures, hillforts, *oppida*, small towns, deserted medieval villages etc. (Figure 5.5).

Figure 5.5 - Large single monument. Deserted medieval village of Calcethorpe, Lincolnshire, under pasture. The site was mainly abandoned by the mid sixteenth century. Enclosures, the main street, churchyard, house platforms, yards and crofts are visible in the area of the former village, with the remains of ridge and furrow cultivation around about. Part of the monument was levelled in the 1970s; a few remaining traces are now visible in the cultivated fields. *[Photograph: RCHME. Crown copyright reserved]*

Linear monuments: long narrow monuments whose length is generally over 300m and whose width is a small fraction of their overall length. Few such monuments exist intact, and most are recorded as a series of units defined on the basis of natural or man-made breaks. Many linear monuments formed, and in some cases still form, boundary features. Examples include cursus monuments, avenues, tracks, roads, linear earthworks, pit alignments, linear boundaries, linear dykes, railways, tramways, canals etc. (Figure 5.6).

Figure 5.6. Linear monument. Wansdyke, Wiltshire, looking east. This medieval boundary is visible as an earthwork mainly under pasture but with other land-uses to both sides. *[Photograph: RCHME. Crown copyright reserved]*

Field systems: tracts of land which fulfilled primarily agricultural purposes, either stock-rearing or arable. The original limits can rarely be precisely defined. Although many field systems include constructed components, much of the physical evidence of their existence is often the product of natural processes of soil movement accelerated by the activities connected with the use of the land. Field systems range in date from the late Neolithic through to the post-medieval period (Figure 5.7).

Standing buildings and structures: masonry or wooden buildings or constructions which are still more or less intact and used in some way, although not necessarily for their original purpose (Figure 5.8). See Chapter 3.5 for exclusions.

Figure 5.7 - Field system. Market Harborough, Leicestershire. Medieval ridge and furrow fields cut by the Grand Union Canal. Modern arable fields have nibbled away some of the earlier system of ridges in the bottom right corner. *[Photograph: Cambridge University Collection of Air Photographs. Copyright reserved]*

Figure 5.8 - Standing building. Seventeenth century manor house near Worth Matravers, Dorset, being surveyed by one of the MARS field survey teams. *[Photograph: MARS Archive]*

Figure 5.9 shows an analysis of the representation of these forms among MARS Monuments nationally. Small single monuments are the largest group, about 56% of the recorded resource. This reflects the strong antiquarian and archaeological tradition of identifying and recording this kind of monument. About 21% of all monuments fell within the MARS definition of standing buildings and structures, again representing a specific focus of interest within archaeology. Large single and linear monuments appear in equal proportions at 9% of the recorded resource. There is possibly some overlap between small single monuments and large single monuments because these two categories are mainly

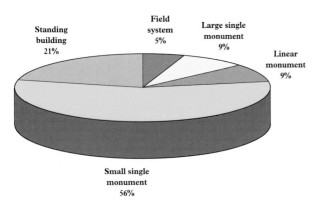

Figure 5.9 - Pie chart showing a breakdown of monument form for MARS Monuments in 1995 quantified by monument count. *[Source: MARS Field Survey Programme. Sample: n= 14,591]*

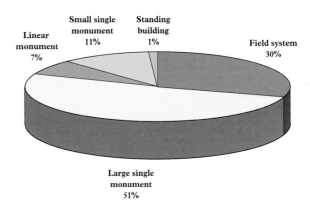

Figure 5.10 - Pie chart showing a breakdown of monument form for MARS Monuments in 1995 quantified by area. *[Source: MARS Field Survey Programme. Sample: n= 14,591]*

distinguished on the basis of size. Moreover, as recorded, some small single monuments are undoubtedly fragments of large single monuments. Numerically, field systems represent the smallest group by form at about 5% of all monuments.

Looked at in terms of the area represented by examples classified as belonging to each form the picture is very different, as Figure 5.10 shows. Large single monuments now represent over 51% of the recorded resource, with small single monuments down to 11% by

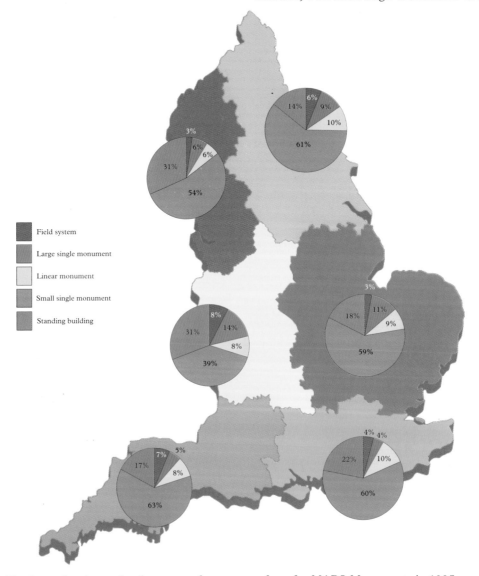

Figure 5.11 - Pie charts showing regional patterns of monument form for MARS Monuments in 1995 quantified by monument count. *[Source: MARS Field Survey Programme. Sample: n= 14,591]*

area, and buildings and structures to just 1%. Linear monuments occupy a similar position in relation to the other forms, but field systems, numerically the smallest group, are the second most extensive form of archaeology in England when quantified in terms of land area.

There are also marked regional variations in the proportion of the resource represented by the different monument forms, as the pie charts on Figure 5.11 demonstrate. These charts were constructed using monument counts. Small single monuments are numerically dominant everywhere, less so in the West Midlands and North West regions. Field systems form a larger percentage of the recorded resource in the South West and West Midlands than elsewhere. In the South West this is explained by the prehistoric examples recorded on Dartmoor and in West Penwith; in the West Midlands by well-preserved medieval systems. Field systems appear poorly represented in the recorded resource of the East Midlands and South East, probably because it is only recently that the work to document them has got underway (Hall 1993). Standing buildings are best represented in the West Midlands and North West. Linear monuments form a consistent percentage of the recorded resource throughout the regions, although generally slightly higher in the east than the west.

5.4 Period and the recorded resource

The distribution of the recorded resource by period is also important. Figure 5.12 shows an overall analysis based on all MARS Monuments subdivided by broad period groupings; Figure 5.13 provides a more detailed breakdown of the prehistoric monuments into recognized cultural-historical phases.

Nearly a quarter of monuments in the recorded resource are of unknown date, while about a third of all monuments are of post-medieval and modern date. This leaves only about 42% of monuments which are of prehistoric, Roman, early medieval or medieval date. Prehistoric monuments, which in chronological terms represent more than 95% of the entire span of human settlement in England, comprise only 12% of the recorded resource.

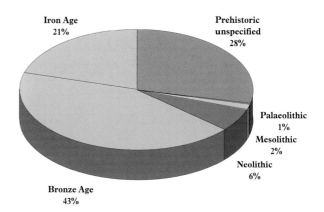

Figure 5.13 - Pie chart showing a breakdown of archaeological period (cultural-historical) for prehistoric MARS Monuments. Quantified by monument count, including multiple entries for multi-period monuments. *[Source: MARS Field Survey Programme and SMR data on dating. Sample: n= 2538 observations]*

Among prehistoric monuments nearly 28% can only be assigned to the prehistoric period in general (these are not included in the percentage of monuments of unknown date on Figure 5.12). The single biggest component of the prehistoric recorded resource consists of monuments dated to the Bronze Age, many of them burial sites.

Prehistoric monuments have an additional implication for the preservation of earlier material, because many are substantial earthworks which seal earlier ground surfaces and structures. Thus, for example, the ramparts of Iron Age hillforts preserve the biggest sample of later Bronze Age ground surfaces currently known; Bronze Age barrows preserve many hectares of late Neolithic land surface; and middle Neolithic long barrows preserve a valuable sample of early Neolithic and Mesolithic land surfaces. Some preliminary work along these lines has been carried out in reviewing prehistoric monuments in south-west Wales (Don Benson pers. comm.).

5.4.1 Monuments and stray finds

Monuments are not the only source of archaeological information about the past; as noted in Chapter 3.5 stray finds are important too. Figure 5.14 compares the period breakdown of monuments to the period breakdown of total records. In general, the difference between the height of the bars reflects the quantity of stray finds for the period. Although the diagram is rather crude in its portrayal, the Neolithic, Romano-British and post-medieval periods in particular have high levels of stray finds such as stone and flint tools, coins and metalwork, and coins and household objects respectively.

5.4.2 Regional patterns of dated monuments

There is marked regional variation in the distribution of dated monuments in the recorded resource. Figures 5.15-5.18 show projections of monument density distributions based on the incidence of MARS Monuments in the sample transects. The plots have been standardized by averaging the density within each transect to a simple monuments per km^2. Although these maps are generalized, clear trends and differences are visible.

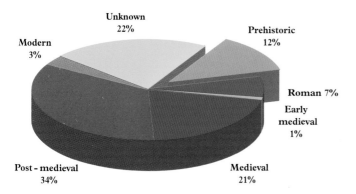

Figure 5.12 - Pie chart showing a breakdown of archaeological period for MARS Monuments. Quantified by monument count, including multiple entries for multi-period monuments. *[Source: MARS Field Survey Programme and SMR data on dating. Sample: n= 20,347 observations]*

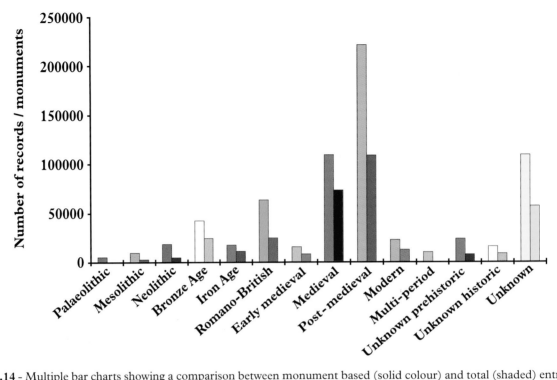

Figure 5.14 - Multiple bar charts showing a comparison between monument based (solid colour) and total (shaded) entries in local SMRs by archaeological period. Quantified by the number of entries, including some multiple entries for multi-period monuments. *[Source: MARS National Survey using SMR data. Samples: Records n= 685,406; Monuments n= 345,763]*

Looked at in sequence, they show a gradual increase through time in the area of land with monument densities higher than the national average. For the prehistoric period (Figure 5.15) there are clear concentrations, for example in Wessex and the traditional heartlands of prehistoric studies by antiquarians and archaeologists; this probably says more about the distribution of effort than the spread of prehistoric settlement. As with the general distribution of monuments (*cf.* Figure 5.2), these apparent imbalances need to be tested by carrying out comparable surveys in what are currently blank areas on the map.

Roman monuments (Figure 5.16) concentrate in quite different areas from the prehistoric example, a general trend towards the south-east and along Hadrian's Wall being noticeable. To some extent this probably reflects accurately the general distribution of Roman occupation and Roman influence on the Romano-British settlement pattern, but it leaves open the question of what happened in the north and west. Here there are difficulties of classification in existing records, early first millennium AD monuments being variously listed as prehistoric, Romano-British, or date unknown. A careful review of the records that may relate to this period would probably redress this imbalance.

In the early medieval and medieval periods, the proportion of monuments in towns and cities increases, and these appear on the maps as numerous localized peaks in monument density (Figure 5.17). The distribution of monuments is much wider than for earlier periods and more indicative of the original resource.

Table 5.2 - Incidence of MARS Monuments by monument form in relation to archaeological period. Quantified by observation, including multiple observations for multi-period monuments. *[Source: MARS Field Survey Programme and SMR data on monument date. Sample: n= 16,488 observations]*

Period	Field system		Large single monument		Linear monument		Small single monument		Standing building		All
	no.	%	no.	%	no.	%	no.	%	no.	%	no.
Prehistoric unspecified	50	5.9	50	3.4	75	5.3	449	4.8	0	0	624
Palaeolithic	0	0	1	<1	0	0	8	<1	0	0	9
Mesolithic	0	0	8	<1	0	0	26	<1	0	0	34
Neolithic	0	0	22	1.5	6	<1	98	1.1	0	0	126
Bronze Age	14	1.6	47	3.2	25	1.8	830	9.0	0	0	916
Iron Age	55	6.5	68	4.6	29	2.1	244	2.6	0	0	396
Roman	40	4.7	96	6.5	265	18.8	601	6.5	6	<1	1008
Early medieval	2	0.2	18	1.2	24	1.7	109	1.2	22	<1	175
Medieval	270	31.7	428	29.2	173	12.3	1540	16.6	776	22.2	3187
Post-medieval	63	7.4	357	24.3	331	23.5	2756	29.7	2358	67.5	5865
Modern	12	1.4	24	1.6	48	3.4	320	3.5	223	6.4	627
Unknown	346	40.6	349	23.8	431	30.6	2288	24.7	107	3.1	3521
Total	**852**	**100%**	**1468**	**100%**	**1407**	**100%**	**9269**	**100%**	**3492**	**100%**	**16488**

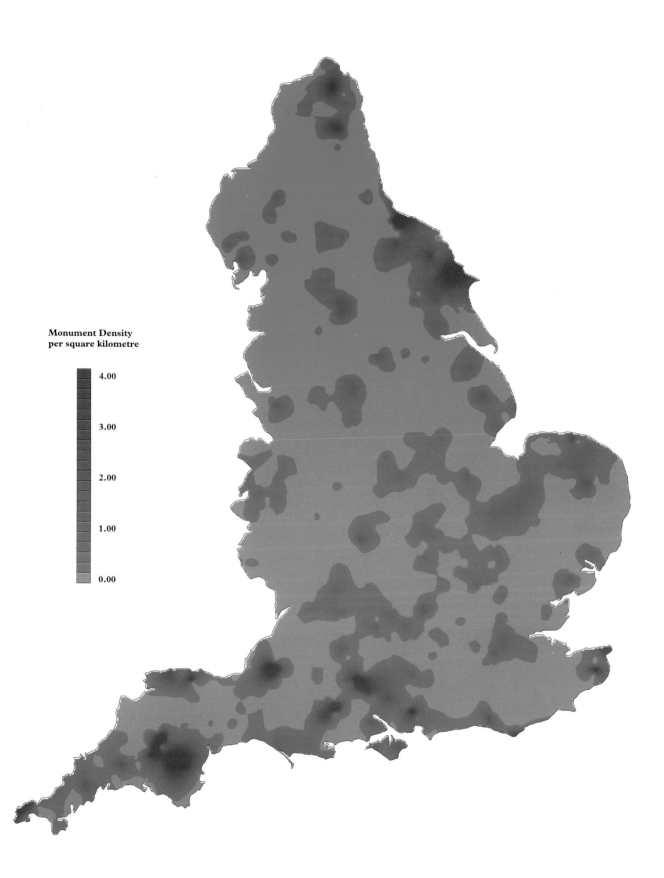

**Monument Density
per square kilometre**

4.00

3.00

2.00

1.00

0.00

Figure 5.15 - Generalized density of prehistoric monuments recorded in England in 1995, extrapolated from the distribution of MARS Monuments. *[Source: MARS National Survey using MARS sample transects. Plot prepared by J Chartrand]*

**Monument Density
per square kilometre**

4.00

3.00

2.00

1.00

0.00

Figure 5.16 - Generalized density of Roman and Romano-British monuments recorded in England in 1995, extrapolated from the distribution of MARS Monuments. *[Source: MARS National Survey using MARS sample transects. Plot prepared by J Chartrand]*

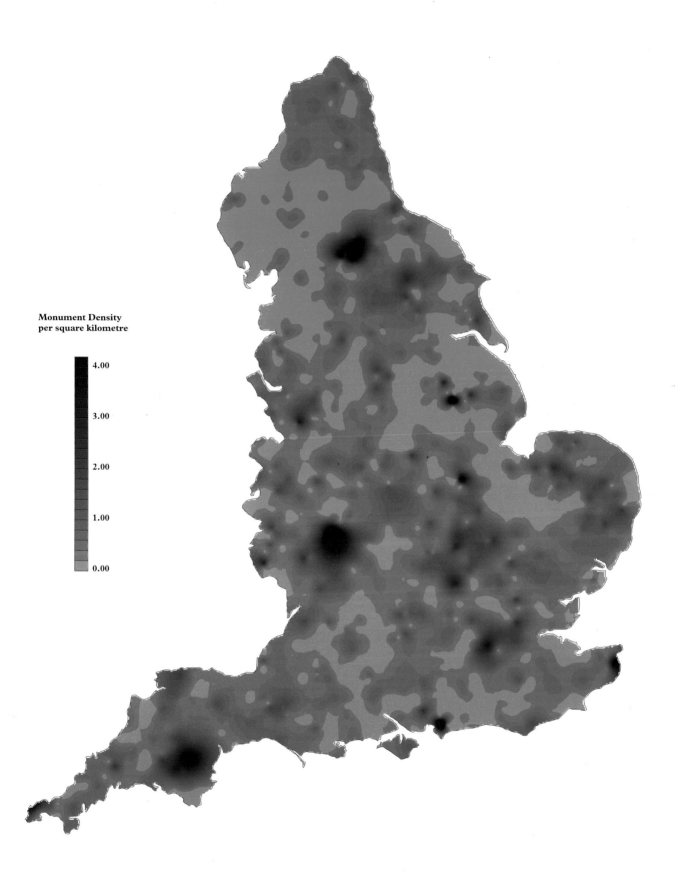

**Monument Density
per square kilometre**

4.00

3.00

2.00

1.00

0.00

Figure 5.17 - Generalized density of early medieval and medieval monuments recorded in England in 1995, extrapolated from the distribution of MARS Monuments. *[Source: MARS National Survey using MARS sample transects. Plot prepared by J Chartrand]*

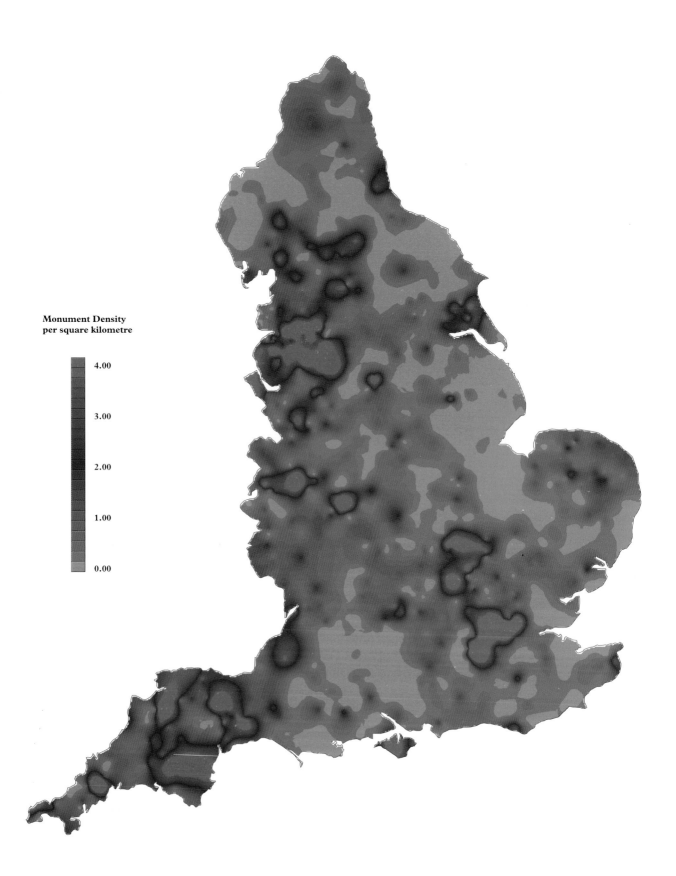

**Monument Density
per square kilometre**

4.00

3.00

2.00

1.00

0.00

Figure 5.18 - Generalized density of post-medieval monuments recorded in England in 1995, extrapolated from the distribution of MARS Monuments. *[Source: MARS National Survey using MARS sample transects. Plot prepared by J Chartrand]*

Upland areas with relatively little medieval settlement, for example the Lake District, show up, as do areas with an abundance of remains of medieval settlement, for example the north Pennines and Midland basin, and including some areas, like Dartmoor, that have been the subject of recent research projects (Fleming and Ralph 1982; Fleming 1988). Similar patterns can be seen in the density of post-medieval monuments, although here the modern settlement pattern and areas of intense industrial activity come to dominate the picture (Figure 5.18).

5.4.3 Monument period in relation to form

Combining monument period and form produces patterns that help to explain some of the geographical differences (Table 5.2). The largest groups of monuments are post-medieval small single monuments and standing buildings, at 16.7% and 14.3% of the recorded resource respectively. Monuments of unknown date, especially small single monuments, are also a large category at 13.8%. These monuments dominate the recorded resource, and some extremely important groups of monuments look insignificant by comparison. The Bronze Age, for example, represents a peak in the extent and density of prehistoric settlement patterns and is mainly known through small single monuments such as barrows and settlements, yet overall these monuments represent only 5% of the recorded resource. Seen in this perspective, there is an obvious need to exercise care in dealing with the earlier elements of the recorded resource, lest they become swamped by the numerically dominant later monuments.

5.5 The extant recorded resource in 1995

Not all monuments in the recorded resource were extant in 1995; some had been destroyed before that time and these now form part of the extinct resource. In all, 11,334 of the 13,488 MARS Monuments which could be field-checked were found to be extant. Thus 84% of the total recorded resource can be characterized as the extant recorded resource and 16% as the extinct recorded resource (*cf.* Figure 2.1). For the purposes of MARS a monument was considered to have been destroyed when 95% or more of its physical extent had been lost. It is recognized that some monuments considered destroyed have been found to retain some vestigial traces when carefully re-examined, but this is relatively rare.

Applying the rate of loss recorded by MARS in the sample transects to the estimates of the total recorded resource discussed above, the size of the extant recorded resource in England in 1995 can be set at approximately 226,680 monuments. Again, however, crude counts hide important characteristics, because the outright loss of monuments is not itself a full representation of the true state of affairs. The 1995 Current Area measurements for 13,488 field-checked monuments totalled 238km². The PAE for these same monuments is 425km², showing that 56% of the areal extent of the recorded resource was extant in 1995. The same constraints apply to these figures as to estimates of the areal extent of the recorded archaeological resource as a whole (above 5.2.2).

In considering these figures it is important to look at

their origins. The creation of the records which represent the recorded resource is heavily reliant on two factors. First, monuments are often recognized visually, which tends to favour the inclusion of the more prominent monuments, probably the best preserved. Second, less well-preserved monuments are often recognized immediately before, or at the time of their destruction or damage, so that the record contains a high proportion of information about monuments that no longer exist or have already been reduced in size: this will affect the scale of the extinct recorded resource as a proportion of the recorded resource.

In Chapter 6 attention focuses on the extinct resource with reference to the loss and damage of monuments; here attention is directed to the general state of the extant resource, and in particular to monument condition.

5.6 The condition of the extant recorded resource

Monument condition is a point-in-time statement of circumstances appertaining to a particular site, mainly the result of changes over time and its prevailing situation. Because condition involves a general assessment of the state of being, circumstances or fitness for purpose, it is difficult to measure objectively. Although an overall impression of condition can be built up it cannot easily be determined with reference to any one variable.

5.6.1 SMR statistics on monument condition

Many local SMRs record a general judgement of monument condition, and condition is one of the four management criteria used in the assessment of monuments within the Monuments Protection Programme (Darvill *et al.* 1987, 399). About one-third of SMRs were able to provide information about condition for a total of 63,473 records (9.7% of all retrievable records at the census date). However, great caution should be exercised in using these data, first because even within the available sample only 30,977 records are usable (about 2884 records related to destroyed monuments and 29,612 records were categorized as 'condition uncertain'), and second because each SMR will have been appraised and recorded condition slightly differently.

Figure 5.19 shows the general picture. Overall, monuments recorded as being in 'good' condition formed 44.6% of the usable sample, and more than 65% of all monuments were in 'medium' condition or better. The monuments for which these data exist probably include all or most Scheduled Monuments. Arguably, these should be in better condition than other monuments (see Chapter 8). There may therefore be some biases in the data.

5.6.2 Monument condition in resource assessments

Some of the many resource assessment surveys undertaken from the 1960s onwards incorporate information about monument condition (see APPENDIX A for listing of reports). As with SMR data there are some problems about how these surveys should be interpreted because they were carried out by many different individuals over a long period of time. Often they were prompted by particular concerns and these became the focus of interest. The most numerous relate to plough

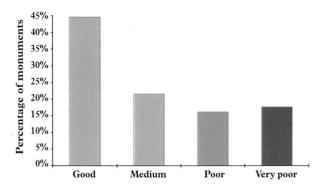

Figure 5.19 - Bar chart showing an analysis of overall monument condition as recorded in 1995 by local SMRs for monuments in their operating area. *[Source: National Survey using SMR data. Sample n= 30,977 observations]*

damage and its effects on monument condition, summary details being presented to a seminar on plough damage and archaeology held in Salisbury in February 1977 (Hinchliffe and Schadla-Hall 1980).

A study of plough damage on the Cotswolds carried out by Alan Saville in 1976-7 (Saville 1990) examined 906 monuments of various classes and periods. Condition here was measured in terms of the extent of agricultural encroachment onto the area of the monument. Overall, 54% of monuments were recorded as being unploughed, 8% part-ploughed, and 38% fully ploughed over. These gross patterns mask considerable complexity in which the larger and more recent classes of monuments seem to suffer less from ploughing than smaller and older classes. None of the 21 medieval moated sites in the survey was found to be ploughed, and only 9% of castle earthworks, 12% of deserted medieval villages and 12% of medieval religious sites were ploughed. This contrasts with ploughing on 60% of Bronze Age round barrows and 54% of long barrows.

The Cotswold figures are very similar to levels of ploughing elsewhere. A study of monuments in Sussex, for example, revealed that in 1975 some 38% of the 660 monuments visited were ploughed (Drewett 1980, 71). Again, high percentages of ploughing were noted among small monuments such as long barrows (40%), Neolithic settlements (94%) and Bronze Age barrows (40%), while no moated sites, castles or major ecclesiastical monuments were ploughed.

Although in many ways atypical, barrows seem to have been the focus of condition studies in several parts of the country. On the Dorset Ridgeway, a study by Peter Woodward between 1977 and 1984 revealed that in lowland areas 36% of barrows were ploughed as against 30% intact, whereas on the higher ground (above the 120m contour), 47% were ploughed and 35% intact (Woodward 1991, 172) In East Anglia, a study of more than 900 recorded possible and certain barrows found that about 20% of examples in Suffolk were ploughed, 22% in Norfolk and 11% in Essex (Lawson *et al.* 1981, 1-2). Further north, a survey of about 100 barrows in Cleveland in 1977-9 (Crawford 1980) revealed that 12 had been ploughed out and a further 10 had been reduced by ploughing.

On a rather different scale, an analysis of deserted medieval village sites in 1965 suggested that of the 2000

or so recorded examples in England, only 250 (12.5%) were of 'first quality', about 1250 (62.5%) being of poor and medium quality, and the remainder totally destroyed (DMVRG 1965). However, like the other studies mentioned here, there is no discussion of the categories used in determining condition.

5.6.3 MARS Monuments and state

Turning to the more detailed evidence available from the MARS Field Survey Programme, one of the most clear and widely applicable indicators of overall condition is the general state of a monument, for example whether it is upstanding or levelled. State was recorded in three broad categories as follows:

Upstanding: a monument with visible surface topography reflecting, in the vertical plane, details of sub-surface features. In this sense, upstanding may include archaeological features that extend downwards into the ground as well as those projecting above ground level.

Flat: a monument in which upstanding features have been peneplained by human or natural agency, thus creating a flat or levelled ground surface that is totally or nearly indistinguishable from the natural topography of its situation. There may be other kinds of surface indications other than topography, for example the presence of distinctive materials or artefacts in the topsoil. It is also likely that archaeological deposits still remain within or below the topsoil at levelled monuments, but, equally, facets of their vertical dimension will have been lost.

Figure 5.20 - Earthwork monuments. Aerial photograph of Knowlton, Dorset, showing the upstanding earthworks of a late Neolithic henge and round barrow (centre), with the cropmark traces of levelled earthworks all around. *[Photograph: RCHME. Copyright reserved]*

Destroyed: a monument at which more than 95% of its recorded physical extent has been lost to a form of land-use whose creation will have removed archaeological deposits (e.g. road-construction, gravel extraction).

State was assessed with reference to monument character, which was itself categorized into three main groupings:

Earthworks: one or more archaeological features, such as a bank, ditch, wall, mound or setting of some kind, that appears in topographical relief in the ground surface, usually as a rise, projection or a series of 'humps and bumps' (Figure 5.20). An earthwork is not necessarily made of soil; it may comprise stones and other materials too. An earthwork normally represents the decayed remains of some kind of structure. Earthworks account for approximately 29% of the extant recorded resource represented by MARS Monuments. (*cf.* RCHME and EH 1995)

Buildings and structures: a permanent fixed construction forming an enclosed space and providing protection from the elements or a construction of some other sort (Figure 5.21). Such monuments may be complete, roofless or ruinous. They are generally made mainly of stone, wood, brick, daub or a combination of these, typically with lesser quantities of other materials too (e.g. iron, steel, cement, plaster etc.). Buildings and structures as a category of monument character account for approximately 35% of the extant recorded resource represented by MARS Monuments. (*cf.* RCHME and EH 1995)

Figure 5.21 - Buildings and structures. View of an L-shaped timber framed building in Weobley, Hereford and Worcester. This Grade II* Listed Building shows evidence of late sixteenth and early seventeenth century construction, with Jacobean gable ends. Recent additions and modifications are also visible. *[Photograph: MARS Archive]*

Landcuts: monuments comprising one or more archaeological features whose creation mainly involved, or resulted from, digging down into the ground, thus forming some kind of hole, void, cavity, shaft or depression (Figure 5.22). Natural holes, caves or depressions which were utilized for some purpose also come into this category. Landcut monuments may contain structures or built-up elements too. Examples include ponds, quarries, wells, mines, shafts and limekilns.

Landcuts account for approximately 36% of the extant recorded resource represented by MARS Monuments.

Figure 5.22 - Landcuts. View of the duck decoy pond at Old Hall Marshes, Essex, showing the partly silted and overgrown decoy arms radiating outwards from the central pond. *[Photograph: Essex County Council. Copyright reserved]*

For earthworks, Figure 5.23 shows a series of bar charts which reflect the situation nationally and by region. The data here are drawn from recorded small single monuments, large single monuments, linear monuments and field systems. At first glance, the distributions of monument state across all regions broadly reflect the national picture, dominated by flattened earthworks but with a low proportion (around 10%) of destroyed examples. There are, however, subtle differences in the East Midlands (lowest portion of upstanding earthworks) and South East (highest portion of destroyed earthworks).

A similar analysis can be carried out for buildings and structures, as shown on Figure 5.24. In contrast to earthworks, a significantly higher proportion of buildings and structures survives in upstanding form, especially in the West Midlands. The trend in each series for each region suggests that these monuments are generally in a better state than earthworks, although the number of destroyed examples in the North West and South East exceeds the percentage of flattened examples. The robustness of the materials used in the construction of these monuments has probably played a major role in their current state, and the converse is perhaps true for earthworks.

One further group of MARS Monuments comprises those defined as landcuts. No analysis is presented for these, however, because a distinction between upstanding or flat is less relevant; few were ever 'upstanding' in the first place.

5.6.4 Visibility and the extant recorded resource

The question of visibility is closely related to state. The popular belief is that if a monument cannot be seen then nothing is or can be known about it, and it probably does not exist. Of course, this is not true. Visibility was measured on a simple scale based on whether or not traces of some or all of the monument could be seen at ground level with the naked eye by the field survey teams, all of whom were reasonably experienced field archaeologists. It is recognized that this is a somewhat crude measure of

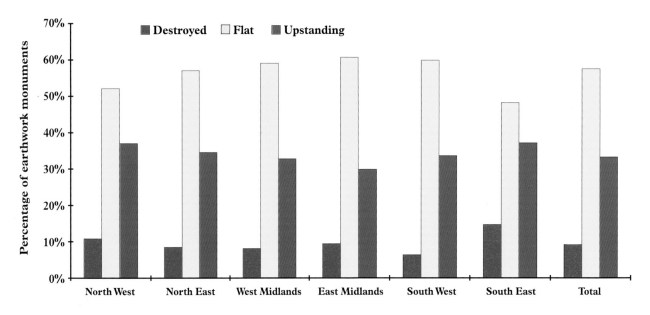

Figure 5.23 - Multiple bar chart summarizing the state of MARS earthwork monuments in 1995 by region and in total. Quantified by count. *[Source: MARS Field Survey Programme. Sample: n= 4230]*

visibility, but given the experience of the teams and the fact that they had with them print-outs of the SMR entries and marked-up maps, together with copies of the NMR entries when they were available, they should have been able to find the monuments and assess this variable fairly consistently. Four categories were used:

Visible: some remains positively identified with the available descriptions of the monument.

Barely visible: possible remains or traces thereof identified with the available description of the monument.

Not visible: no remains or traces found which could be identified with the available description of the monument.

Obscured: dense vegetation cover or structures present which prevented direct observation of the monument and thus prevented a firm statement about visibility.

Figure 5.25 shows an analysis of the overall visibility of MARS Monuments by region. Nationally, nearly half of all MARS Monuments were visible and a further 5% barely visible. 43% were not visible. The North East and East Midlands had slightly lower percentages of visible monuments than the national average (40% and 41% respectively), but the North West and West Midlands apparently had a greater proportion of visible monuments (59% and 60% respectively). The fluctuations in the remaining levels of visibility (barely visible and obscured)

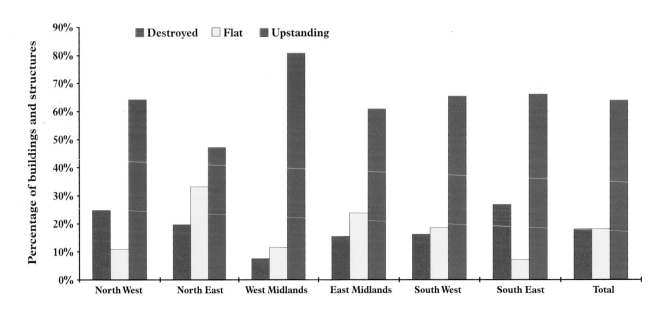

Figure 5.24 - Multiple bar chart summarizing the state of MARS Monuments represented as buildings and structures in 1995 by region and in total. Quantified by count. *[Source: MARS Field Survey Programme. Sample: n= 5171]*

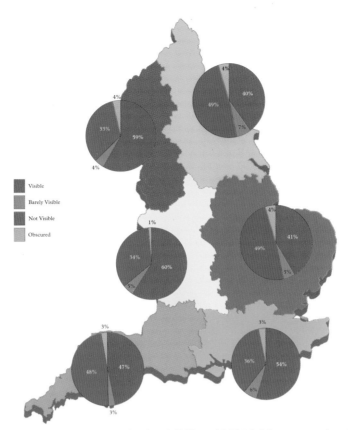

Figure 5.25 - Pie charts showing regional patterns in the visibility of MARS Monuments in 1995. Quantified by monument count. *[Source: MARS Field Survey Programme. Sample: n= 13,426]*

were broadly similar across all regions. Figures for the South West region where 48% of monuments were recorded as not visible may be compared with the results of a survey of monuments on the South Dorset Ridgeway where on the low ground (below the 120m contour) 34% of the sample of 121 monuments were found to be 'not

visible', while on the higher ground only 18% of the 533 monuments in the study were 'not visible' (Woodward 1991, 172).

Table 5.3 presents an analysis of visibility by form. From this it is clear that the most visible monuments are small single monuments, followed closely by standing

Table 5.3 - Incidence of MARS Monuments by monument form in relation to visibility in 1995. *[Source: MARS Field Survey Programme. Sample: n= 11,854]*

Monument Form	Visible		Barely visible		Not visible		Obscured		Total
	no.	%	no.	%	no.	%	no.	%	no.
Field system	170	2.9	75	12.7	470	9.2	17	4.3	732
Large single monument	482	8.3	70	11.9	614	12.1	56	14.1	1222
Linear monument	424	7.3	72	12.2	582	11.4	42	10.6	1120
Small single monument	2269	39.3	355	60.3	3265	64.1	237	59.5	6126
Standing building	2429	42.1	17	2.9	162	3.2	46	11.6	2654
Total	**5774**	**100%**	**589**	**100 %**	**5093**	**100%**	**398**	**100%**	**11854**

Table 5.4 - Incidence of MARS Monuments by broad archaeological period in relation to visibility. Quantified by observation, including multiple observations for multi-period monuments. *[Source: MARS Field Survey Programme and SMR data on monument date. Sample: n= 13,365 observations]*

Period	Visible		Barely visible		Not visible		Obscured		Total
	no.	%	no.	%	no.	%	no.	%	no.
Prehistoric	508	7.8	118	17.5	934	16.5	75	15.8	1635
Roman	92	1.4	49	7.3	522	9.2	29	6.1	692
Early medieval	70	1.1	4	<1	37	<1	4	<1	115
Medieval	1569	24.0	185	27.4	940	16.6	118	24.8	2812
Post-medieval	3312	50.7	151	22.4	1027	18.1	152	32.0	4642
Modern	341	5.2	17	2.5	121	2.1	12	2.5	491
Unknown	646	9.9	151	22.4	2096	36.9	85	17.9	2978
Total	**6538**	**100%**	**675**	**100%**	**5677**	**100%**	**475**	**100%**	**13365**

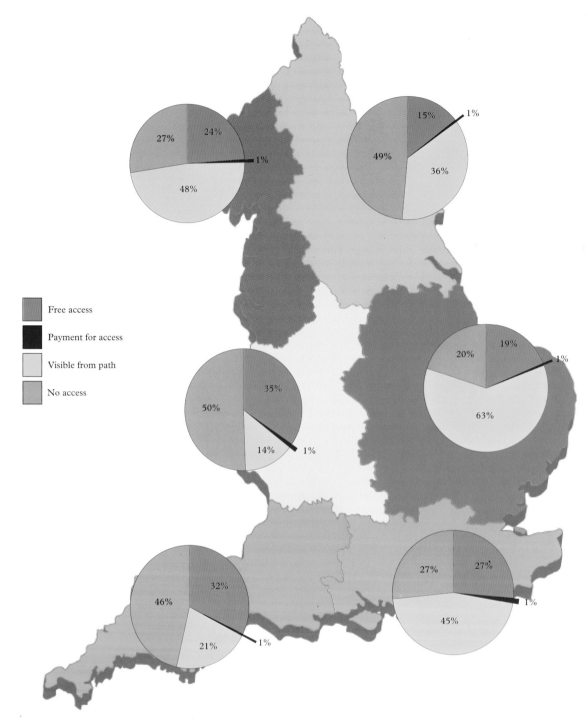

Figure 5.26 - Pie charts showing regional patterns in the accessibility of MARS Monuments in 1995. Quantified by monument count. *[Source: MARS Field Survey Programme. Sample: n= 13,426]*

Table 5.5 - Incidence of MARS Monuments by form in relation to accessibility in 1995. *[Source: MARS Field Survey Programme. Sample: n= 11,343]*

Monument form	Free access		Payment for access		Visible from path		No access		Total
	no.	%	no.	%	no.	%	no.	%	no.
Field system	87	3.1	0	0	273	6.4	328	7.9	688
Large single monument	243	8.6	15	18.3	470	11.0	341	8.2	1069
Linear monument	358	12.7	2	2.4	384	9.0	279	6.7	1023
Small single monument	1349	47.9	28	34.1	2120	49.6	2428	58.2	5925
Standing building	782	27.7	37	45.1	1025	24.0	794	19.0	2638
Total	**2819**	**100%**	**82**	**100%**	**4272**	**100%**	**4170**	**100%**	**11343**

buildings. There are probably two reasons for this. First, small single monuments and standing buildings are relatively easy to identify, even from small traces. Second, forms of monument such as field systems and linear monuments often consist of relatively ephemeral constructions and are therefore more difficult to see.

Table 5.4 presents an analysis of visibility by period, emphasizing the fact that the most visible elements of England's recorded resource are dated to the medieval and post-medieval periods. It is also apparent that monuments dated to earlier periods, and particularly to the prehistoric and Roman periods, are generally much less visible in comparison with examples from later periods. However, the presence of standing buildings in the latter periods does rather distort the picture.

5.7 Accessibility and the extant recorded resource

Visibility is partly related to the question of access to monuments, especially public access and display. There is no advantage in having access to monuments that cannot be seen. Public access is also a factor in the condition of monuments.

Judgements on the matter of access were made by the field teams at the time of their visit, but they cannot be regarded as definitive since no checks have been made on the legal status of footpaths or areas of open land. The judgements made do, however, give a fair indication of accessibility. Four categories were used:

Free access: where monuments were situated in public open space or on land where *de facto* access exists.

No access: for monuments situated on private land with no *de facto* access.

Payment for access: for monuments situated in land for which a fee was charged for public access (usually during restricted opening times), as for example with some National Trust or English Heritage properties in care.

Visible from a public right of way: monuments that could clearly be seen from what appeared to be a public right of way (footpath, bridleway, track or road) without the observer having to leave that right of way (i.e. the monument was within the boundaries of the right of way or immediately adjacent to it, or the right of way passed through or across the monument).

Figure 5.26 shows a breakdown of access by region. Destroyed monuments are excluded from this analysis although it is recognized a few individuals may wish to view the site of a destroyed monument for academic, professional or sentimental reasons. Nationally, about two-thirds of MARS Monuments were found to be accessible to the public, 25% of them freely accessible. It was necessary to pay for access at only 1% of MARS Monuments. About 37% were visible from a public right of way. There was no public access to one-third of the recorded resource represented by MARS Monuments.

There were considerable variations, however, between the regions. There is greatest free access in the West Midlands and the South West, least in the North East. In the South East and the West Midlands a high proportion of monuments are visible from public rights of way. The highest proportions of monuments on private land are in the West Midlands, South West and North East.

Access in relation to monument form (Table 5.5) shows that most small single monuments are inaccessible on private land, but that most of these can be seen from public rights of way. As might be expected, a high proportion of large single monuments and linear monuments are visible from public rights of way, as too are standing buildings.

The relationship between accessibility and visibility is a complicated one, the situation for MARS Monuments being summarized on Table 5.6. Interestingly, a higher proportion of monuments with free access are visible than is the case for monuments where no public access is possible. It may at first sight seem odd that a payment is charged for access to monuments that are not visible, but the reason is that the public are paying for access to features other than archaeological monuments.

Table 5.6 - The incidence of MARS monuments by accessibility in relation to visibility in 1995. *[Source: MARS Field Survey Programme. Sample: n= 6180]*

Access	Visible	Barely visible	Not visible	Obscured
	%	%	%	%
Free access	35.26	16.3	13.08	29.65
Payment for access	1.28	0.34	0.18	0.75
Visible from path	33.41	43.63	43.43	31.91
No access	30.05	39.73	43.31	37.69
Total	**100%**	**100%**	**100%**	**100%**

5.8 Overview

Overall, the general conclusion to be drawn from the limited data available from local SMRs is that the condition of archaeological monuments in England is fairly good (above 5.6.1). Surveys of specific monument classes and local studies of particular environments present a very mixed picture. This seems to be supported by the findings from the MARS Field Survey Programme. Nearly half of the extant recorded resource is visible, and two-thirds is publicly accessible: among earthwork monuments over 30% remain upstanding, and among buildings and structures over 60% remain upstanding. However, these general characteristics need to be set in the context of the more detailed consideration of monument survival which forms the subject of the next chapter, where the situation is far less satisfactory.

6 Monument survival: half a century of change, 1945-95

One must lament too, the destruction of ancient earthworks, especially of the barrows, which is going on all over the downs, most rapidly where the land is broken up by the plough. One wonders if the ever increasing curiosity of our day with regard to the history of the human race in the land continues to grow, what our descendants of the next half of the century, to go no further, will say to us and our incredible carelessness in the matter ... So small a matter to us, but one which will perhaps be immensely important to them.

(W H Hudson 1910, 16)

6.1 Measuring continuous change

England's archaeological resource is constantly changing, not only in its composition and definition, but also in terms of what survives physically and how well. It is a dynamic non-renewable resource. The last chapter provided a snapshot of the condition of England's archaeology as it was found to be in 1995; here the emphasis shifts to the questions of change and the matter of survival. For this, the model of decay trajectories outlined in Chapter 2 becomes crucial, particularly the recognition that all monuments begin to deteriorate from the moment of their creation. If, following its creation, a monument was left entirely alone its deterioration could be described as a natural decay trajectory. The speed of deterioration, the steepness of the decay curve, would be determined by the materials used in construction and the environment in which the monument was set. However, natural decay trajectories seldom if ever occur. There are two opposing forces at work that deflect the course of natural decay trajectories on their inevitable downward path.

First, active curation, whether in the past through repair and reconstruction, or in recent times through conservation and management, may slow down the decay trajectory of a given monument. Second, the effects of hostile land-use or other forms of degradation accelerate the decay process. Because of these forces, the steepness and form of decay profiles, whether natural, semi-natural or accelerated, and the processes that cause decay, are the principal interests of archaeological resource management.

The biggest difficulty in applying the general decay model to actual archaeological monuments is that of knowing where to start measuring the profile: what should be taken as the pristine state from which decay can somehow be measured? For older monuments, in particular those of prehistoric or Romano-British date, this is complicated by the fact that a great part of their decay trajectories lies in the remote past and can only be documented using archaeological evidence. At the outset of MARS it was posited that insights into whole life-cycle decay patterns could be developed by making estimates of the original area (EOA) of monuments as set out in Chapter 2. However, this proved extremely difficult and

early attempts met with an unfavourable reaction when presented at early MARS seminars.

Efforts therefore concentrated on the core aims of the project, namely looking at change over the last five decades, from about 1945 through to 1995. In doing this, considerable use was made of the estimates of Projected Archaeological Extent (PAE) as a crude measure of the horizontal extent of attested archaeological evidence relating to a particular monument.

Focusing on the Projected Archaeological Extent of a monument (based as it is on what is recorded) rather than allowing some estimate of original extent means that the measurable decay profile becomes artificially truncated; the decay model becomes formulated in such a way that the measurable section of the decay curve begins from the position represented by the cumulative sum of available records. In practice, however, the PAE for many monuments is represented by a single set of records, usually the earliest detailed information, and these are often early post-war aerial photographs. Thus estimates of PAE can, for the majority of monuments, be roughly equated with the situation obtaining at the beginning of the five decades under review here. PAE and CA1945 become the same or nearly the same. This does not greatly matter, provided that estimates of survival are recognized as being relative to this arbitrary point rather than being tied into an absolute framework provided by the life-cycles of the monuments themselves.

In this way, PAE values become the baselines from which change is monitored. Since judgements of condition and survival are to some extent subjective, taking an arbitrary but essentially fairly uniform starting date from which the downward trend of decay for all monuments can be measured is both practical and easy to understand.

This chapter begins by looking at the question of monument survival in terms of the gross characteristics of the recorded resource. Two sources are used, data from local SMRs gathered by the National Survey Programme and data from MARS Monuments collected by the Field Survey and Aerial Photographic Survey Programmes. The focus then turns to monument loss as the most visible and pernicious enemy of survival. Two patterns of loss are recognized: wholesale loss in which the whole monument has already disappeared, and piecemeal loss where portions of a partially extant monument have gone. The nature, extent and causes of monument damage and destruction are considered, as too are their combined impact on the recorded resource. The extent to which archaeological information has been recorded in advance of monument destruction (rescue excavation) is briefly addressed before attention focuses on the main hazards linked to the loss and damage of monuments. The last three sections deal with visibility in relation to damage, the spatial characteristics of the impacts of damage recorded at MARS Monuments, and the question of amelioration.

Throughout this chapter comparisons are made between numerical and areal losses. More than 80 years after W H Hudson wrote the words cited at the head of this chapter, it is clear that incredible carelessness continues, but perhaps the importance of what is being lost is now better recognized.

6.2 Survival

Survival is a point-in-time measure of the prevailing state of a monument relative to some former state, a reflection of the cumulative effects of all the natural and human processes that have come to bear on the monument. Survival is one of the factors taken into account in determining the national importance of a monument when considering it for Scheduling (Darvill *et al.* 1987). For this reason, local SMRs are increasingly recording information about monument survival, although since collection is on-going and happens at different times in different places the overall picture is not a point-in-time statement.

6.2.1 The picture from local SMR data

Data on survival were available from 11 SMRs scattered through all the MARS Regions, and relating to 26,130 individual records, 4% of all retrievable records.[1] This is a relatively small sample whose composition and biases are not exactly known so the conclusions that can be drawn from it must be treated with due care. This is especially so given that the data from some counties refer to all records rather than just monuments.

For the purposes of this analysis, survival was categorized on a seven-point scale as follows:

Complete	>99% survival
Almost complete	80-99% survival
Most	60-79% survival
Some	40-59% survival
Little	20-39% survival
Very little	1-19% survival
Destroyed	<1% survival

This scale is based on the survival categories used on the AM107 forms used by English Heritage for the registration of Scheduled Monuments. Where counties did not already use this scheme, their figures have been adapted to fit the scheme as closely as possible.

Figure 6.1 shows a simple bar chart based on the SMR sample. The general picture is clear. Complete monuments account for about 17% of records in the sample, with just over a third of monuments (36%) being recorded as complete or almost complete. The proportion of records assigned to less complete bands decreases down the scale to just 3.6% of records in the lowest band, 'very little' surviving. Within the sample nearly 25% of observations are recorded as 'destroyed'; it is known, however, that at least some of these observations refer to stray finds that have been taken to museums and thus have lost their original archaeological context.

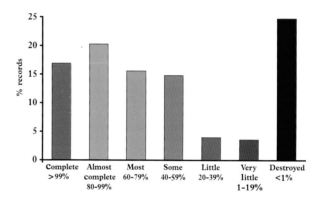

Figure 6.1 - Bar chart showing patterns of monument survival recorded by SMRs for 1995. *[Source: MARS National Survey. Sample: n= 24,741]*

Using the same data a general picture of the period distribution of the different levels of survival can be built up (Table 6.1). For the records relating to 'complete' and

Table 6.1 - The survival of the recorded resource in 1995 by archaeological period. *[Source: MARS National Survey Programme. Sample: n= 26,130 observations]*

	Complete >99%	Almost complete 80-99%	Most 60-79%	Some 40-59%	Little 20-39%	Very little 1-19%	Destroyed <1%
Palaeolithic	0.02	0.04	0	0	0.09	0	0.03
Mesolithic	0.28	0.30	0.07	0.66	0.09	0.10	0.15
Neolithic	0.49	1.56	0.93	0.66	3.07	0.48	0.50
Bronze Age	3.54	11.55	15.60	12.29	12.10	10.55	11.16
Iron Age	0.93	3.84	6.35	6.06	9.76	12.07	5.01
Romano-British	0.63	3.63	4.77	8.11	11.83	12.45	5.36
Early medieval	1.54	2.17	1.77	1.58	1.99	1.62	3.10
Medieval	12.61	18.84	17.28	17.09	21.05	19.30	25.48
Post-medieval	53.66	32.59	29.67	32.69	21.05	26.33	32.69
Modern	21.24	5.00	1.72	1.67	0.90	2.57	6.31
Unknown	5.07	20.49	21.86	19.20	18.07	14.54	10.19
Total	**100%**	**100%**	**100%**	**100%**	**100%**	**100%**	**100%**

'almost complete' survival there are noticeably lower percentages for the early periods than for medieval and later periods. The only exception is the Bronze Age, which accounts for 3.5% of all complete monuments and 11.5% of almost complete monuments. This is probably to be explained by the fact that the present survival of many Bronze Age monuments, especially round barrows, compares well with their state when first discovered and/or the widely held images of what they may have looked like originally. At the other end of the survival spectrum, Bronze Age monuments also account for the third highest percentage of losses.

6.2.2 Survival in resource assessment surveys

A number of resource assessments for particular monument classes or geographically defined study areas have been concerned with the matter of monument survival, although in most cases there is no distinction drawn between survival and condition. APPENDIX A provides a select bibliography of such surveys subdivided according to different kinds of coverage. Attention has already been given to the results of several of these studies in relation to monument condition (Chapter 5.6.2) and those relating to particular kinds of hazard facing archaeological monuments are referred to in more detail below (6.8).

6.2.3 MARS Monuments

Survival among MARS Monuments can be gauged from the data collected by the Field Survey and Aerial Photographic Survey Programmes. Areal survival provides the main measure, as described in Chapter 2, with the calculation of Percentage Area Loss (PAL) values based on the difference between the Projected Archaeological Extent (PAE) and the Current Area (CA) for a defined point in time. The PAE values translate into a series of six bands, survival declining as the PAL increases:

Very good	PAL <20%
Good	PAL 21-40%
Medium	PAL 41-60%
Poor	PAL 61-80%
Very poor	PAL 81-95%
Destroyed	PAL >95%

These categories are similar to the bands used for assessing the survival data held by SMRs and relate closely to the system used by English Heritage for assessing the survival of Scheduled Monuments. For MARS the top two categories of the English Heritage scheme (complete and almost complete) have been

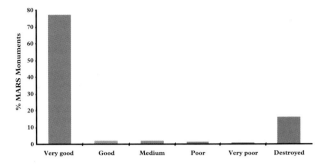

Figure 6.2 - Bar chart showing the areal survival of all MARS Monuments in 1995. *[Source: MARS Field Survey Programme. Sample: n= 13,488]*

amalgamated as 'very good'. It should also be noted, however, that the MARS categorization follows the implications of the decay profile model in being based on the amount of a monument calculated as having been lost; the system used above in 6.2.1 relies on visual estimates of the proportion of a monument believed to be remaining.

Figure 6.2 shows the distribution of MARS Monuments within these six survival categories in 1995. Approximately 77% of all MARS Monuments are included in the 'very good' category, almost double the percentage recorded in the top two categories in the survival estimates obtained from local SMRs. The difference is the product of two factors. First, and probably more significant, are differences in the way survival is perceived. As explained above, MARS used a benchmark provided by the Projected Archaeological Extent for each individual monument against which to measure survival; intuitive estimates of survival are likely to resort to comparisons with a range of known monuments of the same or similar class, perhaps also taking into account some general (if at times subconscious) understanding of how the monument may have looked originally. Second, MARS calculations are based on an examination of horizontal (i.e. areal) survival with little account in this analysis of the vertical dimension. Again, intuitive assessments of survival may take a wider range of dimensions into account.

At the other end of the spectrum, MARS estimates that about 16% of MARS Monuments, in numerical terms, have been destroyed. Estimates based on SMR records suggest that approximately 25% of the recorded resource has been destroyed. However, the difference between these two estimates is not so great when it is recognized that the SMR observations include a wider range of archaeological remains than can be defined as MARS Monuments, notably a percentage of the records

Table 6.2 - The areal survival of MARS Monuments in 1995 by monument form. *[Source: MARS Field Survey Programme with SMR information. Sample: n= 13,488]*

Monument form	Destroyed %	Very poor %	Poor %	Medium %	Good %	Very good %	Total %
Field system	6.4	3.8	4.2	4.1	1.9	79.5	100%
Large single monument	9.2	3.3	2.6	3.0	2.6	79.2	100%
Linear monument	12.1	1.9	3.0	3.2	3.6	76.2	100%
Small single monument	21.1	1.1	1.6	1.7	2.0	72.4	100%
Standing building	9.2	0.3	0.6	0.9	1.1	87.8	100%
All	**15.9**	**1.3**	**1.8**	**1.9**	**2.0**	**77.1**	**100%**

Table 6.3 - The form of MARS monuments by areal survival in 1995. *[Source: MARS Field Survey Programme with SMR information. Sample: n= 13,488]*

Monument form	Destroyed %	Very poor %	Poor %	Medium %	Good %	Very good %	All %
Field system	2.2	15.6	13.1	11.7	5.2	5.6	**5.5**
Large single monument	5.0	21.7	12.7	13.6	11.6	9.0	**8.7**
Linear monument	6.5	12.2	14.8	14.4	15.7	8.5	**8.6**
Small single monument	73.7	45.6	51.7	50.6	55.1	52.3	**55.6**
Standing building	12.5	5.0	7.6	9.7	12.4	24.6	**21.6**
Total	**100%**	**100%**	**100%**	**100%**	**100%**	**100%**	**100%**

which relate to stray finds and single burials, all of which are recorded as destroyed because they have been removed and taken to museums or permanent collections.

In the middle of the spectrum, the MARS data suggest that the bands for 'good', 'medium', 'poor' and 'very poor' each contain about 2% of the extant recorded resource. At first sight this part of the profile may seem rather strange, as greater dispersal might be expected. The problem here is not the sensitivity of the methodology for classifying survival, but rather the difficulty posed by having an arbitrary and relatively recent baseline referred to above (6.1). Decay in archaeological monuments is time-dependent, thus the longer the time-lapse between the initial reference point and observations on survival being made the greater the dispersion there is likely to be within the recorded resource as a whole because individual monuments follow different decay trajectories.

The general patterns of survival modelled on the one hand by available SMR data and on the other by the MARS data are, however, basically the same: relatively high proportions of monuments towards the end of the gradient representing better survival.

Survival in relation to monument form is analysed on Tables 6.2 and 6.3. When the survival pattern for each form is examined separately (Table 6.2) it is clear that standing buildings have the best survival pattern in the sense that the profile is most skewed towards the 'very good' category, while small single monuments have the worst survival pattern with less than three-quarters of examples (72%) in the 'very good' category. Looked at another way, within the recorded resource as a whole more than 52% of monuments rated as having 'very good' areal survival are small single monuments while just over 24% of monuments in the same category are standing buildings (Table 6.3). Rather importantly, both these figures deviate slightly from the actual distribution of these forms within the population as a whole: small single monuments being lower than expected while standing buildings with 'very good' areal survival are higher. One possible explanation for this is quite simply that management and maintenance works to standing buildings are effectively reducing the steepness of the decay trajectory as compared with small single monuments. To see whether this is so requires more attention to the chronological dimensions of survival patterns.

6.2.4 Changes in survival patterns through time

The way in which survival was measured in MARS allows changes over time to be monitored sensitively and accurately. In the analyses discussed above (6.2.3), Current Area 1995 was used in the calculations. A similar

set of calculations can be done for Current Area as recorded or reconstructible for earlier decades. Amongst MARS data the best available earlier sample is for 1945. However, as noted above (6.1), this not only allows the analysis of an earlier point on the decay curve, when the resource as a whole should have better survival, but in this case it also takes the analysis very close to the 'origin' in terms of the baseline from which change is being measured. This does not invalidate the analysis in any way, it only makes the recorded resource superficially appear better than it really is because, to reiterate, the detectable trends are relative to the PAE, not absolute against the actual overall decay trajectory of the monuments. The implications of the categories of survival used here in terms of the actual quality of archaeological information in monuments can be gauged with reference to the case studies presented in Chapter 2.5 and 2.6.

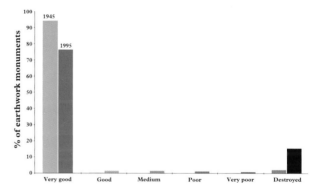

Figure 6.3 - Bar chart showing the areal survival of MARS earthwork monuments in 1945 and 1995. *[Source: MARS Aerial Photographic and Field Survey Programmes. Sample: n= 3880]*

Changes to monument survival patterns over time are illustrated on Figure 6.3 which shows the situation for MARS earthwork monuments. Here the percentage of monuments in each survival band for the mid 1940s, measured again in terms of areal survival, is compared with the situation in the mid 1990s. The pattern is clear. In the 1940s more than 95% of MARS earthwork Monuments in the sample can be assigned to the highest survival band, 'very good'. Over the intervening 50 years nearly 20% of earthwork monuments have slipped out of that band down the decay curve into other bands representing poorer survival. Movement down the gradient will also have happened in other parts of the curve. The loss of examples from the bar at the extreme left-hand end of the chart is balanced by increases in all the bars to the right. The biggest increases are in the

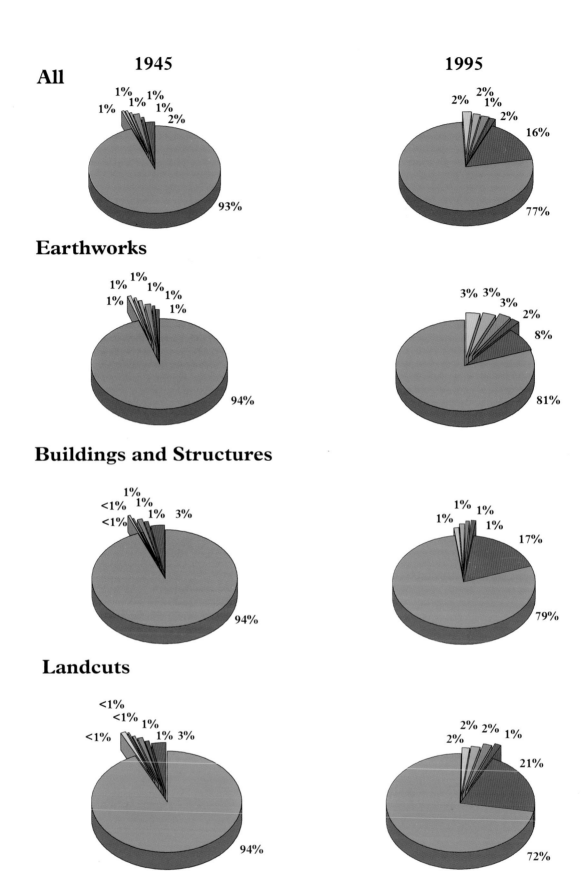

Figure 6.4 - Pie charts showing the patterns of monument survival in 1945 and 1995 for all monuments, earthworks, buildings and structures, and landcuts. *[Source: MARS Aerial Photographic and Field Survey Programmes. Sample: total n= 13,426; earthworks n= 3880; buildings and structures n= 4821; landcuts n= 4725]*

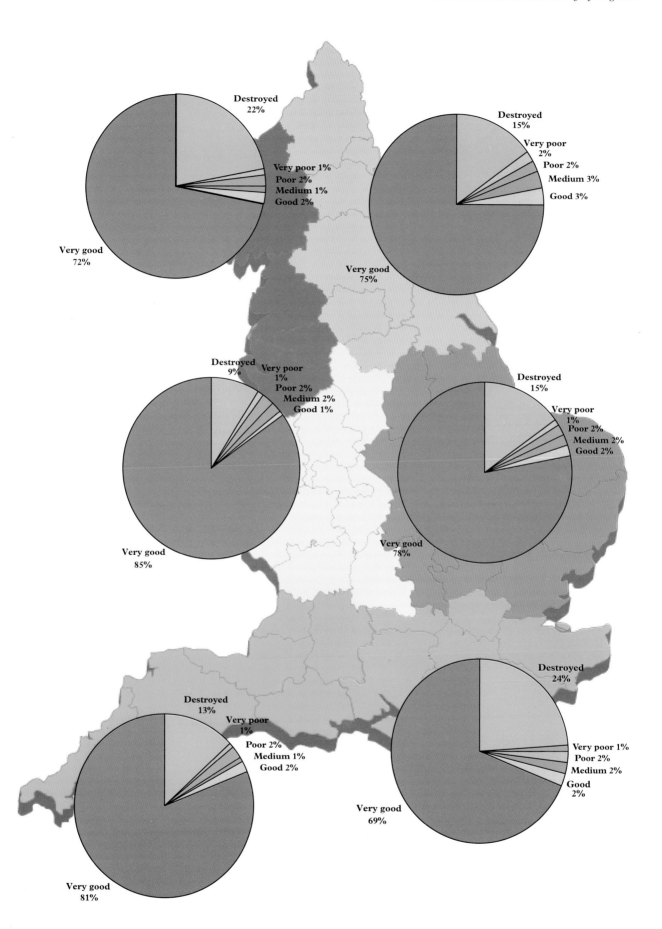

Figure 6.5 - Pie charts showing the regional pattern in areal survival of MARS earthworks monuments in 1995.
[Source: MARS Aerial Photographic and Field Survey Programmes. Sample: n= 3880]

sectors of the chart showing the destroyed monuments, up from 4% to 16% (see below 6.4.1).

Taking a broader perspective, Figure 6.4 shows as a series of pie charts the differences in survival patterns between 1945 and 1995 for all monuments and for all three monument character categories: earthworks, buildings and structures, and landcuts. The losses are not even between character categories and these are considered in more detail below (6.4.1). Earthworks and landcuts both show movements from higher levels of survival down the scale to swell other categories, whereas for buildings and structures movement appears to be more restricted with monuments staying as they are or disappearing altogether.

There are also regional variations in survival, especially in the percentages of 'very good' and 'destroyed' monuments. Figure 6.5 shows the regional pattern for MARS earthwork Monuments in 1995. The national average of 77% of earthwork monuments with 'very good' survival conceals wide regional variations of more than 15% between the highest levels amongst earthworks in the West Midlands (85%) and South West (81%) and the lowest in the South East (69%). The regional differences amongst MARS buildings and structures is even greater (Figure 6.6) with nearly 20% difference in the percentages of examples in the top bands of areal survival as between the West Midlands (88%) and the South East (69%).

Much the same trends can also be seen in earlier survival patterns. Figure 6.7 shows the regional pattern for all MARS Monuments in c.1945. Again the South East and West Midlands represent the extremes, suggesting that the survival patterns are at least influenced by processes extending back before the Second World War.

Tables 6.4 and 6.5 summarize the changes in regional patterns of survival by looking at increases and decreases for earthworks and landcuts respectively. For

earthworks (Table 6.4) all regions have shown a decrease in the number of monuments with 'very good' survival, with the North East losing the most at -5.3% and the North West the least at -0.54%. For landcuts (Table 6.5), the changes are more extreme than for earthwork monuments. Overall, there is a -21% change (i.e. decrease) in the number of monuments regarded as having 'very good' survival. The South West has the greatest change at -5.66%. The South East has the greatest increase in destroyed monuments at 4.81%. The absence of historical information on the condition of buildings and structures means that through-time analysis is not possible in the same way as it is for earthworks and landcuts.

Overall, the best areal survival of monuments tends to be in the west and south-west where development pressures during the present century have generally been fewer. The patterns of areal survival, and of the changes to these patterns over time, are complicated, and while ongoing development is, on the one hand, pushing monuments down the decay profile, the effects of conservatism in relation to land-use and positive conservation measures may, on the other hand, be serving to slow down rates of change in some areas.

The complexity of these survival patterns is also revealed when the data are examined in relation to monument period. There is an apparent trend (Table 6.6) for a higher proportion of later prehistoric, Roman and early medieval monuments to have 'poor' survival than monuments of other periods. In the former, there are proportionally fewer examples with 'very good' areal survival and, conversely, in the latter there are proportionally more examples with 'very good' or 'good' survival. As Table 6.7 shows, the greatest numbers of MARS Monuments with 'very good' survival are of post-medieval date.

Table 6.4 - Changes in the areal survival of MARS earthwork monuments by MARS region 1945 to 1995. *[Source: MARS Aerial Photographic and Field Survey Programmes with SMR information. Sample: 1945 n= 2133; 1995 n= 3880]*

Areal survival	North West %	North East %	West Midlands %	East Midlands %	South West %	South East %
Very good	-0.54	-5.37	-3.24	-2.14	-2.88	-1.09
Good	0.04	0.33	0.07	0.54	0.63	0.48
Medium	0.11	0.71	0.20	0.46	0.38	0.45
Poor	0.19	0.47	0.07	0.53	0.15	0.29
Very poor	0.21	0.23	0.18	0.44	0.18	0.19
Destroyed	0.45	1.17	0.98	2.10	1.27	1.78

Table 6.5 - Changes in the areal survival of MARS landcut monuments by MARS region 1945 to 1995. *[Source: MARS Aerial Photographic and Field Survey Programmes with SMR information. Sample: 1945 n= 1760; 1995 n= 4725]*

Areal survival	North West %	North East %	West Midlands %	East Midlands %	South West %	South East %
Very good	-0.66	-4.83	-2.61	-4.38	-5.66	-3.23
Good	0.08	0.42	0.08	0.20	0.11	0.04
Medium	0.30	0.33	0.07	0.43	0.07	0.06
Poor	0.36	0.32	0.24	0.38	0.14	0.10
Very poor	-0.07	0.15	0.11	-0.02	0.06	0.07
Destroyed	1.70	2.55	1.23	3.73	3.32	4.81

Table 6.6 - Areal survival of MARS monuments by archaeological period in 1995. *[Source: MARS Field Survey Programme with SMR information. Sample: n= 13,488]*

Period	Very good %	Good %	Medium %	Poor %	Very poor %	Destroyed %	Total %
Prehistoric unspecified	85.2	1.9	2.1	2.1	<1	8.1	100%
Palaeolithic	22.2	11.1	11.1	0	0	55.6	100%
Mesolithic	80.0	0	0	0	0	20.0	100%
Neolithic	69.4	<1	<1	2.5	<1	25.6	100%
Bronze Age	75.8	4.8	4.2	2.1	<1	12.4	100%
Iron Age	68.3	2.1	2.1	1.8	1.3	24.3	100%
Roman	63.9	1.6	1.2	1.9	<1	30.6	100%
Early medieval	54.8	3.0	3.6	<1	0	38.1	100%
Medieval	73.9	2.5	2.8	3.1	2.7	14.9	100%
Post-medieval	77.6	1.7	1.2	1.2	1.1	17.1	100%
Modern	81.4	<1	<1	1.2	<1	15.0	100%
Unknown	84.1	1.7	1.7	1.4	1.2	9.9	100%
All	**77.2%**	**2.0%**	**1.9%**	**1.8%**	**1.3%**	**15.8%**	**100%**

Table 6.7 - Archaeological period and MARS monuments grouped by areal survival for 1995. *[Source: MARS Field Survey Programme with SMR information. Sample: n= 13,488]*

Period	Very good %	Good %	Medium %	Poor %	Very poor %	Destroyed %	All %
Prehistoric unspecified	4.1	3.6	4.2	4.4	1.5	1.9	**3.7**
Palaeolithic	0	<1	<1	0	0	<1	**<1**
Mesolithic	<1	0	0	0	0	<1	**<1**
Neolithic	<1	<1	<1	1.1	<1	1.3	**<1**
Bronze Age	5.6	13.4	12.6	6.6	2.9	4.4	**5.7**
Iron Age	2.2	2.6	2.8	2.6	2.4	3.8	**2.5**
Roman	5.1	4.9	3.9	6.6	3.9	11.9	**6.2**
Early medieval	<1	1.6	2.1	<1	0	2.7	**1.1**
Medieval	18.9	24.8	29.8	34.2	39.5	18.5	**19.7**
Post-medieval	35.7	29.0	23.5	24.6	29.3	38.3	**35.4**
Modern	3.9	1.6	1.8	2.6	1.5	3.5	**3.7**
Unknown	22.9	17.9	18.6	16.9	18.5	13.1	**21.0**
Total	**100%**	**100%**	**100%**	**100%**	**100%**	**100%**	**100%**

6.3 Patterns of monument loss

Throughout the foregoing discussion, attention has repeatedly been drawn to the destruction of monuments, 'destroyed' being one of the recognized categories of survival in the MARS approach and elsewhere. It is the loss of monuments that regularly makes headline news in books, archaeological magazines, local newspapers, and sometimes in the national press. These are high-profile and sometimes emotive cases, the public airing of which occasionally means a reprieve for the monument in question.

MARS subdivided monument destruction into two main patterns: first, wholesale destruction where most of a monument disappears, usually in a single event or related series of events. Once lost these monuments become part of the extinct recorded resource and thereafter it is only records of various sorts that provide information about their former extent, date, character and purpose. Second is the piecemeal nibbling away of monuments, either through reducing their vertical dimensions by flattening or sub-surface erosion, or through reducing their horizontal dimensions by slicing away at their physical extent. These monuments remain part of the extant recorded resource even though they may

be seriously reduced in scale. Ultimately, piecemeal loss has the same effect as wholesale loss in the sense that all of the monument disappears. Indeed, the two patterns are really part of the same complicated set of decay processes, the one being what has already gone, the other comprising monuments following along behind at varying speeds. However, the distinction is worth developing through the analyses presented in the following sub-sections because the two patterns can most effectively be quantified in slightly different ways.

6.4 Wholesale monument losses

6.4.1 Counting the losses

To summarize the position already touched upon above (6.3.2), and in Chapter 5.5, out of 13,488 MARS Monuments examined by the Field Survey Programme, 2145 (16%) were found to have disappeared. Examination of available records and work by the Air Photographic Survey Programme revealed that about half of all losses occurred prior to *c*.1945 (8.3% of the MARS sample), the remainder (7.7%) having been lost between *c*.1945 and 1995. With an estimated recorded resource of 300,000 monuments, a 16% destruction means that the extant

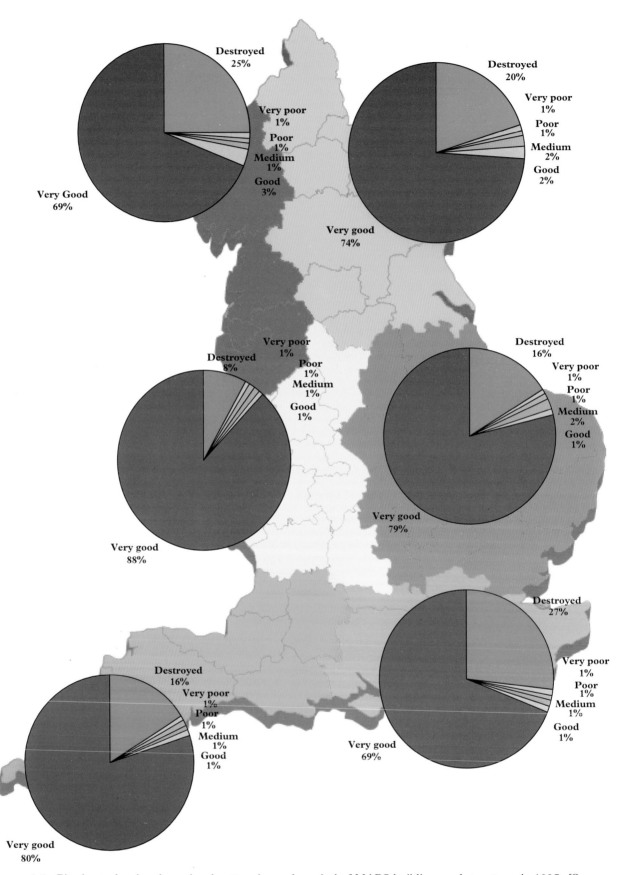

Figure 6.6 - Pie charts showing the regional pattern in areal survival of MARS buildings and structures in 1995. *[Source: MARS Aerial Photographic and Field Survey Programmes. Sample: n= 4821]*

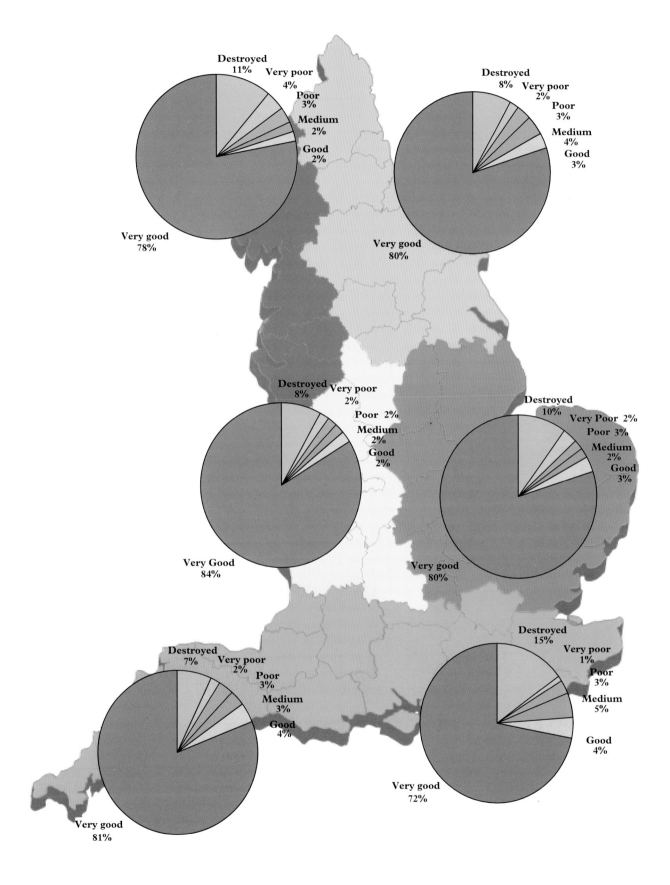

Figure 6.7 - Pie charts showing the regional pattern in areal survival of all MARS Monuments in 1945. *[Source: MARS Aerial Photographic Programme. Sample: n= 4268]*

Figure 6.8 - Pie charts showing the extant and extinct recorded resource by MARS Region in 1945. Quantified by monument count. *[Source: MARS Aerial Photographic Programme. Sample: n= 4225]*

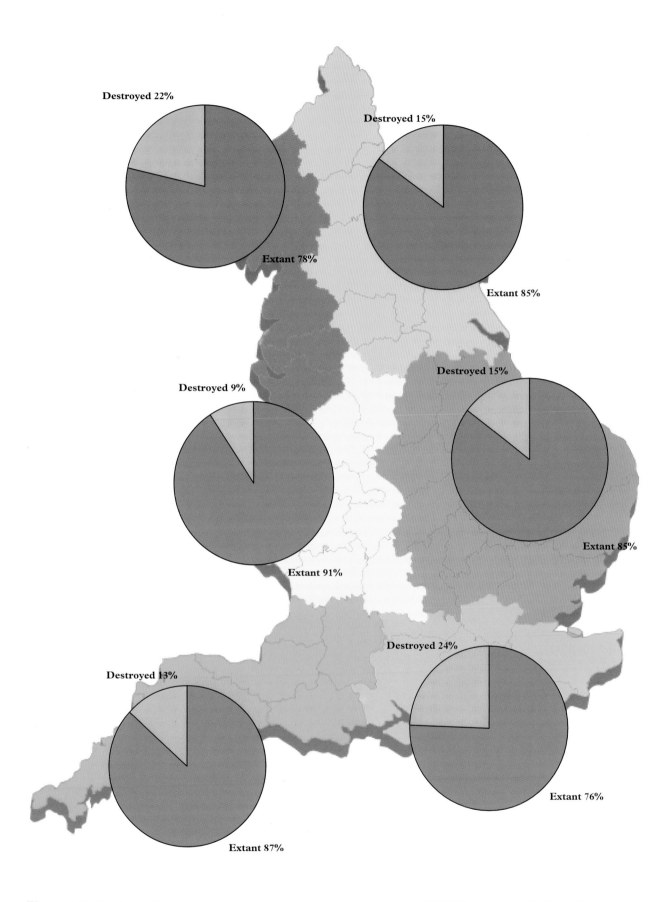

Destroyed 22%

Extant 78%

Destroyed 15%

Extant 85%

Destroyed 9%

Extant 91%

Destroyed 15%

Extant 85%

Destroyed 13%

Destroyed 24%

Extant 76%

Extant 87%

Figure 6.9 - Pie charts showing the extant and extinct recorded resource by MARS Region in 1995. Quantified by monument count. *[Source: MARS Aerial Photographic Programme. Sample: n= 13,426]*

recorded resource in 1995 comprised an estimated 253,000 monuments. Therefore, in numerical terms, the extant recorded resource in 1995 represented 84% of the recorded resource.

There is very little by way of comparative studies available to set these losses into context. In 1965, the Deserted Medieval Village Research Group suggested that of the 2000 deserted medieval villages identified up until that time some 500 (25%) had been totally destroyed (DMVRG 1965). Unfortunately, it is not clear what is meant by 'totally destroyed' in this context, and later sections of the DMVRG's paper suggests that in perhaps half of the cases the monuments have simply be flattened. In a regional study of 116 round barrows in Cleveland, 14 were found to have been destroyed through forestry and quarrying and a further 12 'ploughed out' (Crawford 1980, 76). This total of 26 barrows (22%) is rather similar to the level of losses reported for deserted medieval villages. Again, however, it certainly includes some monuments that have been flattened rather than completely destroyed, lending additional support for the MARS estimate.

6.4.2 Rates and regional patterns of loss

A rate of loss of the scale represented in the MARS sample may superficially look rather low, but in fact it represents a heavy toll on the recorded resource. The loss of an estimated 23,500 monuments in England as a whole over the 50-year period between *c.*1945 and 1995 means an average destruction rate of just over one monument per day. It is of course impossible to say how many monuments which are not within the recorded resource have been lost over the same period.

The rate of losses has not been even throughout England. Figure 6.8 shows a series of pie charts reflecting the balance between the destroyed (i.e. extinct) and the extant resource for all MARS Monuments, as it can be estimated in 1945. Proportional to the recorded resource, the heaviest losses during this phase were in the North West (7%) and the South East (5%). The lowest rates of loss were in the South West and North East. There is a slight general trend to the pattern of destruction reflected in this regional analysis: the percentage of the recorded

resource lost declines northwards and westwards from the South East region, only the North West providing an exception.

During the period *c.*1945 to 1995 the regional patterning becomes stronger. Figure 6.9 shows the situation for the survival of all categories of MARS Monuments in 1995. The South East still has the highest proportion of the recorded resource destroyed: the declining trend northwards and westwards is now, however, strong. Within this it is also noticeable that the increases in the percentage of the resource which has been destroyed differ greatly between regions: a fifteenfold increase in the North East and thirteenfold in the South West, compared with only fivefold in the South East.

6.4.3 Losses by monument character and form

General patterns of monument loss can also be broken down by monument character. Figure 6.5 showed the regional pattern of destruction for earthwork monuments within the context of overall patterns of survival in 1995. The West Midlands has the lowest level of loss, followed by the South West. The heaviest toll is in the South East where the percentage of losses among earthworks in the recorded resource was over two and a half times what it was in the West Midlands. The overall pattern is similar for buildings and structures (Figure 6.6), although the differences between regions are greater.

Analysed by monument form (Table 6.8), the greatest losses have been among small single monuments and buildings (*cf.* Briggs 1952). In numerical terms this is hardly surprising, because removing such monuments takes much less effort than destroying a larger entity such as a large single monument, field system or linear monument. It is therefore important to view the loss of monuments by form in relation to the number of recorded examples of the same form (Figure 6.10). Small single monuments are again ahead of other forms in sustaining the highest levels of loss, but in second place now are linear monuments. Although field systems remain at the bottom end of the spectrum it is important to recognize that while they represent only 2.5% of all monument losses those examples that have disappeared represent over 7% of all field systems.

Table 6.8 - Identified hazards causing wholesale loss of MARS monuments since 1940 in relation to monument form. [Source: MARS Aerial Photographic Programme with SMR information. Sample: n= 2276]

Cause of damage	Field system %	Large single monument %	Linear monument %	Small single monument %	Standing building %	Total %
Development & urbanization	0.62	1.98	1.05	16.34	2.55	**22.54**
Demolition	0	0.40	0.26	8.88	5.54	**15.07**
Unknown	0.22	0.48	1.67	26.53	1.62	**30.52**
Agriculture	0.97	1.41	1.10	5.01	0.04	**8.52**
Road-building	0.26	0.48	2.07	4.26	0.22	**7.29**
Mineral extraction	0.18	0.66	0.48	5.62	0.13	**7.07**
Industry	0	0	0.26	2.11	0.66	**3.03**
Natural process	0.13	0.57	0.35	1.49	0.48	**3.03**
Building alteration	0	0.04	0	1.05	0.57	**1.67**
Forestry	0.09	0.04	0	0.26	0	**0.40**
Military damage	0	0	0	0.22	0	**0.22**
Visitor erosion	0	0.04	0.09	0	0	**0.13**
Vadalism	0	0	0	0.04	0.04	**0.09**
All	**2.46**	**6.33**	**7.34**	**72.01**	**11.86**	**100%**

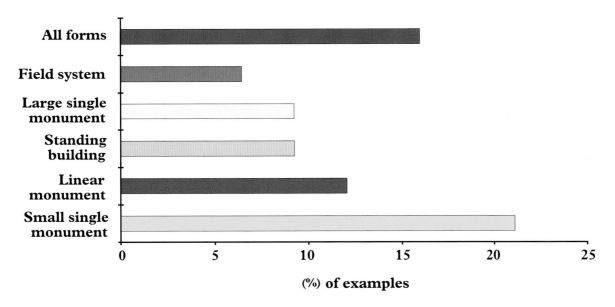

Figure 6.10 - Bar chart showing the loss of MARS Monuments by each recorded form as a proportion of all recorded examples of that form. Quantified by monument count. *[Source: MARS Field Survey Programme. Sample: n= 2448]*

6.4.4 Area losses

Estimates of wholesale monument loss based on numerical counts of the wholesale destruction of monuments tell only part of the story. Estimates of the area of archaeological remains lost are also important; the total area of archaeological remains lost through the wholesale destruction of monuments is considerable.

Within the MARS sample, about 6.5% of the land area, 425km², is known to contain, or has in the past contained, archaeological deposits of one kind or another. This figure represents the sum of the PAE for all monuments in the sample. It does not of course include archaeological monuments or deposits that have not been recorded; it is only what is documented from existing records. The PAE of monuments found by the MARS Field Survey Programme to have disappeared totals 37.7km², 8.9% of the land known to contain archaeological remains within the sample transects.

In percentage terms the simple count of monument losses represents about 16% of the recorded resource while the loss of archaeologically sensitive land represents about 9% of the area of the recorded resource. The

difference between these figures reflects the fact that small single monuments and standing buildings represent, in numerical terms, the majority of monument losses. Their place in the pattern of losses takes on a rather different complexion when considered in terms of area losses.

Figure 6.11 shows an analysis of the estimated losses in square kilometres for the main forms of monument extrapolated out from the MARS sample for the whole of England. Fully apparent here is the impact caused by the loss of relatively few large single monuments and field systems on the recorded resource as a whole as together these account for over three-quarters of the archaeologically sensitive land that has been lost. Buildings and structures have been omitted from this chart because losses here were negligible in terms of area (but *cf.* Table 6.3).

Figure 6.12 presents an analysis of the percentage of land lost as a fraction of the overall land area represented by each form of monument (*cf.* Figure 6.10 for a similar analysis based on monument count). Here it can be seen that fieldsystems represent the greatest losses, large single monuments and linear examples

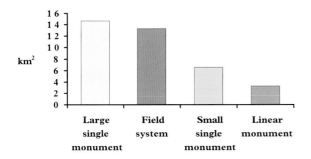

Figure 6.11 - Bar chart showing the total area of destroyed MARS Monuments categorized by the main monument forms. *[Source: MARS Aerial Photographic and Field Survey Programmes. Sample: n= 4001]*

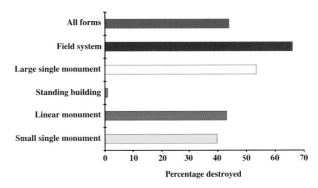

Figure 6.12 - Bar chart showing the loss of MARS Monuments by area as a proportion of the total area recorded for each of the five main monument forms. Quantified by area. *[Source: MARS Field Survey Programme. Sample: n= 14,639]*

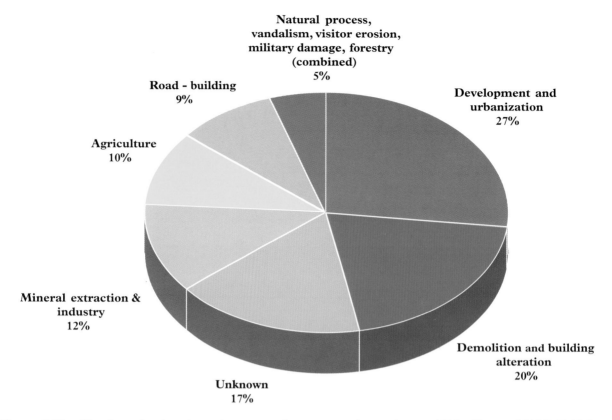

Figure 6.13 - Pie chart showing the main causes of monument destruction to 1995. *[Source: MARS Field Survey Programme. Sample: n= 2145]*

following close behind when losses are quantified in this way.

6.4.5 Forces of wholesale destruction

During the MARS Project 16 different main hazards which gave rise to monument destruction were recognized. As Figure 6.13 shows, five of these hazards account for nearly 80% of all wholesale monument destruction: development and urbanization (27%); demolition and building alteration (20%); mineral

extraction and industry (12%); agriculture (10%); and road-building (9%). Of the remainder, 17% of losses could not be attributed to particular forces, while 5% of losses were attributable to a range of relatively minor factors including natural processes, vandalism, visitor erosion, military damage and forestry operations.

Regional trends are also evident, Table 6.9. Mineral extraction, for example, accounts for a higher percentage of losses in the East Midlands as in the West Midlands. Losses through development and urbanization are highest

Table 6.9 - Identified hazards causing wholesale loss of MARS monuments since 1940 in relation to MARS regions. *[Source: MARS Aerial Photographic Programme with SMR information. Sample: n= 2276]*

Hazard / Cause of destruction	North West	North East	East Midlands	West Midlands	South West	South East	Total
Development and Urbanization	6.46	3.56	1.45	4.79	2.86	3.43	**22.54**
Demolition	5.36	1.1.0	1.49	3.78	1.71	1.63	**15.07**
Agriculture	1.10	1.89	0.57	1.80	1.93	1.23	**8.52**
Road building	1.32	1.54	1.01	1.58	1.27	0.57	**7.29**
Mineral extraction	0.35	1.1.9	0.66	1.49	2.81	0.57	**7.07**
Industry	0.22	0.53	0.40	0.92	0.88	0.09	**3.03**
Natural process	0.48	0.97	0.31	0.53	0.35	0.40	**3.03**
Building alteration	0.09	0.48	0.13	0.70	0.04	0.22	**1.67**
Forestry	0.09	0.26	0	0.04	0	0	**0.40**
Military damage	0	0	0	0.13	0.09	0	**0.22**
Visitor erosion	0	0.04	0	0.04	0	0.04	**0.13**
Vandalism	0	0	0.04	0.04	0	0	**0.09**
Unkown	1.89	4.92	1.84	5.36	4.79	12.12	**30.94**
Total	**17.36**	**16.48**	**7.90**	**21.20**	**16.73**	**20.30**	**100%**

Figure 6.14 - Legbourne Priory, Lincolnshire. Two views of the earthwork remains of the twelfth century Cistercian nunnery looking north-east. The monument, which includes, foundations, enclosures and possible fishponds, was extensively damaged by earthmoving and groundworks. This included the excavation of one of the fishponds to create an ornamental lake, the spoil being dumped over surrounding earthworks. Before, in June 1988 (above), and after, in October 1988 (below). *[Photographs: RCHME. Crown copyright]*

in the North West and East Midlands, lowest in the West Midlands and South West. Some causes of wholesale monument destruction are more evenly spread around the country, for example losses through road-building and natural processes.

6.5 *Piecemeal loss and damage*

Wholesale destruction is only part of the story. The nibbling away of monuments is less noticeable, less sensational, but cumulatively more destructive. Figure 6.14 shows an example of how the extent of monuments can be reduced through piecemeal loss, in this case by extensive groundworks.

6.5.1 Piecemeal area loss

Out of the extant MARS Monuments checked by the Field Survey Programme, 95% were found to have some evidence of damage or destruction. In some cases this was relatively minor, for example animal burrowing; in other cases it was very considerable and involved the disappearance of large parts of the monument. Subtracting the Current Area 1995 (CA95) of extant MARS Monuments from the PAE for the population of extant MARS Monuments reveals that piecemeal loss on extant monuments amounts to 149.3km², 35% of all the land recorded as containing archaeological monuments or deposits in the sample transects. Extrapolated out, this suggests the piecemeal loss of 2975km² square kilometres of recorded archaeology in England to 1995.

6.5.2 *Causes of piecemeal loss and damage*

At any time the recorded resource is vulnerable to damage or destruction from a very wide range of activities: natural and anthropogenic, legal and criminal. Sometimes they can be hard to detect from field observation, and talking to local people and landowners does not always help. The study of aerial photographs sometimes provides valuable clues, especially where they have been taken at or near to the time when monuments were being damaged.

The causes of piecemeal loss to archaeological monuments are numerous and various, with all 16 defined hazards being recorded. Figure 6.15 shows the overall observed incidence of each as a percentage of all recorded observations of damage. At some monuments more than one form of damage was observed. Only 10% of observations could not be tied back to particular hazards or causes.

Four main factors account for nearly 80% of recorded instances of piecemeal loss: agriculture; natural processes and related erosion; building alterations and demolition; and development and urbanization. The balance between these differs considerably from the pattern of forces involved in wholesale destruction. This is because some highly destructive activities such as road-building and mineral extraction do not figure prominently here as their impact is usually wholesale rather than piecemeal. Equally, forces such as agriculture and natural process are well represented here because their effect is accretional and gradual.

The impact of natural and accelerated decay is clear from the figure, with natural processes accounting for

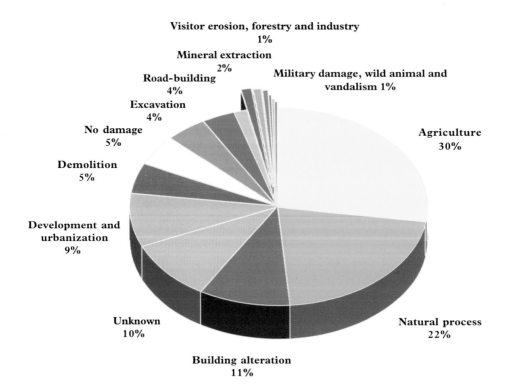

Figure 6.15 - Pie chart showing the main causes of piecemeal loss and damage to MARS Monuments in 1995 including instances where more than one cause of damage was recorded. *[Source: MARS Field Survey Programme. Sample: n= 14,639]*

Table 6.10 - Identified hazards causing piecemeal loss or damage at MARS Monuments in relation to state. *[Source: MARS Aerial Photographic and Field Survey Programmes with SMR information. Sample: n= 14,639]*

Cause of damage	Buildings and Structures				Earthworks				Landcuts				National Average
	Destroyed %	Flat %	Upstanding %	Total %	Destroyed %	Flat %	Upstanding %	Total %	Destroyed %	Flat %	Upstanding %	Total %	%
Agriculture	2.6	24.9	2.5	6.4	22.5	72.7	31.4	53.7	8.5	50.0	13.1	26.5	27.6
Building alteration	3.3	3.1	39.6	27.0	<1	<1	1.0	<1	<1	<1	3.7	1.8	10.1
Demolition	32.5	19.9	3.2	11.1	<1	<1	<1	<1	1.8	2.3	3.1	3.3	5.1
Development and urbanisation	26.1	10.7	3.3	8.5	25.55	4.0	7.9	7.3	18.3	9.2	8.4	10.6	8.9
Excavation	7.0	2.5	<1	1.8	17.3	1.2	6.9	4.6	24.8	2.4	1.1	6.3	4.3
Forestry	0	<1	<1	<1	1.4	1.4	2.6	1.8	<1	1.3	2.0	1.4	1.1
Industry	3.9	<1	<1	<1	3.8	<1	<1	<1	2.0	<1	<1	<1	<1
Military damage	0.0	<1	<1	<1	<1	<1	<1	<1	<1	<1	<1	<1	<1
Mineral extraction	5.1	1.0	<1	1.1	11.0	<1	<1	1.5	7.4	<1	<1	2.1	1.6
Natural process	2.0	5.8	34.0	23.6	4.9	7.4	34.9	17.0	2.8	8.6	42.8	21.7	21.0
No damage	<1	<1	11.6	7.7	0	<1	2.1	1.0	<1	1.3	12.5	5.8	5.1
Road building	4.8	1.0	<1	1.5	5.5	2.0	3.3	2.7	10.1	6.9	4.1	6.4	3.6
Unknown	12.5	29.5	2.6	9.0	5.5	9.2	4.6	7.2	17.9	15.8	5.5	11.9	9.5
Vandalism	<1	0	<1	<1	0	0	<1	<1	<1	0	1.2	<1	<1
Visitor erosion	0	0	<1	<1	<1	<1	1.9	<1	0	0	1.1	<1	<1
Wild animal	0	0	<1	<1	0.0	<1	1.3	<1	0	0	0	0	<1
Total	**100%**	**100%**	**100%**	**100%**	**100%**	**100%**	**100%**	**100%**	**100%**	**100%**	**100%**	**100%**	**100%**

22% of the total incidence of monument loss. The direct effect of anthropogenic causes is clearest, with agriculture and building alteration accounting for 30% and 11% of the total respectively.

At a general level, causes of damage and destruction can be related to the defined monument states, as Table 6.10 shows. Among earthworks, for which there were 4315 observations from 5180 MARS Monuments, agricultural damage was the most frequently reported (53.7% of observations). It is important to recognize, however, that 72% of observations relating to agricultural damage on earthworks relate to flattened monuments whereas only 31% relate to upstanding earthworks. By contrast, 35% of observations related to natural erosion on upstanding earthworks whereas only 7.4% of observations related to natural erosion on flattened earthworks. 2% of observations related to no damage on upstanding earthworks, but only 0.4% of observations recorded no damage on flattened earthworks.

Among buildings and structures, for which there are 5033 observations relating to 5229 MARS Monuments, the two largest causes of reported damage are building alterations (39.6%) and natural processes (34%). No damage was recorded in 11.6% of observations.

Landcut monuments are represented by 5293 observations relating to 5168 MARS Monuments. The pattern here, as with earthworks, is dominated by natural damage to upstanding examples, but this class also has the highest incidence of no recorded damage (12.5%). Road-building, vandalism and development are observed as more frequent causes of damage in this class.

Tables 6.11 and 6.12 show more detailed analyses of damage to MARS Monuments by form, based on 15,963 observations relating to 14,639 monuments. The

Table 6.11 - Identified hazards causing piecemeal loss or damage at MARS Monuments by monument form, summed by hazard. *[Source: MARS Field Survey Programme. Sample: n= 14,639]*

Cause of damage	Field system %	Large single monument %	Linear monument %	Small single monument %	Standing building %	Total %
Agriculture	13.4	15.3	11.9	59.0	<1	100%
Building alteration	<1	1.4	<1	10.9	86.9	100%
Demolition	0	4.0	7.2	60.7	28.1	100%
Development and Urbanization	3.6	19.33	7.9	60.09	9.05	100%
Forestry	9.5	24.4	11.9	53.6	<1	100%
Industry	2.6	11.3	8.7	59.1	18.3	100%
Military damage	9.1	9.1	12.1	60.6	9.1	100%
Mineral extraction	2.2	15.7	7.0	73.5	1.7	100%
Natural process	3.0	7.3	9.4	53.4	26.9	100%
No damage	1.6	17.3	9.3	32.2	39.6	100%
Road-building	5.1	12.9	43.3	36.4	2.3	100%
Unknown	3.56	5.45	5.3	78.69	6.9	100%
Vandalism	0	4.1	0	65.3	30.6	100%
Visitor erosion	3.8	16.3	23.8	51.3	5.0	100%
Wild animal	3.3	10.0	6.7	80.0	0	100%
All	**5.6%**	**10.7%**	**9.7%**	**53.9%**	**20.2%**	**100%**

Table 6.12 - Identified hazards causing piecemeal loss or damage at MARS Monuments by monument form, summed by form. *[Source: MARS Field Survey Programme. Sample: n= 14,639]*

Cause of damage	Field system %	Large single monument	Linear monument	Small single monument	Standing building	National average
Agriculture	65.9	39.5	34.0	30.2	<1	27.6
Building alteration	<1	1.3	<1	2.0	43.5	10.1
Demolition	<1	1.9	3.8	5.8	7.1	5.1
Development and urbanization	5.8	16.1	7.2	9.9	3.1	8.9
Forestry	1.9	2.6	1.4	1.1	<1.0	1.1
Industry	<1	<1	<1	<1	<1	<1
Military damage	<1	<1	<1	<1	<1	<1
Mineral extraction	<1	2.3	1.1	2.1	<1	1.6
Natural process	11.1	14.3	20.5	20.8	28.0	21.0
No damage	1.5	8.2	4.9	3.0	9.9	5.1
Road-building	3.3	4.4	16.3	2.5	<1	3.6
Unknown	8.3	7.0	7.5	20.1	4.6	13.8
Vandalism	<1	<1	<1	<1	<1	<1
Visitor erosion	<1	<1	1.3	<1	<1	<1
Wild animal	<1	<1	<1	<1	<1	<1
Total	**100%**	**100%**	**100%**	**100%**	**100%**	**100%**

Table 6.13 - Identified hazards causing piecemeal loss or damage at MARS earthwork monuments by MARS region. *[Source: MARS Field Survey Programme. Sample: n= 4313]*

Cause of damage	North West %	North East %	West Midlands %	East Midlands %	South West %	South East %	England %
Agriculture	40.5	47.3	48.5	60.6	56.2	57.3	53.7
Building alteration	<1	<1	<1	1.8	<1	<1	<1
Demolition	2.1	<1	<1	<1	<1	<1	<1
Development & urbanization	7.2	8.3	8.1	11.3	3.0	5.6	7.3
Forestry	4.1	3.8	<1	<1	1.6	1.0	1.8
Industry	<1	<1	<1	1.4	<1	<1	<1
Military damage	<1	<1	<1	<1	1.0	<1	<1
Mineral extraction	2.1	1.7	2.1	<1	1.7	1.0	1.5
Natural process	19.5	16.3	10.5	13.8	25.8	13.6	17.0
No damage	4.6	<1	2.9	<1	<1	0.0	1.0
Road building	5.1	5.4	1.1	2.0	1.2	3.4	2.7
Unknown	12.9	14.7	23.8	5.1	7.9	12.4	11.8
Vandalism	<1	<1	<1	<1	<1	<1	<1
Visitor erosion	<1	<1	1.0	<1	<1	2.7	<1
Wild animal	<1	<1	<1	<1	<1	2.6	<1
Total	**100%**	**100%**	**100%**	**100%**	**100%**	**100%**	**100%**

Table 6.14 - Identified hazards causing piecemeal loss or damage at MARS buildings and structures by MARS region. *[Source: MARS Field Survey Programme. Sample: n= 5033]*

Cause of damage	North West %	North East %	West Midlands %	East Midlands %	South West %	South East %	England %
Agriculture	1.8	5.3	3.4	14.4	7.3	3.0	6.4
Building alteration	30.1	12.5	25.3	29.4	22.1	45.7	27.0
Demolition	19.5	7.8	7.4	15.7	6.1	7.7	11.1
Development & urbanization	12.3	11.8	5.5	7.2	7.6	6.4	8.5
Excavation	<1	<1	<1	2.2	<1	8.2	1.8
Forestry	<1	<1	<1	<1	<1	0	<1
Industry	<1	1.7	<1	<1	1.6	<1	<1
Military damage	0	<1	0	<1	<1	<1	<1
Mineral extraction	<1	<1	<1	<1	4.2	<1	1.1
Natural process	15.0	27.5	34.0	15.9	33.9	16.3	23.6
No damage	12.6	2.9	12.7	7.4	6.8	2.6	7.7
Road building	1.3	2.0	1.4	2.0	1.9	<1	1.5
Unknown	4.9	25.2	7.2	3.3	7.6	9.0	9.0
Vandalism	<1	<1	<1	<1	0	0	<1
Visitor erosion	0	<1	1.2	<1	0	<1	<1
Wild animal	0	<1	0	<1	0	0	<1
Total	**100%**	**100%**	**100%**	**100%**	**100%**	**100%**	**100%**

Table 6.15 - Identified hazards causing piecemeal loss or damage at MARS landcuts by MARS region. *[Source: MARS Field Survey Programme. Sample: n= 5173]*

Cause of damage	North West %	North East %	West Midlands %	East Midlands %	South West %	South East %	England %
Agriculture	17.1	23.9	23.5	38.6	25.0	23.4	26.7
Building alteration	<1	<1	1.4	3.4	<1	3.1	1.8
Demolition	6.8	1.2	3.5	3.7	2.3	2.4	3.4
Development & urbanization	19.2	7.1	6.8	10.7	3.2	11.1	10.1
Excavation	1.3	2.0	1.1	7.3	2.7	24.4	6.3
Forestry	2.1	1.7	<1	2.4	<1	<1	1.4
Industry	<1	<1	<1	1.1	1.6	<1	<1
Military damage	0	<1	0	<1	<1	<1	<1
Mineral extraction	1.0	2.3	1.6	2.2	3.5	1.4	2.1
Natural process	21.5	29.1	21.2	14.9	32.3	16.4	22.1
No damage	6.8	4.1	12.9	4.1	5.7	3.5	5.7
Road building	5.2	5.7	7.8	7.8	4.1	5.8	6.1
Unknown	15.3	21.1	17.5	2.6	16.1	6.9	12.1
Vandalism	1.4	<1	<1	<1	<1	<1	<1
Visitor erosion	<1	<1	1.1	<1	<1	<1	<1
Wild animal	0	<1	0	0	0	0	0
Total	**100%**	**100%**	**100%**	**100%**	**100%**	**100%**	**100%**

results highlight the fact that standing buildings suffer from quite different causes of damage from other forms of monument. Agriculture is the single biggest cause of damage to all forms except standing buildings, followed by natural processes.

Agriculture is a particular problem for field systems, and within this class it accounted for 66% of losses through piecemeal destruction. This is borne out by a detailed study of medieval ridge and furrow field systems in Northamptonshire where losses of between 63% and 87% were recorded in six sample parishes (Hall 1993, 25). The impact of road-building is also notable: it accounts for 3.6% of observed losses to monuments taken as a whole, but 16.3% of cases affecting linear monuments. Interestingly, forestry accounts for only 1.09% of all instances of observed destruction, and seems to affect large single monuments more than other forms.

There are also regional differences in the pattern of damaging activities, as Tables 6.13-6.15 show with reference to the three categories of monument character. Among earthworks damage from agriculture is far higher in the East Midlands and South East than in the North West, while natural processes appear to have the greatest effect in the North West and South West. For buildings, natural processes are more prevalent in the West Midlands and South West.

Archaeological excavation is listed as a source of destruction for 4.6% of observations, the excavations usually having taken place in advance of, and prompted by, the threat posed by some other destructive agency. A small portion of these excavations will of course be pure research investigations which have the effect of damaging or nibbling away at a monument just as surely as the other hazards identified here.

6.6 Total area loss

For an overall impression of monument destruction, wholesale losses and piecemeal losses must be added. Numerically, 16% of MARS Monuments have completely

gone and 95% of those extant in 1995 showed signs of some damage, albeit small-scale in some cases. By area, wholesale losses up until 1995 account for the disappearance of about 37.7km² of archaeologically sensitive land within the sample transects while piecemeal loss accounts for a further 149.3km². Together this loss amounts to 187km² or 44% of the archaeological resource by area.

Extrapolating the MARS sample, it can be suggested that nationally some 3740km² of archaeologically sensitive land has already been lost, at least 1799km² of which disappeared between 1945 and 1995. This amounts to an average loss of nearly 10ha per day, every day, over the last 50 years. Put in context, this loss is equivalent to the disappearance of the archaeological equivalent of ten full-sized football pitches.

The Current Area of the extant archaeological resource in England in 1995 is estimated at 4770km², approximately 3.67% of England's land area.

6.7 Recording the losses

It is easy to focus on the loss or disappearance of archaeological monuments without the counter-perspective that, as part of the destruction process, some previously unrecorded monuments are brought to light, while in other cases there is an opportunity to investigate and record the archaeological deposits before they are destroyed. Rescue excavation has been a major part of archaeological work in England since the Second World War (Rahtz 1974; Jones 1984). A survey of rescue excavations carried out between 1938 and 1972 revealed that over 1100 separate pieces of work, ranging in scale from a single trench to the stripping and recording of several hectares, had been undertaken in advance of destruction with central government sponsorship or funding (Butcher and Garwood 1994). Many more projects have been undertaken since the early 1970s, some with central government funding but an increasing percentage through developer funding (Figure 6.16).

The listings in APPENDIX M include a small

Figure 6.16 - Rescue excavation of the medieval and post-medieval street frontage in Friars Walk, Lewes, East Sussex, 1989, prior to redevelopment. Eighteenth century masonry cellars have largely destroyed the medieval buildings, although traces of eleventh to fourteenth century timber structures are visible in the background. *[Photograph: Miles Russell. Copyright reserved]*

selection of reports relating to completed rescue excavation projects prompted by particular kinds of hazards or threats. They provide two kinds of insight: first they show something of the nature and density of archaeological monuments brought to light by these activities, and second they demonstrate the quality of archaeological information generated as a result. In all cases it is important to recognize that rescue excavation and recording take place in relation to a window of opportunity that is presented by and is constrained by the nature of the threats themselves. Thus, for example, the kind of work carried out in relation to extensive threats, such as cultivation or gravel extraction, is rather different from what might be expected from rescue work connected with pipelines or road schemes.

Within the MARS sample transects, about 17% of monuments destroyed prior to 1995 had been excavated under 'rescue' conditions, prior to their destruction, thus allowing a basic record to be made of what was lost. Figure 6.17 shows a simple analysis of the main reasons given in available records for the excavation of destroyed MARS Monuments. Development and utilities predominate. Figure 6.18 shows the same analysis for MARS Scheduled Monuments destroyed prior to 1995.

Figure 6.19 shows an analysis of the changes in the percentage of MARS Monuments excavated in advance of their destruction over time. The four decades 1940s to 1980s are shown; directly comparable data for the 1990s being incomplete at the MARS census date. The trend is clear: by the 1980s, more than 80% of monuments were excavated in advance of being destroyed. However, in very few cases were such excavations total. Entirely typical is the Billingsgate Lorry Park Site beside the Thames in London (Figure 6.20). Excavations here in 1982 were, at that time, the largest and most costly ever undertaken in the capital, funded by the developer. However, the excavation was able to examine only about a quarter of the area eventually destroyed by the development.

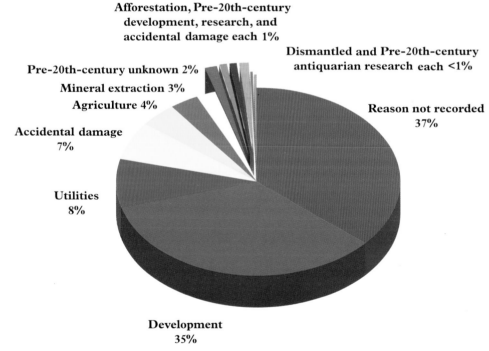

Figure 6.17 - Pie chart showing the main reasons for the excavation of MARS Monuments in advance of their destruction. *[Source: MARS Field Survey Programme. Sample: n= 433]*

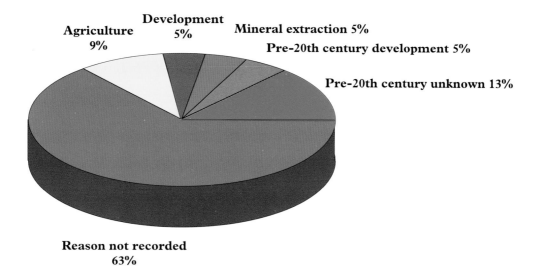

Figure 6.18 - Pie chart showing the main reasons for the excavation of MARS Scheduled Monuments in advance of their destruction. *[Source: MARS Field Survey Programme. Sample: n= 22]*

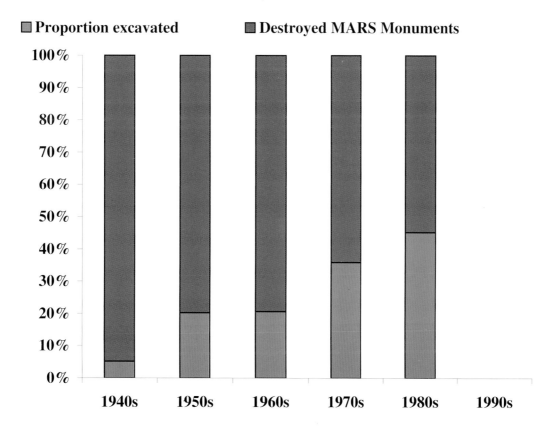

Figure 6.19 - Bar charts showing the percentage of destroyed MARS Monuments excavated in advance of destruction by decade 1940s-1980s. Data for the 1990s not complete at the time of the MARS Project. *[Source: MARS Aerial Photographic and Field Survey Programmes. Sample: n= 445]*

Figure 6.20 - The site of Billingsgate Lorry Park, London, in 1983. In the previous year a large excavation (beneath the piling machines in this picture) had uncovered remains of Roman, Saxon, medieval and post-medieval date, to a depth of 6m; but only investigated a quarter of the site. The other three-quarters were removed by permitted development in 1983. Archaeologists were only allowed a watching brief, and yet recovered over 6000 individual objects, including many rare Saxon coins. *[Reproduced by permission of Museum of London Archaeology Service. Copyright reserved]*

6.8 Principal causes of damage and destruction

Some of the biggest causes of damage to archaeological monuments are at the same time major contributors to the economic and social well-being of people and communities living in England, while others are closely related to particular land-uses. In the following sub-sections consideration is given to the five main causes of destruction and damage affecting archaeological monuments, together with a selection of lesser causes, with particular attention to the overall pattern of these activities and their likely continuation over the next decade or so. APPENDIX M provides a select bibliography of studies and reports dealing with the archaeological side of particular activities linked to the destruction or damage of monuments.

6.8.1 Agriculture/cultivation

Arable agriculture or cultivation is estimated to account for 10% of observed cases of monument destruction and 30% of cases of monument damage. Its impact is especially great for early field systems (66% of recorded destruction) and large single monuments (38% of recorded destruction). It is cited as the reason for archaeological excavation in advance of destruction in 4% of cases among all monuments and 9% of cases involving Scheduled Monuments.

Archaeologically, the problem with cultivation is the process of ploughing and ground preparation, rather than the growing of crops (Figure 6.21). Cultivation is cyclical and repetitive, which exacerbates the problem. In autumn or early spring the land is broken open and turned over by ploughing. Ploughing inverts the topsoil, burying weeds and the remains of crop residues which may hamper subsequent cultivation, presents a fresh soil surface for weathering to produce a new seed bed, and loosens and aerates the soil. Plough depth varies according to soil conditions, but is typically between 150mm and 350mm (Nicholson 1980). Although it is rarely the intention to bring unweathered substrate, subsoil or parent bedrock into the ploughsoil through ploughing, in practice this happens regularly. Uneven soil depths caused by localized soil erosion, the direction of ploughing on slopes and incorrectly set ploughshares are the most common causes. Following ploughing, the land is allowed to weather naturally before being broken up to form a fine seed bed by harrowing and rolling. Some crops can be grown with minimum cultivation, but only in favourable soil conditions. Occasional deep-ploughing or pan-busting to improve soil drainage is closely associated with the process of cultivation.

Not all damage to archaeological monuments from cultivation is recent in date. It is clear that later prehistoric, Roman and medieval cultivation all caused major damage to earlier monuments (Bonney 1980).

Figure 6.21 - The cause and effect of ploughing on ancient monuments. (Top) The process of ploughing. (Right) Typical furrows. (Above) The resultant effect over a Roman mosaic at Stanwick, Raunds, Northamptonshire. *[Photographs: (Top and Right) Timothy Darvill; (Above) English Heritage Central Archaeology Service. Copyright reserved]*

However, the mechanization of arable agriculture this century has allowed the steady expansion of agricultural regimes into land which was formerly untilled and which contained previously unaffected ancient monuments. Moreover, it has led to the creation of larger fields, with reductions in the proportion of land used for boundaries and headlands (Westmacott and Worthington 1997, 109). Steadily increasing tractor-power means that sub-surface obstructions such as archaeological features can be cut through rather than forcing the plough to ride up over them.

Technical studies (Hinchliffe and Schadla-Hall 1980; Lambrick 1977) and simulations (Wainwright 1994; Boismier 1997) show that plough damage varies widely according to the local topography and geology, and that there are few general rules. Where colluvium or alluvium has been deposited the overburden may protect underlying deposits. Equally, however, where the soil cover is thin, for example on slopes, the plough will dig deeper into the underlying layers, and often this can be seen in earthworks as a spreading of material downslope. Systematically predicting where cultivation will be most damaging is not easy, although where it happens its effects are easy to see (Figure 6.21).

Numerous surveys of archaeology in relation to plough damage have been carried out in many parts of England (see APPENDIX M). All demonstrate that ploughing represents the most acute threat to monuments

within arable farmland (for example Hinchliffe and Schadla-Hall 1980; Groube and Bowden 1982), and recognize the intensification of cultivation during the late 1940s and 1950s. Monuments excavated either before the onset of serious plough damage or during the accelerated decay that it produces show that the information yield upon excavation is directly related to the extent of ploughing. This is very clearly illustrated by the three case studies of long barrows considered in Chapter 2.5. It is not, however, confined to substantial upstanding monuments.

At Sancton, Humberside, the re-excavation in 1976-80 of part of an Anglo-Saxon cremation cemetery that had previously been excavated about a century earlier, in 1873, by Canon Greenwell, and again in 1954-8 by W H Southern (Timby 1993, 249-51), provides a rare glimpse of a monument under decay through continuous ploughing. Although Greenwell found that many of the urns he uncovered were broken, most were reconstructible. By the later 1970s

> ploughing has smashed or scattered many of the urns deposited at a higher level or, has broken the upper parts leaving just the base-sherds and lower fill *in situ*. Those urns placed into the natural sand-filled solution hollows in the bedrock have mainly survived but are mostly cracked and highly compressed. (Timby 1993, 253)

Further cases of excavation on plough-damaged sites are included in APPENDIX M.

The RCHME carried out a survey in West Lindsey, Lincolnshire, which showed that between 1946 and 1988 over 50% of the upstanding archaeology of the medieval and later periods had been totally or partially destroyed (Everson *et al.* 1991, 56). This broadly accords with the MARS finding that perhaps as much as 47% of the land area known to have been occupied by monuments has disappeared over more or less this same period. In Sussex, a study of Neolithic flint mine sites revealed that, after 40-50 years of cultivation, monuments were almost unrecognizable, in comparison with their state when first identified (Holgate 1989).

Rates of change have also been examined. A study of Norfolk barrows showed that the annual loss averaged out at 190mm of height per year, and found that 33 out of 162 (20%) Scheduled round barrows had been flattened (Lawson 1981, 34).

Barrows of various sorts have been a favourite subject for study in other agricultural landscapes too. On the Cotswolds, a sample of 906 monuments surveyed in 1976-7 found that 38% were extensively affected by plough damage and a further 8% partially affected (Saville 1980; and see above Chapter 5.6.3). The same picture is repeated in the dozen or so surveys, mainly in southern England, reported in the volume *The past under the plough* (Hinchliffe and Schadla-Hall 1980). These can be supplemented by many others. In a survey of barrows on the south Dorset ridgeway in 1980, it was found that 16% of barrows had been ploughed out between 1954 and the time of the survey (Woodward 1980), a figure which is fairly low compared with other parts of southern England and serves to emphasize the effects of the differential onset of agricultural intensification. Further north, in Cleveland, 10% of round barrows had been ploughed out by the late 1970s (Crawford 1980, 76). Taking a different

approach, a study of archaeological monuments situated within Cambridgeshire County Farms Estate in 1989 (Malim 1990, xxvi) revealed plough damage at 40 out of 113 monuments surveyed (35%).

Figure 6.22 shows a generalized plot of the level of arable cultivation in England since the early 1940s in relation to the destruction of MARS Monuments by agriculture in each decade 1940s to 1990s. Quantification is by monument count (blue bars) and area losses (red bars) where all losses between 1945 and 1995 have been proportioned by decade.

Over the last 50 years the general level of arable cultivation in England has been gradually falling, with minor fluctuations along the way. Set against this, the loss of archaeological monuments has been climbing steadily, more than 25% of all losses through cultivation occurring in the last decade or so. The reason for this pattern is simply that the destructive effect on archaeology of arable cultivation is a cumulative process. Thus the cost now being paid in terms of vanished archaeology is partly the long-term result of heavy cultivation during the early post-war period followed by decades of intensive ploughing.

Currently, there are no effective controls on the incidence of cultivation over archaeological monuments (DoE 1995a). Changes of land-use which involve bringing land into cultivation fall outside the town and country planning system, and for Scheduled Monuments there is a class consent for the continuation of cultivation. Archaeologically, unless monuments are taken out of cultivation, the loss rate will, however, continue to rise because of continuing attrition. Two actions need to be taken in relation to cultivation. First, it is becoming increasingly critical that monuments that are not under cultivation now are prevented from coming into cultivation in the future. It is clear from the numerous resource assessment reports cited above and in APPENDIX A that once cultivation begins the rate of

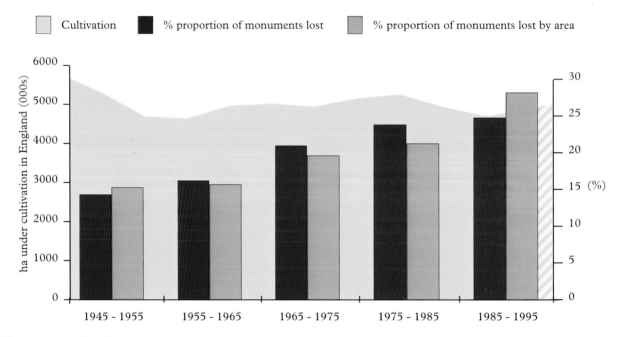

Figure 6.22 - Combination chart showing the outright and cumulative loss of MARS Monuments since 1940 resulting from arable cultivation and related causes. Quantified by gross counts and combined area and set against the changing extent of arable land in England. *[Source: MARS Aerial Photographic and Field Survey Programmes with information from SMRs]*

decay is greatly accelerated. Second, monuments already in cultivation need to be brought into less hostile land-use regimes wherever possible. The land area is not great. Within the MARS sample it is estimated that about 83.3km^2 of archaeologically sensitive land represented within the Current Area of the extant resource was under cultivation in 1995. Extrapolated out this gives a national figure of approximately 16,66km^2. For comparison it may be noted that there was 5449km^2 of agricultural land under Set-Aside in 1995 (MAFF *et al.* 1996, table 3.2). On the basis of the MARS sample, if cultivation continues at present levels it will affect approximately 17% of the total number of monuments in the extant recorded resource, 35% of the land area occupied by the extant recorded resource.

6.8.2 Development and urbanization

The archaeological resource in an urban or developed setting is as diverse as its rural counterpart, and in some cases is simply the rural archaeological resource which has been encroached upon by urban expansion. In addition to the range of above-ground features such as defensive walls, buildings, gates, castles, monasteries and churches, there are likely to be buried deposits and layers many metres thick, as well as anything which stood on the site before the town was built and thus become sealed within or under it (Figure 6.23).

Overall, urban expansion and development are estimated to account for 27% of observed cases of wholesale destruction and 9% of piecemeal loss. To this must be added the effects of building repairs and alterations which account for a further 20% of all monuments destroyed and 16% of piecemeal losses. Building alterations represent the single biggest hazard to standing buildings and structures, accounting for 43% of recorded instances of wholesale or piecemeal loss. Development of various kinds is cited as the reason for archaeological excavation in

Figure 6.23 - Southampton City Walls. The line of the medieval walls on the west side of the town. The adjacent redevelopment programme falls outside the town walls and has been the subject of various archaeological evaluations. *[Photograph: Timothy Darvill. Copyright reserved]*

Figure 6.24 - Excavations in advance of housing development at Dunston Park, Thatcham, Berkshire, in 1991, viewed from the north-west. An early Iron Age round house represented by a circle of postholes can be seen in the centre of the view. *[Photograph by Elaine A Wakefield. Copyright Trust for Wessex Archaeology Limited]*

advance of destruction in 35% of cases among all monuments and 10% of cases involving Scheduled Monuments.

As far as archaeology is concerned, the problem with urban expansion and development is the process of construction and in particular the groundworks associated with it, for example the removal of made-ground (which usually contains the archaeological deposits), foundation construction, and the digging of service trenches, lift-shaft pits and basements. All of these are single events or closely connected chains of events tied to the development or redevelopment of property. Experience suggests that, where development is not intensive, some deposits may remain undisturbed, but as a rule destruction is total unless a mitigation strategy has been implemented (Figure 6.24).

Numerous resource assessment studies for towns and cities across England have been undertaken, many published only as circulated reports. APPENDIX A provides a select bibliography of known examples arranged by Government Office Regions. One of the most influential studies of archaeological losses through urban development was published as a book entitled *The erosion of history* (Heighway 1972). The purpose was to obtain a rough idea of which ancient towns in Britain would be significantly affected by development in the following ten years (i.e. *c*.1972-82). Some 702 towns in England were considered during the survey, which concluded that nearly one-fifth of historic English towns (127 examples) were so seriously threatened that little of their archaeology would remain 20 years hence (i.e. *c*.1992) (Heighway 1972, 30). In the event, the situation was probably less dire than anticipated, not least because the report itself galvanized action which brought about the preservation of at least some areas that would otherwise have been destroyed. There have been losses, of course. In Gloucester, Gloucestershire, for example, one of the towns listed by Heighway and subsequently studied by her in further

detail, some 58% of the historic core had been affected by development by 1974 (Heighway 1974, 2) but relatively few areas, amounting to less than a further 5%, have been affected since. In York approximately 20% of the historic core had been destroyed before 1983 (Andrews 1984).

Figure 6.25 shows how the area of land given over to urban settlement (i.e. built-up land) has increased since 1940, set against the percentage of all MARS Monuments destroyed by urban development of various kinds per decade. The quantification is by monument count (blue bars) and area losses (red bars).

The rate of urban expansion has been steady over the last 50 years, increasing overall from 1.4m hectares in 1945 to nearly 1.9 million hectares in 1995. One major contributor to this expansion has been house construction: between 1984 and 1995, 1,833,300 new dwellings were constructed, the value of this work being £6026 million for 1995 alone (DoE 1995a). In addition, an average of 30 new superstores were opened each year through the 1980s, the total by the late 1980s being well over 500 stores (Dawson 1995). Out of town, and edge of town, development was a major contributor to urban expansion during the 1980s and early 1990s (BDPP 1994). Some indication of the current pace of development can be gauged from the fact that in 1996/7 local planning authorities in England received an estimated 473,000 planning applications, a submission rate of 1300 per day throughout the year (DETR 1998, table 1).

The destruction rate of archaeological monuments is not uniform, however, with relatively small losses until the 1960s, after which the rate of loss seems to have risen more steeply than the increase in urban land-take. The main reason for this trend is probably that urban development from the later 1960s onwards was far more destructive than development of the immediate post-war period, which often had minimal ground penetration.

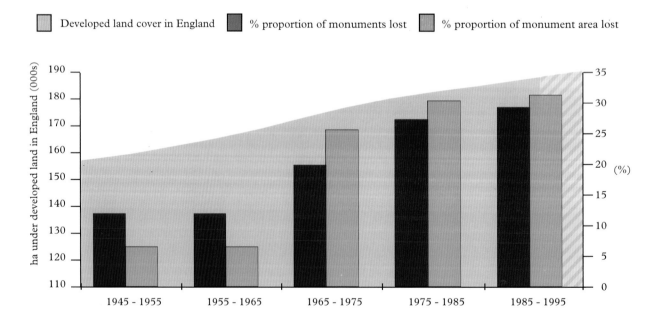

Figure 6.25 - Combination chart showing the outright and cumulative loss of MARS Monuments since 1940 resulting from development and related causes. Quantified by gross counts and combined area and set against the changing extent of urban and developed land in England. *[Source: MARS Aerial Photographic and Field Survey Programmes with information from SMRs]*

Where early post-war developments have been re-excavated in more recent decades, the extent of damage can be gauged.

Urban expansion is set to continue rising over the next decade, with two main foci. First is the continued development of greenfield sites on the edge of urban areas. This affects mostly what is essentially rural archaeology, and is developed for housing and light industry. Second will be brownfield land (urban vacant land) within existing settlements (*cf.* DoE 1992b). However, compared with some periods in history, urban growth is predicted to be relatively modest between 1995 and the year 2001. It is expected that the area of urban land in England will rise to 11% of total land area by 2016 (DoE 1995b). This means that an average of 68km^2 per year between will be developed over that period. Estimates based on MARS figures for the average density of archaeological monuments in England (2.25 per km^2) suggest that this expansion will impact on at least 153 archaeological monuments per year.

Since most urbanization and related development falls within the town and county planning system mechanisms and procedures already exist with PPG16 (DoE 1990a) for a considered archaeological input to the selection of areas for development and the incorporation of suitable responses during the process of design and construction. Studies of the first few years of the operation of PPG16 concluded that it was working well (Pagoda Projects 1992; Roger Tym and Partners 1995).

For archaeology there are two major implications of the anticipated scale of development. First is the continuing need for assessment and evaluation studies in association with the planning process. Second is the need for the development and execution of effective mitigation strategies within urban areas in order to maximize the archaeological return from excavations and watching briefs. Closely associated with these are the need continually to review the effectiveness of PPG16 in providing an appropriate system to integrate archaeology and planning, and the need for urban strategy documents to guide preservation measures, research and public access to archaeology.

6.8.3 Road-building

Road-building is estimated to account for 9% of observed cases of monument destruction and 4% of cases of monument damage. Archaeologically, the problem with road-building is the process of construction itself, together with ancillary works such as landscaping, drainage and screening (Figure 6.26). The average size of new roads or upgrades along the line of earlier roads has increased considerably in the last 20 years, so that the average three-lane motorway corridor (i.e. three lanes in each direction plus verges and fencing) is now 42m wide, a dual carriageway typically has a 28m wide corridor, and even a conventional A-class road will take a strip of land about 14m wide (DTp 1996a). To this must be added the land-take at junctions. For the purposes of environmental assessment, road-building also involves substantial quantities of material, especially aggregates, which have to be quarried and thus have their own impact. Like urban development, the destruction caused by road-building is generally total within the construction corridor unless some specific mitigation is attempted, for example

Figure 6.26 - Road-building on the A27 Westhampnett Bypass near Chichester, West Sussex, in 1992, looking east. The linear extent of the scheme is clearly visible and in its path lies later prehistoric, Romano-British and Anglo-Saxon cemeteries and ritual monuments. *[Photograph: Steve Patterson. Copyright reserved]*

running the road along an embankment over the top of the archaeological remains.

Archaeological interest in road-building programmes has a long history in England, perhaps because of the very public and often controversial nature of the schemes themselves. This has resulted in a large number of excavation and survey programmes prompted by or connected with road-building, a selection of which is listed in APPENDIX M. One of the most significant early examples of archaeology integrated with road-building was during the motorways programme of the 1960s and early 1970s. Fowler (1979; 1980) has reviewed the achievements of work on the M4, M5 and M40, both in terms of the results as a contribution to archaeological knowledge and in terms of the quantity and quality of remains destroyed. What is clear is that destruction frequently involves the total loss of some monuments, mainly small single monuments, and the partial loss of other, larger monuments. In the case of these larger monuments it is not always possible to know how much of the monument has gone, or indeed how the portion that has been destroyed relates to the remainder. Along the 252km of motorway considered by Fowler in his review, some 236 separate monuments were discovered, an average density of roughly one monument per kilometre of road. This average hides a number of localized variations in the incidence of monuments, which range from 0.7 monuments per kilometre along the M4 in Wiltshire to 1.2 monuments per kilometre along the M5 in Somerset. Other road schemes suggest even higher densities of monuments per kilometre in some parts of the country. The M3 in Hampshire, for example, revealed an average density of 4.1 monuments per kilometre along a 19.6km stretch of defined corridor (Biddle and Emery 1973). The same figures apply whether future work applies to new-build or to widening schemes that involve land-take along existing corridors.

In 1990 a study was undertaken by Environmental Resources Limited (ERL 1990) of the potential impact of new road proposals put forward by the Government in a White Paper entitled *Roads for prosperity* (DTp 1989). The White Paper advocated a roads programme costing more than £12bn and involving 21 motorway projects together with nearly 150 trunk road improvements. It was estimated that the combined land-take of the programme would be approximately 14,814ha. The ERL study estimated that the roads programme would involve the total or partial destruction of at least 844 monuments, the archaeological excavation and reporting of which would cost in the order of £73 million at 1990 prices (ERL 1990, 81).

Most of the schemes outlined in *Roads for prosperity* (DTp 1989) and its successor *Trunk roads, England: into the 1990s* (DTp 1990) have since been scrapped, although funding for archaeological work in connection with road schemes has continued for projects in progress. Since 1993 the Department of Transport has taken responsibility for financing assessment programmes and mitigation works for archaeological monuments affected by road schemes. Moreover, guidance on archaeological matters relating to road-building has been published as part of the *Design manual for roads and bridges* (Volume 1)

and under the auspices of environmental assessment regulations (DTp 1993), and the role of tunnels to overcome environmental and archaeological difficulties considered (POST 1997). The Highways Agency spent some £2,245,000 on twelve archaeological projects in 1993-4 (Highways Agency 1995), while in 1994-5 some 15 major archaeological projects connected with road schemes were carried out at a cost of about £800,000 (Highways Agency 1996).

Figure 6.27 shows the increasing level of new road construction from before 1940 to 1995 and beyond on the basis of present estimates outlined in Government expenditure plans. The marked increases in construction after 1960 can clearly be seen. In 1996 there were 280,527km of road in England compared with 238,056km in 1966. The greatest increase had been in the building of motorways, from 618km in 1966 to 2747km in 1995. The current total can be broken down into 2747km of motorway, 5360km of dual carriageway, 28,054km of single carriageway and 82,541km of non-principal routes, mainly B and C class roads (DTp 1996b). Year on year, construction rates vary greatly; in 1990, for example, 263km of motorway and trunk road was started (229km completed) while in 1995 only 151km of the same type was added (DTp 1996b).

Set against this pattern is the loss of archaeological monuments as a result of road-building. The blue bars on Figure 6.27 show losses per decade as a percentage of all MARS Monuments destroyed by road-building; the red bars show the decade by decade losses by land area. In numerical terms the rise seems broadly to parallel the increases in road construction, the changing relative heights of the two bars being a reflection of increasing road size taking larger slices of land.

Tight controls exist over the planning and construction of road schemes. Major schemes are subject to Environmental Assessment procedures and there is good experience within archaeology of dealing with these

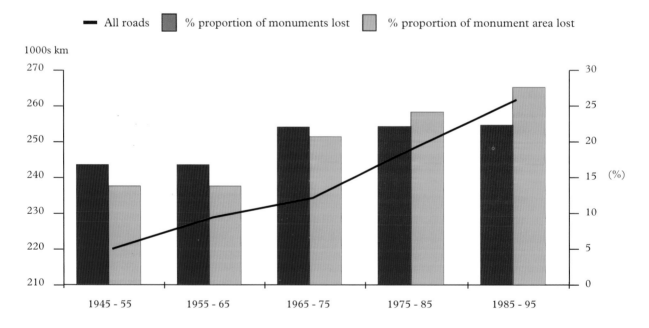

Figure 6.27 - Combination chart showing the outright and cumulative loss of MARS Monuments since 1940 resulting from road-building programmes in relation to the length of road in England (all classes). Quantified by gross counts and combined area. *[Source: MARS Aerial Photographic and Field Survey Programmes with information from SMRs]*

(Ralston and Thomas 1993); smaller schemes fall within the planning system and also the Highway Agency's own development and consultation procedures. In recent years archaeological considerations have become fully integrated into the road-building process.

Road construction will continue over the next decade, although at what scale is not clear. Plans announced in 1990 provided for work on about 4000km of new-build and on-line improvement during the 1990s (DTp 1990). At an average of one monument per kilometre, the proposed programme spread over a 10 year period would impact on about 400 monuments per year.

6.8.4 Mineral extraction

Mineral extraction, especially sand and gravel working in the major river valleys of southern and eastern England, is estimated to account for 12% of observed cases of monument destruction and 2% of cases of monument damage. Mineral extraction is cited as the reason for archaeological excavation in advance of destruction in 2% of cases among all monuments and 5% of cases involving Scheduled Monuments. These figures do not, however, adequately reflect the nature or scale of the archaeology represented in the kind of countryside typically exploited for gravel. What may be treated for record purposes as one monument typically covers several square kilometres and comprise many separate foci (Figure 6.28).

Archaeologically, the problem with mineral extraction is usually the preparatory groundworks (topsoil stripping and the removal of any overburden) and the removal of the mineral and aggregates themselves. The loss is usually total within the area of the quarry, although around the edge the working may slice portions off monuments that extend into unaffected land. Associated tipping and soil storage/disposal are also hazards.

Figure 6.28 - Standlake, Oxfordshire. Aerial view showing excavations by the Oxfordshire Archaeological Unit in August 1986. Within the area stripped for excavation numerous enclosure boundaries and pits can be seen by their dark-coloured fills. The advancing gravel quarry can be seen to the left. *[Photograph: Timothy Darvill. Copyright reserved]*

Archaeological interest in mineral workings in general, and gravel pits in particular, has a long history in England, and the threat posed by this hazard has been recognized from the earliest times. In the 1950s, the Sand and Gravel Association of Great Britain published a pamphlet entitled *Gravel pits and archaeology* which highlighted the need for co-operation between archaeologists and minerals operators. The true magnitude of the problem was not widely appreciated until the publication in 1960 of a study by the RCHME entitled *A matter of time. An archaeological survey of the river gravels of England*. This report highlighted the urgency of

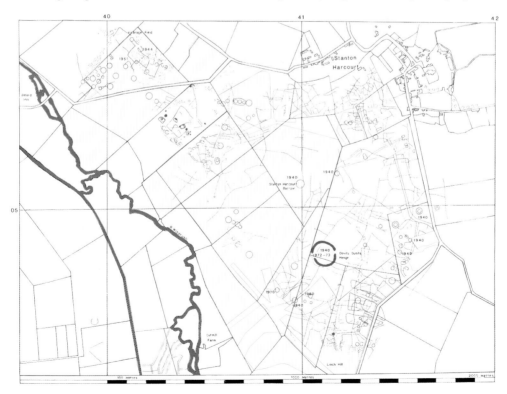

Figure 6.29 - Map showing the extent of gravel extraction around Stanton Harcourt, Oxfordshire, in relation to archaeological features recorded mainly by aerial photography. *[After Benson and Miles 1974, figure 12 with additions. Copyright reserved]*

excavating areas threatened by gravel extraction. Subsequently, detailed surveys of a number of areas where gravel extraction was prevalent were carried out, especially along the Thames valley (see APPENDIX A.3).

One of these resource assessments deals with the upper Thames valley and highlights as a case study the exploitation of gravel around Stanton Harcourt (Benson and Miles 1974). In an area of 168ha known to be rich in cropmark evidence of flattened monuments, quarrying between 1940 and 1970 destroyed outright 57% of the recorded resource and substantially damaged a further 35%. Only 8% of the original extent of the monuments recorded here remained intact in 1974, all of them affected by ploughing (Figure 6.29). Since 1974, further gravel quarrying has taken place in the area, necessitating the removal of the concrete runways of a Second World War airfield as well as archaeological excavations over a wide area (Barclay *et al.* 1995). Much the same can be seen further down the Thames at Dorchester on Thames (Benson and Miles 1974; Whittle *et al.* 1992), and Yarnton, Oxfordshire, where more than 10ha have been fully excavated, 105ha sampled, and a further 182ha examined by field walking (Hey 1997). Similar cases can be identified in most other major river valleys in southern and eastern England (Fulford and Nichols 1992).

APPENDIX M lists a selection of detailed studies into the effects of mineral extraction on particular monuments and areas, and includes some reports on excavations and surveys to illustrate the nature and extent of the archaeological monuments revealed as a result of projects associated with or prompted by mineral extraction programmes. Some of the largest excavations ever carried out in England have been associated with gravel extraction, amongst them: Mucking, Essex (Jones *et al.* 1968; Jones 1974; Clark 1993), Claydon Pike,

Gloucestershire (Miles 1983), and Maxey, Cambridgeshire (Pryor *et al.* 1985) to name but three.

Figure 6.30 shows the pattern of sand and gravel extraction over the period 1945 to 1995 measured in terms of output in relation to estimates of monument loss by decade over the same period. Quantifications are based on raw counts of the number of monuments lost (blue bars) and the land area of recorded archaeology lost (red bars) per decade as a percentage of all losses to this hazard. The scale of losses through mineral extraction, especially in the 1970s and 80s can be clearly seen.

Since the mid 1980s there has been a slight but progressive decline in sand and gravel output (DoE 1994a), although this has yet to come through in the figures for monument losses. The total area of land in England with planning permission for surface mineral workings in 1994 was 94,025ha, covering some 3294 individual extraction sites, 2115ha less than in 1988 (DoE 1991; 1996c). The figure includes all mineral workings and areas for the surface disposal of mineral working deposits which have valid planning permissions, including those operated by virtue of being permitted under General Development Orders and Interim Development Orders (DoE 1998). The six most extensive mineral types - sand and gravel, ironstone, limestone, clay/shale, opencast coal, and peat - account for 80% of the total permitted area (DoE 1996c, ix). In 1994, 50,149ha were worked but not restored (53% of the total permitted area), a reduction of 2438ha since 1988 (71,802ha were recovered by reclamation but by this time they had, of course, been archaeologically sterilized). In terms of surface disposal of mineral working deposits, 14,480ha of land were permitted for disposal of spoil in 1994, 3491ha less than in 1988. Of these, 169 sites were associated with colliery spoil disposal, 113 with sand and gravel, and 99

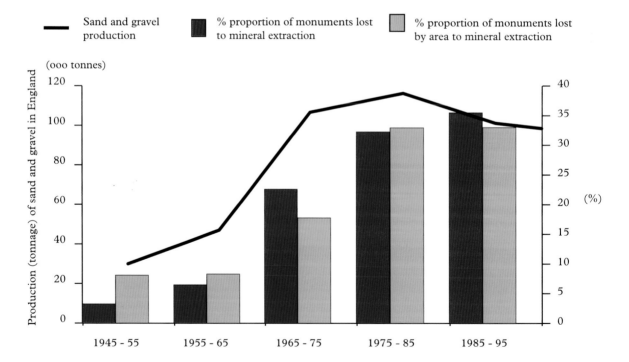

Figure 6.30 - Combination chart showing the outright and cumulative loss of MARS Monuments since 1940 resulting from sand and gravel extraction and related causes. Quantified by gross counts and combined area and set against the changing levels of sand and gravel production in England. *[Source: MARS Aerial Photographic and Field Survey Programmes with information from SMRs. Sample: n= 31]*

with limestone and dolomite. Site aftercare accounted for some 41,132ha in 1994 (an increase of 20,052ha since 1988), with agriculture the most common aftercare use (66%), followed by amenity (27%) and forestry (8%) (DoE 1996b; DoE 1996c, 20 and 22).

Mineral working is a feature of large areas of designated countryside (notably AONBs and NPs). In 1994 some 3909ha were recorded within National Parks (mainly vein minerals, limestone, igneous rock and sandstone) and 4524ha within Areas of Outstanding Natural Beauty (mainly sand and gravel, chalk, limestone and clay/shale). This represents 9% of the total permitted area in England (DoE 1996c, table 8.1).

Mineral extraction is increasingly subject to tight controls through Environmental Assessment and the town and country planning system. Although the areas are large, field evaluation is widely deployed to deal with the assessment of land being considered for mineral working (Darvill *et al.* 1995, 13-15). A Code of Practice on archaeology has been agreed by minerals operators (CBI 1991).

Mineral extraction will continue at fairly predictable levels well into the next century. Projections for the next decade suggest that anticipated demand will cause output to rise again, at least to 2006 (DoE 1994a, paragraph 26). Although there is no simple relationship between output and land-take, an average of 60,000 tons of aggregate per hectare provides a rough guide to the likely impact of sand and gravel workings on the archaeological resource. Using MARS estimates of monument density, anticipated annual outputs of 86m tonnes will impact on, and most likely destroy, at least 32 monuments per year.

Figure 6.31 - Excavations at the Knights Templar preceptory of Temple Newsam, Leeds, West Yorkshire in advance of opencast coal mining. *[Photograph: P. Gwilliam, West Yorkshire Archaeology Service. Copyright reserved]*

Sand and gravel is not the only kind of mineral working with significant archaeological implications. Stone extraction is found in many areas, and open-cast coal-mining in the north Midlands and Yorkshire (Figure 6.31).

6.8.5 Natural erosion and related processes
Action by water, waves, rivers, frost, wind, land-slip, soil-loss, animal activity, visitor erosion, geomorphological and related factors account for up to 5% of observed cases of wholesale destruction and 24% of cases of piecemeal monument loss. Standing buildings and small single monuments have the highest casualty rates from this hazard.

The problem with natural erosion is that it covers a wide range of phenomena. As can be seen from APPENDIX M, very few studies have been carried out in relation to these threats to archaeology, although they have been considered in the context of monument management (Berry and Brown 1994). The only real exception is the investigation of erosion on the coastal fringe and inter-tidal zone undertaken during the 1990s (Fulford *et al.* 1997; Anon 1997d).

Figure 6.32 - Aerial view of Ringborough Battery, Aldbrough, Humberside. The artillery battery was opened in 1941; the gun mountings can now be seen at the foot of the cliff. *[Photograph RCHME. Copyright reserved]*

Coastal erosion is the most widespread form of natural erosion (Figure 6.32) and within the British Isles is by no means confined to the English coastline (e.g. Ashmore 1993). At recorded monuments losses through cliff falls or wave-action can be predicted in terms of the inevitability of loss occurring, although the exact timing is usually uncertain. At major recorded monuments such as Hengistbury Head, Dorset (Cunliffe 1987; Barton 1992), or Belle Tout, East Sussex (Bradley 1970), or Brean Down, Avon (Bell 1990), the loss of areas of monument is an almost daily occurrence. Coastal erosion can also lead to the discovery of previously unrecorded monuments (e.g. Hardie 1994, 6-7), usually at more or less the moment they are destroyed unless special arrangements can be made for conservation and management.

Other geomorphological processes hostile to archaeological monuments include land-slips, soil-cover loss, and meandering watercourses that cut into monuments (Figure 6.33). All of these are relatively rare, although locally significant where they occur. Equally so are the effects of freak atmospheric conditions or weather patterns. Tree throw had widespread effects in southern

Figure 6.33 - Huntspill River, Westhay, Somerset, cutting through Romano-British salterns and settlements in the Somerset Levels. The eroding banks of the river are allowing archaeological layers to be washed away. *[Photograph: Timothy Darvill. Copyright reserved]*

Figure 6.35 - Footpath erosion. Painswick Beacon, Gloucestershire. An Iron Age hillfort now incorporated within a golf-course with public access to trig-point situated on top of the prehistoric ramparts. *[Photograph: Timothy Darvill. Copyright reserved]*

England after the storms of October 1987 and January 1990, damaging ancient woodlands, historic parks and gardens, and even prehistoric barrows (English Heritage 1997c; Cleal and Allen 1994). More unusually still, on 26th October 1996, lightning hit a standing stone on the western fringes of Exmoor in north Devon, shattering it and scattering dozens of pieces all around and up to 20m away (Anon 1997e).

Animal activity, particularly burrowing by rabbits and badgers, is extremely widespread on archaeological monuments (Figure 6.34). In general it is fairly transitory within the life-span of an individual monument, but it does have potentially serious consequences for the integrity of the stratigraphy. At a round barrow near Beckhampton, Wiltshire, the problem of a resident badger population was compounded by illegal digging connected with badger baiting which resulted in a hole 2.1m long by

0.96m wide and 0.58m deep (Anon 1993a, 29-30).

Visitor erosion resulting in the loss of vegetation-cover and downward soil erosion was noted at 37 MARS Monuments, mostly in the form of worn footpaths (Figure 6.35). Studies of this problem have tended to focus on the spectacular monuments, but it is a widespread problem. Headline figures relating to visitor levels for monuments tend to be for heavily promoted sites, mainly within the 1% of monuments for which entrance is charged. These relatively few monuments carry the brunt of visitor use. Some 17.3m tourist arrivals were recorded in the UK in 1989, and 21m in 1994. This equated to an industry-wide income of £12.1m for 1989. It is estimated that 76,000 of the total of 1.5m employed in tourism-related industries were employed specifically in libraries, museums and other cultural activities (Wisniewski 1997, table 6.2).

Archaeological monuments are among the most

Figure 6.34 - Animal erosion on ancient monuments. A Bronze Age bowl barrow under pasture in the Winterbourne Stoke Crossroads Cemetery, south-west of Stonehenge, Wiltshire. This large ditched barrow shows evidence of widespread impact from rabbit infestation. *[Photograph: Timothy Darvill. Copyright reserved].*

Figure 6.36 - Mardale Reservoir, Cumbria, in 1984. Traces of ancient fields, roads and enclosures can be seen below the usual water level. *[Photograph RCHME. Copyright reserved]*

visited places in England, although they are not always promoted as such. In 1994 the Tower of London was the most visited historic site charging admission with 2,407,000 visitors. Other notable sites were Windsor Castle with 1,091,000 visitors and Stonehenge with 607,000 visitors. Of course many visits to archaeological monuments in rural areas are unrecorded, although they could be numerous. Visitor erosion was noted as a cause of damage that accounted for less than 1% of all reported damage. It is, however, a localized problem evident at many popular monuments, particularly those enhanced with tourist facilities. Moreover, visitor numbers for all kinds of archaeological sites look set to remain stable or perhaps rise slightly in line with estimates of increasing leisure time (Potts 1995; Leisure Consultants 1997) and the active promotion of new schemes to make major monuments such as Hadrian's Wall and Stonehenge even more accessible to the public (Fowler 1997).

Natural erosion and related processes will continue over the next decade, and while a certain amount can be predicted with reference to specific monuments, it is in the nature of these hazards that they are unpredictable. They also lie outside any kind of control system that could be conceived, and even monitoring is difficult. Moreover, as already indicated, the research base for describing the problem and identifying possible solutions is not yet fully established, and this needs to be addressed urgently.

6.8.6 *Localized and lesser causes of damage to monuments*

Vandalism and metal-detecting are both very difficult to quantify during a survey like MARS because of their transitory nature. Taken together they appear to affect less than 1% of monuments, but this is certainly an underestimate. A recent detailed study of metal detecting in England concluded that 'archaeological sites are suffering significant damage from unregulated metal

Figure 6.37 - Pipeline archaeology. A section of the Esso Midline near Avebury, Wiltshire. Overall, the pipeline runs for 220km from Fawley, Hampshire to Seisdon, Staffordshire. About 700 archaeological features were investigated during its construction in 1985. *[Photograph: Timothy Darvill. Copyright reserved]*

detecting', and notes that at least 188 Scheduled Monuments are believed to have been damaged by detectorists between 1988 and 1994, when the study was undertaken (Dobinson and Denison 1995). However, 188 Scheduled Monuments represent only just over 1% of Scheduled Monuments, a figure which would not be at odds with the MARS findings.

Archaeological monuments face numerous other hazards too diverse for easy classification: the list is almost endless. Reservoir construction involves the flooding of monuments which sometimes causes their accelerated decay and in other cases preserved them (Figure 6.36). Pipelines and service trenches are well known (Figure 6.37), although once they have been back-filled and covered by vegetation they can be very hard to find as visible causes of damage. A case at Littlejohns Barrow, Cornwall, in 1992 involved both a cable trench and a haul road running right through the barrow (Johns and Herring 1994).

For the period immediately prior to 1945, the impact of war damage on archaeological monuments and historic buildings must also be considered (O'Neil 1948; Anon 1949). Not only was damage wrought by bombing, but the construction of defensive works and military infrastructure such as airfields, ordnance factories, camps and hospitals took its toll too. More than 14,000 separate schemes were put forward by the War Department between 1938 and 1942 (O'Neil 1948, 21). Some sites were destroyed without record, for example a long barrow in Hampshire, parts of Cissbury Camp, West Sussex, and two Saxon cemeteries near Peterborough, Cambridgeshire. Despite the pressures of war, more than 47 monuments were excavated in advance of being damaged or destroyed by military works, 36 of them in advance of airfield developments. During the same period 1943-5 there were a further 12 excavations at monuments threatened by the need to increase outputs from gravel pits, stone quarries, and open cast coal mines. A programme of publication was also set in place (Grimes 1960).

In looking at monument damage and loss it is

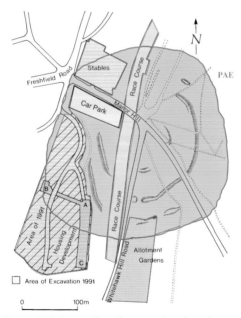

Figure 6.38 - Plan of Whitehawk Camp, Brighton, East Sussex, showing the extent of the Neolithic enclosure (PAE) in relation to various developments that collectively serve to diminish the preserved areal extent of the monument very considerably. See also Figure 1.1. *[After Russell and Rudling 1996, figure 3]*

important to remember that many different hazards may impact on the same monument over the course of time so that piecemeal destruction in particular may have a range of causes. Whitehawk Camp, a Neolithic causewayed enclosure on the outskirts of Brighton, East Sussex, illustrates such a situation very well. Shortly after the enclosure was first discovered, Cecil Curwen noted that

> unfortunately the site has suffered sadly under the encroachment of allotments, and some of it has been levelled in connection with the race-course. being situated, too, right on the edge of a large town, the danger of further destruction by building is ever present. (Curwen 1930, 30)

Figure 1.1 shows an aerial view of the monument soon after the time Curwen was writing and more recently in 1995. The contrast is clear. Figure 6.38 shows a plan of the monument in relation to the intrusions made into it. Since the 1930s, the roads across the monument have been widened, the race-course further extended, new stables built, further allotments added, and in 1991, a housing estate built (Russell and Rudling 1996).

6.9 Visibility and monument damage

Visibility may be a factor in the extent to which monuments are being damaged. Tables 6.16-6.18 show analyses of visibility in relation to the defined causes of damage discussed above for the three main monument character types. Among earthwork monuments over 77% of observations of agricultural damage related to monuments which were not visible at ground level, although more than 14% of observed cases of damage related to earthwork monuments that were either visible or barely visible.

Table 6.16 - Visibility of MARS earthwork Monuments by identified hazards causing piecemeal loss or damage. *[Source: MARS Field Survey Programme. Sample: n= 4392]*

Cause of damage	Visible %	Barely visible %	Not visible %	Obscured %	Total %
Agriculture	14.56	7.60	77.12	<1	100%
Building alteration	57.14	9.52	23.81	90.60	100%
Demolition	13.33	13.33	66.67	6.67	100%
Development and urbanization	18.65	3.60	77.15	6.67	100%
Forestry	16.67	8.97	52.56	21.79	100%
Industry	17.86	0	75.00	7.14	100%
Military damage	27.78	5.56	66.67	0	100%
Mineral extraction	9.38	1.56	89.06	0	100%
Natural process	60.67	7.20	23.07	9.07	100%
No damage	80.95	7.14	9.52	2.38	100%
Road-building	8.33	3.33	87.50	<1	100%
Unknown	27.60	6.00	60.40	6.00	100%
Vandalism	100.00	0	0	0	100%
Visitor erosion	85.29	11.76	2.94	0	100%
Wild animal	91.30	0	4.35	4.35	100%
All	**25.98%**	**6.83%**	**63.93%**	**3.26%**	**100%**

Table 6.17 - Visibility of MARS buildings and structures by identified hazards causing piecemeal loss or damage. *[Source: MARS Field Survey Programme. Sample: n= 5080]*

Cause of damage	Visible %	Barely visible %	Not visible %	Obscured %	Total %
Agriculture	15.62	7.21	76.28	<1	100%
Building alteration	92.95	<1	3.01	3.16	100%
Demolition	14.91	6.67	76.32	2.11	100%
Development and urbanization	19.30	2.52	76.09	2.06	100%
Forestry	7.14	0	57.14	35.71	100%
Industry	7.50	2.50	87.50	2.50	100%
Military damage	60.00	0	20.00	20.00	100%
Mineral extraction	7.02	0	92.98	0	100%
Natural process	89.46	2.82	4.73	2.99	100%
No damage	98.46	<1	1.03	<1	100%
Road-building	26.92	1.28	70.51	1.28	100%
Unknown	12.77	4.01	80.29	2.91	100%
Vandalism	88.24	0	5.88	5.88	100%
Visitor erosion	100.00	0	0	0	100%
Wild animal	100.00	0	0	0	100%
All	**60.87%**	**2.83%**	**33.76%**	**2.54%**	**100%**

Table 6.18 - The visibility of MARS landcuts by identified hazards causing piecemeal loss or damage. *[Source: MARS Field Survey Programme. Sample: n= 5246]*

Cause of damage	Visible %	Barely visible %	Not visible %	Obscured %	Total %
Agriculture	13.19	6.10	79.08	1.63	100%
Building alteration	84.95	2.15	10.75	2.15	100%
Demolition	34.22	5.88	55.08	4.81	100%
Development and urbanization	14.90	1.69	81.30	2.07	100%
Forestry	36.49	5.41	40.54	17.57	100%
Industry	11.11	0	84.44	4.44	100%
Military damage	10.00	10.00	80.00	0	100%
Mineral extraction	12.73	0.91	85.45	<1	100%
Natural process	73.83	4.92	15.46	5.79	100%
No damage	90.54	1.01	7.09	1.35	100%
Road-building	15.09	0.63	80.19	4.09	100%
Unknown	13.50	2.10	83.30	0.93	100%
Vandalism	89.66	0	6.90	3.45	100%
Visitor erosion	96.15	0	0	3.85	100%
Wild animal	100.00	0	0	0	100%
All	**34.46%**	**3.76%**	**58.81%**	**2.97%**	**100%**

6.10 Impact

The effect of damage on archaeological monuments depends on where it occurs, how it occurs, and what it does to the stratigraphy and environment. Whatever the form of a monument, decay processes rarely have equal impact over the entire area, affecting only specific parts. Damage to the structure, fabric or setting of a monument may happen across it, at specific points within its bounds, at the edges, or immediately around about (in the neighbourhood).

Impact is the general term used to describe the way in which actions affect monuments, and for MARS impact was a measure of the extent and position of damage inflicted on archaeological monuments in relation to their size and form. This was examined in two ways: in terms of the spatial distribution of damage across the surface of a monument and in relation to evidence for sub-surface damage.

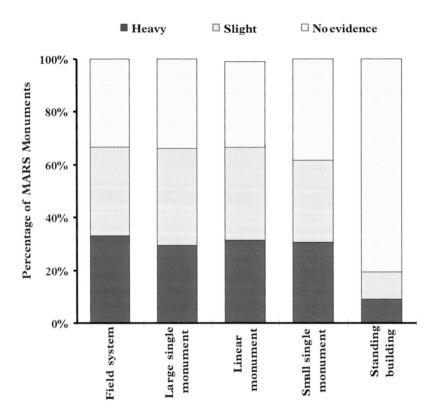

Figure 6.39 - Stacked bar charts showing sub-surface damage to MARS Monuments by monument form. *[Source: MARS Field Survey Programme. Sample: n= 14,164]*

Sub-surface damage is the most difficult to gauge, and as noted in Chapter 1 is mostly beyond the reach of field checking by direct surface observation. However, some indications of sub-surface damage can be seen, and the field surveyors recorded this where they encountered it. Three categories were established for recording:

No evidence: Simple statement of the fact that no evidence of sub-surface damage was visible to the field checking team at the time of visit. This does not mean that no sub-surface damage has taken or is taking place.

Slight: Traces of some sub-surface damage but of limited extent and depth penetration (e.g. tree roots, small-scale animal burrowing, normal ploughing, soil poaching etc.).

Heavy: Extensive traces of damage penetrating to a considerable depth (e.g. deep ploughing, drainage system installation, trenches and holes, tree throw, animal infestation (esp. badgers), scars, pitting).

Overall, no evidence one way or the other was reported for 44% of observations, 26% of observations being of heavy sub-surface damage, and 29% of slight sub-surface damage.

Figure 6.39 shows an analysis of sub-surface damage in relation to monument form. Except for standing buildings, all the forms show remarkably similar profiles, with field systems and linear monuments apparently suffering heavy sub-surface damage only slightly more than small single monuments and large single monuments. As might be expected, standing buildings show little evidence of sub-surface damage,

although this probably reflects in part the kind of work that may give rise to such damage and its relative invisibility to field surveyors (for example the replacement of floors, outside drainage works etc.).

Spatial impact is a factor of land-use. This is clearest in relation to large-scale arable farming (creating a potentially widespread impact), the encroachment of housing estates on monuments (neighbourhood impact), or multiple land-use over large monuments (potentially segmenting impact). Five main forms of impact were recognized for recording MARS Monuments:

Neighbourhood impact: all round rather than over a monument.

Peripheral impact: only the edges affected.

Localized impact: confined to a few discrete places.

Widespread impact: over all or most of a monument.

Segmenting impact: splitting a monument into discrete parts.

During the MARS Field Survey and Aerial Photographic Survey Programmes records were made of the observed impact of visible sources of damage on the monuments inspected. As with recording damage, the assessment of impact involved the careful scrutiny of the monument itself either on the ground or using aerial photographs.

Impact was measured in terms of the extent of decay processes in proportion to the area of the

Table 6.19 - Impact on MARS Monuments by monument form. *[Source: MARS Field Survey Programme. Sample: n= 13,868]*

Impact	Field systems %	Large single monuments %	Linear monuments %	Small single monuments %	Standing buildings %	All %
Widespread	87.3	72.1	79.2	81.0	41.9	**72.1**
Localized	4.3	9.9	6.8	8.7	38.0	**14.6**
No impact	4.4	12.5	8.1	6.8	15.6	**9.2**
Peripheral	1.4	2.9	1.9	1.8	2.0	**1.9**
Segmenting	2.2	1.6	3.3	1.1	1.0	**1.4**
Neighbourhood	<1	1.0	<1	<1	1.6	**<1**
Total	**100%**	**100%**	**100%**	**100%**	**100%**	**100%**

Table 6.20 - Impact on MARS earthwork Monuments by MARS region. *[Source: MARS Field Survey Programme. Sample: n= 4392]*

Impact	North West %	North East %	West Midlands %	East Midlands %	South West %	South East %	England %
Widespread	76.3	80	84.4	85.4	93.6	80.1	85.1
Localized	6.4	11	6.4	7.6	2.5	11.3	7.3
No impact	15	2.5	5.2	2	<1	5.8	3.3
Peripheral	1.7	3.5	<1	1.7	2.4	1.2	2.1
Segmenting	<1	2.9	2.3	2.8	<1	1.2	1.8
Neighbourhood	0	<1	<1	<1	<1	<1	<1
Total	**100%**	**100%**	**100%**	**100%**	**100%**	**100%**	**100%**

Table 6.21 - Impact on MARS buildings and structures by MARS region. *[Source: MARS Field Survey Programme. Sample= 5080]*

Impact	North West	North East	West Midlands	East Midlands	South West	South East	England
	%	%	%	%	%	%	%
Widespread	44.7	69.2	46.8	57.2	78.2	41.1	**57.0**
Localized	32.2	17.6	35.8	26.8	11.0	37.4	**25.3**
No impact	21.0	9.1	14.2	11.9	3.2	19.2	**12.7**
Peripheral	1.0	2.6	<1	1.2	3.6	1.1	**1.7**
Neighbourhood	<1	1.1	1.8	<1	3.4	<1	**1.3**
Segmenting	<1	<1	<1	2.4	<1	<1	**1.0**
Total	**100%**	**100%**	**100%**	**100%**	**100%**	**100%**	**100%**

Table 6.22 - Impact on MARS landcuts by MARS region. *[Source: MARS Field Survey Programme. Sample= xxxxx]*

Impact	North West	North East	West Midlands	East Midlands	South West	South East	England
	%	%	%	%	%	%	%
Widespread	67.5	73.5	68.2	78	89	79.9	**76.7**
No impact	18.7	9.9	13.1	7.1	4.7	12.1	**10.4**
Localized	10.6	9.4	14	10.9	2.2	7.1	**8.9**
Peripheral	1.5	5.4	1.5	1.4	1.9	<1	**2.1**
Segmenting	1.3	1.4	2.2	2.2	<1	0	**1.3**
Neighbourhood	<1	<1	<1	<1	1.1	<1	**<1**
Total	**100%**	**100%**	**100%**	**100%**	**100%**	**100%**	**100%**

monument. Thus the exact form or size of a monument did not matter as much as the precise location within the monument where one or more decay processes had caused a visible effect.

Table 6.19 shows an analysis of impact in relation to monument form. Widespread impact is the most prevalent type of impact on all forms except standing buildings, which are mainly affected by localized impacts. No discernible impact was observed on a small percentage of monuments, but 8% of linear monuments and 12% of large single monuments showed no impacts. There are some regional variations in the way that impacts affect different kinds of monuments, and Tables 6.20-6.22 show analyses of these for earthworks, buildings and structures, and landcuts. It is particularly noticeable that among earthworks widespread impact is very common in relation to other impacts in the South West, whereas in the North West widespread impact is less common and cases of no perceptible impact even more so.

6.11 Amelioration

The concept of amelioration is in almost direct opposition to that of damage. Amelioration occurs when the overall condition of a monument improves slightly over a period of time. This improvement does not refer to the archaeological deposits themselves, only to the circumstances in which a monument is preserved. For example, the abandonment of cultivation over a monument which is turned over to long-term grassland is amelioration, as is the backfilling of a quarry which threatened to swallow up a monument, or the rewatering of a traditionally wet monument that was drying out.

During the Field Survey Programme, evidence of amelioration was recorded as a simple yes/no on the basis of the visible evidence for actions that it was considered would enhance the long-term survival of the monument. Overall, 95% of observations failed to recognize evidence for amelioration. In the 5% of cases where amelioration was recognized, it was mostly among standing buildings and for small single monuments. Regional differences can also be seen, as Figure 6.40 shows. Both the national and regional pictures highlight a simplified view of ameliorative works over monuments. There is apparently more work of this nature taking place in the West Midlands and North West and less in the South West and North East. Ameliorative works clearly represent an element of monument conservation, but unless these are obvious they are difficult to record in the field and often hidden as a by-product of some other land-use process. Although the 'yes' returns are confirmed by observation, the same is not necessarily true of the 'no' returns: the fact that no amelioration was observed does not mean that no amelioration took place. The general picture in all regions is, however, that the majority of sites have not been subject to ameliorative actions in the recent past.

Further work is clearly required to investigate the nature of active processes which assist monument survival. However, the nature and effect of land-use is clearly important both in the processes of amelioration and in the most critical problem of survival and destruction. This is the subject of the next chapter.

Figure 6.40 - Map showing the incidence of amelioration work observed at MARS Monuments within each of the six MARS Regions. *[Source: MARS Field Survey. Sample: n= 13,426]*

7 Land-use change and archaeological monuments

The Wiltshire downs, or Salisbury Plain (as commonly call'd) for extent and beauty, is, without controversy, one of the most delightful parts of Britain. But in late years great encroachments have been made upon it by the plough, which threatens the ruin of this fine champain, and of all the monuments of antiquity thereabouts. Monuments, we can scarce say, whether more wonderful in themselves, more observed, or less understood!

(William Stukeley 1740, 1)

7.1 Land-use and archaeology

Land-use is fundamental to archaeological resource management for three main reasons: first, because it determines the incidence of monument discovery and thus the very nature of the recorded resource (see Chapter 4.6); second, because it is important in dictating the rate at which monuments decay; and third, because the future management of monuments must be tied sensitively to land utilization plans.

It is the last two of these matters that most concerned MARS and they provide the focus of this chapter. The influence of land-use on monuments is profound (Kains-Jackson 1880; Fowler 1977b; Darvill 1987) and well documented (e.g. RCHME 1979). Moreover, it has been recognized for a long time, as can be glimpsed from the words of Britain's first field archaeologist, William Stukeley, written in the eighteenth century at a time of growing agricultural surpluses and falling prices (Mathias 1969, 68), when even tracts of the Wiltshire Downs were brought under cultivation.

Land-use patterns are constantly, kaleidoscopically changing, each land parcel with its own shape and size having a history of change that may or may not match that of adjacent parcels. The documentation and quantification of, and generalization about, land-use change are therefore very complicated. Moreover, with few exceptions, only a little of the land-use history of a given monument can be glimpsed from available records. Evidence for earlier changes, and indeed an understanding of the land-use associated with the construction and use of a monument, can only be gathered by archaeological investigation. Environmental reconstruction work carried out on late Neolithic and Bronze Age ditch fills associated with early Neolithic long barrows shows how complex the picture can be (Evans 1990). Land-use changes at these sites included some which were confined to the monument itself and others of more widespread impact. All the examples studied by Evans developed a woodland cover, followed by episodes of cultivation and pasture. As this and other studies show, the present condition of the archaeological resource is the result not only of recent land-use, but also of practices extending back to the time of construction, use and abandonment of the monuments themselves.

In this chapter, five key dimensions of land-use are explored. First, current land-use patterns over and around monuments as revealed by the MARS Field Survey Programme are described. Second, the changing pattern of land-use on and around archaeological monuments over the last 50 years or so as documented by aerial photography is considered. Third, attention is directed to the five principal land-uses found at archaeological monuments with a view to looking at long-term trends in the incidence of these uses compared with their prevalence on and around the monuments. Fourth, the relationship of land-use to the survival of archaeological monuments is investigated. And, finally, the implications of land-use patterns for visibility and accessibility are considered. However, before turning to these matters, it is necessary to consider briefly the land-use classifications adopted for MARS and their relationship to existing studies.

7.2 Land and its classification

Within the discipline of archaeology there is no generally applicable land classification scheme tailored to the needs of archaeological resource management. Accordingly, extensive use is made of systems developed and established in other related disciplines, many of which have direct application for matters of archaeological concern and can be applied with little modification.

The history of land classification in England goes back to the late eighteenth century, when in 1793 the Government of George III set up the Board of Agriculture and Internal Improvement. One of the first acts of this Board was to commission a series of County Reports on the state of agriculture which included maps of each county showing crude distributions of soil regions and a classification of land based on soil texture (Stamp 1960, 102-3). Classification systems have come a long way since the eighteenth century, developing along several distinct parallel lines. Some of these provide the basis for classifying land-use at MARS Monuments, while others provide comparative data. A detailed examination of the links and relationships between current schemes in use across a wide spectrum of environmental studies has been published (Wyatt *et al.* 1995), although archaeological uses were not explicitly considered. In the following sub-sections, attention is directed to six main recognized types of land classification and their potential use in MARS.

7.2.1 Agricultural land classification

This system may appear to be a direct descendant of the maps produced by the Board of Agriculture and Internal Improvement in the late eighteenth century, but there is no direct connection between them. Between 1967 and 1974 the Research Group of the Land Service of ADAS carried out the first detailed agricultural land classification survey of England and Wales. Five grades of land were recognized, Grade 1 being the best and most versatile down to Grade 5 with severe limitations on use because of soil, relief, climate or a combination of factors. Maps at 1:63,360 scale (113 sheets covering England and Wales) show the provisional extents of these grades, and there are summary maps at 1:250,000 and 1:625,000 scale (ADAS 1968; 1977).

In future, the analysis of monument survival and condition in relation to agricultural land classification will be extremely important, especially at a regional or local scale, for predicting risk environments created by land-use capability (see Chapter 9.5). For MARS however, as the first study of its kind, this land classification was considered too detailed.

7.2.2 Land cover classifications

The classification of land on the basis of vegetation cover has been widely used, especially for biological and botanical studies. Few if any areas of England support wholly natural vegetation patterns, but semi-natural and anthropogenic habitats abound. English Nature has carried out habitat surveys with the aim of mapping semi-natural vegetation types and wildlife habitats over large areas of countryside. The work involves a combination of map inspection and rapid field survey (NCC 1990). Detailed botanical descriptions of each habitat are being prepared. The Institute of Terrestrial Ecology uses a land cover classification with 17 key cover types for its Countryside Surveys in 1978, 1984, 1990 and 2000 (Barr *et al.* 1993, 6).

As with agricultural land classifications, it will be important to consider the distribution of archaeological monuments in relation to land cover at a more detailed level of analysis than was attempted within MARS. As a prelude to this, a check was made to determine the overlap of MARS sample units with the locations of the 1km by 1km units sampled across England by Countryside Survey and its predecessors. Eight MARS sample units lay wholly or partly within the CS units. This was a useful exercise for the future potential integration of archaeological data-sets with information from environmental audits (for example the forthcoming Countryside Survey update, CS 2000).

7.2.3 Natural areas

Building on the experience of land cover classifications, English Nature developed an approach to the definition of natural areas by identifying inland and coastal areas with distinct geological, geomorphological and habitat zones. The work is based on interpreting Land Utilization Maps, Board of Agriculture reports and soil surveys. Ninety-two unique areas have been identified and characterized (English Nature 1993). In 1995, English Nature commissioned a pilot study to characterize farming practices in four Natural Areas with a view to describing and monitoring agricultural change and assessing the opportunities to achieve natural conservation objectives. This work has been reported for two areas: the

Lincolnshire Wolds, and Exmoor and the Quantocks (Cole *et al.* 1996).

Again, these will be of direct interest to archaeological resource management at a more detailed scale of analysis than MARS set out to achieve. Natural areas will be especially important in developing management plans that harmonize with nature conservation and coastal zone management.

7.2.4 Land-type

All land has certain general characteristics that determine, to a greater or lesser extent, the way in which it can be used and what agricultural regimes are possible. The most obvious and long-term restrictions arise from combinations of physical characteristics: topography, geology, pedology, climate, aspect and situation. History, tradition and ownership also impose restrictions on the way some land is used.

Distinctive permutations of physical characteristics can give rise to recognizable landscape types which form general, but not necessarily discrete, regions, for example upland, coastland, wetland, moorland and so on. For archaeological resource management this kind of classification is especially valuable because the categories identified relate closely to the three issues identified above (7.1), namely monument discovery patterns, natural decay trajectories and monument management possibilities. Thus in preparing *Ancient monuments in the countryside* (Darvill 1987) use was made of nine land-type categories: wetland; coastlands and estuaries; rivers, lakes and alluvial spreads; established grassland; woodland; lowland heath; arable land; parkland and ornamental gardens; and upland moor. For a complete coverage of England three further categories need to be added, urban and built-up land, industrial land, and seabed. Although these fell outside the scope of the original report, the complete set of twelve divisions are referred to hereafter as AMIC land-type categories.

Land-types have provided a valuable framework within which to set archaeological investigations and surveys related to monument management and conservation programmes (English Heritage 1991a, 38). APPENDIX O provides a select bibliography of archaeological studies related to particular land-types, illustrating the wide range of work carried out over the last 20 years or so. The projects focusing on wetland, coastland and estuaries and on urban and built-up land are especially significant in terms of their breadth and depth of coverage.

7.2.5 Land-use / land utilization

For archaeological resource management the concept of land-use is very important because it focuses on the dynamics of utilization at one point in time and thus allows a series of 'snap-shot' images to be looked at in sequence to document patterns of change. Moreover, land-use is overtly anthropogenic, the range of options that could potentially be applied to any particular area of ground being restricted only by prevailing physical, social, economic, political and historical factors.

Attempts have been made, quite successfully, to draw on historical sources and early agricultural returns to produce pictures of long term change in the patterns of land-use in Britain (Best and Coppock 1962). However, the earliest really detailed glimpse of land-use patterns in

Britain is Dudley Stamp's magisterial Land Utilization Survey, carried out in the early 1930s, the results of which are presented on a series of 1:63,360 maps (Stamp and Willatts 1935; Stamp 1960, 37-47; 1962). A total of 92 county reports (5800 pages) were published. The basis of this study was a field-by-field survey of the whole country, covering every acre, and recording its current use. Six broad categories of land were defined, some of them subdivided into narrow categories:

- forest and woodland
- meadowland and permanent grassland
- arable or tilled land
- heathland and other forms of rough pasture
- gardens, allotments, orchards and nurseries
- agriculturally unproductive land used for buildings, yards, mines, cemeteries etc.

Areas of open water were also recorded. Information was collected through a network of schoolchildren and university undergraduates who took maps out into the countryside and marked them up with what they saw. Some variability in the quality of observation must be accepted, but the great value of this study lies in the scale and uniformity of the coverage and the fact that it represents the first baseline study for patterns of land-use in England. For all its shortcomings, it is the only general study against which the 1940s information about archaeological monuments recorded by MARS can be compared.

Since the 1930s there have been a number of partial surveys of land-use in England, for example the Second Land Use Survey (Coleman 1961), but attention has increasingly focused on studies of land-use change based on the examination of sample areas, the use of remote sensing, or survey data collected by the Ordnance Survey's surveyors (e.g. Sinclair 1992; DoE 1993; Hunting Surveys 1986; Bibby and Coppin 1994). These studies have all been carried out for slightly different, and often rather particular, reasons which have determined the classifications and methodologies adopted (Wyatt 1991).

Since the late 1980s there has been a growing recognition of the need for a generally applicable land-use classification and monitoring scheme to enhance the information base available for planning and management, both at a national level and within the EU. At the European level land cover and biotype mapping formed part of a programme entitled the 'Co-ordination of Information on the Environment' (CORINE) which was intended to integrate data gathered by each member state (Haigh 1987; Waterton *et al.* 1995). In practice, however, most member states appear to have developed parallel systems for land-use and land cover classification and mapping.

In the UK the Department of the Environment commissioned research on the subject in 1991-2 (Dunn and Harrison 1994), concluding that a National Land Use Stock System (NLUSS) should be established. As envisaged it would comprise a land-parcel-based census of land-use geo-referenced to the National Grid and based on a combination of ground survey and data derived from aerial photographs. The land-use classification would be developed from that used for recording Land Use Change Statistics (Dunn and Harrison 1994, 101). In 1993 the Land Use Statistics Advisory Group (LUSAG) published

a provisional classification based on 12 broad land-use classes, with 53 narrower classes (LUSAG 1993). It is intended that, in due course, this scheme will provide the basis for the national census. The Land Use Statistics Advisory Group was tasked in 1994 with looking at the development of a national stock survey of land-use using the LUSAG classification. In parallel, Coopers and Lybrand (on behalf of DoE) undertook a user-based survey of the classification. A project design for the National Census has since been prepared by a research team based at Bristol University and, at the time of writing this report, was with the Department of the Environment, Transport and the Regions for consideration.

Given MARS's focus on land-use change, the importance of using a land-use classification that was both repeatable and compatible with other systems can hardly be underestimated. It was also important to adopt a scheme which could be applied 'bottom-up' from observations for individual land parcels or blocks of land. The LUSAG scheme was adopted for MARS (see below 7.2.7) because it was broadly based and designed to be widely applicable, and because it was likely that national statistics relating to the defined categories of land-use would be available before long.

7.2.6 Landscape character

The recognition that most existing land classification systems were based wholly or partly on physical attributes such as vegetation cover, soil type and utilization led to attempts to look at the classification of space in a broader way, taking account of both natural and cultural considerations. Beginning as a project called the *New Map of England* and piloted in the south-west of England (Gilder 1994; Herring and Johnson 1997), the full *Character of England Map* was published in 1996 by the Countryside Commission in partnership with English Nature and English Heritage (Countryside Commission 1996a). The map shows 181 discrete character areas (159 inland and 22 coastal), which reflect, among other things, geology, topography, history, architecture, vegetation and public perception. A series of summary statements and character descriptions are also being prepared for each character area.

This important new top-down approach to land classification holds many possibilities for integration with studies of the archaeological resource and its ongoing management, not least because the areas themselves are at least partly influenced by historical and archaeological remains. However, as with some of the other schemes discussed above, the character map is too detailed and the defined areas too small-scale for the kinds of general analysis that form the core of MARS. For reference, however, and as a prelude to future work, APPENDIX J.2 provides a correspondence table linking the MARS regions to the countryside character areas contained within them (and see Figure 3.6).

7.2.7 Classifications for MARS

All of the above-mentioned schemes of land classification have important applications for archaeology in a number of different ways and at different scales. In MARS the detailed recording of individual monuments in the field or from the inspection of aerial photographs was done using the defined LUSAG narrow land-use classes (LUSAG 1993). There are 53 of these and they are listed in

Table 7.1 - AMIC land-type categories in relation to LUSAG narrow land-use classes. *[Source: MARS Case Study Research]*

AMIC land-type category	LUSAG narrow land-uses
Arable land	Allotments
	Fallow land
	Field crop
	Horticulture
Built-up land	Agricultural buildings
	Derelict land
	Educational buildings
	Institutional and communal accommodation
	Institutional buildings
	Leisure and recreational buildings
	Outdoor recreation
	Public car-parks
	Religious buildings
	Residential
	Retailing
	Roads
	Urban land not previously developed
	Vacant land previously developed
Coastlands and estuaries	Coastal rocks and cliffs
	Dunes
	Intertidal sand and mud
	Salt marsh
	Sea/estuary
Established grassland	Improved pasture
	Rough grassland
	Rough pasture
Industrial land	Airports
	Docks
	Industry
	Landfill waste disposal
	Mineral workings and quarries
	Offices
	Railways
	Storage and warehousing
	Utilities
Lowland heath	Heathland
Parkland and ornamental gardens	[Not included in LUSAG types]
Rivers lakes and alluvium spreads	Running water
	Standing water
Unclassified	Unclassified
Upland moor	Bracken
	Inland rock
	Upland grass moor
	Upland mosaic
Wetland	Bog
	Freshwater marsh
Woodland	Broadleaved woodland
	Conifer woodland
	Cropland with woody perennial crops
	Felled woodland
	Land cultivated for afforestation
	Mixed woodland
	Shrub
	Undifferentiated young woodland

Table 7.2 - MARS land-use classes in relation to LUSAG narrow land-use classes. *[Source: MARS Case Study Research]*

MARS land-use class	LUSAG narrow land-uses
Arable land	Allotments
	Fallow land
	Field crop
	Horticulture
Coastal land	Coastal rocks and cliffs
	Dunes
	Intertidal sand and mud
	Sea/estuary
Developed and urban land	Agricultural buildings
	Airports
	Derelict land
	Docks
	Educational buildings
	Industry
	Institutional and communal accommodation
	Institutional buildings
	Landfill waste disposal
	Leisure and recreational buildings
	Mineral workings and quarries
	Offices
	Outdoor recreation
	Public car-parks
	Railways
	Religious buildings
	Residential
	Retailing
	Roads
	Storage and warehousing
	Urban land not previously developed
	Utilities
	Vacant land previously developed
Forestry	Broadleaved woodland
	Conifer woodland
	Cropland with woody perennial crops
	Felled woodland
	Land cultivated for afforestation
	Mixed woodland
	Shrub
	Undifferentiated young woodland
Pasture land	Improved pasture
	Rough grassland
	Rough pasture
Rivers and lakes	Running water
	Standing water
Semi-natural land	Bracken
	Heathland
	Inland rock
	Upland grass moor
	Upland mosaic
Unclassified	Unclassified
Wetland	Bog
	Freshwater marsh
	Salt marsh

APPENDIX H.

As a recently developed scheme, the LUSAG classification is not without some difficulties for archaeology, both in its application and in the way it groups land-uses together for analysis. It is generally more sensitive for built-up and urban situations than for rural areas. Some of the broad groups do not respect general situation (e.g. lowland as against upland), which might have been helpful in view of the differences in economic policy relating to the uplands (Countryside Commission 1983a; 1983b). Some land-uses which are of interest to archaeologists, for example ornamental/designed parks and gardens, do not appear in the classification, and not all the categories are defined according to the 'use' of the land, since some are based on land-cover characteristics rather than use practices. As the scheme develops and finds wider application, it would be useful to modify it slightly by, for example: partitioning the broad category 'agricultural' into 'cultivated land' and 'grazed land'; the addition of a broad category for ornamental and designed parks, gardens and landscapes; the recognition of upland and lowland divisions for heathland, bracken-covered land and rough grassland; the inclusion of golf-courses as a narrow land-use class; and finally separate recognition as narrow land-use classes of mines, quarries and extensive mineral extraction pits.

One of the great strengths of the LUSAG classification is that by recording land-use at this fine level of detail, the narrow classes can be brought together in different combinations to different kinds of analysis. Within the LUSAG scheme there are 12 broad groupings, but these are not used in this report for the analysis of data. Instead, two complementary, and slightly overlapping, approaches are used in this chapter. For a very general picture the AMIC land-type categories were used. Table 7.1 shows the correlations between AMIC land-type categories and the LUSAG narrow land-use classes.

For a more detailed picture a series of land-use groupings based on the LUSAG broad classes were developed and these can be applied at two levels: land-use actually on the monument and land-use around the monument. To avoid confusion these are referred to as the MARS land-use classes as they do differ quite significantly from the LUSAG broad groupings. Table 7.2 shows the correlation between MARS land-use classes and the LUSAG narrow land-use classes from which they are built up.

7.3 Contemporary patterns of land-type and land-use on and around MARS Monuments

7.3.1 Land-type

During the preparation of *Ancient monuments in the countryside* in 1986-5 (Darvill 1987) no baseline statistics on the distribution of archaeological remains within the proposed land-types were available. This situation can now be partly remedied by referring to the MARS data, although one of the themes of the book was that the recognition of archaeological monuments and deposits varied according to the land-type and that, as repeatedly noted in this report, the recorded resource would be an underestimate of what was actually present, in some cases a gross underestimate.

Figures 7.1 and 7.2 show a pair of bar charts representing the distribution of MARS Monuments by AMIC land-types categories. Figure 7.1 is based on simple counts of monuments forming the extant recorded resource in 1995; Figure 7.2 shows the percentage distribution based on the areal extent (CA95). Numerically, the greatest percentage (39%) of MARS Monuments are in built-up land, although this would be equalled if the percentages in established grassland (21%) and arable land (18%) were combined as a single value for agricultural land. The remaining eight AMIC categories each contain relatively small fractions of the extant recorded resource.

The pattern is rather different when the land area of monuments is used as the basis for quantification. As

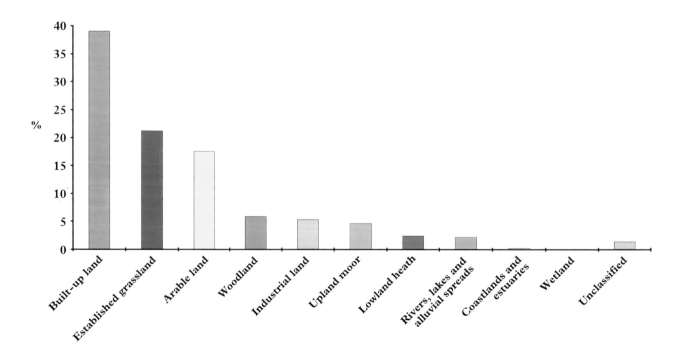

Figure 7.1 - Bar chart showing the distribution of extant MARS Monuments under single land-use regimes in 1995, grouped by AMIC land-type categories. Quantified by count. *[Source: MARS Field Survey Programme. Sample: n= 11,710 observations]*

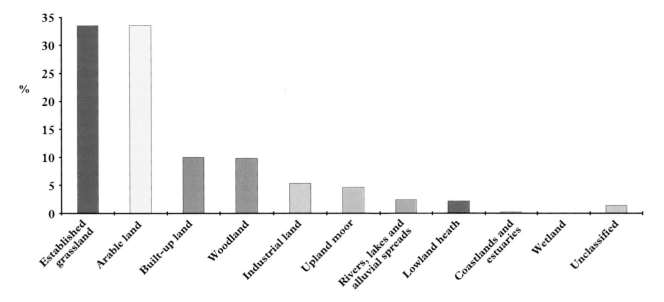

Figure 7.2 - Bar chart showing the distribution of extant MARS Monuments under single land-use regimes in 1995, grouped by AMIC land-type categories. Quantified by area. *[Source: MARS Field Survey Programme. Sample: n= 15,974 observations]*

Figure 7.2 shows, looked at in this way pasture land and arable land both contain equal shares of the extant recorded resource while monuments in built-up land are roughly equal in coverage to monuments in woodland.

A comparison of the distribution of the recorded archaeological resource in relation to the estimated land coverage of AMIC land-type categories is given in Table 7.3. The recorded archaeological resource is subdivided into the three defined monument character sets of earthworks, buildings and structures, and landcuts (see Chapter 5.6.3). From these figures it can be seen that, in total, the extant recorded resource is disproportionately present in certain land-types, mainly built-up and industrial land. Taking earthworks alone, however, the distribution of MARS Monuments is rather closer to the actual breakdown of land-types.

APPENDIX O provides a select bibliography of surveys and detailed studies related to particular land-types. From the listings it is clear that a great deal of attention has been given to three key land-types in recent decades: upland moors, wetland and coastlands. Driven by the recognized potential of these land-types coupled with fears over the impact of perceived and actual risks that they face, a great deal has been achieved and much of importance revealed. Not all of the results of those projects will yet have found their way onto the relevant SMRs to appear as MARS Monuments in this survey, but from Table 7.3 it is clear that archaeology in wetland and upland is fairly well represented in relation to the actual distribution of these land-types. Monuments in coastlands and estuaries, by contrast, appear poorly represented in the extant recorded resource. However, this is almost certainly because information from recent work had not been translated into retrievable records at the MARS

Table 7.3 - Distribution of MARS Monuments in relation to AMIC land-type categories in 1995 by monument character. *[Source: MARS Field Survey Programme. Sample: 15,194]*

AMIC land-type	Approximate % of land in type	Earthworks	Buildings and structures	Landcuts	All monuments
		%	%	%	%
Arable land	39	32.38	4.53	16.03	**16.97**
Built-up land and industrial land	10	13.73	73.53	35.48	**41.93**
Coastlands and estuaries	2.4	<1	<1	<1	**<1**
Established grassland	24	31.91	10.30	24.07	**21.73**
Lowland heath	1.72	4.23	0.49	1.78	**2.08**
Rivers lakes and alluvial spreads	2.5	2.31	3.48	4.00	**3.32**
Unclassified *(includes parks & gardens)*	1.64	<1	<1	2.84	**1.55**
Upland moor	10	6.63	1.34	4.11	**3.92**
Wetland	1.04	<1	<1	<1	**<1**
Woodland	7.7	8.03	5.07	11.25	**8.21**
Seabed (not in MARS)	~	~	~	~	~
Total	**100%**	**100%**	**100%**	**100%**	**100%**

census date.

It may also be noted that many of the surveys and studies related to land-types have focused on the relatively small categories. From Table 7.3 it is clear that there are other land-types that perhaps deserve more attention in future because of the high proportion of the extant recorded resource represented within them. Two seem to stand out for special notice. Pasture land, which is known to contain the highest percentage of recorded archaeology in terms of the area represented, has rarely been recognized for special attention (for example Trueman 1997; Fowler 1970; Sheail and Wells 1970), and not yet fully exploited as a source of quality archaeological information. Similarly, woodlands appears to contain more than 8% of England's extant recorded resource in less than 8% of its land area, emphasizing their very considerable potential (Darvill 1987, 92-104; Beswick *et al.* 1993).

In viewing these AMIC land-type distributions it must be remembered that the classes are not discrete, and although individual monuments have been assigned to one particular class for the purposes of analysis it is possible, for example, for monuments to be within established grassland while simultaneously on an alluvial spread in a river valley. The importance of the AMIC land-types is that for management purposes they broadly reflect the contexts in which conservation and preservation must take place. For management purposes, the large number of small monuments in some land-types contrasts with the relatively small number of large monuments in others. It may be appropriate to establish different strategies in these different land-type sectors, for example whole-estate plans where archaeological remains are extensive, monument-specific plans where they are not.

7.3.2 Land-use patterns on monuments

Figure 7.3 - Single land-use at an ancient monument. Aerial view of Harehough Camp, Coquetdale, Northumberland, under upland grass moor with some rabbit erosion. One of 46 hillforts covered by a strategic study of Iron Age hillforts in the Northumberland National Park. *[Photograph: Tim Gates for Northumberland National Park Authority. Copyright reserved]*

Figure 7.4 - Multiple land-use at an ancient monument. Aerial view of Meon Hill, Warwickshire, under woodland, pasture and arable land *[Photograph: RCHME. Copyright reserved]*

In contrast to the broad-brush approach of land-type studies, consideration of land-use moves closer to the analysis of the processes actually taking place over and around archaeological monuments. However, it also introduces an additional complicating factor from the point of view of analysis because some monuments have multiple land-uses. This was accommodated during data collection by recording multiple land-use entries where necessary, the area of the monument being divided approximately in proportion to each recorded land-use class. As a result, some statistics for land-use are based on observations rather than the number of monuments; in all, 15,964 sets of land-use observations were made over 13,488 MARS Monuments inspected by the field survey teams.

In recording land-use, MARS found that archaeological monuments lie in three main situations: single land-use, where the land parcel, or parcels, in which a monument lay was subject to the same land-use regime throughout (Figure 7.3); multiple land-use where two or more different regimes were present in separate land parcels each covering part of a monument (Figure 7.4); and 'island monuments' where a single land-use was present on the monument itself, but this differed from the

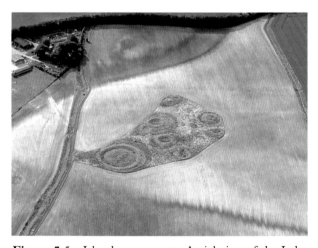

Figure 7.5 - Island monuments. Aerial view of the Lake Down barrow cemetery, Wiltshire, showing a group of Bronze Age barrows left under pasture while the surrounding field is cultivated *[Photograph: RCHME. Copyright reserved]*

Table 7.4 - Incidence of single and multiple land-use on MARS Monuments by decade from 1945 to 1995. *[Source: MARS Field Survey Programme and Aerial Photographic Survey. Samples: as shown]*

Number of land-uses	1945 %	1955 %	1965 %	1975 %	1985 %	1995 %
Sample	4265	2853	3044	3025	1591	13426
1 use	90.46	89.70	89.68	88.23	89.00	87.22
2 uses	5.49	5.85	6.31	6.91	6.41	8.60
3 uses	2.06	2.10	1.91	2.35	2.39	2.82
4 uses	1.03	1.23	1.12	1.32	1.45	<1
5 uses	<1	<1	<1	<1	<1	<1
6 uses	<1	<1	<1	<1	<1	<1
7 uses	<1	<1	<1	<1	<1	<1
8 uses	<1	<1	<1	<1	<1	-
9 uses	<1	-	<1	<1	-	-
10 uses	-	-	-	-	-	-
11 uses	<1	<1	-	-	-	-
Total	**100%**	**100%**	**100%**	**100%**	**100%**	**100%**

Table 7.5 - Incidence of single and multiple land-use on MARS Monuments in 1995 by monument form. *[Source: MARS Field Survey Programme. Sample: n= 13,426 observations]*

Monument form	Single land-use 1995 %	Multiple land-uses 1995 %	All %
Small single monument	57.46	42.95	55.60
Standing building	23.83	6.24	21.58
Large single monument	6.13	26.34	8.71
Linear monument	7.46	16.67	8.64
Field system	5.12	7.81	5.46
Total	**100%**	**100%**	**100%**

Table 7.6 - Matrix showing the incidence of mixed land-use on MARS Monuments in 1995. *[Source: MARS Field Survey Programme. Sample: n= 1012 observations]*

MARS Land-use class	Arable land	Coastal land	Developed and urban land	Forestry	Pasture land	Rivers and lakes	Semi-natural land	Unclassified	Wetland
Arable land		~	137	47	94	20	~	8	~
Coastal land			1	~	~	2	~	1	~
Developed and urban land				93	255	64	10	10	~
Forestry					132	33	7	13	1
Pasture land						38	28	7	7
Rivers and lakes							2	1	~
Semi-natural land								1	~
Unclassified									~
Wetland									

surrounding land-use (Figure 7.5).

At the MARS census date it was found that 87% of MARS Monuments were under a single land-use, with the remaining 13% being under between two and eleven recognized land-uses. Single land-use was defined as meaning that more than 95% of the area of a monument was within the defined land-use class.

Table 7.4 shows an analysis of the extent of multiple land-use through time. Data for earlier decades are derived from the analysis of aerial photographs of MARS Monuments, and for some decades the sample is rather small (and see below 7.3.3 on sample composition). Nevertheless, 10% of monuments are under multiple land-use in every decade since 1945, although they are not necessarily the same monuments through time. The balance between single and multiple land-use on the

MARS Monuments (90% and 10% respectively) is apparently unchanging throughout the 50-year period of the survey, although within monuments under multiple use there has been a slight increase in the incidence of two uses on the same monument.

Table 7.5 shows an analysis of the distribution of single and multiple land-use by form for MARS Monuments. As expected, size is a critical factor, the smaller monuments having a higher incidence of single land-use than the more extensive forms.

There are also some regional differences in the pattern of multiple land-use over monuments. The East Midlands is the only region to have less than 60% of its monuments under one land-use. Only the South East and the North West have sites with more that six land-uses. The South West region has the lowest percentage of

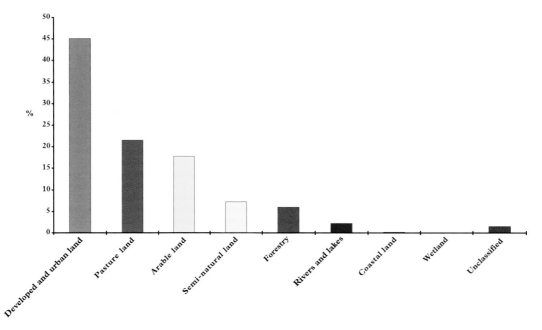

Figure 7.6 - Bar chart showing the distribution of extant MARS Monuments under single land-use regimes in 1995, grouped by MARS land-use classes. Quantified by count. *[Source MARS Field Survey Programme. Sample: n= 11,710 observations]*

monuments under multiple land-uses.

Table 7.6 gives some indication of the combinations of land-uses in a matrix of MARS land-use classes. The incidence rate has been calculated by taking account of all pairs of associated land-use for monuments with three or more land-uses. The three most common combinations are pasture and developed land which is mainly explained by monuments under grass which are partly covered by settlement; arable and developed land which are monuments partly in cultivation and partly covered by settlement; and pasture and forestry which are mainly monuments within and around woodland.

Focusing on those MARS Monuments under a single land-use, Figure 7.6 shows the distribution of MARS Monuments in relation to the MARS land-use classes. The highest percentage of monuments lies under urban and developed land, followed by pasture land, arable land, semi-natural land and forestry, each with over 5% of the extant recorded resource as represented by the MARS sample.

Figure 7.7 shows a series of pie charts representing the patterns of single land-use for the three main subdivisions of the total resource by monument character: earthworks, buildings and structures, and landcuts.

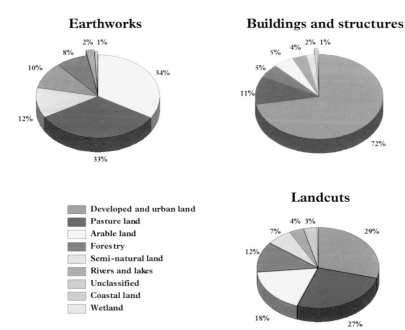

Figure 7.7 - Pie charts showing the patterns of single land-use regimes in 1995, grouped by MARS land-use classes for earthworks, buildings and structures, and landcuts. Quantified by monument count. *[Source: MARS Field Survey Programme. Samples: observations n= 4117 earthworks; n= 4265 buildings and structures; n= 4498 landcuts]*

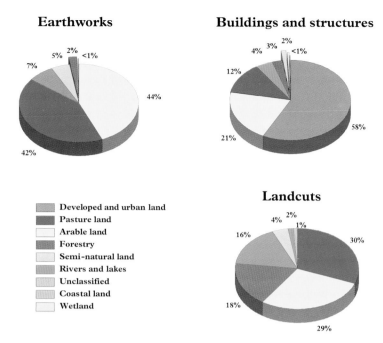

Figure 7.8 - Pie charts showing the pattern of single land-use regimes in 1995, grouped by MARS land-use classes for earthworks; buildings and structures and landcuts. Quantified by area. *[Source MARS Field Survey Programme. Samples: observations n= 3552 earthworks; n= 3985 buildings and structures; and n= 3750 landcuts]*

Quantification is by monument counts. Again, pasture, developed land, arable land, semi-natural land and forestry are the five most frequent single land-uses for earthworks and landcuts, although the exact patterns for each are slightly different and it is always important not to forget the minor land-use classes. Although these each comprise less than 5% of the extant recorded resource, collectively they represent nearly a quarter of all MARS Monuments. The pattern for buildings and structures is rather different from that for earthworks and landcuts, with built-up land dominating the picture (72%) as expected.

Quantified by area (Figure 7.8) the pattern of single land-use on MARS Monuments is rather different. For earthworks, the percentage under pasture and arable is greater than the simpler counts suggest, but the reverse is true for earthwork monuments under forestry and semi-natural land. There is a clear association between earthworks and agricultural land-uses. The proportional areas of buildings and structures under arable (21%) and developed and urban land (58%) are also greater than the simple counts suggest, while for landcuts the patterns of representation are broadly similar.

Comparison between the distribution of MARS Monuments within defined land-use classes and the overall national incidence of those land-use classes is difficult because no national land-use stock statistics are available as yet. However, a number of land-use surveys have been carried out in England during the 1980s and 1990s (see APPENDIX N for details) and the results of these are compared with the distribution of MARS Monuments by MARS land-use classes on Table 7.7. As

Table 7.7- Patterns of land-use on MARS Monuments in 1995 in relation to general estimates of land-use stock in England. *[Sources: MARS Field Survey Programme and as specified in the notes. Sample: n= 13,516 observations]*

Land-use	Percentage of MARS Monuments %	Land-use 1993 (BARR et al[1]) %	CPRE 1992 %[2]
Arable land	25.52	32.4	~
Managed land [3]	~	~	67.8
Coastal land	0.03	2.4	~
Developed and urban land	24.98	10.4	14.9
Forestry	14.09	7.5	8.3
Pasture land	25.36	34.8	9
Rivers and lakes	4.42	0.5	~
Semi-natural land	4.20	9.4	~
Unclassified	1.33	2.4	~
Wetland	0.07	0.2	~
Total	**100%**	**100%**	**100%**

(1) After DOE 1993, 38 (table 3.1)
(2) After CPRE 1992, 80 (table 8.6, appendix 19)
(3) This category is only used by CPRE, it includes cultivated or managed farmland enclosed in fields

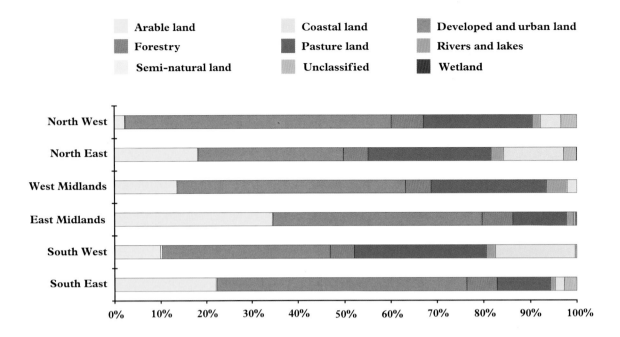

Figure 7.9 - Horizontal stacked bar chart showing regional patterns in the distribution of MARS land-use classes for extant MARS Monuments under single land-use regimes in 1995. Quantified by count for MARS Regions. *[Source: MARS Field Survey Programme. Sample: n= 11,710 observations]*

with the AMIC land-type distributions, it is apparent from these figures that the distribution of archaeological remains as represented by the MARS sample broadly accords with the overall national proportions of sampled rural and urban land-uses, but has a number of discrepancies as a result of over-representation of remains in some small land-use classes, for example developed and urban land and forestry.

There are marked regional differences in the distribution of land-uses and hence in the distribution of MARS Monuments by land-use, as Figure 7.9 shows. Quantification here is based on counts of MARS Monuments under single land-use regimes. The North West has a notably lower percentage of monuments under arable land than all the other regions, and the South East has a proportionally higher than average number of monuments within developed land. Arable land dominates the pattern in the East Midlands. The percentage of monuments in forestry is remarkably even between the MARS Regions.

Figures 7.10-7.12 show regional breakdowns of the five dominant MARS land-use classes for the extant recorded resource subdivided by monument character and quantified by land area.

For earthwork monuments (Figure 7.10) there are two clear patterns of land-use. In the South East, East Midlands and North East, arable land dominates at between 55% and 75%, with pasture land in second position. By contrast, in the West Midlands and South West the situation is reversed: established pasture land dominates in these regions and except in the North West arable land takes second position. In both the North West and the South West, semi-natural land (here mainly upland moor) contain major sectors of the extant recorded resource.

The patterning discernible for earthworks would seem to follow the national pattern of arable land-use and is also perhaps indicative of the highland/lowland zone division. Behind these differences there are of course many other factors, of which two of the most important are farm size and average field size. As a very general principle, areas of intensive arable production have larger farms and higher average field sizes than areas of predominantly pastoral land-uses (Westmacott and Worthington 1997, 110). There are clear implications for resource management planning here, first in terms of the number of owners, tenants and managers who must be accommodated, and second in relation to the economic impact on farm economies caused by prescriptive management for specific monuments. The equation is simple and can be illustrated by a hypothetical example. The average current area of MARS earthwork monuments in England is 0.43ha. For a farm of say 1234ha (500 acres) in East Anglia this represents 0.03% of the productive land area, whereas for a typical small farm unit of say 370ha (150 acres) in Herefordshire the same monument would represent 0.1% of the productive land area. In developing more sensitive management plans and payment schemes (see Chapter 8) attention needs to be given to the gearing of payments in relation to the impact on the farm's economy of the proposed measures.

Regional differences are much less clear for buildings and structures (Figure 7.11) and landcuts (Figure 7.12), because the kinds of land-use involved are themselves less regionally variable: built-up land in Northumberland is more or less the same as built-up land in Cornwall.

Of the 53 defined LUSAG narrow land-use classes (see APPENDIX H), 49 were represented by observations made during the MARS Field Survey Programme. Table

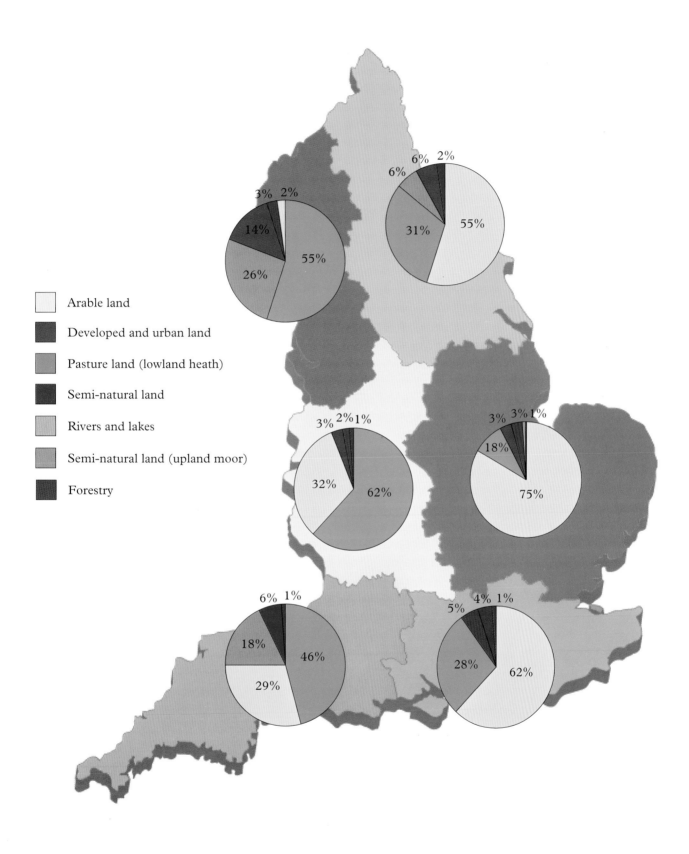

Figure 7.10 - Pie charts showing regional patterns in the five dominant land-use classes for MARS earthworks monuments in 1995. Quantified by count for MARS Regions. *[Source: MARS Field Survey Programme. Sample: n= 4714 observations]*

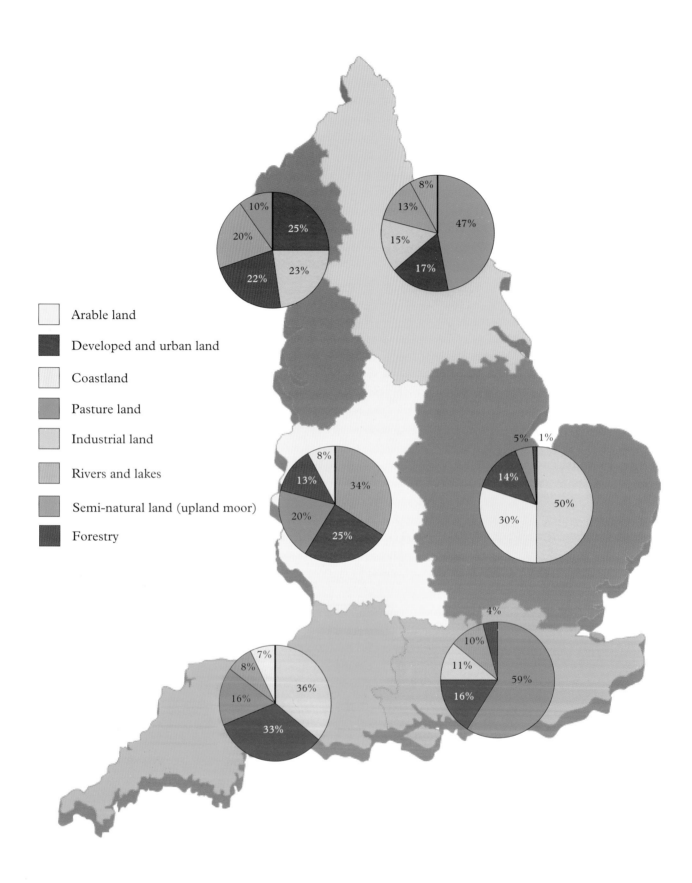

Figure 7.11 - Pie charts showing regional patterns in the top five dominant land-use classes for MARS buildings and structures in 1995. Quantified by count for MARS Regions. *[Source: MARS Field Survey Programme. Sample: n= 5308 observations]*

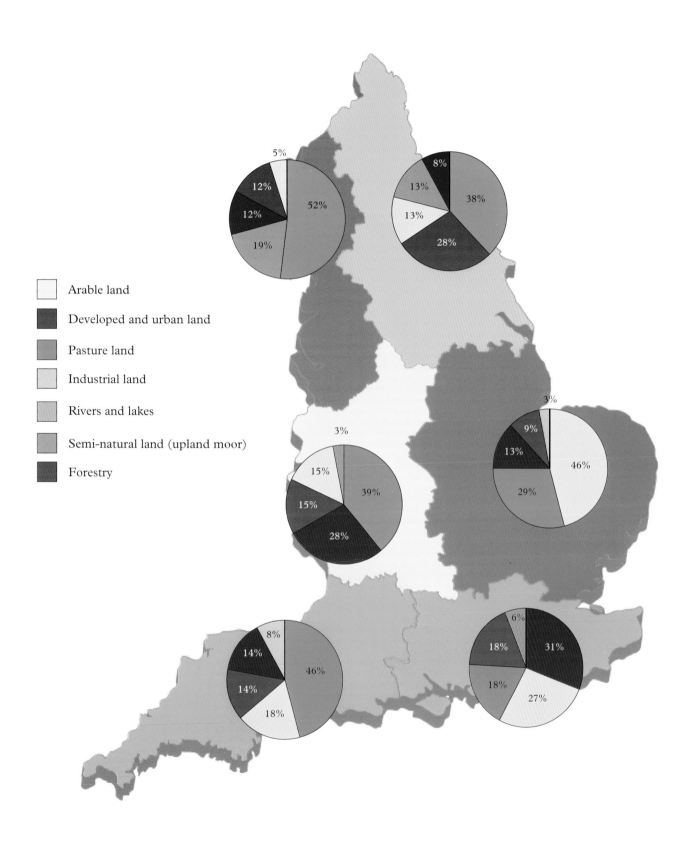

Figure 7.12 - Pie charts showing regional patterns in the top five dominant land-use classes for landcuts in 1995. Quantified by count for MARS Regions. *[Source: MARS Field Survey Programme. Sample: n= 5942 observations]*

Table 7.8 - Incidence of land-use on MARS Monuments in 1995 using LUSAG narrow land-use classes by monument character. Quantified by current area. *[Source: MARS Field Survey Programme. Sample: n= 13,516 observations]*

Land-use on monument	Buildings and structures %	Earthworks %	Landcuts %
Rough pasture	5.9	15.7	13.0
Improved pasture	3.4	13.0	9.5
Residential	29.0	4.6	7.4
Mixed woodland	1.2	2.0	3.4
Fallow land	1.2	6.5	3.6
Broadleaved woodland	1.6	2.0	3.5
Roads	4.3	2.3	7.8
Agricultural buildings	6.9	1.9	1.5
Standing water	1.7	1.6	1.5
Upland grass moor	<1.0	3.7	2.0
Conifer woodland	<1.0	<1.0	<1.0
Outdoor recreation	1.6	<1.0	2.6
Rough grassland	1.2	3.4	2.8
Airports	<1.0	<1.0	<1.0
Unclassified	<1.0	<1.0	3.0
Educational buildings	1.1	<1.0	<1.0
Shrub	2.3	3.0	3.9
Running water	1.7	<1.0	1.4
Railways	<1.0	<1.0	1.1
Heathland	<1.0	4.3	1.8
Retailing	3.7	<1.0	<1.0
Religious buildings	11.7	<1.0	4.3
Bracken	<1.0	2.7	<1.0
Industry	2.1	<1.0	<1.0
Utilities	<1.0	<1.0	<1.0
Mineral workings and quarries	<1.0	<1.0	1.0
Horticulture	<1.0	<1.0	<1.0
Cropland with woody perennial crops	<1.0	<1.0	<1.0
Derelict land	2.8	<1.0	<1.0
Urban land not previously developed	<1.0	<1.0	<1.0
Institutional and communal accommodation	1.5	<1.0	<1.0
Leisure and recreational buildings	1.6	<1.0	<1.0
Landfill waste disposal	<1.0	<1.0	1.7
Inland rock	<1.0	<1.0	1.7
Offices	1.4	<1.0	<1.0
Storage and warehousing	1.3	<1.0	<1.0
Freshwater marsh	<1.0	<1.0	<1.0
Public car parks	<1.0	<1.0	<1.0
Institutional buildings	<1.0	<1.0	<1.0
Docks	<1.0	<1.0	<1.0
Vacant land previously developed	<1.0	<1.0	<1.0
Sea/estuary	<1.0	<1.0	<1.0
Land cultivated for afforestation	<1.0	<1.0	<1.0
Felled woodland	<1.0	<1.0	<1.0
Undifferentiated young woodland	<1.0	<1.0	<1.0
Upland mosaic	<1.0	<1.0	<1.0
Salt marsh	<1.0	<1.0	<1.0
Allotments	<1.0	<1.0	<1.0
Coastal rocks and cliffs	<1.0	<1.0	<1.0
Dunes	<1.0	<1.0	<1.0
Intertidal sand and mud	<1.0	<1.0	<1.0
Total	**100%**	**100%**	**100%**

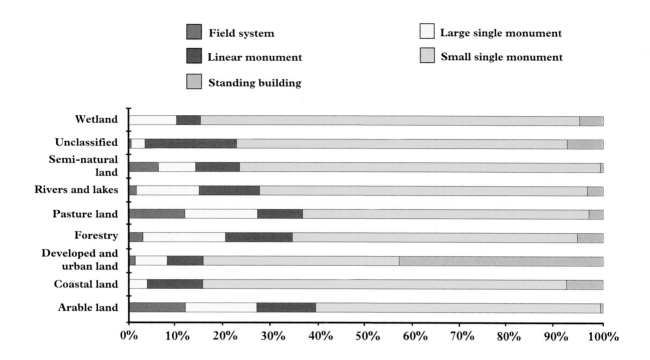

Figure 7.13 - Horizontal stacked bar chart showing the distribution of MARS land-use classes by form for extant MARS Monuments in 1995. Quantified by count. *[Source: MARS Field Survey Programme. Sample: n= 13,532 observations]*

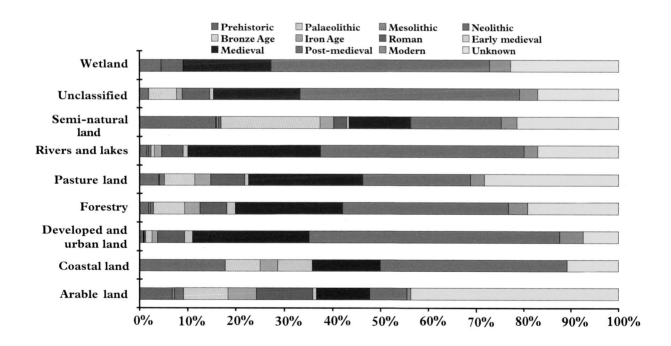

Figure 7.14 - Horizontal stacked bar chart showing the distribution MARS land-use classes by period for extant MARS Monuments in 1995. Quantified by count. *[Source: MARS Field Survey Programme. Sample: n= 17,178 observations]*

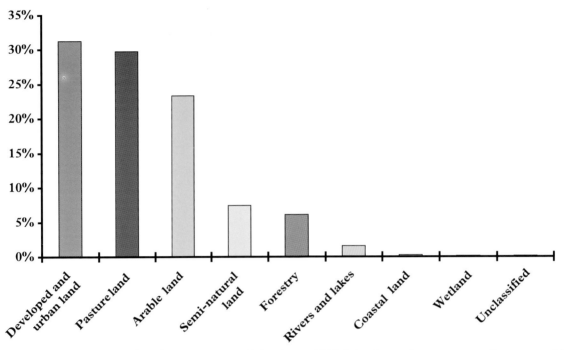

Figure 7.15 - Bar chart showing the percentage of dominant MARS land-use classes surrounding extant MARS Monuments in 1995. Quantified by count. *[Source: MARS Field Survey Programme. Sample: n= 11,861 observations]*

7.8 shows an analysis of the distribution of land-use on the extant recorded resource at the MARS census date by LUSAG narrow land-use class. Quantification is by current area. Each of 22 narrow land-use classes contains 1% or more of the extant recorded resource.

Within these narrow land-use classes, earthworks are clearly more prevalent than other kinds of monument on field crop, pasture and roads. Earthworks are, however, found on fewer land-uses than are other monument classes. Interestingly, where earthworks are under multiple land-use, a far higher proportion (11%) are found partly in residential areas than is the case for earthworks under a single land-use where only 4% are in residential land.

Land-use patterns are also related to other characteristics of the archaeological resource. Figure 7.13 shows an analysis of monument form in relation to land-use. Small single monuments dominate the national picture in most land-use classes, although the percentage of large single monuments, linear monuments, field systems and standing buildings varies considerably between land-uses. Overall there is considerable correlation between land-use classes and monuments.

The distribution of monuments in relation to land-use also varies by period. Figure 7.14 presents a breakdown based on monument counts; earlier monuments appear to the left-hand side of each bar. The most obvious conclusion from the chart is that arable and pasture land have the highest proportions of sites of unknown date. This is partly explained by the problem of dating cropmark sites and low-relief earthworks without excavation. Other patterns are evident too. Semi-natural land has the highest percentage of prehistoric monuments while arable has the lowest percentage of post-medieval and modern monuments. It is not surprising that the majority of monuments on developed land are post-medieval because they are likely to be buildings, and thus

Table 7.9 - Incidence of land-use patterns on and around MARS Monuments in 1995. Quantified by counts. *[Source: MARS Field Survey Programme. Sample: n= 15,964 observations]*

Land-use on monument	Arable land	Coastal land	Developed- and urban land	Forestry	Pasture land	River and lakes	Semi-natural land	Unclassified	Wetland
Arable land	2491	1	58	23	105	4	0	0	2
Coastal land	0	23	2	0	1	0	0	0	0
Developed and urban land	0	10	4834	187	1135	146	55	6	6
Forestry	258	0	164	530	343	21	9	2	1
Pasture land	260	5	215	90	2750	20	28	2	0
Rivers and lakes	72	1	137	75	150	50	18	1	3
Semi-natural land	1	0	10	19	37	4	852	0	1
Unclassified	29	2	87	27	64	3	15	7	2
Wetland	6	0	1	0	6	0	1	0	6

Table 7.10 - Comparison of land-use patterns on and around MARS monuments in 1995 by monument form. Quantified by counts. *[Source: MARS Field Survey Programme. Samples: n= 15,085 observations for land-use on monuments; n= 14,050 observations for land-use around monuments]*

MARS	Field system		Large single monument		Linear monument		Small single monument		Standing building	
	Land-use on %	Land-use around %	Land-use on %	Land-use around %	Land-use on %	Land-use around %	Land-use on %	Land-use around %	Land-use on %	Land-use around %
Arable land	30.36	37.34	21.34	33.60	18.03	33.07	16.11	23.02	<1	2.25
Coastal land	0	<1	0.09	<1	<1	<1	<1	<1	<1	<1
Developed and urban land	9.20	9.15	26.79	18.13	35.20	18.91	32.78	28.11	93.43	79.16
Forestry	3.97	2.76	13.20	6.63	12.14	8.02	8.98	7.08	1.91	2.70
Pasture land	46.92	42.23	28.74	35.59	19.98	30.58	25.63	29.78	3.41	14.14
Rivers and lakes	<1	<1	4.32	<1	4.53	<1	4.60	2.29	<1	1.13
Semi-natural land	8.52	7.64	4.88	4.86	6.72	7.86	9.32	9.01	<1	<1
Unclassified	<1	0	0.53	<1	3.21	<1	2.23	<1	<1	<1
Wetland	0	0	0.11	<1	<1	<1	<1	<1	0	0
Total	**100%**	**100%**	**100%**	**100%**	**100%**	**100%**	**100%**	**100%**	**100%**	**100%**

the land-use is the monument itself. The apparent number of post-medieval monuments on wetland is more surprising, but this is due to small sample size. Palaeolithic and Mesolithic sites are not noticeable because of their small numbers.

7.3.3 Land-use patterns around monuments

The patterns of land-use around archaeological monuments represent a major influence on the range of potential hazards the monuments face, their general decay rate, and the possibility of pursuing particular management regimes. In some cases there are numerous land-uses within the immediate vicinity of a given monument; it can also be difficult to define what represents the neighbourhood of the monument and hence to quantify land-uses. For MARS, neighbouring land-uses were taken to be the dominant land-use that applied in land parcels adjoining or extending beyond the recorded limits of a monument. Since it was not possible to measure neighbouring land-uses in terms of area,

comparisons with the land-use on or over monuments must be based on the frequency of occurrence.

For approximately 58% of MARS Monuments land-use was the same on the monument as around it. Figure 7.15 shows the frequency of land-uses recorded around MARS Monuments. The same four main classes dominate, although their rank order is slightly different in comparison with the incidence of land-use actually on the monument (*cf.* Figure 7.1). It is also notable that pasture, arable and developed land together account for the land-use surrounding more than 80% of the extant recorded archaeological resource. Table 7.9 sets out for comparison the relative incidence of the MARS land-use classes on MARS Monuments and around them. The shaded cells in the matrix show monuments that are situated in the same land-use environment as covers the monument itself. Amongst the major patterns of association in the countryside are semi-natural vegetation on a monument which is situated in arable land.

Table 7.10 shows a breakdown of the patterns of

Table 7.11 - Analysis of the changing percentage of MARS Monuments with single and multiple land-use(s) by decade between the 1940s and the 1990s grouped by monument character. *[Source: MARS Field Survey Programme and Aerial Photographic Survey. Samples: 1940s n= 4265; 1950s n= 2853; 1960s n= 3044; 1970s n= 3025; 1980s n= 1591; 1990s n= 4149]*

Monument Character	Land-use on monument	1940's %	1950's %	1960's %	1970's %	1980's %	1990's %
Building and structure	Single land-use	93.55	92.96	91.91	90.85	94.12	85.25
	Multiple land-use	6.45	7.04	8.09	9.15	5.88	14.75
Building and structure total		**100%**	**100%**	**100%**	**100%**	**100%**	**100%**
Earthwork	Single land-use	89.36	87.95	88.84	87.12	87.59	84.50
	Multiple land-use	10.64	12.05	11.16	12.88	12.41	15.50
Earthwork total		**100%**	**100%**	**100%**	**100%**	**100%**	**100%**
Landcut	Single land-use	90.42	90.12	89.58	88.55	88.69	82.08
	Multiple land-use	9.58	9.88	10.42	11.45	11.31	17.92
Landcut total		**100%**	**100%**	**100%**	**100%**	**100%**	**100%**

land-use on and around monuments in relation to monument form. A number of clear associations can be seen. Most important is the way monuments under pasture seem to lie within pasture, except in the case of linear monuments. The problem here is that the latter often run through or between many different land parcels and thus have more opportunities to be associated with other land-use classes. Arable land shows a less strong pattern of commonality on and around monuments, and it is in arable land that most 'island monuments' are found.

7.4 MARS Monuments and land-use change 1945-95

Land-use change data are not easy to obtain or use. There are four main problems. The first involves the recognition of earlier land-uses from aerial photographs. For large tracts of land this is not generally a problem, and considerable expertise has developed in the field of aerial photographic analysis to support this. The real difficulty comes with small monuments and structures, especially those less than 5m across, and cases where the vegetation cover makes identification and location difficult.

The second problem is that, for the method to be really effective, it is necessary to track land-use changes for each land-use on each individual monument. This is difficult in practice, because changes to land-use often involve changes to the shape, size and boundaries of the land parcel. There are usually gains as well as losses which can balance each other out when blocked together to form the general picture. Much reliance therefore has to be placed on patterns revealed by MARS Monuments with single land-use regimes as opposed to those with multiple land-use, although shifts in the proportion of sites under multiple use are reviewed below.

Third is the problem of sampling. The availability of aerial photographs for earlier decades is variable, and to this must be added constraints represented by the differing quality of the plates and the interpreter's ability to find small monuments on the photographs. The overall effect is that the observations relating to the decades from 1945 to 1985 derive from a smaller sample than observations for 1995, and have a fairly high percentage of non-randomly missing data. The statistical implications of this were reviewed by Mike Baxter (Chapter 3.7). In

practical terms these problems mean that while the trends that can be seen decade on decade for the period 1945 to 1985 are internally fairly consistent, even if not especially robust, they do not always fit comfortably against time-sequence data which include the 1995 observations for the most recent decade. This is especially so for land-uses where the omission of some small single monuments and most standing buildings causes a major distortion of the picture. The best sample for earlier decades is for the 1940s.

The fourth issue is the availability of comparative data to set alongside the patterns revealed for MARS Monuments. This is a problem faced by most environmental resource surveys in recent years and can be met only by using such data as are available. A number of land-use change studies have been undertaken, the most useful to MARS being listed in APPENDIX N. Some of these, like MARS, have relied on aerial photographic evidence (e.g. Bayliss-Smith and Owens 1990; Countryside Commission 1990a), but others have used cartographic sources (e.g. DoE 1989; 1990b; 1992a; 1993) or previous census data (e.g. Sinclair 1992). The Countryside Survey (Barr *et al.* 1993) and its forerunners (e.g. Barr *et al.* 1986) combined a variety of sources including satellite imagery, previous census data, and fieldwork.

Table 7.11 shows an analysis of ways that MARS Monuments have changed in relation to the incidence of single land-uses and multiple land-uses over time. In all three monument character groups there is some evidence to suggest a transfer from single to multiple land-uses through time. The proportion of single land-use for all groups generally decreases as the proportion of multiple land-use increases, in the case of buildings and landcuts nearly doubling over the period. In rural areas, where earthworks and landcuts dominate, these changes can be linked to more general patterns in the fragmentation of land parcels and the increasing diversity of land-uses between the 1940s and the 1990s revealed by other surveys of the changing countryside (e.g. Bayliss-Smith and Owens 1990, 75).

In order to obtain a general picture of changes over the 50-year period 1945 to 1995, Tables 7.12 and 7.13 present an analysis of the differences in the proportions of earthwork monuments, and buildings and structures, respectively for each of the MARS land-use class.

Table 7.12–Changes in land-use on MARS earthwork Monuments between 1945 and 1995. Quantified by count. *[Source: MARS Field Survey Programme and Aerial Photographic Survey. Samples: 1940s n= 2087 observations; 1990s n= 4090 observations]*

| Land-use class | c. 1945 | | 1995 | | % Change |
	No.	%	No.	%	
Pasture land	761	36.46	1354	33.11	-3.36%
Arable land	684	32.77	1385	33.86	1.09%
Semi-natural land	226	10.83	480	11.74	0.87%
Forestry	193	9.25	336	10.10	0.85%
Developed and urban land	184	8.82	413	8.22	0.60%
Rivers and lakes	24	1.15	91	2.22	1.07%
Unclassified	9	0.43	26	0.64	0.21%
Wetland	4	0.19	2	0.07	-0.12%
Coastal land	2	0.10	3	0.05	-0.05%
Total	**2087**	**100%**	**4090**	**100%**	

Table 7.13 - Changes in land-use on MARS buildings and structures between 1945 and 1995. Quantified by count. *[Source: MARS Field Survey Programme and Aerial Photographic Survey. Samples: 1940s n= 699 observations; 1990s n= 4392 observations]*

| Land-use class | c. 1945 | | 1995 | | % Change |
	No.	%	No.	%	
Developed and urban land	276	39.48	3169	72.15	32.67%
Pasture land	168	24.03	463	10.54	-13.49%
Arable land	84	12.01	223	5.08	-6.94%
Forestry	73	10.44	238	5.42	-5.02%
Semi-natural land	46	6.58	96	2.19	-4.40%
Rivers and lakes	35	5.01	151	3.44	-1.57%
Unclassified	7	1	42	0.96	-0.04%
Wetland	7	1	8	0.05	-0.95%
Coastal land	3	0.43	2	0.13	-0.25%
Total	**699**	**100%**	**4392**	**100%**	

Table 7.14 - Changes in land-use around MARS earthwork Monuments between 1945 and 1995. Quantified by count. *[Source: MARS Field Survey Programme and Aerial Photographic Survey. Samples: 1940s n= 1829 observations; 1990s n= 3742 observations]*

| Land-use class | c. 1945 | | 1995 | | % Change |
	No.	%	No.	%	
Arable land	764	41.77	1454	38.86	-2.91%
Pasture land	704	38.49	1256	33.56	-4.93%
Semi-natural land	222	12.14	485	12.96	0.82%
Forestry	79	4.32	195	5.21	0.89%
Developed and urban land	48	2.62	321	8.58	5.96%
Unclassified	5	0.27	4	0.11	-0.16%
Rivers and lakes	3	0.16	19	0.51	0.35%
Wetland	3	0.16	4	0.11	-0.05%
Coastal land	1	0.05	4	0.11	0.06%
Total	**1829**	**100%**	**3742**	**100%**	

Table 7.15 - Changes in land-use around MARS buildings and structures between 1945 and 1995. Quantified by count. *[Source: MARS Field Survey Programme and Aerial Photographic Survey. Samples: 1940s n= 650 observations; 1990s n= 4087 observations]*

| Land-use class | c. 1945 | | 1995 | | % Change |
	No.	%	No.	%	
Pasture land	229	35.23	886	21.67	-13.56%
Arable land	160	24.62	325	7.95	-16.67%
Developed and urban land	84	12.92	2415	59.09	46.17%
Forestry	58	8.92	200	4.89	-4.03%
Rivers and lakes	57	8.77	131	3.21	-5.56%
Semi-natural land	51	7.84	105	2.56	-5.28%
Coastal land	6	0.92	10	0.24	-0.68%
Wetland	5	0.77	8	0.19	-0.58%
Unclassified	0	0	7	0.17	0.17%
Total	**650**	**100%**	**4087**	**100%**	

Table 7.16 -Changes in land-use around MARS buildings and structures between 1945 and 1995. Quantified by count. *[Source: MARS Field Survey Programme and Aerial Photographic Survey. Samples: 1940s n= 650 observations; 1990s n= 4087 observations]*

Land-use class	1940s %	1950s %	1960s %	1970s %	1980s %	1995 %
Arable land	91.4	91.2	92.0	94.2	95.4	92.7
Coastal land	87.5	72.7	77.8	100.0	75.0	90.0
Developed and urban land	33.3	39.9	40.1	41.9	43.4	60.6
Forestry	34.0	36.6	30.4	33.6	30.3	39.3
Pasture land	78.0	76.5	71.7	68.2	62.2	81.5
Rivers and lakes	13.7	6.8	18.3	15.1	14.0	7.1
Semi-natural land	96.4	96.0	97.3	96.5	98.5	92.2
Unclassified	18.4	16.7	26.9	28.6	37.5	3.7
Wetland	42.9	63.6	54.5	40.0	66.7	10.0

Quantification is based on observations of MARS Monuments in single land-use by count. Among earthworks (Table 7.12), changes have been slight and not as marked as those suggested by the national figures for the estimated 18% reduction of cultivated land in general, from 56,046km^2 in 1947 (MAFF Statistics Division, York) to 46,105km^2 in 1995 (MAFF *et al.* 1997, table 3.2).

For buildings and standing structures the changes are more marked and involve a move from pastoral and arable uses to developed land. As noted earlier, the majority of buildings and structures are now found in urban environments and this appears to be a result of their transfer to urban/developed areas over the last 50 years. This shift accords very well with known land-take patterns connected with urbanization (eg. Barr *et al.* 1986).

As far as individual monument classes are concerned, Figure 7.16 shows pie diagrams representing the land-use patterns in *c.*1945 and 1995 for a series of prehistoric and later monument classes. Although the samples are generally quite small, the general trends can be seen. For long barrows there is an increase over time of examples in pasture and arable, mainly as a result of the reduced number under forestry. For round barrows the major change is the percentage found to have been destroyed by 1995, most of which probably come from arable and semi-natural land. Roman villas show the same trend, with apparent stability in the level in pasture land. Deserted medieval villages (DMVs) broadly follow the changes indicated by the national averages in Table 7.12 (for earthworks), concentrating on arable land, urban land, forestry and pasture. A slight increase in arable land-use on DMVs (16% to 17%) is countered by slight decreases in pastoral uses (56% to 42%) and in developed and urban land-use (21% to 20%). Afforestation over these monument classes has apparently increased threefold (3% to 6%).

A similar analysis can be carried out for land-use around monuments. Tables 7.14 and 7.15 show the results, again focusing on earthworks and building and structures respectively. The encroachment of developed land around earthworks is clear in Table 7.14, as is the removal of pastoral and arable land-uses. As with the land-use on and over earthworks, the highest proportions of land-use around monuments continue to be occupied by arable (39%), pasture (34%) and semi-natural (13%), although these land-uses decreased over the 50-year period (by 5% in the case of pasture). Interestingly, although arable land-use on earthworks has apparently increased over the period (albeit by only 2% in terms of the number of earthworks under arable regimes) it has in

fact decreased by 6% as a surrounding land-use.

Changes in land-use types surrounding buildings and structures are as marked as changes to land-uses under them (Table 7.15). Further, Tables 7.13 and 7.15 are broadly similar in showing that the proportions of land-use under and surrounding buildings and structures are comparable and that the patterns of the general shift also match. There has, however, been a greater encroachment of developed land-use (46% compared to 32%) around buildings and structures and a greater shift away from arable use (-17% compared to -7%) over 50 years.

The relationship between land-use on and land-use around a monument is potentially very complicated, but Table 7.16 attempts to simplify the situation. Data are compounded to illustrate the proportion of monuments in each decade which have the same land-use on as around the monument for each of the nine MARS land-use classes. Where there are marked differences between the 1980s and the 1995 figure this is attributable to sample size and monument recognition difficulties. What is clear is the overall stability across the decades, and the contrast between the situation in arable land, coastal land, pasture land and semi-natural land where more than 80% of monuments have the same land-use on as around, and the situation in developed and urban land, forestry, rivers and lakes, and wetland where less than half of the monuments represented have different land-uses on and around.

Continuity of land-use is another important feature of the way that MARS Monuments have survived over the last 50 years. In fact, 59% of the total number of MARS Monuments have not changed land-use over the 50-year period. On the other hand, the rest have changed land-use during this time, and still survive. Of the total, 16% numerically and 10.4% by area have been destroyed (which can also be counted as a change of use). Figures 7.17 and 7.18 show a breakdown of changes and losses between 1945 and 1995 by MARS land-use classes. In Figure 7.17 the quantification is by recorded incidence, in Figure 7.18 as land area. In Figure 7.17 land-use classes with the fewest changes are those with the greatest differences between the first two bars in each cluster. Thus wetland, semi-natural land, rivers and lakes, developed and urban, and arable land show the greatest stability. These are all easy to understand except arable which might be expected to change over the decades more than it does. The explanation is probably in terms of investment in cultivated land: once it has been brought into cultivation is stays that way until something forces it into other uses. Figure 7.18 is more sensitive to the details of

Table 7.17 - Patterns of land-use change by decade 1940s - 1950s. Stable relationships are recorded above the shaded lines, changes below. *[Source: MARS Field Survey Programme and Aerial Photographic Survey. Samples as shown]*

1940	1950	Monuments	%1	%2
Static land-use				
Arable land	Arable land	565	26.68	23.53
Pasture land	Pasture land	534	25.21	22.24
Developed & urban land	Developed & urban land	520	24.55	21.66
Forestry	Forestry	237	11.19	9.87
Semi-natural land	Semi-natural land	183	8.64	7.62
Rivers & Lakes	Rivers & Lakes	54	2.55	2.25
Unclassified	Unclassified	14	0.66	0.58
Coastal land	Coastal land	7	0.33	0.29
Wetland	Wetland	4	0.19	0.17
			100%	
Shifting land-use				
Arable land	Pasture land	88	31.10	3.67
Pasture land	Arable land	86	30.39	3.58
Pasture land	Forestry	26	9.19	1.08
Developed & urban land	Pasture land	9	3.18	0.37
Forestry	Developed & urban land	9	3.18	0.37
Pasture land	Developed & urban land	9	3.18	0.37
Developed & urban land	Arable land	8	2.83	0.33
Developed & urban land	Forestry	8	2.83	0.33
Forestry	Pasture land	7	2.47	0.29
Forestry	Arable land	6	2.12	0.25
Arable land	Developed & urban land	5	1.77	0.21
Rivers & Lakes	Pasture land	3	1.06	0.12
Arable land	Forestry	2	0.71	0.08
Developed & urban land	Rivers & Lakes	2	0.71	0.08
Developed & urban land	Semi-natural land	2	0.71	0.08
Pasture land	Rivers & Lakes	2	0.71	0.08
Arable land	Semi-natural land	1	0.35	0.04
Forestry	Coastal land	1	0.35	0.04
Forestry	Semi-natural land	1	0.35	0.04
Forestry	Unclassified	1	0.35	0.04
Pasture land	Semi-natural land	1	0.35	0.04
Pasture land	Unclassified	1	0.35	0.04
Pasture land	Wetland	1	0.35	0.04
Rivers & Lakes	Developed & urban land	1	0.35	0.04
Rivers & Lakes	Forestry	1	0.35	0.04
Semi-natural land	Forestry	1	0.35	0.04
Semi-natural land	Pasture land	1	0.35	0.04
Total		**2401**	**100%**	**100%**

1950	1960	Monuments	%1	%2
Static land-use				
Arable land	Arable land	463	28.94	25.08
Developed & urban land	Developed & urban land	429	26.81	23.24
Pasture land	Pasture land	318	19.88	17.23
Forestry	Forestry	165	10.31	8.94
Semi-natural land	Semi-natural land	164	10.25	8.88
Rivers & Lakes	Rivers & Lakes	39	2.44	2.11
Coastal land	Coastal land	8	0.50	0.43
Unclassified	Unclassified	8	0.50	0.43
Wetland	Wetland	6	0.38	0.33
			100%	
Shifting land-use				
Pasture land	Arable land	101	41.06	5.47
Arable land	Pasture land	57	23.17	3.09
Arable land	Developed & urban land	14	5.69	0.76
Forestry	Pasture land	14	5.69	0.76
Pasture land	Forestry	12	4.88	0.65
Pasture land	Developed & urban land	10	4.07	0.54
Developed & urban land	Forestry	5	2.03	0.27
Forestry	Arable land	5	2.03	0.27
Developed & urban land	Arable land	4	1.63	0.22
Developed & urban land	Pasture land	4	1.63	0.22
Forestry	Developed & urban land	4	1.63	0.22
Arable land	Forestry	2	0.81	0.11
Pasture land	Rivers & Lakes	2	0.81	0.11
Rivers & Lakes	Forestry	2	0.81	0.11
Semi-natural land	Developed & urban land	2	0.81	0.11
Forestry	Rivers & Lakes	1	0.41	0.05
Forestry	Semi-natural land	1	0.41	0.05
Pasture land	Wetland	1	0.41	0.05
Rivers & Lakes	Developed & urban land	1	0.41	0.05
Rivers & Lakes	Pasture land	1	0.41	0.05
Semi-natural land	Forestry	1	0.41	0.05
Unclassified	Developed & urban land	1	0.41	0.05
Unclassified	Forestry	1	0.41	0.05
Total		**1846**	**100%**	**100%**

1960	1970	Monuments	%1	%2
Static land-use				
Arable land	Arable land	504	33.07	28.95
Developed & urban land	Developed & urban land	385	25.26	22.11
Pasture land	Pasture land	303	19.88	17.40
Forestry	Forestry	150	9.84	8.62
Semi-natural land	Semi-natural land	135	8.86	7.75
Rivers & Lakes	Rivers & Lakes	36	2.36	2.07
Coastal land	Coastal land	4	0.26	0.23
Unclassified	Unclassified	4	0.26	0.23
Wetland	Wetland	3	0.20	0.17
			100%	
Shifting land-use				
Pasture land	Arable land	96	44.24	5.51
Arable land	Pasture land	47	21.66	2.70
Arable land	Developed & urban land	11	5.07	0.63
Developed & urban land	Forestry	11	5.07	0.63
Pasture land	Developed & urban land	9	4.15	0.52
Pasture land	Forestry	7	3.23	0.40
Forestry	Pasture land	6	2.76	0.34
Forestry	Developed & urban land	5	2.30	0.29
Developed & urban land	Arable land	4	1.84	0.23
Developed & urban land	Pasture land	4	1.84	0.23
Forestry	Arable land	4	1.84	0.23
Semi-natural land	Pasture land	3	1.38	0.17
Semi-natural land	Developed & urban land	2	0.92	0.11
Wetland	Arable land	2	0.92	0.11
Arable land	Forestry	1	0.46	0.06
Forestry	Rivers & Lakes	1	0.46	0.06
Forestry	Semi-natural land	1	0.46	0.06
Rivers & Lakes	Forestry	1	0.46	0.06
Semi-natural land	Forestry	1	0.46	0.06
Wetland	Pasture land	1	0.46	0.06
Total		**1741**	**100%**	**100%**

1970	1980	Monuments	%1	%2
Static land-use				
Arable land	Arable land	375	43.50	39.47
Developed & urban land	Developed & urban land	168	19.49	17.68
Pasture land	Pasture land	140	16.24	14.74
Semi-natural land	Semi-natural land	83	9.63	8.74
Forestry	Forestry	71	8.24	7.47
Rivers & Lakes	Rivers & Lakes	17	1.97	1.79
Coastal land	Coastal land	3	0.35	0.32
Unclassified	Unclassified	3	0.35	0.32
Wetland	Wetland	2	0.23	0.21
			100%	
Shifting land-use				
Pasture land	Arable land	34	38.64	3.58
Arable land	Pasture land	19	21.59	2.00
Forestry	Arable land	6	6.82	0.63
Pasture land	Developed & urban land	5	5.68	0.53
Forestry	Developed & urban land	4	4.55	0.42
Arable land	Developed & urban land	3	3.41	0.32
Forestry	Pasture land	3	3.41	0.32
Pasture land	Forestry	3	3.41	0.32
Developed & urban land	Arable land	2	2.27	0.21
Developed & urban land	Forestry	2	2.27	0.21
Developed & urban land	Rivers & Lakes	2	2.27	0.21
Developed & urban land	Semi-natural land	2	2.27	0.21
Developed & urban land	Pasture land	1	1.14	0.11
Forestry	Semi-natural land	1	1.14	0.11
Unclassified	Arable land	1	1.14	0.11
Total		**950**	**100%**	**100%**

1980	1995	Monuments	%1	%2
Static land-use				
Arable land	Arable land	339	40.45	29.58
Developed & urban land	Developed & urban land	165	19.69	14.40
Semi-natural land	Semi-natural land	141	16.83	12.30
Pasture land	Pasture land	119	14.20	10.38
Forestry	Forestry	55	6.56	4.80
Rivers & Lakes	Rivers & Lakes	16	1.91	1.40
Coastal land	Coastal land	2	0.24	0.17
Wetland	Wetland	1	0.12	0.09
			100%	
Shifting land-use				
Arable land	Pasture land	71	22.98	6.20
Arable land	Developed & urban land	27	8.74	2.36
Pasture land	Arable land	25	8.09	2.18
Forestry	Pasture land	22	7.12	1.92
Semi-natural land	Pasture land	20	6.47	1.75
Developed & urban land	Pasture land	15	4.85	1.31
Pasture land	Developed & urban land	14	4.53	1.22
Forestry	Developed & urban land	12	3.88	1.05
Pasture land	Semi-natural land	12	3.88	1.05
Developed & urban land	Forestry	11	3.56	0.96
Pasture land	Forestry	11	3.56	0.96
Semi-natural land	Developed & urban land	7	2.27	0.61
Developed & urban land	Unclassified	6	1.94	0.52
Rivers & Lakes	Developed & urban land	6	1.94	0.52
Semi-natural land	Rivers & Lakes	6	1.94	0.52
Developed & urban land	Rivers & Lakes	5	1.62	0.44
Pasture land	Rivers & Lakes	5	1.62	0.44
Developed & urban land	Arable land	5	1.62	0.44
Unclassified	Developed & urban land	4	1.29	0.35
Arable land	Forestry	3	0.97	0.26
Developed & urban land	Semi-natural land	2	0.65	0.17
Forestry	Arable land	2	0.65	0.17
Forestry	Rivers & Lakes	2	0.65	0.17
Pasture land	Coastal land	2	0.65	0.17
Arable land	Unclassified	1	0.32	0.09
Coastal land	Wetland	1	0.32	0.09
Developed & urban land	Coastal land	1	0.32	0.09
Developed & urban land	Wetland	1	0.32	0.09
Forestry	Semi-natural land	1	0.32	0.09
Forestry	Unclassified	1	0.32	0.09
Pasture land	Unclassified	1	0.32	0.09
Rivers & Lakes	Arable land	1	0.32	0.09
Rivers & Lakes	Semi-natural land	1	0.32	0.09
Semi-natural land	Arable land	1	0.32	0.09
Semi-natural land	Unclassified	1	0.32	0.09
Unclassified	Forestry	1	0.32	0.09
Wetland	Pasture land	1	0.32	0.09
Wetland	Wetland	1	0.32	0.09
Total		**11436**	**100%**	**100%**

Notes: %1 column summed separately for static and shifting land-use
%2 column not summed separately for static and shifting land-use

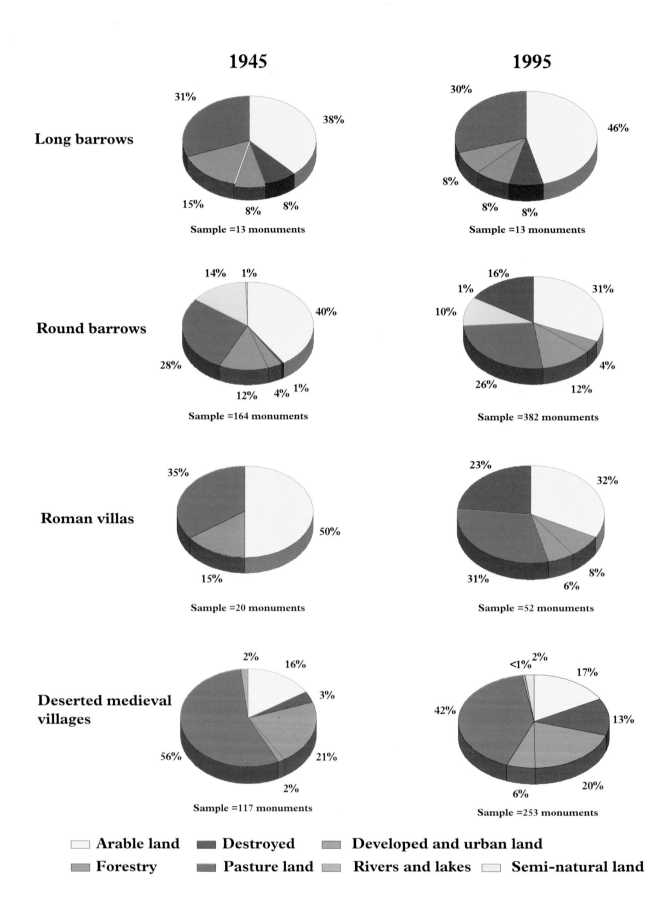

1945

1995

Long barrows

31% 38%
15% 8% 8%

Sample =13 monuments

30% 46%
8% 8% 8%

Sample =13 monuments

Round barrows

14% 1% 40%
28% 12% 4% 1%

Sample =164 monuments

16% 1% 31%
10% 4%
26% 12%

Sample =382 monuments

Roman villas

35% 50%
15%

Sample =20 monuments

23% 32%
8%
31% 6%

Sample =52 monuments

Deserted medieval villages

2% 16%
3%
56% 21%
2%

Sample =117 monuments

<1% 2% 17%
42% 13%
6% 20%

Sample =253 monuments

☐ **Arable land** ▨ **Destroyed** ▨ **Developed and urban land**
▨ **Forestry** ▨ **Pasture land** ▨ **Rivers and lakes** ☐ **Semi-natural land**

Figure 7.16 - Pie charts showing changing land-use patterns between *c*.1945 and 1995 for a selection of four monument classes. Quantified by count. *[Source: MARS Field Survey Programme and Aerial Photographic Programme. Samples: as shown]*

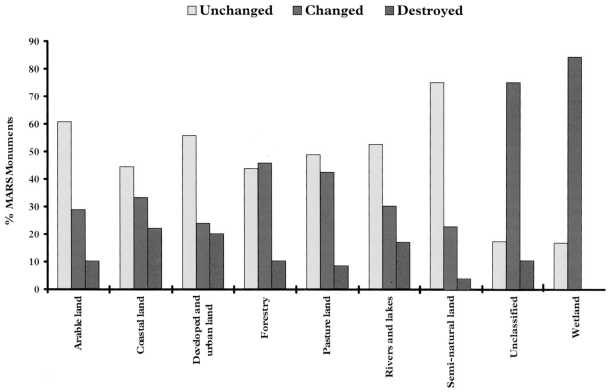

Figure 7.17 - Multiple bar chart showing the percentage of MARS Monuments that remained in a defined land-use class (left-hand bar), changed land-use(centre bar), or were destroyed (right-hand bar) during the period *c*.1945/95. Quantified by count. *[Source: MARS Field Survey Programme and Aerial Photographic Programme. Sample: n= 1201 observations]*

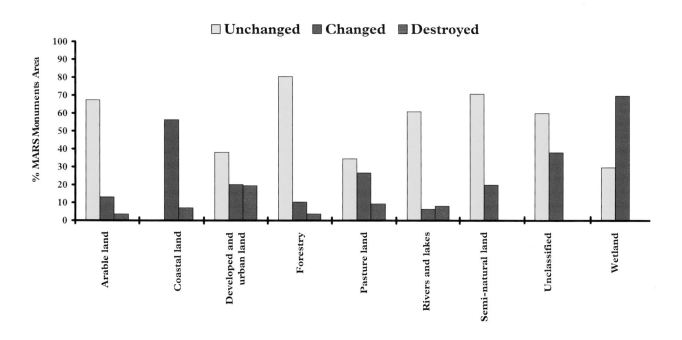

Figure 7.18 - Multiple bar chart showing the percentage of MARS Monuments that remained in a defined land-use class, changed land-use, or were destroyed during the period *c*.1945/95. Quantified by area. *[Source: MARS Field Survey Programme and Aerial Photographic Programme. Sample: n= 1201]*

Figure 7.19 - Multiple bar charts showing regional variations in land-use stability, change and losses *c*.1945-95. Quantified by area. *[Source: MARS Field Survey Programme and Aerial Photographic Programme. Sample: n= 1284 observations]*

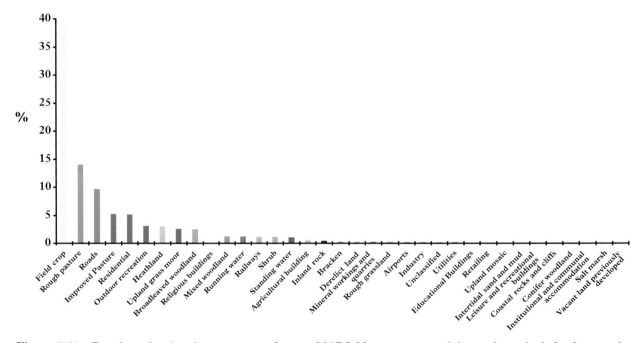

Figure 7.20 - Bar chart showing the percentage of extant MARS Monuments remaining under a single land-use regime (LUSAG narrow land-use classes) over the period 1945-95. *[Source: MARS Field Survey Programme and Aerial Photographic Programme. Sample: n= 1201 observations]*

land-use change and enables partial destruction to be included in the calculations. In terms of area, it is clear that high percentages of archaeological monuments in most land-use classes have remained unchanged.

There are also regional differences in land-use stability. Figure 7.19 shows a series of bar charts for the six MARS Regions showing change, loss and stability among MARS earthwork monuments. The variations show slightly higher rates of change on monuments in the South West and North West than elsewhere.

Figure 7.20 looks in greater detail at the land-use classes that apply to those monuments remaining in the same land-use over the 50-year period. Nearly 40% of those that remained static were under field crop, a point which serves to emphasize both the importance and the stability of this particular land-use regime. Field cropping, together with rough pasture, roads and improved pasture, accounts for about 75% of all observations. This suggests that once a monument falls under any one of these regimes, it is likely to stay under it for a considerable period. This trend will inevitably disguise local variation, but nevertheless the figures remain valid.

Long-term land-uses such as road-building and residential development contribute to the overall proportion of static land-use, and while they represent a virtually irreversible hazard to the archaeological resource anything that is left after the initial impact passes will be subject to relatively low levels of land-use hostility.

Gains and losses are potentially more important for archaeology than for some other environmental resources because losses to hostile land-uses (e.g development or agriculture) cannot be made up by gains moving the other way. Figure 7.21 shows the pattern of changes decade by decade from a baseline in *c.*1945. Totally destroyed monuments have been excluded from these calculations. The actual shifts in land-use represented at the MARS Monuments studied are summarized in Table 7.17, where the before and after land-uses for all those monuments that changed land-use during a given decade are recorded. Above the shaded band in each column the table records stability across the decade, below the shading change. These shifts occur for a variety of reasons, perhaps largely motivated by economic considerations, and for shifts over archaeological monuments this is never more visible than in the contrast between the 1940s and 1950s. Stamp (1962, 1) notes that the factors affecting the pattern of land-use in the 1930s were equally evident in the 1960s, although this and the pace of change were abruptly reversed during the inter-war years by wartime conditions. There were 310 sampled land-use changes between the 1940s and 1950s, of which 31% were from arable to pasture, 30% pasture to arable, and 9% pasture to forestry. Changes in later decades show the increasing movement of arable to pasture as net gains exceed the inevitable movements both ways as land moves in and out of short-ley pasture. Changes from the 1980s to the 1990s are slightly different, and need treating with some caution, because the 1990s are represented by data derived from field survey rather than from aerial photographs.

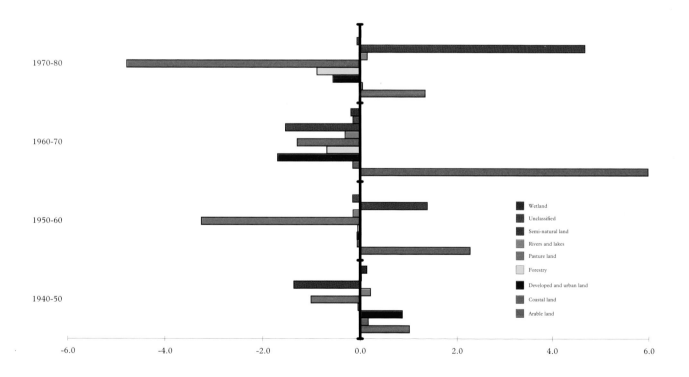

Figure 7.21 - Bar charts showing gains and losses by decade 1940s to 1980s for specified land-use classes over MARS Monuments. Quantified by area. *[Source: MARS Aerial Photographic Programme. Sample: observations 1940s n= 3783; 1950s n= 2493; 1960s n= 2655; 1970s n= 2608; 1980s n= 1397]*

7.5 Five key land-uses: patterns of change and forward projections

In all the foregoing considerations of land-use patterns it is clear that over 96% of the recorded archaeological resource is subsumed within five key land-use classes: pasture land, arable land, developed land, semi-natural land and forestry. Each of these is considered in further detail in the following sub-sections, based on the results from the MARS Field Survey and the Aerial Photographic Programmes.

7.5.1 Pasture land

Long-term pasture is widely recognized as the best possible form of land-use for the preservation of archaeological monuments. During the last 50 years over 28% of MARS Monuments have been under pasture at some stage, 14% of them throughout the period. In 1995 approximately 21% of MARS Monuments with a single

land-use regime, 33% by area, lay under pasture.

Pasture land embraces the following LUSAG narrow land-use classes: improved pasture, rough pasture and rough grassland. This land-use class covered approximately 43% of the land surface of England in 1947, 34% of land area in 1980 (Countryside Commission 1990a), and approximately 33% of land area in 1990 (Environment Agency 1996, 18). Pasture is important for archaeology because, whether it is used for grazing by livestock or as a source of cut grass for hay or silage, the focus of interest is the ground surface itself and the grass sward that forms the vegetation cover. Grass is not deep rooting so there is little ground penetration; a strong and productive sward depends on maintaining a dense surface cover of healthy plants, which means there is little exposed soil, and quality is in large measure determined by the length of time the land is kept under grass without disturbance. Indeed, disturbance of vegetation cover is the greatest problem with grassland

Figure 7.22 - Grassington, North Yorkshire. A prehistoric field system in pasture visible as low-relief earthworks overlain by a post-medieval arrangement represented by stone walls. *[Photograph: Cambridge University Collection of Air Photographs. Copyright reserved]*

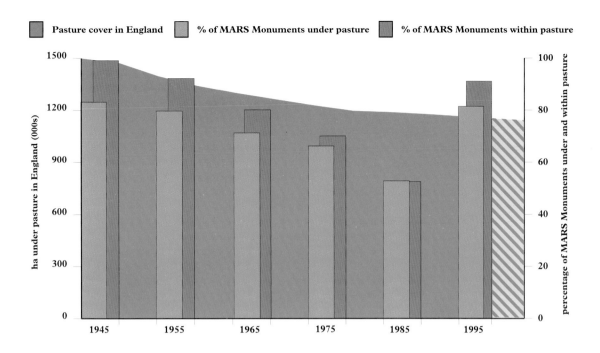

Figure 7.23 - The changing picture of MARS Monuments (excluding buildings) under pasture land. The filled area shows the changing extent of pasture land in England 1945 to 1995 and projected forward in relation to the percentage of MARS Monuments under pasture [blue bars] and situated within pasture [red bars]. *[Sources: MARS Field Survey Programme and Aerial Photographic Programme. Samples: n= 3234 observations for 1945; n= 2123 observations for 1955; n= 2253 observations for 1965; n= 2272 observations for 1975; n= 1192 observations for 1985; n= 7259 observations for 1995]*

management and is therefore guarded against by regulating stock levels and allowing time for regeneration.

Maintenance of grassland requires regular mowing or grazing, occasional aeration of the soil if compaction becomes a problem, weed and scrub control, and the maintenance of nutrient levels through natural manuring as a result of grazing or top-dressing. Pasture land supports substantial earthworm populations (typically 500 per square metre in neutral to alkaline soils) and it has been suggested that the weight of earthworms beneath pasture may equal the weight of animals grazing upon it (Limbrey 1975, 29-30). The worms ensure bioturbation of subsurface materials through worm-sorting of the soil profile and the downward movement of large objects such as stones (Edwards and Lofty 1972). This phenomenon was first studied in detail by Charles Darwin (1888, 151-61), who used the sinkage of some of the fallen sarsens at Stonehenge to illustrate his observations.

The importance of pasture land for the preservation of archaeological monuments is illustrated by the various studies listed in APPENDIX O.4. Figure 7.22 shows an aerial view of extensive prehistoric, Romano-British and later field systems preserved under pasture in the central Pennines near Grassington, in the Yorkshire Dales, North Yorkshire. The early field systems are marked by low banks and earthworks covered by grass, whereas the more recent field walls, which are still in use, are upstanding and have no grass cover. As at Grassington, the existing pattern of fields and walls is itself an archaeological monument. A survey of stone field walls in 700 1km by 1km sample units undertaken in 1994 by ADAS revealed that while 13% of existing walls were basically sound and stockproof, 29% were in derelict of remnant state (Dyson 1995).

Pasture has two critical effects on buried archaeology. First, the use of land as pasture is not itself damaging to the morphology or topography of underlying features and structures, the grass itself providing a robust cover-mat that serves also as a self-regenerating sacrificial layer in the event of surface abrasion. Second, the use of the land as pasture precludes the need for, and indeed positively discourages, the use of heavy ground-disturbing machinery. The only exception to this might be pasture improvement in poorly drained or rocky areas, a process generally too costly to contemplate except where grants and subsidies are available. The result is that in long-term pasture archaeological remains are sealed below the surface, although often visible in favourable conditions as slight relief. The state of preservation at any particular site very much depends on earlier land-use patterns, for example the impact of later prehistoric, Romano-British or medieval ploughing. In cases where pasture has developed immediately after the abandonment of structures preservation can be exceptional, as in the case of some of the remains on Overton and Fyfield Downs in north Wiltshire (Fowler 1967).

Large-scale pasture improvements have not been common in England in recent decades, although some problems have been encountered in Cornwall, where stone-removal has led to the erosion or destruction of some monuments (Johnson and Rose 1983). Similar difficulties have arisen elsewhere in the British Isles, for example in south-west Wales (Benson 1989). It should be borne in mind, however, that stone removal and pasture improvement go back a long way. Corrugation of field surfaces to increase the grazing area of a field by up to 10% is a well-established tradition in England and can give rise to earthworks that look superficially like ridge and furrow. The creation of stone walls during the enclosure movement or before in many parts of western England probably caused the loss or denudation of numerous earlier stone structures such as hut-circles, standing stones and field banks.

Figure 7.23 shows a two-way graph with changes to the overall extent of pasture land in England in relation to the proportion of MARS Monuments recorded as under pasture land in successive decades. Figures for 2000 are projected forwards, assuming a continuation of the same general trend as for recent decades (MAFF and DAFS 1968; MAFF *et al.* 1996). The trends are interesting because the gradual but slowing decrease in area of land under this regime broadly matches the trend of MARS Monuments under pasture. The MARS trendline suggests that monuments are slowly being taken out of pasture.

The rate of decrease in the overall coverage of pasture apparently started to slow after about 1980 and this raises a number of important policy and strategic considerations. First, the move to extensify pasture fits comfortably with the general intention to take archaeological sites into less hostile land-uses. What is needed is some way of targeting the transfer of land into pasture for enhanced benefit, and some means of retaining the land as pasture once it has shifted. The real benefits to the preservation of archaeological remains from being in pasture land take years if not decades to accrue. Second, and in direct opposition to the previous point, it is relatively difficult to undertake extensive surveys based on surface collection on land under pasture, and the potential

of such land for yielding information by aerial reconnaissance is also more restricted.

7.5.2 *Arable land*

Arable land represents the single most extensive land-use in England (39% of land area); 17.5% of monuments in numerical terms under a single land-use regime, 35% by area, lay under arable in 1995, an estimated 12,270ha of archaeology. More importantly, it was recorded as the situational environment for 30% of monuments. Looking back over the last 50 years, 37% of MARS Monuments have been under arable cultivation at one stage or another.

Arable land is here taken to consist of the following LUSAG narrow land-use classes: field crop, horticulture, fallow land and allotments. Historically, the peak year for the extent of arable land was 1871 when as much as 60,000km^2 were cultivated (Best and Coppock 1962, 72). Since that time there as been an overall decline in cultivation, although with a series of ups and downs. It has been estimated that between 1866 and 1966 an average of 67% of all land in England and Wales was under crops and grass, with fluctuations peaking as high as 74% in the period to 1916 (Marks 1989, 130). In 1947 approximately 41,500km^2 of land were under cultivation, 32% of the land area of England. By 1980 this had risen to about 51,600km^2, 40% of England's land area (Countryside Commission 1990a). More recently the amount of land in cultivation has fallen and by 1990 about 32% of land was tilled (Environment Agency 1996, 18).

Arable cultivation is generally hostile to the long-

Figure 7.24 - Colluvium deposit in a valley below the Cotswold escarpment in The Buckles, Frocester, Gloucestershire, in 1983. The excavated surface dates to the middle Bronze Age (*c.*1200 BC), since when it has become sealed beneath up to 2m of colluvium. *[Photograph: Timothy Darvill. Copyright reserved]*

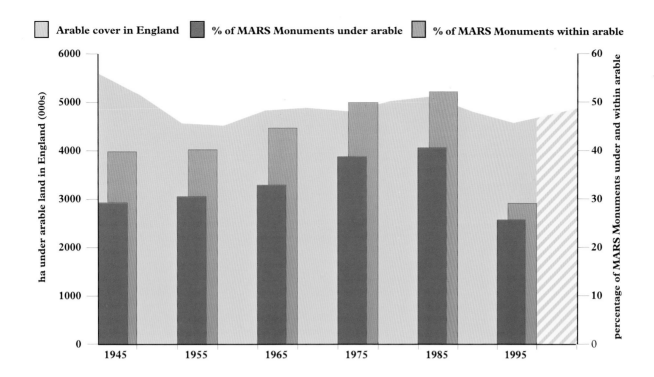

Figure 7.25 - The changing picture of MARS Monuments (excluding buildings) under arable land. The filled area shows the changing extent of arable land in England 1945 to 1995 and projected forward in relation to the percentage of MARS Monuments under arable [blue bars] and situated within arable [red bars]. *[Sources: MARS Field Survey Programme and Aerial Photographic Programme. Samples: n= 3234 observations for 1945; n= 2123 observations for 1955; n= 2253 observations for 1965; n= 2272 observations for 1975; n= 1192 observations for 1985; n= 7259 observations for 1995]*

term preservation of archaeological remains and is widely recognized as one of the most extensive and destructive threats currently known. The problem is caused by the use of the land itself, by the processes involved in cultivation, which works on an annual cycle and makes use of increasingly heavy and powerful machinery. Details of the process of cultivation have been described with reference ·to archaeological remains on several occasions (Lambrick 1977; Hinchliffe and Schadla-Hall 1980), and Chapter 6.8.1 considered in some detail the evidence for damage caused by cultivation. The important factor for archaeology, which is inherent to all arable land-use, is the need to utilize not just the surface of the land but the whole topsoil.

The archaeological implications of ongoing arable land-use can be judged from an examination of the excavation reports and surveys listed in Appendix O (and see Darvill 1987, chapter 12). The damage caused by cultivation has been noted, but archaeology derives two positive benefits from cultivation that should also be noted.

First it makes buried monuments easier to recognize and allows the application of extensive reconnaissance techniques such as fieldwalking and aerial photography (especially monument recognition and mapping based on soilmarks and cropmarks). The current sophistication of these methods is undoubtedly a consequence of the opportunities presented by relatively high levels of arable cultivation in recent decades, the urgency of the need to survey these tracts of countryside before the evidence itself is lost, and the responsiveness (and thus cost-effectiveness) of arable land to the techniques themselves.

As was shown in Chapter 4.8 in recent decades over 7% of additions and more than 3% of enhancements have been based on studies which were possible only as a result of the active erosion of the resource itself.

Second is that downslope soil movement resulting from cultivation of hillsides sometimes results in the development of a cover-layer of colluvium several metres thick that seals and protects valley-bottom monuments and ancient land-surfaces. Investigations of these deposits have been carried out, among other places, in Sussex (Bell 1983), around Avebury, Wiltshire (Evans *et al.* 1993), and below the Cotswold escarpment in Gloucestershire (Figure 7.24). The archaeology represented is among the most intractable in terms of discovering its existence through conventional techniques.

Figure 7.25 shows changes in proportion of MARS Monuments under arable cultivation over the last 50 years in relation to changes in the total area of this land-use over the period. Both figures are projected forward to 2000 on the assumption that recent trends will continue and on the basis of known projections related to European agricultural policy. As already noted, the amount of land in cultivation in England fluctuates within short and medium-term cycles, although since 1945 the overall trend has been downwards, and since the mid 1980s there has been a progressive reduction in arable land. This is, at least superficially, good for the long-term preservation of archaeological remains in regions of the country where arable agriculture is widespread. However, reductions in the area of arable land do not appear to have been translated into any marked change in the representation of archaeological monuments under or within arable.

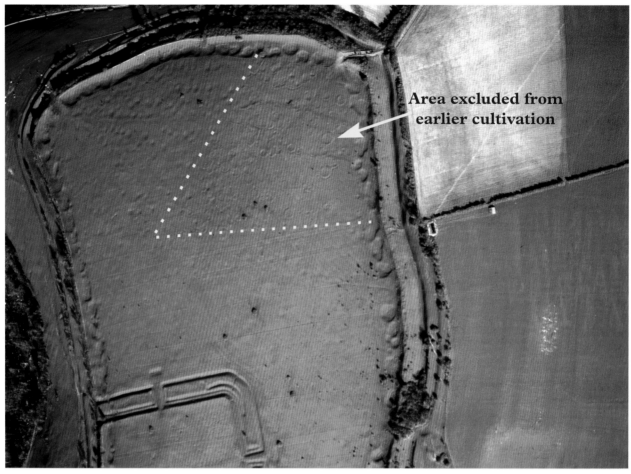

Area excluded from earlier cultivation

Figure 7.26 - Hod Hill, Dorset, aerial view of the Iron hillfort and Roman fort, showing differences in the preservation of archaeological features within the hillfort caused by successive episodes of ploughing in different sectors. *[Photograph: RCHME. Copyright reserved]*

In the face of declining arable land-use, the question that must be asked is what land-use is replacing cultivation. Table 7.17 shows the evidence from MARS Monuments, where switches of land-use out of arable between 1985 and 1995 are mainly accounted for by arable land becoming pasture (23%), developed land (9%) or forestry (1%). The loss of arable land to developed land is the most damaging of these trends.

Not all land in England is capable of being brought into arable cultivation. Climatic and topographical factors limit the extent of arable land-use across England, so that eastern England, from Lincolnshire to Essex, is predominantly an arable landscape, and a band of less intensive cultivation runs across the country from Dorset to Yorkshire. This arrangement has historical antecedents and is visible in the distribution of preserved settlement patterns and field systems (Roberts 1996).

The most problematic relationship between archaeological monuments and arable land-use is in marginal areas which are brought into cultivation for short periods, usually because of specific economic and political circumstances. In the period covered by MARS the expansion of arable cultivation as part of the war effort during the 1940s is the most dramatic and best documented of these events. Many marginal areas were brought into use, especially in southern England (for example west Dorset).

This was not the first time short-term economic

trends had prompted such an endeavour, however, and some archaeological monuments show evidence of several phases of expansion and contraction. A good example is Hod Hill, Dorset, a later prehistoric hillfort and Roman fort covering 21.8ha. Figure 7.26 shows an aerial view of the site. About half of the interior of the hillfort was first ploughed-up in 1858 and continued in cultivation until the later 1890s when it reverted to grassland until the 1940s (Crawford and Keiller 1928). During the Second World War more than three-quarters of the fort was brought into cultivation, including areas formerly ploughed (RCHME 1970, 263-5). The Roman fort in the north-west corner was excavated by Sir Ian Richmond between 1951 and 1958 (Richmond 1968). The early phase of cultivation was prompted by improved techniques of cultivation and economic circumstances which encouraged the ploughing of former grassland, and it continued until increasing imports of cheaper grain from North America late in the nineteenth century made arable cultivation of this land economically unviable. One section in the south-east corner of the Iron Age hillfort has avoided cultivation and here can be found some of the best preserved earthwork remains of houses, boundaries and scoops known at any Iron Age Hillforts in southern England and presumably typical of what must once have been visible in similar monuments.

A similar situation can be found around the most famous prehistoric monument in Europe, the site of

Figure 7.27 - Urban development. Aerial photograph of the city of York, North Yorkshire. The line of the medieval city walls can clearly be seen on both sides of the river, modern development being notable both inside and outside the historic core. *[Photograph: Cambridge University Collection of Air Photographs. Copyright reserved]*

Stonehenge in Wiltshire. Here a survey of monuments and land-use carried out by RCHME in the mid 1970s (RCHME 1979) revealed two main phases of agricultural damage in historic times, although recognized that still earlier cultivation dating back into prehistory had contributed to monument decay. The earliest phase dates to the eighteenth century and is documented by the writings of antiquaries such as William Stukeley (see citation at the head of this chapter) and Richard Colt Hoare. The second phase occurred in the mid twentieth century and can be seen by comparing illustrations made in the nineteenth century with the state of monuments in the 1970s and 1980s. Among the main casualties of this second phase of intensification was the western end of the Stonehenge cursus, flattened by bulldozing in the early 1950s (Christie 1960).

Since 1972 agriculture in England has been strategically controlled through the European Community's Common Agricultural Policy (CAP), and this looks likely to continue for the foreseeable future (EC 1989; Lowe and Whitby 1997; Ritson and Harvey 1997). The increase of agricultural production, mainly cereal production, remains central among the main principles underpinning this policy in the UK. This, it was argued, ensured a fair standard of living for those engaged in farming, reasonable consumer prices and stable markets. The success of the CAP has been mixed, however. Many of the original principles on which it was established have largely been met, but at the cost of food surpluses, increased agricultural expenditure, declining farm incomes and growing public unease about food safety and environmental issues. The environmental effects of implementing the policy have become increasingly clear, and the various policy reviews and reforms from the mid 1980s onwards have been geared specifically to the introduction of set-aside, extensification (support for

cutting output of products in surplus) and diversification (support for non-traditional products). Recognizing that farmers are among the most important stewards of the countryside, the 1992 policy reform went further by suggesting that farmers were also in a prime position to preserve the natural environment and traditional landscapes (Whitby 1994). In the case of Britain the agri-environmental potential of the reform was reinforced with a consultation document (MAFF and DoE 1995) considering the full range of schemes in place. One of the document's main aims was to gauge the success of set-aside up to 1995 and to set out proposals for the transfer of responsibility for set-aside from the Countryside Commission to MAFF. English Heritage also now plays a part in the review and development of agri-environmental issues as part of MAFF's Agri-Environmental Forum (MAFF 1996). The effect of the policy on the archaeological resource has been explored by Owen-John (1994) and Brown (1997), who suggest that the payment schemes often conflict with the needs of monument conservation. The role of payment schemes is considered further in Chapter 8.

7.5.3 Developed and urban land

Developed and urban land is the most rapidly expanding land-use class in England, and like arable land it carries with it an inherent hostility to the long-term survival of archaeological monuments and deposits. It is estimated that in 1945 some 9% of England lay under developed land; by 1995 this had risen to 10% of land area.

In 1995 approximately 44% of recorded monuments under a single land-use regime lay under urban and developed land; 13% by area. About 31% of monuments were situated within such land.

The definition of developed and urban land covers a wide range of individual uses, and LUSAG narrow land-use classes embraced by it are summarized on Table 7.2. Archaeologically, the range of monuments and deposits represented is also extremely diverse. The majority of monuments (60%) recorded on developed land are buildings and structures. The archaeology of such areas is complicated, however, by the fact that many contain a historic core in which archaeological remains are represented as largely undifferentiated (and mainly unrecorded) deposits. Around such a core there is land which during the life of the ancient urban centre was countryside of one sort or another but which has subsequently been drawn into urban use. Moreover, since urban areas are themselves a relatively recent phenomenon (the earliest being Roman), there is as much chance of the existence of prehistoric remains under urban areas as for any comparable area of the countryside.

The differences between historic core areas and more recent additions to urban areas can often be appreciated from street patterns and the effects of earlier defensive lines. Figure 7.27 shows an aerial view of York with its historic centre clearly delineated by the medieval town walls.

Historically, the development of urban deposits has been both good and bad for archaeology. Centuries of settlement activity within the confines of the city walls means that in most cities deep deposits have accumulated. In the City of London, along the rivers Thames and Wallbrook, and in many more localized areas, there is more than 4m of stratification representing the development of this area from early Roman times through to the eighteenth century (Biddle and Hudson 1973). In York the situation is similar, with 5m or more of recorded deposits along the banks of the rivers Foss and Ouse, and between 1m and 3m elsewhere (OAP 1991, 22). The total volume of these deposits has been estimated at 3.8 million cubic metres (Addyman 1974, 153). Even relatively modest historic towns can boast substantial deposits. In a large area of central Cirencester, for example, up to 3m of stratification, mainly representing Roman occupation, has been preserved under the Brewery car park and adjacent streets (Darvill and Gerrard 1994, 76). On the other hand, the density of occupation and pressure on space in urban areas has meant that each new phase of development and rebuilding, whether for a single plot or whole sectors, has had a considerable impact on earlier levels. In early times, for example, foundation trenches, pits and drains cut down into earlier levels. This in turn means that the finds assemblages and environmental sequences of urban deposits contain high levels of residuality.

The urban processes of development and redevelopment represent big threats to the long-term preservation of buried deposits and monuments. Much attention has been given to balancing preservation with development and change in urban areas, especially from the later 1960s (MHLG 1967) and the preparation of conservation studies in four historic towns - Bath (Buchanan and Partners 1968), Chester (Insall and Associates 1968), Chichester (Burrows 1968) and York

(Esher 1968) which can now be seen to have opened the way, and indeed set the pattern, for more detailed archaeological assessments in the 1970s and 1980s (see APPENDIX A.4). Like agriculture, the threats are inherent to the land-use and cannot easily be averted, except by the invention and application of building systems that perpetuate the urban tradition with minimal sub-surface impact. This is possible up to a point, and such techniques have successfully been applied in numerous cases, but deep holes must still sometimes be dug during development. There are also concerns about the real long-term value of some approaches to minimizing impact (e.g. Biddle 1994, 8).

The importance of urban and developed land for the preservation of archaeological monuments is illustrated by the various studies listed in APPENDIX O.11. Special attention needs to be devoted to the fact that some kinds of deposit found in urban areas and developed land occur only very rarely in other land-use classes. This is especially the case for those settlement forms which from Roman times onwards have themselves been urban areas. In most cases the urban role of these settlements has been continuous, but obvious exceptions to this for the Roman period include Silchester, Hampshire, and Wroxeter, Shropshire, which are now situated in open countryside under multiple land-uses.

Figure 7.28 shows a two-way graph reflecting changes to the overall extent of urban and developed land in England in relation to the proportion of MARS Monuments under this land-use in successive decades.

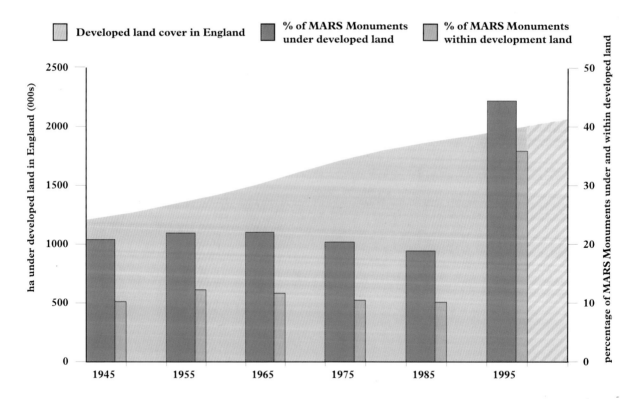

Figure 7.28 - The changing picture of MARS Monuments under urban and developed land. The filled area shows the changing extent of urban and developed land in England 1945-95, and projected forward, in relation to the percentage of MARS Monuments under urban and developed land [blue bars] and situated within urban and developed land [red bars].
[Sources: MARS Field Survey Programme and Aerial Photographic Programme. Samples: Samples: n= 3858 observations for 1945; n= 2559 observations for 1955; n= 2730 observations for 1965; n= 2669 observations for 1975; n= 1416 observations for 1985; n= 11,710 observations for 1995]

The significant increase in urban and developed land since 1945 broadly correlates with an increase in this type of land-use under ancient monuments. There is, however, a sharper increase over the period for monuments surrounded by this land-use than for those subjected to it. Overall, this confirms the largely consistent land-use patterns on and around most monuments in urban and developed environments.

The growth of urban and developed land in England since 1945 has mainly been through planned programmes of development, promoted and controlled through the town and country planning system. Infilling and areal expansion have been the two cornerstones of urban development and redevelopment, the emphasis shifting between them locally and nationally over the decades.

One particularly important contributor to the growth of urban areas between 1946 and 1970 has been the New Towns programme (Ratcliffe 1992; see also Wormell 1978, 49-53). Following the *New Towns Act 1946* twenty-one new towns were established in England with a total land area of 83,129ha: Stevenage (1946), Crawley (1947), Hemel Hempstead (1947), Harlow (1947), Aycliffe (1947), Peterlee (1948), Hatfield (1948), Welwyn Garden City (1948), Basildon (1949), Bracknell (1949), Corby (1950), Skelmersdale (1961), Redditch (1964), Runcorn (1964), Washington (1964), Milton Keynes (1967), Peterborough (1967), Northampton (1968), Warrington (1968), Telford (1968) and Central Lancashire (1970). New towns were also created in Scotland (six) and Wales (two).

Many of these new towns had small historic cores, and at least from the 1960s onwards were the subject of detailed archaeological assessments (see APPENDIX A.4). The concentration of early examples around London is particularly noticeable, although after 1950 the distribution was expanded into the Midlands and north of England.

Since 1970 no New Towns have been designated, and instead the policy has been to increase existing urban areas mainly through outward expansion (green-field

development), although since 1990 increased attention has been devoted to previously developed land within existing urban areas (brown-field development). Despite a number of attempts to reintroduce the idea of new town settlements, notably along the A10 in Cambridgeshire and beside the M3 in Hampshire, they have always been resisted. The basic idea, however, is frequently revived and it is probably only a matter of time before some kind of entirely new settlement is approved (Fyson 1997).

Government statistics show a decrease in the percentage of new urban land being taken from agricultural use from 38% in 1985 to 33% in 1992, accompanied by an increase in the percentage taken from land which was previously developed or was vacant within built-up areas from 51% in 1985 to 58% in 1992 (DETR 1997).

The forward projections for areas in urban and developed land-use shown on Figure 7.28 are based on two factors: recent trends and government statistics showing expected demands. Current projections suggest that by 2016 about 11.9% of England will be urban and developed land. The archaeological implications of this are considered in Chapter 6.8.2.

It is important to emphasize, however, that while urban and developed land allocations for England are established at regional level, the allocations are being passed down to counties, districts and unitary authorities to achieve through their strategic plans. The estimates are based on demographic projections and anticipated demand, and organizations such as the CPRE regularly challenge them (e.g. Sinclair 1992).

7.5.4 Semi-natural land

Semi-natural land is the most diverse and widely scattered land-use class in England. At some stage during the last 50 years over 14% of MARS Monuments have been under semi-natural land, but in 1995 only 7% of monuments under a single land-use regime lay under semi-natural land and 9.05% within areas of semi-natural land.

Semi-natural land occurs mainly in the uplands, but there are also substantial tracts in lowland areas. The broad class embraces the following LUSAG narrow land-use classes: bracken, heathland, inland rock, upland grass moor and upland mosaic. This land-use class covered 13,300km^2, approximately 10% of the land surface of England, in 1949, but by 1980 this had fallen to 9700km^2, 7.4% of land area (Countryside Commission 1990a). These reductions have been documented in more detail for specific areas in connection with archaeological surveys. For example, work in Cornwall has shown that on Bodmin Moor the semi-natural land has declined from 12,200ha in 1946 to 9500ha by 1984, a loss of 16%. In West Penwith, about 20% of the moorland was lost over the same period (Johnson 1986, 226).

Semi-natural land is very important for archaeology because it is not very productive in agricultural terms, and it is not very intensively used. However, its value for other conservation interests is generally high, and its future management is mainly bound up with the need to maintain existing plant and animal habitats. On the whole this is good for the preserved archaeology, although ironically the archaeological remains themselves often represent phases of intensive activity and over-exploitation of fragile ecosystems which were directly responsible for

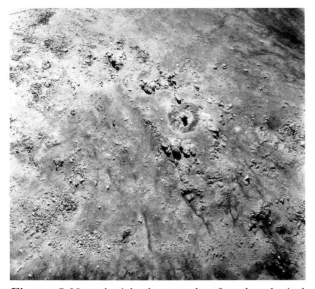

Figure 7.29 - Aerial photograph of archaeological remains preserved at Showery Tor, Bodmin, under semi-natural land-use. The tor and its surrounding tor-cairn can be seen in the centre of the picture. *[Photograph: RCHME. Copyright reserved]*

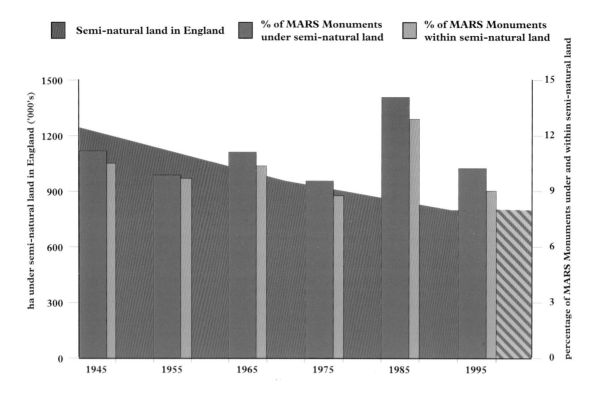

Figure 7.30 - The changing picture of MARS Monuments under semi-natural land. The filled area shows the changing extent of semi-natural land in England 1945 to 1995, and projected forward, in relation to the percentage of MARS Monuments under semi-natural land [blue bars] and situated within semi-natural land [red bars]. *[Sources: MARS Field Survey Programme and Aerial Photographic Programme. Samples: n= 3234 observations for 1945; n= 2123 observations for 1955; n= 2253 observations for 1965; n= 2272 observations for 1975; n= 1192 observations for 1985; n= 7259 observations for 1995]*

the creation of today's environments.

The concept of minimal management is axiomatic to the definition of semi-natural land. This, coupled with the great variability of this type of land, means that little is known about the archaeological remains, and it is very hard to generalize about their quality and condition and the threats they face from this land-use regime. APPENDICES O.6 and O.9 list some of the main surveys and excavations in areas of semi-natural land-use.

Prehistoric (especially Bronze Age) and medieval monuments predominate, but the lesson of all the surveys carried out in recent years is that many traditional assumptions about these areas need to be modified. Two deserve special mention. First, because stone is common and was widely used during some periods there has been a tendency to neglect monuments in other materials which are rarely visible on the surface. The excavation of stone monuments on Dartmoor which revealed timber predecessors is one example of this (Fleming 1988, 78; Wainwright *et al.* 1979, 10).

Second, even the range of monument classes and the distribution of known examples in stone under-represent what was once present. Surveys have revealed many previously unrecognized classes of structure in these semi-natural areas. Figure 7.29 is an aerial photograph of Showery Tor, Bodmin, Cornwall, where a ring of stones has been constructed around a natural rock outcrop. Although undated, it is probably Neolithic or Bronze Age, one of a series of structures where an essentially natural feature has been elaborated through the addition of man-made features. Showery Tor is typical of many areas of semi-natural land-use: the archaeological remains are

either on or above the ground surface or sealed by relatively thin layers of vegetation. Equally, the distribution of monuments such as cup and ring marks is now recognized as being far wider than was once thought; again, they are concentrated in semi-natural land-use areas (Beckensall 1993).

Semi-natural land-use has two critical implications for buried remains. In the first place, the maintenance of semi-natural conditions is rarely damaging to the morphology or topography of underlying features and structures; in many cases the vegetation provides a robust cover-mat that also serves as a self-regenerating sacrificial layer in the event of surface abrasion. In the second place, the very low intensity of land-use and the hostile nature of many tracts of semi-natural land preclude or discourage the use of heavy ground-disturbing machinery, the exception being areas where bracken growth is widespread. Bracken poses a special problem because the root systems penetrate the ground very deeply (in some cases up to 4m; Perring and Gardiner 1976) and can cause considerable disruption to stratification. In addition, bracken clearance is difficult and often involves ground disturbance or chemical treatments (see for example MAFF 1974).

Figure 7.30 is a two-way graph showing changes to the overall extent of semi-natural land in England in relation to the proportion of MARS Monuments (excluding standing buildings) recorded as under and situated within semi-natural land-use in successive decades. A comparison of the two profiles shows identical trends, and of all land-use classes this one is remarkable because, in 1955, 92% of MARS Monuments under semi-natural land-use also lay within areas of semi-natural land-use. As the graph shows, the decline in semi-natural land-use in England since 1945 is not mirrored by a decline in archaeological monuments under semi-natural land-use; indeed the percentage of monuments represented shows a slight increase. One interpretation of this pattern is that the loss of semi-natural environments seems to be inhibited or prevented by the presence of archaeological monuments, and this in turn has the effect of concentrating the monuments into smaller areas under this land-use.

7.5.5 Forestry / woodland

England is not an especially well-wooded country compared with some of its European neighbours, with approximately 8% of its land area covered by forestry in comparison with an average of 36% among all EU countries. France, for example, has 27% of its land under forestry, Germany 31%, Italy 23%, Belgium and Luxembourg 21% (Forestry Commission 1997, table 12). The amount of forested land in England has, however, been rising in recent decades, mainly as a result of deliberate policies introduced in the later years of the Second World War (Forestry Commission 1943; Best and Coppock 1962, 99-117).

Over 11% of MARS Monuments have been under woodland at some stage over the last 50 years, many more no doubt if the a longer time period was considered. In 1995 approximately 7.4% of the extant recorded resource either lay solely under forestry or shared woodland with only one other land-use, and 6.6% of the extant recorded resource lay within a forested environment. The discrepancy between the land area of England occupied by forestry and the lower percentage of MARS Monuments recorded as being in woodland reflects the difficulties of identifying many forms of archaeological monuments under tree cover. Many extensive field survey techniques simply cannot be applied, although with persistence and skill monuments can be located in woodland, as the discovery in 1993 of over 1100 unrecorded monuments in woodland within the North York Moors National Park shows (Anon 1993b). The difference between the percentage of MARS Monuments under woodland and the rather higher number within a woodland environment reflects the fact that positive attempts have been made in recent years to remove tree cover from monuments (see below).

Woodland embraces the following LUSAG narrow land-use classes: broadleaf woodland, conifer woodland, cropland with woody perennial crops, felled woodland, land cultivated for afforestation, mixed woodland, shrub woodland and undifferentiated young woodland. Forestry is the land-use activity that accompanies it. There is considerable diversity among England's woodlands, but change is less common and less visible than in other land-uses. Differences in tree species, woodland composition and management schemes all affect the make-up of woods and forests, but in general the survival of ancient monuments in woodland is subject to two fundamentally different forces. First, the timescale involved, and therefore the potential for land-use continuity, is considerable; even short-term schemes can last for 40 years or more. Second, the impacts are different from those represented by other land-uses, particularly the action of tree roots. There is the natural impact of initial

root development and subsequent growth over the relatively long period of a tree's lifespan, and there are artificial impacts caused by woodland management works with economic or recreational aims.

The value of woodland for preserving archaeological monuments is not well known and is at best only partially investigated. Some light, however, can be shed on its potential effect on the resource. Although root systems penetrate a large volume of soil with their network of tap, lateral and associated roots, they displace only a fraction of the soil they come into contact with. In clayey (plastic) soils these mechanical forces are associated with the indirect action of soil deformation rather than the direct action of the roots themselves (see Biddle 1992). Soil deformation, where it penetrates features, can be destructive, interrupting and complicating stratigraphic sequences, but this should be set against the beneficial effect of the root plate, once established, in stabilizing deposits and stratigraphy. In most tree species, over 90% of structural root growth is within the top 600mm of soil (Dobson 1995). Where archaeological evidence survives ploughing and drainage works or lies below the top metre or so of soil, it is unlikely to be adversely affected by most rooting species.

Previous studies have shown that root growth, although not directly controllable, can be relatively harmless where planting has been, or is, unavoidable. In a number of cases where excavations have been able to explore monuments which were partly within and partly outside woodland it is clear that the woodland helped to stabilize archaeological features and preserved them, whereas the more hostile neighbouring land-uses severely reduced the survival of elements of the same monuments. The Iron Age banjo enclosure excavated at Micheldever Wood in advance of the construction of the M3 through

Figure 7.31 - Aerial photograph of Micheldever Wood, Hampshire, during excavations in 1976. Cropmarks show the position of buried ditches forming the entrance to the enclosure and associated features in the field in the foreground, while within the cleared woodland the main enclosure boundary can be seen preserved as a low earthwork. *[Photograph: RCHME. Copyright reserved]*

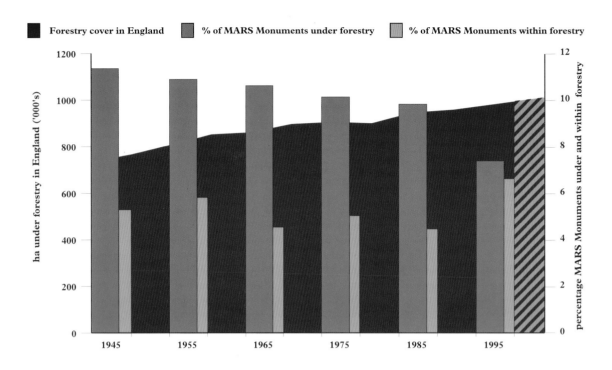

Figure 7.32 - The changing picture of MARS Monuments under forestry. The filled area shows the changing extent of forestry in England 1945-95, and projected forward, in relation to the percentage of MARS Monuments under forestry [blue bars] and situated within forestry [red bars]. *[Sources: MARS Field Survey Programme and Aerial Photographic Programme. Samples: n= 3234 observations for 1945; n= 2123 observations for 1955; n= 2253 observations for 1965; n= 2272 observations for 1975; n= 1192 observations for 1985; n= 7259 observations for 1995]*

Hampshire is an example of this. Figure 7.31 shows an aerial view across the site (Fasham 1980; 1987). The plough-levelled remains of the entrance earthworks and associated features can be seen in the field outside the wood, while in the wood itself the cleared area reveals the presence of upstanding earthworks forming the main enclosure boundary. The entire site has probably been in and out of woodland cover several times since the Roman period, but the main phases of recent regeneration and planting were in 1931, when the north-west corner of the site was planted with beech, and 1963, when the Forestry Commission planted Douglas Fir and Western Red Cedar on the rest of the site.

APPENDIX O.5 lists a number of surveys, studies and excavation reports relating to woodland or to monuments within woodland that have been examined in detail. Barclay *et al.* (1995), Cleal and Allen (1994) and Mercer (1981) in particular provide useful insights into the effect of particular species and planting regimes in woods and forests, drawing on the results of excavations. These studies show that woodlands are important for archaeological remains for three reasons: first because woodland provides long-term protection for monuments that come to be incorporated within this land-use; second because woodlands contain some classes of archaeological monuments that are unique to this land-use (see Darvill 1987, 95-7); and third because some woodlands are themselves archaeological monuments, in the sense that they are of ancient origin and were created and managed in specific ways (Rackham 1980; 1990, 62-152).

MARS shows that the majority (63%) of monuments under woodland are small single monuments

under 3ha in size; large single monuments represent 18% of those recorded, linear monuments 16% and field systems 3%. Most date to the post-medieval and medieval periods.

Figure 7.32 is a two-way graph showing changes to the overall extent of woodland in England in relation to the proportion of MARS Monuments recorded as under and within woodland in successive decades. The two charts show different patterns for archaeological remains under as opposed to within woodland. For monuments within wooded environments, the 1940s, 1950s and 1960s show a broad correspondence between the expansion of woodland and the percentage of archaeological monuments surrounded by trees, while there is a clear downward trend over time for monuments subjected to afforestation. The percentage of monuments within woodland continues to climb at a rate which is broadly in line with the expansion of woodland cover. This is interpreted as evidence for the successful application of a general forestry policy of keeping archaeological monuments free from tree-planting wherever possible (Yarnell 1993; Forestry Commission 1995). In some cases this policy has been implemented by the careful removal of tree cover, as at Bury Ditches, an Iron Age hillfort of 2.6ha in Shropshire (Figure 7.33).

Forest Enterprise (the commercial wing of the Forestry Commission tasked with managing the national stock of public woodland) managed approximately 24% of the 877,000ha of productive woodland in England in 1995, with the remaining 76% in private ownership. This represents a shift in ownership since 1976, when the Forestry Commission directly managed 35% and private forestry accounted for 65%. The trend towards greater private-sector involvement in forestry management looks set to continue. In addition, some 104,000ha of non-productive woodland in England are managed chiefly for amenity and recreation purposes, 15% of which is under the control of Forest Enterprise. There are clear contrasts between the tree species dominating public and privately managed woodland: Forest Enterprise woodland is dominated by coniferous species, mainly planted in the 1920s and 1930s, and private woodlands by deciduous trees introduced in more recent decades as a result of grants and incentives to support deciduous planting.

The Forestry Commission and the Countryside Commission have made forward projections of woodland expansion. The White Paper on *Rural England* (HMG 1996a; 1996b) proposed that woodland cover should double to over 2 million ha, covering some 20% of the land area of England by 2050, an ambitious target given the caution expressed by many about the compromising effect on other environmental concerns (Forestry Commission and Countryside Commission 1996). Much of the new planting will be deciduous trees, a substantial portion of it in at least 12 new Community Forests planned for the fringes of large cities and conurbations and in a new National Forest in the Midlands (Countryside Commission 1993b; Bell 1997).

The implications of new planting proposals for archaeology are very considerable: at an average density of 2.25 monuments per square kilometre, anticipated plantings over an area equivalent to 10,000km^2 over a period of 55 years means that about 400 monuments a year will be affected. Set against this must be the development of increasingly flexible management schemes for planting trees around recorded monuments rather than over them. However, there is no provision in the White Paper for the prior archaeological evaluation of areas earmarked for woodland planting, so successful archaeological management will hinge on the quality of the existing records. This problem has been aired in public in relation to Forestry Commission support for a planting scheme at Birdlip, Gloucestershire, where the County Council, backed by English Heritage, argued that planting should not go ahead without a full archaeological evaluation (Anon 1994). Some desk-based assessment has been carried out for the new National Forest, and this will help to guide planting strategies (Hooke 1992; LUC 1992). Some of the community planting schemes also involve the transfer of undeveloped urban land into woodland schemes.

7.6 Survival and land-use

The relationship between the survival of archaeological monuments and land-use is critical. Which land-uses promote the best survival, and which the worst? Figures 7.34-7.36 show a series of profiles documenting the recorded gross state of monuments (destroyed, flat or upstanding) in relation to LUSAG narrow land-use classes. The charts show separate analyses for earthwork monuments, buildings and structures, and landcuts. Only monuments that have been under the same land-use for all or most of the period between 1945 and 1995 have been included.

For earthwork monuments (Figure 7.34), the general picture is shown by the extreme left-hand column (labelled 'all land uses'). The highest rates of loss occur, as would be expected, in land-use classes such as mineral extraction, roads, airports and utilities. Land-use classes where a higher than average level of upstanding

Figure 7.33 - Bury Ditches, Shropshire, an Iron Age hillfort of 2.6ha cleared of woodland by the Forestry Commission in order to protect the monument following severe storm damage in 1976. *[Photograph: RCHME. Copyright reserved]*

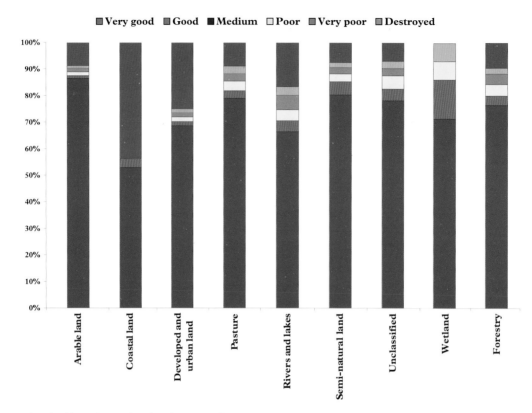

Figure 7.34 - Stacked bar charts showing the state of MARS earthworks in 1995 in relation to land-use by LUSAG narrow class where monuments have stayed under the same land-use class since 1940. Quantified by count. *[Sources: MARS Field Survey Programme and Aerial Photographic Programme. Sample: n= 524]*

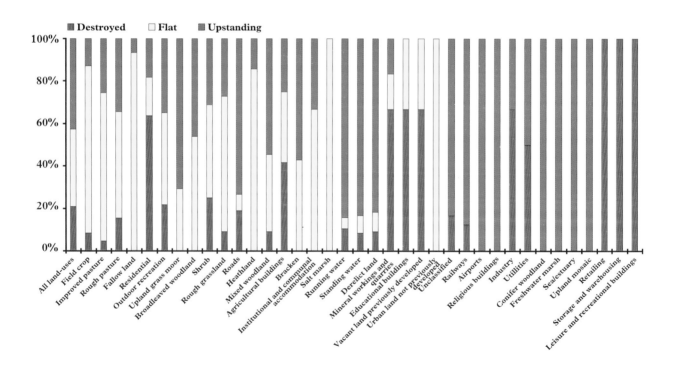

Figure 7.35 - Stacked bar charts showing the state of MARS buildings and structures in 1995 in relation to land-use by LUSAG narrow class where monuments have stayed under the same land-use class since 1940. Quantified by count. *[Sources: MARS Field Survey Programme and Aerial Photographic Programme. Sample: n= 1340]*

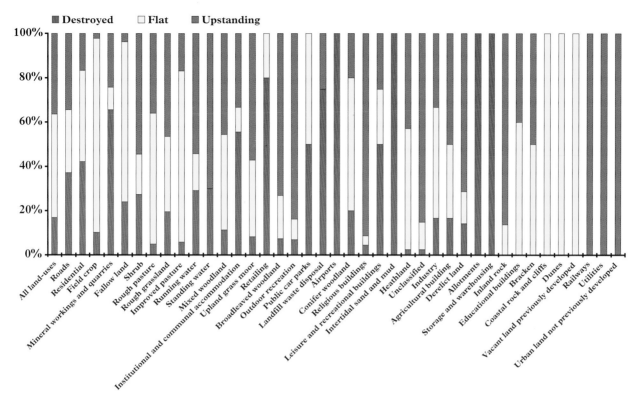

Figure 7.36 - Stacked bar charts showing the state of MARS landcuts in 1995 in relation to land-use by LUSAG narrow class where monuments have stayed under the same land-use class since 1940. Quantified by count. *[Sources: MARS Field Survey Programme and Aerial Photographic Programme. Sample: n= 3194]*

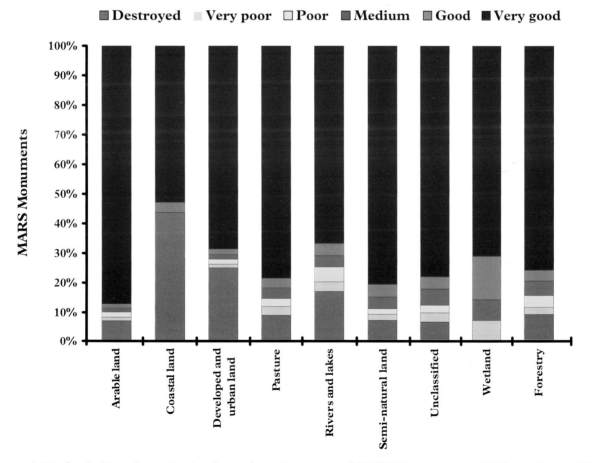

Figure 7.37 - Stacked bar charts showing the areal survival pattern of MARS Monuments in 1995 in relation to MARS land-use classes. Quantified by count. *[Sources: MARS Field Survey Programme. Sample: n= 15,265 observations]*

monuments is represented are more important for the future, however. Those classes for which more than 50% of the sample consists of upstanding monuments are: rough pasture, heathland, upland grass moor, rough grassland, conifer woodland, standing water, inland rock, bracken, shrub, mixed woodland, broadleaved woodland, running water, upland mosaic, coastal rock and cliffs, and religious buildings. It is particularly noticeable that almost all the narrow classes subsumed under the broad class of woodland show high levels of upstanding remains.

Figure 7.35 shows a similar analysis for buildings and structures. Here the picture is far less consistent than for earthworks, probably reflecting the relatively low sample sizes for all land-use classes except those relating to built-up land. The same applies to the results shown on Figure 7.36, which covers landcuts.

These three charts establish a crude hierarchy of the impacts of land-uses on archaeological monuments as a result of continuous operation or implementation. Railways, utilities and urban land not previously developed are at the top of the scale with minimal impact, and allotments, storage and warehousing, airports and intertidal sand and mud extraction are at the bottom with greatest impact.

Figure 7.37 shows an analysis of areal survival in relation to the broad land-use classes. Five classes of survival were used (see Chapter 6.2.2 for definition of classes), and all MARS Monuments extant at the census date were included. A third of all monuments under arable regimes survive in good condition in terms of area, slightly

more than for developed land. Forestry and semi-natural land also enjoy high levels of monuments with very good and good areal survival.

7.7 *Impact and land-use*

The impact of damage is not easy to define for most archaeological monuments, because a lot depends on where it occurs, how it occurs, and what it does to the stratigraphy and environment. Five main forms of impact have been defined for MARS (see Chapter 6.10).

Tables 7.18 and 7.19 show an analysis of impact in relation to broad land-use classes. Most impacts affected the total surface area of the monuments (widespread 73%) or only a few discrete spots (localized 14%). In many cases there is likely to be a link between impact and the type of damage associated with each of the land-uses investigated during field visits and aerial photographic interpretation. For example, damage reported on arable land is mainly widespread (98%), whereas in wetland high levels of localized (30%) and peripheral (20%) damage were noted. Equally, the incidence of peripheral damage is highest at monuments in developed and urban land-use and in pasture land.

On a wider scale, several studies have investigated types of land-use change and the impacts that result on environmental resources. One such study by Bayliss-Smith and Owens (1990) notes that changes over the last 50 years 'may not quite amount to wholesale destruction

Table 7.18 - Patterns of impact on MARS Monuments in 1995 by MARS land-use classes as a percentage for each impact type. *[Source: MARS Field Survey Programme. Sample: n= 15,208 observations]*

MARS land-use class	Widespread impact %	Localized impact %	Peripheral impact %	Segmenting impact %	No impact %	Neighbourhood impact %	Total %
Arable land	22.74	0.81	2.36	2.83	0.82	4.24	**16.96**
Coastal land	0.22	0.10	0.00	0.00	0.00	0.00	**0.17**
Developed and urban land	34.07	69.25	37.16	53.77	61.05	62.71	**41.86**
Forestry	8.53	7.89	13.85	9.43	6.07	3.39	**8.30**
Pasture land	23.99	11.69	31.08	14.15	18.73	15.25	**21.76**
Rivers and lakes	3.39	3.18	8.78	16.04	7.49	10.17	**3.32**
Semi-natural land	6.76	4.09	4.05	2.83	3.30	2.54	**5.94**
Unclassified	1.25	2.71	13.5	0.94	2.47	0.85	**1.55**
Wetland	0.07	0.29	1.35	0.00	0.07	0.85	**0.13**
Total	**100%**	**100%**	**100%**	**100%**	**100%**	**100%**	**100%**

Table 7.19 - Patterns of impact on MARS Monuments in 1995 by MARS land-use classes as a percentage for each land-use class. *[Source: MARS Field Survey Programme. Sample: n= 15,208 observations]*

MARS land-use class	Widespread impact %	Localized impact %	Peripheral impact %	Segmenting impact %	No impact %	Neighbourhood impact %	Total %
Arable land	98.22	0.66	0.27	0.23	0.43	0.19	**100%**
Coastal land	92.31	7.69	0.00	0.00	0.00	0.00	**100%**
Developed and urban land	59.63	22.89	1.73	1.79	12.80	1.16	**100%**
Forestry	75.28	13.15	3.25	1.58	6.42	0.32	**100%**
Pasture land	80.78	7.43	2.78	0.91	7.56	0.54	**100%**
Rivers and lakes	52.67	13.27	5.15	6.73	19.80	2.38	**100%**
Semi-natural land	83.30	9.51	1.33	0.66	4.87	0.33	**100%**
Unclassified	58.90	24.15	1.69	0.85	13.98	0.42	**100%**
Wetland	40.00	30.00	20.00	0.00	5.00	5.00	**100%**
All	**73.27**	**13.83**	**1.95**	**1.39**	**8.78**	**0.78**	**100%**

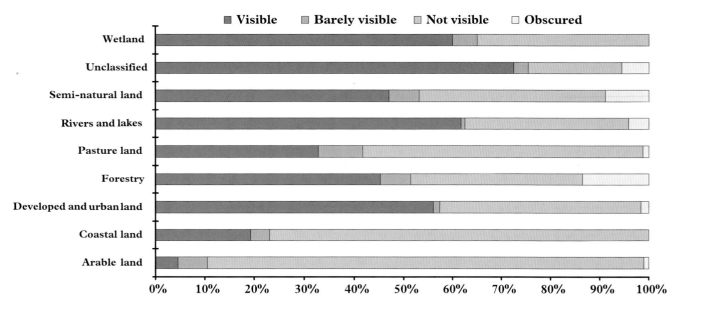

Figure 7.38 - Horizontal stacked bar charts showing the visibility of MARS Monuments in 1995 in relation to by MARS land-use classes. Quantified by count. *[Sources: MARS Field Survey Programme. Sample: n= 15,236]*

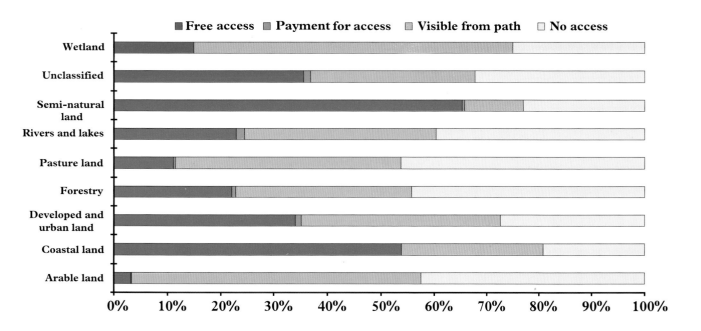

Figure 7.39 - Horizontal stacked bar chart showing access to MARS Monuments in 1995 in relation to MARS land-use classes. Quantified by count. *[Sources: MARS Field Survey Programme. Sample: n= 15,086]*

of the lowland landscape, but they have certainly impoverished its natural components on a massive scale' (Bayliss-Smith and Owens 1990, 75). They then go on to separate these changes into eight broad groups, many of which are analogous with the changes that can be seen to the archaeological resource: massive and general reduction in semi-natural habitats; degradation of remaining semi-natural habitats; loss of historic features as a result of the above two forces; higher levels of drainage and alkalinity in lowland soils; clearer definition of patches in the landscape mosaic; fragmentation and isolation of remaining habitats; loss of habitat corridors; and the creation of fewer diverse new habitats.

7.8 *Visibility and land-use*

The visibility of ancient monuments is determined by a combination of interconnected factors: physical form, survival and the prevailing land-use regime. Under most land-uses upstanding archaeological monuments are visible in some way, although they are not always easy to recognize from ground level. Figure 7.38 shows an analysis of visibility in relation to land-use. The four possible categories of visibility to which monuments were assigned during the Field Survey are described in Chapter 5.6.3.

The only land-use in which more than 30% of the extant recorded resource is visible is developed and urban land. In the remaining eight broad land-use classes less than 30% of the extant recorded resource can be seen from ground level by someone with a reasonable general knowledge of what they are looking for. In the case of arable land, the percentage of monuments that can be seen amounts to less than 5% of all monuments recorded as being under this land-use.

7.9 *Access and land-use*

Access to the countryside in England is not a common right, although the network of public rights of way and public open space means that large areas can be seen if not walked over. The degree of access is heavily influenced by prevailing land-use regimes with, in general, far more freedom of movement in upland areas than in the lowlands. Figure 7.39 shows an analysis of access recorded for MARS Monuments in relation to broad land-use classes. The four classifications for access are described in more detail in Chapter 5.7.

As might be expected, the land-uses with greatest access at the MARS census date were semi-natural land and coastal land. The least accessible were arable land and fallow land, closely followed by wetland. Surprisingly, pasture land had less recorded access than either woodland or river and lake. Combining direct access and visibility of monuments from some public right of way or public open space, between 55% and 80% of monuments can be seen in most land-use classes. The exception is woodland, in which visibility from any distance is inevitably limited; where monuments are not accessible they are difficult to see unless they are in a prominent position such as a skyline.

Entrance charges for access apply to a relatively small percentage of monuments, access arrangements of this sort applying mainly to woodland, semi-natural land, rivers and lakes, pasture and developed land. It should be noted, however, that in many cases payments allow access to the land in general (e.g. a park, garden or estate) rather than to a particular archaeological monument.

The provision of public access to land in general and open countryside in particular is a matter that moved onto the political agenda in the mid 1990s (Payne 1995; DETR and Welsh Office 1998). The issues are complicated and far from clear cut, but one sphere where access is already an issue is in relation to designated sites and areas, the subject of the next chapter.

8 The effects of designation

Gentlemen, I am sure you will agree with me that one of the first subjects on which I ought to congratulate both this Society and the archaeological world of England is the passing into law of the Bill for the Protection of Ancient Monuments ... Perhaps I ought rather to have said a Bill than the Bill, for we all know ... in what a mutilated condition, short of many of its original provisions, crippled in its powers, and limited in its scope, that measure finally became the law of the land ... One illustration of the inadequacy of the Act - through no fault of its promoters - for averting the outrages of the grossest character on the antiquarian remains of this country, was furnished within six months of its being entered on the Statute Book by a project brought before Parliament for handing over the precincts of Stonehenge to the tender mercies of the Bristol and London and South Western Junction Railway.

(Earl of Carnarvon 1883, 293)

8.1 Designation

Since 1882 some archaeological monuments in England have been subject to protective designations of one kind or another. The origins and development of these provisions have been fully described (Harvey 1961; Thompson 1963; Saunders 1983; Champion 1996), and can be seen to stem from an increasing concern for the environment. This radical 'preservationist movement', best exemplified during the nineteenth century in the writings of William Wordsworth, John Ruskin and William Morris, among others, demanded that ancient monuments and venerable buildings should be safeguarded from the builder and speculator and that the countryside in particular should be given special treatment (MacCarthy 1994; Miele 1996). In a sense archaeology was lucky among environmental concerns, as it was the subject of early legislation and there was at least some government support through the appointment of General Pitt Rivers as the first Inspector of Ancient Monuments in March 1883 (Thompson 1960; 1977). This is not to say everything went as planned. As the words of Earl Carnarvon to the Anniversary Meeting of the Society of Antiquaries of London on St George's Day 1883 make clear, the *Ancient Monuments Protection Act 1882* was a pale reflection of what had been intended and its initial operational efficiency was limited.

From these humble beginnings both environmental and ancient monuments legislation have grown considerably in breadth and depth over the last century or so. Today the situation is quite different from the one John Lubbock encountered when steering the first Act through Parliament, although those early foundations are still clear in the current Act. Indeed, it is interesting to note just how far thinking and legislation concerning non-archaeological elements of the countryside and urban areas, both in Britain and other countries, has developed in comparison to those relating to archaeological deposits (Lucas 1992), and how the both the legislation and the practice of monument management encourages more integrated approaches (Berry and Brown 1996). It is also worth reflecting that European conventions and recommendations increasingly provide the wider context for the legislation enacted and implemented in Britain (CoE 1992; O'Keefe 1993).

This chapter attempts to take a broad view of the way in which a wide range of designations affect archaeological monuments. After a brief discussion of the sources of data, and the limitations to their application, the main archaeological and related designations are considered. In general these designations fall into three main groups: site-specific measures, area-based measures and payment schemes. Some measures apply explicitly to archaeological monuments while others, although not conceived with archaeological objectives in mind, nonetheless apply to land which contains archaeological monuments, include archaeological considerations within a broader remit, or have the effect of providing some degree of protection for archaeological remains through conservation and management measures (*cf.* Poore and Poore 1992). Throughout, it should be borne in mind that designations originate from three different levels of government: international, national and local.

Only rather basic analyses can be attempted here because few of the measures and schemes discussed have been running long enough to allow detailed studies of their effect on the archaeological resource in terms of the extent to which they may have altered the rate of monument decay. The main schemes are described and reference made to relevant related studies. The principal aim of this chapter and the data it contains is to establish a baseline statement about the components of the recorded archaeological resource covered by existing designations. There is no attempt to deal in detail with the legislation behind these designations as the law relating to archaeological monuments has competently been summarized in a number of places (Breeze 1993; Pugh-Smith and Samuels 1996) and its origins and context widely discussed (e.g. Kennet 1972; Carman 1996; Champion 1996).

8.2 Data collection and limitations

Some difficulties were encountered in collecting data relating to designations which applied to monuments within the sample transects. In all cases the local SMRs provided the starting point, but in most areas further investigations and the use of complementary sources proved essential to provide a more complete picture. SMRs with the most useful records for this purpose were those integrated with more broadly based environmental records. In the case of Scheduled Monuments further investigation included reference to the county lists published by English Heritage and the English Heritage Records Office. For non-archaeological designations liaison with the authorities responsible for particular designations was necessary.

There were four common problems in trying to assemble and integrate data about designations. The first was in correlating records for individual monuments with site-specific designations: because of the different ways in which records had been drawn up, information about locations was often incompatible, preventing easy comparison and authoritative correlation. Second, the mapping for existing designations was found to be variable in scale, coverage and availability, and overlaying maps showing MARS sample transects with designation maps was not easy. Third, the recording systems relating to some designations were undergoing development or recasting, so that at the time of inquiry there was no single definitive system in operation. And finally, many records relating to designations are held only in the regional offices of lead authorities, which made it difficult to piece together the national picture.

Overall within MARS, the identification of monuments subject to international and national levels of archaeological designation is good, but local archaeological designations and non-archaeological designations are less comprehensively documented.

The MARS National Survey Programme revealed that a minimum of 39,437 archaeological records (6% of the retrievable total in 1995) in local SMRs in England relate to items covered by some kind of archaeological designation, mainly Scheduled Monuments, Guardianship Monuments, World Heritage Sites and county-based archaeological designations. This total excludes entries relating to Listed Buildings. An estimated minimum of 53,000 archaeological records (8% of the retrievable total in 1995) refer to items within areas subject to non-archaeological designations, mainly Areas of Outstanding Natural Beauty, Conservation Areas, Sites of Special Scientific Interest and county-based designations of various sorts.

8.3 Site-specific archaeological designations

At an international level, the World Heritage Convention provides for the designation of World Heritage Sites (UNESCO 1972). However, most of those designated in England cover areas of countryside and townscape rather than individual monuments and are therefore considered below (8.4.1).

At the national level, the main protective designations are established by the *Ancient Monuments and*

Archaeological Areas Act 1979, as amended for England by the *National Heritage Act 1983*. Three main forms of designation, each with different objectives, are represented, and these are discussed in the following sub-sections.

8.3.1 Areas of Archaeological Importance

The purpose of this designation is to allow the definition of Areas of Archaeological Importance (AAIs) within which potential developers are required to give six weeks' notice of any proposals to disturb the ground. Following such notice, a nominated investigating authority has power to enter the site and if necessary carry out a programme of investigation and recording before the development works take place. Only five AAIs have been defined in England since 1979 (Canterbury, York, Chester, Hereford and Exeter), and the intentions implicit in the arrangements have more recently been superseded by normal procedures within the planning process (see McGill 1995, 145 for review of operation). Accordingly, it has been proposed that the relevant sections of the 1979 Act be repealed and that AAIs should cease (DNH 1996, 44). No MARS sample units related to defined AAIs.

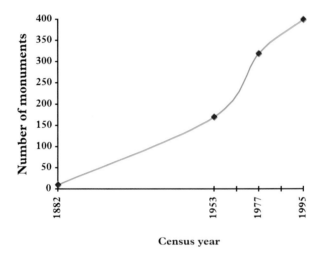

Figure 8.1 - Cumulative increase in the total number of Guardianship monuments between 1882 and 1995. *[Source: MARS National Survey, published lists and English Heritage Records Office data]*

8.3.2 Guardianship Monuments

Guardianship Monuments have been acquired for many different reasons since the 1880s. Today, Guardianship mainly represents a power of last resort for monuments of supreme national importance, whose future cannot otherwise be secured. The number of such monuments has risen steadily since the late nineteenth century (Figure 8.1) so that by 1995 there were approximately 400 monuments in England under State Guardianship, about 80% of them buildings and standing structures of various sorts, the remainder earthworks. This list includes some well-known archaeological monuments, for example Stonehenge, Wiltshire, and Housesteads, Northumberland; many of them are open to the public (Figure 8.2).

Guardianship Monuments represent about 0.1% of the extant recorded resource in England. The MARS sample included no Guardianship Monuments.

Figure 8.2 - Aerial view of Housesteads, Northumberland, a Guardianship Monuments within the Hadrian's Wall World Heritage Site. *[Photograph: RCHME. Copyright reserved]*

In an important change of approach to the management of monuments in State Guardianship, English Heritage announced in 1994 that it would be transferring responsibility for the day-to-day maintenance of some Guardianship monuments to local authorities and public bodies (Page 1994, 24; Young 1995). As a baseline statistic, at the MARS census date such arrangements had been made for 145 Guardianship Monuments, 36% of the total (English Heritage Records Office). Partners in this scheme include the National Trust, National Parks, local authorities, local preservation trusts and parish councils.

The largest single partner is the National Trust with more than 17 agreements covering monuments on their estates all over England, ranging from the massive prehistoric complex at Avebury, Wiltshire, and the extensive area of fields, settlements and ceremonial sites in the Upper Plym Valley, Devon, to the Roman forts at Ambleside and Hardknott in Cumbria. In recent decades the National Trust has developed a high level of expertise in the management of archaeological monuments, and has more than 40,000 monuments, including 1000 Scheduled Monuments and all or part of five World Heritage Sites, on its 234,000ha estate scattered through England, Wales and Northern Ireland (Thackray 1986; Morgan Evans *et al.* 1996).

8.3.3 Scheduled Monuments

Scheduling is the most widely applied site-specific archaeological designation in England. Its purpose is to provide a means of recognizing in law those monuments deemed to be of national importance for which the close controls of Scheduled Monument Consent (SMC) procedures governing all potentially damaging works are appropriate. There are no restrictions on how large or small a Scheduled Monument can be, and a wide range of archaeological monuments are currently included on the Schedule, from single burial mounds up to large tracts of

countryside containing many dozens of individual monuments.

Scheduled Monuments range in date from the Palaeolithic through to the twentieth century AD. Monuments in, on or under the sea bed can be included. Buildings in use as dwellings, other than by a caretaker, and those in regular ecclesiastical use, do not, however, qualify (see Breeze 1993 for a general account of Scheduling).

In 1995 there were approximately 14,478 Scheduled Monuments in England. However, there is no direct link between the number of Scheduled Monuments and the number of elements or components involved; a Scheduled Monument may comprise one round barrow (and be counted as one monument), or it may include an entire barrow cemetery and several other features, not necessarily associated chronologically and still be counted as one monument. It has been estimated that the 14,478 Scheduled Monuments represent approximately 25,000 separate items, many of which correspond to the definition of a monument offered in Chapter 3.2, and almost all of which will correspond to entries in SMRs (G Fairclough pers. comm. April 1997).

The number of Scheduled Monuments in England has grown steadily over the last 113 years, as Figure 8.3 shows. Although the average added each year is about 125, this disguises the rapid expansion of the Schedule over the last 30 years or so. In 1882, the Schedule to the first Act listed just 26 monuments in England. By 1930 this had risen to about 2500, a figure which had almost doubled by 1953. By 1960 there were 7500 Scheduled Monuments, 9500 by 1970 and 12,000 by 1980.

Since 1986 the Monuments Protection Programme (MPP) has been carrying out a review of existing Scheduled Monuments, adding to the Schedule those recorded monuments assessed as being of National Importance which had escaped attention thus far (Startin

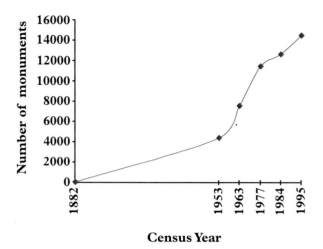

Census Year

Figure 8.3 - Cumulative increase in the total number of Scheduled Monuments between 1882 and 1995. *[Source: MARS National Survey, published lists (MPBW 1953; 1961; 1965; 1969; DoE 1973; 1974a, 1978) and English Heritage Records Office data]*

1987; 1988; English Heritage 1997b). The MPP is systematically tackling the problem from several directions at once, one effect of which has been to increase the number of Scheduled Monuments from 12,500 in 1989-90 to 15,000 in 1995 (English Heritage 1997b).

In total, 820 Scheduled Monuments were represented within the MARS sample units, of which 754 (91%) were visited by the Field Survey teams. This provided a 5% sample of all Scheduled Monuments defined at the census date. The area represented by the Scheduled Monuments in the MARS sample totals 20.5km², suggesting that, overall, Scheduled Monuments in England cover about 409km² or 0.3% of the land area.[1] In the following studies reference is made to patterns revealed by the analysis of Scheduled Monuments in the MARS sample, as well as counts derived from local SMRs through the National Survey Programme and information from the RSM held by English Heritage.

One of the questions often asked about the monuments included on the Schedule is: how representative of the recorded resource are they? In 1983, the then Inspectorate of Ancient Monuments carried out a rapid assessment of the number, range and distribution of monuments that were then Scheduled (IAM 1984). This revealed a number of perceived inadequacies and concluded that (IAM 1984, 47-8):

it is very clear that the schedule of ancient monuments is not a representative sample of the known archaeological sites and monuments of England. In detail:

(i) only 2% of the known sites and monuments are Scheduled.

(ii) the distribution by county of the Scheduled Monuments is seriously unbalanced.

(iii) the distribution by chronological period of the Scheduled Monuments is seriously unbalanced.

(iv) an analysis by monument-type suggests that the schedule contains an inaccurate reflection of the width and depth of monument types in the national archaeological resource.

So how have things changed since 1984? Two parallel processes have been going on in a way that precludes a simple answer. First, the MPP has been tackling the problem of the Schedule and what it contains by updating the existing records, de-scheduling sites that are no longer deemed to be of national importance, and adding monuments that fulfil the criteria of national importance set out by the Secretary of State for the Environment (see DoE 1990a, Annexe 4) and later endorsed by the House of Commons Environment Committee (Environment Committee 1987). Second, there have been additions and improvements to the local SMRs which collectively represent the recorded resource. These latter changes mean that the MPP is operating in a constantly changing environment. All four issues raised by the IAM are, however, being overcome.

In 1983 it was estimated that only 2% of archaeological monuments in Britain were Scheduled, but this must be reviewed in the light of improved understandings of the counts on which these estimates were based. It is now clear (see Chapter 4.4) that the local SMRs include, for good reasons, a lot of records which relate to material not suitable for Scheduling. Estimates discussed above (Chapter 5.2.1) suggest that England's recorded resource currently stands at about 300,000 monuments, of which about 253,000 were extant in 1995. With a total of 14,478 Scheduled Monuments in 1995, it can be estimated that a minimum of 6% of monuments

Table 8.1 - The regional distribution of Scheduled Monuments 1983-1994. *[Source: MARS National Survey, SMR records and English Heritage]*

MARS Region	Scheduled Monuments 1984	Regional proportion %	Scheduled Monuments 1995	Regional proportion %	1984-1995 change %	Regional % of MARS Monuments
North West	770	6.1	896	6.2	16.4	13
North East	2051	16.3	2279	15.7	11.1	18
West Midlands	1869	14.8	2039	14.1	9.1	14
East Midlands	1998	15.9	2204	15.2	10.3	22
South West	4233	33.6	5022	34.7	18.6	20
South East	1679	13.3	2038	14.1	21.4	13
Total	**12600**	**100%**	**14478**	**100%**	**15%**	**100%**

were protected in this way. Nobody knows what the target proportion should be. Morgan-Evans (1985, 93) thought in terms of 10% of the recorded resource being of national importance, although this represented an upper estimate as it included Grade I and II* Listed Buildings. Ultimately, the procedures established for the assessment of archaeological monuments that are being systematically applied by the MPP will define the percentage of the recorded resource that is of national importance.

The definition of MARS Monuments is close to that of the sorts of archaeological evidence that can be considered for Scheduling, but there are differences in the way the definitions are applied. To compare estimates based on MARS Monuments with the scale of the Schedule is to compare two slightly different sets of figures. Looked at another way, the estimated 25,000 recordable items comprising the 14,478 Scheduled Monuments (see above) is very close to the estimate of 21,969 records entries relating to Scheduled Monuments held by local SMRs providing information to the MARS National Survey Programme. Using these figures as a means of establishing the scale of the recorded resource which is Scheduled it can be suggested that approximately 5.0% of all records relate to archaeological monuments that are Scheduled (i.e. 25,000 out of the 493,214 retrievable items (75% of all retrievable items) in SMRs that relate to monuments: see Chapter 4.4).

Table 8.1 presents a breakdown of the distribution of all Scheduled Monuments by MARS Regions for 1984 and 1995. Overall, there has been a 15% increase in the number of Scheduled Monuments over that period, representing the substantial and sustained effort by the MPP. The overall increase does not, of course, reflect the effort put in by the MPP to improving the documentation for existing Scheduled Monuments. The rates of change are likely to reflect the activities of the MPP teams, the greatest increases being in the South East region, up 21.4%, while the West Midlands have to date seen the lowest rate of increase, at about 9.1%. Across the regions, however, the overall balance has changed very little in terms of the percentage of Scheduled Monuments in relation to the recorded resource. This is not surprising, as the breakdowns broadly accord with the national

distribution of monuments, indicating that there is no significant regional bias in the proportion of monuments identified for Scheduling. There may of course be differences between counties in terms of the density of monuments scheduled, or the proportion of the recorded resource protected in this way, but as earlier chapters emphasize there is in any case considerable variation in the character of the recorded resource between counties.

Fraser's 1983 survey suggested that the monuments on the Schedule did not represent a balance of periods and types (IAM 1984, tables 7 and 12). Table 8.2 compares the chronological distribution of Scheduled Monuments with the total recorded population of monuments in England as revealed by MARS. For some periods the match is good, but for others markedly less so. This is largely a reflection of preferential selection. Within the Schedule, Bronze Age monuments are over-represented in relation to the current understanding of the recorded resource, whereas monuments from later periods are proportionately equal to the national average except for post-medieval monuments which are under-represented on the Schedule. As shown in Chapter 4, the recorded resource is constantly changing its complexion in terms of the chronological representation of monuments. The largest groups of Scheduled Monuments date to the medieval period and the Bronze Age.

As a sub-set of the recorded archaeological resource

Table 8.2 - Representation of archaeological period for Scheduled Monuments in the Record of Scheduled Monuments (RSM) in relation to the period breakdown of the recorded resource represented by the MARS sample. *[Source: English Heritage RSM; MARS Field Survey Programme and SMRs]*

Period	Proportion of SMs (EH Records Office) %	Overall proportion %
Prehistoric Unspecified	5.2	4.0
Palaeolithic	1.9	<1
Neolithic	3.6	1.0
Bronze Age	42.4	5.0
Iron Age	3.2	3.0
Roman	6.9	7.0
Early medieval	2.3	1.0
Medieval	24.0	21.0
Post-medieval	7.4	33.0
Modern	<1	3.0
Unknown	3.1	22.0
Total	**100%**	**100%**

Scheduled Monuments

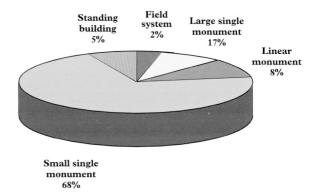

non-Scheduled Monuments

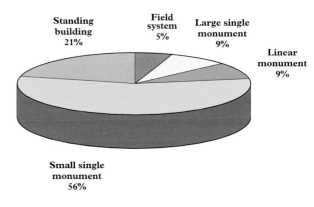

Figure 8.4 - The form of Scheduled Monuments and non-Scheduled Monuments. *[Source: MARS Field Survey Programme. Sample: n= 820 Scheduled Monuments from a total of 14,591 sampled monuments]*

Table 8.3 - Visibility of Scheduled Monuments compared with and non-Scheduled Monuments. *[Source: MARS Field Survey Programme. Samples: n= 830 Scheduled Monuments; n= 13,206 non-Scheduled Monuments]*

| | Scheduled Monuments | | | | non-Scheduled Monuments | | | |
	Earthwork	Building and Structure	Landcut	All	Earthwork	Building and Structure	Landcut	All
Visible	55.90	57.32	51.9	55.06	22.72	61.33	34.27	40.82
Barely visible	7.55	7.60	5.12	6.87	7.14	2.74	3.93	4.40
Not visible	31.60	30.99	39.58	33.73	66.90	33.44	58.65	51.84
Obscured	4.95	4.09	3.40	4.34	3.24	2.49	3.15	2.94
Total	**100%**	**100%**	**100%**	**100%**	**100%**	**100%**	**100%**	**100%**

Scheduled Monuments show some differences in the percentages of different characters and forms represented. Some 51% of Scheduled Monuments in the MARS sample are earthworks, 21% buildings and structures, and 28% landcuts. This is very similar to a sample of 807 Scheduled Monuments examined by Glass (1989) in a study of monument damage based on information recorded by Field Monument Wardens. Here earthwork and cropmark monuments together comprised 50% of the sample.

Looked at by form (Figure 8.4), the Schedule is clearly biased towards single monuments (large and small). This is because such monuments are most likely to be appropriately protected by Scheduling, and comprise the forms most widely addressed by the MPP in its early years. The proportion of linear monuments which are Scheduled is approximately the same as the proportion of linear monuments among the MARS sample. Buildings and structures are often better served by being designated as Listed Buildings. Within the five broad categories of

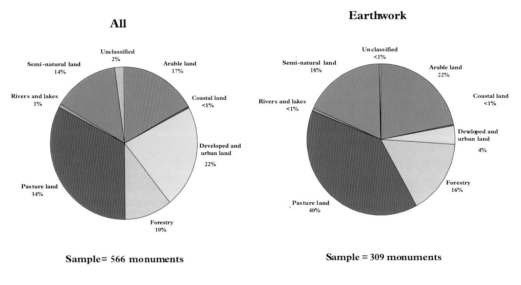

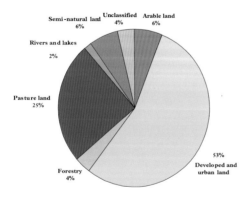

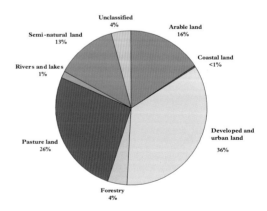

Figure 8.5 - Pie charts showing the single land-use regimes on MARS Scheduled Monuments and by monument character categories: earthworks, buildings and structures, and landcuts. *[Source: MARS Field Survey Programme. Samples as shown]*

monument form there are over 200 different classes of monument needing to be addressed by the MPP (English Heritage 1997b, 13-14).

Overall, therefore, Scheduled Monuments appear to be a better reflection of the recorded resource now than they were in 1983. The proportion of the resource protected in this way has increased considerably, and at a regional level reflects the distribution of recorded archaeology. The chronological distribution of monuments covered by Scheduling is close to the distribution known for the recorded resource, although monuments for some periods are more numerous on the Schedule than within the overall recorded resource. However, there are probably good reasons for this in terms of the quality of survival. The biggest differences lie in the forms of the monuments included on the Schedule, where there is scope for targeting field systems in particular. Throughout, however, it must be recognized that the match between the Schedule and the recorded resource will never be perfect. The applicability of

Scheduling is limited, and it is relevant only to a sub-set of the recorded resource. With buildings and standing structures forming an increasing proportion of the archaeological resource the match will appear to get worse with time even though other kinds of designation apply to these components of the recorded resource.

Results from the MARS Field Survey Programme allows other general characteristics of the population of Scheduled Monuments to be gauged. In total, Scheduled Monuments are more visible than non-Scheduled Monuments, but a slightly higher proportion of them are in fact obscured from view (Table 8.3).

Scheduled Monuments are slightly less accessible than non-Scheduled Monuments (40% and 37% respectively), and they are also less visible from public rights of way or public open spaces (26% and 37% respectively).

Figure 8.5 shows the pattern of single land-use regimes on Scheduled Monuments. The single largest group comprises those under pasture, which account for

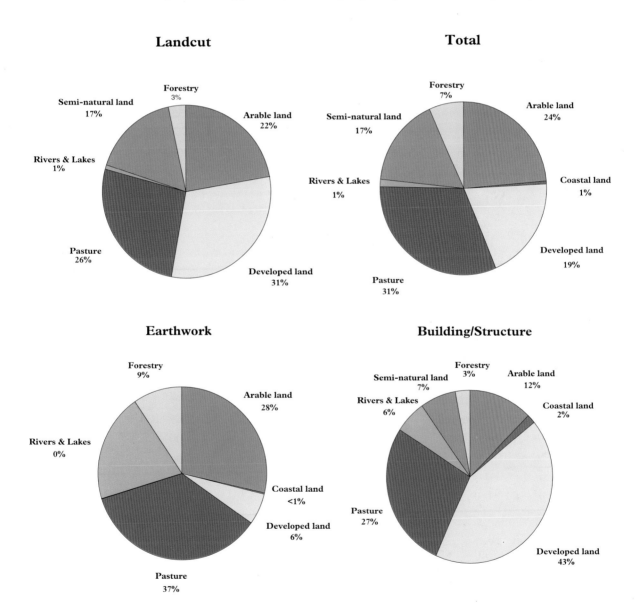

Figure 8.6 - Pie charts showing the single land-use regimes around MARS Scheduled Monuments and by monument character categories: earthworks, buildings and structures and landcuts. *[Source: MARS Field Survey Programme. Sample: n= 566 observations]*

34% of observations, followed by developed and urban (22%), arable (17%) and semi-natural land (14%). This pattern is rather different from the overall distribution of the recorded resource in terms of land-use patterns (*cf.* Figure 7.6), a point which will be explored further below. Figure 8.6 shows the pattern of single land-use around Scheduled Monuments in the MARS sample, in other words the land-use within which Scheduled Monuments sit. Three land-uses are particularly noteworthy: more Scheduled Monuments are surrounded by areas of arable, pasture and forestry than are actually covered by these same land-uses. In the cases of arable and forestry this is probably beneficial for the archaeology, because it means that these monuments are protected from other, relatively hostile land-uses. The picture for pasture around monuments results from the fact that many buildings and standing structures lie within pasture but, because of their nature, are themselves classified as being covered by developed land.

Table 8.4 - The frequency of single and multiple land-use on Scheduled Monuments compared to all monuments in the MARS sample. *[Source: MARS Field Survey Programme. Sample: n= 751 Scheduled Monuments; n= 13,526 all monuments]*

Number of land uses 1995	Scheduled Monuments %	All MARS Monuments %
1	75.4	87.1
2	16.0	8.6
3	5.7	2.8
4	2.1	<1
5	<1	<1
6	<1	<1
7	0.0	0.0
Total	**100%**	**100%**

Multiple land-use on Scheduled Monuments is more common than within the recorded resource as a whole. As Table 8.4 shows, two land-uses were recorded for 16% of Scheduled Monuments compared with only 8.6% of all MARS Monuments. Of these multiple uses, pasture and developed land are the most frequent on Scheduled Monuments, and woodland is more frequent on Scheduled Monuments as a component of multiple land-use than as the sole form of cover (Figure 8.7).

The state of Scheduled Monuments provides a rough measure of condition for comparison with their non-Scheduled counterparts. Overall, 66% of Scheduled Monuments survive in an upstanding state compared to 33% amongst the earthworks represented in the MARS sample and 68% of buildings structures. Figure 8.8 provides a more detailed analysis with a series of pie charts which contrast the situation between Scheduled Monuments and non-Scheduled Monuments in the MARS sample. For all three monument character categories the number of destroyed Scheduled Monuments is less (between one-third and a half) of what it is for non-Scheduled Monuments. For earthwork monuments more than twice as many Scheduled Monuments survive as upstanding remains compared to non-Scheduled Monuments, and the same applies to landcuts. The picture for buildings and structures is comparable for those which are Scheduled and those which are not.

Within the MARS sample, 57 out of 754 Scheduled Monuments inspected (7.5%) were found to have been destroyed. Of these, the majority (68% of those lost) were small single monuments, the remainder linear monuments and large single monuments in equal proportions. This rate of loss is less than half the national average of 16% (see Chapter 6.2.2). The MARS sample can also be compared with regional studies involving Scheduled Monuments. On the Berkshire Downs, Richards (1978, 63) found that two out of 31 separate Scheduled Monuments (6.4%) had been destroyed prior to his visits

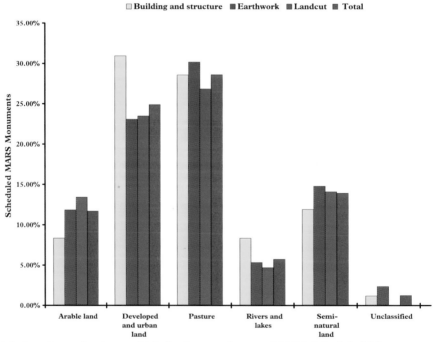

Figure 8.7 - Multiple bar charts showing multiple land-use regimes on MARS Scheduled Monuments and by monument character categories: earthworks, buildings and structures, and landcuts. *[Source: MARS Field Survey Programme. Sample: 402 observations]*

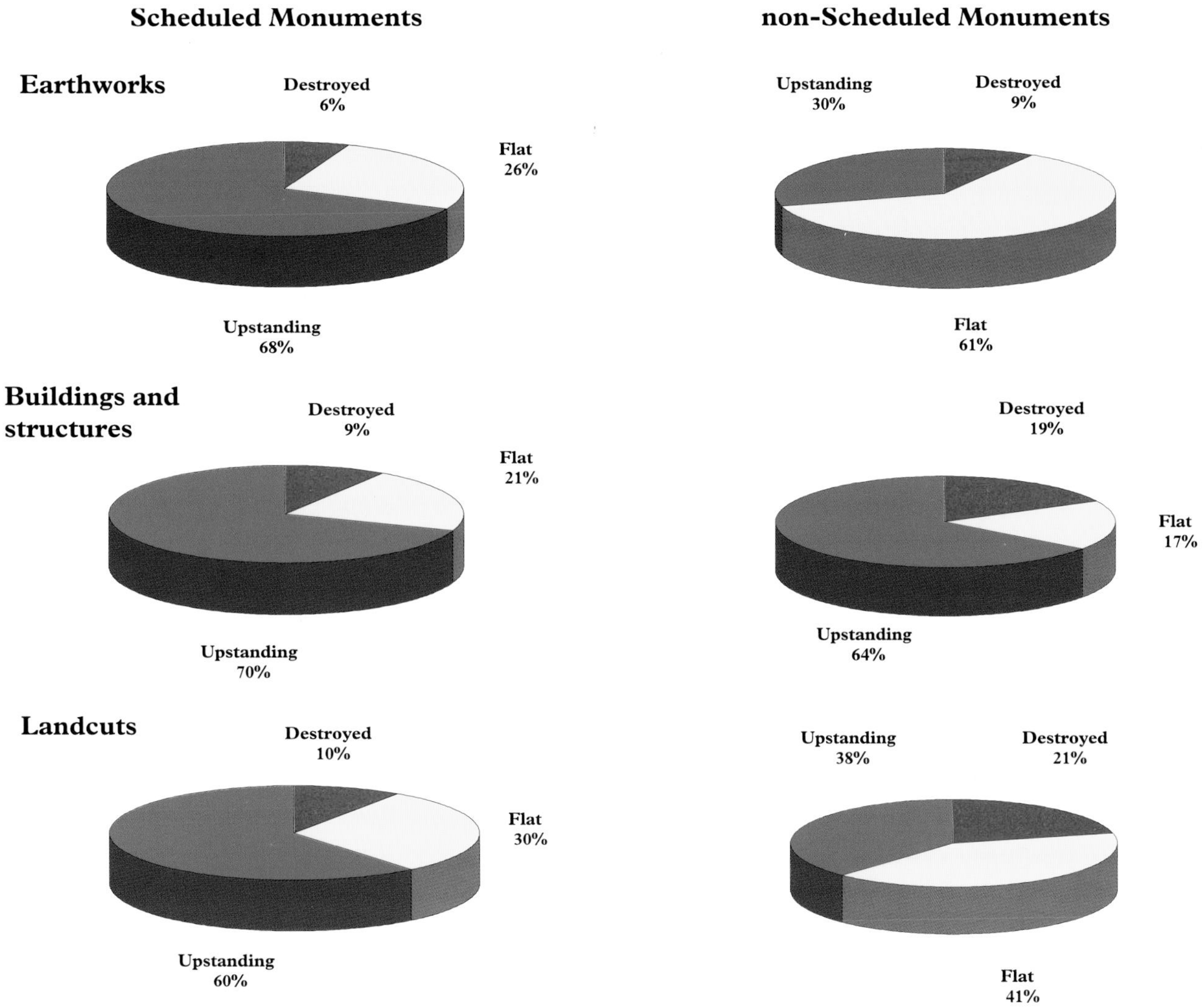

Scheduled Monuments   **non-Scheduled Monuments**

Earthworks

Buildings and structures

Landcuts

Figure 8.8 - Pie charts showing the current state of Scheduled Monuments and non-Scheduled Monuments in 1995 for earthworks, buildings and structures, and landcuts. *[Source: MARS Field Survey Programme. Samples: Scheduled Monuments, earthworks n= 388, buildings and structures n= 151, landcuts n= 210; non-Scheduled Monuments, earthworks n= 3492, buildings and structures n= 4669, landcuts n= 4453]*

in 1976-7. However, the total of Scheduled Monuments here includes 17 items forming the Lambourn Seven barrow cemetery; if this is counted as one monument then the percentage of Scheduled Monuments lost rises to 13% of the local resource. On the South Dorset Ridgeway, Woodward found that 27 of the 405 Scheduled round barrows (6.6%) had disappeared at the time of his visits in 1977-84. This compares with the loss of 109 out of 249 (43%) of non-Scheduled round barrows (Woodward 1991, 172 and fiche 1.8).

Of the extant Scheduled Monuments in the MARS sample in 1995, 85% were found to have very good areal survival, 5.9% good, 4.6% medium, 2.6% poor and 1.9% very poor. Again the percentages of Scheduled Monuments in those categories relating to better areal survival are higher than for the population as a whole. Figure 8.9 provides a breakdown of areal survival by form, emphasizing the way in which standing buildings and small single monuments have the highest proportions of examples with very good areal survival.

In Glass' study of condition and survival among Scheduled Monuments she found that 6% were regarded

as complete, 19% as almost complete, 25% as most surviving, 35% as some surviving, 9% with little surviving, 3% as very little surviving, and 4% as destroyed or unknown (see Chapter 6.2.1 for the scale used). Comparisons may also be made with the results of a survey of Scheduled Monuments in Wales (Burnham 1991). Here 53% of Scheduled Monuments were recorded as being of 'Category A' with no obvious deterioration since the time of Scheduling. Categories B (slight deterioration) and C (serious deterioration) comprised 38% and 8% respectively. In this survey, only 1% of monuments were found to have disappeared.

The nature and extent of hazards facing Scheduled Monuments are very similar to those relating to non-Scheduled Monuments. Table 8.5 provides a comparison of the incidence of factors leading to the wholesale and piecemeal destruction of Scheduled Monuments and non-Scheduled Monuments. The rank order of hazards is very similar to that for all MARS Monuments, although the percentage contributions measured here in terms of observations made at MARS Monuments vary slightly. Agriculture has the highest incidence.

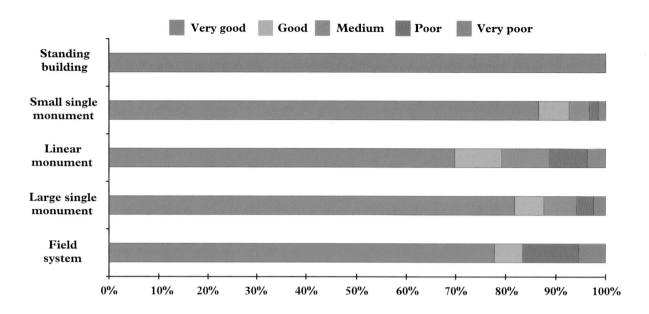

Figure 8.9 - Horizontal stacked bar charts showing the areal survival of Scheduled Monuments by monument form in 1995. *[Source: MARS Field Survey Programme and SMR data. Samples: standing buildings n= 41; small single monuments n= 462; linear monuments n= 53; large single monuments n= 121; field systems n= 18]*

In terms of the extent of this impact, the picture is again very similar for Scheduled Monuments and non-Scheduled Monuments. As Figure 8.10 shows, about three-quarters of monuments, whether Scheduled or not, suffer from widespread impacts.

The results of this analysis of Scheduled MARS Monuments also may be compared with the results obtained by Glass (1989) which showed that in her sample of 807 Scheduled Monuments ploughing, scrub-growth and fabric erosion were the three most frequent causes of damage to Scheduled Monuments, represented by 16%, 13% and 12% of reported cases of damage. Broadly the same problems were encountered in a study of Scheduled Monuments in Wales (Burnham 1991).

All of these characteristics of the resource inevitably lead back to the question: does Scheduling work? Answering this is not easy, because it assumes a straightforward definition of the implications or benefits of Scheduling. Scheduling is a complicated designation; the consequences are manifold. At the heart of Scheduling is the idea of control over the destiny of the monument through the application of a consent procedure (Scheduled Monument Consent) for potentially damaging works. Scheduling will rarely control the incidence or demand for such works, which are influenced by economic and social trends, only their impact and consequences. The legislation supports this control with a stick and a carrot. The stick takes the form of making it a criminal offence to carry out works or cause damage to a Scheduled Monument without prior permission (SMC); the carrot comes in the form of management agreements that encourage owners and occupiers to maintain the monument according to an agreed plan. It is the issue of control of works that provides the means of gauging whether or not Scheduling is working.

Numerous successful prosecutions have been brought over the years, the first in Cumbria in 1907

Scheduled Monuments

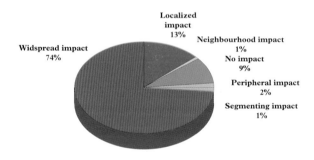

non-Scheduled Monuments

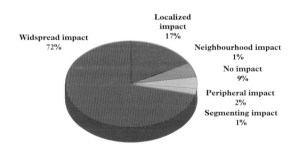

Figure 8.10 - Pie charts showing the impacts recorded on Scheduled Monuments and non-Scheduled Monuments in 1995 *[Source: MARS Field Survey Programme. Sample n= 13,426]*

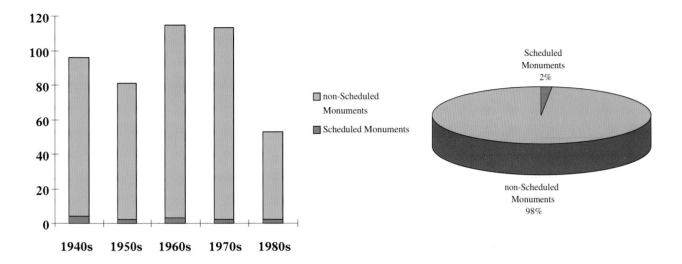

Figure 8.11 - (Left) Stacked bar chart showing losses of Scheduled Monuments in the sample of MARS Monuments by decade 1940s to 1980s; (Right) Pie chart showing the percentage of Scheduled Monuments destroyed to 1995 in relation to losses of non-Scheduled MARS Monuments. *[Source: MARS Field Survey Programme, SMR data, MARS National Survey Programme and English Heritage Records Office data. Sample: bar chart (Left) n= 458; pie chart (Right) n= 2597]*

(Saunders 1983, 16). As an example of the scale of damage to Scheduled Monuments, a total of 37 damage cases were reported to English Heritage in 1986-7. From these, nine prosecutions were made and five resulted in convictions (English Heritage 1987, 23). Carter (1993) discusses a number of cases in detail. This relatively small number of reported damage cases (0.2% of Scheduled Monuments) suggests that either Scheduling is having an effect in reducing the level of damage or that the reporting procedures are not working. MARS cannot address the latter possibility, but in looking at the former five lines of approach can be pursued, all concerned with the matter of

decay. None is conclusive on its own because each looks at a different aspect of the problem. Together, however, these provide a general picture.

First is the question of monument destruction. As already noted, about 7.5% of Scheduled Monuments in the MARS sample have been destroyed and there is no reason to think that this figure cannot be applied more widely. Indeed, comparison with other studies suggest it is a good estimate. At first sight it may seem high, but compared with the 16% rate of destruction within the recorded resource as a whole it is remarkably low. It must also be remembered that this is a cumulative figure built

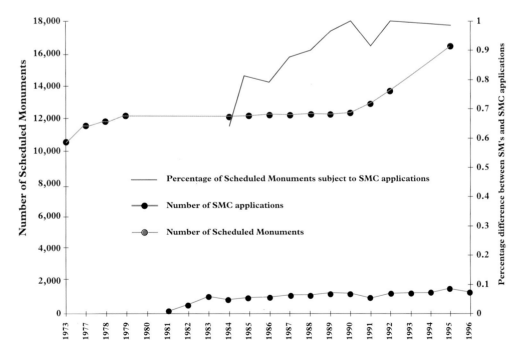

Figure 8.12 - Increases in the number of Scheduled Monument Consent applications 1981-96 in relation to the expanding Schedule between 1973 and 1996. *[Source: MARS National Survey Programme, English Heritage Annual Reports, published lists, and the English Heritage Monitor]*

up over the last century or so, including many decades before Scheduled Monument Consent procedures were introduced. Figure 8.11A shows a bar chart documenting the destruction of Scheduled Monuments per decade as represented by MARS Monuments. Throughout, Scheduled Monuments represent a small percentage of all MARS Monuments destroyed, about 2% of all monuments destroyed (Figure 8.11B). Looked at chronologically, the greatest losses were in the period 1950-80. This is significant because in 1981 the existing ancient monuments legislation was substantially strengthened by a change from notification to formal consent procedures. On the evidence of this analysis, Scheduling as it now applies does appear to be curbing the rate of loss, and the 1979 Act's introduction of the need for consent can be seen to have been effective.

Second, a comparison can be made between the number of Scheduled Monuments and the number of applications for Scheduled Monument Consent. If Scheduling is working to limit and restrict works at monuments then the number of applications should not increase greatly as the size of the Schedule increases. Figure 8.12 shows the trends. Following the introduction of SMC procedures in 1981 the number of applications increased both in absolute terms and in relation to the number of Scheduled Monuments through to 1990. These ten years could be seen as a period of adjustment to the new legislation. Since 1990 the trend shows fewer applications in relation to the scale of the Schedule, suggesting that Scheduling itself may be one of the factors deterring people from proposing works to these monuments.

Third, it is worth looking at the incidence of damage from different causes summarized in Table 8.5. In considering this it is important to recognize that some of these causes are controlled by Scheduled Monument Consent (SMC) procedures and some are not. Surprisingly, perhaps, most agricultural works currently fall outside SMC, since they are covered by a class consent (Class 1, SI 1994, No. 1381) which allows cultivation to continue where it had taken place previously. For the causes of damage controlled by the SMC procedures - building alterations, demolition, development, some elements of forestry, industry, mineral extraction, road-building, and urbanization - the levels of impact for Scheduled Monuments are generally, although not exclusively, lower than or about the same as for non-Scheduled Monuments. For the impacts over which Scheduling has no control - agriculture, some forestry, military damage, natural processes, vandalism, visitor erosion and the effects of wild animals - the levels for Scheduled Monuments are the same as or higher than those for non-Scheduled Monuments. Thus, for impacts

Table 8.5 - Identified hazards causing piecemeal loss of damage to Scheduled Monuments compared with non-Scheduled Monuments and the total sample. *[Source: MARS Field Survey Programme. Samples: Scheduled Monuments n= 873 observations; non-Scheduled Monuments n= 13,766 observations; both from a total sample of n= 14,639 observations]*

Cause of Damage	Scheduled Monuments %	non-Scheduled Monuments %	All MARS Monuments %
Agriculture	30.1	27.5	27.6
Natural process	25.2	20.7	21.0
Building alteration	3.6	10.5	10.1
Unknown	4.4	9.9	9.5
Demolition	3.4	5.2	5.1
No damage	1.9	5.3	5.1
Development and urbanization	7.6	9.0	8.9
Excavation	10.2	3.9	4.3
Road building	4.7	3.6	3.6
Mineral extraction	1.7	1.6	1.6
Forestry	1.4	1.1	1.1
Industry	<1	<1	<1
Military damage	<1	<1	<1
Vandalism	<1	<1	<1
Visitor erosion	2.9	<1	<1
Wild animal	0.9	<1	<1
Total	**100%**	**100%**	**100%**

controllable by SMC procedures, Scheduling appears to be having some effect in reducing the incidence of occurrence.

The fourth approach involves looking at gross changes in the land-use on and around Scheduled Monuments over a period of time, in this case between the 1940s and the 1990s. This study reflects the fact that when monuments are Scheduled a certain 'reverence' attaches to them (or to the threat of the 'stick' being applied through legal action). Thus it might be expected that land-use change over long periods would be less common on Scheduled Monuments than on non-Scheduled Monuments. This could be measured using MARS data from the 1940s and 1995. Since not all monuments currently Scheduled enjoyed the same status in 1940, the list of Scheduled MARS Monuments was compared with the list of Scheduled Monuments in 1953, the first such list to be published after the Second World War, effectively reflecting the situation by the end of the 1940s (MPBW 1953). Some 217 MARS Monuments (1.5%) had been Scheduled by the end of the 1940s, and land-use data for the 1940s were available for 120 of them. Table 8.6 shows an analysis of the available figures which demonstrates that in fact only a relatively small

Table 8.6 - Summary of changes in land-use on Scheduled Monuments and non-Scheduled Monuments 1940-1995. *[Source: MARS Field Survey and Aerial Photographic Survey Programmes. Samples as shown]*

	MARS Monuments Scheduled 1940s		MARS Monuments Scheduled 1950-1995		MARS Monuments (excluding those existing in 1940s)	
	No.	%	No.	%	No.	%
Same land-use 1940 and 1995	11	9.17	25	9.92	781	26.47
Different land-use 1940 and 1995	47	39.17	115	45.63	2169	73.53
Unknown	62	51.67	112	44.44	0	0
Totals	**120**	**100%**	**252**	**100%**	**2950**	**100%**

Table 8.7 - Percentage land-use change values derived from a study of time-sequenced observations for land-use on Scheduled Monuments and non-Scheduled Monuments. *[Source: MARS Field Survey and Aerial Photographic Survey Programmes. Samples as shown]*

	Scheduled before 1940		Scheduled 1940-1995		All MARS Monuments	
	No.	%	No.	%	No.	%
Number of Cases	44		104		2308	
Changed monuments	35	79.55	84	80.77	1591	68.93
1 change	27	61.36	62	59.62	1161	50.30
2 changes	7	15.91	20	19.23	362	15.68
3 changes	1	2.27	2	1.92	68	2.95
Unchanged monuments	9	2.45	20	19.23	717	31.07

percentage of Scheduled Monuments remained under the same land-use throughout the period *c*.1940-95. The same applies to monuments that were Scheduled between 1950 and 1995. Thus although it cannot be certain that these monuments were in the land-use through the period, the fact that fewer Scheduled Monuments than non-Scheduled Monuments appear to have remained constant suggests that, in practice, Scheduling does not minimize land-use change.

Fifth, land-use change can also be explored by considering the number of changes in land-use that have occurred at Scheduled and non-Scheduled Monuments over the last 50 years. One possible explanation of a higher incidence of land-use change on Scheduled Monuments is that changes were made for the good of the monument. One might therefore expect that, if Scheduling were working in this way, the percentage of monuments undergoing a small number of land-use changes would be greater for Scheduled Monuments than for non-Scheduled Monuments. In order to test this proposition a study was made of all MARS Monuments for which there were three sets of land-use observations from aerial photographic sources and one set of land-use observations from field survey. With four sets of time-sequenced observations there is the possibility of a maximum of three and a minimum of zero land-use changes between observations over the whole sequence. Suitable data existed for 2308 MARS Monuments, and Table 8.7 summarizes the results. Again there is no real difference between the behaviour of Scheduled Monuments as against non-Scheduled Monuments.

In the light of these five studies, the answer to the question 'does Scheduling work?' is therefore a clear 'yes' in relation to the aims for which Scheduling was designed; but it is not a simple one-stop solution for all protection, conservation and management issues facing archaeological monuments. On the basis of the MARS sample, Scheduling controls (but does not necessarily totally avert) approximately 40% of the damage observed as having been sustained by Scheduled MARS Monuments; if agriculture could be added to the list of operations fully regulated by Scheduling then it would be capable of controlling more than 70% of observable damage. The remaining 30% of damage is mainly caused by natural processes and related factors and therefore lies beyond any legislative protection.

8.3.4 Listed Buildings

The listing of historic buildings and structures was first established under Section 43 of the *Town and Country Planning Act 1944*, subsequently expanded and improved

upon in several pieces of planning legislation (Harvey 1993; Saint 1996). At the time of the MARS Project approximately 500,000 individual historic buildings, structures and related items (e.g. bridges, milestones etc.) in England were listed as 443,000 entries under Section 1 of the *Planning (Listed Buildings and Conservation Areas) Act 1990* (DoE 1994b, 26).

The number of Listed Buildings in England has increased fourfold since 1970, when there were about 125,000 Listed Buildings. In 1982 Michael Heseltine, then Secretary of State for the Environment, launched a major re-survey of historic buildings which together with earlier work raised the number of entries to approximately 300,919 by the end of 1984 (Robertson 1993). Each building or structure is placed in one of three grades to give an indication of its relative importance. In 1996, 2.5% of entries were Grade I (the highest), 5.5% Grade II* and 92% Grade II (the lowest). The principles of selection and procedures for listing are well established and are summarized elsewhere (DoE 1994b, 26-30).

The purpose of listing is to recognize the special architectural or historic interest of a building and to provide a control over its demolition (in whole or in part) and over any works of alteration or extension which would affect its character as a building of special interest. Controls apply to both internal and external works, and it is a criminal offence to carry out works without Listed Building Consent (see Suddards 1993 for an overview of Listed Building legislation and its application). A sample survey of Listed Buildings at risk was carried out by English Heritage in 1990-1, and a report has been published (English Heritage 1992a). The initiative has since been continued and a further series of studies undertaken (Embree 1995).

There is a significant overlap between what can be regarded as the archaeological resource and the population of historic buildings in Britain; indeed, it could be argued that the latter is simply a sub-set of the former. Among MARS Monuments, approximately 5171, or 35% of the total, are classified as buildings and structures, and this proportion may reasonably be extrapolated to apply to the recorded resource as a whole.

Within the MARS sample, 9.5% of the extant recorded resource is protected by Listed Building designation, most (63%) falling into the Grade II category. Broken down by monument character, 21.3% of buildings and structures are Listed, 0.76% of earthwork monuments and 4.76% of landcuts. Ironically, a higher percentage of the extant recorded archaeological resource is protected through Listing (9.5%) than Scheduling (6%); about 0.2% are subject to both. The matter of

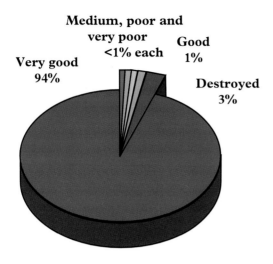

Figure 8.13 - Pie charts showing a comparison of areal survival amongst Listed Buildings and non-Listed Buildings and structures in 1995. *[Source: MARS Field Survey Programme and SMR data. Sample: Listed Buildings n= 1172; non-Listed Buildings and structures n= 3681]*

overlapping designations is being considered by the MPP in an effort to achieve the most appropriate form of protective designation for individual buildings and structures (DoE 1994b, 30).

Figure 8.13 shows the pattern of areal survival for Listed Buildings compared with non-Listed Buildings and structures in the MARS sample. The percentage of destroyed examples is very much lower among Listed Buildings than non-Listed Buildings in the MARS sample, 3% compared to 22%. The levels of buildings with 'very good' area survival are commensurately higher among Listed Buildings than their non-listed counterparts.

8.3.5 *Register of historic parks and gardens*

Since 1984 English Heritage has been compiling a *Register of parks and gardens of special historic interest*, as required under Schedule 4 of the *National Heritage Act 1983*. The first complete set of county lists was published between 1984 and 1988 and contained 1085 entries (English Heritage 1984-8). Since then the original lists have been expanded and upgraded through a series of regional surveys which were in progress at the MARS census date and are expected to be completed in the year 2000 (McRobie 1996b).

Parks and gardens of exceptional historic interest are assessed as Grade I, those of great historic interest as Grade II★ and those of special historic interest as Grade II. The grading system for parks and gardens is independent of the grading of any Listed Buildings within them (Lambert and Shacklock 1995).

The purpose of the register is to recognize and identify the interest attaching to parks and gardens as an aid to planning, and to guide the disbursement of grants. The *Town and Country Planning (General Development Procedure) Order 1995* requires local planning authorities in England to consult English Heritage on any

development likely to affect any park or garden of special historic interest which is classified as Grade I or Grade II★. However, at the time of the MARS Project the register was non-statutory, and no additional planning controls follow from the inclusion of a site in the register. In May 1996 the Department of National Heritage published the consultation paper *Protecting our heritage*, which confirmed that there was no intention to give the register a statutory basis. Local authorities have been enjoined to protect registered parks and gardens when preparing development plans and in determining planning applications. The effect of development proposals on a registered park or garden and its setting is a material consideration in the determination of a planning application (DoE 1994b, 6).

8.3.6 *Register of historic battlefields*

In June 1995 a *Register of historic battlefields* was published by English Heritage. It contained entries for 43 sites. Maps based on the best available evidence show the position and extent of each site (English Heritage 1995a). The use of the Register in the planning process is outlined in PPG15 (DoE 1994b, paragraph 2.25). Publication of the Register was too late for its implications to be included in the MARS Project and no analysis of the sites listed has been undertaken. The Register has, however, already prompted a great deal of debate as many of the examples included, and others beside, are being recognized as at considerable risk from development (Denison 1997; Anon 1997f; Carman 1997; Hargreaves 1998). No doubt the next iteration of MARS will document whether these risks become reality.

8.4 Area-based archaeological designations

8.4.1 World Heritage Sites

The World Heritage Convention, adopted by UNESCO in 1972, was ratified by the United Kingdom Government in 1984 (see Prott 1992 for background and overview). The Convention provides for the identification, protection, conservation and presentation of cultural and natural sites of outstanding universal value (UNESCO 1972). Ten sites in England are currently inscribed on the World Heritage List, all of them cultural sites (date of inscription given in parenthesis): Durham Castle and Cathedral (1986); Ironbridge Gorge (1986); Fountains Abbey and Studley Royal Park (1986); Stonehenge (1986); Hadrian's Wall Military Zone (1986); Blenheim Palace (1987); City of Bath (1987); Westminster Palace, Westminster Abbey and St Margaret's Church (1987); the Tower of London (1988); Canterbury Cathedral, St Augustine's Abbey and St Martin's Church (1988); and Maritime Greenwich (1997).

The World Heritage Convention allows the inscription of 'cultural' or 'natural' sites, the latter where a nomination is considered to be of outstanding universal value for the purposes of the Convention and meets one or more of six inscription criteria (UNESCO 1972). More recently, 'cultural landscapes' have been added to the range of what can be nominated and included on the World Heritage List (Cleere 1995).

Management guidelines have been issued for World Heritage Sites (Fielden and Jokilehto 1993), and work is well advanced with the production of management plans for each of the English sites (e.g. English Heritage 1996b). These serve not only to identify hazards facing components of the site, but also allow risks to be reduced through carefully formulated management and conservation programmes. In the UK inclusion of an area on the World Heritage List serves to highlight the outstanding international importance of the site as a key material consideration to be taken into account by local planning authorities in determining planning and Listed Building consent applications, and by the Secretary of State in determining cases on appeal or following call-in. There are, however, no additional statutory controls relating to designated World Heritage Sites (DoE 1994b, 6).

Altogether, the area of the ten sites amounts to an estimated 500km^2, nearly 0.4% of the land area of England. Four MARS transects fell within or across World Heritage Sites, too few to allow any meaningful separate analysis of the monuments they contain.

8.4.2 Archaeologically Sensitive Areas

At a regional and local level, county councils, National Park Authorities, district councils and unitary authorities can define areas within their administrative jurisdiction as being archaeologically sensitive. Different authorities use different terms for these designations, which can lead to confusion. Their primary purpose is to assist the strategic planning process by supporting the written policies with spatial information consolidated on a Proposals Map (English Heritage 1992b, 2; 1996a; Fairclough 1995). How they are implemented and which policies they are tied to varies from one authority to another. All represent 'constraint' areas, although some authorities define them

with reference to well-established distributions of archaeological monuments or deposits, while others cover areas of archaeological potential. Some define a small number of broad areas, while others focus on a larger number of smaller tracts of land (in some cases better defined as sites than areas). In practical terms this means that the designations guide developers in preparing planning applications, and act as a trigger for local authorities to implement systematic responses such as desk-top assessment or field evaluation (cf. DoE 1990a, paras. 15 and 18).

Table 8.8 shows the range of designations current in each county. The definition and introduction of these areas is a continuing process connected to the revision of the relevant strategic plans, and the table should be seen as a position statement. Spatial designations will no doubt be an increasingly important element of strategic plans in future, especially in relation to the implementation of sustainability, the maintenance of environmental capital and area characterization (English Heritage 1997a; CAG 1997).

A minimum of 11,000 separate areas have been defined to date, but no national record of the position and extent of designations has been assembled. This means that any assessment of differential survival rates within the designated areas is currently impossible. The diversity of the existing designations suggests that further national guidance in this area may be appropriate.

8.5 Non-archaeological site-specific designations

8.5.1 Sites of Special Scientific Interest

The possibility of designating Sites of Special Scientific Interest was introduced in Section 23 of the *National Parks and Access to the Countryside Act 1949* in response to the threats to wildlife habitats, geological exposures or physiographic features posed mainly by urban expansion and industrial development (see Vittery 1985 and Mackay 1985 for general overviews). The early SSSIs, which were mainly blocks of land in private ownership, were notified to local authorities for consideration in the planning process, but were not necessarily notified to owners. By the mid-1960s over 1400 SSSIs had been defined. The *Wildlife and Countryside Act 1981* reformed the system of SSSIs, requiring the NCC (now English Nature) to notify all owners and occupiers that their land had been designated as an SSSI and providing a list of operations that could damage the interest for which the land was notified. Once notified, permission is needed before potentially damaging works can proceed. The purpose of SSSIs has always been the protection of nationally important habitats for fauna and flora, geological exposures and physiographic features, through the control of works and the development of management agreements and appropriate management strategies.

Archaeology is not mentioned as one of the scientific interests for which land can be protected through the SSSI system, although in the case of later Pleistocene and Holocene geological formations there is an obvious overlap of interest, since many such deposits contain archaeological materials and critical evidence for early landforms and environments. Many SSSIs defined to protect flora and fauna contain archaeological monuments; indeed sometimes it is the presence of

Table 8.8 - Summary of local archaeological designations by county in England in 1997. *[Source: MARS National Survey Programme and SMRs]*

County	ASA designation	Number of ASAs	Area covered (km²)	Local designation	Number of locally designated sites
Avon	Under review				
Bedfordshire	AAI	1000	120		
Berkshire	Under review	0	0	N/A	0
Buckinghamshire	ANA	1055	Unknown		
Cambridgeshire	Under review	0	0		
Cheshire	AAP	7	179	N/A	0
Cleveland	SLA				
Cornwall	Under review	0	0	AGHV	22
Cumbria	under review	0	0		
Derbyshire	Under review	0	0		
Devon	N/A			N/A	
Dorset	Under review	0	0		
Durham	Under review	1	<1		
East sussex	ASA	600	N/A		
Essex	Under review	0	0		
Gloucestershire	SAP	3	N/A		
Gtr London	Under review	300			
Gtr Manchester	ASA	100	N/A		
Hampshire	Under review	0	0	N/A	0
Hereford & Worcs	Under review	0	0		
Hertfordshire	AAS	726	159		
Humberside	Under review	0	0		
Isle of Wight	No such areas	0	0	N/A	0
Kent	AAP	2500	Unknown	N/A	0
Lancashire	Under review	0	0		
Leicestershire	Under review	0	0		
Lincolnshire	Under review	0	0		
Merseyside	Under review	0	0	N/A	0
Norfolk	Under review	0	0		
Northamptonshire	Under review	0	0		
Northumberland	Under review	0	0		
North Yorkshire	ASA	4	50	N/A	0
Nottinghamshire	Under review	0	0		
Oxfordshire	Constraint Area & see 2	3261	Unknown	N/A	0
Shropshire	Under review	0	0		
Somerset	OHS				
South Yorkshire	Under review				
Staffordshire	Under review	0	0		
Suffolk	AAI	15 (urban only)	9		
Surrey	AHAP & see 1	1085	23	CSAI	?200
Tyne & Wear	AAI	>20	N/A		
Warwickshire	Under review	0	0		
West Midlands	150				
West Sussex	ASA	1000	N/A		
West Yorkshire	Under review				
Wiltshire	ASAS	39	1575		

Abbreviations:
AAI - Area of Archaeological Interest
AAP - Area of Archaeological Potential
AAS - Area of Archaeological Significance
AGHV - Area of Great Historic Value
AHAP - Area of High Archaeological Potential
ANA - Archaeological Notification Area
ASA - Archaeologically Sensitive Area
ASAS - Area of Special Archaeological Significance

CSAI - County Sites of Archaeological Importance
OHS - Outstanding Heritage Settlement
SAAS - Sites & Areas of Archaeological Significance
SAP - Site of Archaeological Potential
SLA - Special Landscape Area

1. Covers all applications over 0.4 acre or more
2. Excludes Oxford city

Table 8.9 - Distribution of SSSIs by MARS region in relation to recorded archaeology in 1995. *[Source: MARS National Survey Programme and SMRs. Samples as shown]*

Region	Scheduled Monuments in SSSIs[1]	Recorded resource[2]	MARS Monuments
North West	0	77	2
North East	95	541	3
West Midlands	4	146	0
East Midlands	27	269	13
South West	351	2606	26
South East	43	289	41
Total	520	3928	85

1. Data from MARS National Survey
2. Data from MARS National Survey

archaeological remains that has allowed plant and animal communities to survive. The important point here is that management practices which are good for wildlife habitats are also usually good for archaeological remains. A few habitats, for example water-meadows, are often archaeological features in their own right. Moreover, in defining the importance of ground for its nature conservation value, reference is sometimes made to the existence of earthworks and archaeological remains (Ratcliffe 1977, 159).

At the MARS census date there were approximately 3912 SSSIs in England covering about 7% of England's land area. A minimum total of 85 MARS Monuments (0.5%) were recorded as being within SSSIs at the census date. Table 8.9 shows the incidence of archaeological monuments in SSSIs by region. There is clearly an extensive archaeological presence on SSSI sites and a considerable overlap between protection through Scheduling and SSSI designation: according to data obtained by the MARS National Survey, about 3.5% of all Scheduled Monuments are situated within SSSIs. Figure 8.14 shows a breakdown of land-uses recorded on MARS Monuments within SSSIs in comparison with the pattern in other protective designations. It is notable that the patterns for Scheduled Monuments and SSSIs are very similar.

Figure 8.15 shows an analysis of the areal survival of MARS Monuments in SSSIs compared with survival patterns represented within other protective designations. Over 75% of monuments have very good areal survival and only about 9% are recorded as having been destroyed.

8.5.2 National Nature Reserves

The history of National Nature Reserves (NNRs) is very similar to that of SSSIs. Some 67 key areas were identified as potential NNRs in the Huxley Report (WCSP 1947), covering 230km². They were first introduced in Section 16 of the *National Parks and Access to the Countryside Act 1949*, and modified by Section 35 of the *Wildlife and Countryside Act 1981*. The purpose of NNRs was to bring important wildlife habitats under direct protective

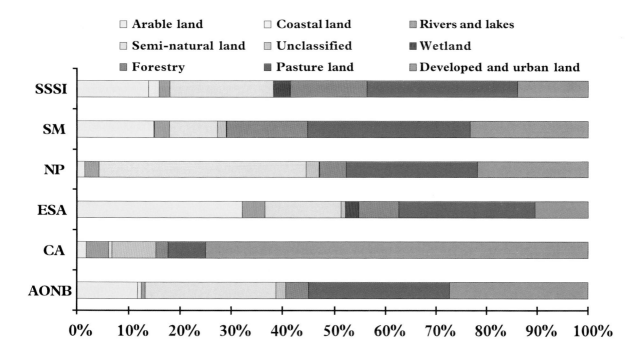

Figure 8.14 - Horizontal stacked bar charts showing land-use on monuments subject to specific protective designations in 1995. *[Source: MARS Field Survey Programme, English Nature, English Heritage Records Office, National Park Authorities, Countryside Commission and MAFF. Samples: n= 94 observations within SSSIs; n= 946 observations for Scheduled Monuments; n= 1267 observations within National Parks; n= 115 observations within Environmentally Sensitive Areas; n= 164 observations within Conservation Areas; n= 593 observations within Areas of Outstanding Natural Beauty]*

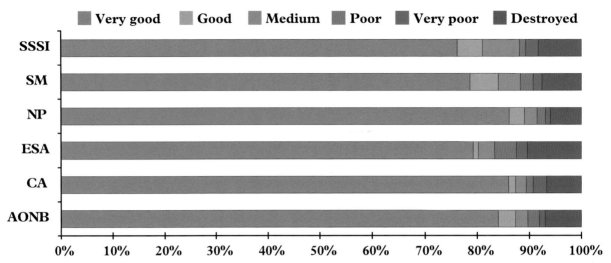

Figure 8.15 - Horizontal stacked bar charts showing the prevailing areal survival of MARS Monuments subject to protective designations in 1995. *[Source: MARS Field Survey Programme, English Nature, English Heritage Records Office, National Park Authorities, Countryside Commission and MAFF. Samples: n= 84 monuments within SSSIs; n= 751 Scheduled Monuments; n= 1206 monuments within National Parks; n= 96 monuments within Environmentally Sensitive Areas; n= 150 monuments within Conservation Areas; n= 544 monuments within Areas of Outstanding Natural Beauty]*

Table 8.10 - Distribution of NNRs by MARS Region in relation to recorded archaeology in 1995. *[Source: MARS Field Survey Programme and English Nature. Samples as shown]*

Region	NNRs	Area of NNRs (km²)	Scheduled Monuments on NNRs[1]	Recorded resource[2]	Density of the recorded resource (monuments per km²)
North West	31	33.19	0	7	0.21
North East	22	26.49	1	25	0.94
West Midlands	22	26.27	0	6	0.22
East Midlands	44	38.28	2	33	0.86
South West	39	61.36	22	66	1.07
South East	35	56.13	0	0	1
Totals	**193**	**241.73**	**25**	**137**	**0.56**

1 Data from MARS National Survey.
2 Data from MARS National Survey

management and to facilitate their use for scientific study. At the MARS census date the number of NNRs in England had risen to 188, covering 712km² or about 0.5% of England's land area.

Table 8.10 shows the distribution of designated NNRs by region in relation to the archaeological resource represented. About 13% of NNRs contain Scheduled Monuments, with perhaps as many as 71% of reserves containing some recorded monuments. Insufficient MARS Monuments were recorded as being within NNRs to allow meaningful analysis of their condition or survival.

8.6 Non-archaeological area-based designations

There are numerous designations of greater or lesser relevance to the protection of archaeological remains that apply in built-up or rural areas, especially at local and regional level. Very few of these can accurately be correlated with archaeological monuments and they have therefore been excluded from this review (for example

Areas of Great Landscape Value, Countryside Heritage Sites, Green Belt land, Heritage Coasts etc.). Approximately 35,000 km² of land in England (27% of land area) is covered by one or more of the following nationally defined area-based designations: National Park, Area of Outstanding Natural Beauty, Conservation Area and Environmentally Sensitive Area (there is an unquantified element of overlap in the total figure). These designations are considered in the following sub-sections.

8.6.1 National Parks

National Parks were first established under Section 5 of the *National Parks and Access to the Countryside Act 1949* for the dual purposes of conservation through preserving and enhancing their natural beauty, and access by promoting their enjoyment by the public. Seven National Parks were designated in England between April 1951 and April 1956 - the Peak District, the Lake District, Dartmoor, the North York Moors, the Yorkshire Dales, Exmoor and Northumberland - covering a total area of 9298 km². In March 1988 an eighth area was added, the Norfolk and Suffolk Broads, bringing the total area

Table 8.11 - Distribution of recorded archaeology in England's National Parks in 1995. *[Source: MARS National Survey Programme, National Park Authorities, and SMRs. Samples as shown]*

National Park	Area of National Parks (km²)[1]	Scheduled Monuments[2]	Density of Scheduled Monuments (monuments per km²)	Area of MARS transects in NPs (km²)	MARS Monuments in NPs	Density of MARS Monuments (monuments per km²)
Dartmoor	945	436	0.46	60	429	7.15
Exmoor	686	151	0.22	32.5	142	4.30
Lake District	2292	135	0.06	155	133	0.85
Norfolk and Suffolk Broads	288	12	0.04	22.5	24	1.06
Northumberland	1031	651	0.63	32.5	107	3.20
North York Moors	1432	300	0.21	47.5	105	2.21
Peak District	1404	199	0.14	55	96	1.74
Yorkshire Dales	1760	114	0.06	100	427	4.27
Totals	**9838**	**1998**	**0.20**	**505**	**1463**	**2.89**

1. Data from Edwards 1991, 2
2. Data from MARS National Survey

covered to 9601km², 7.3% of the land area of England.

Since 1949, the status and operation of National Parks has developed and changed. The *Countryside Act 1968* and the *Wildlife and Countryside Act 1981* both contained major revisions of the way in which National Parks work and the powers available to the committees and authorities that run them. A major review of National Parks was carried out between 1989 and 1991, published as the Edwards Report (Edwards 1991). In it, the review panel recognized that 'archaeology is to some degree a poor relation in the national park world, and has received disproportionately little attention. This is apparent in the inadequacy of archaeological data in National Parks' (Edwards 1991, 23). The panel made a number of recommendations, including that each park should establish an archaeological database in order to integrate the management of archaeological remains with other forms of countryside management, that parks should review their expertise in archaeology, and that they should negotiate access to a representative range of archaeological sites. Progress has been made on most of these recommendations, their importance being made more acute by the fact that the *Environment Act 1995* established the National Park authorities as levying bodies, responsible for the preparation, publication and review of Park Management Plans (their role as planning authorities was also tightened as part of the Act). The history and role of National Parks and their development has been well covered (e.g. TRRU 1981; CNP 1982; Countryside Commission 1991b; Blunden and Curry 1990; MacEwen and MacEwen 1982; DoE 1974b), as have the nature and extent of archaeological monuments represented within the parks (White and Iles 1991) and the approaches to monument management being pursued (e.g. Smith 1986).

With the exception of the recently designated Norfolk and Suffolk Broads, all of England's National Parks are situated in upland areas which are well known for their wealth of preserved archaeological monuments (Darvill 1986). Although National Parks were not selected and defined with reference to the distribution of archaeological remains, they are now collectively recognized as representing one of England's great

archaeological treasure-houses. Moreover, the general lack of development pressure until recent decades, coupled with the robust planning and conservation policies pursued by National Park authorities, has ensured high levels of survival. Table 8.11 summarizes the archaeological resource currently recorded in the eight national parks. In 1990 there were nearly 2000 Scheduled Monuments within National Parks, 14% of the total number of Scheduled Monuments in 7.5% of the land area of England. The overall average density of Scheduled Monuments within National Parks is twice the national average at 0.2 per km², compared with 0.11 per km² elsewhere. Northumberland National Park currently has the highest density of Scheduled Monuments.

A total of 104 MARS sample transects lie wholly or partly within National Parks, providing information for about 1463 MARS Monuments. The density of MARS

Access

Visibility

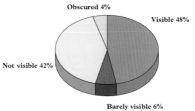

Figure 8.16 - Pie charts showing access and visibility of MARS Monuments in National Parks in 1995. *[Source: MARS Field Survey Programme and National Park Authorities. Samples: n= 1450 access observations; n= 1236 visibility observations]*

Monuments within the sample unit compares favourably with the general picture for National Parks, and numerically MARS has a 5.2% sample of the archaeology of National Parks. Using the MARS sample, National Parks have an overall density of recorded archaeology of 2.89 per km^2, compared with the national average of 2.25 per km^2.

Figure 8.14 shows an analysis of land-use patterns on MARS Monuments within National Parks. The high level of monuments under semi-natural land-use (40%) is especially notable, as too is the low percentage under arable (1.5%).

Figure 8.15 illustrates the analysis of areal survival between different protective designations. National Parks have the highest level of MARS Monuments recorded as having very good areal survival (87%) and the lowest incidence of destruction (7.8%). In this, National Parks perform better than Scheduled Monuments, although the comparison is unfair because of the restricted geographical spread of National Parks and their very special environmental locations. Nonetheless, the completeness of survival singles them out as areas for continued attention and resourcing in future.

Since access is one of the central purposes of National Parks it is pertinent to investigate recorded levels of visibility and access. In Figure 8.16 a pair of pie charts summarize the pattern revealed by MARS Monuments in National Parks. The amount of free access in National Parks is significantly greater at 41% than within the MARS sample as a whole, for which the average is 24%. The percentages of monuments with no access or access only by payment in the National Parks are around the same as the national average. As far as visibility of monuments is concerned, the figures for National Parks are the same as the national average.

8.6.2 Areas of Outstanding Natural Beauty

Section 87 of the *National Parks and Access to the Countryside Act 1949* provided for the designation of Areas of Outstanding Natural Beauty, the primary purposes of which are the conservation and enhancement of natural beauty, including the protection of flora, fauna and geological as well as landscape features. It is recognized that human influences have shaped the landscape as well, and the conservation of archaeological, architectural and vernacular features is also important (Countryside Commission 1990b, 2). Between the mid-1950s and 1988 a total of 32 AONBs were designated in England, the total area covered being about 18,082km^2 or 14% of the land area of England. There are currently 37 such areas, covering approximately 20,400km^2 (15.5% of the total land area). Unlike National Parks, AONBs have no special statutory administrative or financial arrangements and they are operated through the Countryside Commission and Local Advisory Committees (LACs) made up of representatives of the various local authorities whose administrative areas are wholly or partly covered by the designation. A number of general accounts of the nature and operation of AONBs have been published (e.g. Countryside Commission 1989a; 1989b) and the Countryside Commission has a programme to publish landscape assessments for each AONB (*cf.* Countryside Commission 1987). A review of the effectiveness of AONB designation carried out in 1997 argued that some of England's best-loved countryside in existing AONBs was under considerable threat unless new ways were found to manage it and pay for its upkeep (Countryside Commission 1997a).

Table 8.12 presents the extent of the recorded resource in AONBs by MARS Regions as revealed by the National Survey programme. Using data gathered by the National Survey Programme from SMRs the density of the recorded resource in AONBs is estimated at 0.85 per km^2, rather less than the national average of 2.25 per km^2. The MARS sample (see below) is rather higher at 1.48 per km^2. The frequency of Scheduled Monuments is more consistent: an estimated density of 0.12% per km^2 in AONBs against a national average of 0.11% per km^2. As with National Parks, the delineation of AONBs is not based on archaeological criteria, and thus the land which is included must be seen as only a sample of the kind of archaeology represented in the defined areas. Having said this, it is important to recognize that 14% of England's land area is a substantial sample; larger than the sample represented by the National Parks and more widely distributed.

A total of 506 MARS Monuments were recorded as being within AONBs at the census date, a 3.8% sample of the estimated recorded resource within AONBs. Figure 8.14 demonstrates the land-use pattern on MARS

Table 8.12 - Summary of the recorded archaeological resource represented in AONBs in England by MARS Region in 1995. *[Source: MARS National Survey Programme, and SMRs. Samples as shown]*

Region	AONBs	Area of AONBs (km^2)	Recorded resource[1]	Density of recorded resource (monuments per km^2)	Scheduled Monuments[2]	Density of Scheduled Monuments (monuments per km^2)	Area of MARS transects in AONBs (km^2)	MARS Monuments in AONBs	Density of MARS Monuments (monuments per km^2)
North West	3	992	0	–	0	–	20	20	1.00
North East	4	2925	670	0.23	99	0.03	120	73	1.64
West Midlands	5	2144	9	<0.01	136	0.06	10	3	3.33
East Midlands	5	1576	5	<0.01	13	0.01	10	3	3.33
South West	11	5538	13626	2.46	1774	0.32	100	279	0.36
South East	8	4463	666	0.15	178	0.04	80	128	0.62
Totals	**33**	**17638**	**14976**	**0.85**	**2200**	**0.12**	**340**	**506**	**1.48**

1 Data from MARS National Survey. These figures should be regarded as minimum numbers
2 Data from MARS National Survey

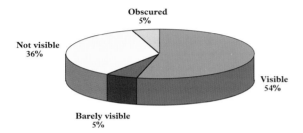

Access

Free access
33%

No access
45%

Visible from path
22%

Visibility

Obscured
5%

Not visible
36%

Visible
54%

Barely visible
5%

Figure 8.17 - Pie charts showing access and visibility of MARS Monuments in AONBs in 1995. *[Source: MARS Field Survey Programme and Countryside Commission. Samples: n= 506 access observations; n= 506 visibility observations]*

Monuments within AONBs. The relatively low percentage under arable cultivation (11.6%) is notable, as too is the relatively high percentage on semi-natural land.

In Figure 8.15 the areal survival characteristics of MARS Monuments in AONBs are compared with the pattern under other designations. The destruction rate (8%) is similar to that represented amongst monuments covered by other designations. The percentage of monuments found to have very good areal survival (83%) is generally a little higher than among monuments within SSSIs and those which are Scheduled.

In Figure 8.17 two pie charts represent the visibility and accessibility of monuments within AONBs.

8.6.3 Conservation Areas

Conservation Areas were first designated under Section 1 of the *Civic Amenities Act 1967*, subsequently modified by Sections 69-80 of the *Planning (Listed Buildings and Conservation Areas) Act 1990*, where they are defined as areas of special architectural or historic interest, the character or appearance of which it is desirable to preserve or enhance. The purpose of Conservation Areas is to control development and provide a framework in which to promote positive measures to maintain, enhance or regenerate the character and amenity of a particular area. The number of Conservation Areas grew rapidly during the 1970s and 1980s to reach 6300 by 1988 and 8435 by 1995 (ETB 1996, 11). Most Conservation Areas lie in built-up areas, but less than 2% are rural non-settlement locations. A full list and accompanying analytical commentary was published in 1990 (Pearce *et al.* 1990), and guidance on Conservation Area practice was issued in 1995 (English Heritage 1995b). Andreae (1996) takes a critical look at the development and effectiveness of Conservation Areas in the light of the kind of development pressures they face.

In defining a Conservation Area it is usual to

identify the special architectural or historical features that give it importance. In about 7% of cases archaeological monuments are included as special features, in many cases moated sites; other archaeological built features are also widely cited as special features, including water mills, bridges and fords, castles and forts, and monastic houses. Topographical features of interest to archaeology such as ponds, commons, greens and woodland are also regularly cited (Hennessey *et al.* 1990, table 9).

The MARS National Survey revealed that numerous archaeological remains have been recorded within Conservation Areas, with over 17,000 records currently in SMRs. At least 244 Scheduled Monuments (1.7% of the national total) lie wholly or partly within Conservation Areas. A total of 140 MARS Monuments in 35 sample transects were found to be within Conservation Areas, most of them buildings and structures (71%). Earthworks and landcuts in Conservation Areas represented 5% and 24% of MARS Monuments respectively. Figure 8.14 shows the pattern of land-use represented by MARS Monuments in Conservation Areas; not unexpectedly, it is dominated by developed land (75%). Figure 8.15 shows areal survival for Conservation Areas compared with survival for monuments in other designations. The picture is very similar to that seen for the National Parks, although the archaeology involved is rather different because the Parks are dominated by earthwork monuments and Conservation Areas are dominated by buildings. In this sense the two might be seen as complementary to one another. Over 85% of MARS Monuments in Conservation Areas have very good areal survival and only 7.5% of the recorded resource has been destroyed to date. Buildings will not be well represented within the sector of the resource recognized as having been destroyed unless they were recorded on archaeological records. The loss of non-archaeologically recorded historic buildings in conservation areas is much greater (see Andreae 1996).

8.6.4 Environmentally Sensitive Areas

Environmentally Sensitive Areas (ESAs) are one of the most recent designations, introduced by Section 18 of the *Agriculture Act 1986*. The purpose of the designation is to conserve and enhance the natural beauty of an area, its flora, fauna, and geological or physiographical features, or to protect buildings or other objects of archaeological, architectural or historic interest through the maintenance or adoption of certain agricultural methods. The designation is therefore very explicit about how its objectives are to be met, and it achieves them through a two-stage process: first, the physical definition and designation of tracts of land which are regarded as Environmentally Sensitive, and second, the conclusion of management agreements with individual owners or users of land within each defined area. Participation in the scheme is optional, and details of the take-up in specific ESAs are confidential to MAFF, which runs the scheme. In 1995/6 MAFF made available £39.5 million for payments to support the ESA scheme (HMG 1997, 8). The operation of the system, and in particular its archaeological aspects, have been described in some detail by Bodrell (1993), while Harvey (1997) provides a critical appraisal, concluding that in some areas farmers find the livestock subsidies more appealing than environmental management payments (Harvey 1997, 89). A more general assessment of the benefits of the scheme has been outlined by Whitby (1994) and reviewed by the Agriculture Committee (1997; and see HMG 1997).

In 1995 there were 22 defined ESAs in England covering a total of 11,492km², 8.8% of the land area of England. This is set to rise considerably before the end of the century (Bodrell 1993, 28). ESAs generally contain relatively high densities of archaeological monuments. A total of 86 MARS Monuments in 25 transects lie within ESAs; this gives an average density of 3.4 MARS Monuments per square kilometre, about one and a half times the national average. However, since the basis of ESA schemes is that, within the defined areas, individual farmers opt into the system it is not known how overall densities relate to land parcels benefiting from the scheme.

The distribution of land-uses recorded on MARS Monuments within ESAs appears in Figure 8.14, a wide spread of different types with a pattern very similar to that of MARS Monuments in SSSIs. The areal survival of MARS Monuments in ESAs is shown in Figure 8.15. About 80% of recorded monuments have very good areal survival, as might be expected given the sort of countryside that is typically represented among ESAs; what is more surprising is the relatively high percentage (10%) of the recorded resource that has been destroyed to date in these areas. Although lower than the national average of 16% it is the highest loss rate among the major designations discussed here. This alone justifies action in these areas.

The first five designated areas (West Penwith, the Pennine Dales, the Somerset Levels and Moors, the South Downs and the Norfolk Broads) have been subjected to intensive monitoring to determine the effects of designation (ADAS 1996a, 1996b; 1996c; 1996d; 1996e). In the case of the archaeological resource, ADAS in association with the relevant county archaeological officers has carried out sample surveys to chart the changing condition of monuments.

In West Penwith, designated in 1987 largely because of its archaeological and historical importance, no damage resulting from agricultural operations was observed at any of the 447 individual monuments within the ESA. However, some evidence of deterioration as a result of natural processes was identified. It was concluded that ESA status was effective in reducing the loss and damage of archaeological and historical features (ADAS 1996a, 24). Similarly, in the Pennine Dales, also designated in 1987 because of its rich archaeological resource, monitoring work increased the number of recorded archaeological monuments and recorded twice as much beneficial change as detrimental change (ADAS 1996b, 22 and 23).

8.7 Payment schemes

Some of the designations discussed above include payment schemes for the support of management agreements or as compensation; other schemes such as set-aside and Countryside Stewardship are based solely on payments and incentives. Whereas during the 1980s attempts to limit agricultural production led to financial aid for agricultural systems, in the 1990s the trend has been towards the recognition of environmental benefit. Grant schemes now

aim to protect and enhance the countryside, the landscape, natural features, wildlife habitats, natural resources (water, air and soil quality), and archaeological and historic features (MAFF 1995, 2). A general review of farming incentive schemes in relation to archaeology by Ian Dormor (1996) found that while such incentive schemes in general help to resolve the conflict between agriculture and environmental conservation archaeology remains a relatively marginal consideration.

The projected levels of grant expenditure for 1996/7 (as estimated at the time of the MARS census) for land management incentive schemes vary significantly between schemes. For example, ESA grants are estimated at £43.1 million, Countryside Stewardship at £11.7 million, archaeological management agreements at a maximum of £200,000, the Woodland Grant Scheme at £18.5 million and SSSI management agreements at £7.8 million. Collectively, these and other schemes represent a total annual spend of about £126.3 million, a large sum of money but only 0.017% of the Gross Domestic Product for the UK.

In the following sub-sections attention is directed to three payment schemes which are directly relevant to archaeology: archaeological management agreements, Countryside Stewardship and set-aside. Others that could have been considered include, for example, the management agreements linked to SSSI designation (English Nature), ESA designation (MAFF), or the grants and support payments under the Moorland Scheme (MAFF), Woodland Grant Schemes (Countryside Commission) and the Conservation Areas Partnerships Scheme (English Heritage).

8.7.1 Archaeological management agreements
Section 17 of the *Ancient Monuments and Archaeological Areas Act 1979* provided for payments to be made in order to assist the active management of archaeological sites. This replaced an earlier system of 'acknowledgement' payments made under the terms of previous legislation. It is estimated that some 1500 management agreements, each lasting for between three and ten years, have been concluded in England, with a heavy regional bias towards the south and south-west of the country, where up to 60% of all archaeological management agreements have been made. Of the remainder, 25% relate to monuments in the Midlands and 15% to the north. There is also significant variation within regions: for example, in the South West, there are 49 such agreements in place in Wiltshire and only 5 in Avon; 21 in Cornwall and 24 in Devon but only 5 in Dorset; 11 in Gloucestershire and 12 in Somerset. Most agreements relate to Scheduled Monuments (less than 10% of all Scheduled Monuments have been subject to such agreements), and where agreements are concluded for non-Scheduled Monuments these are deemed to be of national importance. The annual expenditure on management agreements has gradually increased since 1986 (Figure 8.18), although the overall sums remain small compared with expenditure on management agreements for nature conservation. Expenditure prior to 1986 was mainly connected with the transfer of the old acknowledgement payment schemes to the new pattern of management agreements.

Of the agreements funded, about 1000 remained active at the time of the MARS census, the remainder having lapsed or expired since 1991. The majority of these

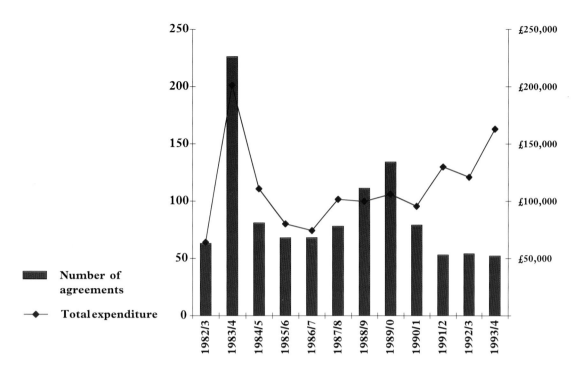

Figure 8.18 - Changes in the funding of archaeological management agreements 1983-95. *[Source: MARS Case Study Research and English Heritage. Sample: n= 1067 agreements]*

agreements are made between English Heritage and occupiers and involve payment in order to secure more appropriate land-use over a monument, for example permanent pasture. Larger payments are commonly made where capital works are necessary, followed by regular maintenance over a longer period. Payments are commonly made for the reduction in stocking levels, the erection of stock-proof fencing, or the transfer of sites from woodland or arable to pasture (G. Friell pers. comm.).

8.7.2 Countryside Stewardship scheme

The Countryside Stewardship scheme was launched by the Countryside Commission in 1991 in partnership with English Heritage and English Nature (Countryside Commission 1992; 1994b); in 1996 responsibility for the scheme was transferred to MAFF (MAFF 1995). Under this scheme specific habitat types and countryside features are targeted, and farmers are able to claim compensation for adopting environmentally friendly measures. The overall aims are: to sustain the beauty and diversity of the landscape; to improve and extend wildlife habitats; to conserve archaeological sites and historical features; to improve opportunities for enjoying the countryside; to restore neglected land or landscape features; and to create new wildlife habitats and landscapes (Countryside Commission 1994b, 3). The workings of the scheme for the management of archaeological sites have been discussed and described by Jago (1995).

Stewardship Areas target a broad range of habitats and landscape forms. Those identified for attention to date include: chalk and limestone grassland; lowland heath; waterside land; the coast; uplands; historic landscapes; old traditional orchards; community forests; the countryside around towns; hedgerows in need of restoration; and old meadows and pasture in Hereford

and Worcester and the Culm Valley in Devon and Cornwall.

As a result of active promotion, it is estimated that 20% of England's lowland heath is now covered by Stewardship agreements, and that agreements are now in place for some 12,000ha of historic parkland (LUC 1995). Although no figures exist nationally, it has been suggested that Stewardship schemes cover a very minor proportion of agricultural land-take (Morris 1997, 21, and see Harvey 1997, 59-61 for critical review). The annual budget for the Scheme was £16.3 million in 1995, with an estimated 5312 agreements in place.

After three years of operation, independent consultants indicated that for some 85% of the sample sites examined there were signs of some positive benefit for one or more of the wildlife, landscape, history and public access objectives (MAFF 1995, 13). Referring specifically to historical and archaeological features within the scope of Stewardship, the review showed that Scheduled Monuments were present on only 9% of all year one to three Stewardship Agreements, and that 90% of management proposals were thought to be wholly appropriate for archaeological and historical features. It was noted, however, that the level of archaeological information was inadequate in several cases and thus objectives could not necessarily be met. A new consultative process involving county archaeological curators was therefore suggested (MAFF 1995, section 36).

There were not enough MARS Monuments within land known to be covered by Stewardship Agreements to make analysis worthwhile, and in any case the scheme is so recent that differences in decay patterns are unlikely to be manifest as yet. However, the investigation of the archaeological resource within the first five of the stewardship target classes has been integral to the Key Habitats Project commissioned by DoE and undertaken by Lancaster University Archaeological Unit. Reports have been prepared for the five key habitats, and there is a summary report (Barr 1997a-f). Monitoring of the effect of the scheme over the period 1991-6 revealed that of the 53 sample sites of historical/archaeological interest, 41 (77% of sample) were meeting the historical conservation objectives set (Countryside Commission 1997b, 69).

8.7.3 Set-aside

Following a period of direct subsidies and price support for agricultural produce under the European Union's Common Agricultural Policy (CAP) throughout the 1970s and 1980s (EC 1989), the CAP reforms of 1992 introduced the idea of taking cultivated land out of production (Whitby 1994; Lowe and Whitby 1997). A number of schemes have been in operation under the general umbrella of set-aside, variously taking field margins, fields and sometimes whole farms out of production. The cost to the taxpayer of set-aside has been estimated at £200 million in 1995 (see chapter 4 in Harvey 1997 for a critical review of the effectiveness of set-aside).

The rules on what could be done with land in set-aside were strictly applied (even carrying out archaeological excavations in set-aside technically required approval), and most farmers have used it as part of a rotation system. The amount of land under set-aside increased in 1992 and 1993 to peak in 1994 when 5.6% of the land area of England was under set-aside.

Because of fluctuations in the area of land under set-aside at any one time it is impossible to relate MARS Monuments to the potential benefits and impacts caused by the scheme. MAFF guidance on the selection of land for set-aside encouraged farmers to take account of archaeology when deciding what to take out of cultivation. Moreover, given the short-term nature of set-aside schemes their impact on reducing damage to monuments through arable agriculture is limited, and it might even be argued that bringing land back into plough again involves more damaging operations than if cultivation had simply continued.

8.8 Multiple designations and overall impacts

As already noted, the range of protective designations and incentive schemes in England is very considerable. Some are grounded in a concern for archaeological monuments, others include archaeology as one of a range of factors, and yet others are not directly related to archaeology but include by default archaeological monuments or deposits within the land that they cover. The result is a mosaic of protective designations, many of them overlapping in their coverage or intentions.

A major advance in the integration of environmental assets and approaches to the operation of designations and management schemes was the creation, in 1996, by MAFF of an Agri-Environment Forum. This group comprises senior representatives from a wide range of statutory organizations and government departments concerned with the physical, cultural and historic environment, among them English Heritage, the Department of National Heritage (now the Department

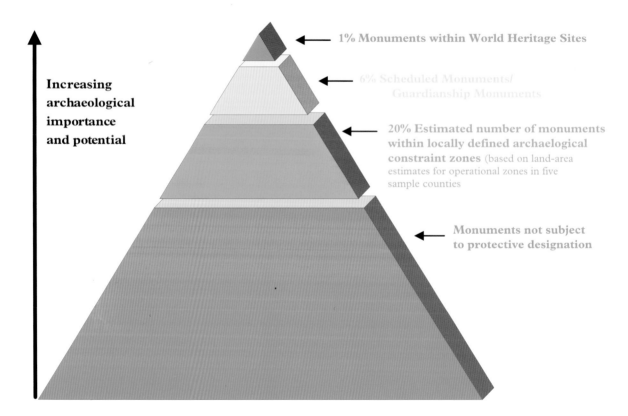

Figure 8.19 - Extent of archaeological designations in England in relation to the scale of the recorded resource in 1995. *[Source: MARS Case Study Research. County and local designations estimated from constraint maps published by authorities with designations already in place]*

of Culture, Media and Sport) and the Institute of Terrestrial Ecology (MAFF 1996).

Looking across the range of designations and their effects, as far as they can be gauged from a sample survey of this type, it seems that all or most fulfil their objectives and purpose. The problem with so many designations is that they are seen as being capable of dealing with every eventuality, and yet manifestly they are not. All designations need to be reviewed from time to time in order to assess their applicability, and revised as necessary. This has happened several times over with, for example, Scheduled Monument and Listed Building designation. It has been recognized that Areas of Archaeological Importance are no longer as relevant as they were in 1979 and they are therefore likely to disappear. It is generally believed that fewer designations would be more effective, and that any new ones need full justification before being introduced. The alternative to designation is the development of broader-based but effective policies dealing with sustainability and the maintenance of environmental diversity (Poore and Poore 1992; Lucas 1992; English Heritage 1997a).

Looking in particular at the archaeological designations it is relevant to ask whether the coverage they provide is appropriate. At one level the answer is 'yes', because substantial parts of England's archaeological resource are covered by one kind of designation or another. Figure 8.19 shows this in diagrammatic form. At the top level, applying to just 1% of England's archaeological monuments, are the ten World Heritage Sites, internationally recognized as of very great importance. A further 6% of monuments are Scheduled as being of national importance or are Guardianship Monuments. Below this a very substantial percentage of England's archaeological resource is covered by regional and local designations where they have been introduced. These comprise areas of high archaeological importance/sensitivity determined on the grounds of what is known to exist or because of high archaeological potential. They are defined by local authorities, mainly county councils, in relation to strategic plans and can be revised at intervals according to the cycle of plan reviews. The remainder of the archaeological resource is not apparently covered by any archaeological designation.

At present there is no Heritage Information Service to map and document all the different forms of designations on a national scale in the way that the Countryside Information Service does for the natural environment. Proposals for such a service are under discussion, and when brought to fruition would undoubtedly help with the integration and harmonization of designations within regions and nationally.

Many non-archaeological designations are clearly important for the overall conservation and management of archaeological monuments, and this is increasingly being recognized in reviews of these measures. National Parks stand out as exceptionally important for the future because of the relatively low destruction rates suffered in recent decades and the high level of areal survival represented. AONBs are also important, and while they do not enjoy quite the same level of protection that National Park status provides they are nonetheless widely distributed across England, extensive in area, and known to contain a wide range of archaeological remains. A pilot scheme carried out by the Dartmoor National Park,

involving delegated responsibilities and the development of pro-active archaeological management schemes (Griffiths 1991), provided the basis for building comparable approaches now in place in other National Parks and local authorities.

All archaeological monuments, whether subject to protective designations or not, remain vulnerable to threats of development or change. This chapter has dealt with the control and avoidance of those threats, and in the next chapter attention is directed to assessing the risk to which monuments are exposed.

9 Monuments at risk

If a site is being destroyed for ever by the removal of soil in bulk, obviously there will be nothing left to dig … Conservation … is the need of the day: conservation not only of purely archaeological features but of the amenities which give them more than half their charm … The need is really urgent; for with the approaching electrification of southern England, the coniferous activities of the Woods and Forests Department and of private planters, the demands of the Services for land for aerodromes and manoeuvres, the spread of bungloid eruptions, and the threat of arterial roads and ribbon development … it is unlikely that any open country or downland will be left … Expensive nibbling at those [ancient sites] which are not threatened is to be discouraged when England's past, and with it much of England's beauty, is perishing before our eyes.

(O G S Crawford 1929, 1-3)

9.1 The idea of risk

The idea of risk has become a fact of life. Every activity can be said to have unpredictable outcomes or consequences, and it is now widely recognized that all archaeological monuments and deposits, whether recorded or not, are at risk in the sense that there is always a chance or possibility of loss, injury damage, or some other adverse consequence as a result of natural processes or the intentional or unintentional actions of individuals. But while risk is by definition the result of erratic processes, the degree of risk faced by individual elements of the archaeological record is not evenly distributed, and can, to some extent, be predicted or anticipated. This is because ancient monuments are not at risk from themselves but from external factors, whose occurrences in many cases follow a pattern as far as the timing and location of their greatest impact are concerned. Crawford, quoted above from an early editorial in the journal *Antiquity*, recognized the risk posed to archaeological remains from the sorts of activities which seemed most threatening in the late 1920s, and advocated directing resources to combat them. The same applies today.

The main hazards that have impacted on archaeological monuments over the last 50 years or so were examined in detail in Chapters 6 and 7. Here, attention focuses on how these hazards combine to create general patterns of risk, and in particular the way in which risk is differentially distributed in relation to the short- and medium-term survival of archaeological monuments. The measures of risk used in MARS are described·and assessed and the results of these studies are then examined with reference to different dimensions of the recorded resource. Inevitably, this kind of risk assessment can apply only to those archaeological monuments that have been recorded and are known about. It needs to be recognized, however, that the hazards posing risks to these monuments apply also to the extant unrecorded resource.

Although the MARS Project did not address it, the question of risk assessment at a scale beyond that of individual monuments is also important, not least because of the blanket effects of some strategic planning decisions.

In April 1997 the European Commission published draft proposals for a wide-ranging directive on strategic environmental assessment under the title *Proposal for a Council Directive on the assessment of the effects of certain plans and programmes on the environment* (EC 1997b). The scope of the proposed directive includes not only structure plans, unitary development plans and local plans, but also programmes in sectors such as transport, energy, waste management, water resource management, industry, telecommunications and tourism. The application of risk management procedures to the archaeological resource for specific proposals and defined subject areas should, in due course, help to predict and overcome the damaging effects of broad policy decisions.

9.2 Measuring risk in archaeology

Risk management has not yet been widely applied in British archaeology, although some work has been done in North America (Dixon 1977). There are no established models for risk assessment of the type being developed with increasing sophistication in other related environmental disciplines (DoE 1996d), mainly through the application of computer simulation and GIS modelling to aggregate and integrate the potential effects of single, chained or parallel events, circumstances and factors (Kumamoto and Henley 1995). Accordingly, a general and highly simplistic model of risk management is used here to provide a context for work already done and the background for the expansion of risk assessment within MARS. Figure 9.1 shows such a general model in schematic form. There are essentially four stages, starting with the identification and perception of risk in terms of the kinds of hazards that might impact on archaeological monuments. Subsequent stages deal with the estimation of risk, the evaluation of incidence, and the development of risk reduction strategies through communicating information about risks related to defined hazards and the executing mitigation strategies. As the diagram shows, in the first two stages it is essentially professional, scientific and analytical judgements that are made, while in the final

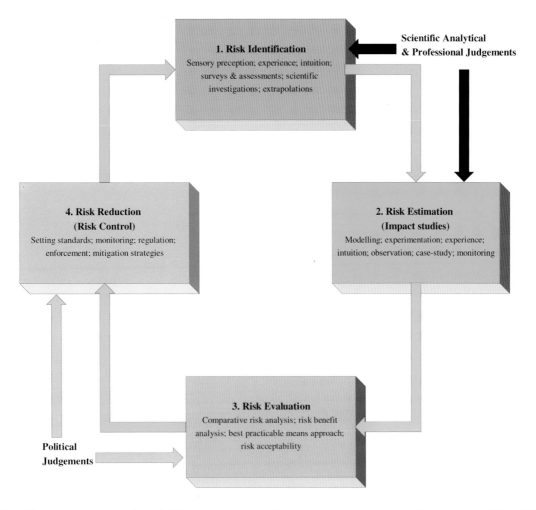

Figure 9.1 - Schematic representation of risk management as four successive processes and procedures. *[After O'Riordan 1979, figure 2]*

stages political judgements are made in relation to acceptability, prevailing legislation and standards (O'Riordan 1979).

There are similarities between this general model of risk management and the more familiar archaeological management cycle articulating assessment, evaluation and mitigation works within archaeological resource management (*cf.* Darvill and Gerrard 1994, 171). There are two places where the risk management scheme and the archaeological management cycle come into coincidence: the risk assessment / identification stage and the risk control stage. Not surprisingly, therefore, much archaeological work that can be seen to have a bearing on the question of risk fits into one or both of these two stages. This is the context for the numerous surveys based on visual inspection that represent resource assessments (APPENDIX A), whether for particular classes of monument, regions, or urban areas. Only in the last decade or so have scientifically based assessment procedures and monitoring programmes become established (see APPENDIX B.6 and B.7 for examples). These hold strong potential for more robust approaches to risk identification and assessment in future.

Two studies of particular land-use classes, wetlands and coastal land, have, unconsciously, begun to move discussions towards issues related to risk estimation, risk evaluation, and risk reduction. In the case of wetlands

(Coles 1995; 1996) the starting point was a review of management systems, building on the very significant and extensive programmes of survey and investigation funded mainly by English Heritage since the early 1980s (see APPENDIX O.1). Wetland was broadly defined as 'those situations where any buried archaeological material would be waterlogged' (Coles 1995, 1). Recognized hazards likely to impact on archaeological remains in these environments included: terrestrialization, climatic change, sea-level change, water abstractions, water pollution, extractive industries, recreation, drainage for agriculture and forestry, and military action. Although no quantification of these hazards was included, and little risk estimation or risk evaluation was carried out, risk control was extensively discussed by reference to the work of other agencies in the field of wetland management on the premise that their considerable expertise in the field could offer appropriate ways forward for the management of the archaeological resource.

The second study dealt with the coastal heritage and focused on archaeological remains in the inter-tidal zone (Fulford *et al.* 1997; English Heritage and RCHME 1996). Although desk-based, it was able to draw on a range of surveys and studies carried out for particular areas of coast in recent years (see APPENDIX O.2 for select listing). The main hazards identified in these environments included: sea-level change, coastal erosion, coastal defence, property development, electricity services, fishing, harbour works, mineral extraction, marine emergencies, military activity, navigation, gas and oil workings, telecommunications, transportation facilities, water supply, and tourism. Some risk estimation and risk evaluation is included; the main recommendations being for future work involving further surveys and closer integration of archaeological issues with more broadly-based approaches to coastal zone management.

Both of these studies address the question of risk in the rather general sense that has also characterized earlier chapters of this report. As such, risk can broadly be equated with the concept of 'vulnerability' included in the criteria for the selection of nationally important monuments for scheduling (DoE 1990a, Annexe 4). However, as outlined above (9.1) and in Chapter 2, MARS attempted to develop the idea of risk in relation to archaeological monuments a little further. The aim was to provided a quantified data-set in relation to risk identification and some preliminary approaches to risk estimation. In doing this MARS adopted a definition of risk based on the one used by the Department of the Environment for contaminated land. Risk is taken to be:

> the combination of the probability or frequency of the occurrence of a recognized hazard in relation to the magnitude of the consequences. (DoE *et al.* 1996, 28)

Within this definition there is a clear contingent relationship between two factors: the probability and magnitude of anticipated hostile events, and the actual impact those events might have on a particular archaeological monument in terms of accelerated decay. The higher the probability of a threat occurring, and the higher the impact that it is expected to have, the greater the risk.

The MARS field survey teams were asked to assess risk for all extant monuments visited. The main sources of information were: visual inspection of the monument and its setting at the time of visit; discussions with landowners and land-users; and information posted at or near the monument (e.g. development control notices) or in the local area. It is acknowledged that these sources have their limitations, for as with gauging damage there are many factors which cannot adequately be identified from visual inspections: below-ground processes such as dewatering are particularly difficult to detect, as is the use of deep ploughing or pan-busting, which leaves surface traces for only a matter of weeks. No attempt was made to contact local planning authorities to document the extent of live planning permissions or allocations made in confirmed strategic plans. Such studies could be undertaken and updated regularly at a regional or local level and would usefully add another dimension to the determination of risk.

The relationship between the kind of archaeological remains represented and the degree of impact posed by anticipated threats is critical to risk identification for monuments. Thus a small number of people walking over a grass-covered earthwork at irregular intervals poses almost no risk at all, but a large number of people using defined routes (e.g. pathways) on a regular basis would put the same monument at a higher level of risk. Moreover, a footpath crossing a small monument, for example a round barrow, constitutes a different scale of risk from a footpath crossing, say, an extensive field system. In the first situation the path might impact on

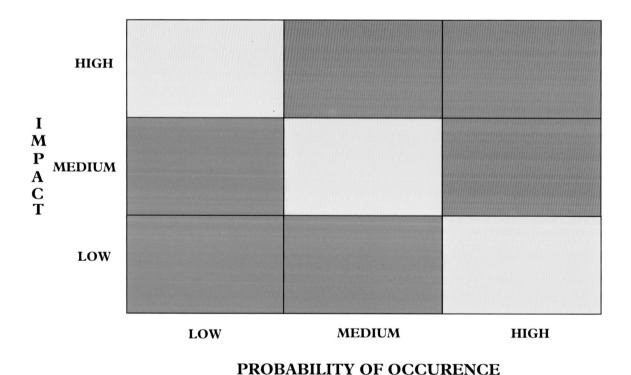

Figure 9.2 - Schematic representation of risk qualified by MARS and in relation to impact and the probability of occurrence. Low risk is zoned green; medium risk is zoned yellow; and high risk is zoned red.

Figure 9.3 - High Risk. Aerial view of a series of later prehistoric enclosures and boundaries near Ashton Keynes in the Cotswold Water Park, Wiltshire, taken in July 1986. The monuments have already been partly destroyed by the construction of houses (bottom right); gravel extraction will remove the remainder in due course *[Photograph: Timothy Darvill. Copyright reserved]*

60% or more of the area of the structure while in the second case damage will be limited to an area representing less than 1% of the total. In considering risk it is necessary to think of monuments as totalities, at least in terms of present understandings of their form and extent.

Time-depth is another important factor relating to risk. Risk can realistically only be identified as a 'snapshot' of known circumstances, yet it must be recognized that the risk environment will constantly be changing. The MARS field survey teams were asked to consider risk in relation to the foreseeable future, defined for practical purposes as the next 3-5 years. Data for these studies derive from 11,287 MARS Monuments; destroyed monuments were excluded from the analyses in this chapter on the grounds that risk relating to any vestigial traces that may remain (and it is recognized that even supposedly destroyed monuments may sometimes retain some archaeological data) would be impossible to assess. No attempt was made to determine risk for earlier decades, as the relevant information sources were not available.

Where possible, MARS Monuments were categorized as being in one of three risk bands - high, medium and low - on the basis of the two factors outlined above. Scoring each of the two factors on a three-point scale produced the MARS risk bands, which can be seen graphically in Figure 9.2. The following notes and examples illustrate how the bands were applied in practice:

High risk: Monuments under imminent threat of wholesale destruction or serious areal or vertical loss, for example through redevelopment, quarrying or road construction (Figure 9.3). Examples taken from MARS records: 'Barrow is situated about 10m from the edge of a limestone quarry: the field is no longer being used for pasture'; 'Timber framed aisled barn in very precarious state. Brick/flint walls, possibly seventeenth century in amongst later agricultural buildings. Roped off by local district council as a dangerous structure'; 'Ring-ditch seen on an aerial photograph. On crest of hill in fallow awaiting development into houses'.

Medium risk: Some chance of the monument being damaged or partly destroyed in the short to medium term, for example by being encroached upon by ploughing, contains unconsolidated masonry or brickwork, or because it is situated within a likely development area (Figure 9.4). Examples taken from MARS records: 'No evidence of this monument on the ground. The field concerned is being left fallow. The whole of the general area around the monument is made up of a mainly disused airfield, with various access roads and runways criss-crossing the area. Any damage that may have been caused by these has been done a long time ago and traffic and road-building no longer appears to be a problem'; 'This moat has been steadily eroded by in-filling to ease farming - much less now survives than is shown on the map we have - only a 70m stretch of the northern side of the moat survives. The moat still holds water in the bit that is left and is being damaged by its use as a watering hole

Figure 9.4 - Medium Risk. Ruinous masonry post-medieval windmill near Spennymoor, County Durham. Without active management monuments like this will continue to decay at a fairly steady rate over a considerable period of time *[Photograph: MARS Archive]*

Figure 9.5 - Low Risk. Pillars forming part of a stone circle under pasture near Lowick Common, Cumbria *[Photograph: MARS Archive]*

by the large numbers of cattle in the field'; 'Barrow suffering from severe mutilation by burrowing, tree rooting and cattle trampling. Trample around the base means that the edges have been distorted. Roughly flat on top. Periphery probable damage from plough'.

Low risk: No perceptible threat to the monument that would effect its survival in the short to medium term, for example a monument on National Trust land under pasture that has been fenced off from human interference (Figure 9.5). Examples taken from MARS records: 'This barn has been very sympathetically restored and is now in use as a private residence. New windows have been inserted on the north-east, south-west and north facing walls together with skylights in the new roof. The cart entrances in the north-east and south-west walls remain as large windows with some brick additions but the original doors. It also has new cross ties, a new chimney and extensive internal alterations'; 'Round barrow extant, well defined and upstanding. The barrow is elongated at one side, almost pear-shaped, and shows little signs of damage. There is one mature tree on the monument, and several at its periphery. A number of trees which once grew on the monument have been felled. The barrow has been excavated in the past and satellite burials were found. There is a large but slight depression at the top of the barrow'.

It proved impossible adequately to assess risk for all MARS Monuments and about 21% of those in the sample considered here, mainly flattened examples with no visible features, could not be assessed. Where relevant, these are quantified as NA (no assessment) on the tables and charts below. Throughout, it is recognized that the MARS data relating to risk are simplistic, impressionistic and subjective, based on observations and judgements made by survey teams. It is clearly impossible to anticipate threats such as those posed by vandalism, programmes of development not yet in the public domain, or natural disasters. Moreover, because of the constantly changing nature of risk, more monuments will fall into the high-risk band over the next few years than can be predicted from present indications. Estimates of high and medium risk should therefore be seen as minimum numbers. Inevitably, monuments that are at high risk of destruction, damage or change tend to come to public attention and take up the time of archaeological curators and contractors. As a result, the predicament of a relatively small number of monuments tends to colour general perspectives of the resource as a whole. Because the MARS data were collected systematically through a sampling scheme that took no regard of the level of threat posed to monuments or areas selected for study, general patterns can be seen.

Table 9.1 Risk to MARS Monuments. *[Source: MARS National Survey Programme, and SMRs. Samples as shown]*

Risk	Count	%
High	226	2.0
Medium	3210	28.4
Low	5470	48.5
N/A	2381	21.1
Total	**11287**	**100%**

9.3 Risk by region, state and form

Table 9.1 presents an analysis of risk levels recorded for the sample of MARS Monuments.

9.3.1 High risk

Nationally, about 2% of MARS Monuments can be regarded as being at high risk, that is in imminent danger of wholesale destruction or extensive loss of area or vertical truncation. Extrapolating from the 226 cases in the MARS sample, it can be estimated that the number of monuments across the country in this category is about 4520. These represent the monuments that will require urgent attention over the next 3-5 years; in many cases this will involve rescue excavation or recording of some kind, in others a mitigation strategy providing preservation in situ will no doubt be possible. In determining risk within MARS no account was taken of the perceived importance or significance of the monument being assessed, so the above estimates include monuments of widely different quality and value.

The distribution of identified high-risk MARS Monuments appears in Figure 9.6, indicating the wide spread across the country, but with concentrations in three areas: the western part of the West Midlands, especially Herefordshire and Shropshire; the south-western counties of the East Midlands, especially Hertfordshire, Cambridgeshire, Buckinghamshire, Bedfordshire and Northamptonshire; and the southern parts of the two northern regions, especially the band across the country from Humberside to Lancashire.

9.3.2 Medium and low risk

The proportion of monuments at medium risk is equally important in the assessment of overall resource requirements. These represent about 28% of the population, about 64,200 monuments nationally, and need to be monitored carefully, perhaps through the implementation of management agreements or protective designations, so that the risks they face can be controlled.

About 48% of monuments in the MARS sample, the largest single group, are regarded as being at low risk under present circumstances. Although they should not be ignored, it is not anticipated that they will require high levels of resource commitment in the near future.

9.3.3 Regional overview

A number of regional trends can be identified. For the MARS Regions, the percentages of MARS Monuments at high risk range from less than 1% in the South East to over 4% in the West Midlands (Figure 9.7). The relatively low percentage of monuments in the South East (bearing in mind that these are recorded monuments only) can be explained by the high prevalence of developed land, which presents a low risk to monuments because damage occurs at the time when land is developed, not later on. Figure 9.8 shows the same data arranged by the Government Office Regions. It is clear that the West Midlands, North East (including Yorkshire and Humberside) and Eastern regions contain the highest levels of monuments at high risk, and this should be taken into account when plans are drawn up for development programmes or countryside management schemes in these areas.

9.3.4 MARS and BARS

General comparisons can be made between the levels of risk facing archaeological monuments and the situation obtaining for Listed Buildings and structures as revealed by the Buildings At Risk Survey (BARS) carried out by English Heritage in 1990-1 (English Heritage 1992a), subsequently enlarged through detailed work undertaken by local authorities and the construction of priority lists (Embree 1995). The original sample survey is the most important for comparison with MARS. It examined some 43,000 Listed Buildings in different parts of England in order to establish a general picture of the condition of the resource. The BARS sample represented about 8.6% of all Buildings Listed at the time of the survey. It is estimated

Figure 9.6 - Map of England showing those MARS Monuments under a high risk within each of the six MARS Regions. *[Source: MARS Field Survey Programme. Sample: n= 226]*

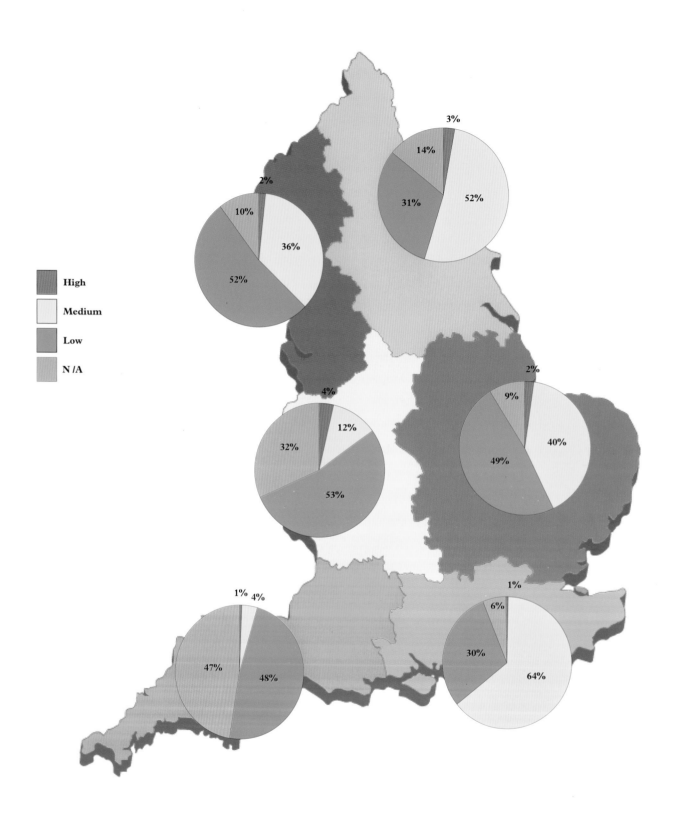

Figure 9.7 - Map of England showing the regional pattern of risk levels affecting MARS Monuments for the six MARS Regions. *[Source: MARS Field Survey Programme. Samples: North West n= 1357; North East n= 1930; West Midlands n= 1715; East Midlands n= 2555; South West n= 2380; South East n= 1350]*

Figure 9.8 - Map of England showing the regional pattern of risk levels affecting MARS Monuments for the Government Office Regions. *[Source: MARS Field Survey Programme. Samples: North West & Merseyside n= 1357; North East & Yorkshire and Humberside n= 1458; West Midlands n= 1149; East Midlands n= 840; Eastern n= 1698; South West n= 2598; South East and London n= 1715]*

Table 9.2 - Risk patterns for MARS Monuments in relation to comparable data for Listed Buildings revealed by the Buildings at Risk Survey 1990-1. *[Source: MARS Field Survey Programme; English Heritage 1992, table 1. Samples: MARS monuments, n= 11,287; Listed Buildings, n= 43,000]*

MARS Risk Categories	BARS Risk categories [1]		% MARS Monuments	% BARS buildings and structures
High Risk	1/1A	Extreme Risk	2.0	2.2
	2	Grave Risk		
Medium Risk	3/3A	At some risk	28.4	19.7
	4/4A	Vulnerable		
Low Risk	5/5A	Not at risk	48.5	78.1
	6	Not at risk		
N/A		Nil	21.1	Nil

(1) English Heritage 1992, table 1

that about 2% of England's building stock was protected by listing at the time. Six risk bands were used in the study, which combined an assessment of condition and occupancy patterns to determine risk. The BARS bands can easily be mapped onto the MARS bands for purposes of comparison (Table 9.2). The top two bands in BARS (1/1A and 2, extreme risk and grave risk) account for 2.2% of the sample, very close to the 2% in the high-risk band used by MARS given that some 21% of MARS Monuments could not accurately be assigned to a risk band at the time of the survey. The percentage of Listed Buildings in the second two bands (3/3A and 4/4A) is slightly lower than for its archaeological counterpart. The lowest bands (5/5A and 6) contain the majority of Listed Buildings, although with a higher proportion of the overall population than the archaeological equivalent. The implication of this comparison is that, nationally, and at a very general level, some sectors of the two resources face similar patterns of risk, but with slightly higher levels of archaeological monuments in the medium-risk band.

Although the characteristics of both resources (historic buildings and archaeological monuments) are similar in terms of their risk profiles, the ways in which risk reduction is approached will be very different.

One major divergence between the buildings considered in BARS and the monuments considered in MARS is the fact that the risks facing many buildings can be overcome by finding new viable uses for the structures themselves (Cunnington 1988; Strike 1994). Archaeological monuments do not lend themselves to this kind of treatment.

Table 9.4 - Risk pattern for MARS earthwork Monuments. *[Source: MARS Field Survey. Sample: n= 2495]*

Risk	High %	Medium %	Low %	Total %
Flat	1.40	39.08	8.42	48.90
Upstanding	1.44	14.91	34.75	51.10
Total	**2.84%**	**53.99%**	**43.17%**	**100%**

Table 9.3 - Risk patterns for MARS Monuments (earthworks and buildings and structures) compared to data for Listed Buildings and Structures revealed by the Buildings at Risk Survey 1990-1. *[Source: MARS Field Survey; English Heritage 1992, table 1. Sample: MARS earthworks, n= 2599; MARS buildings and structures, n= 3985; Listed Buildings, n= 43,000]*

MARS Risk Categories	MARS Monuments Earthworks [1] %	MARS monuments Buildings & Structures [2] %	BAR survey [3] %
High Risk	2.8	2.7	2.2
Medium Risk	43.0	19.3	19.7
Low Risk	54.2	78.0	78.1
Total	**100%**	**100%**	**100%**

1. Sample = 2599 earthworks

2. Buildings and structures calculated excluding buildings and structures whose risk could not be determined. Based on a sample of 3985 MARS Monuments.

3. BARS survey data from English Heritage 1992, table 1. Sample = 43,000 Listed Buildings and structures. See Table 9.2 for correlation of MARS bands with BARS grading.

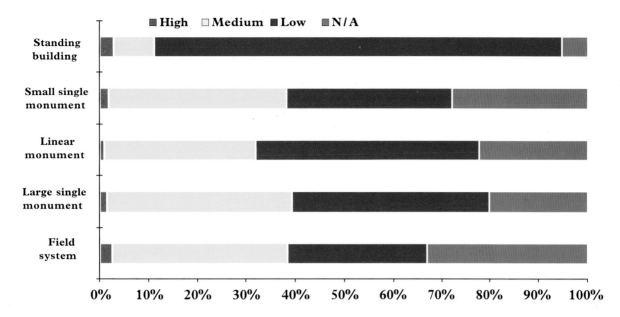

Figure 9.9 - Horizontal stacked bar chart showing the risk patterns for MARS Monuments by monument form. *[Source: MARS Field Survey. Sample: n= 11,287]*

9.3.5 Risk and monument state

Table 9.3 shows MARS Monuments broken into two groups by monument character - earthwork monuments and standing buildings and structures - for which patterns of risk have been calculated. Monuments where no assessment was possible have been omitted from this analysis, it being assumed that the distribution of monuments not assessed was random throughout the sample.

Standing buildings present a rather different picture from other kinds of archaeological monuments. The

percentage of earthwork monuments regarded as being at low risk is considerably smaller the percentage of buildings and structures in the same band. Again, comparison of the MARS sample of buildings and structures with the BARS results reveals an almost identical pattern of risk. This is all the more interesting because the two studies approached the problem from quite different starting positions. It also suggests that the general picture established by the BARS for Listed Buildings applies more widely to all buildings and structures, since the MARS sample was not constituted on the basis of known patterns of protective designation.

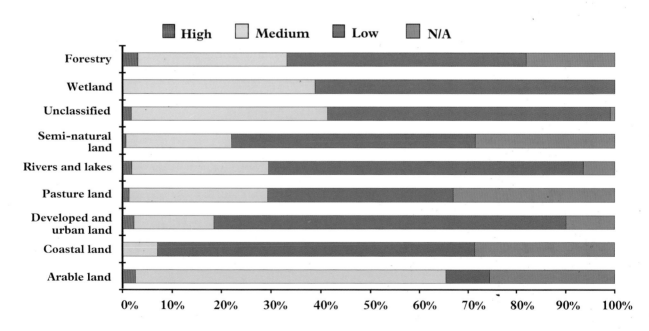

Figure 9.10 - Horizontal stacked bar chart showing the risk patterns for MARS Monuments by land-use class on monuments. *[Source: MARS Field Survey Programme with data for monuments under single land-use regimes. Sample: n= 9793]*

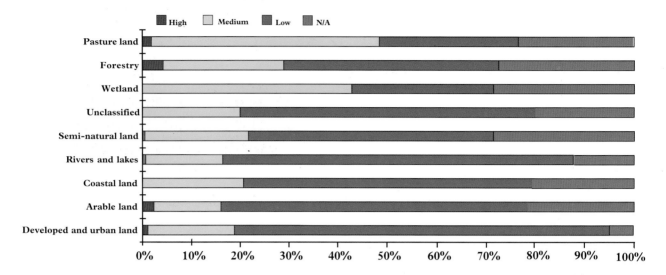

Figure 9.11 - Horizontal stacked bar chart showing the risk pattern for MARS Monuments by land-use class surrounding monuments. *[Source: MARS Field Survey Programme. Sample: n= 9793]*

In fact, 11% of MARS Monuments were Listed Buildings.

For earthwork monuments, Table 9.4 presents an analysis of risk depending on whether the monuments were flat or upstanding. Again, monuments for which no assessment of risk was possible have been excluded from the analysis. It is clear that although the percentages of upstanding earthwork monuments at high risk is the same as for flattened ones, the percentages reported as being at medium and low risk are very different. Over one-third of earthwork monuments are rated as upstanding and at low risk.

9.3.6 Risk and monument form

Figure 9.9 examines the patterns of risk present among all five defined forms of MARS Monuments. Linear monuments have the lowest percentage of recorded examples in the high-risk band (1.1%), and field systems and standing buildings the highest (2.4% and 2.7% respectively). This is probably because many field systems were recorded as at risk from agricultural threats for the simple reason that they have a larger area over which

damage can occur. Standing buildings, for which the converse is true, have the highest percentage of examples at low risk (83%), and field systems have the lowest percentage (29%). On this evidence, attention needs to be directed to risk-reduction strategies for field systems and small single monuments.

9.4 Risk by period

Older monuments appear to be at greater risk than more recent ones. A breakdown of risk patterns by period for MARS Monuments appears in Table 9.5. With a few notable exceptions, the percentage of monuments in the high-risk band increases backwards through time while the percentage in the low-risk band tends to decrease. Mesolithic monuments stand out as having a high percentage in the high-risk band, but this is in part a distortion caused by a relatively low sample size for this group. The percentage of Neolithic monuments in the high-risk band is also more than three times the average.

Table 9.5 - Risk for MARS Monuments by archaeological period. *[Source: MARS Field Survey and SMR records. Includes multiple observations for multi-period monuments. Sample: n= 15,861 observations]*

Risk	High %	Medium %	Low %	N/A %	*Total* %	Sample counts
Prehistoric (unspecified)	2.33	34.28	27.45	35.94	**100%**	601
Palaeolithic	0	50.00	25.00	25.00	**100%**	4
Mesolithic	13.79	20.69	24.14	41.38	**100%**	29
Neolithic	8.18	33.64	33.64	24.55	**100%**	110
Bronze Age	2.29	40.80	37.49	19.43	**100%**	875
Iron Age	2.71	53.93	28.73	14.63	**100%**	369
Roman	2.66	47.04	28.42	21.89	**100%**	827
Early medieval	<1	20.16	67.44	11.63	**100%**	129
Medieval	1.41	21.96	61.81	14.82	**100%**	3401
Post-medieval	2.18	16.97	66.67	14.18	**100%**	5316
Modern	1.17	10.53	68.03	20.27	**100%**	513
Unknown	1.82	50.94	22.46	24.79	**100%**	3687
All periods combined	**2.00%**	**30.28%**	**49.11%**	**18.61%**	**100%**	**15861**

In contrast, the percentage of early medieval and later monuments at high risk is below average.

This pattern can be partially explained by the fact that many of the later MARS Monuments are buildings and standing structures and are therefore at lower levels of risk than earlier earthwork monuments when factors such as the impact of hazards are taken into account.

9.5 Risk by land-use

As Chapter 7 makes clear, land-use is the main determinant of monument survival, and thus one of the principal considerations in assessing risk. Figure 9.10 gives a breakdown of risk in relation to land-use on monuments and Figure 9.11 does the same for surrounding land-use. To simplify these analyses, only single land-use regimes have been used, giving a sample of 9793 observations from MARS Monuments.

For the high-risk cases, the picture is dominated by monuments covered by and set within developed and urban land, arable and forestry. Wetlands and coastal areas appear, from the MARS sample, to have fewer than 1% of monuments at high risk despite the findings of other studies which suggest that monuments in these environments are under very great threat (Coles 1995; 1996; Coles and Coles 1996, 104-132; Fulford *et al.* 1997). There are three main reasons for this apparent discrepancy. First, MARS defines wetland and coastland very precisely with the result that there are relatively few observations in the MARS sample which relate directly to these highly localized land-uses with restricted distributions across England. Monuments at high risk within more broadly defined areas of wetland and coastland will appear under their lost land-use within MARS (e.g. arable land in the case of much land in the Fens of East Anglia). Second, is the fact that within land-use regimes such as wetland the effects of some hazards are hard to see during visual inspection (e.g. dewatering). Third, in the case of land by the coast the processes that represent key hazards tend to be long-term, if progressive; they thus fall into the medium-risk band.

Amongst monuments at medium risk, the highest levels are represented by arable land. Although monuments under cultivation are constantly at risk, and have been for many years, the scale of the impact in relation to the nature of the resource is generally increasing as more powerful tractors are used, whose effect is to cut through or break up deposits that would have been skirted or over-ridden with less powerful machines.

No land-use class contains more than 80% of monuments at low risk. Even pasture land, which is generally reckoned to be most conducive to the long-term stability of archaeological monuments, has only about 55% of monuments at low risk. The reasons for this are two-fold. First, a high percentage in this land-use class could not be assessed for various reasons. Second, threats such as urban development or infrastructure construction cross-cut land-use patterns and thus pose essentially randomized threats in these areas.

Overall, three broad patterns of risk can be recognized on the basis of land-use on recorded monuments. First, arable land has the greatest proportion of monuments reckoned to be at high risk, coupled with a

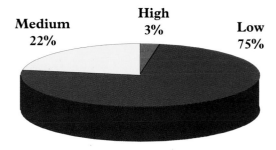

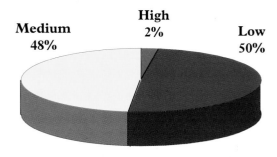

Figure 9.12 - Pie charts showing the risk patterns for Scheduled Monuments and non-Scheduled Monuments (excluding buildings and structures). *[Source: MARS Field Survey Programme. Samples: Scheduled Monuments n= 491; non-Scheduled Monuments n= 5371]*

low percentage of low-risk monuments and a high percentage in the medium-risk band. Semi-natural land, wetlands and coastal land form a second group, characterized by relatively few monuments at high risk and a high percentage at low risk. The third group comprises the remaining land-use classes and is characterized by small but fairly consistent percentages of monuments at high risk, over two-thirds of monuments at low risk, and the remainder at medium risk. The first of these groups requires most attention from archaeological resource managers in future.

It might be expected that the degree of risk attaching to a particular monument should increase in proportion to the number of different land-uses to which it is subject, and up to a point this is the case. Table 9.6 presents a breakdown of risk bands according to the number of land-uses at individual monuments, and the pattern it reveals is relatively consistent. There is a progressive increase in the high- and medium-risk bands as the number of land-uses increases up to three. This is matched by a decrease in the low-risk band. Monuments subjected to more than three land-uses appear to be less at risk than those with less diversity of use. Here, however, small sample sizes may be a factor. There are very few monuments with more than four land-uses.

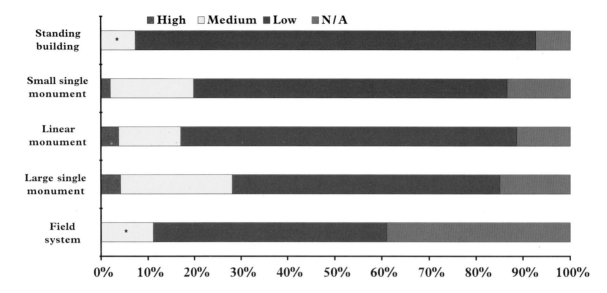

Figure 9.13 - Horizontal stacked bar chart showing patterns of risk to Scheduled Monuments by monument form. * denotes high risk at <1% *[Source: MARS Field Survey Programme. Sample n= 694]*

9.6 *Risk in relation to Scheduled Monuments*

The relationship between risk and protective designations is indirect. There are two key dimensions. First, some designations will be applied to monuments which are perceived to be at medium or high risk in order to monitor and control the hazards that may affect them. Although it is true that many kinds of protective designation should reduce the degree of risk to which a monument is exposed, the reality of most designations is that they exist to control hazards and their impacts rather than to prevent threats arising in the first place. Second, many of the hazards facing monuments are unpredictable in the sense that they are not expected, and in some cases lie outside the scope of protection offered by the designation. Both of these difficulties apply in the case of Scheduling.

Results from MARS suggest that 3% of Scheduled Monuments are at high risk; this compares with the national average of 2% in the sample as a whole (Figure 9.12). The difference is very small, neither is it too surprising when it is realized that Scheduling is sometimes carried out to protect monuments recognized as being at high risk, thus increasing the number in this category. It is also clear that the majority of Scheduled Monuments are at low risk, 75% compared with 50% for non-Scheduled examples. This is almost certainly a reflection of the procedures involved in the selection of monuments for Scheduling which favours the best preserved and most important monuments.

Figure 9.13 analyses Scheduled Monuments in the MARS sample by form; Figure 9.14 gives a comparable breakdown for MARS Monuments which are not Scheduled. There are some differences. Fewer than 1% of Scheduled field systems appear to be at high risk, whereas 3.8% of non-Scheduled field systems are in the high-risk band. Similarly, fewer than 1% of Scheduled standing buildings are in the high-risk band compared with 2.9% of non-Scheduled buildings. Large single monuments, linear monuments and small single monuments reveal a different pattern. Some 4.7% of Scheduled large single monuments are at high risk, but only 2% of non-Scheduled large single monuments. Similar patterns occur for linear and small single monuments. There are more Scheduled Monuments in the low-risk band than non-Scheduled Monuments, but there are also higher proportions in the high-risk band.

Table 9.6 - Risk for MARS Monuments by incidence of land-use regimes on the monument. *[Source: MARS Field Survey. Sample: n= 11,287 observations]*

Number of Land-uses 1995	High %	Medium %	Low %	N/A %	Total %
1	1.9	26.4	49.2	22.5	100%
2	2.6	41.3	43.0	13.0	100%
3	3.7	44.5	42.1	9.8	100%
4	0.9	40.5	51.4	7.2	100%
5 and more	1.8	39.3	50.0	8.9	100%
Observations combined	**2.0%**	**28.4%**	**48.5%**	**21.1%**	**100%**

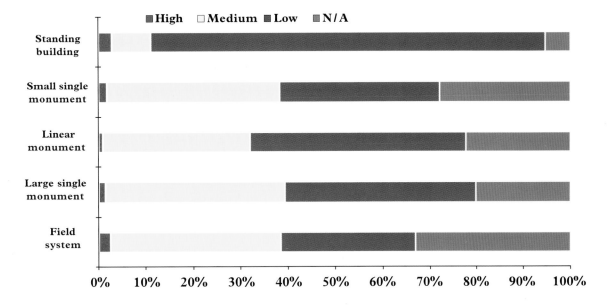

Figure 9.14 - Horizontal stacked bar chart showing patterns of risk to non-Scheduled Monuments by monument form. *[Source: MARS Field Survey Programme. Sample n= 10,593]*

9.7 *The future of archaeological monuments*

At first sight the fact that only 2% of monuments appear to be at high risk looks encouraging. However, it must be remembered that this assessment refers to the near future, 3-5 years hence. Two per cent of the surveyed MARS Monuments represent about 226 monuments, approximately 4520 monuments nationally. These are the archaeological monuments that require urgent attention at any one time. Of course, not all will be completely lost as a result of the hazards impacting upon them, some will suffer piecemeal loss while other will escape loss as a result of negotiated mitigation. It is appropriate, however, to compare the number of monuments at high risk with the documented rates of loss discussed in Chapter 6. The average annual loss of monuments over a 50-year period was found to be 470 monuments. Aggregated over five years this gives an anticipated loss rate of 2350 monuments, about half the number regarded as being at high risk within a similar time-period.

Projected forward, and assuming that the recorded resource remains the same size, a high risk level of 2% and a loss rate of 1.8% of the extant recorded resource per decade (4700 monuments out of an extant recorded resource of 253,000) means that the extant recorded resource is not sustainable over the next millennium. By the year 2015 it is anticipated that the extant recorded resource will comprise about 246,800 MARS Monuments. About half of the present extant recorded resource will have been lost by the year 2375; only a quarter will be left by the year 2755.

9.8 *Monuments at risk: the general pattern*

The risk of accelerated decay taking place on an ancient monument can in part be mapped from the data presented above. Earlier monuments are generally more likely to experience higher levels of risk than later monuments; MARS suggests that Mesolithic and Neolithic monuments are currently at greatest risk. Regionally, monuments are more likely to be at risk the further northwards and eastwards they lie. Physically, there is a graduation of risk according to the form of monuments; field systems are more likely to be at relatively high risk, as are standing buildings, whereas single monuments (both large and small) fall in the middle ground and linear monuments are least likely to be at high risk.

The hazards that lie behind different levels of risk relate to specific land-use regimes on and around monuments. Monuments within urban land not previously developed are among the most likely to be in high-risk bands; monuments within wetlands and on the coast are least likely to be fall in the high-risk band.

These are all generalizations. Risk management needs to take place at a number of different levels and through both local and national studies. In this respect MARS is simply the beginning of the process. The next step in the application of risk assessment in archaeology must be the development of systematic approaches to the examination of risk for individual monuments. This requires high-level research, building on the work done for MARS and drawing on progress made in other environmental disciplines, as well as rigorous testing before it can be widely applied. It could perhaps be applied best at local authority level, so that full account can be taken of strategic planning proposals. However, such considerations involve the application of results and conclusions from MARS to more general themes of archaeological resource management. This is the subject of the final chapter.

10 Summary, conclusions and recommendations

Archaeology, then, being founded on observation, comparison, and inference, it is essential that the material capable of being subjected to examination should be accurately ascertained and carefully protected and preserved.

(David Murray 1896, 17)

10.1 Patterns and baselines

The Monuments At Risk Survey was about England's archaeological resource as it was known and recorded in the mid 1990s. For the first time in the history of archaeological resource management in England it provides a position statement and preliminary analysis of a highly diverse totality as the basis for developing future policy and strategies. The baseline data that have been gathered will serve as the benchmark for monitoring and assessing future change and the efficiency of particular schemes. Through description and preliminary analysis, this report has tried to portray the current scale and extent of archaeological monuments and their survival, and to model patterns of change over the period 1945-95.

The various snapshots taken by MARS reflect the resource's essential character, and have shown how the pressures of modern life in the countryside and the towns of England have largely determined its survival and loss, particularly as a result of land-use, but also through natural decay or neglect. Archaeological monuments are not static entities, they change with the environment in which they lie (Figure 10.1). It is also clear that the scale and breadth of archaeological awareness has increased dramatically over the last 50 years, and that the focus of interest and recording efforts has broadened considerably.

The need accurately to document what is known and the desirability of effective preservation were among the themes addressed a century ago by the Scottish antiquarian David Murray in his prescient proposal for an archaeological survey of the United Kingdom. But Murray could scarcely have anticipated the sheer range and diversity of the material such a survey would have to record, or the urgency of the need for wide-ranging preservation policies; as the first detailed national census of England's archaeological resource MARS has now revealed these issues very clearly, as the preceding chapters show.

This final chapter attempts to summarize the key points set out in earlier chapters and considers the short- medium- and long-term implications of some of the findings of MARS. After a brief résumé of the

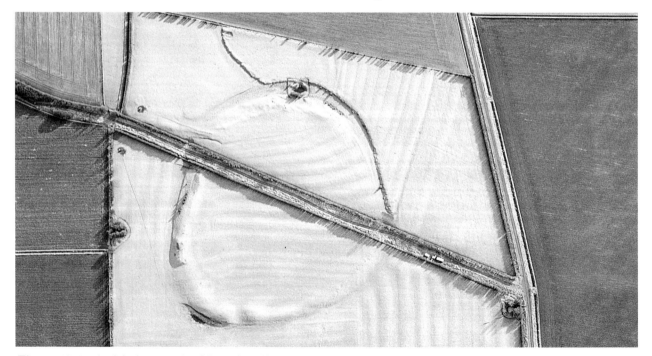

Figure 10.1 - Aerial photograph of Belsar's Hill near Willingham, Cambridgeshire, showing the accumulating layers of history represented at a single monument. In the centre are the ramparts of a roughly circular prehistoric enclosure. These are overlain by the characteristic ridge-and-furrow pattern of medieval strip cultivation. Some groups of strips (furlongs) respect the earlier defences while others run across them. Later still, a trackway bounded by substantial hedges has been constructed across all the earlier features. *[Photograph: Chris Cox, Air Photo Services Ltd. Copyright reserved]*

methodology and approach adopted, a series of ten key themes are explored in terms of what MARS has revealed and how this might be used as the basis for endorsing and developing strategic policy and practical initiatives. Naturally, these themes relate back to the defined objectives of MARS as a whole and must be seen in that context. The aim here, as with the detailed results set out in previous chapters, is to promote and assist informed debate and decision-making at national, regional and local levels. MARS is simply the beginning of a new phase in the development of archaeological resource management in England. It helps put archaeology on the same footing as other environmental disciplines in having a resource census which can inform future decision-making. The context within which the implications of MARS can be carried forward is provided by current framework plans and policy statements. These have been a feature of archaeological work in England since the early years of this century and APPENDIX P provides a select bibliography of published and circulated examples. Strategy documents are also available for other dimensions of the environment, especially the countryside (e.g. Countryside Commission 1991a; 1993a; 1996b) and these are relevant too.

In 1996, a review of extant strategy documents and research frameworks revealed a continuing focus on research-driven, problem-orientated approaches, and reaffirmed the long-term value of such documents (Olivier 1996b). Within such a paradigm it is the definition of topics and issues that forms the crucial step: without good questions there can be no real progress in terms of providing better understandings of the past. Defining worthwhile questions is not easy, and typically relies on a knowledge of what is already known, the broader context of that knowledge in its wider setting, and a degree of inspiration and insight which can be translated into action. Broadly speaking this process has three stages: prior knowledge (the past), relevant questions (the present), projects to generate new knowledge (the future).

This threefold approach can be seen in the many different types of research strategy in circulation, and a vocabulary has been proposed to help identify particular

pieces of work with stages in the process (Figure 10.2). In this, a *Resource Assessment* is defined as a statement of the current state of knowledge and a description of the archaeological resource. An *Agenda* is a list of the gaps in knowledge and of work that could be done to fill such gaps. A *Strategy* is a statement setting out the priorities and methods by which an agenda can be implemented. Together, these three stages can be seen as a framework, of which there are three recognizable types: a *Research Framework* concerned with academic advancement of archaeological knowledge and rooted purely in research; a *Management Framework* concerned with issues of conservation, preservation, and resource management; and a *Universal Framework* which combines research and management frameworks as a single integrated approach. MARS shows very clearly that resource assessment has an established track record within archaeological resource management in England. Many examples have already been referred to in earlier chapters, and APPENDIX A provides a select bibliography by way of a consolidated list of key studies known to the project. Indeed, MARS itself is such a study on a national scale, and is thus the first stage in the process of building frameworks. The results cannot and were never intended to answer all the possible questions relating to archaeological resource management, but they can contribute to the development of agendas and frameworks now being developed, as the following sections show. MARS will have been successful if it poses more questions than its answers.

10.2 MARS: the first archaeological census

For practical and economic reasons, not every archaeological monument in England could be assessed as part of the MARS Project. Accordingly, a sampling scheme was developed which looked at a representative cross-section of England's recorded archaeological resource within a 5% sample of total land area. The MARS field survey teams visited a total of 13,488 recorded monuments in 1297 1km by 5km randomly selected sample transects and recorded, among other items, the circumstances of land-use and extent. A smaller sample, 7005 monuments in 646 transects, was used to look at change over the last 50 years as far as it could be determined from the available aerial photographs. Analysis of the sample and its application suggests that it is robust and that it represents a valid picture of the archaeological resource in the 1940s and mid-1990s.

The archaeological resource which formed the focus of the MARS Project ultimately derived from the archaeological records held in the National Monuments Record and in local Sites and Monuments Records. Because of variations between records in the definition of what constitutes an archaeological monument a lowest common denominator was applied to isolate what are called 'MARS Monuments'. For practical purposes these can be defined as any definable building, structure or work, that has archaeological integrity because it represents the contemporary embodiment of the physical context, setting or result of one or more activities that took place in the past. This includes remains both above and below the surface of the land, caves and excavations, and the remains of vehicles, vessels, aircraft or other movable

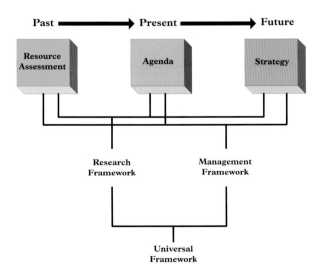

Figure 10.2 - Diagram showing the recognized components of framework documents. *[Source: English Heritage]*

Table 10.1 - England's recorded archaeological resource to 1995.

Characteristics	Records	Monuments	Resource
Original resource			not known
Retrievable records to 1995	657,619		
Anticipated records in 1995	279,865		
All records 1995	937,484		
Number of monuments (broad definition) based on retrievable records in SMRs		328,800	
Estimated number of monuments (narrow definition) based on MARS Monuments		300,000	
Estimated Recorded Resource 1995 (number of monuments)			300,000
Expected additions when anticipated records are incorporated into the record		127,000	
Estimated average density of monuments represented by the Recorded Resource 1995			2.25 per km^2
Estimated land area occupied by the Recorded Resource in 1995			8500km^2
Estimated percentage of England's land area occupied by the Recorded Resource in 1995			6.5%
Estimated number of monuments lost to 1945		23,500	
Estimated number of monuments lost 1945-1995		23,500	
Estimated total number of monuments lost to 1995		47,000	
Estimated area of monument losses (wholesale and piecemeal) to 1995		3750km^2	
Estimated Extant Recorded Resource 1995 (number of monuments)			253,000
Estimated land area occupied by the Extant Recorded Resource 1995			4770km^2
Estimated percentage of England's land area occupied by the Extant Recorded Resource in 1995			3.6%
Estimated Extinct Recorded Resource 1995 (number of monuments)			47,000
Extant Unrecorded Resource 1995			not known
Extinct Unrecorded Resource 1995			not known

Note: all estimates relating to the Resource as a whole are based on the sample of MARS Monuments examined by the Field Survey Programme and Aerial Photographic Survey Programme

structures. However, explicitly excluded were domestic buildings constructed after AD 1700, all buildings constructed after AD 1900, stray finds, miscellaneous non-archaeological records, monuments whose location is not known, and cases where possible archaeological remains are documented only by historical sources, such as place-name evidence or general historical accounts.

This definition covers most of the evidence that is routinely used within the mainstream discipline of archaeology, and a good proportion of the material relevant to related areas of interest such as historical studies of the built environment and historic landscapes. No consideration of underwater archaeology was attempted within MARS, although some coastal material is included by virtue of its appearance on established local Sites and Monuments Records. Other sectors of archaeology, for example industrial archaeology and environmental archaeology, are not specifically addressed, but again the data on which they rely will be represented where incorporated on established records. Throughout this and earlier chapters the term MARS Monument is used to refer to those archaeological monuments embraced by the above definition and situated within the MARS sample transects. The sample of MARS Monuments is robust and allows generalization to the whole population of similarly defined monuments.

A Field Survey Programme and an Aerial Photographic Survey Programme were supported by two further studies, a National Survey Programme which documented the contents of the Sites and Monuments Records in England, and further, a Case Study Research Programme which examined the implications of change for archaeological data. A number of recognized land-types were also examined to investigate monument discovery patterns and decay trajectories. The census date for MARS was taken as 1995, although individual elements of the study were created between September 1994 and August 1996.

Table 10.1 summarizes some of the key characteristics of the archaeological resource, as it can be glimpsed from the data collected by MARS. The data are organized in relation to three main kinds of quantification: records which refer to entries in established Sites and Monuments Records, monuments which refer to definable archaeological entities as discussed above, and the 'resource' which is defined here in terms of the simple model discussed in Chapter 2.2. This basic data-set is a point in time statement of what is known. It will, in due course, be superseded as new data becomes available. Against this summary of England's archaeological assets, some of the finer details revealed by MARS can be explored in a series of ten key themes.

10.3 Key themes

10.3.1 The development and scale of the recorded resource

Interest in the creation of a national register of archaeological material has a long history, but such a register has only been realized in the last 30 years. Today, the most extensive archaeological Sites and Monuments Records exist at a local level, in 92% of cases within county councils, and in the rest at district, borough, city or National Park level.

In 1995 the total number of retrievable records held by the 57 local SMRs covered by the survey was 657,619 entries, an overall increase of 117% on the figures recorded in 1983 when a general assessment of SMR content was carried out. It is important to reiterate that these 657,619 entries do not correspond to more robustly defined entities such as 'monuments' or 'sites' (see Chapter 2). Entries in the record are simply items or units of record and are variously defined. The rate of increase

Figure 10.3 - Different kinds of surviving archaeological evidence at Standlake, Oxfordshire. The two fields in the centre of this aerial photograph display abundant cropmarks in ripening cereals. These result from differential growth and ripening patterns over buried features such as pits and ditches. In the pasture fields above, low relief earthwork remains of enclosures, ditches and cultivation strips can be seen. At the top is part of the village of Standlake with numerous standing buildings, some of considerable antiquity, together with associated gardens, yards and boundary features. *[Photograph: RCHME. Copyright reserved]*

over little more than a decade is impressive, and represents the accumulation of nearly 100 records per day across the country. It is widely recognized that there is a backlog of material awaiting input, and it has been estimated that the total number of records, including those anticipated and those not easily retrievable at present, was 937,484 in 1995. If recent rates of growth continue, then England's Sites and Monuments Records will contain over 1 million entries by the turn of the millennium.

Rates of growth in the recording of different sectors of the archaeological resource vary considerably. Records relating to post-medieval remains have been expanding markedly in recent years, with a 300% increase over the last decade. This compares with a 63% increase in records relating to prehistoric material and 119% for Roman material. Records to which no specific date or archaeological period has been assigned have increased nearly threefold since 1984.

These changes reflect two main trends: an expanding definition of what constitutes archaeological evidence, and changes in the range of sources used in the compilation and updating of records, especially the increasing use of information from early maps to supplement traditional sources of archaeological information such as fieldwork. Records from major recent and ongoing long-term nationwide programmes whose objectives include monument discovery (for example the RCHME National Mapping Programme, and numerous assessment and field evaluation programmes) did not appear to have been incorporated in SMRs at the time of MARS. It is clear that there is still a great deal of information yet to be recorded, and this will require the co-ordinated deployment of a range of appropriate archaeological techniques in order to embrace the diversity of the physical evidence (Figure 10.3).

Recording standards for SMRs are being developed, mainly by the RCHME in association with others, and a programme of SMR audits are being carried out in order to inform future policy. A wide-ranging statement of co-operation has been published by RCHME, English Heritage and ALGAO (RCHME *et al.* 1998). However, at the MARS census date, idiosyncratic and diverse methods of recording were common, and during the later 1980s and early 1990s there has been a trend towards the creation of more smaller record systems rather than the consolidation of what is known in fewer larger ones. The range of systems used is considerable, and becoming greater. Ordnance Survey mapping at 1:10,000 scale currently forms a significant part of archaeological records at local level. Digitized equivalents and the use of GIS were in their infancy at the time of the survey, but looked set to develop rapidly.

A Government consultation document entitled *Protecting our heritage* issued in May 1996 argued that local Sites and Monuments Records should be given a statutory basis (DNH 1996, 46). If this is to be followed through then inter-SMR consistency in matters connected with scope and coverage will need to be strengthened. There is also great potential for networking systems together to provide regional pictures. Changes within the planning system at a national and European level, including a greater emphasis on regional planning, will also have implications for the curation, accessibility and deployment of archaeological data (Darvill 1997b; Anon 1997g; 1998).

On average, each record has been enhanced three times since its creation; the level of record enhancement work is increasing as time goes on. However, duplicate and overlapping records are relatively common within and between SMRs.

The number of records held represent a very crude measure of England's archaeology. About half of all records refer to archaeological monuments in a general sense, the remainder being historic buildings (22%), stray finds (22%) and miscellaneous records (6%). Of these, records of stray finds are likely to increase at a greater rate than other categories in the next few years if reporting procedures currently under trial become more widely applied (Bland 1997).

Using the MARS sample data and the tight definition of monuments outlined above (10.1), it is estimated that there are about 300,000 recorded archaeological monuments in England. These cover approximately 8500km^2 or 6.5% of the land area of England. It is impossible to estimate the number or coverage of monuments not currently catalogued on SMRs.

In the light of these points and the matters discussed more fully in Chapter 4 it is suggested that:

● Following a period of rapid development for SMRs in England, the next step forward must include tighter scoping of what constitutes 'archaeological' material.

● Care must be exercised in the way that sources are exploited so as to ensure balance in the range of material brought onto record systems. A common set of sources could usefully be defined.

● Regular monitoring of the way in which records are defined and structured is needed in order to take account of intellectual and technical advances, and end-user demands. The creation of records relating to historic landscapes is one area for further development.

● Funding should be continued for programmes involving the computerization of records and the reduction of input backlogs, the validation and checking of records, and the integration of data from major survey projects and developer-funded schemes.

● Particular attention should be given to the development of digital mapping systems linked to text-based records where these can include accurate spatial depiction of archaeological monuments.

● Georeferencing archaeological information of all kinds, and defining the spatial extents of archaeological remains, must be a priority for future record enhancement work. GPS now provides a relatively inexpensive and rapid means of achieving this.

● Considering the sharp increase in the number of records held by SMRs since 1983, account needs to be taken of projected future needs. Recent years have seen considerable expenditure on the acquisition of archaeological data and the development of archaeological officer posts to advise local authorities and others. This expansion needs to continue, especially in the light of local government reorganization. Additional resources are therefore required for the active curation and maintenance of the records generated to date.

- New ways of making records easily accessible to those who have to use them should also be explored. New technology will have an increasing role here.

- Joining archaeological data-sets together for easier examination and analysis of patterns and trends should be examined. Both horizontal and vertical linkages need to be explored.

- Flexibility needs to be built into the way local SMRs develop in order to respond to changing needs and new opportunities. With currently available technology, fully networked and properly staffed SMRs could operate perfectly well at a regional or national level. The emerging trend for regional self-determination, the development of Government Office Regions, and greater emphasis on Europe-wide regional planning may provide a framework for the evolution of archaeological record systems.

- Given the likely expansion of records relating to stray finds as a result of reporting procedures set out in the *Code of Practice* for the implementation of the *Treasure Act 1996* (DNH 1997), attention needs to be directed to the rapid integration of appropriate information in local SMRs. If successful, this scheme will lead to very substantial increases in specific types of record.

- Sites and Monuments Records deserve statutory recognition so that the information they contain can be more robustly deployed in the context of strategic planning and development control.

10.3.2 Distribution

Overall, the density of recorded monuments is higher in urban areas than in rural areas. This is not necessarily a true reflection of the distribution of the archaeological resource, especially for earlier periods. The density of recorded archaeological monuments ranges from 1.41 to

Figure 10.4 - A large late Neolithic round barrow standing to a height of about 4m under pasture on Gib Hill, Derbyshire. Although partly excavated by Thomas Bateman in 1848 the monument remains in very good condition. *[Photograph: Timothy Darvill. Copyright reserved]*

Figure 10.5 - Aerial view of flattened medieval ridge-and-furrow field system now under modern arable cultivation near Standlake, Oxfordshire. The cultivation strips are visible as soil-marks reflecting the remnants of richer darker soil in the furrows contrasting with the remains of truncated ridges *[Photograph: Timothy Darvill. Copyright reserved]*

41.78 per square kilometre, although when standing buildings are removed from the calculation the maximum is 16.97 monuments per square kilometre. The average density across England is 2.25 monuments per square kilometre.

As expected, the density of recorded monuments is higher where detailed survey work has been carried out. The cumulative effect of survey work over the past 30 years or so has been to produce overall distributions which contain numerous peaks and troughs, some of which are general while others are period-specific. While the peaks can be substantiated by the surveys themselves, it is not clear to what extent the areas of apparently low density are real or simply the product of differential attention. Especially noteworthy is the apparent poverty of prehistoric remains in three MARS Regions: the North West, West Midlands, and South East. For Roman period remains all the western regions show lower densities than their eastern counterparts. For medieval monuments central southern England, the East Midlands and the North West seem under-represented. A number of areas appear to have less archaeology than surrounding regions for almost all periods. These include: the south Cotswolds, New Forest, South Downs between Portsmouth and Worthing, Weald, Severn Valley and Welsh Marches, south Midlands, north Lancashire and Cumbria, north Lincolnshire and parts of Humberside, and some parts of Northumberland.

In the light of these points and the findings discussed in Chapter 5 it is suggested that:

- Extensive survey programmes, based on coherent sampling strategies, are undertaken in areas where current evidence suggests below-average densities of archaeological monuments. The aims of such projects will include: testing the proposition that these areas were less heavily utilized in the past; and providing a framework for the discovery, mapping and recording of previously unrecognized remains.

- Work on RCHMEs National Mapping Programme is continued in order to provide a consistent retrievable record for the whole country of

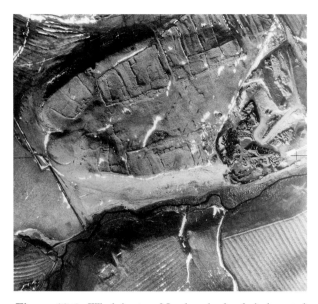

Figure 10.6 - Whelpington, Northumberland. A deserted medieval village with exceptionally clear croft boundaries. The settlement was abandoned before the eighteenth century but is now being lost to stone quarrying which will eventually mean its wholesale destruction. *[Photograph: Cambridge University Collection of Air Photographs. Copyright reserved]*

archaeological remains identifiable through aerial photography.

● Investment in the development of methodologies appropriate to the examination of 'hidden landscapes' is needed. This is especially so for areas covered in peat or alluvium, but also for pasture land and woodland where rather different limitations are found.

10.3.3 Form and period

Numerically, small single monuments under 3ha in area account for 56% of the recorded resource (Figure 10.4), a further 21% being standing buildings and structures. Large single monuments and linear monuments each account for 9%. Field systems account for the remaining 5% of the recorded resource, although in areal terms they represent a far larger proportion of the whole (Figure 10.5).

There are many regional variations in the representation of these main forms; most notable is the apparent concentration of small single monuments in the south and east of England. Large single monuments appear more prevalent in the Midlands.

Although many monuments are of multi-period construction, and therefore span broad chronological periods, about 12% of monuments date mainly to the prehistoric period, of which the largest single group (5% of the total) are classified as being of Bronze Age date. Some 7% of monuments are Roman in date, 22% medieval, and 36% post-medieval and modern. Nearly a quarter of recorded monuments are of unknown date. Arable land contains the highest proportion of undated monuments, mainly because a high proportion were discovered through aerial photography with minimal information about dating unless the morphology of the

features photographed is distinctive.

In the light of these points and findings discussed in Chapter 5 it is suggested that:

● The range of monument classes represented in different regions is reviewed, especially such things as field systems and large single monuments, to determine whether the recorded resource adequately reflects local populations.

● Research into the representation, classification, and recognition of monuments presently in ill-defined classes is needed, building on work already started within the Monuments Protection Programme.

● Better dating of familiar and unfamiliar classes of monument would greatly assist overall assessments of England's archaeological resource and also strengthen local and regional archaeological perspectives. A number of sharply focused small-scale projects aimed at sampling a selection of definable features (especially cropmark features), supported by a programme of scientific dating, would greatly enhance basic knowledge of the recorded resource. Existing museum collections relating to earlier excavations may also help with this problem.

10.3.4 Extent of loss

The MARS Field Survey Programme revealed that 84% of recorded monuments were extant (i.e still in existence) in 1995; 16% of the recorded monuments examined were found to have been destroyed prior to 1995. About half of these losses are known to have occurred since 1945. Looked at another way, on a national scale, in the region of 47,000 recorded archaeological monuments have been destroyed, about 23,500 in the 50 years since 1945. This amounts to the loss of just over one monument per day, every day, over that period. This of course includes monuments of all sorts, but wholesale destruction accounts for the loss of a higher proportion of small single monuments than any other form. Linear monuments are least affected.

There is some regional variability in loss rates, the highest losses being in the South East where, for example, 24% of earthwork monuments are recorded as having been destroyed; the lowest rates being in the South West where only 13% of earthworks have been lost and the West Midlands where just 9% have disappeared. Similar patterns are evident among buildings and structures.

Measured in terms of the area of archaeology lost the figures are more worrying. Out of the total extent of recorded archaeology, 9% has been lost through the wholesale destruction of monuments. To this must be added a further land area, estimated as being approximately 35% of the area covered by the recorded resource, which has been nibbled off the edges of monuments that still remain partly extant. Thus, overall, in areal terms, 44% of the recorded archaeological resource had already been destroyed prior 1995.

Five main hazards together account for most of the wholesale monument destruction and piecemeal loss of sections of monuments since 1945 (Figure 10.6).

Cultivation is the single biggest hazard facing

monuments, accounting for 10% of wholesale monument destruction and 30% of piecemeal loss. Its impact is especially great for early field systems (66% of recorded destruction) and large single monuments (38% of recorded destruction). It is cited as the reason for carrying out the work in 4% of rescue excavations. The problem posed by cultivation has long been recognized, but has now reached a critical point because about one-third of archaeological monuments are affected by it. A two pronged approach is needed: first to prevent any more recorded monuments being brought into cultivation, especially those currently under less hostile land-use regimes such as pasture land; and second to deal with monuments already under cultivation through positive management actions or removing them from cultivated altogether. The first of the these requires the extension of existing mechanisms to control changes to land-use in areas of recorded archaeology (i.e. recorded on local SMRs). The town and country planning system connected to Environmental Assessment procedures is one possible approach (and see NHTPC 1997).

Action by water, waves, rivers, frost, wind, land-slip, soil-loss, animal activity, visitor erosion, and geomorphological factors account for up to 5% of observed cases of wholesale destruction and 24% of cases of piecemeal loss. Standing buildings and small single monuments have the highest casualty rates from this hazard.

Together, property development and urban expansion account for 27% of observed cases of wholesale destruction and 9% of piecemeal loss. To this must be added the effects of building repairs and alterations which account for a further 20% of all monuments destroyed and 16% of piecemeal losses. Building alterations represent the single biggest hazard to standing buildings and structures, accounting for 43% of recorded instances of wholesale or piecemeal loss.

Some 12% of observed cases of wholesale destruction and 3% of cases of piecemeal loss can be attributed to mineral extraction and quarrying, mainly sand and gravel workings in the major river valleys of southern and eastern England. These figures hide the fact that many workings are very extensive and the loss of archaeological deposits within extraction areas is total.

Road-building accounts for 9% of observed cases of wholesale destruction and 4% of cases of piecemeal loss. Always it is the process of road-building itself that is the main problem.

These three last-mentioned causes of damage and destruction, collectively amounting to 30% of all reported cases, fall within the scope of the town and country planning system and therefore within the guidance set out in PPG16 on archaeology and planning. Because this guidance was only published in 1990 its effects cannot be gauged with reference to the MARS data, but other studies suggest it is working well (Pagoda Projects 1992; Roger Tym and Partners 1995). If Government proposals for house-building and urbanization in the period to 2016 are implemented (Leake 1998) it is important that PPG16 is extensively and consistently applied.

The PPG16 era has also seen the widespread application of archaeological mitigation strategies and methods to achieve the *in situ* preservation of important deposits. Surveys of mitigation measures other than archaeological excavation and the impact of construction techniques were commissioned in 1996 (Olivier 1997, 58) and should provide a good general picture. Detailed scientific monitoring of a selection of methods, and their success in securing preservation and identifying risks posed by recognized hazards, is also needed.

In the light of these points and the detailed findings discussed in Chapter 6 it is suggested that:

● The impact of permitted development on the loss of

Figure 10.7 - Aerial views of the remains of a Roman settlement at Hacconby Drove, Lincolnshire. (Left) Taken in 1952 shows the monument under pasture as an upstanding earthwork. (Right) Taken in 1970 shows the same area after extensive ploughing, by this time a flattened earthwork monument. *[Photographs: Cambridge University Collection of Air Photographs. Copyright reserved]*

monuments is reviewed.

- The concept of 'development' is redefined within the town and country planning system in order to include agriculture, perhaps with appropriate permitted development rights.

- The principle that planning permission is needed for changes to the use of land is extended in order to control the transfer of land into cultivation where such land is recorded as containing archaeological monuments.

- The EU directive on Environmental Assessment (EC 1997a) is expanded to include provision for the assessment of archaeologically harmful land-uses where proposals are made for their expansion into areas where archaeological remains are recorded or strongly suspected. The directive already includes discretionary provision for assessments to be carried out where semi-natural landscapes are to be brought into intensive cultivation.

Figure 10.8 - Visibility and accessibility of monuments. Headland Warren, Dartmoor, Devon. A party of visitors on a guided walk is shown a stone cross and ancient field systems. *[Photograph: Timothy Darvill. Copyright reserved]*

- PPG15 and PPG16, and the guidance they contain, continue to be elaborated and promoted, and their full and consistent application encouraged in all development situations where archaeological monuments and historic landscapes are either demonstrably present or might reasonably be expected.

- Research and experimentation is carried out to see how natural erosion can be combated and reduced at archaeological monuments. Novel and innovative measures may be needed in some cases, for example the use of sacrificial layers over eroding surfaces.

- Research and experimentation is carried out to explore positive responses to the threat posed by continuing cultivation. This should include a review

of the impact of currently available machinery and cultivation systems (building on earlier work), the assessment of which areas should be removed from cultivation, and means of lifting the damage-interface away from *in situ* archaeological deposits through modifications to cultivation techniques and ploughsoil environments.

- A programme of monitoring and experimentation is carried out to document the strengths and weakness of current approaches to *in situ* preservation. Technological advances in environmental monitoring should be investigated with a view to developing ways of providing early warnings of defined hazards impacting on the survival of archaeological deposits.

10.3.5 Survival and condition

Measuring the physical extent of a monument in relation to what is recorded about its dimensions in earlier times provides a crude but simple measure of survival, at least in the horizontal plane. Percentage Area Loss (PAL) scores can be calculated, and a scale of loss established to classify changes.

In 1995 approximately 76% of MARS earthwork Monuments were found to have very good areal survival (i.e. PAL less than 20%) while less than 2% of MARS earthwork Monuments were found to have very poor areal survival (PAL of 80-95%). However, the current situation is rather less good than in 1945 when, applying the same criteria, 95% of MARS earthwork Monuments had very good areal survival. What has happened in the intervening 50 years is that the decay of monuments has caused examples to slip down the scale of areal survival. Many of these changes result from the effects of agriculture.

Areal survival was found to be related to archaeological period, monuments of more recent date generally surviving better than those from earlier periods. Small single monuments appear to lose less of their area, and thus survive in a better state, than large single

Figure 10.9 - Prehistoric linear boundary and associated cairnfield near Nether Padley, Derbyshire, under semi-natural land-use. *[Photograph: MARS Archive]*

monuments and field systems.

State provides another measure of condition. Of all MARS earthwork Monuments, for example, only 36% nationally are upstanding; the remaining 64% are now flattened. This erosion, mainly through agriculture, represents the biggest loss to the archaeological resource to date (Figure 10.7). There are marked regional differences: earthworks tend to be flattened in the East Midlands and West Midlands but, conversely, more upstanding in the South West and North West.

As should be expected, far greater numbers of standing buildings and structures (almost 70%) survive in an upstanding state. The West Midlands has proved to be far more sensitive to building survival than earthwork survival.

Only a very small percentage of all monuments (some 5%) display any sort of ameliorative action taken to slow the rate of decay. The highest level of amelioration on a regional level was found in the West Midlands where some 12% of monuments were reported as showing evidence of works which would contribute to their long-term survival.

The implications of these points and findings discussed in Chapters 6 and 7 are considered in Section 10.3.7 below.

10.3.6 Access, visibility and local management

A quarter of monuments are located on publicly accessible land and free of any entry charge. Charging policies are in place at only 1% of monuments.

Approximately 49% of all monuments are visible and only 8% either obscured or barely visible. Certain land-uses, for example forestry, wetland, semi-natural land, and developed and urban land appear to show above-average levels of visible monuments (Figure 10.8). In arable land less than 10% of recorded monuments are visible.

Local management arrangements are already in place at 36% of Guardianship Monuments and there is scope for more. The direct ownership and management of monuments, whether important at a local, regional or national level, is a certain way of reducing risk and providing a secure future. Community action and planning of this sort may be pursued through Local

Figure 10.10 - Aerial view of the Roman forts under forestry at Cawthorn Camps, North Yorkshire. *[Photograph: North York Moors National Park and English Heritage. Copyright reserved]*

Agenda 21 initiatives, and provides a way of promoting sustainability and encouraging local distinctiveness. The National Trust has led the way in this field over recent years (Morgan Evans *et al.* 1996), followed closely by National Parks, local authorities and archaeological trusts (White and Iles 1991; Wade-Martins 1996).

In the light of these points and the findings discussed in Chapter 5 it is suggested that:

- Access plans to enhance public benefit are developed for archaeological monuments wherever possible, for example through community archaeology programmes, archaeological trusts with educational objectives, major landowners and local authorities.

- Public awareness of monuments within a locality is raised through encouraging community involvement in archaeology and its discovery, study and management.

- Where appropriate, local organizations and institutions are encouraged to purchase archaeological monuments for the purposes of conserving, managing and making them accessible to the public.

10.3.7 Land-use and archaeology

The land on which archaeological monuments lie is represented as many differently sized parcels which are widely dispersed. Monuments exist as integral components of working landscapes and townscapes and are thus also very fragile in being subject to the erosive effects of whatever is happening both on the land itself and in surrounding areas. Land-use practices and natural decay are the two key elements which determine the survival and condition of archaeological monuments.

Approximately 87% of monuments lie within a single land-use regime, small single monuments accounting for over half of that total (Figure 10.9). Only 4% of monuments surveyed were found to lie under more than three different land-uses. As a whole, the distribution of monuments by land-use seems to reflect the general proportions of land-use classes, that is, there is little marked clustering of monuments in particular land-use regimes, with the exception of developed and urban land. Agriculture (arable and pasture), developed land and forestry are found on the majority of archaeological monuments. There are both obvious and subtle trends in the types of monument found in each of these broad uses: post-medieval and large monuments are generally found on developed land; small single monuments and those generally dating to earlier periods are found on agricultural land.

Altogether, nearly 80% of monuments lie within agricultural land of various sorts of which 30% are under pasture and 27% under arable. There are of course notable regional variations related to the general distribution of agricultural regimes.

Land-use around monuments is broadly similar in its distribution to that over monuments, but there are frequent mismatches at the level of individual monuments. Approximately 42% of monuments do not experience the same land-use as their surroundings. These are effectively 'island' sites separated from their land-use context.

The distribution of monuments under different land-use regimes has remained fairly constant over the last 50 years, the shifts being from major land-uses such as pasture and arable to small groups such as developed land. Some land-use classes are more persistent over time than others. Looking backwards from the present, 14% of monuments currently under pasture of various sorts were in the same land-use regime in 1940. By contrast 40% of monuments in field crop were in the same usage in 1940.

One exception to the general pattern is that as forestry cover in England has gradually increased over the last 50 years, the portion of the monuments under forestry has decreased. This can be attributed to the development by the Forestry Commission of policies to prevent or limit planting directly over recorded monuments (Figure 10.10).

In the light of the these points and the findings discussed in Chapters 7 and 8 it is suggested that:

- Relevant MARS data is made available to MAFF's Agri-Environment Forum when debating future reforms to the Common Agricultural Policy, especially in relation to arable agriculture.

- Information from MARS is used alongside related insights from, for example, the Character of England Project and historic landscape assessments in the development of strategic approaches to land-use planning at regional and local level.

- The class consent arrangement dealing with

continuing cultivation on Scheduled Monuments needs to be rigorously monitored and resources made available for revocation where significant damage is occurring.

- The evolution and application of targeted initiatives by the Forestry Authority should continue for the management and control of potentially damaging works in forested land and woodland. The need for pre-afforestation assessments and the careful design of planting schemes will be paramount if attempts are made to put ideas of doubling woodland cover into practice.

- There is strict application of the assessment and field evaluation procedures set out in PPG16 in relation to all types of development proposal.

- The programme of compiling Urban Assessments and the associated Urban Strategy Documents should be continued, and include not only urban areas themselves but also land identified for possible residential, commercial or industrial development around about.

- Greater consistency is needed in the formulation of reasonable and viable archaeological constraint areas for inclusion in strategic plans. Two kinds of area need to be identified: first, areas of archaeological significance where land is known to contain important archaeological remains and has the real prospect of revealing more in future.

Figure 10.11 - A high risk monument at Belle Tout, East Sussex, where a Neolithic enclosure and Beaker period settlement are being lost through the erosion of sea cliffs. Monitoring over recent years suggests that between 0.5m and 1m of cliff is lost per year over a distance of 1.2km. *[Photograph: Miles Russell. Copyright reserved]*

Second, areas of archaeological potential which recognize tracts of land within which there is good reason to expect the survival of archaeological remains even though not much has been recorded to date.

● Terminology and definitions relating to local and regional designations of archaeologically important areas need to be standardized and made more consistent between authorities.

● Zones defined for the protection and management of archaeological remains or historic landscapes should, where possible, extend existing designations or link to others.

● Information about the effects of previous land-use regimes on the preservation of archaeological remains should be systematically collected during excavation and fieldwork programmes.

10.3.8 Risk

All archaeological monuments are at risk in terms of potential damage or destruction all the time. What is important is how great that risk is and whether it can be reduced. Overall, 43% of the monuments examined by MARS were considered to be at low risk, while 2% were considered to be at high risk. High-risk monuments are those for which serious damage or destruction within 3-5 years appeared very likely on the basis of information available or visible to the field surveyors. Obvious cases include monuments falling into the sea on eroding cliffs (Figure 10.11) or monuments in the path of a road-building scheme, quarry expansion or proposed urban development.

High risk appears to be most acute among large single monuments and field systems, least so for linear monuments. High risk increases regionally towards the north and east with up to 3% of monuments regarded as being in the high-risk band in the North East and West Midlands. Prehistoric monuments, particularly those dating to the Neolithic, seem to be at greater levels of risk than many more recent monuments. In land-use terms developed and urban land, arable and forestry have the greatest proportion of monuments at high risk.

Although the percentage of monuments regarded as being at high risk seems relatively small, the number of monuments involved is considerable. Multiplied up from the MARS sample approximately 4520 monuments fall into this band and are therefore likely to require some form of investigation and recording within the next decade in connection with the development of a preservation strategy or prior to destruction.

In the long term it is the monuments regarded as being at medium risk which deserve attention now as these are the ones most susceptible to preservation and conservation through careful management; for many of the high-risk cases it is probably too late to take a long-term view. Regionally, medium-risk monuments are most prevalent in the North East (48%), the North West (34%) and the East Midlands (35%). Numerically, small single monuments and field systems represent the biggest groups of monuments under medium risk.

MARS has painted the broad view. The next stage is the development of local risk assessment programmes.

These could usefully be carried out in the context of defining and characterizing the recorded archaeological resource within Character Areas and/or Natural Areas as defined by the Countryside Commission (1996a) and English Nature (1993) respectively.

In the light of these points and the findings discussed in Chapters 8 and 9 it is suggested that:

● A nationwide programme of local monument risk assessments is developed and tied to defined Character Areas. The aim of the work would be the identification of needs in the application of risk-reducing measures and the definition of local action-plans for risk aversion.

● The focus of archaeological survey, recording and investigation programmes is directed to classes of monument, land-use classes and situations where the greatest levels of risk can be identified. Especially important is attention to afforestable land and developable land around existing urban areas.

● The application of archaeological risk assessments to strategic plans is supported, as set out in the recent EU proposal for a directive on strategic environmental assessment (EC 1997b)

● The 'precautionary principle' is applied within development control as the basis for reducing the

Figure 10.12 - The Crippets Long Barrow, Shurdington, Gloucestershire, a Scheduled Monument which still retains a notice erected by the Ministry of Public Building and Works notifying its protected status. *[Photograph: Timothy Darvill. Copyright reserved]*

proportion of high-risk monuments that are destroyed. Sustainability of the recorded resource is the key here.

● Local planning authorities are encouraged to use Environmental Assessment procedures more regularly for the assessment of risks to archaeological monuments. Under the revised directive adopted by the EC in March 1997, local authorities will have greater powers to scope EA programmes.

● The work of the MPP is targeted towards forms of monument, regions and land-use types with the highest levels of medium-risk monuments so that the control of works can be applied to nationally important monuments in these situations before their future is threatened by hazards that place them at high risk.

● More sophisticated, monument-specific, 'risk' assessment simulations are established through the development of GIS-based models which make use of a wide range of factors. These could be tested in regions where risk is currently perceived as being greatest. The application of risk assessment modelling as used in other environmental disciplines may be relevant here.

● Desk-top assessments of Monuments Protection Programme and Scheduled Monument data are carried out to reveal further trends in monument vulnerability and risk levels.

10.3.9 Management measures and information sources

There are many site-specific and area-based designations used with reference to archaeological monuments at international, national, regional and local level. Overall, it is estimated that about 18% of the recorded resource is designated under some form of site- or area-specific status.

Approximately 6% of the extant recorded resource, 14,478 monuments, were afforded protection as Scheduled Monuments in 1995, the work of the Monuments Protection Programme being responsible for recent rises in the proportion of monuments protected in this way. At present, Scheduled Monuments tend to be the small (68%) or large (17%) single forms and most commonly occur under pasture or in developed land (Figure 10.12).

Scheduling is working as a tool to protect monuments, with lower levels of loss amongst Scheduled examples as compared with non-Scheduled Monuments. Although slightly more Scheduled Monuments were found to be at high risk than within the resource as a whole (3% as against 2%), this in part results from the fact that monuments are sometimes Scheduled because they appear to be at risk and therefore need additional protection.

Within National Parks the percentage of MARS Monuments with very high areal survival rates was found to be higher than the gross national picture (94% as against 91%). Monuments in very poor condition were less numerous in National Parks (0.8% as against the national picture of 1.6%). There are probably two main reasons for this, the inherent quality of the archaeological remains found in these areas and the relatively high level of management input over recent years. Monuments also appear to survive well within AONBs.

Approximately 1500 management agreements were recorded for archaeological monuments across England, although there are heavy biases to the South West region with 60% of all recorded agreements. None has been running long enough to indicate whether their long-term effects are beneficial within the parameters measured by MARS. It was found that 5% of monuments with management agreements also had evidence of amelioration recorded.

Information about the extent and coincidence of protective designations and about the nature and extent of archaeological remains within a wide range of designated areas at all scales is poor.

In the light of these points and the findings discussed in Chapter 8 it is suggested that:

● The Monuments Protection Programme is continued to systematically review England's Schedule of monuments as the cornerstone of national conservation policy.

Figure 10.13 - MARS field team measuring a Bronze Age round barrow in a sample transect on Exmoor, Devon. *[Photograph: MARS Archive]*

- The results of MARS and local risk assessment programmes should be used to target the further development of management plans for monuments with special needs, for example those in multiple land-use.

- The monument management practices developed by the National Parks should be continued and their application encouraged in other areas.

- The transfer of designation data from source organizations to SMRs should be investigated as a means of updating current information and creating a unified record.

- Further investigation is made into the effects of environmental land management schemes and designated areas covering the archaeological resource.

- A map-based 'Heritage Information System' should be developed, plans for which have already been drawn-up by English Heritage and RCHME. The system should include mapped information about the nature and extent of designations and constraint zones relevant to archaeology and the historic environment at international, national, regional and local levels. A parallel for such a system is the Countryside Information System (CIS) developed by ITE. Links may usefully be made to the CIS so that a consistent range of data is available in electronic form for all environmental interests.

10.3.10 Further research

The experience gained from MARS provides a number of important pointers for future work. The two main data sources exploited could both be improved before the work is repeated. Because numerous different local SMRs were used as sources for information about the recorded resource there is a certain amount of variation in the quality and definition of the information used as the starting point. In retrospect more attention could have been given to the standardization and validation of these data, especially the detailed mapping of archaeologically sensitive areas. This can be done in preparation for future studies. The second source, aerial photographs, proved its worth, but working with the photographs revealed difficulties connected with available coverage and the recognition of small features. Again, some preparatory work involving the digital mapping of monuments from aerial photographs could be done before MARS is repeated.

The two biggest difficulties with MARS fieldwork were the certain location of monuments, especially where records provided poor information on location in countryside with few reference points, and the objective measurement of archaeological monuments (Figure 10.13). In future, better results should be possible using portable GPS equipment which allows accurate position-finding and the rapid survey of monument extents without the need for local fixed terrestrial reference points. Some experimentation with monument monitoring using these systems would also be appropriate.

One important consideration is that the MARS sample units as now established are not treated differently from the rest of the archaeological resource and the areas in which they lie. In many ways it would be best to forget about MARS sample transects and their location: certainly they should not be used as the basis for any projects likely to preference the enhancement of the recorded resource within the transects in isolation.

In the light of these points and findings outlined in Chapters 4-9 it is suggested that:

- Background studies are carried out to upgrade the information available for MARS Monuments in the sample transects in order to widen the possibilities for supplementary analysis. This should include digitizing of the three main area measurements identified; systematic recording of monument height information from earlier sources; and the validation of sources cited in the original records.

- Further studies of the operation of decay processes are initiated in relation to a range of situations and for a variety of kinds of archaeological evidence.

- The monitoring of change initiated by MARS is repeated in the year 2015, two decades after the census date. Limited monitoring work in 2005 to look at land-use change in relation to monuments in the sample would provide mid-point data to make the next main survey more useful.

- Appropriate methodological improvements for future surveys are investigated, for example the use of satellite imaging for the monitoring of land-use change in relation to recorded archaeological monuments and portable GPS systems for the location and measurement of monuments.

- Use of the MARS transects is actively discouraged for any projects that might preferentially enhance the recorded resource within one or more transects in isolation from the broader populations of which they are a sample.

10.4 Overview

The MARS Project has confirmed that England's extant archaeological resource represented by monuments scattered through the countryside and townscape is extremely diverse in its character and date, and constantly changing in its definition. Considering what it has been through, it is easy to see a number of positive points which give cause for hope. About three-quarters of all monuments survive in very good condition when compared to their known extent 50 years ago. Over 30% of remaining monuments lie in pasture land, which is widely recognized as the best possible land-use for long-term survival, and a further 15% lie in semi-natural environments. Some 36% of earthwork monuments remain upstanding, with nearly half of all monuments visible in some form. A quarter of all monuments are accessible from public rights of way. Only 2% of monuments can be regarded as being at high risk in the sense that their short-term survival is highly unlikely.

But this is only part of the story. All across England archaeological monuments are in a sorry state. There is certainly no scope here for archaeological bodies or other agencies to relax their efforts to improve the conservation of monuments, indeed there is an urgent need to do much more. At least 16% of all recorded monuments no longer exist, nearly half of that loss being attributable to damage and wholesale destruction that has taken place over the last 50 years. In terms of the losses to land area with recorded archaeological deposits the situation is much worse, with approximately 44% of the land known to contain such deposits destroyed by 1995.

This rate of loss cannot continue if communities in the early decades of the next millennium are to have any sort of worthwhile archaeological heritage to enjoy and use as the basis for the development of their history. Of what remains today over one-quarter lies within extremely harsh land-uses, including intensive arable cultivation, and just under half, an estimated 150,000 monuments, is rated as being at medium risk. It is these monuments in particular that require urgent attention in the form of management plans and careful stewardship to ensure long-term survival. This work needs to be added to the short-term requirements of dealing with the 2% of monuments regarded as being at high risk, some of which can no doubt be preserved *in situ* with appropriately constructed mitigation strategies but many of which will require investigation and recording over the next 5-10 years.

All these projections are based on the known and the predictable. As earlier chapters emphasize, archaeological remains are still not widely known and their existence in relation to land-use practices remains unpredictable. There is certainly much more to be found, and the lesson of archaeological programmes connected with development projects is that more is often found as a result of the work than was known about in the first place. Optimists believe that the best archaeology in England has yet to be found; pessimists might argue that the best has yet to be destroyed.

The MARS Project provides clear insights into the nature and state of the archaeological resource, and, while it is not the role of the project to propose specific solutions, a number of areas where resources can be targeted have been identified. Perhaps more than anything else, the survey highlights the need to continue driving ahead in three key areas: strategic policy that is concerted and integrated with other allied interests and at all levels; practical implementation of initiatives at appropriate scales within the range of local, regional, national and international archaeological organizations; and the increasing application of theoretically robust approaches to the formulation, modelling, implementation and monitoring of archaeological resource management in England.

APPENDIX A
Select bibliography of archaeological resource assessments for defined monument classes, geographical regions and urban areas

A.1 Resource assessments for defined monument classes

Field systems
Hall, D, 1993, **The open fields of Northamptonshire: the case for the preservation of ridge and furrow.** Northampton. Northampton Heritage

Flint Mines
Holgate, R, 1989, **The Neolithic flint mines in Sussex: a plough damage assessment and site management report.** London. Field Archaeology Unit, Institute of Archaeology. [Circulated typescript report]

Flint scatters
West Yorkshire Archaeological Service, 1994, **West Yorkshire Mesolithic Project - Marsden Moor, West Yorkshire.** Wakefield. West Yorkshire Archaeological Service. [Project Design document]

Glassworks
Crossley, D, 1994, The Wealden glass industry re-visited. **Industrial Archaeology Review**, 17.1, 64-74

Historic churches
Rodwell, W J, and Rodwell, K A, 1977, **Historic churches: a wasting asset** (= CBA Research Report 19). London. CBA

Long barrows
Brown, L, 1978, A survey of the condition of Oxfordshire long barrows. **Oxoniensia**, 43, 241-5

Drinkwater, J, 1972, Barrows in Gloucestershire, patterns of destruction. In P J Fowler (ed), **Archaeology and the landscape**. London. John Baker. 129-56

Drinkwater, J and Saville, A, 1976, **Gloucestershire long barrows: their condition and future preservation with special reference to plough damage**. Bristol. CRAAGS. [Circulated typescript report]

RCHME, 1979, **Long barrows in Hampshire and the Isle of Wight**. London. HMSO

Roman forts
Welfare, H, and Swan, V, 1995, **Roman camps in England**. London. RCHME and HMSO

Roman pottery kilns
Swan, V, 1984, **The pottery kilns of Roman Britain** (= RCHME Supplementary Series 5). London. HMSO

Round barrows
Allden, A, 1981, **A study of some Devon barrows and their diminishing future** (= DAS/DCRA Occasional Paper 10). Exeter. DAS and DCRA

Crawford, G M, 1980, **Bronze Age burial mounds in Cleveland**. Middlesborough. Cleveland County Council

Lawson, A J, Martin, E A, and Priddy, D, 1981, **The barrows of East Anglia** (= East Anglian Archaeology 12). Norwich. East Anglian Archaeology

Mudd, A, 1984, Round barrows of the Oxfordshire Cotswolds. **Midlands Archaeology**, 14, 1-17

Woodward, P J, 1980, A survey of barrows on the south Dorset Ridgeway: threat, destruction and survival. **Proceedings of the Dorset Natural History and Archaeological Society**, 102, 96-7

Note: Documentation produced for the Monuments Protection Programme in England contains numerous monument class descriptions and resource assessments. A full listing is provided in: English Heritage, 1997, **The Monuments Protection Programme 1986-96 in retrospect**. London. English Heritage

A.2 National and trans-regional resource assessment reports

Darvill, T C, 1986, **The archaeology of the uplands: a rapid assessment of archaeological knowledge and practice.** London. RCHME and CBA

Glass, H J, 1989, **The condition of Scheduled Ancient Monuments: a sample survey of landscapes.** London. English Heritage. [Circulated typescript report]

Heighway, C M (ed), 1972, **The erosion of history. Archaeology and planning in towns: a study of historic towns affected by modern development in England, Wales and Scotland**. London. CBA

Hinchliffe, J, and Schadla-Hall, R T (eds), 1980, *The past under the plough* (= DAMHB Occasional Paper 3). London. DoE

Macphail, R I, 1987, A review of soil science in archaeology in England. In H C M Keeley (ed), *Environmental archaeology: a regional review. Volume II* (= HBMCE Occasional Paper 1). London. English Heritage. 332-79

RCHME (Royal Commission on Historical Monuments, England), 1960, *A matter of time: an archaeological survey of the river gravels of England.* London. HMSO

RCHME (Royal Commission on Historical Monuments, England), 1963, *Monuments threatened or destroyed: a select list.* London. HMSO

Scaife, R, 1987, A review of later quaternary plant microfossil and macrofossil research in southern England: with special reference to environmental archaeological evidence. In H C M Keeley (ed), *Environmental archaeology: a regional review. Volume II* (= HBMCE Occasional Paper 1). London. English Heritage. 125-203

Walsh, 1969, *Report of the Committee of Enquiry into the Arrangements for the Protection of Field Monuments 1966-68.* London. HMSO

A.3 Regional resource assessment reports

(Arranged by Government Office Regions)

North East
Clack, P A G, and Gosling, P F, 1976, *Archaeology in the North. Report of the Northern Archaeological Survey*. Durham. Northern Archaeological Survey

Haselgrove, C, Ferrell, G and, Turnbull, T, 1988, *Durham archaeological survey* (= Department of Archaeology Occasional Paper 2). Durham. University of Durham

Rackham, J, 1984, Environmental work in northern England. In H C M Keeley (ed), *Environmental archaeology. A regional review* (= DAMHB Occasional Paper 6). London. DoE. 134-51

North West
Clack, P A G, and Gosling, P F, 1976, *Archaeology in the North. Report of the Northern Archaeological Survey*. Durham. Northern Archaeological Survey

Clare, T, no date, *Prehistory in north-west England.* Keswick. [Circulated typescript report]

Quatermaine, J (ed), 1994, *Langdale erosion research programme. Project report.* Lancaster. Lancaster University Archaeological Unit and The National Trust. [Circulated typescript report]

Rackham, J, 1984, Environmental work in northern England. In H C M Keeley (ed), *Environmental archaeology. A regional review* (= DAMHB Occasional Paper 6). London. DoE. 134-51

Yorkshire and Humberside
Faul, M L, and Moorhouse, S A, 1981, *West Yorkshire: an archaeological survey to AD 1500.* Wakefield. West Yorkshire County Council (3 vols plus plans)

Kenward, H K, Hall, A R, Jones, A K G, and O'Connor, T P, 1984, Environmental archaeology at York in retrospect and prospect. In H C M Keeley (ed), *Environmental archaeology. A regional review* (= DAMHB Occasional Paper 6). London. DoE. 152-79

Loughlin, N, and Miller, K, 1979, *Survey of archaeological sites in Humberside*. Hull. Humberside Joint Archaeological Committee

Manby, T G, 1980, Yorkshire Wolds: field monuments and arable farming. In J Hinchliffe and R T Schadla-Hall (eds), *The past under the plough* (= DAMHB Occasional Paper 3). London. DoE. 60-8

Merseyside

East Midlands
Hart, C, 1976, *Archaeological survey of Wormill: a Peakland parish under threat.* Chesterfield. North Derbyshire Archaeological Trust

Hart, C J, 1981, *The North Derbyshire Archaeological Survey: to AD 1500.* Chesterfield. North Derbyshire Archaeological Trust

Knight, D, and Howard, A J, 1994, *Archaeology and alluvium in the Trent valley: an archaeological assessment of the floodplain and gravel terraces.* Nottingham. Trent and Peak Archaeological Trust

Liddle, P, 1982, *Leicestershire archaeology. The present state of knowledge.* Leicester. Leicestershire Museums Arts and Records Service. (2 vols)

Robinson, M, and Wilson, B, 1987, A survey of environmental archaeology in the south Midlands. In H C M Keeley (ed), *Environmental archaeology: a regional review. Volume II* (= HBMCE Occasional Paper 1). London. English Heritage. 16-100

Simmons, B, 1980, The Lincolnshire Fens. In J Hinchliffe and R T Schadla-Hall (eds), *The past under the plough* (= DAMHB Occasional Paper 3). London. DoE. 82-9

West Midlands

Bishop, M W, 1973, *A survey of the state of archaeology in Warwickshire.* Warwick. Warwickshire County Council Libraries, Records and Museum Committee

Gaffney, V, and Hughes, G, 1993, *Settlement and environment on the south east Staffordshire gravels: new approaches to a threatened resource.* Birmingham. Birmingham University Field Archaeology Unit

Greig, J, 1987, A review of environmental archaeology in the West Midlands. In H C M Keeley (ed), *Environmental archaeology: a regional review. Volume II* (= HBMCE Occasional Paper 1). London. English Heritage. 101-24

Eastern Region

French, C A I, and Wait, G A, 1988, *An archaeological survey of the Cambridgeshire river gravels.* Cambridge. Cambridgeshire County Council and Fenland Archaeological Trust

Lawson, A J, 1980, Ploughing on archaeological sites in Norfolk: some observations. In J Hinchliffe and R T Schadla-Hall (eds), *The past under the plough* (= DAMHB Occasional Paper 3). London. DoE. 74-7

Malim, T, 1990, *Archaeology on the Cambridgeshire County Farms Estate.* Cambridge. Cambridgeshire County Council and English Heritage

Murphy, P, 1984, Environmental archaeology in East Anglia. In H C M Keeley (ed), *Environmental Archaeology. A regional review* (= DAMHB Occasional Paper 6). London. DoE. 13-42

London

Andrews, G, Hinton, P, and Thomas, R, forthcoming, *London assessment document.* London. English Heritage

Armitage, P, Locker, A, and Straker, V, 1987, Environmental archaeology in London: a review. In H C M Keeley (ed), *Environmental archaeology: a regional review. Volume II* (= HBMCE Occasional Paper 1). London. English Heritage. 252-331

South East

Basford, H V, 1980, *The Vectis Report: a survey of Isle of Wight archaeology.* Newport. Isle of Wight County Council

Benson, D, and Miles, D, 1974, *The upper Thames Valley. An archaeological survey of the river gravels* (= Oxfordshire Archaeological Unit Survey 2). Oxford. Oxfordshire Archaeological Unit

Boismier, W A, 1994, *Archaeological resources on County Council owned farm and recreation land* (= Hampshire County Planning Department Archaeological Report 2). Winchester. Hampshire County Council

Coy, J, and Maltby, M, 1987, Archaeozoology in Wessex. In H C M Keeley (ed), *Environmental archaeology: a regional review. Volume II* (= HBMCE Occasional Paper 1). London. English Heritage. 204-49

Drewett, P L, 1976, *Plough damage to known archaeological sites in East and West Sussex.* London. Institute of Archaeology, University of London. [Circulated typescript report]

Drewett, P L, 1980, Sussex plough damage survey. In J Hinchliffe and R T Schadla-Hall (eds), *The past under the plough* (= DAMHB Occasional Paper 3). London. DoE. 69-73

Ford, S, 1987, *East Berkshire archaeological survey.* Reading. Berkshire County Council

Gates, T, 1975, *The Middle Thames Valley. An archaeological survey of the river gravels* (= Berkshire Archaeological Committee Publication 1). Reading. Berkshire Archaeological Committee

Miles, D, 1980, Some comments on the effect of agriculture in the upper Thames Valley. In J Hinchliffe and R T Schadla-Hall (eds), *The past under the plough* (= DAMHB Occasional Paper 3). London. DoE. 78-81

Perkins, D R J, 1992, *Archaeological sites in Thanet: their need for protection.* Broadstairs. Trust for Thanet Archaeology. [Circulated typescript report]

Richards, J, 1978, *The archaeology of the Berkshire Downs: an introductory survey* (= Berkshire Archaeology Committee Publication 3). Reading. Berkshire Archaeological Committee

Wessex Archaeology, 1993, *The Southern Rivers Palaeolithic Project. Report 1, 1991-2. The Upper Thames Valley, Kennet Valley, and Solent drainage system.* Salisbury. Wessex Archaeology

South West

Balkwill, C J, 1976, *Archaeology and development in rural Devon.* Exeter. Devon Committee for Rescue Archaeology

Bell, M, 1984, Environmental archaeology in south west England. In H C M Keeley (ed), *Environmental archaeology. A regional review* (= DAMHB Occasional Paper 6). London. DoE. 43-133

Bonney, D J, 1980, Damage by medieval and later cultivation in Wessex. In J Hinchliffe and R T Schadla-Hall (eds), *The past under the plough* (= DAMHB Occasional Paper 3). London. DoE. 41-9

Canham, R, 1983, *Archaeology in the Salisbury Plain Training Area*. Trowbridge. Wiltshire County Council Library and Museums Service

Canham, R A, Richards, J, and Schadla-Hall, R T, 1980, Archaeology and agriculture in Wessex. In J Hinchliffe and R T Schadla-Hall (eds), *The past under the plough* (= DAMHB Occasional Paper 3). London. DoE. 49-59

Condick, F, Ellison, A, and Aston, M, 1976, A Somerset field monument and land use survey. *Proceedings of the Somerset Archaeological and Natural History Society,* 120, 85-97

Coy, J, and Maltby, M, 1987, Archaeozoology in Wessex. In H C M Keeley (ed), *Environmental archaeology: a regional review. Volume II* (= HBMCE Occasional Paper 1). London. English Heritage. 204-49

Ellis, P, 1992, *Mendip Hills. An archaeological survey of an AONB*. Taunton and London. Somerset County Council and English Heritage. [Circulated typescript report]

Ellison, A, 1977, *A survey of the archaeological implications of hard-stone quarrying in the counties of Avon, Gloucestershire and Somerset*. Bristol. CRAAGS. [Circulated typescript report]

Ellison, A, 1977, *A survey of the archaeological implications of forestry in the Forest of Dean.* Bristol. CRAAGS. [Circulated typescript report]

Fowler, P J, and Ellison, A, 1977, Archaeology on Exmoor: its nature, assessment and management. *Exmoor Review*, 18, 78-84

Gingell, C, 1971, *A penny for your past: archaeology and the Water Park*. Cheltenham. Committee for Research into the Iron Age in the North West Cotswolds. [Circulated typescript report]

Gingell, C, 1976, *Archaeology in the Wiltshire countryside.* Devizes. Devizes Museum

Groube, L, 1978, Priorities and problems in Dorset archaeology. In T Darvill, M Parker Pearson, R Thomas and R W Smith (eds), *New approaches to our past: an archaeological forum.* Southampton. Southampton University Archaeological Society. 29-52

Groube, L M and Bowden, M C B, 1982, *The archaeology of rural Dorset, past, present, and future* (= DNHAS Monograph 4). Dorchester. DNHAS

Johnson, N, and Rose, P, 1983, *Archaeological survey and conservation in West Penwith, Cornwall.* Truro. Cornwall Committee for Rescue Archaeology. [Circulated typescript report]

Johnson, N, and Rose, P, 1994, *Bodmin Moor. An archaeological survey. Volume 1: the human landscape to c1800* (= HBMCE Archaeological Report 24 / RCHME Supplementary Series 11). London. English Heritage, RCHME and Cornwall Archaeological Unit

Leech, R, 1977, *The Upper Thames Valley in Gloucestershire and Wiltshire: an archaeological survey of the river gravels* (= CRAAGS Survey 4). Bristol. CRAAGS

McDonald, R, 1990, *The Quantock Hills AONB. Summary report of an archaeological survey prepared for Somerset County Planning Department*. Taunton. R McDonald and Somerset County Council. [Circulated typescript report]

McDonald, R, 1990, *The Quantock Hills AONB. Part II. Interim recommendations for management of the archaeological resource prepared for Somerset County Planning Department.* Taunton. R McDonald and Somerset County Council. [Circulated typescript report]

Ratcliffe, J, 1989, *The archaeology of Scilly. An assessment of the resource and recommendations for its future.* Truro. Cornwall Archaeological Unit

RCHME, 1979, *Stonehenge and its environs. Monuments and land-use.* Edinburgh. Edinburgh University Press

Russell, V, 1971, *West Penwith survey.* Truro. Cornwall Archaeological Society

Saville, A, 1979, *Archaeological sites in the Avon and Gloucestershire Cotswolds. An extensive survey of a rural archaeological resource with special reference to plough damage* (= CRAAGS Survey 5). Bristol. CRAAGS

Saville, A, 1980, Archaeology and ploughing on the Cotswolds: the CRAAGS response. In J Hinchliffe and R T Schadla-Hall (eds), *The past under the plough* (= DAMHB Occasional Paper 3). London. DoE. 90-4

Smith, R W, 1981, *Archaeology in the Salisbury Plain Training Areas.* Trowbridge. Wiltshire County Council Library and Museum Service. [Circulated typescript report]

Wilkinson, A J, 1986, *Salisbury Plain Training Area Archaeological Working Party, Report 1984-5.* Bristol. Property Services Agency. [Circulated typescript report]

Woodward, P J, 1991, Appendix 4. The erosion and damage to the archaeological landscape. In P J Woodward, *The South Dorset Ridgeway Survey and Excavations 1977-84* (= DNHAS Monograph 8). Dorchester. DNHAS. 172-3

Notes: (1) The National Trust has an on-going, and very extensive, programme of property surveys that include resource assessment. (2) Desk-top assessments, field evaluation reports, and environmental statements related to particular development proposals or the formulation of management plans, many of which include resource assessments, are not covered here. See: Darvill, T, Burrow, S, and Wildgust, D A, 1994, *The assessment gazetteer, 1982-1991* (= British Archaeological Bibliography Supplement 1). London. CBA

A.4 Resource assessments for built-up land and urban areas

(Arranged by Government Office Region)

North East

Carver, M, and Gosling, P F, 1976, The archaeology of Durham City. In P A G Clack and P F Gosling (eds), *Archaeology in the North.* Durham. Northern Archaeological Survey. 132-45

Ellison, M, 1976, An archaeological survey of Berwick-upon-Tweed. In P A G Clack and P F Gosling (eds), *Archaeology in the North.* Durham. Northern Archaeological Survey. 147-64

Gosling, P F, 1976, An archaeological assessment of Barnard Castle. In P A G Clack and P F Gosling (eds), *Archaeology in the North*. Durham. Northern Archaeological Survey. 207-25

Harbottle, B, and Clack, P, 1976, Newcastle upon Tyne: archaeology and development. In P A G Clack and P F Gosling (eds), *Archaeology in the North*. Durham. Northern Archaeological Survey. 111-31

Lowther, P, Ebbartson, L, Ellison, M, and Millett, M, 1993, The city of Durham: an archaeological survey. *Durham Archaeological Journal*, 9, 27-119

McDougall, J M, and Meyer, G, 1978, *Stockton-on-Tees: an assessment of the archaeological potential*. Middlesborough. Cleveland County Council

Smith, A N, 1984, *The archaeological potential of Stockton-on-Tees.* Middlesborough. Cleveland County Council

Tyson, P, 1976, Morpeth: an archaeological study. In P A G Clack and P F Gosling (eds), *Archaeology in the North*. Durham. Northern Archaeological Survey. 187-205

North West

Gosling, P F, 1976, Carlisle: an archaeological survey of the historic town. In P A G Clack and P F Gosling (eds), *Archaeology in the North.* Durham. Northern Archaeological Survey. 165-85

Hyde, E D, and Grealey, S, 1974, *Warrington New Town development: archaeological survey. Interim report.* Manchester. Archaeological Surveys Ltd

McCarthy, M, and Dodd, V J, 1990, *Carlisle: the historic environment.* Carlisle. Carlisle Archaeological Unit

Powesland, D J, 1974, *Stockport: an archaeological opportunity.* Stockport. Historic Stockport Research Committee

Thompson, P, 1981, *Middlewich: the archaeological potential of a town.* Chester. Cheshire County Council

Williams, B, 1978, *Archaeology in Nantwich.* Chester. Cheshire County Council

Winchester, A J L, 1979, *Cumbria historic towns survey, 1978-79*. Kendal. Cumbria County Council. [Circulated typescript report]

Merseyside

Yorkshire and Humberside

Addyman, P, 1974, York: the anatomy of a crisis in urban archaeology. In P A Rahtz (ed), *Rescue Archaeology.* Harmondsworth. Penguin. 153-62

Addyman, P, and Rumsby, J H, 1971, *The archaeological implications of proposed development in York.* York. York Archaeological Trust

Andrews, G, 1984, Archaeology in York: an assessment. In P V Addyman and V E Black (eds), *Archaeological papers from York presented to M W Barley.* York. York Archaeological Trust. 173-208

Loughlin, N, 1975, *Kingston-upon-Hull: archaeology and redevelopment.* Hull. Hull Museums Service

Magilton, J R, 1977, *The Doncaster District: an archaeological survey*. Doncaster. Doncaster Museums and Arts Service

Ove Arup and Partners, 1991, *York development and archaeology Study.* York. York City Council and English Heritage

Pearson, T, 1987, ***An archaeological survey of Scarborough***. Birmingham. Birmingham University Field Archaeology Unit

Robinson, J F, 1978, ***The archaeology of Malton and Norton***. Leeds. Yorkshire Archaeological Society

East Midlands
Colyer, C, 1975, ***Lincoln: the archaeology of an historic city***. Lincoln. Lincoln Archaeological Trust

Doe, V, Fowkes, D V, and Riden, P, 1973, ***Discovering early Chesterfield: the archaeological implications of redevelopment in central Chesterfield***. Chesterfield. Chesterfield Archaeological Research Committee

Everson, P, 1974, *'A good quick market toune.' Wellingborough: archaeological implications of the central area redevelopment*. Northampton. Northamptonshire County Council

Field, N, 1978, ***Louth: the hidden town. A study of its archaeological potential***. Lincoln. North Lincolnshire Archaeological Unit

Harden, G, 1978, ***Medieval Boston and its archaeological implications***. Boston. South Lincolnshire Archaeological Unit

Hart, C, 1977, ***Bolsover: the archaeological implications of development***. Chesterfield. North Derbyshire Archaeological Trust

RCHME, 1977, ***The town of Stamford***. London. HMSO

West Midlands
Carver, M O H, 1978, Early Shrewsbury: an archaeological definition in 1975. ***Transactions of the Shropshire Archaeological Society,*** 59 (1973-4), 225-263

Carver, M O H, 1981, ***Underneath Stafford town***. Birmingham. Birmingham University Field Archaeology Unit

Carver, M, and Wills, J, 1974, ***Shrewsbury: the buried past. The threatened archaeology of Shrewsbury and its recovery***. Shrewsbury. Shrewsbury Archaeological Unit

Freezer, D F, 1978, ***From saltings to spa town: the archaeology of Droitwich***. Droitwich. Droitwich Archaeological Committee

Gould, J, 1976, ***Lichfield: archaeology and development***. Birmingham. West Midlands Archaeology Rescue Committee

Mytum, H, 1975, ***Warwick archaeology***. Warwick. Warwickshire County Museum

Rylatt, M, 1977, ***City of Coventry: archaeology and redevelopment***. Coventry. Coventry Museums

Sheridan, K, 1971, ***Tamworth development: the archaeological implications***. Tamworth. Tamworth Museum

Shoesmith, R, 1974, ***The city of Hereford: archaeology and development***. Hereford. West Midlands Rescue Archaeology Committee

Slater, T R, and Wilson, C, 1977, ***Archaeology and development in Stratford upon Avon***. Birmingham. University of Birmingham

Eastern Region
Bartlett, R, no date, ***Archaeology in Harlow: a policy for the future***. Harlow. Harlow Museum

Buckley, D, and Hope, J H, no date, ***Archaeology in Braintree: a policy for the future***. Chelmsford. Essex County Council and Brain Valley Archaeological Society

Carr, R D, 1975, The archaeological potential of Bury St Edmunds. ***East Anglian Archaeology***, 1, 46-56

Crummy, P, 1975, ***Not only a matter of time: a survey outlining the archaeology of the Colchester District and methods of counteracting the erosion of its archaeological remains***. Colchester. Colchester Excavation Committee

Eddy, M R, and Petchey, M R, 1983, ***Historic towns in Essex***. Chelmsford. Essex County Council

Essex County Council, 1989, ***Archaeology in Chelmsford: a policy for the future***. Chelmsford. Essex County Council

Hassall, J, and Baker, D, 1974, Bedford: aspects of town origins and development. ***Bedfordshire Archaeological Journal,*** 9, 75-94

RCHME, 1969, ***Peterborough New Town. A survey of the antiquities in the areas of development***. London. HMSO

West, S E (ed), 1973, ***Ipswich: the archaeological implications of development***. Ipswich. SCOLE Committee

London
Andrews, G, Hinton, P, and Thomas, R (eds), forthcoming, ***London assessment document***. London. English Heritage

Biddle, M, Hudson, D, and Heighway, C, 1973, ***The future of London's past: a survey of the archaeological implications of planning and development in the nation's capital***. Worcester. RESCUE

Canham, R, 1978, ***2000 years of Brentford***. London. HMSO

Collins, D, MacDonald, J, Barratt, J, Canham, R, Merrifield, R, and Hurst, J, 1976, *The archaeology of the London area: current knowledge and problems* (= London and Middlesex Archaeological Society Special Paper 1). London. London and Middlesex Archaeological Society

ILAU (Inner London Archaeology Unit), 1976, *The archaeology of Kensington and Chelsea*. London. ILAU

ILAU (Inner London Archaeology Unit), no date, *The archaeology of Hackney*. London. ILAU

ILAU (Inner London Archaeology Unit), no date, *The archaeology of Tower Hamlets*. London. ILAU

ILAU (Inner London Archaeology Unit), no date, *The archaeology of Islington*. London. ILAU

Kingston upon Thames Archaeological Society, 1973, *Archaeology and development: Royal Borough of Kingston upon Thames*. Kingston upon Thames. Kingston upon Thames Archaeological Society

South East
Aldsworth, F, and Freke, D, 1976, *Historic towns in Sussex: an archaeological survey*. London. Sussex Archaeological Field Unit

Andrews, G, 1985, *The archaeology of Canterbury: an assessment*. London. English Heritage

Astill, G, 1978, *Historic towns in Berkshire: an archaeological appraisal*. Reading. Berkshire Archaeological Committee

Benson, D, and Cook, J M, 1966, *City of Oxford redevelopment: archaeological implications.* Oxford. Oxford City Museum

Blair, J, 1976, *Discovering early Leatherhead: a preliminary survey* (Leatherhead and District Local History Society Occasional Paper 1). Leatherhead. Leatherhead and District Local History Society

Champion, S, 1973, *Andover: the archaeological implications of development*. Andover. Andover and District Excavation Committee

Fasham, P, 1972, The archaeological implications of redevelopment in Banbury. *Cake and Cockhorse*, 5.3, 49-56

Gardiner, M, 1992, *An assessment of the archaeological potential of Seaford*. London. South East Archaeological Services

Hughes, M F, 1976, *The small towns of Hampshire.* Winchester. Hampshire County Council

Millard, L, 1975, *A report on the archaeological implications of development in Canterbury* (Second edition). Canterbury. City of Canterbury Amenities and Recreation Department

O'Connell, M G, 1977, *Historic towns in Surrey* (= Research Volume of the Surrey Archaeological Society 5). Guildford. Surrey Archaeological Society

Schadla-Hall, R T, 1977, *Winchester District. The archaeological potential.* Winchester. Winchester District Council

Simpson, C, 1973, *Wallingford: the archaeological implications of development*. Oxford.

Simpson, C, 1973, *Buckingham implication survey*. Buckingham. Buckinghamshire County Museum

Wilkinson, D R P, 1990, *Historic Dover: an archaeological implications survey of the town*. Dover. Oxford Archaeological Unit and Dover District Council

South West
Aldred, D, 1976, *Bishop's Cleeve: archaeology and planning. An assessment of the history and archaeology of the village with planning recommendations to safeguard its historic environment.* Tewkesbury. Tewkesbury Borough Council

Aston, M, and Leech, R, 1977, *Historic towns in Somerset* (= CRAAGS Survey 2). Bristol. CRAAGS

Borthwick, A, and Chandler, J, 1984, *Our chequered past: the archaeology of Salisbury.* Trowbridge. Wiltshire County Council Library and Museum Service

Darvill, T and Gerrard, C, 1994, *Cirencester: town and landscape*. Cirencester. Cotswold Archaeological Trust

Dunning, R (ed), 1977, *Taunton: history, archaeology and development*. Taunton. Taunton Research and Excavation Committee

Ellison, A, 1983, *Medieval villages in south-east Somerset. A survey of the archaeological implications of development within 93 surviving medieval villages in south-east Somerset* (= WAT Survey 6). Bristol. WAT

Haslam, J, 1976, *Wiltshire towns: the archaeological potential*. Devizes. Wiltshire Archaeological and Natural History Society

Heighway, C M, 1974, *Archaeology in Gloucester: a policy for City and District*. Gloucester. Gloucester City Council. [Circulated typescript report]

Leech, R, 1975, *Small medieval towns in Avon: archaeology and planning* (= CRAAGS Survey 1). Bristol. CRAAGS

Leech, R, 1981, *Historic towns in Gloucestershire* (= CRAAGS Survey 3). Bristol. CRAAGS

Miles, D, and Fowler, P J, 1972, *Tewkesbury: the archaeological implications of development*. Tewkesbury. Tewkesbury Archaeological and Architectural Committee

Penn, K J, 1980, *Historic towns of Dorset*. Dorchester. DNHAS

Rodwell, K, (ed), 1975, *Historic towns in Oxfordshire: a survey of the new county*. Oxford. Oxford Archaeological Unit

Saville, A, 1975, *Pre-Regency Cheltenham: an archaeological survey*. Cheltenham. Cheltenham Art Gallery and Museum

Sheppard, P, 1980, *The historic towns of Cornwall*. Truro. Cornwall Committee for Rescue Archaeology

Wingfield, D E V, 1979, *Penryn. Archaeology and development: a survey*. Truro. Institute of Cornish Studies and Cornwall Committee for Rescue Archaeology

Note: In 1996 English Heritage launched two new programmes of resource assessment for urban areas: Intensive Urban Assessments for about 30 or so large towns, and Extensive Urban Assessments for a wide range of other towns. See: Croft, B, Schofield, J, and Webster, C, 1996, Managing archaeology in historic towns. *Conservation Bulletin*, 30, 18-19

APPENDIX B
Select bibliography of scientific and experimental studies relating to decay processes in archaeological materials, sites and structures

B.1 Studies of artefact decay

Andrews, P, 1995, Experiments in taphonomy. *Journal of Archaeological Science*, 22, 147-53

Boddy, L, and Ainsworth, A M, 1984, Decomposition of Neolithic wood from the Sweet Track. *Somerset Levels Papers*, 10, 92-6

Franklin, U M, and Vitali, V, 1985, The environmental stability of ancient ceramics. *Archaeometry*, 27.1, 3-15

Nash, D, and Petraglia, M D (eds), 1987, *Natural formation processes and the archaeological record* (= BAR International Series 352). Oxford. British Archaeological Reports

Newton, R G, 1985, The Ballidon glass burial experiment. *Glass Technology*, 26, 293

Odell, G H, and Cowan, F, 1987, Estimating tillage effects on artefact distributions. *American Antiquity*, 52, 456-84

Pollard, B L, 1994, The disappearing bronze. *Coventry District Archaeological Society Bulletin*, 312, 8

Pryor, J H, 1988, The effects of human trample damage on lithics: a consideration of crucial variables. *Lithic Technology*, 17, 45-50

Reynolds, P, 1989, Sherd movement in the ploughsoil. *British Archaeology*, 13, 24-7

Reynolds, P, 1989, The ploughzone and prehistoric pottery. *British Archaeology*, 12, 24-6

Rick, J W, 1976, Downslope movement and archaeological intra-site spatial analysis. *American Antiquity*, 41, 133-44

Roper, D, 1976, Later displacement of artefacts due to plowing. *American Antiquity*, 41, 372-5

Rottlander, R, 1975 The formation of patina on flint. *Archaeometry*, 17, 106-10

Shackley, M L, 1978, The behaviour of artefacts as sedimentary particles in a fluviatile environment. *Archaeometry*, 20, 55-61

Smith, C S, 1976, Some speculation on the corrosion of ancient metals. *Archaeometry*, 18, 114-16

Stein, J K, and Teltser, P A, 1989, Size distributions of artefact classes: combining macro and micro fractions. *Geoarchaeology*, 4, 1-30

Swain, H, 1988, Pottery survival in the field: some initial results of experiments in frost shattering. *Scottish Archaeological Review*, 5, 87-9

Yorston, R M, Gaffney, V L, and Reynolds, P J, 1990, Simulation of artefact movement due to cultivation. *Journal of Archaeological Science*, 17, 63-83

B.2 Studies of ecofact decay and the degradation of environmental materials

Andrews, P, and Cook, J, 1985, Natural modifications to bones in a temperate setting. *Man* (NS), 20, 675-691

Armour-Chelu, M, and Andrews, P, 1994, Some effects of bioturbation by earthworms (oligochaeta) on archaeological sites. *Journal of Archaeological Science*, 21, 433-43

Atkinson, R J C, 1957, Worms and weathering. *Antiquity*, 31, 219-33

Bell, L S, 1990, Palaeopathology and diagenesis: an SEM evaluation of structural changes using backscatter electronic imaging. *Journal of Archaeological Science*, 17, 85-102

Bell, L S, Boyde, A B, and Jones, S J, 1991, Diagenetic alteration to teeth *in situ* illustrated by backscatter electron imaging. *Scanning*, 13, 173-83

Bethell, P, 1989, The Leverhulme Project on decay and detection on archaeological sites: progress report. *Bulletin of the Sutton Hoo Research Committee*, 6, 21-23

Boddy, L, and Ainsworth, A M, 1984, Decomposition of Neolithic wood from the Sweet Track. *Somerset Levels Papers*, 10, 92-6

Cattaneo, C, Gelsthorpe, K, Phillips, P, and Sokol, R J, 1995, Differential survival of albumen in ancient bone. *Journal of Archaeological Science*, 22, 271-6

Child, A M, 1995, Towards an understanding of the microbial decomposition of archaeological bone in the burial environment. *Journal of Archaeological Science*, 22, 165-74

Evans, J, and Millett, M, 1992, Residuality revisited. *Oxford Journal of Archaeology*, 11, 225-40

Garland, A N, and Janaway, R C, 1989, The taphonomy of inhumation burials. In C Roberts, F Lee and J Binliffe (eds), *Burial archaeology: current research methods and developments* (= BAR British Series 211). Oxford. BAR. 15-37

Gilchrist, R, and Mytum, H, 1986, Experimental archaeology and burnt bone from archaeological sites. *Circaea*, 4, 29-38

Gordon, C G, and Buikstra, J E, 1981, Soil pH, bone preservation and sampling bias at mortuary sites. *American Antiquity*, 116, 566-71

Hedges, R E M, and Millard, A R, 1995, Bones and groundwater: towards the modelling of diagenetic processes. *Journal of Archaeological Science*, 22, 155-64

Hedges, R E M, Millard, A R, and Pike, A W G, 1995, Measurements and relationships of diagenetic alteration of bone from three archaeological sites. *Journal of Archaeological Science*, 22, 201-9

Jambor, J, 1988, Changes in bones of prehistoric populations caused by environmental influence. *Anthropologie*, 26, 55-60

Lubinski, P M, 1996, Fish heads, fish heads: an experiment on differential bone preservation in a salmonid fish. *Journal of Archaeological Science*, 23, 175-81

McNeil, B, and Little, B J, 1992, Corrosion mechanisms for copper and silver objects in near-surface environments. *Journal of the American Institute of Conservation*, 31, 355-66

Mays, S, 1992, Taphonomic factors in a human skeletal assemblage. *Circaea*, 9, 54-8

Millard, A R, and Hedges, R E M, 1995, The role of the environment in uranium uptake by buried bone. *Journal of Archaeological Science,* 22, 239-50

Nicholson, R A, 1992, Bone survival: the effects of sedimentary abrasion and trampling on fresh and cooked bone. *International Journal of Osteoarchaeology*, 2, 79-90

Nicholson, R A, 1996, Bone degradation, burial medium and species representation: debunking the myths and experimental-based approach. *Journal of Archaeological Science*, 23, 513-33

Person, A, Bocherens, H, Saliège, J-F, Paris, F, Zeitaun, V, and Gérard, M, 1995, early diagenic evolution of bone phosphate: an x-ray diffractometry analysis. *Journal of Archaeological Science*, 22, 211-21

Pollard, A M, 1995, Groundwater modelling in archaeology - the need and the potential. In J Beavis and K Barker (eds), *Science and site* (= Bournemouth University School of Conservation Sciences Occasional Paper 1). London. Archetype. 93-8

Price, T D, Blitz, J, Burton, J, and Ezzo, J A, 1992, Diagenesis in prehistoric bone: problems and solutions. *Journal of Archaeological Science*, 19, 513-29

Rink, W J, and Schwarcz, H P, 1995, Tests for diagenesis in tooth enamel: ERS dating signals and carbonate contents. *Journal of Archaeological Science*, 22, 251-5

Robinson, D E (ed), 1990, *Experimentation and reconstruction in environmental archaeology* (= Oxbow Monograph 5). Oxford. Oxbow Books

White, E M, and Hannus, L A, 1983, Chemical weathering of bone in archaeological soils. *American Antiquity*, 48, 316-22

B.3 Studies in monument decay

Clark, R H, and Schofield, A J, 1991, By experiment and calibration: an integrated approach to archaeology of the ploughsoil. In A J Schofield (ed), *Interpreting artefact scatters. Contributions to ploughzone archaeology* (= Oxbow Monograph 4). Oxford. Oxbow Books. 93-105

Nielson, A E, 1991, Trampling the archaeological record: an experimental study. *American Antiquity*, 56, 483-503

Williams, R G B, 1958, Frost and the works of Man. *Antiquity*, 47, 19-31

B.4 Experimental earthworks and features

General

Bell, M, Fowler, P J, and Hillson, S W (eds), 1996, *The Experimental Earthwork Project 1960-1992* (= CBA Research Report 100). London. CBA

Coles, J M, 1973, *Archaeology by experiment*. London. Hutchinson

Coles, J M, 1979, *Experimental archaeology*. London. Academic Press

Crabtree, K, 1990, Experimental earthworks in the United Kingdom. In D E Robinson (ed), ***Experimentation and reconstruction in environmental archaeology*** (= Oxbow Monographs 5). Oxford. Oxbow Books. 225-35

Curwen, E C, 1930, The silting of ditches in chalk. ***Antiquity***, 4, 97-100

Fowler, P J, 1984, Experimental earthworks in England. ***Bulletin of Experimental Archaeology***, 5, 24-32

Fowler, P J, 1989, The experimental earthworks: a summary of the Project's first thirty years. The thirteenth Beatrice de Cardi lecture. ***Annual Report of the Council for British Archaeology***, 39, 83-98

Proudfoot, B, 1964, Experimental earthworks in the British Isles. ***Geographical Review***, 54, 584-6

Reynolds, P J, 1989, Experimental earthworks. ***British Archaeology***, 14, 16-19

Bascomb Earthwork, Hampshire
Reynolds, P J, 1996, The experimental domestic octagonal earthworks. In M Bell, P J Fowler and S W Hillson (eds), ***The Experimental Earthwork Project 1960-1992*** (= CBA Research Report 100). London. CBA. 225-7

Butser Demonstration Area Earthwork and Pits, Petersfield, Hampshire
Reynolds, P J, 1974, Experimental storage pits: an interim report. ***Proceedings of the Prehistoric Society***, 40, 118-31

Reynolds, P J, 1979, ***Iron-Age Farm. The Butser experiment***. London. Colonnade Books

Cranborne Chase, Dorset
Percival, J, 1980, ***Living in the past.*** London. BBC

Fishbourne Earthwork, West Sussex
Reynolds, P J, 1996, The experimental domestic octagonal earthworks. In M Bell, P J Fowler and S W Hillson (eds), ***The Experimental Earthwork Project 1960-1992*** (= CBA Research Report 100). London. CBA. 225-7

Little Butser Earthwork, Hampshire
Reynolds, P J, 1996, The experimental domestic octagonal earthworks. In M Bell, P J Fowler and S W Hillson (eds), ***The Experimental Earthwork Project 1960-1992*** (= CBA Research Report 100). London. CBA. 225-7

Morden Bog, Wareham, Dorset
Evans, J G, and Limbrey, S, 1974, The experimental earthwork on Morden Bog, Wareham, Dorset, England, 1963-1972. ***Proceedings of the Prehistoric Society***, 40, 170-202

Hillson, S W, 1996, The experimental earthwork on Morden Bog, Wareham 1973 (10th year) to 1990 (27th year). In M Bell, P J Fowler and S W Hillson (eds), ***The Experimental Earthwork Project 1960-1992*** (= CBA Research Report 100). London. CBA. 210-24

Overton Down, West Overton, Wiltshire
Ashbee, P, and Cornwall, I W, 1961, An experiment in field archaeology. ***Antiquity***, 35, 129-134

Bell, M, 1996, Overton Down 1992 excavation (32nd year). In M Bell, P J Fowler and S W Hillson (eds), ***The Experimental Earthwork Project 1960-1992*** (= CBA Research Report 100). London. CBA. 66-89

Dimbleby, G W, 1965, Overton Down experimental earthwork. ***Antiquity***, 39, 134-36

Fowler, P J, 1996, The 1968 Overton excavation (8th year). In M Bell, P J Fowler and S W Hillson (eds), ***The Experimental Earthwork Project 1960-1992*** (= CBA Research Report 100). London. CBA. 27-33

Fowler, P J, 1996, The 1976 Overton Excavation (16th year). In M Bell, P J Fowler and S W Hillson (eds), ***The Experimental Earthwork Project 1960-1992*** (= CBA Research Report 100). London. CBA. 34-42

Jewell, P A, (ed), 1963, ***The experimental earthwork on Overton Down, Wiltshire 1960***. London. British Association for the Advancement of Science

Jewell, P A, and Dimbleby, G W (eds), 1966, The experimental earthwork on Overton Down, Wiltshire, England: the first four years. ***Proceedings of the Prehistoric Society***, 32, 313-42

Wroughton Earthwork, Wiltshire
Reynolds, P J, 1985, ***Research earthworks, Wroughton, base data 1985***. Petersfield. Butser Ancient Farm Project Trust

Reynolds, 1996, Experimental domestic octagonal earthworks. In M Bell, P J Fowler and S W Hillson, ***The Experimental Earthwork Project 1960-1992*** (= CBA Research Report 100). London. CBA. 225-7

B.5 Simulation studies

Boismier, W A, 1997, ***Modelling the effects of tillage processes on artefact distributions in the plough zone. A simulation study of tillage induced pattern formation*** (= BAR British Series 259). Oxford. Archaeopress

Wainwright, J, 1994, Erosion of archaeological sites: results and implications of a site simulation model. ***Geoarchaeology***, 9, 173-201

B.6 Site decay monitoring projects

General

Corfield, M, 1994, Monitoring archaeological sites. **English Heritage Scientific Technical Supplement**, 3, 2-3

Corfield, M, no date **Monitoring the condition of waterlogged archaeological sites**. London. English Heritage. [Circulated typescript report]

Brading Roman Villa, Isle of Wight

Knight, B, 1994, **Environmental monitoring at Brading Roman villa, Isle of Wight** (= Ancient Monuments Laboratory Report 57/94). London. English Heritage. [Circulated typescript report]

Trow, S, 1998, Mosaicing the mosaic. **Conservation Bulletin**, 33, 11

Market Deeping, Lincolnshire

Corfield, M, 1994, Monitoring archaeological sites. **English Heritage Science and Technology Supplement**, 3, 2-3

Marks and Spencer, 44-5 Parliament Street, York

Oxley, J, forthcoming, Monitoring archaeological deposit condition in Parliament Street York.

Owmby-by-Spital, Lincolnshire

CAS, 1996, Owmby-by-Spital, Lincolnshire, conservation and management of a plough damaged site. **Archaeology Review 1995-96**, 29

CAS, 1997, Owmby-by-Spital, Lincolnshire, conservation and management of a plough damaged site. **Archaeology Review 1996-97**, 29-30

CAS, 1998, Omby-by-Spital, Lincolnshire, conservation and management of a plough damaged site. **Archaeology Review 1996-97**, 33-4

Rockbourne Long Barrow, Hampshire

Wilson, P R, 1991, Rockbourne. Tenantry Farm long barrow. **Archaeology in Hampshire**, 1991, 54-5

Rose Theatre, Southwark Bridge Road, London

Ashurst, J, Balaam, N, and Foley, K, 1989, The Rose Theatre. **Conservation Bulletin**, 9, 9-10

Somerset Levels, Somerset

Anon, 1998, The Sweet Track, the Brue Valley, Somerset: assessment of *in situ* preservation. **Archaeology Review 1996-97**, 61-2

Brunning, R, 1995, Sweet Track assessment: an interim report. **Archaeology in the Severn Estuary**, 6, 1-3

Brunning, R, 1996, Preservation *in situ* of the Sweet Track. **News WARP**, 20, 34-5

Cox, M J, Jones, E B G, and Hogan, D V, 1995, Wetsite curation and monitoring in the Somerset Levels and Moors. In J Beavis and K Barker (eds), **Science and site** (= Bournemouth University School of Conservation Sciences Occasional Paper 1). London. Archetype. 78-92

B.7 Scientific deposit and artefact assessment methodologies

Grattan, D W, and Mathias, C, 1986, Analysis of waterlogged wood: the value of chemical analysis and other simple methods in evaluating condition. **Somerset Levels Papers**, 12, 6-12

Mouzouras, R, Jones, M A, Jones, E B G, and Rule, M H, 1990, Non-destructive evaluation of hull and stored timbers from the Tudor ship Mary Rose. **Studies in Conservation**, 35, 173-88

Murphy, P, and Wiltshire, P E J, 1994, A proposed scheme for evaluating plant macrofossil preservation in some archaeological deposits, **Circaea**, 11, 1-6

APPENDIX C
Measuring monuments: quantifications of areal extent, height, depth and volume

C.1 Areal extent

Three types of measurements focus on the spatial extent of monuments in the horizontal plane, recognizing that the topography of that plane may affect dimensions. In general they reflect quite distinct facets of the data: the original extent of a monument, the size of a monument as represented by all available archaeological information, and the extent of the physically surviving portions of a monument at some specified time.

Estimated Original Extent (EOE)
Axiomatic to most archaeological work is the idea that some kind of reality existed in the past; it therefore follows that archaeological monuments must at one time have been in some sense 'complete' even if they are now only represented as fragments. In conceiving of the original entity, usually with some knowledge drawn from excavated examples of the same class to suggest what such monuments were like, it should be possible to make an estimate of its original physical extent, usually its maximum physical extent in order fully to take account of multi-period evolving monuments.

Estimating extents means defining boundaries or edges. It is accepted that such edges are often difficult to determine, subjective, and in some cases arbitrary because one monument conjoins another. In some senses the edges can be visualized as fracture-lines in what must, in conceptual terms, be seen as a continuous space representing the environment in which people operated.

For a monument such as a Roman fort, a Bronze Age round barrow or even a deserted medieval village the original edges can be fairly easily projected even if only fragments remain visible. The edges are defined in pragmatic ways based on available interpretations. Thus a Roman fort can be seen as one unit, an adjacent vicus as a second, and perhaps the nearby cemetery as a third. The aim is to produce units for analysis and comparison, not elaborate interpretative statements about what the archaeology means and how it fits together.

Monuments such as prehistoric field systems are more difficult, but the principles remain the same. With a little research it should be possible to come up with some kind of plan of the original monument, at least in broad terms, and this forms the basis for calculating the area. Reconstructing big pictures from small amounts of information is what archaeologists are generally good at, always accepting that the vision which is created is provisional.

Most difficult of all in terms of defining their original extent are extensive areas of overlapping and variously superimposed features such as typically occur with the 'spaghetti-like' blocks of cropmarks in midland and southern England. Much important research has been directed to finding ways of unpicking such tangles of features (Edis et al. 1989; Palmer and Cox 1993), and carefully done this produces useful results both in terms of creating a record of what there is, and as a basis for making interpretative statements.

Projected Archaeological Extent (PAE)
As discussed in Chapter 2, the archaeological record is itself a series of structured observations or events (above referred to as 'sites'). These vary considerably in size and quality, but represent the empirical basis upon which imposed interpretations (monument level) are founded. Some monuments will be known only through data derived from one site; others will be known from many sites, some overlapping and some discrete, and most likely recorded at many different dates (e.g. nineteenth century antiquarian observation, 1940s aerial photography and a 1990s excavation). The cumulative results of all archaeological studies of a monument can be projected to provide an important measure of what is actually known about the extent of a monument. It is a point-in-time measurement because further work may either increase or decrease it.

This measurement is here called the 'Projected Archaeological Extent', although during the early stages of MARS it was referred to as the 'Greatest Recorded Area'. The latter term was dropped because it seemed to cause a degree of confusion with many of those consulted. The main stumbling block was the misapprehension that the measurement was based on whatever record provided the single largest estimate, rather than taking into account all available records. It was also felt that such a measurement involved a degree of 'projection' when trying to combine the implications of several records, and that accordingly this word should be used in the term eventually adopted. However, the key word in the term is 'archaeological' because this measurement is based on the results of archaeological studies rather than on inference and interpretation as in the case of the Estimated Original Extent. Logically, the Projected Archaeological Extent must be the same as or less than the Estimated Original Extent.

Inevitably there are practical limitations on the calculation of the PAE, not least of which are the line thickness and map scales used to depict monuments. A margin of error must be accepted at this stage, and hopefully improved upon in future. Some experiments were carried out with the digitizing of outlines as a series of closed polygons. These can be measured and mapped in great detail, new material being added quickly and easily as it becomes available.

Current Area (CA)
Monuments occupy physical spaces, and thus the amount of space occupied can be measured at any given point in time for which relevant data exist or can be collected.

A prerequisite, however, is some knowledge of where the monument is (an accurate location) and information about its Projected Archaeological Extent. Comparing the PAE with what can be seen on the ground allows a Current Area to be calculated. In this, account must be taken of upstanding and buried remains such as they have been recorded. Since the measurement of Current Area relates to extent, the existence of intact undisturbed land surfaces over buried deposits is taken as evidence for the continued existence of some archaeologically recoverable remains.

In practice, Current Area is the easiest dimension to quantify. Inevitably, these measurements must be regarded as estimates based on the recovery of critical dimensions. In the case of small monuments, these dimensions can be physically measured using hand-tapes or portable EDMs and the areas calculated. Exactly where measurements are taken from and to is a matter of professional judgement, based on a general knowledge of the type of monument in question and any available information about the particular monument being examined. For larger monuments, area can be measured from detailed plans validated by field inspection.

Current Area can also be calculated for earlier times where independent data exist from which measurements can be made. The usual source is vertical aerial photographs. Measurements can be scaled off the prints, and areas calculated. Planimeters can also be used to measure the area of irregular polygons. The Current Area will normally be the same as, or less than, the PAE and EOA, although there may be instances where the decay of a monument involves an increase in physical extent, as when buildings or mounds have gradually spread outwards as their height diminished.

C.2 Height and depth: vertical measurements

A second relevant variable to set alongside area measurements is the vertical dimension in terms of the height and depth of deposit. In their original form, some monuments were predominantly below ground (e.g. flint mines), others were predominantly above ground (e.g. long barrows), while yet others involved a roughly equal proportion of both (e.g. causewayed enclosures). In some cases, of course, the processes of decay will change the balance between above- and below-ground level components. For ease of estimation, maximum height and depth measurements should be considered.

Estimated Maximum Original Height (EMOH)
This can be based on general understandings of the class of monument, construction materials, situation, and other relevant factors. Thus the Maximum Original Height is an estimate of the distance between the ground level (averaged if sloping) and what is believed to have been the highest point.

Estimated Maximum Original Depth (EMOD)
Again this can be based on general understandings of the class of monument, construction materials, situation and other relevant factors. Thus the Maximum Original Depth is an estimate of the distance between ground level (averaged if sloping) to the bottom of what is believed to have been the deepest feature.

Projected Maximum Archaeological Height (PMAH)
This estimate is based on the cumulative record of what has actually been recorded about a monument, in this case its above-ground components. Thus the Projected Maximum Archaeological Height is the greatest observed distance between ground level (averaged if sloping) and the highest recorded point. The PMAH cannot exceed the EOMH.

Projected Maximum Archaeological Depth (PMAD)
This estimate is again based on the cumulative record of what has actually been recorded, in this case for below-ground components. Thus the Projected Maximum Archaeological Depth is the greatest observed distance between ground level (averaged if sloping) and the bottom of the deepest recorded feature. The PMAD cannot exceed the EOMD.

Current Maximum Height (CMH)
This estimate is based on measurements recorded at a particular point in time. Thus the Current Maximum Height is the greatest observed distance between ground level (averaged if sloping) and the highest point surviving on the monument. Current Maximum Height can sometimes be determined for earlier times where authentic records exist. In general, however, these are limited because precise height measurements cannot easily be made from aerial photographs. Earlier surveys are the main source. The CMH measurement cannot exceed the PMAH or the EOMH.

Current Maximum Depth (CMD)
This estimate is again based on measurements recorded at a particular point in time. Thus the Current Maximum Depth is the greatest observed distance between ground level (averaged if sloping) and the bottom of the deepest recorded feature. The CMD measurement cannot exceed the PMAD or the EOMD.

C.3 Volume measurements

Archaeological monuments do not only have horizontal and vertical dimensions, they also have mass or volume. This will include above- and below-ground elements. It is, however, the most difficult measure to estimate; determining the volume of irregular solids is extremely complicated.

Estimated Original Volume (EOV)
This estimate is based on a general understanding of the structure of a monument during its life, accepting that it may change shape through modification and use over time. Account must be taken of all archaeological and structural deposits which comprise the monument.

Projected Archaeological Volume (PAV)
This estimate is based on the cumulative data available about a particular monument, ignoring elements that are thought to exist but for which there is no recorded evidence. Based on what is known, a general indication of volume can be projected. The PAV cannot be greater than the EOV.

Current Volume (CV)

This measure is a point-in-time assessment of the volume of deposits remaining, or believed to remain, *in situ* at a monument. The CV cannot exceed the EOV or the PAV.

APPENDIX D
Archaeological data sources consulted by the MARS Project to obtain information for the National Survey, and local SMR data for sample transects

Avon County Council (Bristol) [+ Bath City*]
Bedfordshire County Council (Bedford)
Berkshire County Council (Reading)*
Buckinghamshire County Council (Aylesbury)
Cambridgeshire County Council (Cambridge)
Cheshire County Council (Chester)
Cleveland County Council (Middlesborough)*
Cornwall County Council (Truro)*
Cumbria County Council (Kendal)
Derbyshire County Council (Matlock)
Devon County Council (Exeter)* [+ Plymouth City*]
Dorset County Council (Dorchester)
Durham County Council (Durham)*
East Sussex County Council (Lewes)*
Essex County Council (Chelmsford)
Gloucestershire County Council (Gloucester) [+ Gloucester City* + Cirencester UAD*]
Greater London (London)
Greater Manchester (Manchester)
Hampshire County Council (Winchester) [+ Winchester City]
Hereford and Worcester County Council (Worcester)*
Hertfordshire County Council (Hertford)*
Humberside County Council (Beverley)
Isle of Wight County Council (Newport)*
Kent County Council (Maidstone)*
Lancashire County Council (Lancaster)*
Leicestershire County Council (Leicester)*
Lincolnshire County Council (Lincoln)* [+ Boston Borough Council (Heckington)* + North Kesteven DC (Heckington)*
        + South Kesteven DC (Heckington)*]
Merseyside (Liverpool)
Norfolk County Council (Dereham)*
Northamptonshire County Council (Northampton)
Northumberland County Council (Morpeth)
North Yorkshire County Council (Northallerton)* [+ Yorkshire Dales National Park (Bainbridge)* + York City *]
Nottinghamshire County Council (Nottingham)*
Oxfordshire County Council (Oxford)*
Shropshire County Council (Shrewsbury)
Somerset County Council (Taunton)*
South Yorkshire (Sheffield)
Staffordshire County Council (Stafford)
Suffolk County Council (Bury St Edmunds)
Surrey County Council (Kingston-upon-Thames)*
Tyne and Wear (Newcastle)
Warwickshire County Council (Warwick)
West Midlands (Solihull) [+ Birmingham City]
West Sussex County Council (Chichester)
West Yorkshire (Wakefield)*
Wiltshire County Council (Trowbridge)*

* Indicates that these organizations were visited by the National Survey Team

APPENDIX E
Data fields used in the MARS National Survey

Survey details:
SMR location [Address]
SMR officer [Name]
Date of survey [Date]
Name of respondent [Name]
System coverage [Type/text]

Composition and period breakdown:
All records [Count for each period]
Monuments [Count for each period, split for monuments and buildings]
Archaeological urban areas [Count for each period]
Archaeological landscapes [Count for each period]
Stray finds [Count for each period]
Miscellaneous records [Count for each period]

Sample monument classes:
Post-medieval [Counts for the following classes: Lime kiln; Bell foundry; Town defences/seige works; Canal; Ice house; Charcoal burning site; Decoy pond; Smelt mill]
Medieval [Counts for the following classes: Deserted/shrunken village; Battlefield; Motte; Windmill mound; Pele tower; Tile kiln]
Early medieval [Counts for the following classes: Cemetery; Settlement]
Roman [Counts for the following classes: Fort; Roman road; Vicus; Villa; Amphitheatre; Colonia; Pottery kiln; Shrine/temple]
Prehistoric [Counts for the following classes: Palisaded settlement; Cursus; Flint scatter; Enclosed settlement; Henge; Stone circle; Chambered tomb; Mortuary enclosure]
Uncertain [Counts for the following classes: Dovecote; Stepping stones; Square barrow; Moot; Hill figure; Dyke; Field system; Burnt mound]

Designations:
Archaeological [Counts for all periods for: SAM; Guardianship; Local authority guardianship; World Heritage Site; County desigation; not designated]
Countryside [Counts for all periods for: AONB; Conservation area; SSSI; County designation; No designation]

Accession status:
All records [Count]
Monuments [Count]
Archaeological urban areas [Count]
Archaeological landscapes [Count]
Stray finds [Count]
Miscellaneous [Count]

SMR history:
Date established [Date]
Initial data format(s) [Format type]
Record development: 1960s, 1970s, 1980s, 1990s [Free text]
Recording criteria [Free text]

Recorded land-use (rural and built up):
All records [Counts for all periods]
Monuments [Counts for all periods. Split between monuments and buildings]
Archaeological urban areas [Counts for all periods]
Archaeological landscapes [Counts for all periods]
Stray finds [Counts for all periods]
Miscellaneous [Counts for all periods]

Monument accessibility:
Monuments on public land with free access [Count]
Monuments accessible for a fee [Count]
Monuments accessible via a right of way [Count]
Total monuments on private land [Count]

Recorded condition and survival:
Recorded monument survival [Counts for all periods and all states]
Survival grading criteria [Free text]
Recorded monument condition [Counts for all periods and all types]
Condition grading criteria [Free text]

APPENDIX F
Fieldwork timetable

Avon	December 1994 to February 1995
Berkshire	February 1996
Buckinghamshire	July 1995 to September 1995
Cambridgeshire	February 1995 to April 1995
Cheshire	October 1995 to December 1995
Cleveland	April 1995
Cornwall	June 1995 to October 1995
Cumbria	July 1995 to December 1995
Derbyshire	July 1995 to October 1995
Devon	October 1995 to January 1996
Dorset	April 1995 to July 1995
Durham	April 1995 to June 1995
East Sussex	May 1995 to August 1995
Essex	September 1995 to November 1995
Gloucestershire	September 1995 to November 1995
Greater London	April 1995 to June 1995
Greater Manchester	January 1996
Hampshire	August 1994 to January 1995
Hereford and Worcester	October 1995 to March 1996
Hertfordshire	November 1994 to February 1995
Humberside	September 1994 to December 1994
Isle of Wight	September 1994
Kent	January 1995 to May 1995
Lancashire	December 1995 to March 1996
Leicestershire	September 1995
Lincolnshire	November 1995 to March 1996
Merseyside	December 1995
Norfolk	April 1995 to August 1995
Northamptonshire	September 1994 to November 1995
Northumberland	May 1995
North Yorkshire	January 1995 to May 1995
Nottinghamshire	October 1995
Oxfordshire	January 1996 to March 1996
Shropshire	January 1995 to May 1995
Somerset	January 1995 to April 1995
South Yorkshire	November 1994 to January 1995
Staffordshire	October 1994 to January 1995
Suffolk	November 1995 to January 1996
Surrey	June 1995
Tyne and Wear	May 1995
Warwickshire	May 1995 to July 1995
West Midlands	September 1994 to November 1994
West Sussex	July 1995 to September 1995
West Yorkshire	June 1995 to August 1995
Wiltshire	September 1994 to December 1994

APPENDIX G
Table of data fields used in the Field Survey and Aerial Photographic Survey Programmes

Field name	Field type	Data source	Recording source
Transect number	I	M	Common
MARS site number	A	S/N	Common
County	A	S	Common
SMR number	I	N	Common
National Grid Reference	A	S/N	Common
Date of photograph	N	NL/C	AP
Photo scale	A	NL/C	AP
Quality	N	NL/C	AP
Vertical/Oblique	L	NL/C	AP
Photograph number/flight line	A	NL/C	AP
Period - SMR & MARS (validated)	A	S/N/M	Common
Type - SMR & MARS (validated)	A	S/N/M	Common
Designation(s) [e.g. SM, AONB]	A	S/N	Common
Date of designation	N	S/N	Common
Estimated original area	N	M	FS
Management agreement?	L	M	FS
Effect of management agreement	M	M	FS
Monument form	A	M	FS
Monument state	A	M	Both
Access	A	M	FS
Dominant geology	A	M	FS
Current Area 1995	N	M	FS
Current Area 1940 - 1980	N	NL/C	AP
Percentage Area Loss	S	M	FS
Percentage Height Loss	S	M	FS
Overall percentage volume loss	S	M	FS
Risk to monument	A	M	FS
Land-use(s) on the monument by %	A	M	Both
Land-use(s) around the monument by %	A	M	Both
Visibility	A	M	Both
Impact	A	M	Both
Subsurface damage visible?	A	M	FS
Cause of damage	A	M	Both
Type of damage (description)	M	M	Both
Conditions for survey	M	M	FS
Amelioration attempted?	L	M	FS
Effect of amelioration	M	M	FS
Recorder/date of interpretation	M	M	Both

Key:

Field type: I= Long integer; A= Alphanumeric; N= Numeric; L= Logical; M= Memo; S= Short integer

Data source: M= MARS; S= SMR; N= NMR; NL/C= NLAP/CUCAP

Recording source: Common= Data created when record established; FS= Field Survey Programme; AP= Aerial Photographic Survey Programme; Both = Field Survey Programme and Aerial Photographic Survey Programme

APPENDIX H
List of LUSAG land-use classes

The following list is taken from lists prepared by the Land Use Statistics Advisory Group (LUSAG 1993, Annexe C)

1. Agriculture
1.1   Field crop
1.2   Horticulture
1.3   Fallow land
1.4   Cropland with woody perennial crops
1.5   Improved pasture
1.6   Rough pasture

2. Woodland
2.1   Conifer woodland
2.2   Mixed woodland
2.3   Broadleaved woodland
2.4   Undifferentiated young woodland
2.5   Shrub
2.6   Felled woodland
2.7   Land cultivated for afforestation

3. Semi-natural vegetation
3.1   Rough grassland
3.2   Heathland
3.4   Upland grass moor
3.4   Bracken
3.5   Upland mosaic

4. Water and wetland
4.1   Sea/estuary
4.2   Standing water
4.3   Running water
4.4   Freshwater marsh
4.5   Salt marsh
4.6   Bog

5. Rock and coastal land
5.1   Inland rock
5.2   Coastal rocks and cliffs
5.3   Intertidal sand and mud
5.4   Dunes

6. Minerals and landfill
6.1   Mineral workings and quarries
6.2   Landfill waste disposal

7. Recreation
7.1   Leisure and recreational buildings
7.2   Outdoor recreation
7.3   Allotments
7.4   Golf courses

8. Transport
8.1   Roads
8.2   Public car parks
8.3   Railways
8.4   Airports
8.5   Docks

9. Residential
9.1   Residential houses and gardens
9.2   Institutional and communal accommodation

10. Community buildings
10.1   Institutional buildings
10.2   Educational buildings
10.3   Religious buildings

11. Industrial and commercial
11.1   Industry
11.2   Offices
11.3   Retailing
11.4   Storage and warehousing
11.5   Utilities
11.6   Agricultural buildings

12. Urban vacant land
12.1   Vacant land previously developed
12.2   Derelict land
12.3   Urban land not previously developed

APPENDIX I
Sites and areas investigated by the MARS Case Study Programme

I.1 Single monument studies

Causewayed enclosures:
    Etton, Cambridgeshire
    Briar Hill, Northamptonshire
    Offham Hill, West Sussex

Henges:
    Mt Pleasant, Dorset
    Devil's Quoits, Oxfordshire
    Mile Oak Farm, East Sussex

Long barrows:
    Hazleton North, Gloucestershire
    Giants' Hills 2, Lincolnshire
    Tiverton, Devon

Bronze Age round barrows:
    West Heath, West Sussex
    Deeping St Nicholas, Lincolnshire
    Cow Common, Gloucestershire

Multi-vallate hillforts:
    Danebury, Hampshire
    Ham Hill, Somerset

Roman forts:
    Ribchester, Lancashire
    Chester-le-Street, County Durham
    Lancaster, Lancashire

Minor Romano-British villas:
    Bancroft, Buckinghamshire
    Gorhambury, Hertfordshire
    Dalton Parlours, West Yorkshire

Roman roads:
    Old Ford, Greater London
    Scaftworth, Nottinghamshire
    East Stratton, Hampshire

Anglo-Saxon cemeteries:
    Apple Down, West Sussex
    Norton, Cleveland
    Christchurch, Dorset

Motte and bailey castles:
    Goltho, Lincolnshire
    Gloucester Old Castle, Gloucestershire
    Bentley Castle, Hampshire

DMVs:
    Thrislington, County Durham
    Caldecote, Buckinghamshire
    Foxcote, Hampshire

Glasshouses:
    Gawber, South Yorkshire
    Catcliffe, South Yorkshire
    Bridgewater, Somerset

I.2 Landscape studies

Arable:
    Skendleby, Lincolnshire

Coastlands and estuaries:
    Belle Tout, West Sussex
    Blackwater Estuary, Essex

Established grassland:	Knighton Down, Wiltshire
Industrial land:	South Shields, Tyne and Wear Castle Bolton and Area, North Yorkshire
Lowland heath:	Hartland Moor, Dorset
Parks and ornamental gardens:	Ashton Court Park, Avon Donnington Park, Leicestershire
Rivers, lakes and alluvian spreads:	Thames, Farmoor, Oxfordshire Ennerdale Water, Cumbria
Upland:	Roughtor Moor, Cornwall
Wetland:	Somerset Levels, Somerset
Woodland:	Kielder Forest, Northumberland New Forest, Hampshire

APPENDIX J
Table showing a comparison of county councils and metropolitan counties (as in 1995) with MARS Regions and regions defined by other authorities

J.1 Correspondence between MARS Regions, Government Office Regions and Government Statistical Regions

County	MARS Region	Government Office Region	Government Statistical Region
Avon	SW	SW	SW
Bedfordshire	EM	E	SW
Berkshire	SE	SE	SE
Buckinghamshire	EM	SE	SE
Cambridgeshire	EM	E	EA
Cheshire	NW	NW	NW
Cleveland	NE	NE	N
Cornwall	SW	SW	SW
Cumbria	NW	NW	N
Derbyshire	WM	EM	EM
Devon	SW	SW	SW
Dorset	SW	SW	SW
Durham	NE	NE	N
East Sussex	SE	SE	SE
Essex	SE	E	SE
Gloucestershire	WM	SW	SW
Greater London	SE	GL	SE
Greater Manchester	NW	NW	NW
Hampshire	SE	SE	SE
Hereford & Worcester	WM	WM	WM
Hertfordshire	EM	E	SE
Humberside	NE	Y&H	Y&H
Isle of Wight	SE	SE	SE
Kent	SE	SE	SE
Lancashire	NW	NW	NW
Leicestershire	EM	EM	EM
Lincolnshire	EM	EM	EM
Merseyside	NW	M	NW
Norfolk	EM	E	EA
Northamptonshire	EM	EM	EM
Northumberland	NE	NE	N
North Yorkshire	NE	Y&H	Y&H
Nottinghamshire	EM	EM	EM
Oxfordshire	WM	SE	SE
Shropshire	WM	WM	WM
Somerset	SW	SW	SW
South Yorkshire	NE	Y&H	Y&H
Staffordshire	WM	WM	WM
Suffolk	EM	E	EA
Surrey	SE	SE	SE
Tyne and Wear	NE	NE	N
Warwickshire	WM	WM	WM

West Midlands	WM	WM	WM
West Sussex	SE	SE	SE
West Yorkshire	NE	Y&H	Y&H
Wiltshire	SW	SW	SW

Summary and abbreviations:

MARS Regions (6):

North West (NW); North East (NE); West Midlands (WM); East Midlands (EM); South West (SW); South East (SE)

Government Regional Areas of Responsibility (10):

North West (NW); North East (NE); West Midlands (WM); East Midlands (EM); South West (SW); South East (SE); Yorkshire and Humberside (Y&H); Eastern (E); Greater London (GL); Merseyside (M)

Standard Statistical Regions (9):

North West (NW); North East (NE); West Midlands (WM); East Midlands (EM); South West (SW); South East (SE); North (N); Yorkshire and Humberside (Y&H); East Anglia (EA)

J.2 Correspondence between MARS Regions and defined Countryside Character Areas

North West

Border Moors and Forests (5); Bowland Fells (34); Bowland Fringe and Pendle Hill (33); Cheshire Sandstone Ridge (62); Cumbria High Fells (8); Cumbrian Coast (180); Eden Valley (9); Howgill Fells (18); Lancashire Coal Measures (56); Lancashire Valleys (35); Lancashire and Amounderness Plain (32); Liverpool Bay (178); Manchester Conurbation (55); Manchester Pennine Fringe (54); Mersey Valley (60); Merseyside Conurbation (58); Morcambe Coast and Lune Estuary (31); Morecambe Bay (179); Morecambe Bay Limestones (20); North Pennines (10); Orton Fells (17); Sefton Coast (57); Shropshire, Cheshire and Staffordshire Plain (61); Solway Basin (6); Solway Firth (181); South Cumbria Low Fells (19); South West Peak (53); Southern Pennines (36); Tyne Gap and Hadrian's Wall (11); West Cumbria Coastal Plain (7); Wirral (59); Yorkshire Dales (21)

North East

Border Moors and Forests (5); Bridlington to Skegness (163); Central Lincolnshire Vale (44); Cheviot Fringe (3); Cheviots (4); Dark Peak (51); Durham Coalfield Pennine Fringe (16); Durham Magnesian Limestone Plateau (15); Holderness (40); Howardian Hills (29); Humber Estuary (41); Humberhead Levels (39); Lincolnshire Coast and Marshes (42); Lincolnshire Wolds (43); Mid Northumberland (12); North Northumberland Coastal Plain (1); North Pennines (10); North Yorkshire Moors and Cleveland Hills (25); Northern Lincolnshire Edge with Coversands (45); Northumberland Coast (160); Northumberland Sandstone Hills (2); Nottinghamshire, Derbyshire and Yorkshire Coalfield (38); Pennine Dales Fringe (22); Saltburn to Bridlington (162); South East Northumberland Coastal Plain (13); Southern Magnesian Limestone (30); Southern Pennines (36); Tees Lowland (23); Tyne Gap and Hadrians Wall (11); Tyne and Wear Lowlands (14); Tyne to Tees Coast (161); Vale of Mowbray (24); Vale of Pickering (26); Vale of York (28); Yorkshire Dales (21); Yorkshire Southern Pennine Fringe (37); Yorkshire Wolds (27)

West Midlands

Arden (97); Black Mountains and Golden Valley (99); Cannock Chase and Cank Wood (67); Clun and North West Herefordshire Hills (98); Cotswolds (107); Dark Peak (51); Derbyshire Peak Fringe and Lower Derwent (50); Dunsmore and Feldon (96); Forest of Dean and Lower Wye (105); Herefordshire Lowlands (100); Herefordshire Plateau (101); Leicestershire Vales (94); Leicestershire and South Derbyshire Coalfield (71); Malvern Hills (103); Manchester Pennine Fringe (54); Mease/Sence Lowlands (72); Melbourne Parklands (70); Mersey Valley (61); Mid Severn Sandstone Plateau (66); Midvale Ridge (109); Needwood and South Derbyshire Coalfield (68); Northamptonshire Uplands (95); Nottinghamshire, Derbyshire and Yorkshire Coalfield (38); Potteries and Churnet Valley (64); Severn and Avon Vales (106); Shropshire Hills (65); South Herefordshire and Over Severn (104); South West Peak (53); Teme Valley (102); Trent Valley Washlands (69); Upper Thames Clay Vales (108); White Peak (52); Yorkshire Southern Pennine Fringe (37); Arden (97); Black Mountains and Golden Valley (99); Cannock Chase and Cank Wood (67); Clun and North West Herefordshire Hills (98); Cotswolds (107); Dark Peak (51); Derbyshire Peak Fringe and Lower Derwent (50); Dunsmore and Feldon (96); Forest of Dean and Lower Wye (105); Herefordshire Lowlands (100); Herefordshire Plateau (101); Leicestershire Vales (94); Leicestershire and South Derbyshire Coalfield (71); Malvern Hills (103); Manchester Pennine Fringe (54); Mease/Sence Lowlands (72); Melbourne Parklands (70); Mersey Valley (61); Mid Severn Sandstone Plateau (66); Midvale Ridge (109); Needwood and South Derbyshire Coalfield (68); Northamptonshire Uplands (95); Nottinghamshire, Derbyshire and Yorkshire Coalfield (38); Potteries and Churnet Valley (64); Severn and Avon Vales (106); Shropshire Hills (65); South Herefordshire and Over Severn (104); South West Peak (53); Teme Valley (102); Trent Valley Washlands (69); Upper Thames Clay Vales (108); White Peak (52); Yorkshire Southern Pennine Fringe (37)

East Midlands

Bedfordshire Greensand Ridge (90); Bedfordshire and Cambridgeshire Claylands (88); Breckland (85); Bridlington to Skegness (163); Central Lincolnshire Vale (44); Central Norfolk Coast (78); Charnwood (73); Chilterns (110); Cotswolds (107); Dunsmore and Feldon (95); East Anglian Chalk (87); Greater Thames Estuary (81); High Leicestershire (93); Humberhead Levels (39); Kesteven Uplands (75); Leicestershire Vales (94); Leicestershire and Nottinghamshire Wolds (74); Leicestershire and South Derbyshire Coalfield (71); Lincolnshire Coast and Marshes (42); Lincolnshire Wolds (43); Mease/Sence Lowlands (72); Melbourne Parklands (70); Mid Norfolk (84); Midvale Ridge (109); North East Norfolk and Flegg (79); North Norfolk Coast (77); Northamptonshire Vales (89); Northern Lincolnshire Edge with Coversands (45); Northern Thames Basin (111); Nottinghamshire, Derbyshire and Yorkshire Coalfield (38); Old Hunstanton to Sheringham (165); Rockingham Forest (92); Sheringham to Lowestoft (166); Sherwood (49); South Norfolk and High Suffolk Claylands (83); South Suffolk and North Essex Clayland (86); Southern Lincolnshire Edge (47); Southern Magnesian Limestone (30); Suffolk Coast (167); Suffolk Coast and Heaths (82); Thames Valley (115); The Broads (80); The Fens (46); The Wash (164); Trent Valley Washlands (69); Trent and Belvoir Vales (48); Upper Thames Clay Vales (108); Yardley-Whittlewood Ridge (91)

South West

Avon Vales (117); Berkshire and Marlborough Downs (116); Blackdowns (147); Blackmoor Vale and Vale of Wardour (133); Bodmin Moor (153); Bridgwater Bay (176); Bristol, Avon Valleys and Ridges (118); Carnmenellis (155); Cornish Killas (152); Cotswolds (107); Dartmoor (150); Devon Redlands (148); Dorset Downs and Cranborne Chase (134); Dorset Heaths (135); Exmoor (145); Hensbarrow (154); Isle of Portland (137); Isles of Scilly (158); Land's End to Minehead (175); Lundy (159); Lyme Bay (173); Marshwood and Powerstock Vales (139); Mendip Hills (141); Mid Somerset Hills (143); Midvale Ridge (109); New Forest (131); Quantock Hills (144); Salisbury Plain and West Wiltshire Downs (132); Severn Estuary (177); Severn and Avon Vales (106); Solent and Poole Bay (171); Somerset Levels and Moors (142); South Devon (151); South Dorset Coast (172); South Purbeck (136); Start Point to Land's End (174); The Culm (149); The Lizard (157); Upper Thames Clay Vales (108); Vale of Taunton and Quantock Fringes (146); West Penwith (156); Weymouth Lowlands (138); Yeovil Scarplands (140)

South East

Berkshire and Marlborough Downs (116); Chilterns (110); East Kent Coast (169); Folkestone to Selsey Bill (170); Greater Thames Estuary (81); Hampshire Downs (130); High Weald (122); Inner London (112); Isle of Wight (127); Low Weald (121); New Forest (131); North Downs (119); North Kent Coast (168); North Kent Plain (113); North Thames Basin (111); Pevensey Levels (124); Romney Marshes (123); Salisbury Plain and West Wiltshire Downs (132); Solent and Poole Bay (171); South Coastal Plain (126); South Downs (125); South Hampshire Lowlands (128); Thames Basin Heaths (129); Thames Basin Lowlands (114); Thames Valley (115); Wealden Greensand (120)

Note: In 32 cases, character zones fall across two or more MARS Regions. Character Area numbers shown in brackets.

APPENDIX K
Project media coverage and consultation 1994-7

K.1 Seminars and presentations

MARS staff attended many seminars and meetings to present papers, deliver seminars or speak about the MARS project, including:

ACAO General Meeting, London (Spring 1994)

Hereford and Worcester Archaeology Day (December 1994)

Bournemouth University Research Seminar (February 1995)

Computer Applications in Archaeology Conference, Oxford (February 1995)

Cheshire Archaeology Day (March 1995)

Computer Applications in Archaeology Conference, Leiden, Netherlands (April 1995)

Standing Conference of Archaeological Unit Managers (April 1995)

Institute of Field Archaeologists, Finds Research Group (May 1995)

Institute of Field Archaeologists, Wessex Regional Meeting, Salisbury (July 1995)

European Association of Archaeologists, First Annual Conference in Santiago de Compostela, Spain (September 1995)

English Heritage (Archaeology Division) Seminar, London (October 1995)

RCHME Staff Seminar, Swindon (October 1995)

MARS Project Seminar, Society of Antiquaries, London (November 1995)

SMR Working Parties: Northern (February 1997), West Midlands (September 1996), South East (August 1996) and South West (June 1996)

English Heritage and MAFF Agri-Environment Forum Seminar, London (June 1996)

Aerial Archaeology Research Group, Chester (September 1996)

SMR Software Users Group, Swindon (November 1996)

Ancient Monuments Advisory Committee, London (July 1997)

K.2 Short articles and press coverage

School of Conservation Sciences Bulletin (January 1994)
Bournemouth Evening Echo (6th June 1994)
Liverpool Echo (12th August 1994)
Planning (12th August 1994)
Swindon Advertiser (13th August 1994)
The Times (17th August 1994)
Bournemouth Advertiser (8th September 1994)
The Times Higher Education Supplement (23rd September 1994)
Hereford Times (29th September 1994)
British Archaeology (September 1994)

English Heritage Conservation Bulletin (October 1994)
Current Archaeology (November 1994, Issue 140)
School of Conservation Sciences Bulletin (December 1994)
Scottish Archaeology (Winter 1994)
Land Rover Fleet World (1995, Issue 13)
Watford Observer (January 1995)
Cambridge Evening News (March 1995)
Cumberland News (22nd September 1995)
Wessex IFA Newsletter (October 1995)
British Archaeology (November 1995)
Heritage Today (December 1995)
The Guardian (January 10 1996)
English Heritage Archaeology Review (1994-5, 44-6)
English Heritage Archaeology Review (1995-6, 59-61)
SMR News (November 1996, Issue 3)

K.3 Refereed papers

Darvill, T, and Wainwright, G, 1994, The Monuments at Risk Survey: an introduction. **Antiquity**, 68, 820-4

Darvill, T, and Wainwright, G, 1995, The Monuments at Risk Survey: an introduction. **Conservation and Management of Archaeological Sites,** 1.1, 59-62

Bell, M, and King, N, 1995, Computing in the MARS project. **Archaeological Computing Newsletter**, 43, 1-5

Bell, M, and King, N, 1996, The MARS Project - an interface with England's past. In H Kamermans and K Fennema (eds), **Interfacing the past. Computer applications and quantitative methods in archaeology CAA95 (= Analecta Praehistorica Leidensia 28**). 87-91

K.4 Television and radio coverage

BBC Radio Cambridge
Radio Five
BBC Breakfast Television News
Meridian News
South Today

K.5 Internal training material, progress reports, and general media items

Press release (June 1994)
Training manuals (June 1994)

Martian Chronicle 1   (June 1994)
Martian Chronicle 2   (December 1994)
Martian Chronicle 3   (November 1995)
Martian Chronicle 4   (April 1996)

MARS, 1994, *MARS: an introduction*. MARS Leaflet

MARS, 1994, *Still standing after all these years*. MARS video

K.6 Displays

MARS Display boards were shown at numerous meetings and events, including:

World Heritage and Museums Exhibition, Earls Court, London (May 1995)

Institute of Field Archaeologists Annual Conference, Bradford (April 1995)

Aerial Archaeology Research Group Annual Conference, Lincoln (September 1995)

Aerial Archaeology Research Group Annual Conference, Chester (September 1996)

APPENDIX L
The MARS Project archive and copy data-sets

L.1 Sample unit archive

Folders for each of 1297 sample units containing NMR and SMR print-outs, index to aerial photographic coverage, field survey notes, 1:10,000 map extracts with located monuments and flightlines plotted, and additional information (leaflets etc).

L.2 Photographic archive

Black and white contact prints, colour transparencies for approximately 400 identified monuments.

L.3 National survey

SMR questionnaire returns. Monument enhancememt programme files including record sheets with enhancement data.

L.4 Case studies

Archive reports for 23 single monument studies, 10 landscape studies. Additional background information including related articles on decay studies, original artwork, maps, plans and reference material.

L.6 Copy data-sets

Database tables comprising field, aerial photographic and national survey data (including record enhancement information).

Copy of field survey, aerial photographic and National Survey database deposited with RCHME NMR.

Digital files of database tables for individual counties deposited with each participating local authority. Second set retained by Bournemouth University.

L.7 Additional archive items

Administrative files; correspondence.

APPENDIX M
Select bibliography of surveys, excavation programmes and studies illustrating archaeological deposit distribution and survival in relation to recognized hazards as sources of damage and destruction

The following sections are intended to provide sources of information about the impact and potential recovery of archaeological information from the main hazards facing the survival of archaeological monuments. The lists are highly selective and attempt to provide information on general background studies, together with examples of regional or local extensive non-invasive surveys and detailed investigations for particular projects. Throughout, the aim is to illustrate the kind of damage done by each hazard, what might be expected as a result of carrying out investigations, and the constraints and potential that apply. Where possible, examples have been selected from different parts of the country and in relation to different periods. Inevitably, some hazards have prompted more work in recent years than others, and this is partly reflected in the quantity and range of sources given. To avoid undue duplication, cross reference is made to other appendices where these include relevant material.

M.1 Ploughing and arable agriculture

General surveys and overviews
Bonney, D J, 1980, Damage by medieval and later cultivation. In J Hinchliffe and R T Schadla-Hall (eds), *The past under the plough* (= DAMHB Occasional Paper 3). London. DoE. 41-8

Hazlegrove, C, Millett, M, and Smith, I (eds), 1985, *Archaeology from the ploughsoil*. Sheffield. Department of Archaeology and Prehistory, Sheffield University

Hinchliffe, J, 1980, Effects of ploughing on archaeological sites: assessment of the problem and some suggested approaches. In J Hinchliffe and T Schadla-Hall (eds) *The past under the plough* (= DAMHB Occasional Papers 3). London. DoE. 11-17

Hinchliffe, J, and Schadla-Hall, R T (eds), 1980, *The past under the plough* (= DAMHB Occasional Papers 3). London. DoE

Lambrick, G, 1977, *Archaeology and agriculture: a survey of modern cultivation methods and the problems of assessing plough damage to archaeological sites.* London and Oxford. CBA and Oxford Archaeological Unit

Richards, J, 1985, Scouring the surface: approaches to the ploughzone in the Stonehenge Environs. *Archaeological Review from Cambridge*, 4, 27-42

Regional and local surveys
See also APPENDIX A.3 for additional regional and local resource assessments which include reports on plough-damage, and papers in Hinchliffe and Schadla-Hall (1980) referred to above.

Buckley, D G, and Clarke, C P, 1979, *Archaeology and agriculture: case studies from Essex.* Chelmsford. Essex County Council Planning Department

Drewett, P L, 1976, *Plough damage to known archaeological sites in East and West Sussex.* London. Institute of Archaeology, University of London. [Circulated typescript report]

Richards, J, 1984, *Stonehenge Environs: a preservation and management policy.* Salisbury. Wessex Archaeology. [Circulated typescript report]

Richards, J, 1990, Death and the past environment: the results of work on barrows on the Berkshire Downs. *Berkshire Archaeological Journal*, 73 (1986-1990), 1-42

Saville, A, 1980, *Archaeological sites in the Avon and Gloucestershire Cotswolds: an extensive survey of a rural archaeological resource with special reference to plough damage* (= CRAAGS Survey Report 5). Bristol. CRAAGS

Shennan, S J, 1981, *Experiments in the collection and analysis of archaeological survey data: the East Hampshire Survey.* Sheffield. Sheffield University Department of Archaeology and Prehistory

Reports on excavation programmes prompted by continuing plough damage
Bell, M, 1977, Excavations at Bishopstone. *Sussex Archaeological Collections*, 115, 1-299

Drewett, P, 1982, Late Bronze Age downland economy and excavations at Black Patch, East Sussex. *Proceedings of the Prehistoric Society,* 48, 321-400

Evans, J G, and Simpson, D D A, 1991, Giants' Hills 2 long barrow, Skendleby, Lincolnshire. *Archaeologia*, 109, 1-45

Gingell, C, 1992, *The Marlborough Downs: a later Bronze Age landscape and its origins* (= Wiltshire Archaeological and Natural History Society Monograph 1). Devizes. Wiltshire Archaeological and Natural History Society

Lawson, A, Brown, J E, Healy, F, Le Hegarat, R, and Petersen, F, 1986, *Barrow excavations in Norfolk, 1950-82* (= East Anglian Archaeology 29). Norwich. East Anglian Archaeology

Richards, J, 1990, *The Stonehenge Environs Project* (= HBMCE Archaeological Report 16). London. English Heritage

Saville, A, 1990, *Hazleton North: the excavation of a Neolithic long cairn of the Cotswold-Severn group* (= HBMCE Archaeological Report 13). London. English Heritage

Stead, I M, 1968, An Iron Age hill-fort at Grimthorpe, Yorkshire, England. *Proceedings of the Prehistoric Society*, 34, 148-190

Wainwright, G J, 1979, *Gussage All Saints: an Iron Age settlement in Dorset* (= DoE Archaeological Report 10). London. HMSO

M.2 Urbanization, property development, building alterations and demolition

General surveys and overviews
Embree, S, 1994, Grade I Buildings at Risk Survey. *Conservation Bulletin,* 23, 32

English Heritage, 1992, *Buildings at Risk: a sample survey.* London. English Heritage

Ottaway, P, 1992, *Archaeology in British towns.* London. Routledge

RCHME (Royal Commission on Historical Monuments, England), 1963, *Monuments threatened or destroyed. A select list: 1956-1962.* London. HMSO

Strong, R, Binney, M, and Harris, J, 1974, *The destruction of the country house 1875-1975.* London. Thames and Hudson

Regional and local surveys
See also APPENDIX A.4 for resource assessment reports relating to historic and modern urban areas.

Croft, R A, and Mynard, D C, 1993, *The changing landscape of Milton Keynes.* Milton Keynes. Buckinghamshire Archaeological Society

RCHME (Royal Commission on Historical Monuments, England), 1969, *Peterborough New Town. A survey of antiquities in the areas of development.* London. HMSO

RCHME (Royal Commission on Historical Monuments, England), 1982, *Beverley. An archaeological and architectural study* (= Supplementary Series 4). London. HMSO

Select reports on excavations prompted by this hazard in historic urban areas (redevelopment)
Addyman, P V (General editor), 1976 - continuing, *The archaeology of York.* Volumes 1-20 some issued in multiple parts. London and York. Council for British Archaeology

Andrews, P (ed), 1997, *Excavations at Hamwic* 2 (= CBA Research report 109). York. CBA

Bateman, N C W, 1997, The London amphitheatre: excavations 1987-1996. *Britannia*, 51-86

Bidwell, P T, 1979, *The legionary bathhouse and basilica and forum at Exeter* (= Exeter Archaeological Report 1). Exeter. Exeter City Council and University of Exeter

Butterworth, C A, and Seager Smith, R, 1997, Excavations at The Hermitage, Old Town, Swindon. *Wiltshire Archaeological and Natural History Magazine*, 90, 55-76

Carver, M O H, 1983, Two town houses in medieval Shrewsbury. *Transactions of the Shropshire Archaeological Society*, 41, 1-140

Chester City Council (various authors), 1978-1996, *Excavations in Chester.* Volumes 1-10. Chester. Chester Archaeology and Grosvenor Museum

Chichester District Council (various authors), 1971-1993, *Excavations in Chichester.* Volumes 1-8. Chichester. Chichester District Council

Cirencester Excavation Committee (various authors), 1982-1998, *Cirencester Excavations* Volumes I-V. Cirencester. Cirencester Excavation Committee and Cotswold Archaeological Trust

Crummy, P (General editor), 1981-1996, *Colchester archaeological reports.* Volumes 1-12. Colchester. Colchester Archaeological Trust

Jones, M (General editor), 1977-1996, *The archaeology of Lincoln.* Volumes I-XVIII, some issued in multiple parts. London and York. Council for British Archaeology and Lincoln Archaeological Trust

McCarthy, M R, 1990, *A Roman, Anglian and medieval site at Blackfriars Street, Carlisle: excavations 1977-9* (= Cumberland and Westmorland Antiquarian and Archaeological Society Research Series 4). Carlisle. Cumberland and Westmorland Antiquarian and Archaeological Society

Maloney, C, 1990, *The upper Wallbrook valley in the Roman period* (= Archaeology on London 1. CBA Research Report 69). York. CBA

Morton, A D (ed), 1992, *Excavations at Hamwic, volume 1: excavations 1946-83, excluding Six Dials and Melbourne Street* (= CBA Research Report 84). York. CBA

Platt, C, and Coleman-Smith, R, 1975, *Excavations in medieval Southampton*. Leicester. Leicester University Press

Shoesmith, R, 1980-85, *Hereford City excavations* (= CBA Research Reports 36, 46 and 56). London and York. CBA. (3 vols)

Williams, J, 1979, *St Peter's Street Northampton: excavations 1973-76.* Northampton. Northampton Development Corporation

Williams, T, 1993, *Public buildings in the south-west quarter of Roman London* (= The Archaeology of Roman London 3. CBA Research Report 88). York. CBA

Woodward, P J, Davies, S M, and Graham, A H, 1993, *Excavations at Greyhound Yard, Dorchester 1981-4* (= DNHAS Monograph 12). Dorchester. DNHAS

Select reports on excavations prompted by this hazard during the expansion of historic urban centres (urbanization)
Moore, J, and Jenning, D, 1994, *Reading Business Park: a Bronze Age landscape* (= Thames Valley Landscapes: the Kennet Valley 1). Oxford. Oxford Archaeological Unit

Nowakowski, J A, 1991, Trethellan Farm, Newquay: the excavation of a lowland Bronze Age settlement and Iron Age cemetery. *Cornish Archaeology*, 30, 5-243

Pryor, F, 1984, *Excavations at Fengate, Peterborough, England: the fourth report* (= Northamptonshire Archaeological Society Monograph 2. Royal Ontario Museum Archaeology Monograph 7). Northampton. Northamptonshire Archaeological Society and Royal Ontario Museum

Wainwright, G, and Davies, S, 1995, *Baulksbury Camp, Hampshire: excavations in 1973 and 1981* (= English Heritage Archaeological Report 4). London. English Heritage

M.3 Road-building

General surveys and overviews
Bevan, B, 1996, Roads to nowhere? Archaeology, landscape and a planning process that by-passes more than towns. *Assemblage*, 21-2 (Internet: http://WWW.shef.ac.uk/uni/union/susoc/assem/bevan.html)

ERL, 1990, *'Roads for prosperity' White Paper 1989: implications for England's archaeological resource*. London. Environmental Resources Limited. [Circulated typescript report]

Highways Agency, 1996, *Trunk roads and archaeology 1994-1995.* London. Highways Agency Environmental Policy Unit

Lawson, A, 1993, The assessment of trunk road schemes. *The Field Archaeologist,* 18, 351-5

POST (Parliamentary Office of Science and Technology), 1997, *Tunnel vision? The future role of tunnels in transport infrastructure.* London. POST

Regional and scheme-specific surveys
See also APPENDIX A.3 for resource assessment reports which include consideration of road schemes.

Bernard, J, 1972, The motorway threat in Surrey. *London Archaeologist,* 1.15, 239-42

Biddle, M, and Emery, V W, 1973, *The M3 extension: an archaeological survey*. Winchester. M3 Archaeological Rescue Committee

Chambers, R A, 1992, The archaeology of the M40 through Buckinghamshire, Northamptonshire and Oxfordshire, 1988-91. *Oxoniensia*, 57, 43-54

Fowler, P J, 1979, Archaeology and the M4 and M5 Motorways, 1965-78. *Archaeological Journal*, 136, 12-26.

Manning, D, 1996, The Norfolk bridge survey. *Industrial Archaeology News*, 96, 3-4

Williams, J (ed), 1973, *Northampton-Wellingborough Express Way: archaeological survey* (= RESCUE Publication 2). Hertford. RESCUE

Reports on excavations prompted by this hazard
Ellis, P, Evans, J, Hannaford, H, Hughes, G, and Jones, A, 1994, Excavations in the Wroxeter hinterland 1988-1990: the archaeology of the A5/A49 Shrewsbury bypass. *Shropshire History and Archaeology*, 69, 1-119

Fasham, P J, 1985, *The prehistoric settlement at Winnall Down, Winchester: excavations of MARC3 Site R17 in 1976 and 1977* (= Hampshire Field Club and Archaeological Society Monograph 2. M3 Archaeological Rescue Committee Report 8). Winchester. Hampshire Field Club

Fasham, P J, and Whinney, R J B, 1991, *Archaeology and the M3: the watching brief, the Anglo-Saxon settlement at Abbots Worthy and retrospective sections* (= Hampshire Field Club and Archaeological Society Monograph 7). Winchester. Hampshire Field Club

Fowler, P J, and Bennett J, 1973, Archaeology and the M5 Motorway: 2nd report. *Transactions of the Bristol and Gloucestershire Archaeological Society*, 92, 21-81

Fowler, P J, and Bennett J, 1974, Archaeology and the M5 Motorway: 3rd report. *Transactions of the Bristol and Gloucestershire Archaeological Society*, 93, 1-1-30

Fowler, P J, and Walters, B, 1980, Archaeology and the M4 motorway, 1969-71: Tormarton, county of Avon, to Ermine Street, Berkshire. *Wiltshire Archaeological Magazine*, 74/5, 69-130

Hinton, D, and Rowley, T, 1974, Excavation on the route of the M40. *Oxoniensia*, 38, 1-183

Smith, R J C, Healy, F, Allen, J, Morris, E L, Barnes, I, and Woodward, P J, 1997, *Excavations along the route of the Dorchester Bypass, Dorset, 1986-8* (= Wessex Archaeology Report 11). Salisbury. Wessex Archaeology

M.4 Mineral extraction, quarrying, peat cutting and dewatering

General surveys and overviews

Anon, 1994, Government says peat-cutting should go on. *British Archaeological News* (NS), 18, 3

Coles, B, 1994, *Wetland management: a survey for English Heritage* (=WARP Occasional Paper 9). Exeter and London. WARP and English Heritage

French, C, and Taylor, M, 1985, Desiccation and destruction: the immediate effects of dewatering at Etton, Cambridgeshire. *Oxford Journal of Archaeology*, 4, 139-56

RCHME (Royal Commission on Historical Monuments, England), 1960, *A matter of time: an archaeological survey of the river gravels of England*. London. HMSO

Schadla-Hall, T, 1986, Wet deposits under threat - losing the early post-glacial. *Rescue News*, 41, 8

Regional and local surveys

See also APPENDIX A.3 for resource assessments which include considerations of this hazard.

Ellison, A, 1977, *A survey of the archaeological implications of hard-stone quarrying in the counties of Avon, Gloucestershire and Somerset*. Bristol. CRAAGS. [Circulated typescript report]

Longley, D, 1976, The archaeological implications of gravel extraction in north-west Surrey. *Surrey Archaeological Society Research Volumes*, 3, 1-35

Reports on excavations prompted by this hazard

Allen, T G, 1990, *An Iron Age and Romano-British enclosed settlement at Watkins Farm, Northmoor, Oxon* (= Thames Valley Landscapes 1). Oxford. Oxford Archaeological Unit and OUCA

Allen, T G, Darvill, T C, Green, L S, and Jones, M U, 1993, *Excavations at Roughground Farm, Lechlade, Gloucestershire: a prehistoric and Roman landscape* (= Thames Valley Landscapes: the Cotswold Water Park 1). Oxford. Oxford Archaeological Unit

Balaam, N, Smith, K, and Wainwright, G J, 1982, The Shaugh Moor Project: fourth report - environment, context and conclusion. *Proceedings of the Prehistoric Society,* 48, 203-278

Barclay, A, Gray, M, and Lambrick, G, 1995, *Excavations at the Devil's Quoits, Stanton Harcourt* (= Thames Valley Landscapes: the Windrush Valley 3). Oxford. Oxford Archaeological Unit

Clark, A, 1993, *Excavations at Mucking. Volume 1. The site atlas. Excavations by M U and T W Jones* (= HBMCE Archaeological Report 20). London. English Heritage

Clay, P, and Salisbury, C R, 1990, A Norman mill dam and other sites at Hemington Fields, Castle Donington, Leicester. *Archaeological Journal*, 147, 276-307

Dawson, M, 1996, Plantation Quarry, Willington, excavations 1988-1991. *Bedfordshire Archaeology,* 22, 2-49

Jarratt, M, 1970, The deserted village of West Whelpington. *Archaeologia Aeliana*, 48, 183-302

Kenyon, K, 1953, Excavations at Sutton Walls, Herefordshire, 1948-1951. *Archaeological Journal*, 110, 1-85

Olivier, A C H, 1987, Excavation of a Bronze Age funerary cairn at Manor Farm, near Borwick, North Lancashire. *Proceedings of the Prehistoric Society*, 53, 129-186

Roberts, M B, 1986, Excavation of the lower Palaeolithic site at Amey's Eartham Pit, Boxgrove, West Sussex: a preliminary report. *Proceedings of the Prehistoric Society*, 52, 215-46

Somerset Levels Project, 1975-1989, *Somerset Levels Papers* (15 volumes). Cambridge and Exeter. Somerset Levels Project

Smith, G, 1991, Excavations at Ham Hill, 1983. *Proceedings of the Somerset Archaeological and Natural History Society*, 134, 27-45

M.5 Forestry

General surveys and overviews
Biddle, P G, 1992, *Tree roots and foundations* (= Arboricultural Research Note). Farnham. DoE Arboricultural Advisory Information Service

Booth, T C, 1967, *Plantations on medieval rigg and furrow cultivation strips: a study in Scoreby Wood, York East Forest* (= Forestry Commission, Forest Record 62). London. HMSO

Cutler, D F and Richardson, I B K, 1989, *Tree roots and buildings*. Harlow. Longman

Everson, P, 1993, Branching out. *British Archaeological News*, 9, 10

Griffiths, F, 1993, Leafing through the past. *British Archaeological News* (NS), 7, 6-7

Jackson, A, 1978, *Forestry and archaeology: a study in survival of field monuments in south-west Scotland*. Hertford. RESCUE

Proudfoot, E (ed), 1987, *Our vanishing heritage: forestry and archaeology* (= Council for Scottish Archaeology Occasional Paper 2). Edinburgh. Council for Scottish Archaeology

Shoesmith, R, 1991, Trees and ancient monuments. *Rescue News*, 53, 8

Regional and local surveys
See also APPENDIX A.3 for resource assessments that may include some consideration of this hazard.

Ellison, A, 1977, *A survey of the archaeological implications of forestry in the Forest of Dean*. Bristol. CRAAGS. [Circulated typescript report]

Whiteley, S P, 1992, Archaeology in South Yorkshire's ancient woodland. In M J Francis, C G Cumberpatch and S P Whiteley (eds), *Archaeology in South Yorkshire 1991-1992*. Sheffield. South Yorkshire Archaeology Service. 25-30

Reports on excavations and studies prompted by or related to woodland change and forestry practice
Cartwright, R, 1991, Cawthorn Roman Camps: protecting an international treasure. In R F White and R Iles (eds), *Archaeology in National Parks. Leyburn.* Yorkshire Dales National Park. 35-38

Cunliffe, B, 1984, *Danebury: an Iron Age hillfort in Hampshire.Volume 1.The excavations 1969-1978: the Site* (= CBA Research Report 52). London. CBA

Cunliffe, B, and Poole, C, 1991, *Danebury: an Iron Age hillfort in Hampshire. Volume 4. The excavations 1979-1988: the Site* (= CBA Research Report 73). London. CBA

Fasham, P, 1987, *A banjo enclosure in Micheldever Wood, Hampshire* (= Hampshire Field Club and Archaeological Society Monograph 5). Winchester. Hampshire Field Club

McOmish, D S, and Smith, N A, 1996, Welshbury hillfort. *Transactions of the Bristol and Gloucestershire Archaeological Society*, 114, 55-64

M.6 Natural processes, vegetation, and related processes

General surveys and overviews
Anon (ed), 1995, *Archéologie and érosion: mesures de protection pour la sauvegarde des sites lacustres et palustres*. Lons-le-Saunier. Centre Jurassien du Patrimoine

Bell, M G, and Boardman J (eds), 1992, *Past and present soil erosion* (= Oxbow Monograph 22). Oxford. Oxbow Books

Berry, A Q, and Brown, I W (eds), 1994, *Erosion on archaeological earthworks: its prevention, control and repair*. Mold. Clwyd County Council

Hamel, G and Jones, K, 1982, *Vegetation management on archaeological sites*. Wellington. New Zealand Historic Places Trust

Thompson, F H (ed), 1980, *Archaeology and coastal change* (= Society of Antiquaries Occasional Paper (NS) 1). London. Society of Antiquaries

Trow, S, 1994, Archaeology at the edge ... the coastal resource. *Conservation Bulletin*, 23, 24-5

Regional and local surveys
See also APPENDIX A.3 for resource assessments that may include some consideration of this hazard, and APPENDIX O.1-2 for surveys of land-types in which natural erosion is widespread.

Webber, M, 1996, Thames foreshore: pilot study reveals extent of destruction. *Rescue News*, 68, 4

Reports on detailed surveys and excavations prompted by these hazards
Barton, R N E, 1992, *Hengistbury Head, Dorset. Volume 2: the late upper Palaeolithic and early Mesolithic sites* (= OUCA Monograph 34). Oxford. OUCA. [coastal erosion]

Bell, M, 1990, **Brean Down: excavations 1983-1987** (= HBMCE Archaeological Report 15). London. English Heritage [coastal erosion]

Cardwell, P, 1995, Excavation of the hospital of St Giles by Brompton Bridge, North Yorkshire. **Archaeological Journal**, 152, 109-245 [river erosion]

Cherry, J, 1982, Sea cliff erosion at Drigg, Cumbria: evidence of prehistoric habitation. **Transactions of the Cumberland and Westmorland Antiquarian Society**, 82, 1-6

Cleal, R, and Allen, M J, 1994, Investigation of tree-damaged barrows on King Barrow Ridge, Amesbury. **Wiltshire Archaeological and Natural History Magazine**, 87, 54-84 [storm damage]

Harry, R, and Morris, C, 1997, Excavations on the lower terrace, site C, Tintagel Island, 1990-4. **Antiquaries Journal**, 77, 1-143 [fires and peat/soil loss]

Howard-Davis, C, 1996, Seeing the sites: survey and excavation on the Anglezarke uplands, Lancashire. **Proceedings of the Prehistoric Society**, 61, 133-166 [peat erosion]

Neal, D S, 1983, Excavation of a settlement at Little Bay, Isles of Scilly. **Cornish Archaeology**, 22, 47-71. [coastal erosion]

Pickin, J, 1991, Staple Crag, Upper Teesdale: site consolidation and recording. **Archaeology North,** 2, 10-11 [ground-cover and soil erosion]

Steane, J, 1994, Stonor - a lost park and a garden found. **Oxoniensia**, 59, 449-70 [storm damage]

Todd, M, 1992, The hillfort of Dumpton. **Proceedings of the Devon Archaeological Society**, 50, 47-52 [storm damage]

Warren, S H, Piggott, S, Clark, J G D, Birkitt, M C, Godwin, H, and Godwin, M E, 1936, Archaeology of the submerged land-surface of the Essex coast. **Proceedings of the Prehistoric Society**, 2.2, 178-210 [marine inundation]

M.7 Vandalism, looting and metal detecting

General surveys and overviews
Addyman, P, 1997, As looted antiquities keep pouring in. **British Archaeology**, 22, 11

Baker, D, 1993, Arson threat increasing. **British Archaeological News** (NS), 7, 3

Cleere, H, 1984, Editorial: Cadbury's get egg on their faces. **CBA Newsletter and Calendar**, 8.3, 41

Crowther, D R, 1983, Swords to ploughshares: a nationwide survey of archaeologists and treasure-hunting clubs. **Archaeological Review from Cambridge**, 2.1, 9-19

Dobinson, C, and Denison, S, 1995, **Metal detecting and archaeology in England.** York and London. CBA and English Heritage

Gregory, T, 1986, Whose fault is treasure-hunting? In C S Dobinson and R Gilchrist (eds), **Archaeology, politics and the public** (= York University Archaeology Publication 5). York. Department of Archaeology, University of York. 25-7

Wainwright, G J, 1995, Metal detecting and archaeology in England. **Conservation Bulletin,** 26, 13

Regional and local surveys and reported instances
See also APPENDIX A.3 for resource assessments that may include some consideration of this hazard.

Cleere, H, 1982, Editorial: vandals at Sutton Hoo. **CBA Newsletter and Calendar**, 6.2, 25 and 36

Gregory, T, 1991, Metal detecting on a Scheduled Ancient Monument. **Norfolk Archaeology**, 41, 186-96

Jenkins, R, 1996, Prehistoric stone circle damaged by vandals. **The Times**, 20th June, 7

Wilkinson, P, 1990, Stonehenge scarred by graffiti artists. **The Times**, 20th March, 22

Reports on excavations and surveys prompted by this hazard
Anon, 1985, Detector looting results in rescue excavation. **CBA Newsletter**, 9.7, 55-6

Fitzpatrick, A P, 1996, A 1st-century AD 'Durotrigian' inhumation burial with a decorated Iron Age mirror from Portesham, Dorset. **Proceedings of the Dorset Natural History and Archaeological Society,** 118, 51-70

Stead, I M, 1991, The Snettisham Treasure: excavations in 1990. **Antiquity**, 65, 447-65

Woodward, A, and Leach, P, 1993, **The Uley Shrines. Excavation of a ritual complex on West Hill, Uley, Gloucestershire: 1977-9** (= HBMCE Archaeological Report 17). London. English Heritage

M.8 Tourism, recreation, traffic and visitor erosion

General surveys and overviews
Ardito, A J, 1994, Reducing the effects of heavy equipment compaction through a program of in-situ archaeological site preservation. **Artefact**, 17, 23-5

Berry, A, and Brown, I W (eds), 1994, *Erosion on archaeological earthworks: its prevention, control and repair*. Mold. Clwyd County Council

Bonsey, C, 1970, The problems of recreation on sites of archaeological and ecological interest. In J Sheail and T C E Wells (eds), *Old grassland: its archaeological and ecological importance.* Abbots Ripton. Monks Wood Experimental Research Station. 73-9

Cleere, H, 1978, Editorial: tourist erosion. *CBA Newsletter and Calendar*, 2.1, 1-2

Regional and local surveys
See also APPENDIX A.3 for resource assessments that may include some consideration of this hazard.

Frodsham, P, 1994, Monument management in Berkshire. In A Berry and I W Brown (eds), *Erosion on archaeological earthworks: its prevention, control and repair.* Mold. Clwyd County Council. 57-69

Griffiths, D, 1994, Dartmoor: erosion on open moorland. In A Berry and I W Brown (eds), *Erosion on archaeological earthworks: its prevention, control and repair.* Mold. Clwyd County Council. 81-6

Taylor, A, 1994, Flat-earth erosion control: caring for archaeological monuments in Cambridgeshire. In A Berry and I W Brown (eds), *Erosion on archaeological earthworks: its prevention, control and repair.* Mold. Clwyd County Council. 71-80

White, R, 1994, Combating erosion in the Yorkshire Dales National Park. In A Berry and I W Brown (eds), *Erosion on archaeological earthworks: its prevention, control and repair.* Mold. Clwyd County Council. 93-101

Reports on excavations and detailed site-based surveys prompted by this hazard
Claris, P, and Quartermaine, J, 1989, The Neolithic quarries and axe factory sites of Great Langdale and Scafell Pike: a new field survey. *Proceedings of the Prehistoric Society*, 55, 1-25

Preston-Jones, A, 1993, The Men an Tol reconsidered. *Cornish Archaeology*, 32, 5-16

M.9 War damage and military works etc.

General surveys and overviews
Anon, 1994, MoD under fire over historic sites. *British Archaeological News* (NS), 14, 1

Ministry of Works, 1949, *War and archaeology in Britain.* London. HMSO

O'Neil, B H St.J, 1949, War and archaeology in Britain. *Antiquaries Journal,* 28, 20-44

Regional and local surveys
Canham, R, 1993, Assault course for archaeology. *British Archaeological News* (NS), 8, 5

Canham, R, and Chippindale, C, 1988, Managing for effective archaeological conservation: the example of Salisbury Plain Military Training Area, England. *Journal of Field Archaeology*, 15, 53-65

Morgan Evans, D, 1992, The paradox of Salisbury Plain. In L Macinnes and C R Wickham-Jones (eds), *All natural things: archaeology and the Green debate* (= Oxbow Monograph 21). Oxford. Oxbow Books. 176-9

Reports on excavations prompted by these hazards
Anon, 1996, Salisbury Plain Training Area Wiltshire. *Wessex Archaeology Annual review 1995-6,* 6-7

Christie, P M, 1988, A barrow cemetery on Davidstow Moor, Cornwall. Wartime excavations by C K Croft Andrews. *Cornish Archaeology,* 27, 27-170

Grimes, W F, 1960, *Excavations on defence sites 1939-1945. I. Mainly Neolithic and Bronze Age* (= Ministry of Works Archaeological Reports 3). London. HMSO

Smith, G, 1988, Excavation of the Iron Age cliff promontory fort and of a Mesolithic and Neolithic flint working areas at Penhal point, Holywell Bay, near Newquay, 1983. *Cornish Archaeology*, 27, 171-99

M.10 Reservoirs, water catchment schemes, pipelines, airports etc.

General surveys, statements and overviews
Catherall, P D, 1980, Archaeology and gas pipelines. *Gas Engineering and Management*, 20, 471-6

Pearson, N, and Brinklow, D, 1997, Pipelines and archaeology: one approach. *The Archaeologist,* 30, 18-19

Reports on excavations and surveys prompted by this hazard
Allen, T, 1995, *Lithics and landscapes: archaeological discoveries on the Thames Water pipeline at Gatehampton Farm, Goring, 1985-92* (= Thames Valley Landscapes 7). Oxford. Oxford Archaeological Unit. [pipeline construction]

Bennett, P, 1988, Archaeology and the Channel Tunnel. *Archaeologia Cantiana*, 106, 1-24. [tunnel building and associated works]

Brooks, H, and Bedwin, O, 1989, *Archaeology at the airport: the Stanstead archaeological project 1985-89*. Chelmsford. Essex County Council. [airport construction]

Catherall, P D, Barnett, M, and McClean, H (eds), 1984, ***The Southern Feeder: the archaeology of a gas pipeline (from Wisbech to Mappowder)***. London. British Gas Corporation. [pipeline construction]

Coggins, D, Gidney, L J, 1988, A late prehistoric site at Dubby Sike, Upper Teesdale, Co Durham. ***Durham Archaeological Journal***, 4, 1-12. [water erosion in bed of modern reservoir]

Garton, D, 1987, A pilot archaeological field survey of Tintwistle Moor, North Derbyshire. ***Derbyshire Archaeological Journal***, 107, 5-12. [reservoir construction]

Griffiths, F M, 1984, Archaeological investigations at Colliford Reservoir, Bodmin Moor, 1977-78. ***Cornish Archaeology***, 23, 47-140. [reservoir construction]

Grimes, W F, 1993, The excavation of Caesar's Camp, Heathrow, Harmondsworth, Middlesex, 1944. ***Proceedings of the Prehistoric Society***, 59, 303-360. [airport construction]

Jobey, I, and Jobey, G, 1988, Gowanburn River Camp: an Iron Age, Romano-British and more recent settlement in North Tynedale. ***Archaeologia Aeliana,*** 16, 11-28. [reservoir construction]

Rahtz, P A, and Greenfield, E, 1977, ***Excavations at Chew Valley Lake, Somerset*** (= Department of the Environment Archaeological Reports 8). London. HMSO. [reservoir construction]

Rawlings, M, 1995, Archaeological sites along the Wiltshire section of the Codford to Ilchester water pipeline. ***Wiltshire Archaeological and Natural History Magazine***, 88, 26-49. [pipeline construction]

Smith, R, and Cox, P, 1986, ***The past in the pipeline: archaeology of the Esso Midline***. Salisbury. Wessex Archaeology. [pipeline construction]

Timby, J, 1996, ***The Anglo-Saxon cemetery at Empingham II, Rutland*** (= Oxbow Monograph 70). Oxford. Oxbow Books. [reservoir construction]

APPENDIX N
Select bibliography of studies dealing with land-use and land-use change

N.1 European

Brouwer, F M, Thomas, A J and Chadwick, M J (eds), 1991, *Land use changes in Europe: processes of change, environmental transformations and future patterns*. Dordrecht. Kluwer

Commission of the European Communities, 1990, *Corine: examples of the use of the results of the programme 1985-1990*. Brussels. Directorate-General for the Environment, Consumer Protection and Nuclear Safety

Stanners, D and Bourdeau, P (eds), 1995, *Europe's environment: the Dobris Assessment.* Luxembourg. Office for Official Publications of the European Communities

Wateron, C, Grove-White, R, Rodwell, J, and Wynee, B, 1995, *CORINE: databases and nature conservation. The new politics of information in the European Union*. (= Report of the Centre for the Study of Environmental Change and the Unit of Vegetation Science). Lancaster. Lancaster University

N.2 England

Barr, C, Benefield, C, Bunce, B, Ridsdale, H, and Whittaker, M, 1986, *Landscape changes in Britain.* Manchester. ITE

Barr, C J, Bunce, R G H, Clarke, R T, Fuller, R M, Furse, M T, Gillespie, M K, Groom, G B, Hallam, C J, Hornung, M, Howard, D C, and Ness, M J, 1993, *Countryside Survey 1990: main report* (= Countryside 1990 Series: Volume 2). London. DoE

Best, R H, and Coppock, J T, 1962, *The changing use of land in Britain*. London. Faber and Faber

Coleman, A, 1961, The second Land Use Survey: progress and prospect. *The Geographical Journal*, 127, 168-86

Countryside Commission, 1990, *Changes in landscape features in England and Wales 1947-1985* (= CCD 44). Cheltenham. Countryside Commission

Countryside Commission and English Nature, 1997, *The character of England: landscape, wildlife and natural features*. Cheltenham. Countryside Commission

DoE (Department of the Environment), 1986, *Land-use change in England number 1* (= Department of the Environment Statistical Bulletin (86)1). London. DoE

DoE (Department of the Environment), 1987, *Land-use change in England number 2* (= Department of the Environment Statistical Bulletin (87)7). London. DoE

DoE (Department of the Environment), 1988, *Land-use change in England number 3* (= Department of the Environment Statistical Bulletin (88)5). London. DoE

DoE (Department of the Environment), 1989, *Land-use change in England number 4* (= Department of the Environment Statistical Bulletin (89)5). London. DoE

DoE (Department of the Environment), 1990, *Land-use change in England number 5* (= Department of the Environment Statistical Bulletin (90)5). London. DoE

DoE (Department of the Environment), 1992, *Land-use change in England number 6* (= Department of the Environment Statistical Bulletin (92)3). London. DoE

DoE (Department of the Environment), 1992, *Land-use change in England number 7* (= Department of the Environment Statistical Bulletin (92)4). London. DoE

DoE (Department of the Environment), 1993, *Land-use change in England number 8* (= Department of the Environment Statistical Bulletin (93)1). London. DoE

DoE (Department of the Environment), 1994, *Land-use change in England number 9* (= Department of the Environment Statistical Bulletin (94)1). London. DoE

DoE (Department of the Environment), 1995, *Land-use change in England number 10* (= Department of the Environment Statistical Bulletin). London. DoE

DoE (Department of the Environment), 1996, *Land-use change in England number 11* (= Department of the Environment Statistical Bulletin). London. DoE

DoETR (Department of the Environment, Transport and the Regions), 1997, *Land-use change in England No.12* (= DoETR Statistical Bulletin). London. DoETR

Environment Agency, 1993, *The environment of England and Wales: a snapshot*. Bristol. Environment Agency

ITE (Institute of Terrestrial Ecology), 1986. *Landscape changes in Britain*. Huntingdon. ITE

Moore, J, 1982, *Historical change in the physical environment*. Butterworth. London

NCC (Nature Conservancy Council), 1984, *Nature conservation in Great Britain*. Peterborough. NCC

SERRL (South East Regional Research Laboratory), 1994, *Analysis of land-use change statistics*. London. SERRL and Birkbeck College

Spedding, C, 1988, Land use change in Britain. In H Talbot-Ponsonby (ed), *Changing land use and recreation*. London. Countryside Recreation Research Advisory Group.

Stamp, D L, 1962, *The land of Britain: its use and misuse* (3rd edition). London. Longmans

Stott, A P (ed), 1993, *Countryside Survey 1990: summary report*. London. DoE

LUC (Land Use Consultants), 1997, *Characterization of farming in natural areas* (= English Nature Research Report 205). Peterborough. English Nature, Land Use Consultants, Entec, and Countryside Planning and Management. [Circulated typescript report]

N.3 Methodological

Bunce, R G H, Barr, C J, and Fuller, R M, 1992, Integration of methods for detecting land use change, with special reference to Countryside Survey 1990. In M C Whitby (ed), *Land use change: the causes and consequences* (= ITE Symposium 27). London. HMSO. 69-78

Cole, L, Kernon, T, and Knightbridge, R, 1996, *Identifying and describing farm character and structure in the Natural Areas* (= English Nature Research Report 206). Peterborough. English Nature

Dunn, R, and Harrison, A, 1994, *Feasibility study for deriving information about Land Use Stock*. London. Department of the Environment Planning Research Programme

Hooper, A J, 1992, Field monitoring of environmental change in the Environmentally Sensitive Areas. In M C Whitby (ed), *Land use change: the causes and consequences* (= ITE Symposium 27). London. HMSO. 52-9

APPENDIX O
Select bibliography of surveys and studies illustrating archaeological deposit distribution, character, survival and potential in relation to major land-types and land-use regimes

The following sections are intended to provide sources of information about the nature and extent of archaeological remains in different kinds of land-type or land-use environment. The lists are highly selective and attempt to provide information on general background studies, together with examples of extensive non-invasive surveys and detailed investigations such as excavations. Throughout, the aim is to illustrate the kind of thing that might be expected and the constraints and potential that apply to archaeological work in these different environments. Where possible, examples have been selected from different parts of the country and in relation to different periods. Inevitably, some land-types have been subject to more intensive study in recent years than others, and this is partly reflected in the quantity and range of sources given (see also Darvill 1987, chapters 6-14). To avoid duplication, cross reference is made to other appendices where these include relevant material.

O.1 Wetland

General studies and overviews

Coles, B, 1990, Wetland archaeology: a wealth of evidence. In M Williams (ed), **Wetlands: a threatened landscape**. Oxford. Basil Blackwell. 145-80

Coles, J, 1984, **The archaeology of wetlands**. Edinburgh. Edinburgh University Press

Coles, J, and Coles, B (eds), 1989, **The archaeology of rural wetlands in England** (= WARP Occasional Papers 2). Exeter and London. Wetlands Archaeological Research Project and English Heritage

Purdy, B A (ed), 1988, **Wet site archaeology**. New Jersey. Telford Press

Rowley, T (ed), 1981, **The evolution of marshland landscapes**. Oxford. Oxford University Department of External Studies

Williams, M (ed), 1990, **Wetlands: a threatened landscape**. Massachusetts

Regional and local wetland surveys

Anon, 1995, **First Annual Report: Humber Wetlands Survey (1994-5)**. Hull. Humber Wetlands Survey

Cowell, R W, and Innes, J B, 1994, **The wetlands of Merseyside** (= Lancaster Imprints 2). Lancaster. Lancaster Imprints

French, C A I, and Pryor, F M M, 1993, **The South West Fen Dyke Survey Project 1982-86** (= East Anglian Archaeology 59). Norwich. East Anglian Archaeology

Hall, D, 1987, **The Fenland Project, number 2: Cambridgeshire survey. Peterborough to March** (= East Anglian Archaeology 35). Norwich. East Anglian Archaeology

Hall, D, 1992, **The Fenland Project, number 6: the south-western Cambridgeshire Fenlands** (= East Anglian Archaeology 56). Norwich. East Anglian Archaeology

Hall, D, 1996, **The Fenland Project, number 10: Cambridgeshire survey, Isle of Ely and Wisbech** (= East Anglian Archaeology 79). Norwich. East Anglian Archaeology

Hall, D, Wells, C E, and Huckerby, E, 1995, **The wetlands of Greater Manchester** (= Lancaster Imprints 3). Lancaster. Lancaster Imprints

Hall, D, and Coles, J, 1994, **Fenland Survey: an essay in landscape and persistence** (= English Heritage Archaeological Report 1). London. English Heritage

Hayes, P P, and Lane, T W, 1992, **The Fenland Project, number 5: Lincolnshire survey, the south-west fens** (= East Anglian Archaeology 55). Norwich. East Anglian Archaeology

Healy, F, 1996, **The Fenland Project, number 11: the Wissey Embayment: evidence for pre-Iron Age occupation prior to the Fenland Project** (= East Anglian Archaeology 78). Norwich. East Anglian Archaeology

Howard-Davies, C, Stocks, C, and Innes, J, 1988, **Peat and the past: a survey and assessment of the prehistory of the lowland wetlands of north-west England**. Lancaster. Lancaster University

Lane, T W, and Hayes, P, 1993, ***The Fenland Project, number 8: Lincolnshire Survey, the northern fen-edge*** (= East Anglian Archaeology 66). Norwich. East Anglian Archaeology

Leah, M, Wells, C E, Appleby, C, and Huckerby, E, 1997, ***The wetlands of Cheshire*** (= Lancaster Imprints 5). Lancaster. Lancaster Imprints

Leah, M, Wells, C E, Stamper, P, and Welch, C, forthcoming, ***The wetlands of Shropshire and Staffordshire***. Lancaster. Lancaster Imprints

Middleton, R, and Tooley, M, forthcoming, ***The wetlands of south-west Lancashire.*** Lancaster. Lancaster Imprints

Middleton, R, Wells, C E, and Huckerby, E, 1995, ***The wetlands of North Lancashire*** (= Lancaster Imprints 4). Lancaster. Lancaster Imprints

Pryor, F, French, C, Crowther, D, Gurney, D, Simpson, G, and Taylor, M, 1985, ***The Fenland Project, number 1: The lower Welland Valley*** (= East Anglian Archaeology 27). Norwich. East Anglian Archaeology. (2 vols)

Silvester, R J, 1988, ***The Fenland Project, number 3: Marshland and the Nar Valley, Norfolk*** (= East Anglian Archaeology 45). Norwich. East Anglian Archaeology

Silvester, R J, 1991, ***The Fenland Project, number 4: the Wissey Embayment and the Fen Causeway, Norfolk*** (= East Anglian Archaeology 52). Norwich. East Anglian Archaeology

Van de Noort, R, and Davies, P, 1993, ***Wetland heritage: an archaeological assessment of the Humber wetlands***. Hull. University of Hull, School of Geography and Earth Resources

Van de Noort, R, and Ellis, S (eds), 1995, ***Wetland heritage of Holderness: an archaeological survey (1994-1995)***. Hull. University of Hull School of Geography and Earth Resources

Van de Noort, R, and Ellis, S (eds), 1997, ***Wetland heritage of the Humberhead Levels: an archaeological survey***. Hull. Humber Wetland Project, University of Hull School of Geography and Earth Resources

Waller, M, 1994, ***The Fenland Project, number 9: Flandrian environmental change in Fenland*** (= East Anglian Archaeology 70). Norwich. East Anglian Archaeology

Reports on excavations
Bulleid, A, and Gray, H StG, 1911 and 1917, ***The Glastonbury Lake Village***. Glastonbury. Glastonbury Antiquarian Society. (2 volumes)

Clark, J G D, 1954, ***Excavations at Star Carr***. Cambridge. Cambridge University Press

Coles, J, and Minnitt, S, 1995, **'*Industrious and fairly civilized': the Glastonbury Lake Village***. Taunton. Somerset Levels Project and Somerset County Council Museums Service

Pryor, F, French, C, and Taylor, M, 1985, An interim report on excavations at Etton, Maxey, Cambridgeshire, 1982-84. ***Antiquaries Journal,*** 65, 275-311

Pryor, F, French, C, and Taylor, M, 1986, Flag Fen, Peterborough I: discovery, reconnaissance and initial excavation (1982-85). ***Proceedings of the Prehistoric Society,*** 52, 1-24

Somerset Levels Project, 1975-1989, ***Somerset Levels Papers*** (15 volumes). Cambridge and Exeter. Somerset Levels Project

Turner, R C, and Scaife, R G (eds), 1995, ***Bog bodies: new discoveries and new perspectives.*** London. British Museum

O.2 Coastland and estuaries

General studies and overviews
Fulford, M, Champion, T, and Lang, A, 1997, ***England's coastal heritage: a survey for English Heritage and the RCHME***. London. English Heritage and RCHME

Thompson, F H (ed), 1980, ***Archaeology and coastal change*** (= Society of Antiquaries of London Occasional Paper (NS) 1). London. Society of Antiquaries

Regional and local surveys
Allen, J R L, and Fulford, M G, 1990, Romano-British wetland reclamations at Longney, Gloucestershire, and evidence for the early settlement of the inner Severn Estuary. ***Antiquaries Journal,*** 70, 288-326

Brooks, I P, 1990, ***The Lindsey Coastal Survey 1989-1990.*** Lincoln. Lindsey Archaeological Services

Eddison, J, and Green, C (eds), 1988, ***Romney Marsh: evolution, occupation and reclamation*** (= OUCA Monograph 24). Oxford. OUCA

McDonald, R, 1985, ***Archaeological survey of the Somerset claylands: report of survey work 1985-6.*** Taunton. Somerset County Council

Marshall, G, 1995, Redressing the balance: an archaeological evaluation of North Yorkshire's coastal alum industry. ***Industrial Archaeology Review,*** 18.1, 39-62

Rippon, S, 1997, *The Severn Estuary: landscape evolution and wetland reclamation.* Leicester. Leicester University Press

Thomas, C, 1985, *Exploration of a drowned landscape.* London. Batsford

Wilkinson, T J, and Murphy, P, 1984, Archaeological survey of an inter-tidal zone: the submerged landscape of the Essex coast, England. *Journal of Field Archaeology*, 13, 177-94

Wilkinson, T J, and Murphy, P L, 1995, *The archaeology of the Essex Coast. Volume 1. The Hullbridge Survey* (= East Anglian Archaeology 71). Chelmsford. Essex County Council

Reports on excavations
Bell, M, 1990, *Brean Down: excavations 1983-1987* (= HBMCE Archaeological Report 15). London. English Heritage

Cunliffe, B, 1987, *Hengistbury Head, Dorset. Volume 1: the prehistoric and Roman settlement 3500 BC - AD 500* (= OUCA Monograph 13). Oxford. OUCA

Warren, S H, Piggott, S, Clark, J G D, Birkitt, M C, Godwin, H, and Godwin, M E, 1936, Archaeology of the submerged land-surface of the Essex coast. *Proceedings of the Prehistoric Society,* 2.2, 178-210

Wright, E V, 1990, *The Ferriby boats: seacraft of the Bronze Age*. London. Routledge

O.3 Rivers, lakes and alluvium spreads

General studies and overviews
Brown, T, 1997, *Alluvial archaeology.* Cambridge. Cambridge University Press

Ehrenburg, M, 1980, The occurrence of Bronze Age metalwork in the Thames: an investigation. *Transactions of the London and Middlesex Archaeological Society,* 31, 1-15

Evans, J, 1992, River valley bottoms and archaeology in the Holocene. In B Coles (ed), *The wetland revolution in prehistory* (= WARP Occasional Paper 6). Exeter. WARP

Fulford, M, and Nichols, E (eds), 1992, *Developing landscapes of lowland Britain. The archaeology of the British gravels: a review* (= Society of Antiquaries Occasional Paper (NS) 14). London. Society of Antiquaries

Good, G, Jones, R, and Ponsford, M (eds), 1991, *Waterfront archaeology* (= CBA Research Report 74). London. CBA

Graham-Campbell, J (ed), 1997, *Riverine archaeology* (= World Archaeology 29.1). London. Routledge

Milne, G, and Hobley, B (eds), 1981, *Waterfront archaeology in Britain and northern Europe* (= CBA Research Report 41). London. CBA

Needham, S, and Macklin, M (eds), 1992, *Alluvial archaeology in Britain* (= Oxbow Monograph 27). Oxford. Oxbow Books

RCHME (Royal Commission on Historical Monuments, England), 1960, *A matter of time: an archaeological survey of the river gravels of England*. London. HMSO

Regional and local surveys
Benson, D, and Miles, D, 1974, *The upper Thames Valley. An archaeological survey of the river gravels* (= Oxfordshire Archaeological Unit Survey 2). Oxford. Oxfordshire Archaeological Unit

French, C, 1988, *An archaeological survey of the Cambridgeshire river gravels.* Cambridge. Cambridgeshire County Council and Fenland Archaeological Trust

Gates, T, 1975, *The middle Thames Valley. An archaeological survey of the river gravels* (= Berkshire Archaeological Committee Publication 1). Reading. Berkshire Archaeological Committee

Knight, D, and Howard, A J, 1994, *Archaeology and alluvium in the Trent Valley: an archaeological assessment of the floodplain and gravel terraces*. Nottingham. Trent and Peak Archaeological Trust

Leech, R, 1977, *The upper Thames Valley in Gloucestershire and Wiltshire. An archaeological survey of the river gravels* (= CRAAGS Survey 4). Bristol. CRAAGS

Webster, G, and Hobley, B, 1964, Aerial reconnaissance over the Warwickshire Avon. *Archaeological Journal,* 121, 1-22

White, A J, 1984, Medieval fisheries in the Witham and its tributaries. *Lincolnshire History and Archaeology,* 19, 29-35

Reports on excavations
See also APPENDIX M.4 for excavations at gravel extraction sites in major river valleys.

Lambrick, G, and Robinson, M, 1979, *Iron Age and Roman riverside settlements at Farmoor, Oxfordshire* (= CBA Research Report 32. Oxfordshire Archaeological Unit Report 2). London and Oxford. CBA and Oxford Archaeological Unit

Longley, D, 1980, ***Runneymede Bridge 1976: excavations on the site of a late Bronze Age settlement*** (= Research Volume of the Surrey Archaeological Society 6). Guildford. Surrey Archaeological Society

Millett, M, and McGrail, S, 1987, The archaeology of the Hasholme logboat. ***Archaeological Journal,*** 144, 69-155

Taylor, F, and Woodward, P J, 1985, A Bronze Age barrow cemetery, and associated settlement, at Roxton, Bedfordshire. ***Archaeological Journal,*** 142, 79-149

O.4 Established grassland

General studies and overviews
Fowler, P J, 1970, Old grassland: its archaeological significance and ecological importance. ***Antiquity,*** 44, 57-9

Moore, I, 1966, ***Grass and grasslands.*** London

Sheail, J, and Wells, T C E (eds), 1970, ***Old grassland: its archaeological and ecological importance***. Abbots Ripton. Monkswood Experimental Research Station

Regional and local surveys
Bradley, R, Entwistle, R, and Raymond, F, 1994, ***Prehistoric land-divisions on Salisbury Plain: the work of the Wessex Linear Ditches Project*** (= English Heritage Archaeological Report 2). London. English Heritage

Eagles, B N, 1991, A new survey of the hillfort on Beacon Hill, Burghclere, Hampshire. ***Archaeological Journal,*** 148, 98-103

Canham, R, 1983, ***Archaeology in the Salisbury Plain Training Area.*** Trowbridge. Wiltshire County Council Library and Museums Service

Wildgoose, M, 1991, The drystone walls of Roystone Grange. ***Archaeological Journal,*** 148, 205-240

Reports on excavations
Andrews, D D, and Milne, G, 1979, ***Wharram. A study of settlement on the Yorkshire Wolds. I. Domestic settlement, 1: areas 10 and 6.*** (= Society for Medieval Archaeology Monograph 8). London. Society for Medieval Archaeology

Bowen, H C, and Fowler, P J, 1961, The archaeology of Fyfield and Overton Downs, Wiltshire (interim report). ***Wiltshire Archaeological and Natural History Magazine,*** 58 (1961-63), 98-115

Dixon, P, 1994, ***Crickley Hill. Volume 1. The hillfort defences.*** Nottingham. Crickley Hill Trust and University of Nottingham

Haselgrove, C C, Lowther, P C, and Turnbull, P, 1990, Stanwick, North Yorkshire, part 3: excavations on earthwork sites 1981-86. ***Archaeological Journal,*** 147, 37-90

Sharples, N M, 1991, ***Maiden Castle. Excavations and field survey 1985-6*** (= HBMCE Archaeological Report 19). London. English Heritage

O.5 Woodland

General studies and overviews
Barclay, G J, 1992, Vegetation management on ancient monuments in forestry and other areas. ***Aspects of Applied Biology,*** 29, 105-111

Barclay, G J, 1992, Forestry and archaeology in Scotland. ***Scottish Forestry,*** 46, 27-47

Bell, M, and Limbrey, S (eds), 1982, ***Archaeological aspects of woodland ecology*** (= BAR International Series 146). Oxford. BAR

Beswick, P, Rotherham, I D, and Parsons, J (eds), 1993, ***Ancient woodlands: their archaeology and ecology.*** Sheffield. Landscape Conservation Forum

Lee, G, 1995, Forestry management and archaeology. In A Q Berry and I W Brown (eds), ***Managing ancient monuments: an integrated approach.*** Mold. Clwyd County Council. 97-104

Rackham, O, 1980, ***Ancient woodland.*** London. Edward Arnold

Regional and local surveys
Fasham, P J, 1983, Fieldwork in and around Micheldever Wood, Hampshire, 1973-1980. ***Proceedings of the Hampshire Field Club,*** 39, 5-45

Hayes, T, 1976, A survey of Wark Forest. In P Clack and P Gosling (eds), ***Archaeology in the North.*** Durham. Northern Archaeological Survey. 247-53

Hendry, G, Bannister, N, and Tom, J, 1984, The earthworks of an ancient woodland. ***Bristol and Avon Archaeology,*** 3, 47-53

Hooke, D, 1992, ***The historical study of the New National Forest Area.*** Birmingham. University of Birmingham

LUC (Land Use Consultants), 1992, ***New National Forest: archaeological and historical study - a summary report.*** London. LUC

McCrone, P, 1985, The archaeology of the Dartmoor woodlands. ***Devon Archaeological Society Newsletter,*** 31, 11

Smith, N, 1995, Military training earthwork in Crowthorne Wood, Berkshire: a survey by the Royal Commission on the Historical Monuments of England. ***Archaeological Journal,*** 152, 422-40

Sumner, H, 1917, *The ancient earthworks of the New Forest.* London. Chiswick Press

Reports on the excavation of sites under woodland
Cleal, R, and Allen, M J, 1994, Investigation of tree-damaged barrows on King Barrow Ridge, Amesbury. *Wiltshire Archaeological and Natural History Magazine,* 87, 54-84

Fasham, P J, 1979, The excavation of a triple barrow in Micheldever Wood, Hampshire. *Proceedings of the Hampshire Field Club,* 35, 5-40

Fasham, P J, 1987, *A banjo enclosure in Micheldever Wood, Hampshire* (= Hampshire Field Club and Archaeological Society Monograph 5). Winchester. Hampshire Field Club and Archaeological Society

O.6 Lowland heath

General studies and overviews
Dimbleby, G W, 1962, The development of British heathlands and their soils. *Oxford Forestry Memoirs,* 23

Dimbleby, G W, 1976, The history and archaeology of heaths. In J H P Sankey and H W Mackworth (eds), *The southern heathlands: symposium held at Rogate Field Centre 4-6th October 1974.* London.

Surveys
Sussans, K, 1996, *The Breckland Archaeological Survey 1994-6.* Bury St Edmunds. Suffolk County Council, Norfolk Museums Service and English Heritage

Reports on excavations
Ashbee, P, and Dimbleby, G W, 1974, The Moor Green Barrow, West End, Hampshire, excavations 1961. *Proceedings of Hampshire Field Club and Archaeological Society,* 31, 5-18

Cox, P W, and Hearne, C A, 1991, *Redeemed from the heath: the archaeology of the Wytch Farm Oilfield* (= DNHAS Monograph 9). Dorchester. DNHAS

Petersen, F F, 1981, *Excavation of a Bronze Age cemetery on Knighton Heath, Dorset* (= BAR British Series 98). Oxford. BAR

Piggott, C, 1943, Excavation of fifteen barrows in the New Forest 1941-2. *Proceedings of the Prehistoric Society,* 9, 1-27

Smith, G, 1996, Archaeology and environment of a Bronze Age cairn and prehistoric and Romano-British field system at Chysauster, Gulval, near Penzance, Cornwall. *Proceedings of the Prehistoric Society,* 62, 167-219

O.7 Arable land

General studies and overviews
Hazlegrove, C, Millett, M, and Smith, I (eds), 1985, *Archaeology from the ploughsoil.* Sheffield. Department of Archaeology and Prehistory, University of Sheffield

Lambrick, G, 1977, *Archaeology and agriculture: a survey of modern cultivation methods and the problems of assessing plough damage to archaeological sites.* London and Oxford. CBA and Oxford Archaeological Unit

Schofield, A J (ed), 1991, *Interpreting artefact scatters: contributions to ploughzone archaeology* (= Oxbow Monograph 4). Oxford. Oxbow Books

Regional and local surveys
Stoertz, C, 1997, *Ancient landscapes of the Yorkshire Wolds.* Swindon. Royal Commission on the Historical Monuments of England

Reports on excavations
See APPENDIX M.1 for reports of excavations within arable land.

O.8 Parkland and ornamental gardens

General studies and overviews
Brown, A E (ed), 1991, *Garden archaeology* (= CBA Research Report 78). London. CBA

McRobie, L, 1996, Garden archaeology. *Conservation Bulletin,* 28, 14-15

Taigel, A, and Williamson, T, 1994, *Parks and gardens.* London. Batsford

Taylor, C, 1983, *The archaeology of gardens.* Princes Risborough. Shire

Surveys and gazetteers
Bond, J, and Tiller, K, 1987, *Blenheim: landscape for a palace.* Gloucester. Alan Sutton and Oxford University Department of External Studies

Everson, P, 1989, The gardens of Campden House, Chipping Campden, Gloucestershire. *Garden History,* 17, 109-21

English Heritage, 1984-88, *Register of Parks and Gardens of special historic interest in England.* London. English Heritage. (46 vols in 4 parts)

Reports on excavations
Currie, C K, 1996, Archaeological excavations at Leigh Park, Havant, Hampshire, 1992. *Hampshire Studies (= Proceedings of the Hampshire Field Club and Archaeological Society),* 51, 201-32

Currie, C K, and Locock, M, 1993, Excavations at Castle Bromwich Hall gardens, 1989-91. *Post Medieval Archaeology*, 27, 111-199

Dix, B, 1995, Kirby Hall and its gardens: excavations in 1987-1994. *Archaeological Journal*, 152, 291-380

O.9 Upland moor

General studies and overviews
Darvill, T, 1986, **The archaeology of the uplands: a rapid assessment of archaeological knowledge and practice**. London. CBA and RCHME

Darvill, T, 1986, **Archaeology in the uplands: what future for our past?** London. CBA

Surveys
Charlton, D B, and Day, J C, 1978, Excavation and field survey in upper Redesdale. *Archaeologia Aeliana* (ser 5), 6, 61-86

Fleming, A, 1978, The prehistoric landscape of Dartmoor. Part 1. South Dartmoor. *Proceedings of the Prehistoric Society*, 44, 97-124

Fleming, A, 1983, The prehistoric landscape of Dartmoor. Part 2. North and east Dartmoor. *Proceedings of the Prehistoric Society*, 49, 195-242

Fleming A, and Ralph, N, 1982, Medieval settlement and land-use on Holne Moor, Dartmoor: the landscape evidence. *Medieval Archaeology*, 26, 101-37

Hayes, R H, 1983, **Levisham Moor: archaeological investigations 1957-1978**. Helmsley. North York Moors National Park Committee and Scarborough Archaeological and Historical Society

Johnson, N, and Rose, P, 1994, **Bodmin Moor. An archaeological survey. Volume 1: the human landscape to c1800** (= HBMCE Archaeological Report 24 / RCHME Supplementary Series 11). London. English Heritage, RCHME and Cornwall Archaeological Unit

Reports on excavations
Barnett, J, 1994, Excavations of a Bronze Age unenclosed cemetery, cairns, and field boundaries at Eagleston Flat, Curbar, Derbyshire 1984, 1989-90. *Proceedings of the Prehistoric Society*, 60, 287-370

Beresford, G, 1979, Three deserted medieval settlements on Dartmoor: a report on the late E Marie Minter's excavation. *Medieval Archaeology*, 23, 98-158

Harding, A F, and Ostoja-Zagórski, J, 1994, Prehistoric and early medieval activity on Danby Rigg, North Yorkshire. *Archaeological Journal*, 151, 16-97

Hewitt, I, and Beckensall, S, 1996, The excavation of cairns at Blawearie, Old Bewick, Northumberland. *Proceedings of the Prehistoric Society,* 62, 255-274

Smith, K, Coppen, J, Wainwright, G J, and Beckett, S, 1981, The Shaugh Moor Project: third report. Settlement and environmental investigations. *Proceedings of the Prehistoric Society,* 47, 205-276

Wainwright, G J, Fleming, A, and Smith, K, 1979, The Shaugh Moor Project: first report. *Proceedings of the Prehistoric Society,* 45, 1-34

O.10 Industrial land

General studies and overviews
Alfrey, J, and Clark, C, 1993, **The landscape of industry.** London. Routledge

Hudson, K, 1984, **Industrial history from the air.** Cambridge. Cambridge University Press

Palmer, M, 1993, Mining landscapes and the problems of contaminated land. In H Swain (ed), **Rescuing the historic environment: archaeology, the Green movement and conservation strategies for the British landscape.** Hertford. RESCUE. 45-50

Surveys
Giles, C, and Goodall, I H, 1992, **Yorkshire textile mills: the buildings of the Yorkshire textile industry 1770-1930.** London. RCHME and HMSO

Gould, S, and Ayris, I, 1995, **Colliery landscapes. An aerial survey of the deep-mined coal industry in England.** London. English Heritage

GMAU (Greater Manchester Archaeological Unit), 1990, **Reversion areas: the identification and survey of relict industrial landscapes in Greater Manchester.** Manchester. GMAU

Pye, A, and Woodward, F, 1996, **The historic defences of Plymouth.** Truro, Cornwall Archaeological Unit

RCHME, 1989-1993, **An architectural survey of Urban Development Corporation Areas** (seven volumes: Leeds (1989); Sheffield (1989); Tyne and Wear I - Tyneside (1990); Bristol (1991); The Black Country (1991); Tyne and Wear II - Wearside (1992); Teeside (1993)). London. RCHME.

Sharpe, A, 1989, **The Minions survey.** Truro. Cornwall Archaeological Unit. (2 vols)

Impact studies and reports on excavations
Crossley, D, 1995, The blast furnace at Rockley, South Yorkshire. *Archaeological Journal*, 152, 381-421

Davies, S M, 1995, Cattledown Reclamation Scheme, Plymouth. An archaeological impact study. In K Ray (ed), ***Archaeological investigations and research in Plymouth. Volume 1*** (= Plymouth Archaeological Association Occasional Publication 2). Plymouth. Plymouth Archaeological Association. 9-17

O.11 Built-up land and urban areas

General studies and overviews

Aston, M, and Bond, J, 1976, ***The landscape of towns.*** London. Dent

Carver, M, 1987, ***Underneath English towns.*** London. Batsford

Heighway, C M (ed), 1972, ***The erosion of history. Archaeology and planning in towns: a study of historic towns affected by modern development in England, Wales and Scotland.*** London. CBA

Schofield, J, and Leech, R (eds), 1987, ***Urban archaeology in Britain*** (= CBA Research Report 61). London. CBA

Surveys

See APPENDIX A.4 for list of resource assessments and detailed surveys of the archaeology of particular urban areas.

Reports on excavations

See APPENDIX M.2 for reports on excavations arising from the destruction of archaeological deposits through urbanization and property development.

APPENDIX P
Select bibliography of published policy statements, codes of practice, research frameworks and strategies relating to the treatment and management of the archaeological resource

P.1 Policy statements and codes of practice

BADLG (British Archaeologists and Developers Liaison Group), 1991, *The British Archaeologists' and Developers' Liaison Group code of practice (first pubished 1986)*. London. BADLG

CBI (Confederation of British Industry), 1991, *Archaeological investigation: code of practice for mineral operators* (first published 1981). London. CBI

DoE (Department of the Environment), 1986, *Conservation and development: the British approach*. London. DoE

DoE *et al.* (Department of the Environment, Ministry of Agriculture Fisheries and Food, and Welsh Office), 1989, *The Water Act 1989: code of practice on conservation, access and recreation*. London. DoE

DoE (Department of the Environment), 1990, *Planning policy guidance: archaeology and planning* (= PPG16). London. HMSO

DoE and DNH (Department of the Environment and Department of National Heritage), 1994, *Planning policy guidance: planning and the historic environment* (= PPG15). London. HMSO

DNH (Department of National Heritage), 1997, *The Treasure Act 1996: code of practice (England and Wales)*. London. DNH

HMG (Her Majesty's Government), 1994, *Sustainable development: the UK strategy* (= Command Paper 2426). London. HMSO

JNAPC (Joint Nautical Archaeology Policy Committee), 1995, *Code of practice for seabed developers*. London. JNAPC

RESCUE, 1991, Archaeological funding and legislation: a manifesto for the 1990s. *Rescue News,* 54, 45

RESCUE, 1997, *A new manifesto for British archaeology (draft)*. Hertford. RESCUE. (Circulated typescript report)

P.2 National research frameworks and strategies

AIA (Association for Industrial Archaeology), 1990, *A policy for industrial archaeology*. London. AIA

AIA (Association for Industrial Archaeology), 1991, *Industrial archaeology: working for the future*. London. AIA

CBA (Council for British Archaeology), 1988, A policy for the countryside. *British Archaeological News*, 3, 57-60

CBA (Council for British Archaeology), 1993, *The past in tomorrow's countryside*. York. CBA

CIA (Council for Independent Archaeologists), 1994, *The role of local societies in PPG 16*. Northampton. CIA

DMVRG (Deserted Medieval Village Research Group), 1969, memoranda on the preservation of deserted medieval village sites. Reproduced as Appendix I, In M Beresford and J G Hurst (eds), 1989, *Deserted medieval villages* (2nd Edition). Gloucester. Alan Sutton. 303-12

English Heritage, 1991, *Exploring our past: strategies for the archaeology of England*. London. English Heritage

English Heritage, 1996, *Frameworks for our past: a review of research frameworks, strategies and perceptions*. London. English Heritage

English Heritage, 1997, *English Heritage Archaeology Division Research Agenda (Draft)*. London. English Heritage

Forestry Commission, 1995, *Forests and archaeology: guidelines*. Edinburgh. Forestry Commission

Hawkes, C, and Piggott, S (eds), 1948, *A survey and policy of field research in the archaeology of Great Britain. I. Prehistory and early historic ages to the seventh century AD*. London. Council for British Archaeology

Peers, C A, 1929, A research policy for fieldwork. *Antiquaries Journal*, 9, 349-53

Prehistoric Society, 1981, *National priorities for prehistoric archaeology*. London. Prehistoric Society

Prehistoric Society, 1984, *Prehistory, priorities and society: the way forward*. London. Prehistoric Society

Prehistoric Society, 1988, *Saving our prehistoric heritage: landscapes under threat*. London. Prehistoric Society

Society for Medieval Archaeology, 1987, Archaeology and the middle Ages. *Medieval Archaeology*, 31, 1-12

Society for Post-Medieval Archaeology, 1988, *Research priorities for post-medieval archaeology*. London. Society for Post-Medieval Archaeology

Society for the Promotion of Roman Studies, 1985, *Priorities for the preservation and excavation of Romano-British sites*. London. Society for the Promotion of Roman Studies Advisory Committee for the Roman Period to the English Heritage Commission

Thomas, C (ed), 1983, *Research objectives in British archaeology*. London. CBA

P.2 Regional research frameworks and strategies

(By Government Office Region)

North East
Hadrian's Wall Advisory Commitee, 1988, *Academic priorities for work on Hadrian's Wall*. London. Hadrian's Wall Advisory Committee

Northumberland County Council, 1995, *A strategy for coastal archaeology in Northumberland*. Morpeth. Northumberland County Council

North West
Cheshire County Council, 1991, *An archaeological strategy for Cheshire*. Chester. Cheshire County Council

Chester Archaeological Service, no date, *Chester Archaeological Service: draft research guidelines*. Chester. Chester City Council

Greater Manchester Archaeological Unit, 1994, *Research frameworks for Greater Manchester (draft)*. Manchester. Greater Manchester Archaeological Unit

Yorkshire and Humberside
Halkon, P, and Millett, M, 1994, *The Holme Project: research framework*. Durham. Department of Archaeology, University of Durham

South Yorkshire Archaeological Service, 1994, *A research strategy for the Yorkshire Archaeological Service*. Sheffield. South Yorkshire Archaeological Service

Sumpter, A B, 1987, *An assessment of priorities for the Roman period in West Yorkshire*. Wakefield. West Yorkshire Archaeological Service

Whitwell, B, no date, *The future of Humberside's past*. Beverley. Humberside County Council

York City Council, 1992, *Conservation Policies for York: archaeology*. York. York City Council Directorate of Development Services

Merseyside

East Midlands
Derbyshire Archaeological Advisory Committee, 1986, *Archaeology in Derbyshire: research potential*. Derby. Derbyshire Archaeological Advisory Committee

Derbyshire Archaeological Advisory Committee, 1987, *Archaeology in Derbyshire: a proposed programme of research*. Derby. Derbyshire Archaeological Advisory Committee

Derbyshire Archaeological Advisory Committee, 1994, *Archaeology in Derbyshire: a proposed second programme of research*. Derby. Derbyshire Archaeological Advisory Committee

Foard, G, 1979, *Archaeological priorities: proposals for Northamptonshire* (= Archaeology Occasional Paper 4). Northampton. Northamptonshire County Council

Hannan, A, 1994, *Research frameworks for archaeology in Northamptonshire*. Northampton. Northampton Heritage

Jones, M J and Vince, A G, 1992, *Academic priorities: ideas for future research*. Lincoln. City of Lincoln Archaeological Unit

Mahany, C M (ed), 1977, *Priorities 1977*. East Midlands Committee of Field Archaeologists

Brown, A, 1993, *Priorities for the East Midlands: some suggestions.* London. English Heritage

West Midlands

Boland, P, and Collins, P A, 1994, Strategy for industrial archaeology in the Black Country. *Industrial Archaeology Review,* 14, 157-69

Brown, D, Buteux, V, *et al.,* 1993, *Post-medieval archaeology: towards a co-ordinated approach.* Worcester. Hereford and Worcester County Archaeological Service

Buteux, S, 1994, *The archaeology of the West Midlands: overview and research strategies. Prehistory.* Birmingham. Birmingham University Field Archaeology Unit

Carver, M O H (ed), 1980, Medieval Worcester - an archaeological framework. *Worcester Archaeological Society Proceedings* (3rd Ser), 7, 1-356

Carver, M O H, 1991, A strategy for lowland Shropshire. *Transactions of the Shropshire Historical and Archaeological Society,* 67, 1-8

Graig, J, and Moffett, L, 1992, *Environmental archaeology in middle England: research directions for projects funded by English Heritage.* Birmingham. Birmingham University Field Archaeology Unit

Eastern Region

Ayers, B, Glazebrook, J, and Rogerson, A, 1994, *An outline research framework for Norfolk (draft).* Norwich. Norfolk County Council

Brown, N, 1995, *Regional research framework: East Anglia (Palaeolithic, Mesolithic, Neolithic and Bronze Age).* Chelmsford. Essex County Council

Bryant, S, 1994, *Research frameworks for Hertfordshire.* Hertford. Hertfordshire County Council

Bryant, S, 1996, *An archaeological strategy for Hertfordshire.* Hertford. Hertfordshire County Council

Buckley, D G, 1994, *East Anglia archaeology regional research agenda: current research priorities in Essex.* Chelmsford. Essex County Council

Cambridge Archaeological Field Group, 1994, *Cambridge Archaeological Field Group Research Plan.* Cambridge. Cambridge Archaeological Field Group

Cambridgeshire County Council, 1994, *Exploring Cambridgeshire's past: strategies for a County Archaeological Service.* Cambridge. Cambridgeshire County Council

Carr, B, Martin, E, Pendleton, C, Plouviez, J, and Wade, K, 1994, *Archaeological research priorities in Suffolk.* Ipswich. Suffolk County Council

Hedges, J D, 1975, *The archaeological heritage: a policy for Essex.* Chelmsford. Essex County Council

Huggins, P J, 1994, *Waltham Abbey five-year research programme.* Waltham Abbey. Waltham Abbey Historical Society

Luff, R, 1994, *New perspectives and directions in the zooarchaeology of East Anglia and environs.* Cambridge. Cambridge Faunal Remains Unit

Mays, S A, 1994, *Archaeological research priorities for human remains in East Anglia* (= Ancient Monuments Laboratory Report 94/30). London. English Heritage

Niblett, R, 1994, *Research objectives: St Albans District.* St Albans. St Albans District Council

SCOLE Committee, 1973, *The problems and future of East Anglian archaeology.* Norwich. SCOLE Committee

London

Biddle, M, 1973, *The future of London's past* (= Rescue Publication 14). Hertford. RESCUE

Canham, R, 1978, Some priorities and problems in the prehistoric archaeology of the Thames Basin. In *London and Middlesex Archaeological Society Special Paper 2.* London. London and Middlesex Archaeological Society. 32-8

South East

City of Winchester Archaeology Office, 1981, *Excavation and fieldwork policy.* Winchester. Winchester City Council Archaeoloy Office

East Sussex County Council, 1993, *Strategy for archaeology in East Sussex.* Lewes. East Sussex County Council

Ellison, A, 1981, *A policy for archaeological investigation in Wessex.* Salisbury. Trust for Wessex Archaeology

Forum for Archaeology in Wessex, 1994, *Wessex and archaeology: opportunities, priorities and management in the 1990s and the new millennium.* Southampton. Forum for Archaeology in Wessex

Gardiner, M, 1994, *Further research directions for archaeology on Romney Marsh*. London. South Eastern Archaeological Services

Hampshire County Council, 1979, *Hampshire's heritage and a policy for its future*. Winchester. Hampshire County Council Planning Department

Hinton, D A, and Hughes, M (eds), 1996, *Archaeology in Hampshire: a framework for the future*. Salisbury. Hampshire County Council

Lawson, A, 1986, *Rescue and research in Wessex*. Salisbury. Trust for Wessex Archaeology

Mays, S A, 1991, *Research priorities for human remains in Wessex* (= Ancient Monuments Laboratory Report 128/91). London. English Heritage

Mays, S A, and Anderson, T, 1995, *Archaeological research priorities for human remains from South East England (Kent, East and West Sussex and Surrey)* (= Ancient Monuments Laboratory Report 56/94). London. English Heritage

Winchester Museums Service, 1985, *Research priorities in fieldwork*. Winchester. Winchester City Museum

South West

Bath Archaeological Trust, no date, *Academic priorities for archaeological research in Bath and the surrounding area*. Bath. Bath Archaeological Trust

Bath Archaeological Trust, 1994, *Academic priorities for archaeological research in Bath and its region*. Bath. Bath Archaeological Trust

Cotswold Archaeological Trust, 1996, Research objectives. *Cotswold Archaeological Trust Annual Review*, 6, 18-20

Darvill, T C, and Gerrard, C M, 1994, Appendix C: research objectives. In T Darvill and C Gerrard, *Cirencester: town and landscape*. Cirencester. Cotswold Archaeological Trust. 195-7

Davison, A, 1995, *Research priorities: Gloucestershire, Somerset and Avon*. London. English Heritage

Ellison, A, 1981, *A policy for archaeological investigation in Wessex*. Salisbury. Trust for Wessex Archaeology

FAW (Forum for Archaeology in Wessex), 1994, *Wessex and archaeology: opportunities, priorities and management in the 1990s and the new millennium*. Southampton. FAW

Groube, L M, and Bowden, C B, 1982, *The archaeology of rural Dorset: past, present and future* (= DNHAS Monograph 4). Dorchester. Dorset Natural History and Archaeological Society

Hingley, R, no date, *An archaeological strategy for the Upper Thames Gravels in Gloucestershire and Wiltshire*. Gloucester and Trowbridge. Gloucestershire County Council and Wiltshire County Council

Lawson, A, 1986, *Rescue and research in Wessex*. Salisbury. Trust for Wessex Archaeology

Mays, S A, 1991, *Research priorities for human remains in Wessex* (= Ancient Monuments Laboratory Report 128/91). London. English Heritage

Piggott, S, 1971, An archaeological strategy and policy for Wiltshire. Part III. Neolithic and Bronze Age. *Wiltshire Archaeological Magazine*, 66, 47-57

Roe, D, and Radley, J, 1969, An archaeological survey and policy for Wiltshire. Parts I and II. *Wiltshire Archaeological Magazine*, 64, 1-20

Straker, V, 1989, *Archaeobotany in south west England: research directions for HBMCE-funded projects*. Bristol. English Heritage

SWAF (South-West Archaeological Forum), 1996, *Towards a regional research strategy, papers presented on 20th March 1996. County Hall Exeter*. SWAF. Taunton. (Circulated typescript report)

Woodward, P J, 1994, *Research frameworks*. Dorchester. Dorset Archaeological Committee

P.3 Topic-based or theme-specific research frameworks

Blick, C, Standing, I J, and Cranstone, D, 1991, *Metallurgical sites in Britain: priorities for research and preservation*. London. Historical Metallurgy Society

Carruthers, W, 1993, *A review of archaeobotanical research priorities* (= Ancient Monuments Laboratory Report 16/93). London. English Heritage

CBA (Council for British Archaeology), 1997, *Themes for urban research, c100 BC to AD 200*. York. CBA.

Chadburn, A, 1994, *Research frameworks: round barrows*. London. English Heritage

Coles, J M, 1986, Precision, purpose amd priorities in wetland archaeology. *Antiquaries Journal*, 66, 227-47

Cranstone, D, 1991, *Mining sites in Britain: priorities for research and preservation*. London. Institute of Mining History and Archaeology

Croft, R, and Williamson, T, 1988, Statement of excavation policy. *Medieval Settlement Research Group Annual Report*, 3, 8

Firth, A, 1995, *Research frameworks in maritime/underwater archaeology*. Birmingham. IFA Maritime Affairs Group

Kinnes, I, Mercer, R J, and Smith, I F, 1976, *Research priorities in the British Neolithic*. London. Prehistoric Society

Lambrick, G, and Robinson, M A, 1988, *Research directions for HBMCE-funded environmental archaeology at Oxford*. Oxford. Oxford Environmental Archaeology Committee

Mellars, P A, 1975, *Palaeolithic and Mesolithic sites in Britain: priorities for research and conservation*. London. CBA

Mellars, P (ed), 1987, *Research priorities for archaeological science*. London. Council for British Archaeology

MSRG (Moated Sites Research Group), 1983, *Policy for the preservation and excavation of moated sites*. London. MSRG

Payne, S, 1992, *Review of academic priorities for work on animal bones funded by English Heritage*. London. Ancient Monuments Laboratory, English Heritage

PCRG (Prehistoric Ceramics Research Group), 1991, *The study of later prehistoric pottery: general policies* (= PCRG Occasional Paper 1). Oxford. PCRG

Robinson, M A, 1986, *Research directions for HBMCE-funded environmental archaeology on plant remains, invertebrate remains and soils/sediments at Oxford*. Oxford. Oxford Environmental Archaeology Committee

Roebuck, J, 1995, *Medieval estates: priorities for research*. London. English Heritage

Roebuck, J, and Davison, A, 1995, *Medieval monastic sites: priorities for research*. London. English Heritage. [Circulated typescript report]

Notes

Chapter 2

1. This case study is based on research by Hugh Beamish.

2. This case study is based on research by Karen Gracie-Langrick.

Chapter 4

1. This section is based on research carried out by Nicola King and drafted by her.

2. This case study draws heavily on a document researched and written by Nicola King and Karen Gracie-Langrick.

Chapter 5

1. Within the MARS sample, PAE data are missing for 718 observations (about 5% of the total), the distribution and causes of which are unknown. It is assumed to be randomly missing data, and should not adversely affect the calculation.

Chapter 6

1. The counties providing data were: Avon (excluding Bath City), Cheshire, Cornwall, Cumbria, Durham, Essex, Hertfordshire, Lincolnshire, Merseyside, Norfolk, and Warwickshire.

Chapter 7

1. In the event, it seems that MARS has collected the largest sample of modern land-use for some years (15,964 observations), albeit based on point-data within a spatially defined sampling frame.

2. There was a difference in the sample sizes used by MARS for the Field Survey and Aerial Photography Survey Programmes because of one of the features of the MARS database and its relational structure. The difference occurs because a site can have more than one value for some classifications such as land-use, and thus the number of entries in the relevant database tables may appear to be greater than the number of MARS Monuments. (Land-use and related data are stored in the 'cond.db' database table). In most cases data are presented in terms of MARS Monuments (14,591 examples), but where there is the possibility of multiple entries for one monument, the unit of presentation is an 'observation', and the appropriate number of observations is noted.

Chapter 8

1. Great care must be exercised in using these estimates because Scheduled Monuments do not constitute from a statistically random sample.

Bibliography

Aberg, F A, and Leech, R H, 1992, The national archaeological record for England. Past, present, and future. In C U Larsen (ed), *Sites and monuments. National archaeological records.* Copenhagen. Nationalmuseet. 157-69

ACAO (Association of County Archaeological Officers), 1978, *A guide to the establishment of SMRs.* Bedford. ACAO

ADAS (Agricultural Development Advisory Service), 1968, *Agricultural land classification map of England and Wales. Explanatory note.* London. MAFF

ADAS (Agricultural Development Advisory Service), 1977, *1:250,000 series agricultural land classification of England and Wales. Explanatory note.* London. MAFF

ADAS (Agricultural Development Advisory Service), 1996a, *Historical monitoring in West Penwith ESA 1993-1995.* London. ADAS [Circulated typescript report]

ADAS (Agricultural Development Advisory Service), 1996b, *Historical monitoring in the Pennine Dales ESA 1987-1995.* London. ADAS [Circulated typescript report]

ADAS (Agricultural Development Advisory Service), 1996c, *Historical monitoring in South Downs ESA 1987-1995.* London. ADAS [Circulated typescript report]

ADAS (Agricultural Development Advisory Service), 1996d, *Historical monitoring in the Somerset Levels and Moors ESA 1987-1995.* London. ADAS [Circulated typescript report]

ADAS (Agricultural Development Advisory Service), 1996e, *Historical monitoring in The Broads ESA 1987-1995.* London. ADAS [Circulated typescript report]

Addyman, P, 1974, York: the anatomy of a crisis in urban archaeology. In P A Rahtz (ed), *Rescue archaeology.* Harmondsworth. Penguin. 153-162

Agriculture Committee, 1997, *Environmentally Sensitive Areas and other schemes under the agri-environment regulation. Volume I. Report, together with the proceedings of the committee* (= HC 45-I). London. The Stationery Office

Alexander, P, 1998, Onwards with a stronger regional focus. *Conservation Bulletin*, 33, 1-2

ALGAO (Association of Local Government Archaeological Officers), 1998, *Protecting our heritage: archaeology in local government 1997.* Chelmsford. ALGAO

Allcroft, A H, 1908, *Earthwork of England.* London. Macmillan

Allden, A, 1984, The County Sites and Monuments Record. *Glevensis,* 18, 7

Allison, G, Ball, S, Cheshire, P, Evans, A, and Stabler, M, 1996, *The value of conservation? A literature review of the economic and social value of the cultural built heritage.* London. English Heritage

Andreae, S, 1996, From comprehensive development to Conservation Areas. In M Hunter (ed), *Preserving the past. The rise of heritage in modern Britain.* Stroud. Alan Sutton. 135-55

Andrews, G, 1984, Archaeology in York: an assessment. In P V Addyman and V E Black (eds), *Archaeological papers from York presented to M W Barley.* York. York Archaeological Trust. 173-208

Anon, 1949, *War and archaeology in Britain: the excavation of ancient sites and the preservation of historic buildings.* London. HMSO

Anon, 1993a, Beckhampton, barrow reinstatement. *Wessex Archaeology Annual Review 1992-3*, 29-30

Anon, 1993b, New sites found in forest survey. *British Archaeological News* (NS) 1, 7

Anon, 1994, Forestry proposals test case for archaeology. ***British Archaeological News*** (NS), 12, 1

Anon, 1995a, Stonehenge houses. ***British Archaeology***, 8, 4

Anon, 1995b, Best year ever. ***British Archaeology***, 8, 5

Anon, 1997a, New 7th century remains found at Ripon. ***British Archaeology***, 24, 5

Anon, 1997b, Sussex 'Flag Fen' decays without record. ***British Archaeology***, 24, 5

Anon, 1997c, Hedgerow legislation introduced. ***Devon Archaeological Society Newsletter***, 68, 14

Anon, 1997d, Erosion places coastal sites in danger. ***British Archaeology***, 22, 5

Anon, 1997e, Thunderstruck (or a Devon Millennium event). ***Devon Archaeological Society Newsletter***, 66, 10

Anon, 1997f, First Tewkesbury, now Stamford Bridge. ***British Archaeology***, 27, 5

Anon, 1997g, Regional Development Agencies: the implications for planning. In M Grant (ed), ***Encyclopedia of Planning Law and Practice Monthly Bulletin***, December, 1-2

Anon, 1998, Modernising planning: what's happening? In M Grant (ed), ***Encyclopedia of Planning Law and Practice Monthly Bulletin***, February, 3-7

Ashbee, P, 1966, The Fussell's Lodge Long Barrow excavations 1957. ***Archaeologia***, 100, 1-80

Ashbee, P, 1972, Field archaeology: its origins and development. In P J Fowler (ed), ***Archaeology and the landscape***. London. John Baker. 38-74

Ashmore, P J, 1993, ***Archaeology and the coastal erosion zone. Towards a Historic Scotland Policy***. Edinburgh. Historic Scotland

Baker, D, 1983, ***Living with the past. The historic environment***. Bedford. David Baker

Baldwin Brown, G, 1905, ***The care of ancient monuments. An account of the legislative and other measures adopted in European countries for protecting ancient monuments and objects and scenes of natural beauty, and for preserving the aspect of historical cities***. Cambridge. Cambridge University Press

Barclay, A, Gray, M, and Lambrick, G, 1995, ***Excavations at the Devil's Quoits, Stanton Harcourt, Oxfordshire 1972-3 and 1988*** (= Thames Valley Landscape: the Windrush Valley, Volume 3). Oxford. Oxford Archaeological Unit

Barclay, G J, Maxwell, G S, Simpson I A, and Davidson D A, 1995, The Cleaven Dyke: a Neolithic cursus monument/bank barrow in Tayside Region, Scotland. ***Antiquity***, 69, 317-26

Barr, C J (ed), 1997a, ***Current status and prospects for key habitats in England. Part 1. Lowland heath landscapes***. London. DETR

Barr, C J (ed), 1997b, ***Current status and prospects for key habitats in England. Part 2. Calcareous grassland landscapes***. London. DETR

Barr, C J (ed), 1997c, ***Current status and prospects for key habitats in England. Part 3. Upland landscapes.*** London. DETR

Barr, C J (ed), 1997d, ***Current status and prospects for key habitats in England. Part 4. Coastal landscapes.*** London. DETR

Barr, C J (ed), 1997e, ***Current status and prospects for key habitats in England. Part 5. Waterside landscapes.*** London. DETR

Barr, C J (ed), 1997f, ***Current status and prospects for key habitats in England. Part 6. Summary report.*** London. DETR

Barr, C J, Benefield, C, Bunce, B, Ridsdale, H, and Whittaker, M, 1986, ***Landscape changes in Britain***. London. ITE

Barr, C J, Bunce R G H, Clarke, R T, Fuller, R M, Firse, M T, Gillespie, M K, Groom, G B, Hallam, C J, Hornung, M, Howard, D C and Ness, M J, 1993, *Countryside Survey 1990: main report*. London. DoE

Barton, R N E, 1992, *Hengistbury Head, Dorset. Volume 2. The later Upper Palaeolithic and early Mesolithic sites* (= OUCA Monograph 34). Oxford. OUCA

Bayliss-Smith, T, and Owens, S (eds), 1990, *Britain's changing environment from the air*. Cambridge. Cambridge University Press

BDPP and OIRM (BDP Planning and Oxford Institute of Retail Management), 1994, *The effects of major out of town development. A literature review for the Department of Environment*. London. HMSO

Beckensall, S, 1993, What future for our cup and rings? *British Archaeological News* (NS), 6, 3

Bell, M, 1983, Valley sediments as evidence of prehistoric land-use on the South Downs. *Proceedings of the Prehistoric Society*, 49, 119-150

Bell, M, 1990, *Brean Down excavations 1983-1987* (= HBMCE Archaeological Report 15). English Heritage. London

Bell, M, Fowler, M J, and Hillson, S W (eds), 1996, *The Experimental Earthwork Project 1960-1992* (= CBA Research Report 100). York. CBA

Bell, S, 1997, The National Forest. From planning to implementation. *Report of the Proceedings of the Town and Country Planning Summer School 1997*. London. Royal Town Planning Institute. 32-3

Bender, B, Hamilton, S, and Tilley, C, 1997, Leskernick: stone worlds; alternative narratives; nested landscapes. *Proceedings of the Prehistoric Society*, 63, 147-78

Benson, D, 1972, A Sites and Monuments Record for the Oxford Region. *Oxoniensia*, 37, 226-37

Benson, D, 1985, Problems of data entry and retrieval. In I Burrow (ed), *County archaeological records: progress and potential*. Taunton. ACAO

Benson, D, 1989, *Upland archaeology in Dyfed. A preliminary assessment*. Carmarthen. Dyfed Archaeological Trust

Benson, D, and Miles, D, 1974, *The upper Thames Valley. An archaeological survey of the river gravels* (= Oxfordshire Archaeological Unit Survey 2). Oxford. Oxfordshire Archaeological Unit

Berry, A Q, and Brown, I W (eds), 1994, *Erosion on archaeological earthworks: its prevention, control and repair*. Mold. Clwyd County Council

Berry, A Q, and Brown, I W (eds), 1996, *Managing ancient monuments: an integrated approach*. Mold. Clwyd County Council

Best R H, and Coppock, J T, 1962, *The changing use of land in Britain*. London. Faber and Faber

Beswick, P, Rotherham, I D, and Parsons, J (eds), 1993, *Ancient woodlands. Their archaeology and ecology*. Sheffield. Landscape Conservation Forum

Bibby, P, and Coppin, P, 1994, *Analyses of land-use change statistics* (= SERRL Occasional Monograph 1). London. SERRL

Biddle, M, 1989, The Rose reviewed: A Comedy (?) of Errors. *Antiquity*, 63, 753-60

Biddle, M, 1994, *What future for British archaeology?* (= Oxbow Lecture 1). Oxford. Oxbow Books

Biddle, M, and Emery, V W, 1973, *The M3 Extension: an archaeological survey*. Winchester. M3 Archaeological Rescue Committee

Biddle, M, and Hudson, D M, 1973, *The future of London's past: a survey of the archaeological implications of planning and development in the nation's capital*. Worcester. RESCUE

Biddle, P G, 1992, *Tree roots and foundations* (= Arboricultural Research Note). Farnham. DoE Arboricultural Advisory and Information Service

Bland, R, 1997, New definition for archaeological finds. *Conservation Bulletin*, 32, 22-23

Blunden, J and Curry, N (eds), 1990, *A people's charter? Forty years of the National Parks and Access to the Countryside Act 1949.* London. HMSO

Bodrell, C R, 1993, The influence of MAFF policies. In H Swain (ed), *Rescuing the historic environment. Archaeology, the Green movement and conservation strategies for the British landscape*. Hertford. RESCUE. 27-28

Boismier, W A, 1997, *Modelling the effects of tillage processes on artefact distributions in the plough zone. A simulation study of tillage induced pattern formation* (= BAR British Series 259). Oxford. Archaeopress

Bonney, D J, 1980, Damage by medieval and later cultivation in Wessex. In J Hinchliffe and R T Schadla-Hall (eds), *The past under the plough* (= DAMHB Occasional Paper 3). London. DoE. 41-9

Bradley, R, 1970, The excavation of a Beaker settlement at Belle Tout, East Sussex, England. *Proceedings of the Prehistoric Society*, 36, 312-79

Breeze, D J, 1993, Ancient Monuments legislation. In J Hunter and I Ralston (eds), *Archaeological resource management in the United Kingdom. An introduction*. Stroud and Birmingham. Alan Sutton and the Institute of Field Archaeologists. 44-55

Briggs, M S, 1952, *Goths and Vandals: a study of the destruction, neglect and preservation of historical buildings in England*. London. Constable

Bromley, D W (ed), 1995, *The handbook of environmental economics*. Oxford. Blackwell

Brown, I, Burridge, D, Clarke, D, Guy, J, Hellis, J, Lowry, B, Ruckley, N, and Thomas, R, 1995, *20th century defences in Britain. An introductory guide* (= Practical Handbooks in Archaeology 12). York. CBA

Brown, M, 1997, Protecting the historic environment. *Rescue News*, 72, 7

Bryson, B, 1996, *Notes from a Small Island*. London. Black Swan

BTA (British Tourist Authority), 1996, *Visits to tourist attractions 1995*. London. British Tourist Authority and English Tourist Board Research Services

Buchanan, R A, and Partners, 1968, *Bath: a study in conservation.* London. HMSO

Buchanan, R A, 1972, *Industrial archaeology in Britain*. Harmondsworth. Penguin

Burnham, B, and Wacher, J, 1990, *The small towns of Roman Britain*. London. Batsford

Burnham, H, 1991, *A survey of the condition of Scheduled Ancient Monuments in Wales. Part 7. Overall review.* Cardiff. CADW. [Circulated typescript report]

Burrow, I (ed), 1985, *County archaeological records: progress and potential*. Somerset. ACAO

Burrows, G S, 1968, *Chichester: a study in conservation.* London. HMSO

Butcher, S, and Garwood, P, 1994, *Rescue excavation: 1938 to 1972*. London. English Heritage

CAG (CAG Consultants), 1997, *What matters and why. Environmental capital: a new approach*. Cheltenham. CAG Consultants and the Countryside Commission

Carman, J, 1996, *Valuing ancient things: archaeology and the law*. London. Leicester University Press

Carman, J, 1997, Interpreting the landscapes of battle. *British Archaeology*, 21, 8-9

Carnarvon, Earl, 1883, Anniversary Address. ***Proceedings of the Society of Antiquaries of London*** (2nd Ser), 9, 292-303

Carter, H, 1993, Ancient monuments on trial. ***Conservation Bulletin***, 20, 15-16

Carver, M O H, 1987a, ***Underneath English towns***. London. Batsford

Carver, M O H, 1987b, The nature of urban deposits. In J Schofield and R Leech (eds), ***Urban archaeology in Britain*** (= CBA Research Report 61). London. CBA. 9-26

Carver, M, 1994, Putting research back in the driving seat. ***British Archaeological News*** (NS), 13, 9

Carver, M O H, 1996, On archaeological value. ***Antiquity***, 70, 45-56

CAS (Congress of Archaeological Societies), 1910, ***Scheme for recording ancient defensive earthworks and fortified enclosures*** (Revised edition). London. Congress of Archaeological Societies in union with the Society of Antiquaries of London

CAS (Congress of Archaeological Societies), 1926, ***Report of the special committee on the cataloguing of local antiquities.*** London. Congress of Archaeological Societies

CAS (Congress of Archaeological Societies), 1927, ***Report on linear earthworks***. London. Congress of Archaeological Societies

CAS (Congress of Archaeological Societies), 1931, ***Report on lynchets and grass ridges.*** London. Congress of Archaeological Societies

CAS (Congress of Archaeological Societies), 1938, ***Report of the forty-fifth Congress and of the Research Committee for the year 1937***. London. CAS

CBA (Council for British Archaeology), 1952, ***Report for the year ended 31 July 1952.*** London. CBA

CBA (Council for British Archaeology), 1975, ***Report of the working party on archaeological records to the RCHM(E)***. London. CBA. [Circulated typescript report]

CBA (Council for British Archaeology), 1978, Survey and archaeology. ***Report No 28 of the Council for British Archaeology for the year ended 30 June 1978.*** London. CBA. 55-62

CBA (Council for British Archaeology), 1984, ***Possible outputs from a National Archaeological Database (NADB)***. London. CBA. [Circulated typescript report]

CBA and RESCUE (Council for British Archaeology and RESCUE), 1974, ***Archaeology and government: a plan for archaeology in Britain.*** London and Worcester. CBA and RESCUE

CBI (Confederation of British Industry), 1991, ***Archaeological investigation: code of practice for mineral operators***. London. CBI

Chadburn, A, 1989, Computerised county sites and monuments records in England. An overview of their structure, development and progress. In S Rahtz and J Richards (eds), ***Computer applications and quantitative methods in archaeology*** (= BAR International Series 548). Oxford. BAR. 9-18

Champion, T, 1996, Protecting the monuments: archaeological legislation from the 1882 Act to PPG 16. In M Hunter (ed), ***Preserving the past: the rise of heritage in modern Britain***. Stroud. Alan Sutton. 38-56

Chapman, S B, Clarke, S T, and Webb, N R, 1989, The survey and assessment of heathland in Dorset, England, for conservation. ***Biological Conservation***, 47, 137-52

Cherry, J F, Gamble, C, and Shennan, S (eds), 1978, ***Sampling in contemporary British archaeology*** (= BAR British Series 50). Oxford. BAR

Christie, P M, 1960, The Stonehenge cursus. ***Wiltshire Archaeological and Natural History Magazine***, 58, 370-82

Clark, A, 1993, ***Excavations at Mucking.Volume 1. The site atlas. Excavations by M U and T W Jones*** (= HBMCE Archaeological Report 20). London. English Heritage

Cleal, R M J, and Allen, M J, 1994, Investigation of tree-damaged barrows on King Barrow Ridge and Luxenborough Plantation, Amesbury. *The Wiltshire Archaeological and Natural History Magazine,* 87, 54-84

Cleere, H (ed), 1982, *Archaeology in Britain 1981*. London. CBA

Cleere, H (ed), 1983, *Archaeology in Britain 1982*. London. CBA

Cleere, H (ed), 1984, *Approaches to the archaeological heritage*. Cambridge. Cambridge University Press

Cleere, H (ed), 1989, *Archaeological heritage management in the modern world* (= One World Archaeology Series 9). London. Unwin Hyman

Cleere, H, 1995, Cultural landscapes as World Heritage. *Conservation and Management of Archaeological Sites*, 1, 63-8

Clubb, N, and James, P, 1985, A computer record for Greater London. *London Archaeologist*, 5, 38-9

Clubb, N, and Lang, N, 1996, A strategic appraisal of information systems for archaeology and architecture in England - past, present and future. In H Kamermans and K Fennema (eds), *Interfacing the past: computer applications and quantitative methods in archaeology. CAA 95 (= Analecta Praehistorica Leidensia, 28)*. 51-72

CNP (Council for National Parks), 1982, *National Parks and the rural economy. Summary of proceedings of a conference held in London 8th March 1982*. London. CNP

Cochran, W G, 1977, *Sampling techniques* (Third edition). New York. Wiley

CoE (Council of Europe), 1992, *European Convention on the Protection of the Archaeological Heritage (Revised)* (= Treaty Series 143). Strasbourg. Council of Europe

Cole, L, Kernon, T, and Knightbridge, R, 1996, *Identifying and describing farm character and structure in the Natural Areas* (= English Nature Research Report 206). Peterborough. English Nature

Coleman, A, 1961, The Second Land Use Survey: progress and prospect. *The Geographical Journal*, 127, 168-86

Coles, B, 1995, *Wetland management. A survey for English Heritage* (= WARP Occasional Paper 9). Exeter. WARP

Coles, B, 1996, Wetlands in danger. *Conservation Bulletin,* 28, 11-13

Coles J, and Coles, B, 1996, *Enlarging the past: the contribution of wetland archaeology* (= Society of Antiquaries of Scotland Monograph 11. Wetland Archaeology Research Project (WARP) Occasional Paper 10). Edinburgh. Society of Antiquaries of Scotland

Colt Hoare, R, 1810, *The ancient history of Wiltshire. Part 1*. London. Privately published

Colt Hoare, R, 1819, *The ancient history of Wiltshire. Part 2*. London. Privately published

Comeren, C M, 1994, The destruction of the past: nonrenewable cultural resources. *Nonrenewable Resources*, 3.1, 6-24

Copinger, W A, 1907, *On a scheme for rendering the charters and MSS in the various repositories available for county purposes*. London. Congress of Archaeological Societies

Countryside Commission, 1983a, *What future for the uplands?* (= CCP 149). Cheltenham. Countryside Commission

Countryside Commission, 1983b, *The changing uplands?* (= CCP 153). Cheltenham. Countryside Commission

Countryside Commission, 1987, *Landscape assessments: a Countryside Commission approach* (= CCD 18). Cheltenham. Countryside Commission

Countryside Commission, 1989a, *Areas of Outstanding Natural Beauty in England and Wales* (= CCP 276). Cheltenham. Countryside Commission

Countryside Commission, 1989b, *Directory of Areas of Outstanding Natural Beauty* (= CCD 54). Cheltenham. Countryside Commission

Countryside Commission, 1990a, *Changes in landscape features in England and Wales 1947-1985* (= CCD 44). Cheltenham. Countryside Commission

Countryside Commission, 1990b, *Areas of Outstanding Natural Beauty: a policy statement 1990* (= CCP 302). Cheltenham. Countryside Commission

Countryside Commission, 1991a, *Caring for the countryside: a policy agenda for England in the nineties* (= CCP 351). Cheltenham. Countryside Commission

Countryside Commission, 1991b, *Landscape change in the National Parks. Technical report* (= CCP 359). Cheltenham. Countryside Commission

Countryside Commission, 1992, *Application pack for Countryside Stewardship* (= CCP 345). Cheltenham. Countryside Commission

Countryside Commission, 1993a, *Sustainability and the English countryside* (= CCP 432). Cheltenham. Countryside Commission

Countryside Commission, 1993b, *The National Forest strategy: draft for consultation*. Cheltenham. Countryside Commission

Countryside Commission, 1994a, *Views from the past. Historic landscape character in the English countryside.* Cheltenham. Countryside Commission. [Draft policy statement]

Countryside Commission, 1994b, *Countryside Stewardship: handbook and application form* (= CCP 453) Cheltenham. Countryside Commission

Countryside Commission, 1996a, *The character of England: landscape, wildlife and natural features* (= CCX 41). Cheltenham. Countryside Commission

Countryside Commission, 1996b, *A living countryside: our strategy for the next ten years* (= CCP 492). Cheltenham. Countryside Commission

Countryside Commission, 1997a, *Areas of Outstanding Natural Beauty: providing for the future* (= CCP 523). Cheltenham. Countryside Commission

Countryside Commission, 1997b, *Countryside Stewardship: monitoring and evaluation of the pilot scheme 1991-96* (= CCWP 05). Cheltenham. Countryside Commission

Cox, P W, and Hearne, C M, 1991, *Redeemed from the heath: the archaeology of the Wytch Farm Oilfield (1987-90)* (= DNHAS Monograph Series 9). Dorchester. DNHAS

Crawford, G M, 1980, *Bronze Age burial mounds in Cleveland.* Middlesborough. Cleveland County Council

Crawford, O G S, 1922, *Notes on archaeological information incorporated in the Ordnance Survey Maps. Part 1: the long barrows and stone circles in the area covered by sheet 8 of the 1/4-inch map (the Cotswolds and Welsh Marches)* (= Ordnance Survey Professional Papers (NS) 6). Southampton. HMSO

Crawford, O G S, 1925, *The long barrows of the Cotswolds.* Gloucester. John Bellows

Crawford, O G S, 1926, Archaeology and the Ordnance Survey. In *The work of the Ordnance Survey* (= Professional Paper (NS) 10). London. HMSO. 9-11

Crawford, O G S, 1929, Editorial. *Antiquity,* 3, 1-4

Crawford, O G S, 1955, *Said and done: the autobiography of an archaeologist.* London. Weidenfeld and Nicholson

Crawford, O G S, 1960, *Archaeology in the field* (4th impression). London. Phoenix

Crawford, O G S, and Keiller, A, 1928, *Wessex from the air.* Oxford. Oxford University Press

Croad, S J, 1992, The National Monuments Record: the early years. ***Transactions of the Ancient Monuments Society,*** 36, 79-98

Croad, S J, and Fowler, P J, 1984, RCHME's first 75 years: an outline history, 1908-83. ***Royal Commission on Historical Monuments (England) Annual Review 1983-84***, 8-13

Croft, B, Schofield, J, and Webster, C, 1996, Managing archaeology in historic towns. ***Conservation Bulletin***, 30, 18-19

Cunliffe, B, 1987, ***Hengistbury Head, Dorset. Volume 1. The Prehistoric and Roman Settlement, 3500 BC-AD 500*** (= OUCA Monograph 13). Oxford. OUCA

Cunnington, P, 1988, ***Changes of use: the conversion of old buildings***. London. A C Black

Curwen, E C, 1930, Neolithic camps. ***Antiquity***, 4, 22-54

Daniel, G, 1978, Editorial. ***Antiquity***, 52, 1-6

Dannell, G B, and Wild, J P, 1987, ***Longthorpe II. The military works-depot: an episode in landscape history*** (= Britannia Monograph Series 8). London. Society for the Promotion of Roman Studies

Darvill, T, 1986, ***The archaeology of the uplands: a rapid assessment of archaeological knowledge and practice***. London. RCHME and CBA

Darvill, T, 1987, ***Ancient monuments in the countryside: an archaeological management review*** (= HBMCE Archaeological Report 5). London. English Heritage

Darvill, T, 1989, England's archaeological resource: the Survival Assessment Programme. Project design for the Wiltshire Pilot Study. London and Woodchester. English Heritage and Timothy Darvill Archaeological Consultants. [Circulated typescript report]

Darvill, T, 1991, ***England's archaeological resource: the Survival Assessment Programme. Report on the Wiltshire Pilot Study***. London and Woodchester. English Heritage and Timothy Darvill Archaeological Consultants. [Circulated typescript report]

Darvill, T, 1992a, ***Monuments Protection Programme: monument evaluation manual. Part III. Relict cultural landscapes***. London. English Heritage. [Circulated typescript report]

Darvill, T, 1992b, ***Monuments Protection Programme: monument evaluation manual. Part IV. Urban areas.*** London. English Heritage. (2 vols). [Circulated typescript report]

Darvill, T, 1993a, ***England's archaeological heritage: the state of the resource. Briefing paper, method appraisal and outline proposal for implementation***. Bournemouth. Bournemouth University. [Circulated typescript report]

Darvill, T, 1993b, ***Valuing Britain's archaeological resource*** (= Bournemouth University Inaugural Lecture). Bournemouth. Bournemouth University

Darvill, T, 1995, Value systems in archaeology. In M A Cooper, A Firth, J Carman and D Wheatley (eds), ***Managing archaeology***. London. Routledge. 40-50

Darvill, T, 1997a, Landscapes and the archaeologist. In K Barker and T Darvill (eds), ***Making English landscapes*** (= Bournemouth University School of Conservation Sciences Occasional Paper 3). Oxford. Oxbow Books. 70-91

Darvill, T, 1997b, Archaeology and Europe: an update. ***The Archaeologist***, 29, 15-17

Darvill, T, Burrow, S, and Wildgust, D A, 1995, ***Planning for the past. Volume 2. An assessment of archaeological assessments 1982-91***. London and Bournemouth. English Heritage and Bournemouth University

Darvill, T, and Fulton, A, 1998, ***MARS: the Monuments at Risk Survey of England, 1995. Summary report***. Bournemouth and London. Bournemouth University and English Heritage

Darvill, T, Fulton, A, and Bell, M, 1994, ***Monuments at Risk Survey: project design***. Bournemouth. Bournemouth University. [Circulated typescript report]

Darvill, T, and Gerrard, C, 1994, *Cirencester: town and landscape*. Cirencester. Cotswold Archaeological Trust

Darvill, T C, Parker Pearson, M, Smith, R, and Thomas, R (eds), 1978, *New approaches to our past*. Southampton. Southampton University Archaeological Society

Darvill, T, Saunders, A, and Startin, B, 1987, A question of national importance: approaches to the evaluation of ancient monuments for the Monuments Protection Programme in England. *Antiquity*, 61, 393-408

Darwin, C, 1888, *The formation of vegetable mould through the action of worms, with observations on their habits*. London. John Murray

Dawson, A, 1995, *Grocery retailing 1995. The market review*. Watford. IGD Business Publications

Denison, S, 1997, The sad tale of Tewkesbury battlefield. *British Archaeology*, 25, 11

DETR (Department of the Environment, Transport and the Regions), 1997, *Land-use change in England number 12* (= DETR Statistical Bulletin). London. DETR

DETR (Department of the Environment, Transport and the Regions), 1998, *Statistics of planning applications. October to December 1997*. London. DETR

DETR and Welsh Office (Department of the Environment, Transport and the Regions and Welsh Office), 1998, *Access to the open countryside in England and Wales*. London and Cardiff. DETR and Welsh Office

DMVRG (Deserted Medieval Village Research Group), 1965, Memoranda on the preservation of deserted medieval village sites. Reproduced as Appendix I, in M Beresford and J G Hurst (eds), 1989, *Deserted medieval villages* (Second edition). Gloucester. Alan Sutton. 303-12

Dixon, K, 1977, Forecasting impacts. In M Schiffer and G J Gumerman (eds), *Conservation archaeology: a guide for cultural resource management studies*. London. Academic Press. 292-301

DNH (Department of National Heritage), 1996, *Protecting our heritage: a consultation document on the built heritage of England and Wales*. London and Cardiff. DNH and Welsh Office

DNH (Department of National Heritage), 1997, *The Treasure Act 1996: code of practice (England and Wales)*. London. DNH

Dobinson, C and Denison, S, 1995, *Metal detecting and archaeology in England*. London and York. English Heritage and CBA

Dobson, M, 1995, *Tree root systems* (= Arboricultural Research Note). Farnham. DoE Arboricultural Advisory and Information Service

DoE (Department of the Environment), 1972, *Field monuments and local authorities* (= Circular 11/72). London. DoE

DoE (Department of the Environment), 1973, *Ancient monuments in England: a list prepared by the Department of Environment corrected to 31st December 1971*. London. HMSO

DoE (Department of the Environment), 1974a, *List of ancient monuments in England and Wales: first supplement to the 1971 list*. London. HMSO

DoE (Department of the Environment), 1974b, *Report of the National Park Review Committee*. London. HMSO

DoE (Department of the Environment), 1978, *List of ancient monuments in England as at 31st December 1977*. London. HMSO. (3 vols)

DoE (Department of the Environment), 1981, *Ancient monuments manual and county sites and monuments records* (= DoE IAM Advisory Note 32). London. DoE

DoE (Department of the Environment), 1989, *Land-use change in England number 4* (= Department of the Environment Statistical Bulletin (89)5). London. DoE

DoE (Department of the Environment), 1990a, ***Planning policy guidance: archaeology and planning*** (= PPG 16). London. HMSO

DoE (Department of the Environment), 1990b, ***Land-use change in England number 5*** (= Department of the Environment Statistical Bulletin (90)5). London. DoE

DoE (Department of the Environment), 1991, ***Survey of land for mineral workings in England 1988. Volume 2. Survey tables***. London. HMSO

DoE (Department of the Environment), 1992a, ***Land-use change in England number 6*** (= Department of the Environment Statistical Bulletin (92)3). London. DoE

DoE (Department of the Environment), 1992b, ***The national sample survey of vacant land in urban areas of England 1990***. London. HMSO

DoE (Department of the Environment), 1993, ***Land-use change in England number 8*** (= Department of the Environment Statistical Bulletin (93)1). London. DoE

DoE (Department of the Environment), 1994a, ***Minerals planning guidance. Guidelines for aggregate provision in England*** (= MPG 6). London. HMSO

DoE (Department of the Environment), 1994b, ***Planning policy guidance: planning and the historic environment*** (= PPG 15). London. HMSO

DoE (Department of the Environment), 1994c, ***Land-use change in England number 9*** (= Department of the Environment Statistical Bulletin (94)1). London. DoE

DoE (Department of the Environment), 1995a, ***Housing and construction statistics for Great Britain 1985-1995***. London. HMSO

DoE (Department of the Environment), 1995b, ***Planning controls over agriculture and forestry development and rural building conversions***. London. HMSO

DoE (Department of the Environment), 1995c, ***Rates of urbanization in England 1981-2001*** (Department of the Environment Planning Research Programme). London. HMSO

DoE (Department of the Environment), 1996a, ***Digest of environmental statistics Number 18 1996.*** London. DoE

DoE (Department of the Environment), 1996b, ***Results and progress. No. 3. Restoration and aftercare of land worked for minerals*** (= Planning Research Programme. Geological and Minerals Planning Research). London. DoE

DoE (Department of the Environment), 1996c, ***Survey of land for mineral workings in England 1994. Volume 1. Report on survey results***. London. HMSO

DoE (Department of the Environment), 1996d, ***A guide to risk assessment and management for environmental protection***. London. HMSO

DoE (Department of the Environment), 1998, ***Minerals planning guidance. Minerals planning and the general development order*** (= MPG 5). London. HMSO

DoE *et al.* (Department of the Environment, Y Swyddfa Gymreig / Welsh Office, and Scottish Office), 1996, ***Environmental Protection Act 1990 Part IIA: contaminated land. Consultation on draft statutory guidance on contaminated land***. London, Cardiff and Edinburgh. DoE

Dormor, I, 1996, An appraisal of the archaeological potential of farming incentive schemes. In J Grenville (ed), ***Archaeological heritage management and the English agricultural landscape*** (= York Archaeological Heritage Studies Occasional Paper 1). York. York University, Department of Archaeology. 13-59

Drewett, P, 1980, Sussex plough damage survey. In J Hinchliffe and T Schadla-Hall (eds), ***The past under the plough*** (= DAMHB Occasional Paper 3). London. DoE. 69-73

DTp (Department of Transport), 1989, ***Roads for prosperity*** (= Command Paper 693). London. HMSO

DTp (Department of Transport), 1990, *Trunk roads, England: into the 1990s.* London. HMSO

DTp (Department of Transport), 1993, Cultural heritage. *Design manual for roads and bridges* (Section 11.3, Part 2). London. DTp

DTp (Department of Transport), 1996a, Cross sections and head rooms. *Design manual for roads and bridges* (Section 1, Part 2). London. DTp

DTp (Department of Transport), 1996b, *Transport statistics, Great Britain. 1996 edition.* London. DTp

Dunn, R, and Harrison A R, 1994, *Feasibility study for deriving information about land-use stock.* London. Department of Environment

Dyson, J, 1995, Tumbledown heritage. *Countryside,* 75, 4-5

EC (European Commission), 1989, *A Common Agricultural Policy for the 1990s* (= Periodical 5/1989). Luxembourg. Office for Official Publications of the European Communities

EC (European Commission), 1997a, Council Directive 97/11/EC of 3 March 1997 amending Directive 85/337/EEC on the assessment of the effects of certain public and private projects on the environment. *Official Journal of the European Communities,* 14 March 1997, L73/5

EC (European Commission), 1997b, Proposal for a Council Directive on the assessment of the effects of certain plans and programmes on the environment. *Official Journal of the European Communities,* 25 April 1997, C129/14

ECVST (European Council for the Village and Small Town), 1991, *A strategy for rural Europe*. Strasbourg. ECVST

Edis, J, MacLeod, D, and Bewley, R, 1989, An archaeologist's guide to the classification of cropmarks and soilmarks. *Antiquity*, 63, 112-26

Edwards, C A, and Lofty, J R, 1972, *The biology of earthworms*. London. Chapman and Hall

Edwards, R, 1991, *Fit for the future: report of the National Parks Review Panel* (= CCP 334). Cheltenham. Countryside Commission

Embree, S, 1995, Buildings at Risk Survey: a success story. *Conservation Bulletin,* 25, 7-8

English Heritage, 1984-8, *Register of historic parks and gardens of special historic interest in England.* London. English Heritage. (46 vols in 4 parts)

English Heritage, 1985, *An analysis of support from central government (DAMHB) and the Historic Buildings and Monuments Commission (HBMC) for the recording of archaeological sites and landscapes in advance of their destruction between 1982 and 1984.* London. English Heritage. [Circulated typescript report]

English Heritage, 1986, *Annual Report 1985-86*. London. English Heritage

English Heritage, 1987, *Annual Report 1986-87*. London. English Heritage

English Heritage, 1991a, *Exploring our past: strategies for the archaeology of England.* London. English Heritage

English Heritage, 1991b, *Management of archaeological projects*. London. English Heritage

English Heritage, 1992a, *Buildings at risk: a sample survey*. London. English Heritage

English Heritage, 1992b, *Development plan policies for archaeology*. London. English Heritage

English Heritage, 1992c, *Managing the urban archaeological resource.* London. English Heritage

English Heritage, 1995a, *Register of historic battlefields in England*. London. English Heritage

English Heritage, 1995b, *Conservation Area practice*. London. English Heritage

English Heritage, 1996a, *Conservation issues in local plans*. London. English Heritage

English Heritage, 1996b, ***Hadrian's Wall World Heritage Site. Management Plan***. London. English Heritage

English Heritage, 1997a, ***Sustaining the historic environment: new perspectives on the future.*** London. English Heritage

English Heritage, 1997b, ***The Monuments Protection Programme 1986-96 in retrospect***. London. English Heritage

English Heritage, 1997c, ***After the storms***. London. English Heritage

English Heritage and RCHME, 1996, ***England's coastal heritage. A statement on the management of coastal archaeology.*** London. English Heritage and RCHME

English Nature, 1993, ***Strategy for the 1990's: Natural Areas.*** Peterborough. English Nature

Environment Agency, 1996, ***The environment of England and Wales: a snapshot.*** Bristol. Environment Agency

Environment Committee, 1987, ***First Report from the Environment Committee Session 1986-87. Historic Buildings and Ancient Monuments.*** London. HMSO. (3 vols)

ERL (Environmental Resources Limited), 1990, *'Roads for prosperity' White Paper 1989: implications for England's archaeological resource*. London. ERL. [Circulated typescript report]

Esher, L B, 1968, ***York: a study in conservation***. London. HMSO

ETB (English Tourist Board), 1996, ***English heritage monitor 1995***. London. ETB

Evans, D, 1984, A national archaeological archive - computer database applications. ***Computer Applications in Archaeology***, 12, 112-18

Evans, D, 1985, Computerisation of sites and monuments records: the development of policy. ***Computer Applications in Archaeology***, 13, 62-74

Evans, J, 1892, An archaeological survey of Hertfordshire. ***Archaeologia***, 53, 245-62

Evans, J G, 1990, Notes on some later Neolithic and Bronze Age events in long barrow ditches in southern and eastern England. ***Proceedings of the Prehistoric Society***, 56, 111-16

Evans, J G, Limbrey, S, Máté, I and Mount, R, 1993, An environmental history of the upper Kennet valley, Wiltshire, for the last 10,000 years. ***Proceedings of the Prehistoric Society***, 59, 139-196

Evans, J G, and Simpson, D D A, 1991, Giants' Hills 2 Long Barrow, Skendleby, Lincolnshire. ***Archaeologia***, 109, 1-45

Everson, P L, Taylor, C, and Dunn, C J, 1991, ***Change and continuity: rural settlement in north-west Lincolnshire***. London. HMSO

Fairclough, G, 1995, Archaeology in development plans. ***Conservation Bulletin***, 19, 24

Fasham, P, 1980, Archaeology in wood and field. In J Hinchliffe and R T Schadla-Hall (eds), ***The past under the plough*** (= DAMHB Occasional Paper 3). London. DoE. 114-22

Fasham, P, 1987, ***A banjo enclosure in Micheldever Wood, Hampshire*** (= Hampshire Field Club and Archaeological Society Monograph 5). Winchester. Hampshire Field Club

Fawcett, J (ed), 1976, ***The future of the past: attitudes to conservation 1147-1974***. London. Thames and Hudson

Fielden, B M, and Jokilehto, J, 1993, ***Management guidelines for World Heritage Cultural Heritage Sites***. Rome. ICCROM

Fleming, A, 1988, ***The Dartmoor Reaves: investigating prehistoric land divisions***. London. Batsford

Fleming, A, and Ralph, N, 1982, Medieval settlement and land-use on Holne Moor, Dartmoor: the landscape evidence. ***Medieval Archaeology***, 26, 101-37 ·

Foard, G, 1997, What is a site event? **SMR News**, 3, 4 (Internet: http://www.rchme.gov.uk/smrnews3.html#event)

Forestry Commission, 1943, **Post-war forestry policy** (= Command Paper 6447). London. HMSO

Forestry Commission, 1995, **Forests and archaeology: guidelines**. Edinburgh. Forestry Authority

Forestry Commission, 1997, **Facts and figures 1996-1997**. Edinburgh. Forestry Commission

Forestry Commission and Countryside Commission, 1996, **Woodland creation: needs and opportunities in the English countryside - a discussion paper** (= CCP 507). Northampton. Forestry Commission and Countryside Commission

Fortlage, C A, and Catharine, A, 1990, **Environmental assessment**. London. Gower

Fowler, P J, 1967, The archaeology of Fyfield and Overton Downs, Wiltshire. **Wiltshire Archaeological and Natural History Magazine**, 62, 16-33

Fowler, P J, 1970, Old grassland: its archaeological significance and ecological importance. **Antiquity,** 44, 57-9

Fowler, P J, 1977a, **Approaches to archaeology**. London. A C Black

Fowler, P J, 1977b, Land management and the cultural resource. In R T Rowley and M Breakell (eds), **Planning and the historic environment II**. Oxford. Oxford University Department of External Studies. 131-42

Fowler, P J, 1978, The business of archaeology. In T C Darvill, M Parker Pearson, R W Smith and R M Thomas (eds), **New approaches to our past: an archaeological forum.** Southampton. Southampton University Archaeological Society. 1-10

Fowler, P J, 1979, Archaeology and the M4 and M5 Motorways, 1965-78. **Archaeological Journal**, 136, 12-26

Fowler, P J, 1980, Tradition and objectives in British field archaeology, 1953-78. **Archaeological Journal**, 137, 1-21

Fowler, P J, 1981, The Royal Commission on Historical Monuments (England). **Antiquity,** 55, 106-14

Fowler, P J, 1984, Secretary's report to commissioners. **Royal Commission on Historical Monuments (England): Annual Review 1983-84**. London. RCHME. 2-6

Fowler, P J, 1989, The thirteenth Beatrice de Cardi Lecture - the experimental earthworks 1958-88. **Council for British Archaeology Annual Report 39 for the year ended 30th June 1989**, 83-98

Fowler, P J, 1997, Why public access must be controlled. **British Archaeology**, 23, 11

Fox, C, 1945, Anniversary address. **Antiquaries Journal**, 25, 107-116

Fulford, M, Champion, T C, and Lang, A, 1997, **England's coastal heritage: a survey for English Heritage and the RCHME**. London. English Heritage and RCHME

Fulford, M, and Nichols, E (eds), 1992, **Developing landscapes of lowland Britain. The archaeology of the British gravels: a review** (= Society of Antiquaries Occasional Paper (NS) 14). London. Society of Antiquaries

Fulton, A K, 1996, **Monuments at Risk Survey Project Design: interim revision 1**. Bournemouth. Bournemouth University. [Circulated typescript report].

Fyson, A, 1997, New settlements back on the agenda. **Countryside**, 85, 7

Gilder, P, 1994, Completing the landscape jigsaw. **Countryside**, 65, 4-5

Glass, H J, 1989, **The condition of Scheduled Ancient Monuments: a sample survey of landscapes**. London. English Heritage [Circulated typescript report]

Greeves, T, 1989, Archaeology and the Green movement: a case for perestroika. **Antiquity,** 63, 659-66

Griffiths, D, 1991, The English Heritage - Dartmoor National Park Pilot Scheme. In R F White and R Iles (eds), **Archaeology in National Parks**. Leyburn. Yorkshire Dales National Park. 11-17

Grimes, W F, 1960, *Excavations on defence sites 1939-1945. I. Mainly Neolithic and Bronze Age* (= Ministry of Works Archaeological Reports 3). London. HMSO

Grinsell, L V, 1959, *Dorset barrows*. Dorchester. DNHAS

Groenewoudt, B J, and Bloemers, J H F, 1997, Dealing with significance: concepts, strategies and priorities for archaeological heritage management in the Netherlands. In W J H Willems, H Kars, and D P Hallewas (eds), *Archaeological resource management in the Netherlands: fifty years of state service for archaeological investigations*. Assen. Van Gorcum. 119-172

Groenewoudt, B J, Hallewas, D P, and Zoetbrood, P A M, 1994, *De degradatie van de archeologische betekenis van de Nederlandse bodem* (= Interne Rapporten ROB 33). Amersfoort. Rijksdienst voor het Oudheidkundig Bodemonderzoek

Groube, L M, and Bowden, M C B, 1982, *The archaeology of rural Dorset, past, present and future* (= DNHAS Monograph 4). Dorchester. DNHAS

Haigh, N, 1987, *EEC environmental policy and Britain*. London. Longman

Hall, D, 1993, *The open fields of Northamptonshire. The case for the preservation of ridge and furrow*. Northampton. Northampton County Council

Hardie, C, 1994, Bodies on the beach. In C Hardie (ed), *Archaeology in Northumberland 1993-1994*. Morpeth. Northumberland County Council. 6-7

Hargreaves, P, 1998, Strategic advances on the English field. *Planning*, 2nd January, 14-15

Harley, J B, 1975, *Ordnance Survey maps: a descriptive manual*. Southampton. Ordnance Survey

Hart, J and Leech, R, 1989, The National Archaeological Record. In S Rahtz and J Richards (eds), *Computer applications and quantitative methods in archaeology 1989* (= BAR International Series 548). Oxford. BAR. 57-67

Harvey, G, 1997, *The killing of the countryside*. London. Jonathan Cape

Harvey, J, 1961, The origin of official preservation of ancient monuments. *Transactions of the Ancient Monuments Society* (NS), 9, 27-31

Harvey, J, 1993, The origins of listed buildings. *Transactions of the Ancient Monuments Society* (NS), 37, 1-20

Heighway, C M (ed), 1972, *The erosion of history. Archaeology and planning in towns: a study of historic towns affected by modern development in England, Wales and Scotland*. London. CBA

Heighway, C M, 1974, *Archaeology in Gloucester: a policy for City and District*. Gloucester. Gloucester City Council. [Circulated typescript report]

Hennessy, B, Hems, L, and Pearce, G, 1990, *Conservation Areas in London and the South East*. London. English Heritage

Herring, P, and Johnson, N, 1997, Historic landscape character mapping in Cornwall. In K Barker and T Darvill (eds), *Making English landscapes* (= Bournemouth University School of Conservation Sciences Occasional Paper 3 and Oxbow Monograph 93). Oxford. Oxbow Books. 46-54

Hey, G, 1997, Neolithic settlement at Yarnton, Oxfordshire. In P Topping (ed), *Neolithic landscapes* (= Neolithic Studies Group Seminar Papers 2 and Oxbow Monograph 86). Oxford. Oxbow Books. 99-112

Highways Agency, 1995, *Trunk roads and archaeology*. London. Highways Agency

Highways Agency, 1996, *Trunk roads and archaeology 1994-1995*. London. Highways Agency

Hinchliffe, J and Schadla-Hall, R T (eds), 1980, *The past under the plough* (= DAMHB Occasional Paper 3). London. DoE

Hingley, R, 1991, The purpose of cropmark analysis. *AARGnews,* 2, 38-43

HMG (Her Majesty's Government), 1994, *Sustainable development: the UK strategy* (= Command Paper 2426). London. HMSO

HMG (Her Majesty's Government), 1996a, *Rural England: the rural White Paper. Volume I. Report together with proceedings of the committee*. London. HMSO

HMG (Her Majesty's Government), 1996b, *Rural England: the rural White Paper. Volume II. Minutes of evidence and appendices*. London. HMSO

HMG (Her Majesty's Government), 1997, *Environmentally Sensitive Areas and other schemes under the agri-environment regulation: response of the Government to the second report (1996-97) from the Agriculture Committee* (= Command Paper 3707). London. HMSO

Hodder, I, 1992, Theory, practice and praxis. In I Hodder (ed), *Theory and practice in archaeology*. London. Routledge. 1-10

Holgate, R, 1989, *The Neolithic flint mines in Sussex: a plough damage assessment and site management report*. London. Field Archaeology Unit, Institute of Archaeology. [Circulated typescript report]

Hooke, D, 1992, *The historical study of the New National Forest Area*. Birmingham. University of Birmingham. [Circulated typescript report]

Hudson, W H, 1910, *A shepherd's life: impressions of the south Wiltshire downs*. London. Methuen

Hunter, J, and Ralston, I, 1993, *Archaeological resource management in the UK. An introduction*. Stroud and Birmingham. Alan Sutton and the Institute of Field Archaeologists

Hunting Surveys, 1986, *Monitoring landscape change*. Hemel Hempstead. Hunting Surveys and Consultants Ltd

IAM (Inspectorate of Ancient Monuments), 1984, *England's archaeological resource: a rapid quantification of the national archaeological resource and a comparison with the Schedule of Ancient Monuments*. London. DoE

Insall D W, and Associates, 1968, *Chester: a study in conservation*. London. HMSO

Jago, M, 1995, The Countryside Stewardship Scheme: testing the way forward for integrated countryside management. In A Q Berry and I W Brown (eds), *Managing ancient monuments: an integrated approach*. Mold. Clwyd County Council

Jewell, P A (ed), 1963, *The experimental earthwork at Overton Down, Wiltshire, 1960*. London. British Association for the Advancement of Science

Johns, C, and Herring, P, 1994, Littlejohns Barrow: the damage and re-profiling of the round barrow west of Hensbarrow, Roche. *Cornish Archaeology,* 33, 22-35

Johnson, N, 1985, Archaeological field survey: a Cornish perspective. In S Macready and F H Thompson (eds), *Archaeological field survey in Britain and abroad* (= Society of Antiquaries Occasional Paper (NS) 6). London. Society of Antiquaries. 51-66

Johnson, N, 1986, The historic heritage: present and future attitudes. *Cornish Archaeology,* 25, 221-32

Johnson, N, and Rose, P, 1983, *Archaeological survey and conservation in West Penwith, Cornwall*. Truro. Cornwall Committee for Rescue Archaeology. [Circulated typescript report]

Johnson, N, and Rose, P, 1994, *Bodmin Moor. An archaeological survey. Volume 1: the human landscape to c1800* (= HBMCE Archaeological Report 24. RCHME Supplementary Series 11). London. English Heritage, RCHME and Cornwall Archaeological Unit

Jones, B, 1984, *Past imperfect: the story of Rescue archaeology*. London. Heinemann

Jones, M U, 1974, Excavations at Mucking, Essex: a second interim report. *Antiquaries Journal,* 54, 183-99

Jones, M U, Evison, V I, and Myres, J N L, 1968, Crop-mark sites at Mucking, Essex, *Antiquaries Journal*, 48, 210-30

Judge, W J, Ebert, J I, and Hitchcock, R K, 1975, Sampling in regional archaeological survey. In J W Mueller (ed), *Sampling in archaeology.* Tucson. University of Arizona Press. 82-123

Kains-Jackson, C P, 1880, *Our ancient monuments and the land around them.* London. Elliot Stock

Kennet, W, 1972, *Preservation.* London. Temple Smith

Kristiansen, K, 1993, The strength of the past and its great might: an essay on the use of the past. *Journal of European Archaeology,* 1, 3-32

Kumamoto, H, and Henley, E J, 1995, *Probabilistic risk assessment and management for engineers and scientists.* London. IEEE

Lambert, D, and Shacklock, V, 1995, Historic parks and gardens: a review of legislation, policy guidance and significant court and appeal decisions. *Journal of Planning and Environmental Law,* July, 563-73

Lambrick, G, 1977, *Archaeology and agriculture: a survey of modern cultivation methods and the problems of assessing plough damage to archaeological sites.* London and Oxford. CBA and Oxford Archaeological Unit

Lambrick, G, 1993, Environmental assessment and the cultural heritage: principles and practice. In I Ralston and R Thomas (eds), *Environmental assessment and archaeology* (= IFA Occasional Paper 5). Birmingham. Institute of Field Archaeologists. 9-19

Lang, N A R, and Stead, S, 1992, Sites and monuments records in England - theory and practice. In G Lock and J Moffett (eds), *Computer applications and quantitative methods in archaeology 1991* (= BAR International Series 577). Oxford. Tempus Reparatum. 69-76

Law, W, 1914, Archaeological record and registration. *Brighton and Hove Archaeologist,* 1, 61-71

Lawson, A, 1981, The barrows of Norfolk. In A J Lawson, E A Martin and D Priddy, *The barrows of East Anglia* (= East Anglian Archaeology 12). Norwich. East Anglian Archaeology. 32-63

Lawson, A J, Martin, E A, and Priddy, D, 1981, *The barrows of East Anglia* (= East Anglian Archaeology 12). Norwich. East Anglian Archaeology

Leake, J, 1998, Labour to bulldoze green belt for millions of homes. *The Sunday Times*, 18th January, Section 1 (News), 5

Leech, R, 1986, Computerisation of the NAR. *Computer Applications in Archaeology,* 14, 29-37

Leisure Consultants, 1997, *Leisure forecasts 1997-2001: leisure away from the home.* Sudbury. Leisure Consultants

Limbrey, S, 1975, *Soil science and archaeology.* London and New York. Academic Press

Lowe, P, and Whitby, M, 1997, The CAP and the European environment. In C Ritson and D R Harvey (eds), *The Common Agricultural Policy* (Second edition). Wallingford. CAB International. 285-304

Lowenthal, D, 1990, *The past is a foreign country*. Cambridge. Cambridge University Press

LUC (Land Use Consultants), 1992, *New National Forest: archaeological and historical study - a summary report.* London. LUC

LUC (Land Use Consultants), 1995, *Countryside Stewardship monitoring and evaluation. Third interim report.* London. LUC

Lucas, P H C, 1992, *Protected landscapes: a guide for policy-makers and planners.* London. Chapman and Hall

LUSAG (Land Use Statistics Advisory Group), 1993, *Preparatory work for Land Use Stock System (Stage 1)*. London. LUSAG. [Circulated typescript report]

MacCarthy, F, 1994, *William Morris: a life of our time.* London. Faber

MacEwen, A, and MacEwen, E, 1982, *National Parks: conservation or cosmetics?* London. George Allen and Unwin

Macinnes, L, and Wickham-Jones, C R (eds), 1992, *All natural things: archaeology and the Green debate* (= Oxbow Monograph 21). Oxford. Oxbow Books

Mackay, K F, 1985, SSSIs and the use of management agreements. In G Lambrick (ed), *Archaeology and nature conservation*. Oxford. Oxford University Department of External Studies. 39-43

McGill, G, 1995, *Building on the past. A guide to archaeology and the development process.* London. E & FN Spon

McGimsey, C R, 1972, *Public Archaeology.* New York and London. Seminar Press

McRobie, L, 1996a, Garden archaeology. *Conservation Bulletin*, 28, 14-5

McRobie, L, 1996b, The Gardens Register. *Conservation Bulletin*, 29, 18

MAFF (Ministry of Agriculture Fisheries and Food), 1974, *Bracken and its control* (= MAFF Advisory Leaflet). London. MAFF

MAFF (Ministry of Agriculture Fisheries and Food), 1990, *Agricultural Statistics United Kingdom 1988.* London. HMSO

MAFF (Ministry of Agriculture Fisheries and Food), 1995, *New funds for Countryside Stewardship Scheme* (= MAFF Press release 423/95, 28th November 1995). London. MAFF. [Circulated typescript paper]

MAFF (Ministry of Agriculture Fisheries and Food), 1996, *New Agri-Environmental Forum launched* (= MAFF Press Release 35/96). London. MAFF

MAFF and DAFS (Ministry of Agriculture Fisheries and Food, and Department of Agriculture and Fisheries for Scotland), 1968, *A century of agricultural statistics: Great Britain 1866-1966.* London. HMSO

MAFF *et al.* (Ministry of Agriculture Fisheries and Food, Scottish Office Agriculture and Fisheries Department, Department of Agriculture for Northern Ireland, and Welsh Office), 1996, *The digest of agricultural census statistics: United Kingdom 1995.* London. HMSO

MAFF *et al.* (Ministry of Agriculture Fisheries and Food, Scottish Office Agriculture and Fisheries Department, Department of Agriculture for Northern Ireland, and Welsh Office), 1997, *The digest of agricultural census statistics: United Kingdom 1996.* London. HMSO

MAFF and DoE (Ministry of Agriculture Fisheries and Food, and the Department of the Environment), 1995, *Environmental land management schemes in England.* London. MAFF and DoE. [Circulated typescript report]

Major, J K, 1975, *Fieldwork in Industrial archaeology.* London. Batsford

Malim, T, 1990, *Archaeology on Cambridgeshire County Farm Estate.* Cambridge. Cambridgeshire County Council

Manning, P, and Leeds, E T, 1921, An archaeological survey of Oxfordshire. *Archaeologia*, 71, 227-65

Marks, H F, 1989, *One hundred years of British food and farming: a statistical survey.* London. Taylor and Francis

Marsden, B, 1983, *Pioneers of prehistory: leaders and landmarks in English archaeology (1500-1900).* Ormskirk and Northridge. G W & A Hesketh

Mathias, P, 1969, *The first industrial nation.* London. Methuen

Mercer, R, 1981, The excavation of an earthwork enclosure at Long Knowe, Eskdale, Dumfriesshire. *Transactions of the Dumfriesshire and Galloway Natural History and Antiquarian Society,* 56, 38-72

MHLG (Ministry of Housing and Local Government), 1967, *Historic towns: preservation and change.* London. HMSO

Miele, C, 1996, The first conservation militants: William Morris and the Society for the Protection of Ancient Buildings. In M Hunter (ed), *Preserving the past: the rise of heritage in modern Britain*. Stroud. Alan Sutton. 17-37

Miles, D, 1983, An integrated approach to the study of ancient landscapes: the Claydon Pike Project. In G S Maxwell (ed), *The impact of aerial reconnaissance on archaeology* (= CBA Research Report 49). London. CBA. 74-84

Moore, M, 1992, The National Monuments Branch of the Office of Public Works. In C U Larsen (ed), *Sites and monuments: national archaeological records*. Copenhagen. National Museum of Denmark. 223-30

Morgan Evans, D, 1985, The management of historic landscapes. In G Lambrick (ed), *Archaeology and nature conservation.* Oxford. Oxford University Department of External Studies. 89-94

Morgan Evans, D, Salway, P, and Thackray, D (eds), 1996, *'The remains of distant times': archaeology and the National Trust.* London. Boydell Press for the Society of Antiquaries of London and the National Trust

Morris, C, 1997, Effete or effective stewardship. *Landscape Design,* May, 19-23

Morris, R, 1994, Taking archaeology into a new era. *British Archaeological News* (NS), 18, 9

MPBW (Ministry of Public Building and Works), 1953, *List of ancient monuments in England and Wales: a list prepared by the Ministry of Public Building and Works.* London. HMSO

MPBW (Ministry of Public Building and Works), 1961, *List of ancient monuments in England and Wales: a list prepared by the Ministry of Public Building and Works*. London. HMSO

MPBW (Ministry of Public Building and Works), 1965, *List of ancient monuments in England and Wales: a list prepared by the Ministry of Public Building and Works*. London. HMSO

MPBW (Ministry of Public Building and Works), 1969, *Ancient monuments in England and Wales: fifth supplement to the 1963 list.* London. HMSO

Murray, D, 1896, An archaeological survey of the United Kingdom. The preservation and protection of our ancient monuments. *Transactions of the Glasgow Archaeological Society* (NS), 3, 1-76

NCC (Nature Conservancy Council), 1990, *Handbook for Phase 1 habitat survey: a technique for environmental audit.* Peterborough. JNCC

NCC (Nature Conservancy Council), 1991, *A review of Phase 1 habitat survey in England.* Peterborough. NCC. (Reprinted 1993)

Neal, D S, Wardle, A, and Hunn, J, 1990, *Excavation of the Iron Age, Roman and medieval settlement at Gorhambury, St Albans* (= HBMCE Archaeological Report 14). London. English Heritage

Nesbit, R C, 1996, *Eyes of the RAF*. Stroud. Alan Sutton

NHC (National Heritage Committee), 1994, *National Heritage Committee Third Report. Our heritage: preserving it, prospering from it*. London. HMSO. (2 vols)

NHTPC *et al*. (National Housing and Town Planning Council, Council for the Protection of Rural England, and Association of District Councils), 1997, *Planning control over farmland: reforming permitted development rights in the countryside.* London. Association of District Councils

Nicholson, R J, 1980, Modern ploughing techniques. In J Hinchliffe and R T Schadla-Hall (eds), *The past under the plough* (= DAMHB Occasional Paper 3). London. DoE. 22-5

Nickens, P R (ed), 1991, *Perspectives on archaeological site protection and preservation* (= Technical Report EL-91-6). Washington DC. Department of the Army, US Army Corps of Engineers

OAP (Ove Arup and Partners and York University), 1991, *York development and archaeology study.* English Heritage and York City Council

O'Keefe, P J, 1993, The European Convention on the Protection of the Archaeological Heritage. *Antiquity,* 67, 406

Olivier, A C H (ed), 1995, *Archaeology review 1994-95.* London. English Heritage

Olivier, A C H (ed), 1996a, *Archaeology review 1995-96.* London. English Heritage

Olivier, A C H, 1996b, *Frameworks for our past: a review of research frameworks, strategies and perspectives.* London. English Heritage

Olivier, A C H (ed), 1997, *Archaeology review 1996-97.* London. English Heritage

O'Neil, B H St. J, 1946, The Congress of Archaeological Societies. *Antiquaries Journal,* 26, 61-6

O'Neil, B H St. J, 1948, War and archaeology in Britain. *Antiquaries Journal,* 28, 20-44

O'Neil, H, and Grinsell, L V, 1960, Gloucestershire barrows. *Transactions of the Bristol and Gloucestershire Archaeological Society,* 79, 1-149

Ordnance Survey, 1951, *Ordnance Survey Policy Statement. September 1951.* Unpublished document. [Public Record Office: Correspondence and Papers of the Ordnance Survey Office (OS 1): 11/38 PS 26 Archaeology]

Ordnance Survey, 1965, *Ordnance Survey Policy Statement. August 1965.* Unpublished document. [Public Record Office: Correspondence and Papers of the Ordnance Survey Office (OS 1): 11/38 PS 26 Archaeology]

Ordnance Survey, 1966, *Ordnance Survey: Correspondence and Papers.* Unpublished document. [Public Record Office: Correspondence and Papers of the Ordnance Survey Office (OS 1): 1/1276, no 14a]

Ordnance Survey, 1975, *Archaeology. Policy Statement 10. March 1975.* Unpublished document. [Public Record Office: Correspondence and Papers of the Ordnance Survey Office (OS 1): 11/38 PS 26 Archaeology]

Ordnance Survey, 1986, *1:625,000 scale map of Great Britain (Local Government Areas).* Southampton. Ordnance Survey. (2 sheets)

Ordnance Survey, 1995, *Statlas UK: a statistical atlas of the United Kingdom.* Southampton and Norwich. Ordnance Survey and HMSO

O'Riordan, T, 1979, The scope of environmental risk management. *Ambio,* 8.6, 260-64

Owen-John, H, 1994, Archaeology and agriculture: some current issues. *Conservation Bulletin,* 14, 18-20

Page, J A, 1994, Opportunity and challenge. *Conservation Bulletin,* 24, 1-2

Pagoda Projects, 1992, *An evaluation of the impact of PPG16 on archaeology and planning.* London. Pagoda Projects for English Heritage. [Circulated typescript report]

Palmer, R, 1991, Approaches to classification. *AARGnews,* 2, 32-7

Palmer, R, and Cox, C, 1993, *Uses of aerial photography in archaeological evaluations* (= IFA Technical Paper 12). Birmingham. Institute of Field Archaeologists

Payne, M, 1995, Roaming the hills. *Countryside,* 73, 4-5

Pearce, G, Hems, L, and Hennessy, B, 1990, *The Conservation Areas of England.* London. English Heritage

Perring, F H, and Gardiner, B G (eds), 1976, *The biology of bracken.* London. Academic Press

Phillips, C W, 1949a, The Ordnance Survey and archaeology, Part I. *The Archaeological Newsletter,* 2.1, 1-3

Phillips, C W, 1949b, The Ordnance Survey and archaeology, Part II. *The Archaeological Newsletter,* 2.2, 23-5

Phillips, C W, 1961, The Ordnance Survey and archaeology, 1791-1960. *The Geographical Journal,* 127, 2-9

Phillips, C W, 1980, *Archaeology in the Ordnance Survey 1791-1965.* London. CBA

Piggott, S, 1974, The origins of the English county archaeological societies. *Transactions of the Birmingham and Warwickshire Archaeological Society*, 86, 1-15

Poore, D and Poore, J, 1992, *Protected landscapes in the United Kingdom* (= CCP 362). Manchester. Countryside Commission

Popper, K, 1959, *The logic of scientific discovery*. London. Routledge and Kegan Paul

POST (Parliamentary Office of Science and Technology), 1997, *Tunnel vision? The future role of tunnels in transport infrastructure*. London. POST

Potts, K, 1995, *UK leisure and recreation. 1995 market review*. Hampton. Key Note

Prott, L V, 1992, A common heritage: the World Heritage Convention. In L Macinnes and C R Wickham-Jones (eds), *All natural things: archaeology and the Green debate* (= Oxbow Monograph 21). Oxford. Oxbow Books. 65-86

Pryor, F, 1984, *Excavation at Fengate Peterborough, England: the fourth report* (= Northamptonshire Archaeological Society Monograph 2 and Royal Ontario Museum Archaeology Monograph 7). Northampton. Northampton Archaeological Society and Royal Ontario Museum

Pryor, F, French, C, Crowther, D, Gurney, D, Simpson, G, and Taylor, M, 1985, *Archaeology and environment in the Lower Welland Valley: the Fenland Project 1* (= East Anglian Archaeology 27). Norwich. East Anglian Archaeology. (2 vols)

Pugh-Smith, J, and Samuels, J, 1996, *Archaeology in law*. London. Sweet and Maxwell

Rackham, O, 1980, *Ancient woodland*. London. Edward Arnold

Rackham, O, 1990, *The history of the countryside*. London. Dent

Rahtz, P A (ed), 1974, *Rescue archaeology*. Harmondsworth. Penguin

Ralston, I, and Thomas, R (eds), 1993, *Environmental assessment and archaeology* (= IFA Occasional Paper 5). Birmingham. Institute of Field Archaeologists

Ratcliffe, D A (ed), 1977, *A nature conservation review*. Cambridge. Cambridge University Press. (2 vols)

Ratcliffe, J, 1992, *An introduction to town and country planning*. London. UCL Press

RCHME (Royal Commission on Historical Monuments, England), 1910, *An inventory of the historical monuments in Hertfordshire*. London. HMSO

RCHME (Royal Commission on Historical Monuments, England), 1960, *A matter of time: an archaeological survey of the river gravels of England*. London. HMSO

RCHME (Royal Commission on Historical Monuments, England), 1963, *Monuments threatened or destroyed. A select list: 1956-1962*. London. HMSO

RCHME (Royal Commission on Historical Monuments, England), 1969, *Peterborough New Town. A survey of antiquities in the areas of development*. London. HMSO

RCHME (Royal Commission on Historical Monuments, England), 1970, *An inventory of historical monuments in the county of Dorset. Volume three. Central Dorset*. London. HMSO. (2 vols.)

RCHME (Royal Commission on Historical Monuments, England), 1978, *Survey of surveys 1978. A review of local archaeological field survey and recording*. London. RCHME

RCHME (Royal Commission on Historical Monuments, England), 1979, *Stonehenge and its environs: monuments and land-use*. Edinburgh. Edinburgh University Press

RCHME (Royal Commission on the Historical Monuments of England), 1992, *Thesaurus of archaeological site types*. London. RCHME and English Heritage

RCHME (Royal Commission on the Historical Monuments of England), 1993a, *Recording England's past: a review of national and local sites and monuments records in England*. London. RCHME

RCHME (Royal Commission on the Historical Monuments of England), 1993b, *Recording England's past: a data standard for the extended National Archaeological Record.* London. RCHME

RCHME (Royal Commission on the Historical Monuments of England), 1993c, Launch of heritage database and report on SMRs. *RCHME Newsletter,* 10, 1

RCHME (Royal Commission on the Historical Monuments of England), 1996a, *Strategic plan.* Swindon. RCHME

RCHME (Royal Commission on the Historical Monuments of England), 1996b, *Annual Report 1995/6.* Swindon. RCHME

RCHME (Royal Commission on the Historical Monuments of England), 1997, *Annual Report 1996/7.* Swindon. RCHME

RCHME (Royal Commission on the Historical Monuments of England), 1998, *MIDAS. A manual and data standard for monument inventories.* Swindon. RCHME

RCHME and EH (Royal Commission on the Historical Monuments of England and English Heritage), 1995, *Thesaurus of monument types. Standard for use in archaeological and architectural records.* Swindon and London. RCHME and English Heritage

RCHME *et al.* (Royal Commission on the Historical Monuments of England, English Heritage, and Association of Local Government Archaeological Officers), 1998, *Unlocking the past for the new millennium: a new statement of co-operation on sites and monuments records between the Royal Commission on the Historical Monuments of England, English Heritage, and the Association of Local Government Archaeological Officers.* Swindon. RCHME

Rees, S, 1994, Erosion in Wales: the extent of the problem. In A Q Berry and I W Brown (eds), *Erosion on archaeological earthworks: its prevention, control and repair.* Mold. Clwyd County Council. 29-36

Reynolds, P J, and Schadla-Hall, R T, 1980, Measurement of plough damage and the effects of ploughing on archaeological material. In J Hinchliffe and R T Schadla-Hall (eds), *The past under the plough* (= DAMHB Occasional Paper 3). London. DoE. 114-22

Richards, J, 1978, *The archaeology of the Berkshire Downs: an introductory survey* (Berkshire Archaeological Committee Publication 3). Reading. Berkshire Archaeological Committee

Richards, J, 1998, Meeting the ancestors? *The Archaeologist,* 31, 25-6

Richmond, I, 1968, *Hod Hill. Volume 2. Excavations carried out between 1951 and 1958.* London. British Museum

Riley, D N, 1983, The frequency of occurrence of cropmarks in relation to soils. In G S Maxwell (ed), *The impact of aerial reconnaissance on archaeology* (= CBA Research Report 49). London. CBA. 59-73

Ritson, C and Harvey, D R, 1997, *The Common Agricultural Policy* (Second edition). Wallingford. CAB International

Roberts, B K, 1996, *Landscapes of settlements: prehistory to the present.* London. Routledge

Roberts, H E, 1949, *Notes on the medieval monasteries and minsters of England and Wales.* London. Society for the Promotion of Christian Knowledge

Robertson, M, 1993, Listed buildings: the national resurvey of England. *Transactions of the Ancient Monuments Society* (NS), 37, 21-94

Roger Tym and Partners, 1995, *Review of the implementation of PPG16: archaeology and planning.* London. Roger Tym and Partners and Pagoda Associates for English Heritage

Russell, M, and Rudling, D, 1996, Excavations at Whitehawk Neolithic enclosure, Brighton, East Sussex: 1991-93. *Sussex Archaeological Collections,* 134, 39-61

Saint, A, 1996, How listing happened. In M Hunter (ed), *Preserving the past: the rise of heritage in modern Britain.* Stroud. Alan Sutton. 115-134

Saunders, A D, 1983, A century of Ancient Monuments legislation 1882-1982. *Antiquaries Journal,* 63, 11-33

Saville, A, 1980, *Archaeological sites in the Avon and Gloucestershire Cotswolds* (= CRAAGS Survey 5). Bristol. Committee for Rescue Archaeology in Avon, Gloucestershire and Somerset

Saville, A, 1990, *Hazleton North, Gloucestershire, 1979-82: the excavation of a Neolithic long cairn of the Cotswold-Severn group* (= HBMCE Archaeological Report 13). London. English Heritage

Schiffer, M B, 1976, *Behavioral archaeology*. Academic Press. New York and London

Schiffer, M B, 1987, *Formation processes of the archaeological record*. Albuquerque. University of New Mexico Press

Schiffer, M, and Gumerman, G J, 1977, *Conservation archaeology: a guide for cultural resource management studies*. London. Academic Press

Schofield, J, 1987, Recent approaches to urban archaeology. In J Schofield and R Leech (eds), *Urban archaeology in Britain* (= CBA Research Report 61). London. CBA. 1-8

Schofield, J, and Lake, J, 1995, Defining our defence heritage. *Conservation Bulletin,* 27, 12-13

Serpell, D, 1979, *Report on the Ordnance Survey Review Committee*. London. HMSO

Sheail, J, and Wells, T C E (eds), 1970, *Old grassland: its archaeological and ecological importance*. Abbots Ripton. Monks Wood Research Station

Shennan, S, 1985, *Experiments in the collection and analysis of archaeological survey data: the East Hampshire Survey*. Sheffield. University of Sheffield Department of Archaeology and Prehistory

Sinclair, G, 1992, *The lost land: land-use change in England 1945-1990*. London. Council for the Protection of Rural England

Smith, G, 1990, A Neolithic long barrow at Uplowman Road, Tiverton. *Proceedings of the Devon Archaeological Society*, 48, 15-26

Smith, K, 1986, Monument management in the Peak District National Park. In M Hughes and L Rowley (eds), *The management and presentation of field monuments*. Oxford. OUDES. 71-6

Speorry, P, 1992, *The structure and funding of British archaeology: the RESCUE questionnaire 1990-1*. Hertford. RESCUE

St Joseph, J K S (ed), 1977, *The uses of air photography*. London. John Baker

Stamp, L D, 1960, *Applied geography*. Harmondsworth. Penguin

Stamp, L D, 1962, *The land of Britain: its use and misuse* (Third edition). London. Longmans, Green and Co

Stamp, L D, and Willatts, E C, 1935, *An outline description of the first twelve one-inch maps* (Second edition). London. Land Utilization Survey

Startin, B, 1987, The Monuments Protection Programme. *Conservation Bulletin,* 1, 8

Startin, B, 1988, The Monuments Protection Programme. *Conservation Bulletin*, 6, 1-2

Steer, K, 1947, Archaeology and the National Air-Photographic Survey. *Antiquity,* 21, 50-3

Strike, J, 1994, *Architecture in conservation: managing development at historic sites*. London. Routledge

Stukeley, W, 1740, *Stonehenge: a temple restor'd to the British druids*. London. W Innys and R Manby

Suddards, R W, 1993, Listed buildings. In J Hunter and I Ralston (eds), *Archaeological resource management in the UK: an Introduction*. Stroud and Birmingham. Alan Sutton and Institute of Field Archaeologists. 77-88

Swain, H (ed), 1993, *Rescuing the historic environment: archaeology, the Green movement and conservation strategies for the British landscape*. Hertford. RESCUE

Taylor, C, 1983, *The archaeology of gardens*. Princes Risborough. Shire

Thackray, D W R, 1986, Care and management of National Trust properties. In M Hughes and L Rowley (eds), *The management presentation of field monuments.* Oxford. OUDES. 63-8

Thompson, M W, 1960, The first Inspector of Ancient Monuments in the field. *Journal of the British Archaeological Association* (3rd Ser), 23, 103-24

Thompson, M W, 1963, The origin of scheduling. *Antiquity*, 37, 224-5

Thompson, M W, 1977, *General Pitt-Rivers: evolution and archaeology in the nineteenth century.* Bradford-on-Avon. Moonraker Press

Timby, J, 1993, Sancton I Anglo-Saxon cemetery excavations carried out between 1976 and 1980. *Archaeological Journal*, 150, 243-365

Timms, S, 1993, From ancient monuments to historic landscapes: the quest to conserve Devon's archaeological heritage. *Proceedings of the Devon Archaeological Society,* 51, 1-16

Toman, M A, and Walls, M, 1995, Nonrenewable resource supply: theory and practice. In D W Bromley (ed), *Handbook of environmental economics.* Oxford. Blackwell. 182-201

Toulmin Smith, L, 1906-10, *The itinerary of John Leland in or about the years 1535-1543.* London. G Bell

TRRU (Tourism and Recreational Research Unit), 1981, *The economy of rural communities in the National Parks of England and Wales* (= TRRU Research Report 47). Edinburgh. Edinburgh University Press

Trueman, M, 1997, Historical characteristics of the calcareous grassland mask. In C Barr (ed), *Current status and prospects for key habitats in England. Part 2. Calcareous grassland landscapes.* London. DETR. 46-9

UNESCO (United Nations Educational, Scientific and Cultural Organization), 1972, *Convention concerning the protection of the world cultural and natural heritage.* Paris. UNESCO

Vittery, A, 1985, Wildlife and the countryside. In G Lambrick (ed), *Archaeology and nature conservation.* Oxford. Oxford University Department of External Studies. 19-21

Wacher, J, 1974, *The towns of Roman Britain.* London. Batsford

Wade-Martins, P, 1996, Monument conservation through land purchase. *Conservation Bulletin*, 29, 8-11

Wainwright, G J, 1984, The pressure of the past: presidential address. *Proceedings of the Prehistoric Society,* 50, 1-22

Wainwright, G J, 1989, Saving the Rose. *Antiquity* 63, 430-35

Wainwright, G J, 1993, Managing change: ancient monuments in the countryside. In H Swain (ed), *Rescuing the historic environment: archaeology, the Green movement and conservation strategies for the British landscape.* Hertford. RESCUE. 17-18

Wainwright, G J, Fleming, A, and Smith, K, 1979, The Shaugh Moor Project: first report. *Proceedings of the Prehistoric Society,* 45, 1-34

Wainwright, J, 1994, Erosion of archaeological sites: results and implications of a site simulation model. *Geoarchaeology,* 9, 173-201

Walsh, D, 1969, *Report of the Committee of Enquiry into the Arrangements for Protection of Field Monuments 1966-8* (= Command Paper 3904). London. HMSO

Waterton, C, Grove-White, R, Rodwell, J, and Wynee, B, 1995, *CORINE: databases and nature conservation. The new politics of information in the European Union* (= Report of the Centre for the Study of Environmental Change and the Unit of Vegetation Science). Lancaster. Lancaster University. [Circulated typescript report]

WCSP (Wildlife Conservation Special Committee), 1947, *Conservation of nature in England and Wales: Report of the Wildlife Conservation Special Committee* (= Command Paper CMD 7122). London. HMSO

Westmacott, R, and Worthington, T, 1997, *Agricultural landscapes: a third look* (= CCP 521). Cheltenham.

Countryside Commission

Whimster, R, 1989, *The emerging past: air photography and the buried landscape*. London. RCHME

Whitby, M, 1994, *The European environment and CAP reform: policies and prospects for conservation.* Wallingford. CAB International

White, R F and Iles, R (eds), 1991, *Archaeology in National Parks*. Leyburn. Yorkshire Dales National Park

Whittle, A, Atkinson, R J C, Chambers, R, and Thomas, N, 1992, Excavations in the Neolithic and Bronze Age complex at Dorchester-on-Thames, Oxfordshire, 1947-1952 and 1981. *Proceedings of the Prehistoric Society,* 58, 143-201

Wildgoose, M, 1991, The drystone walls of Roystone Grange. *Archaeological Journal*, 148, 205-40

Willems, W J H, Kars, H, and Hallewas, D P (eds), 1997, *Archaeological resource management in the Netherlands: fifty years of state service for archaeological investigations*. Assen. Van Gorcum

Williams, R J, and Zeepvat, R J, 1994, *Bancroft: a late Bronze Age / Iron Age settlement, Roman villa and temple-mausoleum* (= Buckinghamshire Archaeological Society Monograph 7). Aylesbury. Buckinghamshire Archaeological Society

Wisniewski, D (ed), 1997, *Annual abstract of statistics. 1997 edition. Number 133*. London. The Stationery Office

Witts, G B, 1883, *Archaeological handbook of the county of Gloucester.* Cheltenham. G Norman

Woodward, P J, 1980, A survey of barrows on the South Dorset Ridgeway: threat, destruction and survival. *Proceedings of the Dorset Natural History and Archaeological Society*, 102, 96-7

Woodward, P J, 1991, *The South Dorset Ridgeway. Survey and excavations 1977-84* (= DNHAS Monograph 8). Dorchester. DNHAS

Wormell, P, 1978, *Anatomy of agriculture: a study of Britain's greatest industry*. London. Harrap

Wrathmell, S, and Nicholson, A (eds), 1990, *Dalton Parlours Iron Age settlement and Roman villa* (= Yorkshire Archaeology Reports Series 3). Wakefield. West Yorkshire Archaeology Service

Wyatt, B K, Greatorex-Davies, J N, Hill, M O, Parr, T W, Bunce, R G H, and Fuller, R M, 1995, *Comparison of land cover definitions* (= Countryside Survey 1990 Series 3). London. DoE

Wyatt, G, 1991, *A review of Phase 1 Habitat Survey in England: field manual.* Peterborough. Nature Conservancy Council

Yarnell, T, 1993, Archaeological conservation in woods and forests. In H Swain (ed), *Rescuing the historic environment: archaeology, the Green movement and conservation strategies for the British landscape.* Hertford. RESCUE. 29-30

Young, C, 1995, Putting more local muscle into site management. *Conservation Bulletin*, 25, 3-4

Index *by Susan Vaughan*

Figures are indicated by page numbers in *italics* or by (*illus*) where figures are scattered throughout the text. The following abbreviations have been used in this index: C - century; DMV - deserted medieval village; *illus* - illustrated; PPG - Planning Policy Guidance; RCHME - Royal Commission on the Historical Monuments of England; SMR - Sites and Monuments Record.